LESSONS LEARNED IN THE WILDERNESS SERIES: BOOKS 4-6

THE LESSONS LEARNED IN THE WILDERNESS COLLECTION - VOLUME 2

KENNETH A. WINTER

JOIN MY READERS' GROUP FOR UPDATES AND FUTURE RELEASES

Please join my Readers' Group so i can send you a free book, as well as updates and information about future releases in the series.

See the back of the book for details on how to sign up.

* * *

Lessons Learned In The Wilderness Series: *Books 4-6*

(The Lessons Learned In The Wilderness Collection - *Volume 2* ***)***

A collection, including:
Walking With The Master
Taking Up The Cross
Until He Returns

Published by:

Kenneth A. Winter

WildernessLessons, LLC

Richmond, Virginia

United States of America

kenwinter.org / wildernesslessons.com

Cover Design: Melanie Fisher-Wellman

ISBN 978-1-7341930-8-4 (soft cover)

ISBN 978-1-7341930-7-7 (ebook)

CONTENTS

BOOK FOUR

BOOK FIVE

BOOK SIX

BEFORE YOU GO...

A WORD OF EXPLANATION

For those of you who are new to my writing.

* * *

You will notice that whenever i use the pronoun "I" referring to myself, i have chosen to use a lowercase "i". It is not a typographical error. i know that is contrary to proper English grammar and accepted editorial style guides. i drive editors (and "spell check") crazy by doing this. But years ago, the LORD convicted me – personally – that in all things i must decrease and He must increase. And as a way of continuing personal reminder, from that day forward, i have chosen to use a lower case "i" whenever referring to myself. Because of the same conviction, i use a capital letter for any pronoun referring to God. The style guide for the New Living Translation (NLT) does not share that conviction. However, you will see that i have intentionally made that slight revision and capitalized any pronoun referring to God in my quotations of Scripture from the NLT. If i have violated any style guides as a result, please accept my apology, but i must honor this conviction.

Lastly, regarding this matter – this is a personal conviction – and i share it only so that you will understand why i have chosen to deviate from normal editorial practice. i am in no way suggesting or endeavoring to have anyone else subscribe to my conviction. Thanks for your understanding.

* * *

BOOK FOUR

WALKING WITH THE MASTER

LESSONS LEARNED IN THE WILDERNESS

WALKING WITH THE MASTER

KENNETH A. WINTER

CHAPTER SCRIPTURE LISTING

Chapter 1 *In the Beginning* (John 1:1-14)
Chapter 2 *Run, Don't Walk* (Luke 2:8-18)
Chapter 3 *MAGI - Men on a Mission* (Matthew 2:1-11)
Chapter 4 *The Son Needed a Father* (Matthew 2:13-23)
Chapter 5 *A Trip to the Temple* (Luke 2:41-52)
Chapter 6 *Fully Pleasing* (Matthew 3:13-17)
Chapter 7 *Then the Devil* (Matthew 4:1-3)
Chapter 8 *What's So Special About Cana?* (John 2:1-11)
Chapter 9 *From Darkness Into Light* (John 3:1-21)
Chapter 10 *A Journey to the Well* (John 4:3-39)
Chapter 11 *A Journey Back Home* (Luke 4:16-30)
Chapter 12 *Fishers of Men* (Mark 1:16-18)
Chapter 13 *What Happens When the Water is Gone?* (John 5:1-9)
Chapter 14 *All of Nothing (Simon Peter)* (Luke 6:13-16)
Chapter 15 *In the Shadow of Peter (Andrew)* (Luke 6:13-16)
Chapter 16 *A Family Affair (James)* (Luke 6:13-16)
Chapter 17 *A Unique Perspective (John)* (Luke 6:13-16)
Chapter 18 *Even a Tax Collector (Matthew)* (Luke 6:13-16)
Chapter 19 *Along for the Ride, Not for the Journey (Judas)* (Luke 6:13-16)
Chapter 20 *All the Rest (the remaining six)* (Luke 6:13-16)
Chapter 21 *Plucking the Grain* (Mark 2:23-28)
Chapter 22 *Sermon of Sermons* (Matthew 5:1 – 7:29)
Chapter 23 *Faith Like This* (Matthew 8:5-13)
Chapter 24 *Arise!* (Luke 7:11-17)
Chapter 25 *Even John Doubted* (Matthew 11:2-6)
Chapter 26 *Who Dared to Anoint Jesus* (Luke 7:36-50)

PREFACE

Your attitude should be the same that Christ Jesus had. Though He was God, He did not demand and cling to His rights as God. He made Himself nothing; He took the humble position of a slave and appeared in human form. And in human form He obediently humbled himself even further by dying a criminal's death on a cross. Because of this, God raised Him up to the heights of heaven and gave Him a name that is above every other name, so that at the name of Jesus every knee will bow, in heaven and on earth and under the earth, and every tongue will confess that Jesus Christ is Lord, to the glory of God the Father.
Philippians 2:5-11

* * *

He was and is the Son of the Living God. There has never been another like Him and there never will be. He is God incarnate. He is God Who took on flesh so that we might <u>know how</u> to live a life that glorifies the Father and that we might <u>be able</u> to live a life that glorifies the Father. Jesus didn't need to walk on this earth for His own sake; He did so for our sake. He did so in obedience to the Father so that all who believe in Him and follow Him might be saved and so the Father might be glorified. Jesus called His disciples to follow Him – to walk with Him.

A relationship with Jesus is never static – it entails moving and growing. Jesus was constantly on the move, carrying out the Father's work and His will. He was continuously surrendered and submitted to the Father and the will of the Father. He humbled Himself – even to the point of dying a criminal's death on the cross. And as Paul wrote, because of the humility of Jesus, the Father exalted Him. Jesus humbled Himself in ways that our finite, unrighteous minds can never understand, and in so doing the Father has exalted Him above all else. To walk with the Master means we must walk surrendered and submitted to the Father – Jesus would never walk any other way. To walk with the Master means we must walk in the humility of a servant – a servant who is willing to get up from the table, put on a towel and wash the dirty feet of those around him. To walk with the Master means we must walk according to the Father's will, wholly devoted to Him and the accomplishment of His work – whatever the cost.

A walk with Jesus isn't a "cakewalk". It is not a walk that is promised to be trouble-free. It is not a walk that promises to be replete with physical comforts and financial prosperity. The Master did not have a pillow on which to lay His head; He had no earthly home to call His own – why should we think that we should be otherwise entitled? It is not a walk that insures the acceptance and support of all of those around you. As a matter-of-fact we can be certain that we will be ridiculed, misunderstood and possibly persecuted if we are truly walking with the Master. It happened to Him – why shouldn't it happen to us? A walk with the Master has no promise of the absence of pain and suffering – but through it all the Master does promise to give us the grace that is sufficient – His grace – and the strength – His strength – to walk through those times of pain and suffering.

A walk with the Master is a walk with purpose. Everything that transpires, everyone we encounter and every trial we walk through is for the purpose of the Father's glory (Romans 8:28). He has permitted it. Therefore we can walk with confidence when we are walking with the Master. But the reverse of that promise is also true – we cannot walk with confidence when we are not walking with the Master. We don't get to decide what is for our good any more than we get to decide what is for God's glory.

Our choice then is - will we walk with the Master? Not how or where or when, but if! If you have surrendered your life to Christ, He has invited you to follow Him – but that invitation is not a suggestion. Following Jesus is not a part-time vocation. His invitation is not one that we can compartmentalize for when it is convenient to our schedules or lines up with our desires. The Master is not looking for weekend followers. He has called us to follow Him 24/7. He has called us to walk with Him. And as we walk with the Master, He will call us to climb higher, to walk farther and to draw nearer to Himself. He has much to teach us in the journey – teach us about the Father, teach us about Himself and teach us about ourselves. You will encounter uncertainties in the journey – there will be turns in the path that are unclear; there will be circumstances that seem unbearable. But remember you can journey with the Master with certainty and with confidence. He will not leave you or abandon you in the journey. There is nothing you will encounter that He is not able to overcome. The journey will lead to God's glory and your ultimate good (because the Master will use it to make you more and more like Him).

The Master has extended His invitation – "Come and follow Me!" There are lessons to be learned and there is a Master to know, to know more and to know more intimately. Walk with the Master in His journey for your life. There is no greater journey on which you can embark.

* * *

1

IN THE BEGINNING

In the beginning the Word already existed. He was with God, and He was God. He was in the beginning with God. He created everything there is. Nothing exists that He didn't make. Life itself was in Him, and this life gives light to everyone. The light shines through the darkness, and the darkness can never extinguish it. ...But although the world was made through Him, the world didn't recognize Him when He came. Even in His own land and among His own people, He was not accepted. But to all who believed Him and accepted Him, He gave the right to become children of God. ...So the Word became human and lived here on earth among us. He was full of unfailing love and faithfulness. And we have seen His glory, the glory of the only Son of the Father.

John 1:1-5, 10-12, 14

* * *

The journey with the Master in some respects is a journey that has no beginning, because in the beginning He was. He was with God. He was God. He was the Creator of all things and in Him and for Him were all things created. He was Life and from Him life was given. He was Light and from Him light was given to the world. He was Light and through Him darkness was extinguished. He always was, and He forever will be.

Though He has no beginning, through Him was the beginning and in Him is the beginning. Through Him the world was created. Through Him the world was redeemed. Through Him the world was given the right to become children of God. He always was, and He forever will be.

. . .

Jesus was the Word of God. Jesus was the Truth of God. Jesus was the glory of God. Jesus was the love of God. Jesus was the faithfulness of God. He always was, and He forever will be.

However, the journey with the Master in other respects is a journey that does have a beginning - not a beginning for Him, but a beginning for us. It is a journey that begins with the creation of this world and it is a journey that begins with His incarnation. On that day two thousand years ago, God sent His Son to take on flesh that His Word, His Truth, His glory, His love and His faithfulness might be revealed. God sent His Son to take on flesh that His work of redemption might be made complete. God sent His Son so that His creation could be reconciled unto Him.

Imagine the stirrings in heaven that day.

Before creation, the Father had known that we would need a Redeemer.
Before creation, He had put in place His plan of redemption.
Before creation, plans were made for Jesus to take on flesh
to live on earth among His creation.
Before creation, plans were made for Jesus to suffer and
die on a cross as the sacrifice for our sin.
Before creation, plans were made for Jesus to arise from the dead,
conquering sin and death.
Before creation, plans for His journey had already been established.

From the days in the Garden of Eden, His coming had been foretold.
From the days of the flood, His coming had been promised.
From the day when God stayed Abraham's hand from slaying Isaac
on Mount Moriah, His coming had been assured.
From the days of the prophets, His coming had been anticipated.
And now that day had arrived!

All that needed to be completed prior to His arrival on earth had now been fulfilled. The days prior to His arrival had now been accomplished. Eyes that had longed to see this day would now be rewarded. All that remained was for Jesus to begin His journey.

. . .

We often look at what our sin cost Jesus at Calvary (and rightly so), but what about the cost at Bethlehem? As He began His journey, Jesus arose from His seat at the right hand of the Father; a crude manger was the throne that now awaited Him. As He stood, Jesus gazed into His Father's eyes; an earthly mother and "father" now awaited Him. Jesus removed His heavenly robe; a swaddling cloth was the garment that now awaited Him. A heavenly host gathered at His feet in worship and in praise as He left, as a small number of shepherds unknowingly were preparing to gather and worship Him in a stable. A journey that would begin and end on streets of gold would include many miles on paths of dust. Voices that were lifted in adoration and praise would be exchanged in the days to come for voices of ridicule and contempt.

He Who was and is the Light of the world was about to be heralded by the light of a star. He Who was and is the Way was about to be announced in a place where there was no room for Him to stay. He Who was and is the Truth was about to begin a journey that would be <u>the</u> defining moment in history.

And He began the journey – because He loves the Father; and the Father so loves us that He sent the Son. He began the journey so that we would know how to live – a purpose-filled life. He began the journey so that we might be able to live – an everlasting life. He began the journey so that we might be empowered to live – an abundant life.

On July 21, 1969 Astronaut Neil Armstrong spoke those now-memorable words as he was the first man to set foot on the surface of the moon, "One small step for man, one giant leap for mankind." Well, two thousand years ago, Jesus began His journey with a step, and we cannot fully grasp the gigantic leap for mankind that resulted. His journey began; and because His journey began, our journey can begin. Let us now heed the lessons to be learned walking with the Master.

* * *

2

RUN, DON'T WALK

That night some shepherds were in the fields outside the village, guarding their flocks of sheep. Suddenly, an angel of the Lord appeared among them, and the radiance of the Lord's glory surrounded them. They were terribly frightened, but the angel reassured them. "Don't be afraid!" he said. "I bring you good news of great joy for everyone! The Savior--yes, the Messiah, the Lord -- has been born tonight in Bethlehem, the city of David!" ...They ran to the village and found Mary and Joseph. And there was the baby, lying in the manger. Then the shepherds told everyone what had happened and what the angel had said to them about this Child. All who heard the shepherds' story were astonished.

Luke 2:8-11, 16-18

* * *

God will never lead us on a journey that does not bring glory to His Name. He has purposed to draw all men, all tongues, all tribes and all peoples to Himself that we might glorify Him. He sent Jesus to pay the price and make the way. And He has sent us, that through us He will make a global impact. As we saw in the first chapter the journey began with Jesus stepping from heaven to earth. If we would walk with the Master, we must in turn step from where we are to journey with Him.

The first men to take that step were the shepherds. A recurring theme we see throughout Scripture is that God's invitation to them came to them right where they were. They were in the fields. That's what shepherds do; they watch over their sheep while they are grazing in the fields. The men were not in the synagogue. They were not already at the stable. They weren't even inside of Bethlehem. They were in the fields outside the village. Now that's not to say that God couldn't have spoken to them in the synagogue, at the stable or inside of Bethlehem; rather, it is to say that God will invite us right where we are to come to Him from right where we are.

i believe that some of us miss out on walking with Jesus because we have a mindset that says, "One day I'll get dressed up and go to the synagogue at Bethlehem, and then I'll be ready for God to invite me to come to the stable." As if God couldn't possibly speak to me right where i am! Or some of us have an urge to go to Bethlehem, but we're delaying our departure because we're too busy – "there is no way I can go; I'm too busy guarding the sheep." Well that urging that you sense, that voice that you hear, is God inviting you to come from right where you are.

How do we know that it is God's invitation? How do we know that it is His voice? Well, look at the shepherds. We read, *"the radiance of God's glory surrounded them."* Everything that God does radiates His glory! They saw His glory and they knew! What's that you say – you've never seen the radiance of God's glory? God knew their hearts. He knew before he invited them that they would respond. He knew that they had ears to hear and eyes to see. He knew that as He revealed His glory they would respond to His glory. Could it be that God knows our heart as well? Of course He does! And He knows how we will respond. If you have not seen the radiance of His glory, could it be because you have not been prepared to respond to His glory? The Lord didn't come to them that night because they were watching for Him – they didn't have a clue that the angel would appear that night or any night. But they had hearts that were willing to respond. Jesus said, *"Anyone who is willing to hear should listen and understand"* (Matthew 11:15). We don't set the time or the place that He comes to us – He does; but we must have hearts that are willing to respond.

How did they at first respond when the Lord revealed His glory through the angel? With fear – they were *"terribly frightened"*. Now, I'm going to categorize fear in three ways – one that I will call "unhealthy fear", one that I will call "healthy fear" and the other that I will call "reverent fear". "Unhealthy fear" is that apprehension, anxiety, dread or despair that we allow to paralyze us or plague us – the fear of what other people will think or do or say, or how a possible or probable situation or event will unfold. "Healthy fear" is that emotion that is responding to evil or the expectation of it, or the apprehension of impending danger or wrong-doing or the consequence of it, that then in turn causes us to avoid that evil or danger, or confront it in an appropriate manner. "Reverent fear" is that reverence and awe that overshadows us when we come into the presence of the Sovereign and Almighty God, and having encountered His holiness and majesty we are now confronted with our own sinfulness and unworthiness. We are then compelled to walk in the awareness that our every thought, attitude and action is being observed by Him. Abraham and Moses, the only two men recorded in Scripture to be the "friends" of God, walked in that kind of fear before Him. It is that kind of fear, the writer of Proverbs says, that leads to knowledge of Him, and wisdom and understanding. The angel declared to the shepherds to not be paralyzed by "unhealthy fear" but to be propelled by "reverent fear".

And i love how Scripture records their response – *"they RAN to the village"*. When the Lord has invited us to join Him on the journey, we are to go without hesitation – to go "full out" – not allowing anything to detract us or distract us in or from the journey.

And after having seen Jesus they *"told everyone what had happened"*. As we go, we will tell – we will tell everyone we encounter of the One we have seen and heard and the One with Whom we have walked.

Are you ready for an evening run? He's invited us to go. Let's not just walk; let's run to Jesus – and let's run with the Master.

* * *

3

MAGI – MEN ON A MISSION

Now after Jesus was born in Bethlehem of Judea in the days of Herod the king, behold, magi from the east arrived in Jerusalem, saying, "Where is He who has been born King of the Jews? For we saw His star in the east, and have come to worship Him." And when Herod the king heard it, he was troubled, and all Jerusalem with him. And gathering together all the chief priests and scribes of the people, he began to inquire of them where the Christ was to be born. And they said to him, "In Bethlehem of Judea, for so it has been written by the prophet...." Then Herod secretly called the magi... and having heard the king, they went their way; and lo, the star, which they had seen in the east, went on before them, until it came and stood over where the Child was. And when they saw the star, they rejoiced exceedingly with great joy. And they came into the house and saw the Child with Mary His mother; and they fell down and worshiped Him; and opening their treasures they presented to Him gifts of gold and frankincense and myrrh.

Matthew 2:1-5, 7, 9-11 (NASB)

* * *

We've already looked at the fact that God is on mission to make a global impact. In doing so, He desires to work through men and women – MAGI – wise men and women who desire to be used by Him to Make A Global Impact. If we are to be those modern-day MAGI who journey on mission with the Master, we must learn from our first century forerunners.

. . .

First, they had a desire to seek Him. Like the shepherds, God had given the magi that desire long before the star appeared. Many saw the star, but Scripture records only the magi following the star. God, having placed that desire in their hearts, was able to call them from right where they were. You see, if you are looking for His star, you will see it, no matter where you are. Like the shepherds, the magi were doing what magi do. They were in their homes in their own countries watching and studying the stars. God called them in the midst of their day-to-day lifestyles. They were magi when He called them, and they were magi when they went. Don't miss this – God's call to them to step out on the journey didn't require them to change their profession, only their purpose! **God's call is never to a place and never to a position; God's call is always to move from where we are unto Himself!**

But in order for them to heed God's call, they first had to "hear" God's call. And in order for them to "hear" God's call, they had to be alert for His call. God chose few people to encounter Jesus when He was born, revealing His Son only to those whose hearts were faithful and pure. As I've already said, the star was there for everyone to see, but only the magi saw it – because they were watching. And the God that led them to go, led them all the way. He did not lead them to begin and then leave them to "figure out" the way, He journeyed with them all the way. Just as He led His people to the Promised Land by means of a pillar of fire, He led the magi to His Promised Seed by means of a brilliant star – and He will lead us all the way in our journey with Him as well.

How did God call them? Through the stars – the Father used a brilliant light burning in the darkness to announce the birth of The Light to a very dark world. These men were astronomers and astrologers – God spoke to them in a language they would understand. There wasn't any question for them as to what the star meant, or if there was, they quickly researched and studied the prophecies to remedy their concern. And when He spoke, they knew that they must respond. As Dr. Henry Blackaby says, "You can't stay where you are and go with God." It will require an adjustment. These men were not embarking on a short trip; it was a journey. It probably took at least a year. They did not start out together; they set out from different countries. Matthew Henry writes, "Those who truly desire to know Christ, and find Him, will not regard pains or perils in seeking after Him." But those who don't have that desire can be right in the midst of His activity and miss it. Look at the religious leaders of the day – they knew the prophecies, but they were not looking. The magi sought the King, Herod rejected the King, and, perhaps the greater tragedy, the Jewish priests ignored the King. They were *five miles* from the very Son of God, yet they did not go to see Him. I am encouraged that despite the apathy, pride and resentment they encountered, the magi were not discouraged, distracted or detracted from their mission.

Scripture never tells us that there were three magi; Scripture records that when their caravan arrived in Jerusalem there were enough of them to "disturb" the whole city. I am convinced that if the church of Jesus Christ will make the adjustment He has called us to make and journey with Him, the kingdoms of this earth will be disturbed, and the Good News of the Kingdom of Heaven will be seen and heard.

But not only did they have a desire to seek Him; secondly, they had a heart to worship Him. When they encountered the Living Lord Jesus they fell to the ground. They did not solely honor Him as the King of Kings; they worshipped Him as the Son of God. Having then presented themselves to Him, they next presented their gifts. They knew, as we should, that our gifts will never be acceptable to God until first we have presented ourselves to Him as living sacrifices. But also conversely, if we truly surrender ourselves to Him, we will never be unwilling to part with the things of this world – those things that we value and hold dear – bringing them to Him and for Him. Worship begins as we present ourselves and continues as we present all that we possess. That with which God has given us favor is that with which we must honor Him. The magi presented gold symbolizing His royalty, frankincense symbolizing His deity and myrrh symbolizing His humanity. Their gifts acknowledged to Whom they were giving. I wonder if our checkbooks would reflect that we as modern day MAGI have or have not lost sight of to Whom we are giving. Are we giving Him our best that is commensurate with His Royalty as the King of Kings, His Deity as the Son of God and His Humanity as the Son of Man, or are we giving Him the leftovers? These magi gave of their best because they gave out of a heart to worship Him.

Thirdly, their journey led to a greater intimacy with Him. On more than one occasion i have pondered what it must have been like at that moment in that place. Imagine the intimacy of that moment – the Lord Jesus, Mary, Joseph, the magi – the holy hush - a scene that you'd like to observe but you fear that even your presence would be an intrusion on the intimacy and the tenderness of the moment. As i have traveled overseas with mission teams, i often endeavor to capture images on video to show our church family back home. On many occasions i have found myself in the midst of "a moment" – one of those times when God's spirit is conspicuously at work in the hearts of people. But in those moments, as much as i would like to capture them on video, i hesitate for fear that i will disturb the intimacy and the tenderness that is being expressed. That is but a hint of what i think it must have been like that day.

Though Scripture does not record the events of their lives after this journey, i am convinced that the effect of the intimacy of that moment with Jesus transformed them for eternity. Just as i believe that as we experience a greater intimacy with the Master we too can, and will, never be the same.

God used this entourage and their journey to announce the birth of His Son to a world that was not looking for Him and had not otherwise seen. If we will be faithful to be modern-day MAGI responding to His call with hearts that desire to seek Him and worship Him, God will use us to accomplish His mission – to make a global impact – to carry the Good News to a world that may otherwise not see Him. And in the process He will draw us to a greater level of intimacy with Himself that we might know Him more and know Him more intimately. James wrote, *"Draw near to God and He will draw near to you"* (James 4:8 NKJ). **Be that modern-day MAGI – walk with the Master on mission with Him to make a global impact.**

* * *

4

THE SON NEEDED A FATHER

After the wise men were gone, an angel of the Lord appeared to Joseph in a dream. "Get up and flee to Egypt with the child and his mother," the angel said. "Stay there until I tell you to return, because Herod is going to try to kill the child." That night Joseph left for Egypt with the child and Mary, his mother, and they stayed there until Herod's death. This fulfilled what the Lord had spoken through the prophet: "I called my Son out of Egypt." ...When Herod died, an angel of the Lord appeared in a dream to Joseph in Egypt and told him, "Get up and take the child and his mother back to the land of Israel, because those who were trying to kill the child are dead." So Joseph returned immediately to Israel with Jesus and his mother. But when he learned that the new ruler was Herod's son Archelaus, he was afraid. Then, in another dream, he was warned to go to Galilee. So they went and lived in a town called Nazareth. This fulfilled what was spoken by the prophets concerning the Messiah: "He will be called a Nazarene."
Matthew 2:13-15, 19-23

* * *

The English translators did Joseph an injustice when they translated this particular passage, because ALL of the wise men were not gone. The magi may have been gone, but one wise man remained – and his name was Joseph. Over the course of Jesus' earthly ministry, a number of men had the privilege of journeying with Him, but only one man had the privilege of journeying with Him as His earthly father.

Just as the Heavenly Father chose John the Baptist to be the forerunner of

Jesus, and He chose Mary to be the mother of Jesus, He chose Joseph to be the earthly father of Jesus. Do not think that the Father chose Mary to be the mother of Jesus, and then left the selection for the role of earthly father up to Mary. God ordered the steps of this woman and this man to be the earthly parents of Jesus. He graced Joseph with the awesome privilege and responsibility of parenting the Son of Man.

Soon after our children were born, my wife and i modified our wills to include a guardian for our children in the event something happened to us and we could no longer care for them. i remember the process we went through in making that determination. We did not make it quickly or casually; we entered into it prayerfully and carefully. And i am certain that the Heavenly Father chose the earthly father for His Son with even greater deliberation; as a matter of fact God created him for that intended purpose.

There is much more written in Scripture about Mary than there is about Joseph. But knowing that God made Joseph for the purpose of parenting His only Son, there are certain aspects of His character that we can know with certainty. Repeatedly the earthly father allowed the Heavenly Father to guide and direct his steps. We see that demonstrated before the birth of Jesus when the angel of the Lord revealed in a dream to Joseph that the baby Mary carried within her was conceived by the Holy Spirit. We see Joseph's responsiveness again, three times in this passage: God directs him to go to Egypt, God directs him to return to Israel, and God directs him to relocate to Nazareth. And in each instance, Joseph knew the voice of God then Joseph obeyed the voice of God. There is no record that he ever questioned or debated the word of the Father; he heard, and he obeyed. Even when i am sure he did not understand – there had never been a baby born of a virgin and conceived by the Holy Spirit, and neither has there been since – but Joseph didn't keep asking questions until he understood, he just obeyed. The Father said it; that settled it. He knew God; he knew His voice and he obeyed Him.

Joseph was a man of conviction. When Joseph learned that Mary was pregnant, before he had heard from the angel of the Lord, he intended to break their engagement - he could not be a party to anything that dishonored God. But he was also a man of compassion – he had chosen to break their engagement in a manner that did not bring public shame or humiliation to Mary. He was prepared to be honorable, even when, according to the world's standard, he had been dishonored. And he was a man of courage – he disregarded the ridicule of those who assumed the worst about Mary's pregnancy, he protected his Son from the plot of Herod, and he left his lifetime home and livelihood in Judea and started all over again in Galilee. Custom and tradition would tell us that Joseph was probably in his middle-aged years, if not his later years, and Mary in her early teens when they were betrothed (sorry to shatter the mental image you may have had of this young newlywed couple). So Joseph was walking away from everything he owned (albeit the meager lot that it was) and everything he knew, for the sake of his family and in obedience to the Father. But he could do that, because Joseph was a man of confidence – confidence in GOD.

The Father is calling us to be men and women who walk with the Son with that same conviction, compassion, courage and confidence. Even the Son needed a father - and the father, like you and me, definitely needed the Son. Just as the Father worked through Joseph to fulfill His purpose through the Son, so does He intend to do so through us. You didn't choose Him, He chose you. Whether you are in those teen years or in your later years, He has an assignment for you. Come – walk with the Master – with conviction… with compassion… with courage… and with confidence.

* * *

5

A TRIP TO TEMPLE

Every year Jesus' parents went to Jerusalem for the Passover festival. When Jesus was twelve years old, they attended the festival as usual. After the celebration was over, they started home to Nazareth, but Jesus stayed behind in Jerusalem. His parents didn't miss Him at first, because they assumed He was with friends among the other travelers. But when He didn't show up that evening, they started to look for Him among their relatives and friends. When they couldn't find Him, they went back to Jerusalem to search for Him there. Three days later they finally discovered Him. He was in the Temple, sitting among the religious teachers, discussing deep questions with them. And all who heard Him were amazed at His understanding and His answers.

His parents didn't know what to think. "Son!" His mother said to Him. "Why have you done this to us? Your father and I have been frantic, searching for you everywhere." "But why did you need to search?" He asked. "You should have known that I would be in My Father's house." But they didn't understand what He meant.

Then He returned to Nazareth with them and was obedient to them; and His mother stored all these things in her heart. So Jesus grew both in height and in wisdom, and He was loved by God and by all who knew Him.

Luke 2:41-52

* * *

This is the only event recorded in Scripture that took place during that thirty-year period between the Master's birth and His baptism. And in light of the theme of this book, it is appropriate that it also was a journey. Now as we look at this passage i want us to be mindful of the premise of our study. Jesus came and journeyed on this earth so that we might know how to live, might be able to live and might be empowered to live. The truth of what took place on this journey goes a long way toward teaching us how to live in our life journey. As such, we will look at this passage, as we will often do throughout this book, through the eyes of Jesus' traveling companions.

As a part of the Law handed down through Moses, the children of Israel were commanded to celebrate three festivals each year (Deuteronomy 16:16). Many chose to travel to Jerusalem to observe those celebrations. Joseph being poor was probably unable to make that trip three times per year; but he faithfully did so once each year to celebrate the Passover. Every year he would take Mary and Jesus and the rest of the family and travel the sixty miles from Nazareth in Galilee to Jerusalem in Judea. And they did not travel alone. Often entire villages would make this annual pilgrimage together. As was the custom, the women and children would walk in the front of the entourage and the men and their teenage sons would follow, discussing politics and religion. They would not travel as a family, but as a village; and the family would not come together until it was time to stop for the evening.

At the age of twelve, Jesus was no longer a child, but He was not yet considered a man. So on this trip, Jesus probably spent time bouncing from one group to another, as well as with friends. So, on the return trip to Nazareth that first day, it is not surprising that Mary and Joseph did not discover that Jesus was missing until the evening hours. Besides, they had been busy finalizing any business they needed to conduct in Jerusalem while they were there, as well as making preparations for the four to five day journey back home. In the midst of their busyness, it would have been easy to lose sight of Jesus. But in the evening when the pace slowed, the busyness stopped, and the distractions subsided, they began to become acutely aware of His absence.

How many of us have journeyed with Jesus, only to discover that in the middle of the busyness of our journey He has become absent in our midst? How many of us have become so preoccupied with what we were doing and/or the people around us, that we didn't even think to look for Him? Well, that's what happened to Mary and Joseph. And in their hearts, His absence and their separation from Him turned into sorrow, a sorrow that led them to stop traveling in the direction they were going – to turn around – and seek Jesus.

If you have found yourself journeying in the wilderness without Jesus, take heart in the truth of this account: **if you seek Him, you will find Him**. Respond to the sorrow of your separation, turn from the direction you were headed and turn back to where He is.

It took one day for them to get back to Jerusalem and they searched for two more days before they found Him. Be mindful that even though they were the earthly parents of Jesus, they still didn't understand all that was going on. They knew that Jesus was the Messiah; the angel had told them that. But remember the Jews thought the Messiah would come as the King to the palace, not as the Son of Man to the temple … and the cross. Joseph and Mary may have been more impressed to first seek Jesus in the palace then they were to look for Him in the temple.

Perhaps you too are seeking Jesus, but not sure where to look. Heed the lesson of Joseph and Mary: **go back to the last place you saw Him**. He will be there; He will be waiting for you.

And when Joseph and Mary came upon Him, what did they see? They saw Him listening to the teaching of God's Word. They saw Him asking questions to clarify God's Word. And they saw Him answer the teachers with the God-given wisdom and understanding of God's Word. As you return and find Him, listen to His teaching. Don't be fearful to ask questions to clarify. And then respond – in word and in action – with the wisdom and understanding that He has given you through His Word. **Don't be so excited by the emotion of finding Him that you miss His teaching. And don't be in such a hurry to get back on your journey that you fail to respond to Him.**

The one tragedy of the day surrounded the teachers with whom He sat. Because there He was in their presence, speaking the Truth of the Father and they did not know Him. They marveled at His understanding and missed the reality of His Person. Do not solely seek Jesus as your Teacher; seek Him as your Savior and your Master – as the Son of the Living God.

. . .

And one more truth, as we prepare to start back on our journey, remember that Jesus told Mary that He was "about the Father's business" (Luke 2:49 NKJ). Let us be mindful that we too must make the Father's business our priority. Let us heed these lessons from a trip to the temple with the Master.

* * *

6

FULLY PLEASING

Then Jesus went from Galilee to the Jordan River to be baptized by John. But John didn't want to baptize Him. "I am the one who needs to be baptized by You," he said, "so why are You coming to me?" But Jesus said, "It must be done, because we must do everything that is right." So then John baptized Him. After His baptism, as Jesus came up out of the water, the heavens were opened, and he saw the Spirit of God descending like a dove and settling on Him. And a voice from heaven said, "This is my beloved Son, and I am fully pleased with Him."
Matthew 3:13-17

* * *

The time had come, and Jesus would not delay. At some point prior to this, Joseph had died. For some time now Jesus had continued in the carpentry trade of Joseph caring for His mother and his younger half-siblings. But then in accordance with His Heavenly Father's timetable the time had come for Him to step out from obscurity.

His first step was into the Jordan River. It is significant to me that Jesus was baptized in the Jordan River, the river through which the Israelites crossed as they journeyed from the wilderness to the land of God's promise. Jesus is the fulfillment of the Father's promise. Everything is in Him, for Him, through Him and by Him. Jesus is The Way through which the Father's promise is fulfilled and realized. His baptism in the Jordan symbolizes that turning point – our ability to cross from the wilderness of sin into the land of God's promise – through Him. He has been made our Jordan – there is no other way for us to enter into God's land of promise.

Not only was the place where He was baptized significant, so was the person whom He permitted to baptize Him. Jesus came to John to affirm the ministry of John. John was six months older than Jesus, and had probably begun his earthly ministry just six months earlier. He had been sent by God to *"prepare a pathway for the Lord's coming"* (Matthew 3:3). Jesus later affirmed the ministry of John when He declared, *"Of all who have ever lived, none is greater than John the Baptist"* (Matthew 11:11), but on this day, Jesus affirmed John through His action. It was a living illustration of God's promise that those who honor Him, He will honor (John 12:26).

But let us also learn from John's response to the Master's affirmation. Too often, we can allow God's expression of honor upon our lives to cloud our vision of who He is and who we are apart from Him. Like King Saul, we can allow a spirit of pride to well up in our souls and blind us from Him. John did not allow the honor of God to displace the primacy of God in his life.

- John, who had been full of the Holy Spirit from his mother's womb, in the Master's presence became aware of his need for even a greater filling,
- John, who preached the message of repentance to the multitudes, in the Master's presence had a greater view of his own sinfulness,
- John, who had been sent to prepare the way for Jesus, in the Master's presence had a greater view of his own need for Jesus, and
- John, who that day was ministering to the multitude on the riverbank, in the Master's presence did not miss his own need to personally and publicly confess Jesus as the Christ.

But Jesus did not only come to the river to affirm John, He came to be identified with sinners. He who knew no sin came to be baptized by a sinner as a sinner among sinners. Baptism in one word is that – identification. Through baptism we are identified with Christ. On that day He came as King of Kings to be identified with His subjects. The Father *"made Him who knew no sin to be sin for us, that we might become the righteousness of God in Him"* (2 Corinthians 5:21 NKJ). As we have already said several times thus far, Jesus came to teach us how to live, to enable us to live and to empower us to live. In order to teach us how, He was baptized in the Jordan, in order to enable us, He was baptized on the cross and in order to empower us, He has become our High Priest *"who understands our weaknesses, for he faced all of the same temptations we do"* (Heb 4:15) and intercedes on our behalf. Jesus never taught His disciples to do anything that He did not first model. He did not set Himself here as an example – He was holy, without sin – while we walk on this earth we will never be without sin; but He came to identify Himself with us. Let me illustrate the point. John's baptism was a baptism of repentance of sin. After someone was baptized they would then immediately publicly confess their sin right there in the water. But in the New American Standard Bible we read, *"After being baptized, Jesus went up IMMEDIATELY from the water…."* (Matthew 3:16 NASB, emphasis added). Jesus did not need to remain in the water and confess His sin; He had no sin to confess! He had been baptized to be identified with us.

And thirdly, Jesus came to be baptized that day because baptism symbolized death. It was a picture of His future baptism on the cross. Just as He became identified with us through baptism, we become identified with Him – His death, His burial and His resurrection. We are raised out of the waters of baptism to walk in new life in Him and with Him.

And on that day all of heaven affirmed Jesus. The heavens opened to encourage Him in His going and to encourage us to receive Him. The Holy Spirit descended upon Him as a dove. It is interesting that the dove is the only bird that was permitted to be offered as a sacrifice (Leviticus 1:14) and it was the sacrifice that was presented at the temple on the eighth day when Jesus was circumcised in obedience to the Law (Luke 2:24). And it was a dove that God directed Noah to release from the ark that returned with the olive leaf in her beak (Genesis 8:11), symbolizing the peace and the promise of God.

Then the Father, Himself, affirmed Jesus on that day. He affirmed His relation as His Son, His affection as His beloved and His affirmation as the One in whom He is "fully pleased". You see, the fourth reason – but most important reason – Jesus came to the Jordan that day was in obedience to the Father. Jesus came to do the will of the Father – in all that He did. And His baptism that day was the Father's will.

• • •

What would the Master teach you beside the waters of the Jordan? Several years ago the Lord gave me an opportunity to visit the Jordan River and there be baptized in those same waters. Though i had been baptized at age 10 in my local church, i truly did not surrender my life to Christ until over two decades later. The Lord had brought me to the realization that my baptism needed to be on the right side of my salvation – truly identifying with Him. And He ordered my steps so that it could take place in the Jordan River. On that day, in that place, i was reminded that Jesus had allowed Himself to be identified with me as a sinner. And now i had the opportunity to be identified with Him as my Savior. And in both instances the Father is pleased, and the Father is glorified.

Now we don't need to physically travel to the Jordan River, we can come to that place right in our own hometowns. Wherever you are, if you have not yet taken that step of obedience, i encourage you to wait no longer. Follow our Master in what He modeled – remember that was Jesus' first step – the Father will be pleased, and the Father will be glorified as you walk with the Master in baptism.

* * *

7

THEN THE DEVIL CAME

Then Jesus was led out into the wilderness by the Holy Spirit to be tempted there by the Devil. For forty days and forty nights He ate nothing and became very hungry. Then the Devil came….
Matthew 4:1-3

* * *

At the Jordan, Jesus identified with us through His baptism; in the wilderness, Jesus identified with us through His temptation. Do not miss this – the Father ordered His steps into the wilderness, just as He had ordered His steps to the Jordan, that He might there be tempted, tested and proven. Not proven to the Father; the Father knew that He could not fail. Jesus was led into the wilderness to prove to us that He could not fail. Another important distinction that we must understand before we look at the events that unfolded is that Jesus was not tempted as the Son of God; He did not use His divine power to overcome the temptation. If He had, there would be nothing for us to learn. Remember, He came to teach us how to live, to enable us to live, and to empower us to live. You and I will never have divine power; we're not God! We have access to divine power, but we do not ourselves possess it. Therefore if Jesus had responded to Satan as the Son of God, He would not have taught us how to respond to temptation. Rather, He responded – and was proven – as the Son of Man using the same spiritual resources that are available to us in our journey today: the power of the Holy Spirit (Matthew 4:1) and the power of the Word of God.

. . .

J. Vernon McGee told a story that beautifully illustrates this idea of His being "proven".

> *"The Santa Fe Railroad crossed the left fork of the Brazos River near our town in West Texas. One winter we really had a flood, and it washed out the rail bridge over the Brazos River. One day, after they completed building the new bridge, they brought in two engines and stopped them in the middle of the bridge, and tied down their whistles. When we ran to the bridge to see what all the noise was about, one brave citizen asked the engineer in charge, 'What are you doing?' The engineer answered, 'Testing the bridge.' The brave citizen countered, 'Are you trying to break it down?' 'Of course not', the engineer sneered. 'We're testing it to prove that it can't be broken down.'"*

Now that is exactly what the Father was doing; He was proving that Jesus couldn't be broken down – He could not (and cannot) fail! And the Father permitted Him to be tested in ways greater than any limit we could bear.

The Father also ordered Jesus' journey into the wilderness that the Devil's tactics might be exposed. Satan is a predictable foe. His pattern has remained unchanged since the days in the Garden of Eden. His temptations will come on three fronts. First, **he will tempt us according to our physical needs**. He will call into question the Father's care and concern for our physical well-being. He will tempt and test us through the senses. He appealed to Eve through the physical appearance of the fruit on the tree (the fruit looked fresh and delicious). He appealed to Jesus' physical hunger after forty days of fasting. In both instances, Satan's implication was that God's provision was unreliable.

Second, **he will tempt us according to our "soulish" desires.** He will tempt and test us to exercise our own will and desires, instead of those of the Father. He will test us to presume upon the Father's power and protection in order for us to do things our way. When we attempt to do God's work man's way, we are succumbing to this temptation. When we fail to seek the Lord and instead make our own plans and then ask God to bless them, we are succumbing to this temptation. When we are driven by selfish ambition based upon "what's-in-it-for-me", we are succumbing to this temptation. He tempted Eve, that disobeying God and eating the fruit would make her wise; and Jesus, that He could redeem Himself and the world without the suffering of the cross. In both instances, Satan's implication was that God's will was fallible and His character was undependable.

. . .

Third, **he will tempt us to deify ourselves.** The second temptation is disregarding the Father's will; the third temptation is to elevate our will over the Father's. He will tempt us to supplant the Father's honor and homage in a feeble attempt to gain glory for ourselves. When I was ordained a wise man told me that if I was faithful to pass on all the glory to God, that when the suffering comes along I can confidently pass that on to Him as well. **You see, if we would share in the honor, we must share in the suffering.** Satan tempted Eve, that by disobeying God she would become like God; Jesus, that by worshipping Satan He would be the God of this world. The honor is not Satan's to give; it is God's, and His alone. Satan's implication was that God's glory was undue.

Yes, the Father led Jesus into the wilderness that Jesus might be proven, Satan might be exposed, and to reveal that Satan is a defeated foe. The answer to temptation is ALWAYS in the Word. We don't have to depend upon what we think, we can trust and stand confidently on what God has said. And apparently that was good enough for the Devil, because after Jesus responded with the Word of the Father ... Satan left. He left with his tail between his legs as a defeated foe. He didn't leave for good – that hasn't happened yet – he would return to tempt Jesus another day. But each time he did, he did so as one who is defeated; one that cannot be victorious. And he will return to tempt us, time and again, but remember the answer is ALWAYS in God's Word.

The Father led the Master into the wilderness to be tempted, and as you walk with the Master, the Father will permit you to be tempted that you might be proven, and Satan might be exposed and revealed to be a defeated foe. Paul wrote, *"No temptation has overtaken you except such as is common to man; but God is faithful, who will not allow you to be tempted beyond what you are able, but with the temptation will also make the way of escape, that you may be able to bear it"* (1 Corinthians 10:13 NKJ). Jesus told His disciples, *"Here on earth you will have many trials... but take heart, because I have overcome the world"* (John 16:33). No man has the right to call others to obey until he has obeyed himself. When the Father led the Son of Man into the wilderness, the Master obeyed. Yes, the devil came... but then he left as a defeated foe. Our Master has called us now to obey. He has shown us how, He has enabled us, and through God's Spirit and God's Word He has empowered us.

* * *

8

WHAT'S SO SPECIAL ABOUT CANA?

The next day Jesus' mother was a guest at a wedding celebration in the village of Cana in Galilee. Jesus and His disciples were also invited to the celebration. The wine supply ran out during the festivities, so Jesus' mother spoke to Him about the problem. "They have no more wine," she told Him. "How does that concern you and Me?" Jesus asked. "My time has not yet come." But His mother told the servants, "Do whatever He tells you." Six stone water pots were standing there; they were used for Jewish ceremonial purposes and held twenty to thirty gallons each. Jesus told the servants, "Fill the jars with water." When the jars had been filled to the brim, He said, "Dip some out and take it to the master of ceremonies." So they followed His instructions. When the master of ceremonies tasted the water that was now wine, not knowing where it had come from (though, of course, the servants knew), he called the bridegroom over. "Usually a host serves the best wine first," he said. "Then, when everyone is full and doesn't care, he brings out the less expensive wines. But you have kept the best until now!" This miraculous sign at Cana in Galilee was Jesus' first display of His glory. And His disciples believed in Him.

John 2:1-11

* * *

It was an obscure corner of Galilee. Very few people knew where it was, let alone traveled to it. Cana is never mentioned in the Old Testament, and it is only referred to three times in the New Testament - this being the first and most significant. Most people only passed through Cana on their way to some other place. In its day it was a place of little notoriety. It wasn't a center of activity like Jerusalem or even Capernaum. But Cana became significant that day, not because of what it was, but because of what took place there. It became significant because Jesus came there. It became significant in light of Who He is and what He did.

Jesus came to the village and the celebration at the request of His mother. She was the guest; He was also invited. You know the routine – "Oh, and Mary, bring Jesus with you too." He was not the guest of honor. He wasn't yet known for His miracles or His teaching. To that point He had lived an obscure life. He was there because He was "Mary's son", perhaps her escort on that day, not because He was God's Son. The bride or bridegroom or both were probably somehow related to Mary; her instructions in the household seemed to carry weight and have influence. And no one seemed to care that Jesus had brought along a group of His friends.

But then something happened. In the scope of eternity, it was pretty minor; but to the family of the bride and groom, it was a big deal. The attendance at the wedding was apparently larger than expected. The guests were reveling in the hospitality and the celebration of the moment. And all of a sudden someone realized that the supply of wine had run out. The shame and embarrassment to the host would be huge. Running out of refreshments for your guests is always a concern for hosts, but for Middle Easterners in the first century this would have tarnished their image and their standing as a family in their community for years to come. This was not only a social "pho-pa"; this would impact their influence, their livelihood and their respect among the people of their village, their synagogue and that entire region. Somehow the matter came to Mary's attention – either she was told or she observed it. Understanding the implications, she turned to Jesus. She understood that though the implications were huge, the problem was minor. And she knew that, no matter how big, or how small, the problem was, she could bring it to Jesus.

To that point, Jesus' time had "not yet come"; His public ministry had not yet begun. But this would be that day; this would be that place. The Father had ordered His steps to begin His earthly ministry at this wedding feast. Isn't it interesting that He will continue His earthly ministry when He returns again at a wedding feast – the wedding feast of the Lamb – when He unites with His bride – the church? And on that day He will not be a "tag-along" guest, He will be the Guest of honor – the

Bridegroom. But on this day in Cana, He honored the bridegroom of that feast.

Why did He at first answer His mother, "What has this concern of yours to do with Me"? He was not disrespecting Mary, rather first, He was making it clear that He was absolutely bound to the Father's will in heaven and to no one on earth – not even His mother. *"The Son can do nothing of His own accord, but only what He sees the Father doing"* (John 5:19). His miracles were not at His mother's disposal – or anyone else's, but entirely at the direction – and in the midst of the activity – of the Heavenly Father. Jesus and the Father are one, and have one will. It is important for us to remember that we are not to ask God to join us in our activity – rather for us to seek to join Him in His.

Secondly, in the midst of the Father's activity, He desired, even for His mother to communicate to Him what she was asking Him to do. Repeatedly we see Jesus asking those who have come to Him, "What would you have Me to do"? He was teaching them, as He is teaching us, that they (and we) must ask – and must ask according to God's will. On that day, Jesus responded to the faith of His mother as it aligned with the will of the Father – and that faith was communicated to Him by her asking. The same is true for each of us.

As a result, He then invited the servants to be a part of the miracle He was about to perform. The invitation came through a word of instruction from Mary to the servants. She said, "Do whatever He tells you." The servants needed a miracle – not only would the hosts pay the price for this oversight, so would the servants – someone had failed to properly plan. Incidentally, that's always true of miracles – you won't experience one until you truly need one. And that was true in Cana – people who lived in a little-known place needed a miracle and, as they obediently responded to what Jesus told them to do, Jesus did that which only He could.

Jesus told the servants to use the six earthen vessels that were standing there – the ones that were used for the washing of hands and feet. There wasn't anything special about those water pots – as a matter of fact they had been crafted by the potter to be used for the mundane and the routine. But in the hands of The Master Potter they would be used for God's glory. That which had up to that point only been used for the natural would now be used by the Master for the supernatural. The issue wasn't the pot – it never is; it was the Potter. The pots had no ability to transform water into wine, only the Potter did. And in His hands, "any old pot" will do.

And Jesus told them to fill the pots to the brim – with water. I have a lot of admiration for the faith of those servants. Their jobs were on the line – maybe their very lives. And this Man, who they didn't know, told them to fill the ceremonial washing pots with water – and what they needed was wine! Wouldn't it have made more sense for Him to give them a few shekels and send them by a back way to the local 7-Eleven to pick up a few gallons of wine? But no, He told them to fill the water pots with water – to the brim, I might add. He didn't tell them to do anything halfway. His instruction was to go all of the way - just like His instruction is to us. Understand that these pots held twenty to thirty gallons of water, and there were six of them. This required quite a few trips to the well. And as each moment went by, the servants were rapidly approaching the humiliation of their master and themselves.

Now here came the real faith-tester. Next He told them to withdraw some of the water back out of the pot and take it to the master of ceremonies to taste. Imagine what was going through their minds! It's one thing to fill the pots with water, it's quite another to reach in and draw it back out. And yet they never questioned Him! i often wonder – when was the water transformed – when they filled the pots – or when they drew it out? I believe the bigger step of faith was in drawing it out. And they never hesitated! And because it aligned with the will of the Father, and because of the faith of Mary, and the faith of those servants, He transformed the water into wine. Not just any wine – but the best anyone had ever tasted! Whatever Jesus does will ALWAYS be the best!

I am mindful that every guest at the feast benefited from the miracle that day; but Mary and the servants – they <u>experienced</u> the miracle that day. Through their faith and obedience they became instruments that God used to bring glory to His Name. It had nothing to do with their ability; they truly contributed nothing more than those clay water pots. But they were faithful and obedient. And as a result, they – and the disciples – saw Jesus for Who He was.

So do you see the "formula" for a miracle? It will occur at the place and time of God's choosing – usually an obscure place, at an unexpected time, as a result of an invitation that is compelling, through servants who are obedient, by a Savior Who is able. So, do you need a miracle? **Do whatever He tells you!** And watch Him take this place that isn't very special and use it as a platform for a miracle to His glory!

9

FROM DARKNESS INTO LIGHT

After dark one evening, a Jewish religious leader named Nicodemus, a Pharisee, came to speak with Jesus. "Teacher," he said, "we all know that God has sent You to teach us. Your miraculous signs are proof enough that God is with You." ... Jesus replied, "You are a respected Jewish teacher, and yet you don't understand these things? ...For God so loved the world that He gave His only Son, so that everyone who believes in Him will not perish but have eternal life. God did not send His Son into the world to condemn it, but to save it. There is no judgment awaiting those who trust Him. But those who do not trust Him have already been judged for not believing in the only Son of God. Their judgment is based on this fact: The light from heaven came into the world, but they loved the darkness more than the light, for their actions were evil. They hate the light because they want to sin in the darkness. They stay away from the light for fear their sins will be exposed and they will be punished. But those who do what is right come to the light gladly, so everyone can see that they are doing what God wants."

John 3:1-2, 10, 16-21

* * *

Nicodemus was a Pharisee and a member of the Sanhedrin. Pharisees were zealous in their keeping of the Laws of Moses, to the extreme of straining the letter of the Law over the Spirit of the Law (2 Corinthians 3:6). (For example, the Pharisees developed such detailed rules for the observance of the Sabbath that they missed the whole purpose for God's designation of the Sabbath. – Matthew 12:1-8) The Sanhedrin was the ruling council and court of justice among the Jewish people in Judea. Presided over by the high priest, the Sanhedrin was granted limited authority by the Romans over certain religious, civil and community matters. There was no higher position of political power for a Jew in the time of Christ, but their power was always subject to the authority of the Roman government and never extended outside of Judea. Nicodemus is considered by many to have been Nicodemus ben Gorion, the brother of Josephus the historian. He was considered to be one of the three wealthiest men in Jerusalem of his day.

The overturning of the money changers' tables and the scattering of the merchants in the Temple by Jesus just a few days earlier had created quite a stir among the Sanhedrin (John 2:13-22). Who was this upstart Galilean that dared to question their authority and their practice? But the miracles that He was performing were gaining Him great notoriety among the people of Jerusalem. And the Sanhedrin understood the axiom of leadership that says, "you are truly only leading if others are following". The people were beginning to follow this One from Nazareth. Before the Sanhedrin openly opposed Him, perhaps it would be in their best interest to investigate Him a little further.

Nicodemus – this ruler, this teacher, this Pharisee – came to Jesus that night. The poor were flocking to Him by day, but Nicodemus came to Him under the cloak of darkness. There are three possible explanations for the time of his visit. Perhaps he was an anxious inquirer drawn to Jesus by the miracles that He performed, and he did not want others in the Sanhedrin to know of his visit. Word of his visit could greatly affect his reputation and position on the council. Or perhaps, he came in his capacity as a member of the Sanhedrin, though perhaps self-appointed, to investigate Jesus further and he did not want to lend credence to Jesus by making his visit public knowledge. Or maybe, as is my conviction, it was a combination of both.

When Nicodemus arrived, he believed, or at least so he declared, Jesus to be inspired like the prophets of old – on a divine mission, but not having a divine nature. This would explain the source of His power, but deny the authority of His Person. But Jesus immediately declared to him that His mission and His nature could not be separated. He declared that He was not only sent by God, He was also the Son of God, sent not to condemn the world, but so that the world through Him might be saved (John 3:17).

Jesus began to show Nicodemus that not only had he come to Jesus in the cover of the darkness of nightfall, but he was blinded from seeing Jesus for who He truly is by the cover of the darkness of sin. "You are a teacher," Jesus said, "and yet you do not understand." And to paraphrase, "You do not understand, because you do not see"; and "You do not see, because you are blinded." But God sent the Light of heaven in the form of His Son into the world to expel the darkness. And yet many denied the Light because they loved the darkness and they hated the Light because it exposed their darkness. The very religious hierarchy of which Nicodemus was a part existed and thrived because of that darkness. Their power and their authority came from the fear of that darkness. Eradicating that darkness was tantamount to unmasking the fallacy of their teachings and eroding their basis of power. Those that resist the Light are therefore not condemned by Jesus; they are condemned by their own action. They alone are responsible for their own unbelief. And those who come to the Light gladly are doing what God wants – experiencing their redemption and receiving their salvation.

Nicodemus is only mentioned in the Gospel of John; all the others are silent on this account. We see in John 18:15 that John was acquainted with the high priest. John more than likely knew other members of the Sanhedrin as well, including Nicodemus. He would therefore have had more than a passing interest in the journey to salvation of this Pharisee. Some believe that John helped arrange this meeting between Nicodemus and Jesus, perhaps in the home of one of John's relatives. John goes on to record the continuation of the journey that Nicodemus made from **anxious inquiry** here to **sincere belief** – when Nicodemus defended Jesus among the Sanhedrin (John 7:50-53); and then his **bold profession** when he and Joseph of Arimathea claim the body of Jesus for burial (John 19:39-40).

Tradition tells us that Nicodemus was later baptized by Peter. Having boldly declared himself to be a follower of Jesus, he was removed from his office in the Sanhedrin and expelled from Jerusalem. Josephus wrote that he became so poor as a result of the persecution he received for having embraced Christ, that "his daughter was seen gathering barley corn for food from under the horses' feet."

Nicodemus is a picture of that man who steps from darkness into Light. He moved from anxious inquiry to bold profession. Yes, in doing so he stepped from being one of the three wealthiest men in Jerusalem, a man of worldly prestige and authority, and became a man without any worldly possession or position. But in doing so he knew that he was "giving up that which he could not keep, to gain that which he could not lose". Nicodemus counted the cost to follow the Master. And He heeded the Master's teaching that the darkness will perish, but the Light will abide forever. If we would walk with the Master, we too must first step from the darkness into the Light. May God give each one of us the strength, the grace and the courage to "do what is right" and step from the darkness into His Glorious Light.

* * *

10

A JOURNEY TO THE WELL

So Jesus left Judea to return to Galilee. He had to go through Samaria on the way. Eventually He came to the Samaritan village of Sychar, near the parcel of ground that Jacob gave to his son Joseph. Jacob's well was there; and Jesus, tired from the long walk, sat wearily beside the well about noontime. Soon a Samaritan woman came to draw water, and Jesus said to her, "Please give Me a drink." ...The woman left her water jar beside the well and went back to the village and told everyone, "Come and meet a man who told me everything I ever did! Can this be the Messiah?" So the people came streaming from the village to see Him. ...Many Samaritans from the village believed in Jesus because the woman had said, "He told me everything I ever did!"

John 4:3-7, 28-30, 39

* * *

Jesus was traveling north from Judea to Galilee. John writes *"He had to go through Samaria on the way."* Don't skip over what John said. Those words are not inserted as filler. Neither is John giving us a geography lesson. It is true that if you look at a map of that region during the time of Christ, you will see that Samaria was bordered by Judea to the south and Galilee to the north. So following the theory that "the shortest distance between two points is a straight line", you would concur that to make that trip you *"had to go through Samaria"*. But if you were a Jew in the first century you might see things a little differently. Samaria was a territory to be avoided by Jews if at all possible.

. . .

Let's look at the history. Following the death of King Solomon, the kingdom of Israel split into two kingdoms: the southern kingdom of the tribes of Judah and Benjamin called Judea, and the northern kingdom of the other ten tribes called Israel. Jeroboam, the king of Israel, in order to keep the citizens of the northern kingdom from traveling to Jerusalem (in the southern kingdom) to offer sacrifices in the Temple, designated shrines in the northern kingdom by placing calf idols in two cities in that region. He then instituted religious festivals that were "counterfeits" of those commanded by God. Then in 722 BC the region fell to the Assyrians. The region was then repopulated by people from Assyria who brought their pagan idolatries with them. Intermarriage among the Jews led to a mixed race – called Samaritans – that was despised by full-blooded Jews. And in the first century, the Jews and Samaritans still contended over what they each believed to be the acceptable place of worship – Jerusalem or Mount Gerizim.

In Jesus' day, Jews traveling north from Judea would frequently travel the western route along the Mediterranean Sea or the eastern route on the east side of the Jordan River to avoid traveling through Samaria. Though the journey would be longer, a Jew would consider this to be a small price to pay to avoid being "defiled" by the dust of Samaria. But Jesus would not be detoured by the prejudices and the hatred of the day. *"He had to go through Samaria"* because the Father would have Him go through Samaria. Later in this same chapter Jesus told His disciples, *"My food is to do the will of Him who sent Me, and to finish His work"* (John 4:34 NKJ). None of Jesus' journeys were by chance or of His own design; all of His journeys were by the Father's design. Thus Jesus HAD to go through Samaria. (Quick side road: If we would journey with the Master, we too must understand that our journey is designed by the Father. Nothing in the journey is by chance or by our own design. We are compelled by the cross of our Master to obey the direction of our Father!) On this particular day it was the Father's will that Jesus journey to Samaria, and in His sovereignty, it was the Father's will that the woman journey to the well. And it was a blessed day for the people of Samaria that they both obeyed.

What is the Samaria that the Father has put before you in your journey? It may be across the world. It may be across the street. Samaria is that place or those persons or that person that you have avoided due to resentment, bigotry, pride or prejudice. Hear me; the Lord would have you go through Samaria on your journey.

. . .

Let us look at the woman that Jesus encountered at the well as He obeyed the Father. She had come with an empty bucket. She came because she needed water and she didn't have any. The Father used her physical need to bring her to the well. But He also used her emotional need to direct the timing of her journey to the well. As we read the account, it is easy to see that her life was hard. She had been married five times, probably divorced, and was now living with a man who was not her husband. Though she was seeking love and fulfillment, she hadn't found it and she felt like her life was a downward spiral. She was an outcast in her own village; possibly she felt as if she didn't have a friend in the world. Look at when she came to the well – she came at the sixth hour – midday. The busy time at the well had been first thing in the morning, when everyone collected the water they would need for the day. But not this woman, she came when the others would probably not be there. And look where she came. Archaeologists tell us that her village – Sychar – had its own well right there in the village. But she had come to the well outside of the village. She wanted to avoid running into anyone. She was tired of their hurting remarks and their judgmental looks. She came to the well wounded that day – cut to the heart by the rejection she had experienced throughout her life. She came to the well living a life of quiet desperation – shutting out the world around her on the outside and raging on the inside. And though she came to the well with an empty bucket, she came full of questions. She knew the religious teachings of her day, but she knew in her heart that there had to be more. There had to be an answer to the pain that she felt.

As she approached the well, she saw the Man. He was a stranger here. She had never seen Him before. On closer inspection she realized He was a Galilean. "O great, not only someone to have to encounter at the well, but a Galilean Jew no less!" In addition to everything else in her life, she expected this Galilean to deride her just for being a Samaritan. Galilean and Judean Jews made no secret of their contempt for Samaritans (and vice versa, though she probably wouldn't have admitted that!). And then He did something that astounded her – He spoke to her – but without ridicule or derision. As a matter of fact, He asked her for a favor – a drink from the well. And His speech and His demeanor did not reflect arrogance and contempt, they evidenced humility and compassion. He spoke to her in a way that no one had ever spoken to her before. Perhaps this was a "religious" man. She had encountered Rabbis and Pharisees before, and they had been just as cruel and self-centered as the rest. But from the onset, she could sense that this Man was different. Though He was well-meaning – offering to give her water, what He called "living water" – He obviously didn't have the means to deliver what He was offering – He had no means to draw from the well. (Another side road: How often do we also allow our senses to limit our understanding of the means and the power of the Living God? We look at His hands and not seeing what we might expect, we assume that He is unable or unwilling to meet our need.)

But then, her eyes were opened, and she saw the Master for Who He was. Here was One Who could look in her eyes and see her heart; here was a Man Who knew all about her. Here was a Man that wanted to give her life – not this miserable existence that the world called life – but a life of integrity, a life of purpose – abundant life. She saw and heard the Father and His love revealed through this One – this Stranger, this Rabbi – The Messiah. (One last side road: Do the people we encounter see a stranger, an enemy or a "religious" person? Or do they see Jesus in us? If so, they will be drawn to Him and the Living Water that He has to offer.)

Look at the exchange that occurred at the well that day. The Samaritan woman came with an empty bucket, but left with the spring of Living Water. She came rejected by most, but left accepted by God Himself. She came wounded, but left having been made whole. She came living a life of quiet desperation, but left overflowing with hope. She came full of questions, but left as a source of answers – now knowing The Answer.

Now don't misunderstand, when she left the well that day people probably still treated her rudely. She was still poor. The circumstances of her life were still hard. But now a love relationship with God gave meaning to her life. She knew He loved her, and by His grace she was His child. Nothing and no one could take that away. And she was so full of joy that she forgot about her waterpot and ran into the village to tell others about the Master at the well. And we read that many others believed because she told. The faithfulness of this woman in telling her testimony may very well have been the spark that God used to later ignite the fires of spiritual awakening in Samaria (Acts 8:5-7).

i don't know what brought you to journey to the well today, but i do know Who brought you. He wants to fill your bucket to overflowing. Don't leave the well with that same old empty bucket, or filled only with those things that won't last. The Father brought you here to encounter the

Master, and He brought the Master that He might encounter you. Allow the Master to fill you up, to make you whole and give you hope for the journey. And as you journey with the Master to the next well, allow Him to enable you to point the one that you meet there to Him. Who knows – God could use you to ignite the fires of revival in that Samaria!

* * *

11

A JOURNEY BACK HOME

When [Jesus] came to the village of Nazareth, His boyhood home, He went as usual to the synagogue on the Sabbath and stood up to read the Scriptures. The scroll containing the messages of Isaiah the prophet was handed to Him, and He unrolled the scroll to the place where it says: "The Spirit of the Lord is upon Me, for He has appointed Me to preach Good News to the poor. He has sent Me to proclaim that captives will be released, that the blind will see, that the downtrodden will be freed from their oppressors, and that the time of the Lord's favor has come." He rolled up the scroll, handed it back to the attendant, and sat down. Everyone in the synagogue stared at Him intently. Then He said, "This Scripture has come true today before your very eyes!" ...Jumping up, they mobbed Him and took Him to the edge of the hill on which the city was built. They intended to push Him over the cliff, but He slipped away through the crowd and left them.

Luke 4:16-21, 29-30

* * *

Only Dr. Luke records this account of Jesus' journey back to His hometown. By this time, Jesus' notoriety had spread regarding the healings and miracles He had performed. He came home to praise and honor from his neighbors who fully expected Him to perform His miracles for their benefit as well. Not unlike Nicodemus, they could not deny His divine mission, but they had no interest in His "claim" of a divine nature. Unfortunately, their response to Jesus was unlike that of Nicodemus. The picture of His return to His hometown is very similar to His return to Jerusalem three years later – the people gathering to shout His praises on Palm Sunday and yet shouting to crucify Him on Friday. This hometown crowd was also just that fickle.

(Let's start off with a side road: It is worthy of note that Jesus went as usual to the synagogue on the Sabbath. Again, remember that Jesus came so that we might know how to live. If I had a dollar for everyone who has ever told me that they don't need to go to church on Sunday to have a relationship with God, I would be a very wealthy man. And that statement is partially true – we don't have a relationship with God because we go to church; but the fact is, we go to church because we have a relationship with God and He desires that we gather corporately with His people to worship Him. Jesus, who knew far better than anyone the corruptness of the religious system of that day and had absolutely no need to receive any instruction from any of its teachers, faithfully went to synagogue every Sabbath to honor and worship the Father. How much more of a reason do we need?)

Jesus taught in many synagogues, but it is only recorded that He "read" the Scripture in one – this synagogue in Nazareth. It was His "home church" – the place He had been a "member" since His youth. Every Sabbath the tradition was that the Priest, a Levite and five other members would read from the Scripture. Jesus did on that day what He had done on many previous occasions, He served as one of the five. Though Scripture is silent on how He spent most of the days of His first thirty years, one thing is certain – on the Sabbath He was in synagogue, and at numerous times, He was one of the men reading from the Scriptures. Like all of those previous occasions, He read one of the passages selected by the priest. And He stood in honor of the reading of God's Word, as He was taught and as was appropriate.

As Jesus read from the prophet Isaiah (Isaiah 61:1-2), the people knew that this passage was referring to the Messiah. Many times they had read it, and many times they had prayed for its advent and the coming of God's promised Messiah. After Jesus read the passage, He sat down and began to teach, as was also the custom. We don't have the full discourse of His teaching, but through His words He made it very clear to everyone gathered as they listened and watched intently, that He was the One of whom Isaiah had written. And at first the people were attentive and affirming, even amazed at the clarity of His words and His teaching. But wait a minute – "Jesus just said that He is the Messiah! This is Jesus; He's one of us. We've known Him since He was a child. This is Joseph's son; the son of a poor carpenter. He can't be the Messiah; the Messiah is a King. And the little house that He grew up in is DEFINITELY not a palace! There is no question that God has given Him the power to perform miracles. The stories are too widespread and too well known to refute. Jesus has healed many people. And now that He has come back home we will experience some of those same miracles ourselves. If He healed people in Judea and even Samaria, can you just imagine what He is going to do right here in His hometown! But let's not take this to the extreme! The Messiah? Jesus hasn't even attended rabbinical school. He has no credentials. He was a good boy and a fair man, and there is no question that He is a captivating speaker and teacher – but the Messiah? From Nazareth?"

But Jesus knew what they were thinking and how they would respond. *"No prophet is accepted in his own hometown."* Those who have known your extraction and your education are reluctant to receive your edification. Those who have known you in the rank of "private" are unwilling to honor you as a prophet. It is said that "familiarity breeds contempt". I'm not sure if that is true, but our tendency is to receive the council of those we don't know over the council of those we do know, especially if they qualify as an "expert" – which means they come from at least one hundred miles away.

Jesus also knew that He would not perform miracles in Nazareth. The works of healing were a physical manifestation of the person's faith in Who Jesus was; those that could not believe Him to be the Messiah could not be healed. As He taught, He gave examples of Elijah and Elisha and the ministry God had called them to among the Gentiles and even the enemies of the Jews. He was telling them that they, His own people, were apt to miss a great blessing because of their refusal to accept Him for who He was. And though Jesus had come to bring salvation to the Jew and through them to the world, He knew that His own would refuse Him the most.

His statements regarding God's favor to the Gentiles through Elijah and Elisha provoked those gathered. Jesus was comparing Himself to these great prophets and was comparing them to the evil men of that corrupt age – those that had worshipped Baal. The idea that the God of Israel desired a relationship with anyone, other than themselves as Jews, infuriated them.

• • •

Jesus had come to His own and His own received Him not (John 1:11).

They rebuked Him,
they rose up against Him,
they rejected Him, and
they rebelled against Him with fury and frenzy.

He would have gathered them to Himself, but instead their rejection and rebellion caused Him to pass through them and pass from them.

So what are the lessons we can learn from walking back home with the Master? First, our Lord has given us the mission to carry the Good News to the entire world, beginning in our hometown and extending to the uttermost parts of the earth. As we carry that message, we must understand that there will be those who reject our Master; they did it then, they will do it now. We, too, may not be received, even in our hometown, but we cannot let that distract us from the mission that our Master has given us. Second, imagine the Master's heartbreak. Those He knew the best, rejected Him the most. Those He desired to bless the greatest, turned from Him with the greatest fury. Do not allow "familiarity" with your Lord to cause you to miss out on what He wants to do in your life. Sometimes, because we've heard so much about Jesus – at church, at home or elsewhere – we relate to Him as a story and not as a Person. In so doing, out of familiarity, we off-handedly reject Him for Who He is and miss the reality of what He desires for our lives. Take a journey back home with the Master, but allow the journey to turn you back to Him, not away from Him.

After all:

The Spirit of the Lord is upon Him,
for He has appointed Him to preach Good News to the poor.
He has sent Him to proclaim that captives will be released,
that the blind will see and the downtrodden will be freed…,
and the time of the Lord's favor has come.

We are those captives. We are the poor, the blind and the downtrodden. The Master has journeyed back home to tell us that the time of His favor has come!

* * *

12

FISHERS OF MEN

And as He walked by the Sea of Galilee, He saw Simon and Andrew his brother casting a net into the sea; for they were fishermen. Then Jesus said to them, "Follow Me, and I will make you become fishers of men." They immediately left their nets and followed Him.
Mark 1:16-18 (NKJ)

* * *

Growing up in South Florida, you would think that i would have learned to be a fisherman – but alas, that wasn't to be. So when my son, at the age of three, became infatuated with the idea of fishing, i had no experience from which to draw. One day, he saw an advertisement on television for fluorescent-colored fishing lures that were "guaranteed" to attract fish – and plenty of them! As his birthday approached, this was the "only gift" he wanted. i will never forget the look of delight in his eyes as he unwrapped that gift and announced with excitement, "let's go fishing!" He knew that he was about to have the greatest fishing experience of his life.

With fishing gear in hand and those brand new fishing lures guaranteed to attract fish, off we headed to the intracoastal waterway. We hadn't been fishing along the seawall very long when Justin's pole arced, and his line started to rapidly run out – he had a fish on his line – and it was a whopper! His eyes widened like saucers as he saw the biggest "fish" he had ever seen swimming away with the lure in his mouth. Unfortunately, the thrill was short-lived as what turned out to be a manatee made short work of snapping that ten-pound test line and continued to swim away. Justin didn't catch any fish that day, but boy, did he ever have a story to tell about the one that got away!

The day Jesus was walking by the Sea of Galilee wasn't His first encounter with Simon and Andrew. Andrew had been with John the Baptist in Bethany the day that Jesus returned from His forty days in the wilderness. Andrew had heard John declare Jesus to be the Lamb of God. And Andrew had immediately gone to find his brother, Simon, so that he too could meet Jesus. They had accompanied Jesus to the wedding feast in Cana when He transformed the water into wine. And we read that they "believed in Him". But sometime soon thereafter they had returned to their fishing boat to be about their day-to-day lives.

The first time these men had encountered Jesus, He had said, "Come and you will see." This time Jesus was saying, "Follow Me." His invitation to them was progressive. His first invitation had been for them to observe; this invitation was to abandon – to abandon their work – their very livelihood – and follow Him. He never told them where He was going. He was telling them to abandon all that they knew and all that they did. He was telling them to leave their responsibilities to the family business. He was telling them to be away from their families for an extended period of time. He was telling them to do things that would not only cost them personally, but would cost their family as well. He was telling them to step out by faith and trust Him completely – for their livelihood, for their families and for their very lives.

Over the years, the Lord has given me many opportunities to invite many people to join me on a short-term overseas mission experience. There are always many details surrounding those trips, and most of the people i have invited have had <u>many</u> questions about what all is involved – from where we are going, to how we will get there, to what we will wear, what we will say, what we will eat and where we will sleep – to just name a few. And it has always been interesting to watch how the answers – and the subsequent experiences – have moved the individuals out of their respective comfort zones. i can honestly say that i have never had anyone join me on a trip and not ask any questions. But look at Simon and Andrew – they didn't ask Him any questions – they just stepped out in abandon and followed Jesus.

. . .

Jesus told them that He would make them become "fishers of men". Jesus didn't invent that term; it was actually a common description used by philosophers of the day who "captured men's minds" through their persuasive teaching. They would "bait the hook" with their captivating words and "catch" disciples. Perhaps, Simon and Andrew had that concept in mind when they heard Jesus utter those words.

But, of course, Jesus was using a term these professional fishermen would understand. They were part of a successful fishing enterprise. They knew all the right things to do, and the right order in which to do them that would result in the greatest harvest of fish. They knew how and where to cast their nets that would yield the greatest result. So perhaps when Jesus told them He would make them fishers of men their minds immediately went to techniques He was going to show them. In our modern day vernacular – perhaps He had a new evangelism method or the latest discipleship study.

But the reality was that Jesus' plan did not involve the learning of persuasive words or new techniques. If Jesus had wanted scholars of the faith, He would have established a school. If He had wanted soldiers, He would have set up a code of conduct. If He had merely wanted practitioners of the faith, He would have simply established standards. But Jesus was seeking men and women with hearts surrendered to follow Him – wherever and however He leads. So His invitation was simple – "Follow Me!" But the response required total surrender. And the promise that He would make them "fishers of men" was that they would become His followers who would lead others to follow Him, who would lead others to follow Him. Unlike a harvest of fish in the net, it would be a harvest of followers that would multiply exponentially to become a multitude from every language, people, tribe and nation following Christ to the glory of the Father. Now that's some promise that Jesus made to them!

And get this, they didn't stop to think about what He said. They didn't even stop to ask Zebedee if it was alright if they left their nets and boat behind – they IMMEDIATELY followed Him! The passage says that they had just cast their net into the sea; it doesn't tell us that they even took the time to draw in the net! We will talk more about Simon Peter in a couple of chapters – but my personal prayer is that i will respond to whatever Jesus tells me to do in the way that Peter did (and in this case, Andrew did). Peter rarely hesitated – he was always jumping out of the boat –

either to walk on water or wade to the shore – he acted immediately to follow Jesus!

As we walk with the Master, He will make us fishers of men (and women and children) if we will but follow Him as wholeheartedly and unreservedly as Simon and Andrew did on that day – and the days that would follow.

* * *

13

WHAT HAPPENS WHEN THE WATER IS GONE?

Afterward Jesus returned to Jerusalem for one of the Jewish holy days. Inside the city, near the Sheep Gate, was the pool of Bethesda, with five covered porches. Crowds of sick people—blind, lame, or paralyzed—lay on the porches. One of the men lying there had been sick for thirty-eight years. When Jesus saw him and knew he had been ill for a long time, He asked him, "Would you like to get well?"
"I can't, Sir," the sick man said, "for I have no one to put me into the pool when the water bubbles up. Someone else always gets there ahead of me."
Jesus told him, "Stand up, pick up your mat, and walk!"
Instantly, the man was healed! He rolled up his sleeping mat and began walking!
John 5:1-9

* * *

In the 8th century BC, as the Assyrians were approaching to capture Jerusalem, King Hezekiah commissioned that a dam be built across the Beth Zeta valley, turning it into a reservoir for rain water. A channel cut in the rock was used to bring water from the reservoir into the city of Jerusalem. In the 2nd century BC, a second reservoir (or pool) was added and the channel was enclosed. In the 1st century BC, natural caves to the east of the reservoirs were turned into small baths and cisterns. Under Roman rule, the city walls were extended to include the pools, and five porticos were added to surround this labyrinth of pools and baths. The Romans also brought their pagan beliefs with them and likely incorporated them around parts of the Pool of Bethesda. Many historians believe this site was an "*asclepieion*" (a healing place) where a temple to the god Asclepius was located. Considered the god of healing, Asclepius carried a serpent entwined on a staff (the symbol of medicine today). This god was also worshipped as *"soter"* or savior. It is likely the Roman soldiers who were quartered in the Fortress Antonio carried on their pagan rituals alongside the infirm Hebrews at these healing pools.

At some point the legend grew that from time to time, an angel would visit the pool and stir the waters – giving the waters healing powers. The first person to then enter the pool once the waters had been stirred would be healed. As you can imagine, the blind, the lame and the paralyzed from all over either came or were brought by family or friends so that they might experience the mercy of this miraculous healing. The place came to be called "Bethesda", meaning *"house of mercy"* or *"house of grace"*.

One day Jesus, entering Jerusalem through the Sheep Gate, came to this place filled with a crowd of the sick and infirm. And one man in that crowd would be changed for eternity – not because of a stirring of the waters, rather because of a stirring of his heart through a personal encounter with Jesus.

As a result of a 19th century archaeological dig, the pools and cisterns which had long been hidden from view were unearthed and identified. Today, though the broken down remnants of the pools and the porches are again visible, the cisterns have all dried up. This "house of mercy (or grace)" no longer draws the crowds of the blind, lame or paralyzed to wait beside its waters. The hope of the healing power of the bubbling water has faded – the water is gone. The reservoir that once was the source of the pool has dried up. The crowds – still seeking a cure – are now gathered at some other modern day source of hope – whose healing powers are truly no greater than the waters that once filled this pool. How willing we are to seek and trust in sources that at their best can only provide temporary relief – and in most instances provide none!

But the same question to those who are broken and hurting remains – as relevant today as it was when Jesus first asked it – "would you like to get well?"

The man had not come to the pool that day expecting to encounter Jesus. He was hopeless. He had been sick for thirty-eight years. Even though he was at this place of hope – this house of mercy -- he was fretful that even that hope was beyond his grasp because he had no one to put him "into the pool when the water bubbles up". He had never heard of Jesus. He didn't even know His name. His response to Jesus wasn't one of faith or understanding. In his hopelessness, the man didn't even know what to ask --- BUT – Jesus KNEW what to answer! His compassion fails not! Jesus responded to his hopelessness. And when Jesus spoke to him, and the man obeyed, he was immediately healed.

He learned an important truth that day – his source of hope was never in a temporal place – it was never in the water. It was never in a person coming to his aid. It was never in a possession that he could ever have. His hope could only be found – only be realized – in the Person of Jesus Christ.

Before his encounter, this man didn't know to look to Jesus. How many of us who do know Jesus are seeking a cure by going to a place that will provide a change of scenery or momentary relief? As i write this, LaVonne and i are here in Jerusalem for a time of spiritual renewal. Yesterday we visited the site of the pools. Am i seeking to be refreshed by this unique place, or through a personal encounter with the Master, as i spend time with Him? Our surroundings will constantly change. Even the very places themselves will change over time. People will fail us – even unintentionally. Possessions will never satisfy – the polish will quickly disappear. The water will eventually dry up. But the Person of grace and mercy will remain – fresh and new and relevant each and every day.

But, gratefully the story doesn't stop with his miraculous physical healing. Though we read that Jesus immediately withdrew from the crowd, He soon thereafter sought out the man. Because Jesus' compassion and purpose went well beyond his crippled body – His concern was for "something even worse" – the consequence of NOT believing and NOT following Jesus. Let's not lose sight, that Jesus' mission was to seek and save those that are lost. As a matter of fact, Jesus was surrounded by "crowds of sick people", and yet He only healed one man that day. He had knowledge of all, compassion for all, and power over all – and yet He healed only one. He could have stayed there healing the masses, but He didn't. Because He never lost sight that His mission was – and is – to be about the Father's business – seeking and saving those that are lost. His mission was not focused on physical healing, but rather spiritual healing. That's an important reminder for us. Is our primary prayer focus on physical healing (keeping folks out of heaven) – or is our prayer focus on the salvation of the lost (discipling them into heaven)? Our prayer lists say a lot.

So, here's the question as we walk with the Master – "would you like to get well?" Are you stuck in a place waiting for a miracle – or are you looking to the "Miracle Worker"? Whatever it is that is going on in your life, you can trust Him. "Stand up, pick up your mat, and walk" – with the One who is inviting you to follow Him. He is the One who extends true mercy and grace. He is the One and only true Source of hope! Roll up your sleeping mat and begin walking… with Him.

* * *

14

ALL OR NOTHING

At daybreak He called together all of His disciples and chose twelve of them to be apostles.
Here are their names:
Simon (He also called him Peter), Andrew (Peter's brother), James, John, Philip, Bartholomew, Matthew, Thomas, James (son of Alphaeus), Simon (the Zealot), Judas (son of James), Judas Iscariot (who later betrayed Him).
Luke 6:13-16

* * *

Three of the Gospel accounts indicate that Simon Peter was the first disciple to be chosen by Jesus and his name heads every list of the Twelve in the New Testament. He was first to be named an apostle by Jesus, he was first to confess Jesus as the Messiah, and he was the first man (and thus far the only as far as we know) to walk on water. He was the recognized leader of the disciples and frequently served as their spokesman.

But prior to any of that, Simon was a Galilean fisherman. He and his wife lived in the town of Capernaum on the north shore of the Sea of Galilee. He had grown up there. He and his younger brother, Andrew, were partnered with a man by the name of Zebedee, together with his two sons, James and John, in a successful fishing enterprise; an enterprise that had been passed on to Simon, as the eldest son, by his father, John. Simon probably came from a long line of fishermen. He had that tanned and ruddy appearance that comes from spending each day under the hot sun. Years of repeated casting and drawing of fishing nets had enabled him to develop a strong muscular frame. Simon was a man's man who worked hard to earn a living and to care for his family. Like the others in his family, he traveled to Jerusalem at least one time each year – to celebrate the Passover. But other than that, he spent his days on the sea gathering fish and on the shore attending the tools of his trade - cleaning, mending and preparing his nets and maintaining his boat. He knew the bounty of a plentiful harvest, but he also knew the disappointment of a day's labor with nothing to show for it. Simon's life was "normal", predictable and relatively uneventful – **until that day** – the day he met Jesus!

Andrew came running to Simon insisting that Simon come with him to meet a man; but not just any man – a man who Andrew purported to be the Messiah. I'm not sure whether Simon believed Andrew at first, but nonetheless he went with Andrew to meet Jesus. And as they came to Jesus, Andrew said, *"Master, this is my brother Simon."* Scripture records that Jesus *"looked intently at Simon"* (John 1:42). Imagine that look! Jesus looked at Simon as One who knew him – and knew him better than Simon knew himself. He looked at Simon as if He had always known him – because He had. And He knew not only Simon's life of days past, He knew what lay ahead. As Jesus looked at Simon, He saw Simon's faithfulness as well as Simon's faithlessness; Jesus saw his moral victories, as well as his moral failures. And Jesus saw a "rock" – not the "rock" that he was, but the "rock" he would become by God's grace – and Jesus called him "Peter" – the rock. Peter would be the leader of that elite group of intimates called the apostles. He would walk, sleep and eat with the Master. Jesus would literally pour his life into Peter and these men for over three years, and then He would send them forth.

In order to walk with Jesus, Peter had to leave much behind. He left his family; and having walked away from his livelihood, he left his wife without a visible source of financial provision. He gave up the comforts of his home along the seaside and exchanged it for the hardships of the Judean and Galilean wilderness. Many nights a rock was his pillow and the stars were his blanket. All to walk with the Master. All to sit under His teaching. All to know the Messiah.

That's how Peter was; he didn't do anything halfway – it was all or nothing. Months later, walking toward Jesus on the water didn't require Peter to daintily dangle his legs; it required him to jump out of the boat wholeheartedly. That night in the upper room when Jesus wanted to wash his feet and Jesus told him that otherwise he could *"have no part with Me"* (John 13:8 NASB), Peter immediately responded, *"Not my feet only, but also my hands and my head"* (John 13:9 NASB). Peter never followed Jesus partially; he was prepared to follow Him all the way.

And that is how it started. One day soon after Andrew had taken Peter to meet Jesus that first time, Jesus walked to the water's edge of the Sea of Galilee and saw Peter and Andrew casting a net into the sea and said to them *"Follow Me, and I will make you fishers of men"* (Matthew 4:19 NASB). And Scripture records that they *"**immediately** left their nets and followed Him"* (Matthew 4:20 NASB). Peter didn't hesitate; he didn't look back. He didn't even pause to think about it. As a matter of fact this fisherman who earned his living with his nets, left his net in the sea right where he had cast it. Peter **immediately** followed Jesus.

There are many lessons we can learn from Peter, but the first is **immediate** obedience. There is no such thing as "delayed obedience"; as Dr. Henry Blackaby writes *"delayed obedience is disobedience"*. Jesus Himself taught that *"anyone who puts a hand to the plow and then looks back is not fit for the Kingdom of God"* (Luke 9:62). When Jesus calls us to follow Him, there can be no looking back, there can be no gathering in of the nets and there can be no delay. Peter didn't want to miss a moment of following Jesus. He didn't want to miss a moment of being in the presence of Jesus. He didn't want to miss a moment of hearing from Jesus. Peter never asked Jesus where they were going. He was content to follow Him wherever He went – as a matter of fact he was more than content, he was exuberant about following him wherever He went!

The Master has invited you to walk with Him – to follow Him. Learn this lesson from Peter – follow the Master without hesitation – follow Him immediately; follow the Master without restriction – follow Him whole-heartedly; and follow the Master without reservation – follow Him exuberantly. It's all or nothing!

* * *

15

IN THE SHADOW OF PETER

At daybreak He called together all of His disciples and chose twelve of them to be apostles.
Here are their names:
Simon (He also called him Peter), Andrew (Peter's brother), James, John, Philip, Bartholomew, Matthew, Thomas, James (son of Alphaeus), Simon (the Zealot), Judas (son of James), Judas Iscariot (who later betrayed Him).
Luke 6:13-16

* * *

Simon and Andrew were brothers. Andrew was the younger of the two. Together, they had grown up in Bethsaida on the northwest coast of the Sea of Galilee. John, their father, had raised both of his sons to honor their God as whole-hearted worshipers, to provide for their families as industrious fishermen, and to love those around them as selfless servants. Andrew had lived his life in the shadow of his big brother Simon. He was often referred to as Andrew, the brother of Simon. But that fact never bothered Andrew. He loved, respected and looked up to his brother.

One day Andrew heard of a man teaching a message of repentance in the wilderness of Judea. After obtaining his brother's permission to leave his responsibilities in the family fishing business, he embarked on a pilgrimage to Bethany, beyond Jordan, where John was baptizing. Andrew hungered to know more of God and to hear first hand this message of the Kingdom of God. Perhaps he was even sent as an emissary for the family to glean the truth of this message. Having once heard John, his heart resonated with the truth of God being declared through him and he became a disciple of this "voice crying in the wilderness."

He and John (the son of Zebedee) were standing with John (the Baptist) when the wilderness preacher looked upon Jesus and declared Him to be the Lamb of God. Immediately, with the full blessing of John the Baptist, Andrew and John turned to follow Jesus. As they did, Jesus asked them, "What do you want?" Their simple reply was, "Teacher, where are you staying?" From that moment on their lives would never be the same. Jesus invited them to "Come and see" and for the rest of that day they remained with Him. Scripture does not record all that they saw or all that they heard Jesus say that day. But by day's end, Andrew and John knew firsthand that Jesus was the Messiah – the Chosen One of God!

At this moment, in light of what Andrew does next, we are shown three important truths about his character. First, he was a man of integrity. He had been sent with his brother's blessing to glean the truth. And now having discovered The Truth, in the form of Jesus, his first action – without delay – was to honor his commitment and carry that report back to his brother and family. He could have selfishly chosen to stay right where he was – there at the feet of Jesus. How many of us would have been tempted to do just that? But that wasn't an option for Andrew; he had given his brother a promise.

Second, he loved his brother. He was under the care and authority of his older brother. Simon apparently did not lord that authority over him, rather he selflessly and affectionately desired the best for Andrew. And Andrew reciprocated that affection by demonstrating that his first priority was to bring Simon to meet Jesus. What greater expression of love can there be than introducing those we love to Jesus?

Third, he did not have a personal agenda – he was Kingdom-focused. That characteristic is not only evidenced in his action to immediately find his brother and bring him to Jesus, it is evidenced wherever we see him mentioned in the Gospels.

Before we look at those examples, let's look at where he is not mentioned.

His brother, Simon Peter, and his other two fishing partners, James and John, are the three apostles that had the most intimate relationship with Jesus throughout His earthly ministry. But Jesus chose not to include Andrew in that group, perhaps because He had a different assignment for him (even though he and John had been the first two apostles to follow Jesus). The Master, in fact, saw within Andrew not only a desire for a deeper knowledge of God, but also a missionary spirit to bring others to Him.

After bringing his brother to Jesus, Andrew had accompanied the Master to Galilee. He had witnessed the miracle at the wedding feast (John 2:2). Also, more than likely, he was traveling with Jesus when they encountered the Samaritan woman at the well (John 4:8). And Andrew would have learned an important life lesson through both of those experiences. First, that Jesus could do the "impossible" – He had turned water into wine! There was no limitation on what Jesus could do. Second, on that day in Samaria, Andrew would have been with the other disciples that went into the village to buy food. As they walked along the path from the well to the village, they would have passed a woman who was traveling in the other direction toward the well. There wouldn't have been many traveling the path toward the well at that time of day, so she would have stood out. But since they were a group of Jewish men, they ignored that Samaritan woman. Imagine Andrew's surprise when the group returned to the well and he watched Jesus speaking with that very woman! i don't believe that the lesson of that day was lost on Andrew. Jesus had come to seek and to save all people – no one was to be ignored, cast aside or walked by. From that moment on, Andrew was watchful for those who were on the path toward an encounter with Jesus.

So, on the day that the apostles were trying to figure out how to feed the large crowd that had gathered to hear Jesus, it was Andrew that introduced the young boy with five barley loaves and two fish to Jesus (John 6:8-9). Though he had no idea what difference that modest lunch could make, he knew that he could not ignore the lad – and he knew that he had seen Jesus do much more… with much less!

Several years later, toward the end of Jesus' earthly ministry, there was a group of Greeks who had come to Jerusalem for the Passover celebration (John 12:20-22). The original text indicates that they "were accustomed to come and worship at the feast." They were not curious visitors or casual observers. These men were truth seekers, and "kept asking" the apostle

Philip for an interview with Jesus. They weren't seeking signs like the Jews; they were seeking truth. It's interesting that Philip didn't immediately take them to Jesus, rather he told Andrew about them. i believe that by then Andrew had become recognized by the other apostles as the one who was continually introducing others to Jesus. There is also a good possibility that even Philip himself had first been introduced to Jesus by Andrew (John 1:44). So, whether it was due to that firsthand experience, or do to what Philip had seen modeled, it apparently felt very appropriate to enlist Andrew's help in bringing them to Jesus.

You see, the apostle that grew up in the shadow of his older brother, Simon Peter, now was casting quite a shadow himself – a shadow that led others to Jesus. A shadow that was never about him – but was all about Jesus. As we walk with the Master, i pray that each one of us will cast a shadow that points those around us to Jesus!

* * *

16

A FAMILY AFFAIR

At daybreak He called together all of His disciples and chose twelve of them to be apostles.
Here are their names:
Simon (He also called him Peter), Andrew (Peter's brother), James, John, Philip, Bartholomew, Matthew, Thomas, James (son of Alphaeus), Simon (the Zealot), Judas (son of James), Judas Iscariot (who later betrayed Him).
Luke 6:13-16

* * *

My paternal great-great-grandfather died soon after his 49th birthday. His widow was left to raise their seven children who were still living at home, ranging in ages from 3 to 17 years. My great-grandfather, John Calvin Winter, at age 13, together with his elder 17-year-old brother, assumed much of the responsibility in caring for the family farm in Central Pennsylvania and otherwise assisting their mother in the support of the family. In 1906 a local historian wrote of John Calvin, *"it was through this that he developed those traits of persistency and industry which afforded him an equipment for his subsequent useful and successful career."* As the years went by, he formed a *"general contracting and building business"* that achieved considerable success and, to quote the historian, *"the fruits of his labors are visible in the many ornamental edifices, business and residential, which adorn the city, and have given it the modern air which attracts the gratified attention of the visitor."* (i love the style of writing in the early 20th century!) His sons joined him in the enterprise, as did his grandsons (which included my father). It was a family affair, that not only enjoyed commercial success, but also was *"among the foremost in the advancement of every worthy enterprise"* – including higher education and the furtherance of the gospel message.

Such was the pedigree of the apostle James, the elder brother of the apostle John. James grew up along the Sea of Galilee, probably in the town of Capernaum. His father, Zebedee, led a successful fishing enterprise which included both of his sons, as well as hired men. James and John were not the only members of Zebedee's family that chose to follow Jesus that day. We read in Matthew 27:56, Mark 15:40 and John 19:25, that their mother (Zebedee's wife) – Salome – also was among those who traveled with Christ – following Him even to the cross. Salome was probably one of the women mentioned in Luke 8:3 *"who were contributing from their own resources to support Jesus and His disciples."* And those resources, more than likely, came from Zebedee's fishing enterprise.

The family apparently not only had financial means, but they were also a family of influence that even extended to Jerusalem. The fact that the apostle John was permitted access into the home of Caiaphas the high priest (John 18:15-16) is indicative of the position that the family enjoyed among Jewish society.

James walked intimately with Jesus. He, together with his brother John and Simon Peter, were the three apostles that Christ often drew aside to join Him up close and personal. It was those three that He permitted to enter into the home when He raised the daughter of Jairus from the dead (Mark 5:37-42). On the Mount of Transfiguration, only they were invited to witness His conversation with Moses and Elijah (Matthew 17:1-7). And it was these three that Jesus chose to draw nearer with Him in intercession that night at the Garden of Gethsemane (Matthew 26:36-46) before His betrayal and arrest.

The special relationship that James (and John) had with Jesus prompted Salome to ask if her sons might sit in places of honor on the right and left hand sides of Jesus. Little did she know what she was asking, for James would, in fact, be the first apostle to be martyred as a follower of Christ by King Herod Agrippa (Acts 12:1-2).

Even his martyrdom underlines that he walked steadfastly with Jesus. He walked with Him not only when Jesus said "Yes" – "walk with Me to Jairus' home", "join Me on the Mount of Transfiguration", etc.; but perhaps even more importantly, he walked with Jesus when He said "No" – "I will not prevent you from being martyred". James was prepared to follow Jesus no matter where He led and no matter the cost.

James followed Jesus with his whole heart, as did the other members of his family. He followed Him with passion. As a matter of fact, Jesus referred to James and his brother, John, as "*Boanerges*" translated "sons of thunder" (Mark 3:17) in light of their fiery eloquence and quick temper. Perhaps it was His loving rebuke to their impassioned plea to "call down fire from Heaven" to destroy the people of a Samaritan village who had snubbed Jesus (Luke 9:44-45). In this instance they were allowing their fiery passion for Jesus to blind them from the mission of Jesus – a mission that unbeknownst to them would subsequently lead to a spiritual awakening across Samaria soon after Pentecost.

Yes, James experienced a unique relationship with Jesus as an intimate as he responded to the call to follow Him. But it was a family affair. God's call on His life was not only for him personally; it was a call on the entire family – each one ministering in a unique way – each one fulfilling their respective part in the mission of Christ.

And that is a truth we must hold onto today. Just as my great-grandfather was uniquely equipped and gifted for the work for which God created and called him, that work and that calling was not in a vacuum – it involved his entire family. It had implications which led to specific assignments for each of them – and in many respects still does.

How is the Lord leading you to follow Him? It will never be in isolation. It will always be in the broader context of the body of Christ – and will include those who are closest to you. God's call on you will require you to make adjustments – and most likely will require those around you to make adjustments as well. So watch, not only how He is leading you, but also how He is leading those who are close to you. And follow Him **intimately**, follow Him **steadfastly**, and follow Him **wholeheartedly**. The impact will be much further reaching than you can ever imagine – reaching to the generations that follow – even those (if Jesus tarries) you will never know on this side of eternity.

17

A UNIQUE PERSPECTIVE

At daybreak He called together all of His disciples and chose twelve of them to be apostles.
Here are their names:
Simon (He also called him Peter), Andrew (Peter's brother), James, John, Philip, Bartholomew, Matthew, Thomas, James (son of Alphaeus), Simon (the Zealot), Judas (son of James), Judas Iscariot (who later betrayed Him).
Luke 6:13-16

* * *

Each one of the four Gospel accounts have a different perspective on the earthly ministry of Jesus, and thus their presentation of the Gospel message. One Gospel, but four different accounts. Two are written by apostles – Matthew and John; two are written by men who were sharing accounts given to them by others. Matthew is primarily speaking to the Jew, and emphasizes that Jesus came as Messiah, fulfilling the promises of God prophesied in the Old Testament. Mark is primarily speaking to those people in the Roman Empire with little or no understanding of the beliefs of the Jews. Mark speaks to the acts and actions of Jesus as a Servant. Dr. Luke is primarily speaking to those more intellectually minded – primarily Greeks – emphasizing the humanity of Jesus as the Son of Man. John was the last to write his gospel account and it reflects the unique perspective he had as the writer of the account… and as an apostle.

. . .

John outlived the other eleven apostles. He was in his nineties when he died. As a matter-of-fact, excluding Judas Iscariot, he was the only apostle that did not die a violent death as a follower of Jesus. Everything that he recorded in the Gospel of John is a firsthand account. He is truly describing only that which he personally observed and helps us as readers understand that though he is a disciple "whom Jesus loved", he truly did not fully understand who Jesus is – the Son of God – until He had risen from the dead (John 2:22).

But i am getting ahead of myself. John's perspective begins in a way very similar to the apostle Andrew. John was the younger son of Zebedee and the younger brother of James. Zebedee had permitted his younger son to leave his responsibilities in their family fishing business to follow after John the Baptist. John was there when Jesus came to John the Baptist to be baptized (John 1:15). He was there when the Holy Spirit descended like a dove and rested upon Jesus (John 1:32). When John the Baptist told both he and Andrew that Jesus is "the Lamb of God", he also immediately turned to follow Jesus. But unlike Andrew, we do not read that John immediately returned home to tell his brother James and father Zebedee about Jesus. They would have heard about Jesus from their fishing partners, Andrew and Simon Peter; and at some point, John did return home.

John was one of the disciples that accompanied Jesus at the wedding feast in Cana. He followed Jesus to Jerusalem, and observed as Jesus passionately cleansed the Temple (John 2:17). More than likely, due to his family's influential relationship in Jewish society (see chapter 16, *A Family Affair*), Nicodemus called upon John to help arrange his private meeting with Jesus (John 3), at which there were probably only three people in the room – Jesus, Nicodemus and John (thus such a detailed account of the Gospel, even though John truly did not understand it at the time). John would have followed Jesus back into the Judean countryside, and would have been one of His disciples that was baptizing (John 3:22). He was also at Jacob's well, and saw the multitude of Samaritans that came to Jesus as a result of the testimony of the Samaritan woman. And he was back in Cana with Jesus, when He performed His second miraculous sign in Galilee – the healing of the government official's son. Soon thereafter, John returned to his family, working alongside of his father and brother, until the day Jesus called all four (Peter, Andrew, James and John) to follow Him and become fishers of men.

John, together with Peter and James, formed an inner circle that Jesus chose to walk with Him in a more intimate relationship. As a result, he experienced a bird's eye view of Jesus on the Mount of Transfiguration (Matthew 17:1-9) and at the Garden of Gethsemane (Mark 14:33-42). His family's influence enabled him to gain admittance into Jesus' trial in the High Priest's home, and protected him from retribution as he stood as the only apostle there at Calvary, as Christ was being crucified. Jesus entrusted His mother Mary into John's care – which given the fact that she had other sons – speaks volumes about the relationship between John and Jesus. John was the first disciple to see the empty tomb (John 20:2-9), though Peter was the first to enter. And it was at that moment he (and Peter) truly believed (John 20:9 and John 2:20-22).

John was there when Jesus ascended. He was there in the upper room when the Holy Spirit came upon them, and he was one of the first two disciples to be taken into custody after Pentecost. And through it all, he came to know, follow and love the Son of God personally… and intimately.

John wrote his Gospel account through that lens. He does not want the readers of his Gospel to come to the understanding of Who Jesus is as a conclusion from reading through his account. Rather, he has written the first eighteen verses of his Gospel as a prologue so that we might truly know Who Jesus is from the very beginning. The Gospel message is encapsulated in those eighteen verses. He wants us to look at what Jesus did through the lens of Who He is. He wants us to follow Him because of Who He is and not what He will do for us. He wants us to surrender our lives to Him, not out of some self-seeking motivation, but because of Who He is. He wants us to submit our lives to Him, not commit to Him. He wants us to love Him with all of our heart, soul and mind because of Who He is. He wants us to worship Him because He is worthy of worship.

As you walk with the Master, heed this reminder from the disciple who Jesus loved:

He is The One who is the true light, who gives light to everyone.
He came into the very world He created, but the world didn't recognize Him.
He came to His own people, and even they rejected Him.
But to all who believed Him and accepted Him,
He gave the right to become children of God.
From His abundance we have all received one gracious blessing after another.
God's unfailing love and faithfulness came through Jesus Christ.

(John 1:9-12, 16-17)

18

EVEN A TAX COLLECTOR

At daybreak He called together all of His disciples and chose twelve of them to be apostles.
Here are their names:
Simon (He also called him Peter), Andrew (Peter's brother), James, John, Philip, Bartholomew, Matthew, Thomas, James (son of Alphaeus), Simon (the Zealot), Judas (son of James), Judas Iscariot (who later betrayed Him).
Luke 6:13-16

* * *

So far each of the apostles we have looked at – Simon Peter, Andrew, James and John – have been men who were seeking the Messiah. They knew the Scriptures. They knew the prophecies. They were watchful and expectant that the Messiah would one day come – perhaps in their lifetime. They had been greatly influenced by the ministry of John the Baptist. They were influential members of their community. And though they were not religious leaders, they were respected and trusted within their religious community (at least we know that John was). Though they may not have been learned men (Acts 4:13), in many respects they had a great pedigree to be followers of Jesus! Besides – they had great early training to be fishers of men!

But now we come to Matthew, also known as Levi. He was a tax collector. The tax collector's role was to collect duties and customs on imported goods crossing the Sea of Galilee or passing along the Damascus road that ran along the shore between Bethsaida and Capernaum. Everyone knew that tax collectors were notoriously corrupt. They had the reputation of being dishonest and greedy men. They made their living extorting far and above what was due in order to line their own pockets, let alone the coffers of Rome. As such they were protected by Roman soldiers to insure that Rome received its duties. Thus the tax collectors were untouchable.

We first see him in his booth along the lakeshore of Capernaum. Jesus is back in Galilee and has been staying in a house in Capernaum. Quickly news spread that He was there, and the house became so packed that there was no room for anyone else to enter. While Jesus was preaching, four men arrived carrying their paralyzed friend on a mat (Mark 2:1-12). Seeing that they could not enter the house, they dug a hole in the roof above Jesus and lowered their friend (no subtle distraction here). And Jesus, seeing the faith of the friends, says, *"My child, your sins are forgiven."*

As you will recall, the religious teachers "threw a fit", saying, *"How can this Man forgive sins?"* Jesus, knowing their hearts, immediately replied, *"I will prove to you that the Son of Man has the authority on earth to forgive sins."* Turning to the paralyzed man, He said, *"Stand up, pick up your mat and go home!"* And Scripture says that not only did the man get up, he <u>jumped</u> up, grabbed his mat and walked out through that stunned, packed crowd. That group of onlookers were amazed. Even the religious leaders must have been amazed. Imagine the exclamations from the crowd that spread immediately around that village.

On the heels of that moment, Jesus begins to walk along the lakeshore, teaching the crowd as He walks. As He does, He encounters Levi. There is no indication that they had ever met before. But as a resident of Capernaum, Levi most probably had knowledge of the miracles Jesus had performed, including more than likely the one that had just occurred. Jesus looks at him and says, *"follow Me and be My disciple"*. He doesn't say, "Hi. I'm Jesus. Tell me your name. Tell me about yourself. What can I do for you?" Jesus didn't have time for small talk. He was on a mission! And there wasn't anything that Levi could say about himself that Jesus didn't know already. Jesus knew him… just like He knew the woman at the well, and Nicodemus, and the four friends of the paralyzed man… just like He knows you… and me. What did Jesus see in him? Sure, his profession gave him a good understanding of human nature and behavior – and accurate business habits – and a unique understanding of how to make a way to the hearts of many publicans and sinners not otherwise easily reached. He was probably a man of good education. But that is NOT what Jesus saw. He saw the same thing He sees in us – a man… or woman… or child – dead in our sin, separated from our Creator, unable to save ourselves. And at that moment, Jesus extended an invitation to Levi – *"Follow Me and be My disciple."*

To his credit, Levi IMMEDIATELY got up, walked away from everything and followed Jesus. Remember, Levi would have been a wealthy man – albeit from ill-gotten gain. But he knew that there was nothing he had that could ever compare with having a personal relationship with the One who was standing before him at that moment! And Levi became Matthew ("gift of God"). In an instant transformed by the saving power of Jesus – the Messiah – the Son of the Living God. He was radically – and eternally – changed.

Either that night or soon after, Matthew invited Jesus to his home for a banquet held in His honor, attended by many other tax collectors, former companions and friends. Matthew wanted to introduce them to Jesus! He wanted them to experience the same saving grace that he had received. He wasn't about to keep the change in his life a secret. He was like the woman at the well. He wanted to immediately tell everyone he knew about Jesus.

The Pharisees and religious teachers predictably said, "Why do you eat and drink with such scum?" (Luke 5:30) Jesus replied, "Healthy people don't need a doctor – sick people do. I have come to call not those who **think** they are righteous, but those who **know** they are sinners and need to repent." (Luke 5:31)

It's interesting that this account is given almost verbatim in the Gospels of Matthew, Mark and Luke. But only Matthew adds Jesus saying to the religious leaders, *"Now go and learn the meaning of the Scripture: 'I want you to show mercy, not offer sacrifice'"* (Matthew 9:13 quoting Hosea 6:6). You see, the real corrupt tax collectors were the religious leaders – taxing the people with laws and requirements that they could never live up to and would never lead to salvation. And they failed to point the people to the mercy of God and to extend that mercy to a sick and dying world. Matthew understood in a moment what the religious leaders had failed to learn and failed to receive from Jesus.

The questions to us as we journey with the Master are:

1. How have we responded to the Master's invitation? Have we immediately forsaken all else and followed Him?
2. Are we following Matthew's lead and inviting all of our coworkers, companions and friends to meet the One who has transformed our life?
3. Are we walking in a way that reflects and magnifies the mercy of God, or are we merely following religious practice and tradition?

Matthew is listed as being in the upper room In Acts 1 – but we don't see any further reference to him in Scripture after that. Historians indicate that he stayed in Jerusalem another fifteen years after Pentecost before going out as a missionary to the Persians, Parthians and Medes. According to legend, he died a martyr for the gospel in Ethiopia.

But if you remember nothing else about him, remember that on that day when Jesus said, "follow Me," he immediately got to his feet, and left all that he had to follow Jesus. You see, Jesus had a purpose and a plan for even a tax collector. Just as He does for you… and for me.

* * *

19

ALONG FOR THE RIDE, NOT FOR THE JOURNEY

At daybreak He called together all of His disciples and chose twelve of them to be apostles.
Here are their names:
Simon (He also called him Peter), Andrew (Peter's brother), James, John, Philip, Bartholomew, Matthew, Thomas, James (son of Alphaeus), Simon (the Zealot), Judas (son of James), Judas Iscariot (who later betrayed Him).
Luke 6:13-16

* * *

Having looked at the roster of the notables, let's look at the one who is "despicable" – let's look at Judas Iscariot. If you look up the name Judas in the dictionary, you will find *"one who betrays another under the guise of friendship; a deceiver or traitor"*. As a result, the name "Judas" is no longer a popular choice among parents determining the name for their bouncing baby boys. That wasn't always the case. In the first century A.D. it was a name synonymous with honor, and therefore a very popular name (two of the twelve disciples were named Judas). The name was given in recognition of Judas Maccabaeus, one of the great generals in Jewish history. He and his followers defeated the Syrian armies in 165 BC, restored the religious rites and rededicated the Temple in Jerusalem. The Jews, through their observance of Hanukah, celebrate this victory to this day. Simon Iscariot named his son Judas in the hope that he would be a man of honor in the tradition of Judas Maccabaeus.

. . .

Simon made sure that his son attended synagogue and sat under the teachings of the rabbis. Judas knew the Scriptures. He knew the prophecy of the Messiah. He probably was faithful to pray for the coming of the Messiah, so that the people of God – the children of Israel – might be freed from the tyranny of their foreign conquerors. He prayed and waited, believing that the Messiah would come and establish His kingdom and the bonds of tyranny and oppression would be broken once and for all. Judas was zealous in his belief and was dedicated to the cause.

Judas also had a good head for business. We see that demonstrated by the fact that he was chosen by the other disciples to be their treasurer – the keeper of the purse. They would not have made that selection lightly. As we have seen, several were successful fishermen and Matthew was a tax collector; but together they perceived Judas to be the best educated, the most astute and sufficiently trustworthy to handle the group's finances. He continued in that role for almost three years which indicates that the performance of his duty was satisfactory to the rest.

One day, Judas met a man named Jesus. He had heard rumors of healings performed by this man. He heard that Jesus taught as one with authority. And one day Judas heard Jesus in person. He watched in amazement as the blind were made to see and the lame to walk. He followed Jesus at a distance and continued to observe Him in His teaching and His practice. Judas began to ask himself if this was their Messiah – the One for whom they had waited and prayed. And if this was the Messiah, he wanted to be a part of His inner circle. Judas saw an opportunity not only to experience the freedom of the Messiah's reign, he also saw the opportunity to be a part of the Messiah's government. Judas drew closer; and Jesus chose him to become one of the twelve. He sat beside Jesus. Wherever Jesus was, he was there. And he watched. And he waited. His wait would soon be over.

Each day as he traveled with Jesus, he saw more of the oppression being experienced by the people – and he became more zealous for the cause. Each day as he traveled with Jesus, he saw the Master perform great miracles – the feeding of the five thousand, Peter walking on water, the storm stilled, and the miracle of miracles, Lazarus raised from the dead! And he became more convinced of the opportunity for personal gain. He would be a lieutenant to the Messiah – imagine the power and the prestige. He could very easily become the treasurer of the kingdom! He began to see this journey with Jesus as a ticket to ride to all that he could ever desire – freedom for his people, and personal gain for himself. And he was prepared to tolerate the trip to the "pot of gold" that awaited him at the end of the journey – the nights without a roof over his head, the long journeys, and the masses that just came for what they could receive.

But as days became months and months turned into years, Judas began asking himself why Jesus was not making His move. Everywhere they went the masses shouted praises to His Name. His popularity was increasing daily. Now was the time for Jesus to make His move. Why wasn't He? To delay any longer would be counter-productive. Couldn't Jesus see that the time was right? There was no question that Jesus had been sent by God; He was the Messiah! Why wouldn't He take the step to become the rightful ruler of Israel? Maybe Judas would have to help Him take that step. After all, he was the keeper of the purse; He was the one with the best head for business. Maybe Jesus was just waiting for one of His lieutenants to step out and do something. Surely it wasn't going to happen on its own. And we couldn't wait for this rabble of poor to lead the charge. The time had come to make it happen. The people would be free, Jesus would be in power and Judas would be rich. There is no downside to that business proposition. Everybody wins! Yes this "ride" with Jesus would turn out just right. Judas would get just what he wanted. Now all he needed to do was watch for the right time and the right opportunity. Obviously Jesus was being patient; he would be also. After all, Jesus had brought him along for the ride, there was no way Judas could fail.

Then, he saw the moment and the opportunity. The religious leaders had been seeking to trap Jesus for years, but He was just too smart for them. What if someone helped them corner Jesus and bring Him before a public trial? Jesus would be left with no choice but to finally establish His "kingdom" and step into the position for which He had been born. The wait would be over. It was within Judas' grasp. He would help tip the scales. And the thirty pieces of silver – that was just a signing bonus.

But imagine the horror as night turned into day, and he realized things were not going the way he planned. Jesus didn't declare Himself. He didn't marshal the troops to establish His kingdom. Rather, all was lost – Jesus was to be crucified. All that Judas had worked for and waited for wasn't going to happen. And instead of "helping" Jesus, he had betrayed Him. He had become merely a device that the religious leaders – and the enemy – used to accomplish what they thought would be their victory.

The demons of hell were ecstatic – Jesus was about to die – and Judas had become a pawn in their scheme.

How many of us are like Judas? Oh we hear his name and we shudder, but we're just like him. We too have come along side of Jesus for the ride. We're looking around to see what's in it for us. Oh yes, we know that the Messiah will bring victory over our oppression, but then we're looking at the opportunities that victory will create for us – health, wealth, prosperity, position, et al. And somewhere along the line, we miss the Master's purpose for the journey and get sidetracked by our own. At that moment, we just continue to go along for the ride.

Don't miss the lesson from Judas. Don't settle for a ride of selfish ambition that merely seeks what Jesus can do for you. Join Him in His journey. The journey is not about you and it's not about me – it never has been. The journey is about the Master – His plan, His mission, His purpose, His gospel. The journey leads to His glory. The journey may pass through the valley of death, poverty, illness – perhaps even persecution, before we arrive at the journey's end. We don't get to set the course or the timetable. Only the Master does. But trust Him – He knows exactly what He's doing! Don't join Him for the ride; join Him for the journey!

* * *

20

ALL THE REST

At daybreak He called together all of His disciples and chose twelve of them to be apostles.
Here are their names:
Simon (He also called him Peter), Andrew (Peter's brother), James, John, Philip, Bartholomew, Matthew, Thomas, James (son of Alphaeus), Simon (the Zealot), Judas (son of James), Judas Iscariot (who later betrayed Him).
Luke 6:13-16

* * *

On occasion i find myself praying, "LORD, grant me the boldness of Peter" or "the passion of James", the "compassion of Andrew", the "love of John", even "the urgency to tell others about YOU of Matthew." Scripture so clearly tells us about these men and their walk with Christ. But we know very little about the rest of the men listed in Luke 6 that Jesus called to be His apostles. The very fact that Jesus chose them tells us that He could entrust them (except Judas Iscariot) empowered by the Holy Spirit to carry out His mission to make disciples. They weren't "superstars"; they were more like the rest of us. They were flawed, quirky, imperfect sinners. They didn't merit salvation. Nothing about them qualified them to be apostles, other than the grace that Jesus extended to them. When He met them, He didn't see them for who they were, He saw them for who they would become in Him. As Jesus said to Nathanael the day they met, *"I tell you the truth, you will all see heaven open and the angels of God going up and down on the Son of Man, the one who is the stairway between heaven and earth"* (John 1:51).

. . .

Let's take a minute and look at these remaining six:

Philip

The day after Andrew brought Simon Peter to meet Jesus, we read that Jesus "found" Philip as He was traveling to Galilee. It is highly probable that Andrew and John were traveling with Jesus. Philip was from Bethsaida (Andrew & Peter's hometown). Philip was more than likely a fellow fisherman, and a friend of Andrew's. Quite possibly, Andrew helped Jesus "find" Philip, just as he had helped his brother "find" Jesus the day before. And i love that Scripture records that Jesus found Philip (John 1:43) and Philip found Jesus (John 1:45). That is such a great picture of salvation – when we were dead in our sin Jesus "found" us, and as we repented and surrendered our lives to Him, we "found" Him.

The other great picture is – that just like Andrew – on that very same day – Philip went to find his friend, Nathanael – to introduce him to Jesus. He didn't require six weeks of evangelism training – he just went out and immediately introduced his friend to the One he had met that day.

Philip was a part of the growing entourage that witnessed Jesus transform the water into wine at the wedding feast in Cana. So it was appropriate that the Master turned to him the day when that great crowd was before them, and asked, "Where can we buy bread to feed all these people?" As a matter of fact, we read in John 6:5-7 that Jesus was "testing" Philip. What did he learn from the miracle in Cana? Philip replied, "Even if we worked for months, we wouldn't have enough money to feed them!" Wrong answer! But Jesus lovingly again taught him – as well as the rest of the disciples and the multitude – that He is Lord over all – and He is our sufficiency!

Soon after Jesus' triumphal entry into Jerusalem, a group of Greek pilgrims came to Philip asking, "Sir, we want to meet Jesus" (John 12:20-22). They may have been drawn to him because Philip is a Greek name; he may have even spoken Greek. Philip tells his friend, and fellow disciple, Andrew – and together they go to ask Jesus.

The last recorded statement by Philip is at the last supper, just before they head to the Garden (John 14:8—11). Jesus was teaching His disciples about the unity of the Father and the Son. But Philip's statement – "Lord, show us the Father, and we will be satisfied" – again demonstrates that he didn't quite yet get it. But then, neither did the rest of the disciples. So once more, Jesus lovingly teaches them that He and the Father are One.

Bartholomew (aka Nathanael)

We read in John 1 that when Philip came to Nathanael (Bartholomew) to tell him about Jesus, Nathanael's immediate reply was *"Can anything good come from Nazareth?"* Philip replied, *"Come and see for yourself."* To Nathanael's credit, he did just that. And as they approached, Jesus said, *"Now here is a genuine son of Israel—a man of complete integrity."* To which Nathanael replied, *"How do you know about me?"* Jesus answered, *"I could see you under the fig tree before Philip found you."* Then in a reaction very similar to the Samaritan woman at the well, Nathanael exclaimed, *"Rabbi, you are the Son of God—the King of Israel!"* To which Jesus replied, *"Do you believe this just because I told you I had seen you under the fig tree? You will see greater things than this."* Immediately Nathanael left where he was to follow Jesus – and he never looked back.

Thomas (aka Didymus – "the twin")

After learning that Lazarus has died, Jesus declares, *"Let's go see him"* (John 11:1-16). (Note: He doesn't say, *"Let's go see his body."* He says, *"Let's go see him."* But we'll talk more about that in chapter 57.) Despite the fact that Jesus and all the disciples knew the Pharisees were determined to stone Him, He was resolved to go to Bethany. Thomas speaks up and says to his fellow disciples, *"Let's go, too – and die with Jesus."* Peter and Andrew tended to most often see the glass as half-full, whereas Thomas – "bless his heart" – appears to have often seen the glass as half-empty. His was not necessarily the voice in the group that inspired confidence, but nevertheless, he went.

Not long after that – the disciples were gathered in the upper room – as Jesus assured them, *"…I am going to prepare a place for you…. When everything is ready, I will come and get you, so that you will always be with Me where I am."* Again, it was Thomas who spoke up and said, *"We have no idea where You are going, so how can we know the way?"* (John 14:2-5) Bear in mind that the disciples had been walking with Jesus for three years. And yet, Thomas – and the rest of them – still did not understand.

• • •

But he is best known for his statement to the other disciples after the risen Christ has appeared to them in his absence. *"I won't believe it unless I see the nail wounds in His hands, put my fingers into them, and place my hand into the wound in His side"* (John 20:25). From that moment, he became "Doubting Thomas" – to this day defined as "a skeptic who refuses to believe without direct personal experience." His skepticism and faithlessness robbed him of joy for eight long days before Jesus again stood among them, this time including Thomas. And Jesus admonished him with a truth that we would do well to embrace – don't believe because you see; believe because of Who I am and what I have said" (paraphrase John 20:29).

James – son of Alphaeus (aka Clopas)

This James also came to be known as James the Less, making a distinction between him and James, the son of Zebedee, and James, the half-brother of Jesus. But like the sons of Zebedee, following Jesus was apparently a family affair for this James as well. His mother, Mary was one of the women who traveled with the disciples. She was there at the foot of the cross when Jesus was crucified (Matthew 27:56, Mark 15:40, John 19:25), and she was one of the women who came to the tomb to anoint Jesus' body (Matthew 28:1, Mark 16:1, Luke 24:10). His father, Alphaeus (also known as Clopas) was possibly one of the two disciples to which Jesus appeared on the road to Emmaus (Luke 24:13-35, Mark 16:12-13).

Simon the Zealot

Probably the only thing we know about Simon is that he was zealous – but we don't know for sure whether his zeal was directed toward his faith in Christ, or the political movement of the day to be freed from the rule of Rome, or both. If the latter is the case, more than likely he was the second apostle carrying a sword that night at the Garden of Gethsemane. Either case would have given him a unique perspective as a disciple of Christ. And he is another reminder to each of us that followers of Christ come from all circles and all backgrounds.

Judas (aka Thaddeus) – son of James

With little being known about Judas, son of James, there is much confusion. Is he the brother of James the Less, or is he in fact the brother of James, the half-brother of Jesus and therefore the writer of The Epistle of Jude? Regardless, he does appear to be the apostle that spoke up that night as they gathered with Jesus for the Last Supper. All of them knew that Jesus was the Messiah. And He had just told them that He was going to die, and that one of them would betray Him, one would deny Him, and all would abandon Him. So Judas speaks out with a question that must have been on all of their minds, "Lord, why are You going to reveal Yourself only to us and not to the world at large?" (John 14:22) or in other words, "Jesus, why don't You publicly declare Yourself to be the Messiah so that the people will follow YOU?" Though they had been with Jesus for the last three years, they were still a few days away from truly understanding His mission.

Just like the others, these six fled and deserted Jesus after His arrest. After His crucifixion they all huddled in fear together. But as the resurrected Christ appeared before them, their eyes were finally opened, and they truly believed!

Soon after, they were all together in the upper room on the Day of Pentecost when the Holy Spirit came upon them. Now they were fully empowered for the mission to which their Lord had called them. Scripture records the journey of many of the disciples after that day (and historians also bear witness) that each of these men were true to their Master's command to go out into the world and make disciples:

Peter went to Antioch and then on to Rome.
Andrew preached throughout Asia Minor, including modern day Turkey and Greece.
James preached the gospel in Judea before he was beheaded by Herod.
John traveled to Rome and Ephesus, and was exiled on Patmos.
Matthew preached the gospel in Persia and Ethiopia.
Philip went to Carthage, and then Asia Minor.
Nathanael went to Armenia, Ethiopia and Southern Arabia.
Thomas went to Syria, and then to what is now India.
James the Less went to Syria.
Simon the Zealot went to northern Africa and parts of Europe.
Judas, the son of James, preached in Armenia and Persia.
And the gospel began to spread to the ends of the earth.

Not one of them was anyone special on their own merit. They were just like the rest of us. But as they walked with the Master, He transformed them into His image and empowered them for His mission. And He'll do the same in us and through us – as we walk with Him!

21

PLUCKING THE GRAIN

One Sabbath day as Jesus was walking through some grain fields, His disciples began
breaking off heads of grain to eat. But the Pharisees said to Jesus,
"Look, why are they breaking the law by harvesting grain on the Sabbath?"
...Then Jesus said to them, "The Sabbath was made to meet the needs of people, and not people to meet the requirements of the Sabbath. So the Son of Man is Lord, even over the Sabbath!"
Mark 2:23-28

* * *

This will show my age. i remember the day when the only establishments open for business on Sunday were the restaurants and emergency services. The opening of the restaurants must have come about because everyone knows that good food – and in particular the gospel bird – is essential for good fellowship and rest on the Lord's Day. My family tells me that when i was a child, i would often say "Chicken on Sunday is what keeps you flying all week!" i'm not quite sure where that came from, but it gave a little boy a lot of laughs. I'm also not totally sure how it was that restaurants were the permissible business to be open, but someone somewhere had made that "pronouncement" and given them "special dispensation". Chick-fil-A didn't exist back then!

i can remember going to the cafeteria at our local mall, and it was the only storefront open. People would walk around the mall after their Sunday dinner looking in the windows of the seventy plus closed storefronts. Sunday didn't look like any other day of the week. It was set aside for going to church, being with family, and resting. Those Sundays are fond memories of simpler days. Interestingly, that Sabbath rest was not just enjoyed by churchgoers, it was enjoyed by everyone across our nation. It was a weekly Sabbath for everyone (except for those who worked in the restaurants). It was a "national" observance of a weekly Sabbath that thousands of years prior, God had given to one nation – the nation of Israel.

God gave the Sabbath to the people of Israel right after they came out of their bondage in Egypt. The Sabbath was a gift from God, intended for the blessing of His people. It was given as an expression of freedom. But the religious leaders over time had turned this blessing from God into a crushing burden by heaping on traditions and restrictions that equated to nothing more than religious bondage. A day intended for rest and worship had become a day of confinement and duty. The religious leaders of the day had long since turned from leading the people to worship the Lord of the Sabbath, and had become the "Sabbath enforcers" – determining what could and could not be done on that day – and making sure that everyone abided by their mandates. It had changed from being a day of rest and had become a day of rules. In many respects the Sabbath was no longer about worshiping the Father, it was more about the religious leaders and obeying their rules.

This day, as Jesus and His disciples walked through the grainfield, was not His first act of "Sabbath defiance". You will recall the kafuffle He stirred by healing the crippled man at the Pool of Bethesda on the Sabbath (chapter 13). Now His disciples were wantonly disregarding "the rules" by plucking off the heads of grain, rubbing them between their hands, and eating the grain.

Thus we see the clash – that continues today – the religious traditions of men versus an authentic relationship with a Holy God. God is surely more concerned with bringing glory to His Name, than He is with protecting religious tradition. The religious leaders had their priorities confused. So Jesus told them to get their priorities right -- *"The Sabbath was made to meet the needs of people, and not people to meet the requirements of the Sabbath. So the Son of Man is Lord, even over the Sabbath!"*

. . .

Was Jesus saying disregard the Sabbath? Of course not! He told them that He is Lord, even over the Sabbath. Sabbath was created for the rest of man and the worship of God, not for the worship of Sabbath. Jesus was admonishing them to take everything that they had added to the Word of God in their practices and expressions of worship – including those rules they had added to Sabbath – and strip them away!

The Pharisees are not the only ones that have developed traditions and placed them above the Word of God – whether it be about Sabbath – or worship – or our day-to-day walk with the Master. We, too, have created our traditions and given them a high place in what it means to worship and be a follower of Christ. You see those traditions demonstrated across our churches – what style of clothing is acceptable to wear when we gather to worship, what style of music is acceptable to sing in worship, how and how often we observe the Lord's Supper, and on and on. And that's just the beginning. On top of that, we have added programs and events and practices that have become such a part of our lives that we would consider it to be heresy to strip them away. And that's not just true of long-standing traditional churches; that's also true of more recently planted churches that also have developed newly formed traditions and practices that are dangerously close to eclipsing the very gospel itself.

As missionaries prepare to be sent overseas as church planters, an important element of their training is to help them strip away from their idea of "church" every element that we in the west have added – from the place that we worship, to the way it is appointed, to the order and style of our worship, and so on. We need to be careful that we don't add anything that would prevent anyone from "plucking" the grain of the gospel and feeding on His Word, and worshiping our Lord authentically with their whole heart, soul and mind.

We must turn our walk from being about what we are against to Who we are for – from being about a list of do's and don'ts, to being followers of Jesus, and lovers of our neighbors.

As you walk with the Master today, be sure to pluck some grain off the stalks if you're hungry – physically, emotionally or spiritually. But also – make sure you don't set any rules – or elevate any traditions – that keep others that are hungering or thirsting for our Father from doing the same.

22

SERMON OF SERMONS

One day as He saw the crowds gathering, Jesus went up on the mountainside and sat down. His disciples gathered around Him, and He began to teach them.... When Jesus had finished saying these things, the crowds were amazed at His teaching, for He taught with real authority — quite unlike their teachers of religious law.
Matthew 5:1 – 7:29

* * *

Over the years, God has used many preachers to teach me His Word. Some were at a distance, like John Piper, Warren Wiersbe, Chuck Swindoll and John MacArthur. Some have been close and personal, like Henry Blackaby, Keith Thomas, Mark Becton and David Platt. Some have spoken through the ages, like Charles Spurgeon, Jonathan Edwards, D. L. Moody and A. W. Tozer. Others date back to the New Testament, like Paul, John, Peter and James, as well as the Old Testament prophets like Moses, Isaiah, Jeremiah and Zechariah. But as greatly as the Father has used each and every one of these men – and so many more – to be heralds and teachers of His Word, all of them pale in comparison with Jesus.

One day He gathered the multitude that had come out into the countryside to hear Him, and He began to teach... the greatest sermon that ever was – the sermon of all sermons. Jesus taught:

God blesses those
... who are poor and realize their need for Him,
... who mourn and are in need of comfort,
... who are humble,
... who hunger and thirst for righteousness,
... who are merciful,
... whose hearts are pure,
... who work for peace,
... who are persecuted for doing right,
... who are mocked or maligned for following Him,
... who are the salt of the gospel,
... whose good deeds shine for the glory of the Father,
... who are righteous according to the Father's purpose,
... who are not angry and do not vilify others,
... who seek forgiveness and reconciliation,
... who settle their differences with others quickly,
... who do not lust,
... who honor their spouse, as Christ honors His bride,
... whose "yes" means yes, and their "no" means no, and do not make vows,
... who do not seek revenge,
... who love their enemy,
... who give to those in need,
... who seek the Father in prayer,
... who seek the Father through fasting,
... who store their treasures in heaven,
... who do not covet,
... who do not worry,
... who are not judgmental,
... who are neither critical or hypocritical,
... who allow the Holy Spirit to guide them,
... who pray without ceasing and seek the Father in all things,
... who extend grace in the measure they desire it be extended to themselves,
... who seek the way of the Father,
... who do the will of the Father, and
... who hear and heed the teaching of Jesus.

Gratefully, Jesus was not delivering a message of new commandments that we are to keep. The reality is that there is only One Man who could ever measure up to these standards. Jesus is the only One who has ever had a heart that is pure. No, this is not a path through which we can enter into salvation. If it was, the cause would be lost for each and every one of us. Rather, it is about the character that will be reflected in the lives of those who truly follow Christ. Later, John will record in John 15 that Jesus said, "... *Those who remain in Me, and I in them, will produce much fruit. For apart from Me you can do nothing.*" If you will permit me to paraphrase, Jesus is saying, "If you remain in Me, I will produce the character that I taught about that day in the Sermon on the Mount. And know, that apart from Me, you can never even hope to reflect that character."

Jesus was describing His character and the character that should be reflected through each of His true followers. The character He described was very different from that reflected by the religious leaders of the day – and different from that reflected through the lives of many who proclaim to be followers of Christ today. But He was also describing the character and the characteristics of His Kingdom. Remember that many within the sound of His voice, including the apostles, had already come to see Him as the Messiah. But what view did they have of the Messiah? Most of them saw the Messiah as one who would come and establish a material kingdom that would throw off the yoke of bondage to Rome and restore the nation to the prominence it had under King David. They believed that the Messiah's kingdom would be a political and military kingdom like that of their early kings. So imagine their confusion when He speaks of humility, mercy, peace, and "loving your enemy".

Perhaps the most disconcerting idea – both then and now – was that of "storing up treasures in heaven". The vast majority of those listening to His voice then – and listening today – were highly motivated to build their own earthly treasures. For many, it was (and is) their primary life purpose. So though it was the greatest sermon ever preached, very few would actually take the sermon to heart.

But it was never Jesus' purpose of the sermon to rally the multitudes and to sway them into believing in Him. His purpose was to clearly define His Kingdom – and to clearly show the difference between His Kingdom and the religious practice of the day – the day then – and in many instances, the day now.

As we continue our walk with the Master:

He will teach us more about His Kingdom.

He will continue to mold and shape our lives, and remove

every part that doesn't reflect His Kingdom and His character.

He will expose self-righteousness and make a clear distinction between it and His true righteousness.

He will expose our selfish pride and reveal it as filthy rags in clear contrast to a selfless, sacrificial humility that does not call attention to itself.

He will expose our soulish kingdom ambition and lead us to seek His Kingdom and His righteousness first.

And as He does, He will transform our lives into a sermon of sermons that brings glory to Him.

* * *

23

FAITH LIKE THIS

When Jesus returned to Capernaum, a Roman officer came and pleaded with Him,
"Lord, my young servant lies in bed, paralyzed and in terrible pain."
Jesus said, "I will come and heal him."
But the officer said, "Lord, I am not worthy to have You come into my home. Just say the word
from where You are, and my servant will be healed. I know this because I am under the authority
of my superior officers, and I have authority over my soldiers. I only need to say,
'Go,' and they go, or 'Come,' and they come. And if I say to my slaves, 'Do this,' they do it."
When Jesus heard this, He was amazed. Turning to those who were following Him, He said,
"I tell you the truth, I haven't seen faith like this in all Israel! And I tell you this, that many
Gentiles will come from all over the world—from east and west—and sit down with Abraham,
Isaac, and Jacob at the feast in the Kingdom of Heaven. But many Israelites —those
for whom the Kingdom was prepared—will be thrown into outer darkness, where there
will be weeping and gnashing of teeth." Then Jesus said to the Roman officer, "Go back home.
Because you believed, it has happened." And the young servant was healed that same hour.
Matthew 8:5-13

* * *

Jesus was amazed by the faith of a man – and this man wasn't one of His closest followers..., he wasn't a devout religious leader..., he wasn't even a Jew. He was a Roman soldier. It was highly unusual for the Son of God to be amazed. He knew what was in man, so very little would amaze Him. But Scripture records that He was amazed twice – the first in Mark 6:6 – by the <u>un</u>belief of the Jews in His hometown of Nazareth; and the second – by the faith of this Roman officer.

Whenever i think about a "man of faith", i think of George Müller. Müller was an evangelist in the mid-1800's and the founding director of the Ashley Down orphanage in Bristol, England. During his lifetime he cared for 10,024 orphans in 5 orphanages and established 117 schools. It is said that Müller never made requests to anyone for funding, and he never went into debt. The only One to whom he ever made his requests known was his Lord. Often he would receive unsolicited food donations only hours or minutes before they were needed to feed the children. On one well-documented occasion, thanks was given for breakfast when all the children were sitting at the table even though there was nothing to eat in the house. As they finished praying, the baker knocked on the door with sufficient fresh bread to feed everyone, and the milkman gave them plenty of fresh milk because his cart broke down in front of the orphanage.

In this autobiographical entry on February 12, 1842, Müller wrote:

> *"A brother in the Lord came to me this morning and, after a few minutes of conversation gave me two thousand pounds for furnishing the new Orphan House ... Now I am able to meet all of the expenses. In all probability I will even have several hundred pounds more than I need. The Lord not only gives as much as is absolutely necessary for His work, but He gives abundantly. This blessing filled me with inexplicable delight. He had given me the full answer to my thousands of prayers during the [past] 1,195 days."*

Müller knew that his Lord was able and sufficient to meet every need. There was never any question of "if"; it was merely a question of "when". And even in that question, Müller knew that the Lord's timing was perfect. i don't know if Jesus was ever amazed by Müller's faith – but i know i am. But a significant difference between Müller and this Roman officer is the fact that Müller was a follower of Jesus. He had long before surrendered his life to Christ. But the day the Roman officer approached Jesus – though he believed Jesus was able – he had yet to trust Him with his eternal soul.

In the parallel account in Luke 7, we read that he had devised a plan for approaching Jesus. Though he had faith, he thought he could approach Jesus on his own terms. First, he sent emissaries on his behalf – making a case as to why Jesus should help him. Surprisingly, it was a group of Jewish leaders – and in that day, Jews were not in the habit of advocating for Roman soldiers. He presumed he could leverage relationships to gain the favor of Jesus. But he wasn't going to use relationships as his only strategy. Second, the emissaries endeavored to merit the favor of Jesus on the officer's behalf, by telling Him about the officer's good works. As they pled that the officer deserved Jesus' help, they underscored that "he loves the Jewish people, and even built a synagogue for us." (Luke 7:5). Again, just like Jews were not in the habit of helping the Roman soldiers, soldiers were not in the habit of helping the Jews.

But it was his personal appeal that caused Jesus to respond. It wasn't about who he knew, or the works he had done, it was his faith – his wholehearted confidence in who Jesus was and his firm conviction that Jesus was able. Billy Graham once said, "God will not reward fruitfulness; but He will reward faithfulness."

And that's true for each one of us – whether we are a follower of Christ like Müller, or an unrepentant sinner like the officer. It's not about who we know or what we have done. We are not able to come to Him because we are worthy. We are able to come to Him by faith, purely because of His grace and His mercy. And Jesus is a Rewarder of faith. The writer of Hebrews says, *"it is impossible to please God without faith. Anyone who wants to come to Him must believe that God exists and that He rewards those who sincerely seek Him."* That is true whether we are seeking Him as a sinner seeking salvation, or as His child seeking His answer.

Just before Jesus ascended to heaven, He reminded His disciples that *"I have been given <u>all</u> authority in heaven and on earth."* Unlike most of the Jews, and even the disciples of Jesus at that moment in time, the Roman officer recognized Jesus' <u>absolute</u> authority. He knew that only He who has

Supreme authority can *"by the mere expression of His will, restore health to men"* (John Calvin) – physical, emotional and spiritual health.

"And the young servant was healed that same hour." The officer's request was answered. In response to his faith and according to God's will, the servant was healed. Does that mean that whatever we ask – if we ask in faith – like Müller or the Roman officer, God will give it to us? No. Faith acts in alignment with God's purpose and His will. Faith is not the proverbial "rubbing of the genie's lamp" to receive whatever we want. It is a recognition that He has all authority, and His purpose and plan will be accomplished. The apostle John was a first-hand witness of the Roman officer's encounter with Jesus that day. i can't help but wonder if he was remembering that very day, when later he wrote, *"This is the confidence which we have before Him, that, if we ask anything according to His will, He hears us. And if we know that He hears us in whatever we ask, we know that we have the requests which we have asked from Him"* (1 John 5:14-15 NASB).

As we close out this account of the officer's encounter with Jesus, i am mindful that this is a first fruit among Gentiles. As Jesus was commending the officer's faith, He was also emphasizing that salvation does not come from our good works or "who" we are. Salvation comes by faith – like the faith demonstrated by this Gentile officer. Jesus said, *"Gentiles will come from all over the world—from east and west"* and enter into *"the Kingdom of Heaven. But many Israelites—those for whom the Kingdom was prepared—will be thrown into outer darkness…."* And because of that faith, there will be a multitude of believers from every language, people, tribe and nation gathered around God's throne in heaven worshiping Him.

As you walk with the Master, walk with Him with a "faith like this!"

* * *

24

ARISE!

Soon afterward Jesus went with His disciples to the village of Nain, and a large crowd followed Him. A funeral procession was coming out as He approached the village gate. The young man who had died was a widow's only son, and a large crowd from the village was with her. When the Lord saw her, His heart overflowed with compassion. "Don't cry!" He said. Then He walked over to the coffin and touched it, and the bearers stopped. "Young man," He said, "I tell you, get up." Then the dead boy sat up
and began to talk! And Jesus gave him back to his mother.
Great fear swept the crowd, and they praised God, saying, "A mighty prophet has risen among us," and "God has visited His people today."
And the news about Jesus spread throughout Judea and the surrounding countryside.
Luke 7:11-17

* * *

To this point in Jesus' earthly ministry, people had seen Him perform many miracles – from the transformation of water to wine, to the healing of lepers, cripples and even the blind. The people marveled – even His disciples – at this One who could make the lame to walk and the blind to see. And the multitudes began to flock to Him to witness, and for many, to experience – His healing touch. But they were about to see something that they had NEVER seen – and something that they could not even imagine. They were about to see Jesus raise a young man from the dead!

. . .

This day was no different – a large crowd was following Him. But what they didn't know was that Jesus was on His way to another divine appointment. Please remember that none of our Lord's encounters were by chance. Each and every one of them was ordered in such a way as to fulfill His purpose and bring the greatest glory to the Father. That was true at a well in Samaria – and it was true at this village gate at Nain. It was true with a Samaritan woman at mid-day – and it was true with a grieving mother and her dead son as dusk approached. The Lord Jesus knew before time began that those encounters would take place with those people… at those times… in those places. And He ordered His steps accordingly… just as He ordered theirs.

There are some personal parallels here with Jesus that we can't ignore. The writer of Hebrews wrote, *"This High Priest of ours* (Jesus) *understands our weaknesses, for He faced all of the same testings we do…"* (Hebrews 4:15). As He encountered this grieving widow, He had to be mindful of His own earthly mother – Mary. By this time in Jesus' life, His earthly father, Joseph, had been dead for some time. He had witnessed the grief of His widowed mother at Joseph's passing. Though Mary had multiple sons, and perhaps daughters, she had but one son who was the only Son of God. And Jesus knew that one day soon, His widowed mother would be grieving the death of her only Son, just as this widow was grieving the death of her only son. We read that *"His heart overflowed with compassion."* Though i know that the Son of God has compassion for all, i do believe that the Son of Man had a special place in His heart for this grieving mother.

No one asked Jesus to bring this young man back from the dead. The grieving widow did not plead with Him for a miracle. Those in the crowd didn't begin to wonder out loud among themselves as to what Jesus would do. Raising this young man from the dead was not a thought on anyone's mind. He was dead. His mother was grieving. Nothing else could be done… even by Jesus (or so they thought). So no one even thought to ask. No one knew what to ask. But Jesus knew… and He knew what needed to be done… and He was able to do it. So He intervened, and He interceded. There will be times in our lives when we won't know what to ask. We won't know to expect anything different. Gratefully – and graciously – our Lord has given us His Holy Spirit, who *"helps us in our weakness. For we do not know what to pray for as we ought, but the Spirit Himself intercedes for us…"* (Romans 8:26 ESV). Trust Him to intercede, even when we don't know.

• • •

The first thing Jesus did was to offer the mother comfort. We don't know if she knew who He was – but regardless, He spoke comfort into her life. Knowing she needed mercy and tenderness, He spoke consolation to her.

Next, He did the unthinkable – He touched the bier (or "coffin"). The religious leaders of the day believed that to touch a bier rendered you unclean for days and unable to perform your religious duty. But Jesus didn't hesitate. *He walked over to the coffin and touched it, and the bearers stopped.* Has the Lord ever told you to "touch a coffin"? Has He ever brought someone into your life who seemed like a hopeless cause or a waste of time? Has He ever directed you to get involved in ministry that may cause you to be "unclean"? Remember, Jesus didn't hesitate. He walked over and did what needed to be done!

Then He spoke to him who was dead, *"Young man, I tell you get up."* Jesus spoke. In every instance that Jesus raised the dead to life, He did so by speaking. And we read in Scripture that when He returns, He will do so again. *"For the Lord Himself will descend from heaven with a shout… and the dead in Christ will rise first* (1 Thessalonians 4:16 NASB). As in all things, Jesus has but to speak it! He spoke, *"Let there be light"* (Genesis 1:3) and there was light. He spoke, *"Peace! Be still!"* (Mark 4:39) and the wind stopped. He spoke, *"Get up"* and the dead boy sat up and began to talk! At the very *name of Jesus every knee will bow… in heaven and on earth and under the earth* (Philippians 2:10 NASB), and at the very voice of Jesus, the dead will rise.

Scripture records that Jesus raised three people from the dead (in addition to Himself). In this case, He says *"Young man, get up!"* In the case of Jairus' daughter, He said, *"Little girl, get up!"* (Mark 5:41) And in the case of Lazarus, He said, *"Lazarus, come forth!"* (John 11:43) i am convinced that in each instance He addressed them specifically. Otherwise, all the dead bodies within the sound of His voice would have arisen! Because at His very voice, the dead will arise!

And we read that *"great fear swept the crowd"* and *"the news about Jesus spread…."* The people marveled. And though, regrettably, many chose NOT to follow Him, the Good News about Jesus spread.

As you walk with the Master, be mindful that His Good News is still being spread through His followers. We are to be His hands and feet. We are to be a reflection of Him in all that we do. Remember that not one of your encounters is by chance. He has a purpose and a plan in each and every one. Follow His lead and listen to His voice. You may be there to provide comfort. He may even direct you to "touch a coffin". But whatever the circumstance, He has you there to speak truth and life.

So, arise!

* * *

25

EVEN JOHN DOUBTED

John the Baptist, who was in prison, heard about all the things the Messiah was doing. So he sent his disciples to ask Jesus, "Are You the Messiah we've been expecting, or should we keep looking for someone else?"
Jesus told them, "Go back to John and tell him what you have heard and seen — the blind see, the lame walk, those with leprosy are cured, the deaf hear, the dead are raised to life, and the Good News is being preached to the poor." And He added, "God blesses those who do not fall away because of Me."
Matthew 11:2-6

* * *

John the Baptist had now been imprisoned for some time by Herod Antipas for denouncing the tetrarch's adulterous marriage to Herodias (Luke 3:19-20). You would have thought that the Jewish leaders would have been up in arms defending John's position and denouncing Herod's action. Yet, they were silent. Most likely their attitude toward Jesus is what resulted in their lack of action on John's behalf. After all, John had honored Jesus and proclaimed Him to be the Messiah. But then again John was also not popular with them by his own right. He didn't cater to the crowds, let alone the Pharisees. He was a man of conviction and courage – the greatest of the prophets (Matthew 11:11).

He came in the spirit and power of Elijah (Luke 1:17) and even dressed and ministered like him (2 Kings 1:7-8, Matthew 3:4). Like Elijah, John had a message of judgment for the apostate nation of Israel. The prophet

Isaiah had announced John's coming (Isaiah 40:3). John's ministry was to prepare the nation for Jesus and present Jesus to the nation.

But now his voice had been silenced. He could not preach to the crowds from a jail cell. This voice with a divine mandate to proclaim was being muffled in prison. And he became discouraged, and perhaps broken.

John's disciples had been watching Jesus and keeping John apprised of His movements, His miracles and His message. It's very probable that John was expecting Jesus to, at any moment, declare His authority as the Messiah, establish His kingdom and His government, and free the nation from Roman rule. John was anticipating that any day now the Messiah would begin His reign and the door of John's prison cell would be opened and he would be set free. John was probably trying to understand why Jesus was taking so long to assume the throne. More than likely, this was his context when he asked, *"Are You the Messiah we've been expecting, or should we keep looking for someone else?"* As we have traveled through the previous chapters in this book thus far, we have seen that common thread running through the minds of the disciples and the followers of John. Now we see it expressed by John himself. Even the way the Pharisees felt threatened by who Jesus was, largely resulted from the fact that He didn't look anything like the Messiah they were selfishly expecting! Everyone had a picture in their mind of who and what the Messiah would look like – and Jesus didn't look like that picture! Even John was beginning to doubt!

So Jesus tells John's messengers, *"Go back to John and tell him what you have heard and seen...."* Tell him, *"... the blind see, the lame walk, those with leprosy are cured, the deaf hear, the dead are raised to life, and the Good News is being preached to the poor."* Jesus was using the very words of the prophet Isaiah – *"Say to those with fearful hearts, 'Be strong, and do not fear, for your God is coming to destroy your enemies. He is coming to save you. And when He comes, He will open the eyes of the blind and unplug the ears of the deaf. The lame will leap like a deer, and those who cannot speak will sing for joy!'"* (Isaiah 35:4-6). Jesus is sending John a word of encouragement – not a word of rebuke. And when He adds, *"God blesses those who do not fall away because of Me"*, He is reminding John of what Isaiah also wrote:

> *He will keep you safe. But to Israel and Judah, He will be a stone that makes people stumble, a rock that makes them fall. And for the people of Jerusalem, He will be a trap and a snare. Many will stumble and fall, never to rise again. They will be*

snared and captured." Preserve the teaching of God; entrust His instructions to those who follow me. I will wait for the Lord, who has turned away from the descendants of Jacob. I will put my hope in Him.

(Isaiah 8:14-17)

Though God Himself would be a stumbling stone to Israel and Judah, He would not cause those to stumble who trust Him! Songwriters Babbie Mason and Eddie Carswell communicated that message well when they wrote, *"when you can't trace His hand, trust His heart."*

As we walk with the Master, we, too, will encounter circumstances that we never expected, and we certainly don't understand. We were expecting the Lord to do one thing in our life – and He does something totally different – or He allows something totally different – at best, disappointing – or at worst, tragic. He doesn't look anything like we think God should look like. He hasn't done what we think He should do. We're like John – we know the Scriptures – we know the promises of God – but we just got "sucker-punched" – and we don't understand! The pain, the sorrow, the devastation, or even the disappointment will more than likely cause us to question Jesus. It could cause us to ask, *"Jesus, are You really who I think You are? If so, how could you allow this to occur? Are You the One to follow or should we keep looking for someone else?"*

In that moment, Jesus has a message for us as well.

All things work for our good
Though sometimes we don't see
How they could
Struggles that break our hearts in two
Sometimes blind us to the truth

Our Father knows what's best for us
His ways are not our own
So when your pathway grows dim
And you just don't see Him,
Remember you're never alone

God is too wise to be mistaken
God is too good to be unkind
So when you don't understand
When you don't see His plan

When you can't trace His hand
Trust His Heart
Trust His Heart

He sees the master plan
And he holds our future in His hand,
So don't live as those who have no hope,
All our hope is found in Him

We see the present clearly
But He sees the first and the last
And like a tapestry He's weaving you and me,
To someday be just like Him

God is too wise to be mistaken
God is too good to be unkind
So when you don't understand
When don't see His plan
When you can't trace His hand
Trust His Heart

He alone is faithful and true
He alone knows what is best for you

God is too wise to be mistaken
God is too good to be unkind
So when you don't understand
When you don't see His plan
When you can't trace His hand
Trust His Heart

When you don't understand
When you don't see His plan
When you can't trace His hand
Trust His Heart
Trust His Heart

SONGWRITERS: BABBIE Y. MASON / EDDIE CARSWELL

* * *

26

WHO DARED TO ANOINT JESUS

Then He turned to the woman and said to Simon, "Look at this woman kneeling here. When I entered your home, you didn't offer Me water to wash the dust from My feet, but she has washed them with her tears and wiped them with her hair. You didn't greet Me with a kiss, but from the time I first came in, she has not stopped kissing My feet. You neglected the courtesy of olive oil to anoint My head, but she has anointed My feet with rare perfume.
Luke 7:36-50

* * *

Simon was a Pharisee. We're not told Simon's purpose for inviting Jesus into his home. We don't know if Simon was a sincere seeker like Nicodemus, wanting to truly get to know Jesus, or whether he had some ulterior motive in mind. Regardless, he extended an invitation to Jesus – and Jesus chose to accept. Remember, nothing about Jesus' journey was random. It was a part of the Father's plan for Jesus to dine with Simon.

In that day, it was customary for outsiders to hover around a banquet in order to watch the "important people" and listen in on the conversation. The dinner did not take place behind closed doors, so it was very easy for anyone to gain access. But also bear in mind that Jewish rabbis did not speak to or dine with women in public. And in that day no woman would have been invited to the banquet – and particularly not one of ill-repute.

. . .

We read that the woman knelt behind Jesus at His feet (Luke 7:38). For those of us used to dining as we sit in a chair at a table, it is difficult to understand how she could have been doing that. But it makes more sense if we understand that Jesus would have been reclining on a couch, leaning on His arm with His feet sticking out in back. And the woman had positioned herself in that place – kneeling at Jesus' feet as she wept.

She had brought an offering to Jesus. Not a financial offering – it was of greater value than mere money. It was a "beautiful alabaster jar filled with expensive perfume." But of even greater value she offered her tears. The perfume and her tears mixed as a sweet expression of repentance and thanksgiving to the One who had enabled her to lay down her heavy burden of sin and receive forgiveness. Her weight had been lifted by the only One who could lift it. And there she knelt expressing her thanksgiving and joy as she proffered her tears mixed with perfume and kissed His feet as an act of worship.

When Simon saw what was happening, *"he said to himself, 'If this man were a prophet, He would know what kind of woman is touching Him. She's a sinner!"* (Luke 7:39). Simon's action was in essence to be repulsed by the woman and critical of Jesus. How could she, an immoral woman, dare to do what she was doing; and how could Jesus dare to permit her to do so?

But Jesus knew exactly what Simon was thinking. After all, Jesus never entrusted Himself to any man, *"because He knew all people and… He knew what was in man"* (John 2:24-25).

Jesus told Simon this story: *"A man loaned money to two people — 500 pieces of silver to one and 50 pieces to the other. But neither of them could repay him, so he kindly forgave them both, canceling their debts. Who do you suppose loved him more after that?"* Simon replied, *"I suppose the one for whom he canceled the larger debt."*

At that point, we pick up with the verses at the top of this chapter. This is the first time Jesus has actually acknowledged the woman at His feet. But His remarks are not to her; they are to Simon. Simon had invited Jesus to come to his home, but he had never welcomed Jesus into his home. He had not even bestowed a customary welcome to Jesus as his guest. He had not provided water for Jesus to wash His feet as a common courtesy.

Neither had he greeted Jesus with a kiss on the cheek or anointed His head with oil, which would have been the customary greeting of a guest. Simon, who had the most to offer, offered nothing.

The woman, who had the least to give, gave all that she had. She knew that she had much for which to be forgiven. And she had released that heavy burden to Jesus. And now she offered all that she had in worship and thanksgiving. But Simon mistakenly believed that he had nothing for which to be forgiven. And what's more, he remained blinded to the Savior who was in his midst. So he gave nothing; there was nothing in his heart to give. He didn't give out of thanksgiving and love; he didn't even give out of common courtesy.

And when Jesus said to the woman, *"Your sins are forgiven"*, all Simon and his other guests could say among themselves was *"Who is this Man, that He goes around forgiving sins?"* (Luke 7:48-49).

The evening ended very differently for this woman and Simon. The woman who had dared to anoint the feet of Jesus and give all that she had out of a repentant, forgiven heart had walked away in peace, saved by her faith. But alas, Simon who sat there with a cold, indifferent heart remained unchanged and dead in his sin.

As you walk with the Master, take care that you do not walk as Simon did – with Jesus, but unaffected by Jesus. Be sure that you're not simply walking through the motions of following Jesus without a repentant and surrendered heart. Make certain that you're not just giving the outward appearance of following Jesus when there has been no inward change in your life. Rather, dare to anoint the One who has forgiven your sins and paid your sin debt. Dare to show Him the worship, thanksgiving and love that He is due – with all of your heart, soul, mind and possessions. Don't remain where you are – unchanged. Dare to walk with Him in peace.

* * *

27

YOUR FAMILY IS LOOKING FOR YOU

Then Jesus' mother and brothers came to see Him. They stood outside and sent word for Him to come out and talk with them. There was a crowd sitting around Jesus, and someone said, "Your mother and Your brothers are outside asking for You." Jesus replied, "Who is My mother? Who are My brothers?" Then He looked at those around Him and said, "Look, these are My mother and brothers. Anyone who does God's will is My brother and sister and mother."

Mark 3:31-35

* * *

As many of you know, most of my life, i lived in South Florida. I attended school there from the age of 12. LaVonne and i met there. Our children were born there. God called us into ministry there. Though we are delighted to now call Virginia our home, we savor every opportunity we have to return to South Florida for a visit. People frequently ask us if our family is there – to which we reply that though no "blood relatives" live there any longer, our ties there are to long-time friends (brothers and sisters in the Lord) who have become family through the years. That bond has become just as strong – if not, in some ways, stronger. So periodically, as the sun and surf call out to us to return and get some rest, our visits to South Florida have become a respite and a retreat from the busyness of life and the pressing pace of the day-to-day, as we reconnect with our family of friends.

Earlier in this passage (Mark 3:20-21), Mark records that the crowds were pressing in on Jesus so greatly that He and His disciples couldn't find time to eat. *When His family heard what was happening, they tried to take Him away* because they feared *"He was out of His mind."* His family had traveled thirty miles from Nazareth to plead with Him to come home and get some rest.

As we look at this passage, Jesus is not being disrespectful to His family. He knows that their concern for Him is genuine. You'll remember that at the wedding feast in Cana, Mary (the mother of Jesus) had turned to Jesus when she learned that the wine was becoming depleted. As we discussed in chapter 8, Mary was either a member of the family or a close personal friend of the wedding party. By association, therefore, so was Jesus. She was genuinely concerned for the family that day, and was certain that Jesus would also be concerned. But He had patiently – and firmly – reminded Mary that He was absolutely bound to the Father's will – and the Father's will took precedent even over His mother. Even at age 12, Jesus had explained to His mother that He must be about His Father's business (though Mary didn't fully understand what He meant).

Jesus was not suggesting that His followers ignore or abandon their families in order to serve the Father. Rather, He was modeling that they put His will above all else in life. Another time when Jesus was teaching His disciples about the cost of following Him, He said, *"If you want to be My disciple, you must, by comparison, hate everyone else—your father and mother, wife and children, brothers and sisters—yes, even your own life. Otherwise, you cannot be My disciple'* (Luke 14:26). Though it is certainly the Father's will that we honor and care for our families (Exodus 20:12; 1 Timothy 5:8), we must never allow our loved ones to detour us from pursuing the Father's will, no matter how well-intentioned their motivation. That was a radical position for Jesus to take in first century Jewish society. In many respects, it's still a radical position today!

But Jesus was also reinforcing the truth that, as followers of Christ pursuing the Father's will, we are family. *"Anyone who does God's will is My brother and sister and mother."* We have become brothers and sisters in Christ! We are to love one another, encourage one another and lift one another up. We're going to spend eternity together, so let's learn how to live as family in the here and now!

But regrettably, that is not always the way we treat one another. Too often, instead of lifting up, we are tearing down; and instead of encouraging, we are criticizing – and not in a godly way! That too, then detours us from being about the Father's will. And trust me – no matter how much we may want to dress up our actions in "godly" jargon, there is no good motivation involved! The result is that the body is injured, our testimony is tarnished, the devil is delighted, the mission is set back, and we detract from the glory of God.

It is worthy to note that the very discussion Jesus was engaged in that day when Mary and His half-brothers came to see Him, was with the Pharisees. They had just accused Jesus of being possessed by Satan (Mark 3:20-30). And in His response, He admonished them that *"a family splintered by feuding will fall apart."* There can be no health in feuding, no matter how well-intentioned.

As you walk with the Master, be mindful of your family. Children, treat your parents with the honor they are due. Parents, nurture and cherish your children. Husbands, love your wives as Christ loves the church. Wives, submit to your husband as you do to the Lord. Brothers and sisters, love and edify one another. But above all else, love the Lord your God with all your heart, soul and mind. Seek Him first. Honor Him above all else and all others. And as you do, He will enable you to honor your family as you should.

Your family is looking for you! Whether it be the family of your household, your extended family, or your church family — they are looking for you – to honor them rightly and well. Honor them in the way Jesus would!

* * *

28

SIMPLE STORIES, IMPORTANT TRUTHS

Later that same day Jesus left the house and sat beside the lake. A large crowd soon gathered around Him, so He got into a boat. Then He sat there and taught as the people stood on the shore. He told many stories in the form of parables….
Matthew 13:1-43

* * *

We're going to start off this chapter with a "spoiler alert". The content is a little bit longer, but also a little bit harder. Often when Jesus spoke to the multitudes, He would use simple stories (parables) to communicate important truths about the Kingdom of God. Once the disciples asked Him, *"Why do You use parables when You talk to the people?"* Jesus replied, *"To those who listen to My teaching, more understanding will be given, and they will have an abundance of knowledge. But for those who are not listening, even what little understanding they have will be taken away from them"* (Matthew 13:12-13). He went on to say, *"I use parables because they look, but don't really see. They hear, but don't really listen or understand."* And Jesus explained that, through parables, the prophecy recorded in Isaiah 6:9-10 was being fulfilled:

"When you hear what I say, you will not understand.
When you see what I do, you will not comprehend.
For the hearts of these people are hardened, and their ears cannot hear,
and they have closed their eyes— so their eyes cannot see,
and their ears cannot hear, and their hearts cannot understand,

and they cannot turn to Me and let Me heal them" (Matthew 13:14-15).

Jesus was communicating this important truth:

There is a difference between looking and seeing.
There is a difference between hearing and listening.
There is a difference between knowledge and understanding.
And the difference is not an issue of the eyes, ears or mind; it's an issue of the heart.

One more thing, before we look at the parables, let's remember this about the Kingdom. Jesus said, *"The Kingdom of God can't be detected by visible signs. You won't be able to say, 'Here it is!' or 'It's over there!' For the Kingdom of God is already among you"* (Luke 17:20-21). Jesus was correcting a misunderstanding of the Kingdom. The people of that day had been expecting the arrival of a Messiah that would overturn Rome, vindicate the people of Israel and establish an earthly government and kingdom. And Jesus was teaching them that that was not how the Kingdom was to come. The Kingdom was already among them, because Jesus was among them. He was and is the arrival of the Kingdom. It is all about Him. It is all about the gospel. But there are elements of the Kingdom that are here and now, then there are other elements that we will not see until He returns.

So let's take a look at some of those simple stories, and ask the Father to open our hearts so that we might hear His truth about His Kingdom.

The Sower and the Soils

This parable does not begin with "The Kingdom is like..." because it sets the stage for how the Kingdom begins in the hearts and lives of followers. Jesus knew as He was speaking to the multitudes that the majority of the people would not follow Him. He knew that the soils of this parable described the hearts of those that were hearing Him then... and many hearing today. It must have broken His heart to know that the people represented by three out of the four soils would never bear fruit – because, as Jesus said in Matthew 7:16, *"you can identify them by their fruit."*

A farmer sowed life-giving seed. Some of the seed fell on the footpath and was carried away by the birds. Some fell on rocky soil and, though it sprouted quickly, the soil was shallow, and the seedlings died quickly in the hot sun. Some fell among thorns which "choked out the tender plants." And some fell on fertile soil and produced a crop a hundred times as much as had been planted.

The seed in all four instances represents the life-giving seed of the gospel. The soils represent the various conditions of the hearts in which the seed is sown. The footpath is a heart that is hard, unreceptive, and preoccupied with the comings and goings of life, and the gospel is never given any opportunity to penetrate the heart. The evil one is there to rob the seed before it can be planted into their heart. The rocky soil and the thorny soils are hearts that "believe" but are never surrendered. They "prayed a prayer" but there never was a heart transformation so their faith "fizzled" or their other life pursuits "choked" it out.

As some of you know, i would describe my first thirty years as a "Christian" as being in that shallow or thorny soil. i had "prayed a prayer" at age 6, but as i grew into adulthood it became obvious that i had never truly surrendered my life. i believe that we make a mistake when we invite people to make a commitment to Christ. Because a commitment only lasts until i make my next commitment to whomever or whatever i choose to pursue. A commitment is usually based upon my own terms, therefore, i can change the terms or the duration. That's why i prefer the idea of "surrender". i don't get to choose the terms of my surrender, my Captor does – and i can't change them down the road. i fear that too many of us in the church today are "planted" in one of these two soils, having never truly surrendered our lives to Christ, and it is proven by "our fruit" – or the lack thereof.

The fourth soil represents a heart that has been surrendered and a life that has been transformed by the power of the gospel from which fruit is being multiplied. In such soil, the Kingdom of Heaven has been birthed and is being multiplied.

From there, Jesus continues with parables that describe Satan's opposition to the Kingdom. Remember, Satan is a counterfeiter; he is not a creator. So his attacks will come in the way of false imitations. His goal is to deceive, to distract and divide, and he will plant false Christians, encourage false growth and introduce false doctrine.

. . .

The Wheat and the Weeds (false Christians)

The farmer (the Son of Man) has planted good seed (His Word) that has produced wheat (followers of Christ) in his field (the world). He planted His followers in His world – for the purpose of spreading His gospel and multiplying disciples. But the enemy (Satan) has planted "weeds" (false Christians) among the wheat. The weeds, by outward appearance, may look like followers but they subscribe to a counterfeit gospel and do not truly follow Jesus. Most often, they are the product of seed that fell upon rocky or thorny soil. They subscribe to religious practice and tradition, and speak using religious jargon, but are guided by soulish, man-made interpretations instead of a true faith in God. Jesus often referred to the religious leaders of His day as blind guides – "weeds" who elevated the practice of tradition over true worship of the Father. At harvest time (the return of Christ), God Himself will separate these weeds from the wheat, gather them together and burn them (casting them into eternal hell). Be mindful that Jesus said, *"Not everyone who calls Me Lord will enter into God's Kingdom"* (Matthew 7:21). Jesus told His disciples to not spend their time on trying to pull out the weeds, rather to concentrate on planting and multiplying the wheat.

The Mustard Seed (false growth)

Jesus did not give us an explanation of this next parable about the mustard seed. He said that the Kingdom is *"like a mustard seed planted in a field. It is the smallest of all seeds, but it becomes a large plant"* – not a stately tree, but a large shrub. Birds then come and nest in its branches. Earlier in the parable of the sower and the soils, the birds represented the evil one that snatches away the seed. Bible scholars tell us that in passages like Daniel 4:12 and Ezekiel 17:23 the tree is used as a symbol of a world power. i believe that this parable is a continuation of what Jesus is teaching in the parable of the wheat and the weeds. Because, though the Kingdom work began just like a tiny mustard seed, over the centuries it has grown taking on many forms – some of it "wheat-like" and some of it "weed-like". It has grown to the point that now even the evil one "nests" in some of its branches.

Please allow me to illustrate. In much of the world, including the U.S., if you are a follower of Christ, it is problematic to identify yourself as a Christian. Not because of persecution for genuine faith, rather because "Christian" has come to mean so many things – much of which looks nothing like Jesus or His teachings – and in many instances is a perversion of the gospel. Just as weeds continue to be planted and grow, these false branches will continue to grow until Jesus returns. i am reminded of the axiom – "everything that is healthy grows; but not everything that grows is healthy." This parable is a reminder that not everything that is a part of the plant is truly what Jesus planted. We must always test everything we see and hear against God's Word.

The Yeast (false doctrine)

Jesus did not explain this parable either – and i have heard it explained in different ways. Jesus said, the Kingdom is *"like the yeast a woman used in making bread. Even though she put only a little yeast in three measures of flour, it permeated every part of the dough"* (Matthew 13:33). Some talk about the gospel being that yeast (leaven) that spreads and permeates. The problem with that interpretation is that leaven is never used anywhere else in the Bible as being a "good" thing – it is a symbol of "evil". Jesus used leaven to symbolize hypocrisy (Luke 12:1) and false teaching (Matthew 16:6-12). Even the apostle Paul used leaven as a symbol for sin (1 Corinthians 5:6-7). i believe that the leaven Jesus is talking about in this parable is false teaching.

Today there is an ever-growing movement within the church toward compromising Biblical truth with the politically correct views of our day. Truth has moved from being absolute (what God has said in His Word) to relative (whatever current society says that it is). Let us heed the apostle Paul's admonition to the believers in Thessalonians 5:21 to *"test everything"* and only *"hold on to what is good."* Because even a little leaven spoils the whole loaf.

Though these are simple stories, they are important truths. Hold on to them as you continue in your day-to-day journey. Satan is at work opposing the work of the Master by sowing counterfeit Christians, encouraging false growth and introducing false doctrine. When our Lord returns, all will be exposed and all will be judged. Until then, test everything, and only hold on to what is good!

* * *

29

EVEN THE WIND OBEYS

As evening came, Jesus said to His disciples, "Let's cross to the other side of the lake." So they took Jesus in the boat and started out, leaving the crowds behind (although other boats followed). But soon a fierce storm came up. High waves were breaking into the boat, and it began to fill with water. Jesus was sleeping at the back of the boat with His head on a cushion. The disciples woke Him up, shouting, "Teacher, don't You care that we're going to drown?" When Jesus woke up, He rebuked the wind and said to the waves, "Silence! Be still!" Suddenly the wind stopped, and there was a great calm. Then He asked them, "Why are you afraid? Do you still have no faith?" The disciples were absolutely terrified. "Who is this man?" they asked each other.
"Even the wind and waves obey Him!"
Mark 4:35-41

* * *

Walking with the Master does not mean that we will not go through storms – just ask the disciples! They learned, as must we, that storms are a part of the journey. The storms of our life, at the very least, are permitted by our Sovereign Lord and, in some instances, are orchestrated by Him. All for the purpose that He desires to accomplish in and through our lives for His glory. So here are four lessons to be learned from this experience for the next time your journey takes you into a storm.

<u>Remember His promise that He gave you before you encountered the storm</u>. As they all got into the boat, Jesus said, *"Let's cross to the other side*

of the lake." He did not say, *"Let's go out to the middle of the lake... and there we will sink."* We must hold on to His promise before the storm, in the midst of the storm, and after the storm has passed. He is trustworthy! What He says will be accomplished! He never promised the disciples an easy trip, but He did guarantee that they would arrive at their destination.

The disciples were in the storm because of their obedience to Jesus. Unlike Jonah, who had encountered a storm to redirect him due to his disobedience to God, these guys were doing exactly what Jesus told them to do. They started well. Jesus gave them a word and, by faith, they obeyed. They trusted His word to start out when it was smooth sailing. What they needed to learn was to trust His word when the storm came upon them.

You may be going through a storm right now. It may be health-related... or financial... or you may find that you are unemployed. Whatever the storm is, hold on to His promise. At the very least – even if He has not given you a specific promise about this particular storm – whatever it is – Jesus has promised you that He will never fail you or abandon you (Hebrews 13:5)! i am often reminded of His promise of provision through the shepherd David in Psalm 37:25 – *"Once I was young, and now I am old. Yet I have never seen the godly abandoned or their children begging for bread."* Whatever the promise, hold on to it! Because He is true to His word!

Take comfort in His presence in the midst of the storm. Now granted, we can only take strength from that fact if we are truly walking in His presence, and we haven't headed off doing our own thing. i can do that really easily. i can head off in my own direction, trusting in my own wisdom and my own strength. i can ignore what the Master has told me to do and be walking in disobedience. In those times, it's difficult to take comfort in His presence. But the good news is if i repent of my disobedience and seek His forgiveness, i have then entered back into His presence. Just ask Jonah – the Lord may not have been right there with him in the hold of the ship, but He sure was there in the belly of the big fish.

As you take comfort in His presence, take a cue from His demeanor. He was at peace in that boat – sleeping soundly. Allow His peace to rule over you, even when the waves are breaking around you. i agree that is more easily said than done, but keep your eyes on Him and do not let your circumstances distract you. The reality of your situation is dependent upon what Jesus says it is, not based on the circumstances you are seeing. It was the unbelief of the disciples that caused their fear, not the storm and not their circumstances. So take comfort in His presence.

Your Master is more powerful than your storm. When we're in the midst of the storm, we, too, have a tendency to ask, *"Master, don't You care that we're going to drown?"* We act as if our Lord is off doing something else and has no idea what we are facing, or if He knows, that He doesn't care. Our God is omniscient – which means He has "infinite awareness, infinite understanding and infinite insight". There is not anything outside of His view. There is not anything taking place in our lives that is beyond His capacity to know what needs to be done to make it right. AND, there is nothing beyond His capability to make it right. He is all powerful. *"The LORD hasn't lost His powerful strength; He can still hear and answer* prayers" (Isaiah 59:1 CEV).

He is the Lord God Creator who created all things.
He is the Great Physician who is able to bring healing.
He is Jehovah Jireh who is able to provide all that is needed.
He is the Great I Am.
He speaks… and even the wind obeys and the storm calms!

Your Master will use your storm to bring Himself glory. The disciples had no idea what Jesus would do. They didn't know to ask Him, *"Jesus, would you still the storm?"* They had an advantage over us in that regard. They didn't really know Who He was. They had an idea, but they didn't have the full picture. They didn't comprehend the magnitude of Who He was and what He could do. Therefore all they could do was call out to Him in desperation. Whereas we, knowing that He is the Almighty God, have it in our minds to tell Him what we would like Him to do. We have thought through the best solution to our storm – *"so Jesus, we've already figured it out; we just need You to do this, that, or the other thing!"* Wrong! *"'My thoughts are nothing like your thoughts,' says the LORD. 'And My ways are far beyond anything you could imagine.'"* More than likely, He will not still your storm in the way you expected – or perhaps in the way you would have preferred. But one fact stands above all the rest – He will still the storm in the way that brings Him the greatest glory! And we may not understand what that is on this side of heaven. But we will hold to His promise that He *"causes everything to work together for the good of those who love God and are called according to His purpose for them."*

. . .

Jesus rebuked the wind, and then He rebuked the disciples – *"Do you still have no faith?"* Then we read *"The disciples were absolutely terrified."* The disciples were not terrified by what He asked; they were terrified by what they had just seen Him do. They somewhat had an excuse – they hadn't seen Jesus do that before. We don't have that excuse. We have it on the authority of good and faithful firsthand reports, as well as in our own lives.

So what storm have you encountered as you walk with the Master? Do you still have no faith? Trust Him – even the wind and waves obey Him!

* * *

30

JESUS DOESN'T DO RANDOM

...They arrived in the region of the Gerasenes, across the lake from Galilee. As Jesus was climbing out of the boat, a man who was possessed by demons came out to meet Him. For a long time he had been homeless and naked, living in the tombs outside the town. As soon as he saw Jesus, he shrieked and fell down in front of Him. Then he screamed, "Why are You interfering with me, Jesus, Son of the Most High God? Please, I beg You, don't torture me!" For Jesus had already commanded the evil spirit to come out of him. This spirit had often taken control of the man. Even when he was placed under guard and put in chains and shackles, he simply broke them and rushed out into the wilderness, completely under the demon's power. Jesus demanded, "What is your name?" "Legion," he replied, for he was filled with many demons. The demons kept begging Jesus not to send them into the bottomless pit. There happened to be a large herd of pigs feeding on the hillside nearby, and the demons begged Him to let them enter into the pigs. So Jesus gave them permission. Then the demons came out of the man and entered the pigs, and the entire herd plunged down the steep hillside into the lake and drowned....

Luke 8:26-39

* * *

As you walk with the Master, you will move from one experience to the next. Jesus will be teaching you through each one, and always His next teaching will be building on what He just taught you. As you read this passage, don't lose sight that the disciples have just gone through a harrowing ride. They have just seen Jesus, through His spoken word, still the winds and calm the waves. Matthew writes that the disciples were amazed. Mark says they were absolutely terrified. Luke, ever the one to include all the details, says they were amazed AND terrified. They had seen Jesus heal the sick. They had even witnessed Jesus through His spoken word raise a young servant from the dead – though they had not actually seen the dead boy arise since he was miles away. But now they had seen creation itself obey! Their emotions had made the journey from fearing for their lives to terrified amazement in just one instant. If i had gone through that experience, i know that i would still have been processing it. It's not an experience that you go through and then just turn it off and go forward to the next thing. Remember – they knew Jesus was the Messiah – but they had never envisioned a Messiah like this! And they were still asking, *"Who is this Man?"* (Luke 8:25).

As soon as they arrive on the other side, just as Jesus is getting out of the boat, the men are there at the shore to meet them. One other thing to remember – the night before, as they got into the boat, Jesus had told them, *"Let's cross to the other side of the lake"* (Luke 8:22). The disciples had no idea why they were going to the other side of the lake. They had no idea what Jesus' purpose was or who they would encounter. But Jesus did! Nothing with Jesus is random! He doesn't waste an experience or an encounter. Nothing is inconsequential. So, on your journey, don't try to come up with your own next step. Follow the example of the disciples. Keep following Him wherever He goes. As you do, you will be right where He wants you to be – in the midst of His activity – and His purpose – for His glory!

Matthew reports that there were two men who were possessed by demons (Matthew 8:28). Apparently one was the spokesman, because Mark and Luke only reference the one. They were homeless, naked and living in tombs. They were strong and violent, able to break their chains and shackles, and escape those who were guarding them. With a shriek, the one screamed, *"Why are you interfering with me, Jesus, Son of the Most High God?"* Even before Jesus had said or done anything, they had come to the shore to meet Him. They were there as He arrived. The demons within the men knew more than the disciples did. They knew who Jesus was. They knew He was the Son of the Most High God. They knew His power. They knew His mission. They knew that one day He alone would judge them and cast them into eternal damnation. Their plea was not about <u>what</u> He would do – that was a foregone conclusion. Their plea was about <u>when</u> He was going to do it. *"Have You come here to torture us before God's appointed time?"* (Matthew 8:29)

. . .

These men were controlled by a legion of demons. (For reference, a Roman legion was as many as 6,000 men.) And that multitude of demons not only knew who Jesus was – they believed! They believed Who He was, in the authority that was His, and in the judgment that was to come and the torment they faced. They even believed in prayer! They were begging Jesus not to send them into the abyss. Jesus had already commanded them to come out of the men. Their plea was that Jesus would allow them to enter into a herd of 2,000 pigs, because they knew that Jesus would not permit them to enter into anyone else that was there on the shore.

Please understand this. The demons knew Who Jesus was. They knew the prophecies that they would one day be judged by Him. They also knew that the day of judgment had not yet come. But keep in mind that the demons can no more see into the future than you or i can. Their knowledge and beliefs were founded in what God had said through His prophets. Beyond that, they do not have foreknowledge.

So when Jesus granted their plea and gave them permission to enter into that herd of pigs, they had no idea what was coming next! But Jesus did! And that entire herd of pigs bolted for the lake and drowned. Remember, Jesus doesn't "do" random! He has a purpose and a plan in everything that He does!

Before you get too sympathetic about those 2,000 pigs, i want you to be mindful of how much Jesus valued those two possessed men. He valued them over the lives of those pigs. Be mindful of how much He values you and me. He values us so much that He was willing to lay down His own life for us. The Father gave His Son so that we might have everlasting life. What's that compared to 2,000 pigs?

At least one of the men who had been set free from the bondage of the demons (Luke 8:38) begged Jesus to allow him to go with Him. But Jesus told him to go back to his family *"and tell them everything God has done for you."* And Mark tells us that the man went all through the ten towns of that region proclaiming, *"the great things Jesus had done for him"* (Mark 5:20).

It is sad to note that the herdsmen and the people of that nearby town were more concerned about the pigs that had died than the men who had been delivered. Jesus was in their midst, but sadly the demons believed in Him much more than the townspeople. As a result, Jesus left them and crossed back to the other side.

Imagine what the disciples were thinking through all of this and as they continued on their journey with Jesus. Not only does the wind obey, but the demons believe. Not only does He still the storm, He sets captives free. And there is nothing random about anything He does! Remember that!

* * *

31

SENT FROM THE CLASSROOM INTO THE LAB

Then Jesus went from village to village, teaching the people. And He called His twelve disciples together and began sending them out two by two, giving them authority to cast out evil spirits. He told them to take nothing for their journey except a walking stick—no food, no traveler's bag, no money. He allowed them to wear sandals but not to take a change of clothes. "Wherever you go," He said, "stay in the same house until you leave town. But if any place refuses to welcome you or listen to you, shake its dust from your feet as you leave to show that you have abandoned those people to their fate." So the disciples went out, telling everyone they met to repent of their sins and turn to God. And they cast out many demons and healed many sick people, anointing them with olive oil.
Mark 6:6-13

* * *

To this point, the disciples had been following Jesus, watching Jesus and providing a helping hand to Jesus whenever He required them to do so. They had been in observation mode in the "classroom". On this day, Jesus was sending them from the classroom into the lab. He was sending them out – as Mark records *"two by two"* – to "teach and do" what they had been observing Jesus "teach and do". He was sending them out into the villages of Judea to preach the Good News. He was now teaching them an important Kingdom truth that, if they truly were going to follow Him, it would involve leading others to follow Him. He wanted them to fully understand that the truths He was entrusting to them, they in turn were to entrust to others.

. . .

This is a truth that i fear many of us as followers of Jesus have yet to learn and practice. How many of us have heard the Good News and Message of Jesus and have never shared it with anyone else? How many of us have lost sight of the truth that a follower of Jesus is a disciple who is making other disciples who are making other disciples?

At this moment in their journey, the disciples were learning that following Jesus meant that they must live as those who have been sent. Jesus' last words to His disciples before He ascended to Heaven (Matthew 28:18-20; Mark 16:16-18; Luke 24:48-49; John 20:21; Acts 1:8) were that they were to share the Good News and make disciples among every people (as are we). Each one of us as followers is to live as one who has been sent. As we walk with the Master, we must walk as one who has been sent by the Master. And the same truths that He spoke to the disciples here apply to us as well.

As we look at these truths, let's first remember that these were ordinary men. As we saw in chapters 14-20 of this book, these men did not have special powers or abilities. Most of them were uneducated and were from very humble backgrounds. They were no different from you and me. And i have to believe, when Jesus told them that He was sending them out into the villages, most of them – if not all of them – were apprehensive. They'd never done anything like this before! It's one thing to tag with Jesus when He is teaching and healing – but it's quite another matter for Him to send us out to do so without Him. Remember, at this point, they didn't fully understand that He was the Son of God, but they believed He was the Messiah. And they knew they weren't. So how could they possibly do what they had seen Jesus do?

First, Jesus sent them out with His power and His authority. Their ability and their calling came from Jesus. All that they would do would be the result of Jesus working through them. The Spirit of God was going before them, with them and behind them. And the Son of God was working through them. He gave them the power to cast out demons and to heal the sick. Matthew, in his account (Matthew 10:1-15), includes that Jesus gave them the power to cure those with leprosy and raise the dead. They were not sent out to go work on their own. They were ambassadors of Christ (2 Corinthians 5:20). And He gave them the power to accomplish whatever would be needed for the fulfillment of His mission.

. . .

Second, Jesus sent them out with a clear purpose – to tell *"everyone they met to repent of their sins and turn to God."* Don't lose sight that Jesus' purpose was not to heal physical sicknesses, it was to see sinners set free from their sin. And the missional purpose He gave the disciples was to be about that clear message.

Third, Jesus sent them with an urgency. He told them to go now – to take what they had on them. They were not to go out and acquire anything else for the trip. They were to go with a sense of urgency for the mission and a complete dependence on God that He would provide whatever they needed to fulfill that mission. Jesus wanted them to be adequately supplied, but not to the point that they ceased to live by faith. The Father would provide whatever they needed – including food and lodging through willing hosts.

He told them that, as they went, they would encounter hospitality from some… and hostility from others. That was the case for Jesus. Why would it be any different for those He sent? But He reminded them that if a village or a home refused to welcome them, it was not them who were being refused or rejected – it was Jesus. And the disciples were not to let it discourage them or keep them from continuing in the mission for which He had sent them. Rather they were to *"shake {the} dust from your feet as you leave to show that you have abandoned those people to their fate."*

In all three Gospel accounts – Matthew, Mark and Luke (Luke 9:1-6) – we read that the Good News was preached, the sick were healed, and demons were cast out. We don't actually read as to whether or not anyone repented and believed. The "success" of their mission as sent ones was not to be measured based upon how many people responded, rather by their obedience and faithfulness to the One who had sent them. Today, we most frequently evaluate the effectiveness of a ministry or mission by the number of people who have made "decisions for Christ". It's important to remember that Jesus never used that criteria, His focus was always on the faithfulness and obedience of those He had sent.

So, as we walk with the Master, the reminder for you and me is that, if we are followers of Jesus, we too have been sent. We have been sent out with His power and authority – throughout our traffic patterns of life – as well as to every corner of the world. We have been sent with a clear purpose to make disciples. And we have been sent with an urgency. Isn't about time we ventured out of the "classroom" and into the lab?

* * *

32

MORE THAN ENOUGH, WITH PLENTY LEFT OVER

After this, Jesus crossed over to the far side of the Sea of Galilee, also known as the Sea of Tiberias. A huge crowd kept following Him wherever He went, because they saw His miraculous signs as He healed the sick. Then Jesus climbed a hill and sat down with His disciples around Him. (It was nearly time for the Jewish Passover celebration. Jesus soon saw a huge crowd of people coming to look for Him. Turning to Philip, He asked, "Where can we buy bread to feed all these people?" He was testing Philip, for He already knew what He was going to do. Philip replied, "Even if we worked for months, we wouldn't have enough money to feed them!" Then Andrew, Simon Peter's brother, spoke up. "There's a young boy here with five barley loaves and two fish. But what good is that with this huge crowd?" "Tell everyone to sit down," Jesus said. So they all sat down on the grassy slopes. (The men alone numbered about 5,000.) Then Jesus took the loaves, gave thanks to God, and distributed them to the people. Afterward he did the same with the fish. And they all ate as much as they wanted. After everyone was full, Jesus told His disciples, "Now gather the leftovers, so that nothing is wasted." So they picked up the pieces and filled twelve baskets with scraps left by the people who had eaten from the five barley loaves. When the people saw him do this miraculous sign, they exclaimed, "Surely, He is the Prophet we have been expecting!" When Jesus saw that they were ready to force Him to be their king, He slipped away into the hills by Himself.

John 6:1-15

* * *

The disciples had just returned from their time in the villages. They were excited to tell Jesus everything they had done and experienced

(Luke 9:10). If you have ever been a part of a short-term mission team that has been sent out to carry the Good News to another part of the nation or the world, you can probably relate somewhat to the disciples. Like them, you probably saw the transforming work of the gospel and the leadership of the Spirit. You may have witnessed miraculous healing. But one thing is for sure, you experienced the awesome privilege of joining with God in His activity – and now, you want to tell everyone about the experience. And hopefully, you and your team had an opportunity to debrief the experience. That's how it was for the disciples. They wanted Jesus to hear all about their time, and He wanted to debrief them.

So Jesus pulled away from the crowds with the disciples to do just that. He climbed a hill and sat down with His disciples and began to hear about their experiences. But the masses kept following, and a huge crowd had gathered. Jesus *"welcomed them and taught them about the Kingdom of God, and He healed those who were sick"* (Luke 9:11). Late in the afternoon the disciples said to Jesus, *"Send the crowds away to the nearby villages and farms, so they can find food and lodging for the night. There is nothing to eat here in this remote place"* (Luke 9:12). But Jesus had a different plan – His perfect plan. He always has a perfect plan!

One other side road: when Jesus sent out the twelve, He told them not to take food with them. Rather, they were to depend on the hospitality of those they encountered. I can't help but wonder if Jesus was preparing to return the favor – to provide hospitality to this crowd – and at the same time bring glory to the Father.

Jesus turned to Philip and asked him, *"Where can we buy bread to feed all these people?"* John tells us that Jesus was testing Philip. Why Philip? To this point, all of the disciples had seen Jesus perform many miracles – most recently the calming of the storm and the healing of the demon possessed men. (Forgive the quip: but where are those 2,000 pigs when Jesus needs them now?)

But Philip had been one of the handful with Jesus that day at the wedding feast in Cana. He had been one of those who "believed in Jesus" as a result of that miracle (John 2:11). John also had been there. And that's why i believe he mentions this conversation between Jesus and Philip – whereas none of the other Gospels make mention of it. Philip had seen Jesus transform water into wine. Couldn't that same Jesus transform anything into food? Had Philip learned a truth that day? And could he apply it here? This was Philip's big opportunity to shine. But alas, he missed it! He had already worked out what was needed (even *"two hundred denarii worth of bread is not sufficient"* – John 6:7 NKJ). Incidentally i wonder if Judas had given the treasurer's report that morning and reported that they had two hundred denarii in their treasury.

But then Andrew, who had also been at the wedding feast, steps up and says, *"There's a young boy here with five barley loaves and two fish."* Andrew would have been the prize pupil if he had stopped there. But he went on to say, *"But what good is that with this huge crowd?"* He forgot to Whom he was speaking. And that is an important reminder for us. Whatever God entrusts to us is sufficient for His purpose – no matter how inconsequential it may appear to us.

Jesus told the disciples to have the crowd sit down – and watch the difference a little can make in the hands of the Master? After thanking the Father for the provision, Jesus took a young boy's lunch and transformed it into a feast for five thousand men, plus women and children – probably fifteen thousand or more people. And everyone ate until they were full! The Master's provision will always be enough when it is presented in His way for His glory!

So that there would be a visual reminder, Jesus had the leftovers gathered. Imagine seeing twelve baskets filled with barley loaves and fishes, having earlier seen a "tiny sack lunch". And the people who had come that day to see Jesus perform miracles were by no means disappointed. They were ready to declare Him King. Regrettably, they weren't ready to follow Him as Lord and Savior. They witnessed the miracle, but totally missed the Miracle Worker. And John writes that Jesus *"slipped away into the hills by Himself."*

What went through the disciples' minds that day? Specifically, what went through Philip's and Andrew's minds? Were they focused on what Jesus had done? Or were they in awe of Who He was? Did they see Jesus based upon what He had done – that day and in days past – or Who He was?

And what about us – as we walk with the Master? Do we look at Him and evaluate Him based upon what He has done for us – this day or in days past – or based upon Who He is? What He does will constantly be changing – and He will always know what is best. But Who He is – the Almighty God – will never change. Trust Him! He is trustworthy! And He is worthy to be followed – not only as King, but also as Lord and Savior! He is more than enough – with plenty left over!

* * *

33

TAKE A WALK ON THE WATER

When Jesus saw that they were ready to force Him to be their king, He slipped away into the hills by Himself. That evening Jesus' disciples went down to the shore to wait for Him. But as darkness fell and Jesus still hadn't come back, they got into the boat and headed across the lake toward Capernaum. Soon a gale swept down upon them, and the sea grew very rough. They had rowed three or four miles when suddenly they saw Jesus walking on the water toward the boat. They were terrified, but He called out to them, "Don't be afraid. I am here!" Then they were eager to let Him in the boat, and immediately they arrived at their destination!

John 6:15-21

* * *

Three of the Gospel writers give an account of this night – Matthew (14:22-34), Mark (6:45-53) and John. Jesus had just performed the miracle of feeding the five thousand men, plus women and children. As the crowd watched the disciples collect the twelve baskets of leftovers, the significance of what Jesus had just done with five loaves and two fishes began to sink in with the crowd. They had come with the expectation of seeing Jesus perform a miracle, and He had not disappointed them. The crowd became frenzied. They were *"ready to force {Jesus} to be their king."* i'm certain that some of the disciples, most notably Judas Iscariot, were rejoicing that finally Jesus would be raised into His rightful position as the Messiah, and they, as His faithful followers, would receive their reward of power and position. The crowd and, even at least some of, the disciples were stirred with excitement.

. . .

Matthew and Mark tell us that Jesus "insisted that His disciples get back into the boat" and cross to the other side of the lake. He knew that they were in danger of being caught up in the frenzy, so He was getting them away from the harmful influence of the crowd. Let's stop and apply this. As we walk with the Master, there will be times when Jesus redirects us with urgency. More than likely, we will not fully understand why Jesus is being so emphatic. He is doing so in light of two possible reasons – and maybe both – one, to protect us from harm in our immediate circumstance (most often a harm we don't see or comprehend) and two, to redirect us to another work that He is orchestrating (again, most often, outside of our line of sight). In this case, for the disciples it was both.

The disciples got in the boat and waited. Jesus had told them to go to the other side, but they didn't want to abandon Him to the crowd or leave Him behind. Again, there is a question as to their motivation. Was it a sincere concern for Jesus and His safety, or was it to protect their soulish ambition if He was about to step into His rightful position of power? Regardless, while they waited, Jesus slipped away from the crowd and had gone into the hills to spend time with His Father in prayer. As darkness fell, the crowd was dispersing, and the moment appeared to have passed. The disciples began to wonder if Jesus had found another way to get to the other side. They decided that they needed to do what the Master had instructed them to do; they needed to cross back over the lake to Gennesaret, near Capernaum.

As their journey across the lake begins, continue to be mindful that at least half of these guys had grown up on this lake. They had been fishing on boats on this lake since they were old enough to throw a net. This was a familiar place for them. Also, just a few days before, they had made a similar journey to Gennesaret. That time Jesus had been in the boat with them – and had calmed the storm. So now, in the midst of something very familiar, comes "the lesson in the boat 2.0".

They were out in the middle of the lake, and they were besieged by heavy waves and a strong wind. Unexpected wind and waves were not unusual on the lake, but they can come upon you suddenly and require all of the attention and skill of experienced seamen. All of a sudden, all of their thoughts and conversation about what they had just witnessed Jesus do ceased, and their complete attention turned to the storm surrounding them. A few years ago, my wife and i were crossing the Sea of Galilee with a group in a boat similar to the one the disciples would have been on. When we left shore, the day was still and sunny and the sea was calm. We were thoroughly enjoying the sights and experience of the crossing with our fellow passengers. Thirty minutes into the journey, the waves began to pound, and the winds began to blow. At that moment, our attention quickly turned to staying out of the spray of the sea and keeping our excellent lunches in our bellies. Our experienced boat captain and crew craftily navigated our boat through the storm to the other side, where we arrived soaked from head to toe, but safe – and with a great story to tell! i can tell you first hand, that when the waves and wind arose, the focus of the disciples was turned to *"rowing hard and struggling against the wind and waves."*

Did Jesus know that He was sending the disciples into a storm? Of course He did! The disciples had just experienced tremendous exhilaration in being part of such a great miracle. But what had they learned? And would they apply what they learned in this storm? Was the same Jesus – who just a few days before had spoken and calmed these very seas -- and a few hours before had fed a multitude with a little boy's lunch – able to deliver them from a storm in the midst of a journey He had directed them to take? And did they have the faith to trust Him to do so? Mark writes that their hearts were still *"too hard"* to take in the significance of the miracle of the loaves. (Remember that Simon Peter is Mark's source for what he writes. So this truly is a confession from Peter!)

The disciples had only traveled three to four miles over many hours as they struggled against the storm. It was now three o'clock in the morning when Jesus came toward them, *"walking on the water."* All three Gospel writers write that the disciples *"were terrified"*. They all thought Jesus was a ghost! Then Jesus called out to them, *"Don't be afraid! Take courage. I am here!"*

Matthew records that Simon Peter called out, *"Lord, if it's really You, tell me to come to You, walking on the water."* Perhaps it was at this moment that Peter truly began to understand what they had witnessed Jesus do with the five thousand. Because it prompted an expression of faith from him, unlike any of the other disciples. So that when Jesus said, *"Come!"*, Peter jumped over the side of the boat and *"walked on the water toward Jesus."*

. . .

i would contend that only One walked on the water that night, and that One was Jesus. **Peter didn't walk on the water..., he walked on a word from Jesus – *"Come!"*** It wasn't water he was trusting in. He was trusting in the word that had been spoken to him, and the One who had spoken it. The impossible – feeding five thousand with a boy's lunch, or walking on water – becomes possible only when Jesus says so! We can't wish it into existence; we can only experience it becoming so, because Jesus has said it is so! And once He does, we must step out on faith, keeping our eyes on Him, His word, and His promise. Because the moment we divert our eyes to the circumstances surrounding us, we will "sink" just like Peter did. But let's be careful to not judge Peter too harshly – he was the only one with the faith to get out of the boat!

John records that as soon as Jesus and Peter got back into the boat, they *"immediately arrived at their destination."* The lesson was over. The truth had been taught. The purpose for that leg of the journey was complete.

As you walk with the Master, be mindful that every leg of the journey has purpose. Jesus has designed and directed your path for His divine purpose in and through your life. Peter may have witnessed a miracle when Jesus fed five thousand, but he experienced the miracle when he stepped out by faith. What word has Jesus given you to step out on today? If you don't have one, have you asked Him for one? And once He has given it to you, be prepared to step out on it by faith – without delay. Today's a good day to take a walk on the water – if that's what Jesus has planned!

* * *

34

THE BREAD OF LIFE

The next day the crowd that had stayed on the far shore saw that the disciples had taken the only boat, and they realized Jesus had not gone with them.... When the crowd saw that neither Jesus nor His disciples were there, they got into the boats.... They found Him on the other side of the lake and asked, "Rabbi, when did You get here?" Jesus replied, "I tell you the truth, you want to be with Me because I fed you, not because you understood the miraculous signs. But don't be so concerned about perishable things like food. Spend your energy seeking the eternal life that the Son of Man can give you. For God the Father has given Me the seal of His approval." ...They answered, "Show us a miraculous sign if You want us to believe in You. ... After all, our ancestors ate manna while they journeyed through the wilderness! The Scriptures say, 'Moses gave them bread from heaven to eat.'" Jesus said, "I tell you the truth, Moses didn't give you bread from heaven. My Father did. And now He offers you the true bread from heaven. The true bread of God is the One who comes down from heaven and gives life to the world." "Sir," they said, "give us that bread every day." Jesus replied, "I am the bread of life. Whoever comes to Me will never be hungry again. Whoever believes in Me will never be thirsty. But you haven't believed in Me even though you have seen Me.... Anyone who eats this bread will not die as your ancestors did (even though they ate the manna) but will live forever."

John 6:22-59

* * *

The day before, this crowd had been fed until they could eat no more, out of a young boy's meager lunch. They had been in a frenzy to force Jesus to be their king (John 6:15). But that was yesterday. Today, they wanted another miraculous sign in order to believe in Jesus (John 6:30). And tomorrow, they would seek another. Because if all you are seeking is a miracle, it will never be enough.

Throughout their journey in the wilderness, the Israelites saw God single-handedly destroy the mightiest army on the face of the earth, after He had made a way for the Israelites' escape through a parted Red Sea. But it was only a matter of days before they were again grumbling and complaining, and seeking another miracle. That pattern would be repeated time and again throughout that forty-year journey. And it wouldn't stop there… and it didn't stop only with the people of Israel. It was true of this crowd in Capernaum… and it is true of you and me. Miracles are like manna. They are only sufficient for the day. **If all we seek is a miracle, we'll always be looking for the next one.**

As i read this account, two other previous encounters come to mind. The first is the wedding feast at Cana. The wedding guests – the "crowd" at the wedding – experienced the "fruit" of the miracle, but only the servants had seen and experienced the Miracle Worker. And as a result, the crowd was unchanged, but the servants knew and believed. The second is the Samaritan woman. She came to the well solely looking for water, but she ended up seeing and experiencing the Miracle Worker. And as a result, she – and many of her neighbors – knew and believed.

But this crowd at Capernaum only saw the miracle. And even though at one point they wanted to make Him their king, they never truly saw the Miracle Worker. The Samaritan woman sought water and ended up with Living Water. This crowd sought more bread but rejected the Bread of Life. The Samaritan woman saw past her prejudice toward a Jewish man, and she walked away redeemed. This crowd couldn't see past their familiarity with Him as the son of Joseph and Mary (John 6:42), and they walked away unchanged.

Those who come to Jesus as the Bread of Life *"will never be hungry again."* And those who come to Him as Living Water *"will never be thirsty."* But regrettably, neither was true of that crowd. Jesus said to them, *"You haven't believed in Me even though you have seen Me"* (John 6:36).

At that point, Jesus begins to teach them some of the most profound truth about salvation that He ever spoke. He explains that salvation involves both divine sovereignty and human responsibility – the sovereignty of God and the free will of man. These are two truths that to our finite minds seem contradictory to one another. But to a sovereign God they work together in perfect harmony. Jesus said,

"Those the Father has given Me will come to Me, and I will never reject them" (vs. 37)
– divine sovereignty
"It is My Father's will that all who see His Son and believe in Him should have eternal life" (vs. 40)
– human responsibility
"No one can come to Me unless the Father who sent Me draws them to Me..." (vs. 44)
– divine sovereignty
"Everyone who listens to the Father and learns from Him comes to Me" (vs. 45)
– human responsibility
"I am the Living Bread.... Anyone who eats this Bread will live forever..." (vs. 51)
– human responsibility

Charles Spurgeon was once asked how he reconciled these two truths. He replied, simply, *"I never try to reconcile friends."* It is the Father's will that none should perish (2 Peter 3:9). The Father draws. The sinner repents and believes. Those who come to Jesus are eternally secure in their salvation. Warren Wiersbe writes, *"The sinner hears, learns and comes as the Father draws him. A mystery? Yes! A blessed reality? Yes!"*

As we close out this chapter of our journey with the Master, be mindful of these truths:

- There was no cost to the Father in sending manna each day, but there was great cost to the Father to give His Son as the Bread of Life!
- The Jews had to eat manna daily, but the Bread of Life only needs to be received once, and whoever receives it will hunger no more.
- Manna was the gracious gift of God given to an undeserving, obstinate, rebellious people. The Bread of Life is the gracious

> gift of God to an undeserving, obstinate, rebellious people who believe in Him.

Heed this word of encouragement from this psalm of David: *"Taste and see that the LORD is good. Oh, the joys of those who take refuge in Him!"* (Psalm 34:8)

* * *

35

WHO DO YOU SAY JESUS IS?

One day Jesus left the crowds to pray alone. Only His disciples were with Him, and He asked them, "Who do people say I am?" "Well," they replied, "some say John the Baptist, some say Elijah, and others say You are one of the other ancient prophets risen from the dead." Then He asked them, "But who do you say I am?" Peter replied, "You are the Messiah sent from God!" Jesus warned His disciples not to tell anyone who He was.
Luke 9:18-21

* * *

If i was to ask you. "who do you say i am?", you would be correct to immediately question my motive. Am i seeking approval or affirmation? Does my self-worth rest on who others believe me to be? Where am i headed with this question? Am i intending to manipulate your thinking? We could come up with a variety of possible reasons, most of which would reflect poorly on me.

But i cannot think of a more pivotal question to ask someone than "who do you say Jesus is?" It is a question that immediately gets to the heart of who we are. The answer immediately expresses one's religious beliefs, personal convictions, life trajectory, and eternal destiny.

. . .

Every major world religion acknowledges Jesus. Muslims believe He was a prophet. Jews believe He was a teacher and a miracle worker. Hindus believe He was a holy man, even a "god". Buddhists believe He was an enlightened man and a wise teacher. Baha'is believe that Jesus came from God and was a wise teacher with a divine nature. Even the New Age movement believes that Jesus was a wise moral teacher.

Even within those beliefs that are often included under the umbrella of Christianity, there are differing views. The Jehovah's Witnesses believe Jesus was God's first creation, separate from God. Though Mormons believe that Jesus is the Son of God, they believe that the Father and Jesus are two distinct beings and that Jesus began as a spirit child of God. Christian Scientists view Jesus as a "way-shower" between humanity and God.

When Jesus walked on the earth, there also were a myriad of views. "*Some say John the Baptist, some say Elijah, others say… one of the ancient prophets risen from the dead.*" The Pharisees called Him "Teacher". Those from Nazareth called Him "Jesus the Carpenter, the son of Joseph".

By this point, the disciples had been following Jesus through at least two Passovers. Jesus was about to tell them that He would be killed and He would rise from the dead on the third day. So before He begins to describe <u>what</u> He is going to do, He wants to make certain that His disciples understand <u>Who</u> He is. When Peter responds, he is doing so both out of personal conviction and belief, and also as a spokesperson for the entire group. The disciples had spent much time together discussing this very question ever since they had first begun to follow Jesus. Some had been there at the baptism of Jesus when the Father declared Him to be His Beloved Son (Matthew 3:17). Given all that they had seen Jesus do, all that they had heard Him teach, and what the Father Himself had revealed, Peter boldly proclaimed, "*You are the Messiah, the Son of the Living God*" (Matthew 16:16).

But Jesus then did something that was curious. He "*sternly warned the disciples not to tell anyone that He was the Messiah*" (Matthew 16:20). Having seen how the crowd reacted at the feeding of the five thousand, Jesus knew that if the apostles began to publicly preach that He was indeed the Messiah, it would lead to a popular uprising against Rome. And, of course, that was not His mission. But once Jesus rose from the dead, the apostles were no longer under that restriction to not tell. As a matter of fact, they were given a mandate – sent out on a mission – to tell everyone Who Jesus was and the Good News of the gospel.

And we, too, have been sent out on that mission to tell the world Who Jesus is and what He has done. And each person on this planet needs to hear that Good News and answer for themselves Who they say Jesus is.

Was He merely sent by God, or is He the Son of God?
Was He merely a good man, or is He the Son of Man?
Was He a crucified martyr, or is He the crucified and risen Savior?
Was He simply a miracle worker, or is He the Giver of Life?
Was He simply a teacher and a prophet, or is He the Word Who became flesh?
Was He simply one of many ways to the Father, or is He the One and Only Way?
Was He simply a teacher of truths, or is He the living absolute Truth?

Then each one, must go one additional step with their answer:

Is He simply the Savior of the world, or is He also my Savior?
Is He simply the Lord over all, or is He also the Lord of my life?

The reality is that you can't be neutral about who Jesus is. He was clear about Who He is. Whether i accept Him or reject Him doesn't change Who He is. It only changes who i am! My answer to that question will determine Who i follow in this journey of life…, what my purpose will be…, and what my eternal destiny will be.

i pray that each of you reading this, will join with Peter in saying, "Jesus, You are the Messiah, the Son of the Living God!" And join with me in saying, "And You are my Lord and my Savior, and i will follow You!"

* * *

36

A CHANGE IN OUR POINT OF VIEW

"The Son of Man must suffer many terrible things," he said. "He will be rejected by the elders, the leading priests, and the teachers of religious law. He will be killed, but on the third day He will be raised from the dead."
Then He said to the crowd, "If any of you wants to be My follower, you must give up your own way, take up your cross daily, and follow Me. If you try to hang on to your life, you will lose it. But if you give up your life for My sake, you will save it. And what do you benefit if you gain the whole world but are yourself lost or destroyed? If anyone is ashamed of Me and My message, the Son of Man will be ashamed of that person when He returns in His glory and in the glory of the Father and the holy angels."
Luke 9:22-26

* * *

Jesus has just underscored Who He is, and Peter, on behalf of the rest of the disciples, has declared their acknowledgement and belief that He is the Messiah, the Son of the Living God. Jesus knew that it was one thing for them to declare Who He was, but it was quite another for them to understand and follow Him in His mission. Remember, they are still thinking that He is soon going to establish His kingdom, overthrow Rome, and elevate them to their positions of power.

So Jesus tells them the mission, as plainly as He possibly can. The Son of Man will suffer. He will be rejected, and He will be killed, all at the hands of the elders, leading priests and teachers of the religious law. And on the third day He will rise from the dead. Though the disciples heard what He said, they didn't comprehend it. i believe they thought He was speaking metaphorically, not literally. Because He was the Messiah! He was the Son of God! He couldn't die!

And they were partially correct. None of that could occur in His life if He was solely the Son of God. The Son of God cannot die. He is eternal. He always was, and He always will be. Only as the Son of Man could He die. And only as the Son of Man could He suffer, carry our sorrows, and pay the price for our sins, fulfilling the prophecy through Isaiah:

> *He was despised and rejected — a Man of sorrows, acquainted with deepest grief.... He was despised, and we did not care. Yet it was our weaknesses He carried; it was our sorrows that weighed Him down....He was pierced for our rebellion, crushed for our sins. He was beaten so we could be whole. He was whipped so we could be healed. All of us, like sheep, have strayed away. We have left God's paths to follow our own. Yet the Lord laid on Him the sins of us all. He was oppressed and treated harshly, yet He never said a word. He was led like a lamb to the slaughter. And as a sheep is silent before the shearers, He did not open His mouth. Unjustly condemned, He was led away.... But He was struck down for the rebellion of My people. He had done no wrong and had never deceived anyone.... It was the Lord's good plan to crush Him and cause Him grief.... And because of His experience, my Righteous Servant will make it possible for many to be counted righteous, for He will bear all their sins* (Isaiah 53:3-11).

But the disciples had not yet made that connection. John the Baptist had already presented Him as *"the Lamb of God"* (John 1:29) and Jesus had predicted the "destruction " of the temple of His body (John 2:19). But they still hadn't put all the pieces together. Also, it may have still been hard for the disciples to hear that their Jewish leaders would be the ones to do all of this to their Master. They had grown up under their teaching.

As a matter of fact, Mark records that Peter reprimanded Jesus for having said such things (Mark 8:32). Again, as a reminder, Mark's Gospel is in fact an account from Peter. So Peter obviously clearly remembers how he foolishly contradicted and reprimanded Jesus that day. And he still "feels" the sting of the reprimand he received back from Jesus – *"Get away from Me, Satan! You are seeing things merely from a human point of view, not from God's"* (Mark 8:33).

. . .

i don't know about you, but that last part – *"you are seeing things merely from a human point of view, not from God's"* – is a constant battle for me – and i am too often in need of that reminder and reprimand from the Master!

But Jesus didn't stop with what His mission meant for Him, He went on to tell the disciples – and the crowd – what it meant for them to be His followers. As we already said, the disciples thought that they were getting ready to step into positions of power. For those in the crowd who were beginning to see Jesus as the Messiah, they thought they would soon be out from underneath the rule of Rome and would be their own masters. To which Jesus says (paraphrased), "if you want to follow Me, you must give up your right to be your own master, and you must take up an instrument of death." That was not the message they were expecting! And Jesus goes on and says (paraphrased), "if you try to keep your life, you'll lose it. *But if you give up your life for My sake, you will save it.*" Here the people are thinking about what the Messiah is going to do for them, and Jesus is telling them they must die to themselves. And folks, they aren't any different from many of us today. When we look at Jesus from our point of view, we're expecting Him to do things for us – heal us, bless us, provide for us, etc. What is Jesus going to do for us? Now, does Jesus heal, bless and provide? Of course He does. But that can't be our focus. Jesus said that day, *"What do you benefit if you gain the whole world but are yourself lost?"* We must die to our point of view and turn to Him!

And Jesus says, (paraphrased) "Furthermore, that Kingdom that you are expecting Me to establish – I will establish it when I return. But there will not be any place in it for you, if you have not died to yourself and to your own point of view and turned to Me!"

You and i both know that yes, there is a Kingdom that He will establish upon His return, but He has already begun His Kingdom. Turning to Him and following Him is not solely for the hereafter; it's also for the here and now!

As you walk with the Master on this journey, it's time to do some soul-searching on why you are following Him. Are you following Him for what He can do for you? Or are you following Him for Who He is and what He has already done for you… on a cross? Make sure you have the right point of view!

37

A DAY TO REMEMBER

"I tell you the truth, some standing here right now will not die before they see the Kingdom of God." About eight days later Jesus took Peter, John, and James up on a mountain to pray. And as He was praying, the appearance of His face was transformed, and His clothes became dazzling white. Suddenly, two men, Moses and Elijah, appeared and began talking with Jesus. They were glorious to see. And they were speaking about His exodus from this world, which was about to be fulfilled in Jerusalem. Peter and the others had fallen asleep. When they woke up, they saw Jesus' glory and the two men standing with Him. As Moses and Elijah were starting to leave, Peter, not even knowing what he was saying, blurted out, "Master, it's wonderful for us to be here! Let's make three shelters as memorial — one for you, one for Moses, and one for Elijah." But even as he was saying this, a cloud overshadowed them, and terror gripped them as the cloud covered them. Then a voice from the cloud said, "This is my Son, my Chosen One. Listen to Him." When the voice finished, Jesus was there alone. They didn't tell anyone at that time what they had seen.

Luke 9:27-36

* * *

A few years ago, the Lord permitted LaVonne and i to enjoy ten days of extended quiet time with Him in an upper room in Jerusalem. It was not "the" upper room where the apostles gathered; but for me personally, it was "my" upper room. It was a place where the Lord permitted us to wait before Him, to hear His voice, to experience His presence and to be renewed through the filling of His Spirit. Though i know that He is able to do those things in my life wherever i am – whenever i am willing to be still before Him – it was an added blessing to do so there in Jerusalem where the Lord Himself says that He will make His home among His people (Joel 3:21). i could hear the joy of children laughing and playing in the near distance, mixed with the sounds of gentle breezes and the chirping of birds. i envisioned – as best i could – what that day will be like when our Lord returns to make His home there among His people.

As the time drew to a close, i knew that we could not tarry there – any more than Peter, James and John were able to tarry in His presence on the Mount of Transfiguration. The time quickly arrived for us to come "down from the mountain" or (if you will permit) from our "upper room". Life awaited at the base of the mountain – the day-to-day demands of life, the many opportunities of ministry, and the activities that i can so easily allow to distract me. As it turned out, in less than two weeks, the Lord would call my mother home to glory. But as i remember those days with Him in that upper room, i am mindful that He not only allowed us that special opportunity to taste and see His glory, but He also allowed us to walk down the mountain and into the day-to-day with Him.

This account on the Mount of Transfiguration is described in the Gospels of Matthew (16:28 – 17:13), Mark (9:1-13) and Luke. In all three instances, it begins with a preface. As we saw prior to this account, Jesus had just challenged the disciples' view of the Kingdom of God. He had given them an explanation of what the Kingdom is – and what it will be upon His return. Then He tells the disciples that *"some standing here right now will not die before they see the Kingdom of God."* He's talking about the Kingdom of God that will come upon His return. And He is about to give Peter, James and John an opportunity to taste and see what that day will be like. Not only will they taste and see the glory of God, but they will have the opportunity to bear witness of all that they see and experience to the other disciples – and to each of us as followers. Unquestionably, it was to be a day to remember!

All three accounts record that as Jesus prayed, His appearance "was transformed" *"and His clothes became dazzling white."* Jesus experienced this transformation, not as the Son of God, but as the Son of Man. When the three disciples saw Jesus there on the mount, they saw Him experience the exact same transformation that we as followers will one day experience. The apostle Paul described it as, *"…we will all be transformed! It will happen in a moment, in the blink of an eye, when the last trumpet is blown. For when the trumpet sounds, those who have died will be raised to live forever. And we who are living will also be transformed. For our dying bodies must be transformed into bodies that will never die; our mortal bodies must be transformed into immortal bodies"* (1 Corinthians 15:51-53). And the reason for that transformation is because *"...our physical bodies cannot inherit the Kingdom of God. These dying bodies cannot inherit what will last forever"* (1 Corinthians 15:50). Then Moses and Elijah appeared in much the same way. The light that radiated was not external; it was internal. The light shined brightly and radiantly, because the glory of God reflected in and through them. They were clothed in His glory – just as we will be.

Luke records that Jesus, Moses and Elijah *"were speaking about His {upcoming} exodus from this world, which was about to be fulfilled in Jerusalem."* Think about it! There stands Moses – representing the Law, and Elijah – representing the Prophets, bearing witness to Jesus – the fulfillment of them all! The very Gospel to which the Law and Prophets bore testimony was about to be fulfilled. That to which Moses and Elijah had looked forward by faith was now soon to become sight. Yes, they were there to encourage Jesus as the Son of Man – but i think the greater purpose was that the Father was bearing witness to His Kingdom and all that Jesus was teaching. Remember, Jesus doesn't "do" random. Peter, James and John were there for a purpose – to bear witness. Peter would later write, *"... we were not making up clever stories when we told you about the powerful coming of our Lord Jesus Christ. We saw His majestic splendor with our own eyes when He received honor and glory from God the Father.... We ourselves heard that voice from heaven when we were with Him on the holy mountain"* (2 Peter 1:16-18).

But unfortunately on that day on the mountain, Peter was not quite as clear as to what he was witnessing. He hastily blurted out, *"let us make three tabernacles: one for You, and one for Moses, and one for Elijah"* (Luke 9: 33 NASB). He said it, *"not realizing what he was saying"* (NASB). Peter did what many of us do – he spoke without first thinking. He was placing Moses and Elijah on par with Jesus, as if mere men were worthy of worship. His statement conveyed what many religions do today. But Jesus didn't come to form a religion, He took on flesh as the Son of Man – to die on a cross as our Savior. It could be said that He has not only saved us from our sin, but also from religion.

And the Father was not going to let Peter's comment go unrebuked. Immediately a cloud engulfed them. And from within the cloud, the voice of the Father rang out, *"This is my Son, my Chosen One. Listen to Him."* The

Father will not permit anything or anyone to rob Him of the glory that is due Him.

When the Father stopped speaking, Jesus led the disciples back down the mountain. And He told the three *"not to tell anyone what they had seen until the Son of Man had risen from the dead"* (Mark 9:9).

Ministry awaited them. Crowds were expecting them. The Cross was before them. But the Master had given them a special opportunity – a day to remember – and a day of which to bear witness to His glory. Soon they would have that opportunity.

As you walk with the Master, He has permitted you to have a day like that as well. More than likely, it wasn't at the Mount of Transfiguration, and perhaps not an upper room. But He has given you the opportunity to see His glory on display. His purpose was to encourage you, but it was also for you to bear witness to His goodness and His glory. For some of us, that day was longer ago than others. Perhaps a lot of "life" has happened between then and now. I want to encourage you to take a few moments to remember that day, reflect on His glory and His goodness, be reminded that He's coming back soon – and bear witness of what you have seen.

* * *

38

FROM THE MOUTH OF A FISH

On their arrival in Capernaum, the collectors of the Temple tax came to Peter and asked him, "Doesn't your Teacher pay the Temple tax?" "Yes, He does," Peter replied. Then he went into the house. But before he had a chance to speak, Jesus asked him, "What do you think, Peter? Do kings tax their own people or the people they have conquered?" "They tax the people they have conquered," Peter replied. "Well, then," Jesus said, "the citizens are free! However, we don't want to offend them, so go down to the lake and throw in a line. Open the mouth of the first fish you catch, and you will find a large silver coin. Take it and pay the tax for both of us."

Matthew 17:24-27

* * *

It is not surprising that Matthew, the tax collector, is the only Gospel writer that records this conversation and miracle. The temple tax was a law of God instituted through Moses (Exodus 30:11-16). It was a required offering given by each person twenty years of age and over for purification. Each person was to give half a shekel regardless of whether they were rich or poor. The offering was then to be used for the care of the tabernacle, and later the temple.

Capernaum was the hometown of Peter, Andrew, James, John and Matthew. After Jesus was rejected in Nazareth (Luke 4:28-30), Capernaum had become the center of Jesus' activities whenever He returned to

Galilee. He taught in the local synagogue, so the locals now considered it to be His hometown. As a Jew living in Capernaum, it would have been expected of Him to now pay a tax to the temple in that town.

The collectors of the tax came to Peter, the "hometown boy" to inquire about Jesus paying the tax. Though it would have been an appropriate question for them to ask, the way they asked it infers their intent to find "another infraction" with which to accuse Jesus. Peter, who had been paying the tax since he had turned twenty, hastily speaks before he thinks... again. He blurts out "yes" without first having asked Jesus. There is a part of me that believes that he did so because he wanted to defend Jesus against another slanderous accusation. Peter's outbursts were often done with the best intentions, though they were most often ill-conceived.

As he approached Jesus to ask about the tax, he didn't even have time to get the words out. Jesus already knew what he was going to ask. Let's pause here for an important truth. There is nothing that we will ever come to ask Jesus that He doesn't know already. That should never preclude us from asking, but it should give us great confidence. He knows everything that concerns us, and He has truth for our every situation. He just desires that we ask Him. And He desires that we learn from Peter to ask Him first – before we speak – and before we act.

Jesus walked Peter through an important truth that he had not considered – and we need to understand. It is about the notion of "purification". The offering of purification was given to enable the people of Israel to enter into the presence of a holy God. Allow me to add two other terms – justification and sanctification. If we are followers of Jesus, our hearts are purified by faith – and faith alone. He has paid the price of our sin debt. He has paid our "temple tax", if you would. Like justification, it is not a process; it is a one-time act. At the moment of my salvation, God declared me to be purified and justified – to no longer be a sinner, but to be perfectly righteous before His high bar of justice. God credits us with the righteousness of Jesus, by His grace. Then because we are justified (and purified), He is continually working in our lives to "sanctify" us – to conform us more into the image of Jesus through His Holy Spirit.

So the reality is, as Jesus explained to Peter, He did not have to pay the temple tax. He is the Son of the King – and most definitely did not need purification. And Peter was a child of the King by virtue of his faith in the Son – and as Peter would later write, Jesus was about to pay his ransom with His "precious lifeblood" as the Lamb of God (1 Peter 1:18-19). But as the Son of Man, Jesus did not want to offend the people. Being a Jew, He did not want the people to perceive that He was violating God's Law. Bear in mind, Jesus had no reluctance to challenge the traditions of men that the Pharisees were placing as burdens on the people. But this was the Father's Law, and though He knew it did not apply to Him, He also knew that those around Him could not immediately comprehend that truth… even Peter.

So He taught Peter another important truth. **We can never use our freedom in Christ to hurt or destroy others.** The apostle Paul would later teach the believers living in Rome "*to live in such a way that you will not cause another believer to stumble and fall*" (Romans 14:13).

With that in mind, Jesus sent Peter out to make a withdrawal from the first "Fish Bank and Trust Company". It is significant that Jesus chose to provide the silver coin that was needed through a fish. He had turned five loaves and two fish into a feast for five thousand men. He could have used anything to provide the silver coin that was needed. But He chose a fish. Peter had been fishing all his life. He had probably harvested hundreds, if not thousands, of fish. And i would venture that not one of them ever had a silver coin in its mouth. But give Peter credit, he never questioned Jesus.

You may recall that the day Jesus came to Peter and told him to "Follow Me", Peter had been fishing all night and hadn't caught a thing (Luke 5:2-11). Jesus told him to go out into the deep water and let down the nets. And when they did, their nets were so full of fish they began to tear! So Peter had already seen enough examples from Jesus to know that He had dominion over all of creation. If Jesus said the silver coin would be in the mouth of the fish – that's exactly where it would be!

It would be interesting to know the events that our Lord orchestrated for that fish to end up with a coin in its mouth. And how He orchestrated for that one fish to be the first fish that Peter caught that day. We don't know the details. We rarely do. What we do know is that our Master is able to accomplish His purpose, His plan, and even provide the needed resources through any means He chooses.

As you walk with the Master, remember Who He is. He is our Purifier and our Justifier. He is our Savior and our Lord. He is our Provider. Take it, not only from Matthew…and Peter…, but also from a fish… that i'm sure has quite a story to tell!

* * *

39

WHO IS THE GREATEST?

After they arrived at Capernaum and settled in a house, Jesus asked His disciples, "What were you discussing out on the road?" But they didn't answer, because they had been arguing about which of them was the greatest. He sat down, called the twelve disciples over to Him, and said, "Whoever wants to be first must take last place and be the servant of everyone else." Then He put a little child among them. Taking the child in His arms, He said to them, "Anyone who welcomes a little child like this on My behalf welcomes Me, and anyone who welcomes Me welcomes not only Me but also My Father who sent Me."
Mark 9:33-37

* * *

Before we look at this passage, let's get some context. Peter, James and John have just recently fallen asleep "on the job" as they accompanied Jesus to the Mount of Transfiguration. Then Peter riled the Father by foolishly making a statement that diverted glory from Jesus. Afterwards, Jesus, Peter, James and John descended from the Mount and came upon the other disciples at the foot of the mountain. A large crowd was surrounding them, and some of the religious teachers were arguing with the disciples. When Jesus asked what they were arguing about, one of the men in the crowd responded, *"Teacher, I brought my son, so You could heal him. He is possessed by an evil spirit….* {Since You weren't here,} *I asked Your disciples to cast out the evil spirit, but they couldn't do it…. Have mercy on us and help us, if You can"* (Mark 9:14-29). After Jesus cast the evil spirit out of the boy, His disciples asked, *"Why couldn't we cast out that evil spirit?" "'You don't have enough faith,' Jesus told them. 'I tell you the truth, if you had faith even as small as a mustard seed... nothing would be impossible"* (Matthew 17:20-21).

As they left that region, heading toward Capernaum, Jesus again told His disciples that soon He would be *"betrayed into the hands of His enemies"* and then killed. But three days later He would rise from the dead. Mark writes, *"they didn't understand what He was saying, however, and they were afraid to ask Him what He meant"* (Mark 9:32).

So recapping these recent events: the three that were closest to Jesus fell asleep on the job. The de facto leader of the group blurts out a totally inappropriate statement. The remaining nine are rebuked by Jesus for their lack of faith. And now, when Jesus is sharing this most intimate detail of what He is about to endure, the entire group is unable to comprehend what He is saying. What's more, they are afraid to ask Him what He means. Instead, after demonstrating such stellar followship, they turn their attention to *"arguing {with one another} about which of them {would be} the greatest* in the Kingdom." You almost want to ask them, "the greatest what?"

See how easily they missed the moments, the opportunities and the lessons that Jesus had for them. See how easily they could become so distracted by their own selfish ambition. Peter was the leader of the twelve, so surely he would become the prime minister. Judas Iscariot was the treasurer of the group, so he was a shoo-in to become the minister of the treasury. Andrew was very adept at shuttle diplomacy, so he would more than likely be the minister of foreign affairs. And the sons of thunder – James and John – without a doubt Jesus would choose to be His ministers of defense. Can you just imagine the conversation? These guys are still thinking that Jesus is about to establish His earthly kingdom and they are preoccupied with what their roles will be in His new government.

Then they got caught! Jesus asked them, *"What were you discussing out on the road?"* Give them credit, they at least knew not to answer the question – because they at least had learned that Jesus never asks a question for which He doesn't already know the answer.

i am struck by the gracious and patient way that Jesus called the disciples over to Him, sat them down, and said, *"Whoever wants to be first must take last place and be the servant of everyone else."* At that moment, by that criteria, not one of them would qualify for "greatest", because all of them had been seeking first place, not last place. Each of them was seeking to be served – not to be a servant of others.

And it's telling that Jesus used a little child as the visual example of the humility and lack of pretense of the Kingdom. I wonder if the child was the same age of the young boy from whom Jesus had just cast out the demon. Jesus said to them, *"I tell you the truth, unless you turn from your sins and become like {this little child}, you will never get into the Kingdom of Heaven"* (Matthew 18:3), let alone aspire to be the greatest in the Kingdom (my paraphrase).

After this rebuke, i don't believe the disciples ever – at least openly – discussed positions in the Kingdom, though Judas Iscariot still clearly had his sights on a role. Soon after, Salome, the mother of James and John, would ask Jesus about positions for her two sons (Matthew 20:20). I tend to think that James and John just silently stood by, embarrassed that their mother would even think about asking the question again.

So enough about the disciples – what about us? How many of us are more concerned about our "kingdoms" on this earth than the Kingdom? How many of us are seeking the approval of the crowd? How many of us are living "as unto the Lord" for the whole world to see, so that we might receive recognition from others for the "godly things" we do? How many of us want to impress those around us with our biblical knowledge, our generosity or our "selfless" service? How many of us are seeking a seat at the head table instead of serving at tables? How many of us have become so distracted by our own selfish ambition that we are no longer useful to the Master for His purpose and His Kingdom (2 Timothy 2:21)?

As you continue in your walk with the Master, remember His words: *"Whoever wants to be first must take last place and be the servant of everyone else."*

* * *

40

PROVE IT!

After this, Jesus traveled around Galilee. He wanted to stay out of Judea, where the Jewish leaders were plotting His death. But soon it was time for the Jewish Festival of Shelters, and Jesus' brothers said to Him, "Leave here and go to Judea, where Your followers can see Your miracles! You can't become famous if You hide like this! If You can do such wonderful things, show Yourself to the world!" For even His brothers didn't believe in Him. Jesus replied, "Now is not the right time for Me to go, but you can go anytime. The world can't hate you, but it does hate Me because I accuse it of doing evil. You go on. I'm not {yet} going to this festival, because My time has not yet come." After saying these things, Jesus remained in Galilee.

John 7:1-9

* * *

About six months has passed since Jesus fed the five thousand. It's now October, and it's about six months until His crucifixion. Jesus has continued to teach and minister in Galilee. The religious leaders in Jerusalem are plotting to kill Him. But the Father has His divine timetable, and these men cannot touch Jesus until His time has come.

It was time for the annual Festival of Tabernacles. This feast celebrates Israel's deliverance out of Egypt. Since they lived in tents during the wilderness journey, this feast is characterized by tents, or shelters. During the festival, the inner court of the temple is illuminated with torches. These torches represent the pillar of fire that guided the Israelites by night. It is a reminder that the Messiah will take up residence in His temple (Malachi 3:1). And when Jesus returns, that is exactly what He will do! But it wasn't yet the time.

Jesus' half-brothers were headed to the festival in Jerusalem, as was the practice of Jewish men. Their names as listed in Matthew 13:55 were James (who subsequently became a leader of the church, and writes the Epistle of James), Joseph, Simon and Judas (who subsequently wrote the Epistle of Jude). At this point, however, none of them believed Jesus to be the Son of God. They believed He had a special anointing and gift to perform miracles, but that's all. Thus the advice that they had come to give Him flowed out of their unbelief.

They counseled Jesus to go to Jerusalem and prove Himself to the world by putting His miracles on display for everyone to see! Jerusalem would be crowded with religious pilgrims, and this would give Jesus a tremendous opportunity to enlist many more disciples and gain the approval of the crowd. (The brothers may have been mindful that many of Jesus' disciples had recently abandoned Him – John 6:66.) They did not desire for Jesus to be harmed in any way. They wanted Him to be honored – and that couldn't happen if He stayed here in Galilee. They truly desired the world's best for Him. And surely His notoriety and success wouldn't hurt them any either. There was "gain" to be shared all the way around. It was a great marketing strategy! But Jesus knew that their counsel was anything but wise. It was contrary to His wisdom and the will of the Father.

Here is a significant takeaway for us. As we walk with the Master, He will sometimes lead us on a path that makes absolutely no sense to those who aren't His followers. And sometimes, even some of His followers may not truly understand. With a sincere desire to be helpful, family and friends will come to you and give you counsel to pursue a different path. It's not because they don't have your best interest at heart – they do! The problem is that they are relying on human wisdom. Don't misunderstand me, not all human wisdom is wrong. **But we do not know the truth and wisdom of any situation until we have heard God's truth and His wisdom!** When God has given you a clear word and direction, do not allow even well-intentioned counsel to the contrary to cause you to change course. Stick with the Master's word! Just a reminder – it made absolutely no sense for Peter to get out of the boat and walk on the water to Jesus. But when Jesus said "Come!", it would have been absolutely wrong for him not to do so – no matter what his brother or friends might have told him.

So here is an important question – "how do I know what God's truth and wisdom is in every situation?" First, let's use the example of Peter. He had spent time with Jesus. Because of that, Peter knew His voice. He also knew Jesus was trustworthy. And he knew that, whatever Jesus told him to do, Jesus would enable him to accomplish. How can we have that same confidence? By walking with Him daily. By spending time with Him in His word. By allowing the truth of His word to guide us in every aspect of our lives. Yes, by surrounding ourselves with other godly believers, who God will use to speak into our lives with godly counsel. Just be sure it's godly counsel!

One other thought – and it comes a few verses later in this passage. After Jesus' half-brothers left for the festival, Jesus also went to the festival, but stayed out of public view. Midway through the festival, He went up to the Temple and began to teach this truth. Jesus told them, "*Anyone who wants to do the will of God will know whether My teaching is from God or is merely My own. Those who speak for themselves want glory only for themselves, but a person who seeks to honor the One who sent him speaks truth, not lies*" (John 7:17-18).

Jesus was clearly saying that it is a question of motive. Is our desire to honor the Father, or is our desire to honor ourselves? The Father does not need us to prove Him right. He promises that if we seek Him, we will find Him. If we sincerely seek His truth in His Word, and His will, we will find it. He's not in His heavens just hoping we figure it out. He will make it abundantly clear. And once He does, our only response is to immediately obey Him by faith. It's not our responsibility to prove His truth, His word or His will. He will prove Himself. Because at the end of it all… it's all about His glory.

Jesus didn't need to be concerned about proving anything to anyone; He just needed to be faithfully obedient to the Father. And as we walk with the Master, so do we!

* * *

41

HE SET HIS FACE

As the time drew near for Him to ascend to heaven, Jesus resolutely set out for Jerusalem. He sent messengers ahead to a Samaritan village to prepare for His arrival. But the people of the village did not welcome Jesus because He was on His way to Jerusalem. When James and John saw this, they said to Jesus, "Lord, should we call down fire from heaven to burn them up?" But Jesus turned and rebuked them. So they went on to another village.
Luke 9:51-56

* * *

The New King James translation of verse 51 is *"Now it came to pass, when the time had come for Him to be received up, that He steadfastly set His face to go to Jerusalem."* We sometimes fall into a trap of thinking of Jesus' crucifixion as the result of Judas' betrayal, the Sanhedrin's envy, Pilate's spinelessness and the soldiers' cruelty. We can be lulled into thinking His death was involuntary. And salvation is the result of God taking something that the enemy meant for evil and using it for His glory and our good. Now, don't misunderstand me, the enemy had evil intentions. But Jesus' death on the cross was not God's afterthought resulting from the enemy's plan. The cross was a part of the Father's redemptive plan from the very beginning. As John Piper wrote, *"Jesus was not accidentally entangled in a web of injustice. He was the very embodiment of His Father's love for sinners."* And the cross was to be the instrument of that mission. So, in this passage, Jesus sees that the time is drawing near, and He has "steadfastly set His face" toward that moment that would occur at that place. Jesus later says, *"No one can take My life from Me. I sacrifice it volun-*

tarily.... For this is what My Father has commanded" (John 10:18). His face is set to fulfill the mission that the Father has given Him.

In the course of this journey, He and His disciples were taking the direct route through Samaria. In an earlier chapter (chapter 10), we talked about the enmity that existed between Samaritans and Jews, and the normal practice for Jews to bypass Samaria in their travels. But Jesus was not making any detours. Obviously the Samaritan village He was approaching was not Sychar. If it had been Sychar, they would have rolled out the red carpet of welcome. But this unnamed village in Samaria would do no such thing. Jesus' fame was spreading throughout the region, including reports that He was the Messiah. And if Jesus *"was on His way to Jerusalem"* to establish His kingdom, instead of doing so there in Gerizim (the location of the Samaritans' temple), they would have no part in providing Him with hospitality in their village. Thus they refused Jesus entry.

James and John, the "sons of thunder" (Mark 3:17), took this affront toward Jesus very personally. Bear in mind that the two of them, together with the rest of the disciples, still thought Jesus was going to declare Himself and establish His kingdom in Jerusalem. Though Jesus had told them about His upcoming betrayal and death, the disciples still did not understand. For James and John, this was a victory march. The Conqueror was going to Jerusalem to claim His reward – and the disciples were part of that conquering army. Who did this insignificant village think they were – and how could they possibly treat the Messiah in such a way? James and John were ready to wipe them off of the face of the earth! And, oh by the way, word of that judgment would get to Jerusalem before they arrived. And even Jerusalem would tremble! Great plan... only, it was the wrong plan and Jesus rebuked them, and they simply went to another town.

Let's stop and apply this. The disciples had a mistaken view of what their journey was all about. They still had a wrong view of the Kingdom and of Jesus' mission. Therefore, they had a wrong view of their role as His disciples in the Kingdom. If Jesus' mission was to judge, then the disciples' role would have been to execute judgment. However, if His mission was to be a sacrifice for the salvation of the lost, before He comes again to reign in glory and in power, then their role was to follow Him for the salvation of the lost. The former road leads to position, prestige and power; the latter to the glory of the Father by way of Calvary.

. . .

What James and John had to learn, you and i must also learn. Jesus' journey to Jerusalem is our journey. If He has set His face to that mission, we must set our face to follow Him in that mission. Be careful that you don't get lulled into a notion that Jesus suffered and died so that we could have comfort and treasure and privilege. Earlier in this passage He had already taught, *"If any of you wants to be My follower, you must give up your own way, take up your cross daily, and follow Me. If you try to hang on to your life, you will lose it. But if you give up your life for My sake, you will save it."* Walking with the Master is a journey on the Calvary Road. As John Piper wrote, *"When Jesus set His face to walk the Calvary Road, He was not merely taking our place; He was setting our pattern. He is our substitute and our pace-setter."* The Calvary Road is not the road of material prosperity; it is a road of selfless sacrifice. It is a road on which we are to follow Him wherever He leads and however He leads. It is a journey that is characterized by loving our neighbor – whoever they are – and making disciples – wherever they are… and all else is loss.

As you continue on your walk with the Master, be careful that your heart hasn't become hardened like the villagers in Samaria, failing to grant any room or place in your life to Jesus. But also, make sure that your focus is not like James and John, sanctimoniously conveying judgment and spiritual piety – but failing to be about the Father's business. Set your face like the Master on His mission and follow Him on His Calvary Road.

* * *

42

THE COST OF DISCIPLESHIP

As they were walking along, someone said to Jesus, "I will follow You wherever You go." But Jesus replied, "Foxes have dens to live in, and birds have nests, but the Son of Man has no place even to lay His head." He said to another person, "Come, follow Me." The man agreed, but he said, "Lord, first let me return home and bury my father." But Jesus told him, "Let the spiritually dead bury their own dead! Your duty is to go and preach about the Kingdom of God." Another said, "Yes, Lord, I will follow You, but first let me say good-bye to my family." But Jesus told him, "Anyone who puts a hand to the plow and then looks back is not fit for the Kingdom of God."

Luke 9:57-62

* * *

Years ago, the Lord used a dear brother in Christ by the name of Bryan, to speak truth into my life. Bryan was at times my Paul and at others my Barnabas. i often heard him share a story that had great impact on my life. There was a man who owned a large beautiful land tract, comprised of 1,000 acres. One day, he made the decision to deed all but one acre of the land to a ministry, who in turn would use the tract as the site for a training and retreat center. As a condition of the deed transfer, he required that the ministry grant him the right of ingress and egress through the donated property to his one acre. Neither the man nor the ministry thought the request was unreasonable in light of the man generously surrendering all of his property, except for this one acre. The ministry took possession of its 999 acres and constructed its training and retreat facilities on the property. It was a peaceful, out of the way site, that worked perfectly.

But as time went on, the man decided to use his one acre to host loud musical concerts once a month and he invited the public to attend. Unfortunately, the concerts were loud and so were the concert goers, and they littered and destroyed some of the surrounding property as they accessed the site. Over time, the noise volume, attendance, and frequency of the concerts all increased. The concerts became weekly events – and soon they were every night. The amount of damage to the surrounding property continued to increase, and the entire tract was no longer conducive for the ministry's purpose. The ministry was forced to abandon the site, all because the man held on to one inconsequential acre to use for his own purpose.

Regrettably, this is all too often reflective of our "commitment" to follow Christ. We tell Him, *"LORD, I give you my life to use as you will wherever You go."* But secretly, we hold on to one little acre in the middle of the tract. Surely, the Master will be okay with me holding on to this one little thing in my life. The reality is that one little thing is the foothold that the enemy uses to get us off track from following Jesus. As we look at this passage in Luke, we will see three men who attempted to hold on to "just one acre".

Now bear in mind, this passage is not about salvation. The question being asked is not "what must I do to be saved?". That is a question of unmerited favor by grace through faith (Ephesians 2:8-9). The question being posed by these men, as believers in Jesus whose sins have been forgiven, is "what do we need to do to follow You as Your disciple". Let me hasten to say that i believe it is a hard distinction to make between the two questions because, i can't imagine receiving His unmerited favor, mercy and forgiveness, and not surrendering all of my life as His follower. But there were years of my life when that was true for me. Thus the reason for Bryan sharing his story with me!

Dietrich Bonhoeffer, in his book "The Cost of Discipleship", contrasts what he calls "cheap" grace and "costly grace":

> ***Cheap grace*** *is grace without discipleship, grace without the cross, grace without Jesus Christ.*

> ***Costly grace*** *confronts us as a gracious call to follow Jesus. It comes as a word of forgiveness to the broken spirit and the contrite heart. It is costly because it compels a man to submit to the yoke of Christ and follow Him; it is grace because Jesus says: 'My yoke is easy, and my burden is light.'"*

Earlier in Luke, we see that Jesus said, *"If any of you wants to be My follower, you must give up your own way, take up your cross daily, and follow Me"* (Luke 9:23). It is a conditional "if… then" statement. IF we don't give up our own way, die to ourselves, take up the cross He has set before us and follow Him, THEN we are NOT His follower. The pre-condition is our salvation. But this statement is about what we do once we are saved. Jesus lays down His conditions for us being His disciples. And there is no wiggle room. There is no acre excluded. There are conditions, but it is not conditional. If we would walk with the Master, our full surrender and discipleship CANNOT be conditional. We either are His disciple, or we are not.

Though this passage is not clear on whether all of these men turned away from following Jesus, my fear and my belief is that they did. If i am mistaken, i am grateful that i am in error. But i will use the perspective that they turned away as i write this.

The first man in verse 57 makes the declaration, *"I will follow You {Jesus} wherever You go."* But Jesus knew his heart. I fear that he was prepared to follow Jesus wherever Jesus went, as long as he did not need to leave his comfortable bed. How many of us have made that same statement? In fact, how many of us have expressed that same statement in song – "Wherever You lead, I'll go"? But do we really mean it?

Over the years, God has blessed me with the opportunity to accompany many people as they have traveled overseas on a short term mission experience. i can tell you that two questions that i have been commonly asked are, "where will we be sleeping?", and "what are the bathroom facilities like?" Folks can really get out of their comfort zones in those two arenas! How many of us are prepared to follow Him wherever He goes… as long as it's not ________________ (you fill in the blank with the name of that part of the world where you flat out would not want to go)?

. . .

Matthew tells us (Matthew 8:19) that this first man was a Pharisee. He was a teacher of the Word, but his concern about his accommodations kept him from following Jesus. That was the "one acre" in his life.

The second man in verse 59 tells Jesus that before he can follow, he first needs to go home and attend to his ailing father. Jesus wasn't forbidding him from going to his father's funeral. This son was headed home to take care of his father until he died. The man was saying that after his father was gone, he would be free to follow Jesus. Over the years, i have known missionaries and those serving in ministry who have had to make difficult decisions regarding ailing and aging family members. LaVonne and i also have needed to make decisions regarding moves with those considerations in mind. So i can in particular relate to this man. And i know for us, and for many others we know, this has been an earnest matter of seeking the Master on what He would have us do. Sometimes the answer is to stay; sometimes the answer is to go. The important fact is to do what the Master tells you!

In this instance, i believe that Jesus knew his heart, and his reality was that his love for family surpassed his love for Jesus. And Jesus was clearly showing him that our human affections must take second place to the Master. He claims and is due "first place". If He leads us to leave a family member, we can trust them to His care. He loves them even more than we do!

Jesus could see that the third man in verse 61 kept looking back instead of ahead. i am not a farmer, but i tend to believe that it's impossible to plow as you are looking back instead of ahead. This man was only committed halfway and half-heartedly. He wanted to be a disciple without making a sacrifice. His face was not set to follow; he couldn't truly let go of what he had. Over the years, i have talked with a number of missionaries serving overseas who have dealt with that struggle. All of the technological advancements in global communication have enabled folks serving in the far corners of the world to stay connected in wonderful ways with family, friends and supporters. And it is a huge blessing! But sometimes, it has become an impediment for missionaries truly letting go of their home culture and connecting with their host culture. Jesus is clearly saying that we need to let go of that which is behind us and look to Him and where He is leading. The apostle Paul would later write, "*… brothers and sisters, … focus on this one thing: Forgetting the past and looking forward to what lies* *ahead, I press on to reach the end of the race and receive the heavenly prize for which God, through Christ Jesus, is calling us"* (Philippians 3:13-14).

The cost of our salvation was high. It cost the Father the death of His Son. The cost of discipleship is high. Christ demands all with which He has entrusted us, including our very lives. Every acre… with none held back.

* * *

43

A LEDGER IN THE SAND

Then the meeting broke up, and everybody went home. Jesus returned to the Mount of Olives, but early the next morning He was back again at the Temple. A crowd soon gathered, and He sat down and taught them. As He was speaking, the teachers of religious law and the Pharisees brought a woman who had been caught in the act of adultery. They put her in front of the crowd. "Teacher," they said to Jesus, "this woman was caught in the act of adultery. The law of Moses says to stone her. What do You say?" They were trying to trap Him into saying something they could use against Him, but Jesus stooped down and wrote in the dust with His finger. They kept demanding an answer, so He stood up again and said, "All right, but let the one who has never sinned throw the first stone!" Then He stooped down again and wrote in the dust. When the accusers heard this, they slipped away one by one, beginning with the oldest, until only Jesus was left in the middle of the crowd with the woman. Then Jesus stood up again and said to the woman, "Where are your accusers? Didn't even one of them condemn you?" "No, Lord," she said. And Jesus said, "Neither do I. Go and sin no more."

John 7:53 – 8:11

* * *

Your Bible translation may indicate that this passage was omitted from some of the early manuscripts. Augustine wrote that the reason for its omission was because of a prudish fear that it would encourage adultery. However, the passage, as we will see, clearly condemns sin; it doesn't condone it.

. . .

The night before this confrontation, John records that there had been a meeting of the Sanhedrin. The members of the Sanhedrin were divided in their opinion as to whether or not Jesus was the Messiah. Nicodemus had spoken up on Jesus' behalf, but was abruptly belittled as one of Jesus' fellow Galileans, and pointedly reminded that no prophet could possibly come from Galilee.

This particular morning Jesus was back teaching in the Temple – and as usual, a crowd had gathered. At an optimum time to create the greatest spectacle, the scribes and Pharisees brought this woman before Jesus. They had caught the woman in the act of adultery – but where was the man? The Law (Leviticus 20:10) required that both the adulterer and the adulteress be put to death. The very fact that they had not brought the man before the crowd makes it apparent that they were not seeking to enforce the Law; they were seeking to trap Jesus so that they could accuse Him. Their goal was not to stone the woman as the Law required, rather their goal was to stone Jesus.

The religious leaders smugly said, *"Teacher, this woman was caught in the act of adultery. The law of Moses says to stone her. What do You say?"*

Picture the scene. There stood the woman. Having been abruptly dragged before Jesus, she would have been disheveled and disarrayed with a posture that conveyed a mixture of defiance, embarrassment, fear and remorse. Behind her stood her accusers – the religious leaders – with an air of superiority, stiffneckedness, smugness and contempt – probably more directed toward Jesus than even the woman. Surrounding them all was the crowd – leering at the woman and craning their necks to see what was going to happen. In the midst of them all, Jesus stooped down and wrote in the dust. He clearly took a posture that distanced Himself from her accusers and did not add to her humiliation. And He began to write, as if He wasn't paying any attention to what was going on in front of Him and around Him. Talk about peace in the midst of a storm! That time on the boat with the disciples doesn't even begin to compare with this!

As we look through Scripture, this is the only time we ever see Jesus writing. And we do not know what He wrote. He intended it to be that way. If He had wanted us to know, He would have had John record it. But the prophet Jeremiah may have given us a clue when he wrote, *"O LORD, the Hope of Israel,* ***All who forsake You*** *shall be ashamed. Those who depart from*

Me ***shall be written in the earth****, because they have forsaken the LORD, the fountain of Living Waters"* (Jeremiah 17:13 NKJ, emphasis added).

Who in His midst had forsaken the Lord? The woman? Yes. The religious leaders? Yes. The crowd? Yes. Every one of them! (Every one of us!) And i believe that Jesus began to write – in the form of a ledger, if you will – the very specific sins of those who were now standing there in judgement of the woman. They would have been "secret" sins committed in private that the religious leaders believed no one knew anything about. Sins, that if they were made publicly known, would not only have been a great source of embarrassment, but would have cost these men their position of influence. It may have even cost some of them their lives.

As the religious leaders again pressed the question, Jesus replied, *"All right, but let the one who has never sinned throw the first stone!"* And one-by-one, as they looked more closely at the "ledger" that Jesus had written, they began to realize that Jesus knew! It wasn't repentance that overtook them. It was fear! And they turned around one-by-one and left under some pretense. Again, i don't believe they left out of remorse. I believe they left out of fear. And they left even more motivated to destroy this Jesus – this One who knew everything they had ever done (John 4:29).

Jesus was the only One in the midst of that crowd who was qualified to judge that day – or any day for that matter. He met the qualification – He was sinless. And when He returns, He will return as Judge! But on that day, He was in their midst as Savior. Yes, the woman was guilty. But Jesus had come that day to put the cross between her and her sin. Jesus had once told the Pharisee Nicodemus that *"God sent His Son into the world not to judge the world, but to save the world through Him"* (John 3:17). Yes, He will return as the Judge. But by God's grace – to that woman – and to you and me – He first came as the Savior to pay our sin debt – so that when He returns as Judge our debt in the ledger can be marked "paid in full".

So what is our role as we walk with the Master? Has He called us to be judges of those around us – belittling, accusing, showing disdain and being judgmental? Our name and our sins would be written there in that ledger in the sand if it wasn't for His saving grace. And as recipients, we are to take the posture of our Savior and be His ambassadors of the gospel of His saving grace. There are multitudes waiting to have their sin debt marked paid in full. Let's not make them continue to wait!

44

THE LIGHT OF THE WORLD

Jesus spoke to the people once more and said, "I am the light of the world. If you follow Me, you won't have to walk in darkness, because you will have the light that leads to life." The Pharisees replied, "You are making those claims about Yourself! Such testimony is not valid." Jesus told them, "These claims are valid even though I make them about Myself. For I know where I came from and where I am going, but you don't know this about Me. You judge Me by human standards, but I do not judge anyone. And if I did, My judgment would be correct in every respect because I am not alone. The Father who sent Me is with Me. Your own law says that if two people agree about something, their witness is accepted as fact. I am one witness, and My Father who sent Me is the other." "Where is Your father?" they asked. Jesus answered, "Since you don't know who I am, you don't know who My Father is. If you knew Me, you would also know My Father." Jesus made these statements while He was teaching in the section of the Temple known as the Treasury. But He was not arrested, because His time had not yet come.

John 8:12 - 20

* * *

Jesus was still in the treasury section of the Temple (vs. 20), which was in the women's court. This was where the religious leaders had just brought the woman caught in the act of adultery before Him. At the well, Jesus had declared Himself to be the Living Water. Following the feeding of the five thousand men, Jesus had declared Himself to be the Bread of Life. Now having just brought the sins of these religious leaders who had brought the woman before Him into the light, He refers to

Himself as the Light of the World. The sin that the men had thought was well hidden had now been illuminated by the Light. And like rats and cockroaches, they had scattered to get away from the Light.

Darkness cannot exist in the light, because darkness is the absence of light. Darkness cannot put out the light, for it is light that eradicates the darkness. Unholiness and unjustness cannot survive in the light. Jesus is absolute holiness and justness because He is the Light. There is no beauty or color without light. However He has made all things beautiful in their time (Ecclesiastes 3:11), because He alone is the Light. And if we follow Him, we have the Light. But apart from Him, we walk in darkness. The Light leads to life; darkness leads to death.

Remember, Jesus was in Jerusalem for the Feast of Tabernacles. As we have already seen in chapter 40 of this book, that celebration included the use of torches in the inner court of the Temple and the parade of torches as a reminder that, as light, God led the children of Israel as a pillar of fire. Whenever and wherever the pillar of fire led, the Israelites followed. It is not "coincidental" that Jesus is using this analogy of light in the midst of that celebration. And it wasn't lost on the Pharisees either! It was yet another declaration by Jesus of Who He is.

One quick side road: as we've already seen, John has now recorded Jesus using three wilderness images – the water from the rock (Exodus 17:6), the manna (Exodus 16:14-15) and the pillar of fire (Exodus 13:21) – reflecting that He is the Living Water, the Bread of Life, and now, the Light of the World.

It's ironic that the Pharisees' response to His declaration is to accuse Him of bearing witness to Himself. *"You are making those claims about Yourself! Such testimony is not valid."* The religious leaders who had just had their sins exposed could easily have borne witness! But they had scattered like the "rats" they were. And the whole group was now becoming even more fearful of Jesus.

Jewish courts did not permit a person to bear witness to himself. But *light* does bear witness to itself, and the only ones who cannot see it are those who are blind! Jesus made it clear that they were unable to see because their judgment was faulty. It is tragic that these religious experts in the

Law did not even know their own Messiah as He stood before them. They truly were "blind guides" (Matthew 15:14).

As the Pharisees attempted to take Jesus down a path to detour Him from the truth He had just spoken, Jesus used it as an opportunity to reinforce that very truth:

"I know where I came from and where I am going, but you don't know this about Me" (vs. 14). He knows where He came from. He was there. He always was. He had no beginning. His authority is not from human origin. He is the Light of the World because He is one with the Father. He comes from the Father, speaks for the Father and is going to the Father. Jesus was there at the beginning. He has always been the Light of the World. He is not just becoming the light. The world has no other light than Him. He is the light that our Creator intended. There is either darkness or Jesus; there is not a third option.

"You judge Me by human standards, but I do not judge anyone. And if I did, My judgment would be correct in every respect because I am not alone" (vs. 15-16). His judgment is not limited – by time or space or human knowledge. Everything looks different in the light of Christ – disasters, disease, suffering, even death. One day His light will cover the earth – and when it does – disaster, disease, suffering and death will be banished to outer darkness. Until then His light enables us to bear the sorrows of darkness. It is a comforting glow in the midst of devastating loneliness. It is the lamp that illumines our troubling path.

"The Father who sent Me is with Me. Your own law says that if two people agree about something, their witness is accepted as fact. I am one witness, and My Father who sent Me is the other" (vs. 16-18). The Father has borne witness to His testimony and to Who He is. But just as the Pharisees were blinded to the Son, they were blinded to the Father. *"If you knew Me, you would also know My Father"* (vs. 19). *"No one comes to the Father except through Me"* (John 14:6). As Warren Wiersbe wrote, *"They claimed to know the Law of God, but they did not know the God of the Law."*

As we walk with the Master, we will encounter those who use some of these same arguments in an attempt to refute the fact that Jesus is the Light of the World. Do not be surprised. The same author of lies that spoke through the Pharisees speaks through those who are blinded today. But Jesus is still in the business of making the blind to see. His Light still completely destroys the darkness. His light is able to lead the way for the captives to be set free. Allow His light to shine through you, so others see the goodness of God, just as *"He called you out of the darkness into His wonderful light"* (1 Peter 2:9).

* * *

45

ONE BORN BLIND SEES

As Jesus was walking along, He saw a man who had been blind from birth. "Rabbi," His disciples asked Him, "why was this man born blind? Was it because of his own sins or his parents' sins?" "It was not because of his sins or his parents' sins," Jesus answered. "This happened so the power of God could be seen in him.... Then He spit on the ground, made mud with the saliva, and spread the mud over the blind man's eyes. He told him, "Go wash yourself in the pool of Siloam...." So the man went and washed and came back seeing! His neighbors and others who knew him as a blind beggar asked each other, "Isn't this the man who used to sit and beg?" ... He told them, "The man they call Jesus made mud and spread it over my eyes and told me, 'Go to the pool of Siloam and wash yourself.' So I went and washed, and now I can see!" ... Then the Pharisees again questioned the man who had been blind and demanded, "What's your opinion about this man who healed you?" The man replied, "I think He must be a prophet." ... So for the second time they called in the man who had been blind and told him, "God should get the glory for this, because we know this man Jesus is a sinner." "I don't know whether He is a sinner," the man replied. "But I know this: I was blind, and now I can see!" "...Look!" the man exclaimed. "I told you once. Didn't you listen? Why do you want to hear it again? Do you want to become His disciples, too?" Then {the Pharisees} cursed him and said, "You are His disciple, but we are disciples of Moses! We know God spoke to Moses, but we don't even know where this man comes from." ... When Jesus heard what had happened, He found the man and asked, "Do you believe in the Son of Man?" The man answered, "Who is He, Sir? I want to believe in Him." "You have seen Him," Jesus said, "and He is speaking to you!" "Yes, Lord, I believe!" the man said. And he worshiped Jesus....

John 9:1-41

* * *

The prophet Isaiah wrote, *"And when He {the Messiah} comes, He will open the eyes of the blind and unplug the ears of the deaf. The lame will leap like deer, and those who cannot speak will sing for joy!"* (Isaiah 35:5-6) Blindness, deafness, lameness and muteness are not conditions that are orchestrated by God. They did not exist when God created the heavens and the earth. Rather, they are products of the fall of man that resulted from human sin. God had nothing to do with their creation, but He has everything to do with their cure.

The disciples asked Jesus the cause for this man being born blind. Most often when we witness or experience loss of this nature – whether it be loss of sight or hearing, or the loss of life, or the loss of position or possession – due to disaster, disease, violence or some unexplainable reason – we want to know what caused the pain. But most often even knowing the cause doesn't provide us with a decisive explanation – let alone an explanation that satisfies us. Because we will never be satisfied with pain or loss – no matter the cause – nor should we!

However, if we are following Jesus, we can take strength from the Lord's assurance that He *"causes everything to work together for the good of those who love God and are called according to His purpose for them"* (Romans 8:28). That means that ultimately it will be worth all that we have endured because God will use it for His good purpose. If being loved by God and being used by Him for His purpose has greater value to us than our sight, our lives, or virtually everything else, then His promise in Romans 8:28 will provide us with great comfort. However, none of this will make sense or be of any comfort to us if God, and the glory of His works, is not our greatest treasure.

Jesus answered His disciples with *"It was not because of his sins or his parents' sins. This happened so the power of God could be seen in him."* God wasn't the cause of his blindness, but He was about to be the cure in a way that brought great glory to the Father and the Son. God was going to use his healing to further reveal the Light of the World. In so doing, some like the blind man would be drawn to worship Jesus in the Light, but unfortunately others, like the Pharisees, would be blinded to the grace and truth of Jesus by their own darkness.

. . .

The blind man could see more in his blindness than the Pharisees could see with their sight. Just like light reveals the condition of the eye, the Light of the World reveals the condition of the soul. The Pharisees thought they saw, but they were blind. And just like the lack of sight does not mean light is not there, their spiritual blindness did not mean that the Light of the World was not in their midst. There are none so blind as those who will not see!

The healing of this man is a great picture for us of a life transformed by the power of the gospel:

1. The man was blind (he was separated from the Light of the World).
2. He was blind from birth (like each of us, he was born in sin).
3. He was beyond human help (there is no human remedy for sin).
4. He was a beggar (there is no way he could help / save himself).
5. He wasn't looking for Jesus (Jesus sought him out).
6. The disciples wanted to analyze the man. Jesus alone felt compassion for this man (He is our only solution).
7. Jesus made mud and spread it over his eyes and told him, *"Go to the pool of Siloam and wash"* (Jesus made the way for our salvation).
8. In order to receive his sight, he needed to do what Jesus had told him (we, too, must respond by faith).
9. He who was blind, now sees (we who were lost are now saved).
10. Jesus sent him to the Pool of Siloam to wash. John tells us that Siloam means "sent". (This is a picture of how the glory of God is seen through our lives as we go in obedience.)
11. He told others about what had happened – "I was blind, Jesus touched me, I obeyed by faith, now I see" (I was lost and now I am found).
12. His neighbors knew something had happened to him. (If there is no evidence of change, then something is wrong.)

The Pharisees could not contest the miracle that had occurred. The man and his parents were well known within their community. Everyone in the community knew he had been blind from birth. So they chose to try to discredit the Miracle Worker. They did so by changing the narrative from a miracle of sight to one about Jesus violating their man-made sabbath rules. The logic went something like this:

All people from God keep the sabbath. Jesus does not keep the sabbath. Therefore, Jesus is not from God.

Jesus had performed three unlawful "works" according to their rules: He made the clay, He applied the clay, He healed the man. They looked to their rules and their traditions instead of looking to their Scripture. For if they had, they would have known:

Only people from God can open the eyes of a man born blind. Jesus opened the eyes of the blind man.
Jesus is from God.

The irony is that the more they tried to discredit Jesus, the closer the man was drawn to Him. A further irony is that the Pharisees' arguments ultimately convinced the man that Jesus is the Son of God. The religious leaders officially excommunicated the man from the synagogue. And when he was presented with the choice between religion and Jesus – he chose Jesus. He chose well!

So here are three take-aways, as we continue in our walk with the Master:

1. God has a good, Father-honoring, Christ-exalting purpose for everything that happens in your life.
2. Jesus is the only path through which the Father's purpose will be fulfilled.
3. When everyone else ignores or rejects you – just like they did the blind man – be assured that Jesus is seeking you out… to enable you to see more of Him… and to draw you closer to Him.

* * *

46

THE GOOD SHEPHERD

"I tell you the truth, anyone who sneaks over the wall of a sheepfold, rather than going through the gate, must surely be a thief and a robber! But the one who enters through the gate is the shepherd of the sheep. The gatekeeper opens the gate for him, and the sheep recognize his voice and come to him. He calls his own sheep by name and leads them out. After he has gathered his own flock, he walks ahead of them,
and they follow him because they know his voice. They won't follow a stranger; they will run from him because they don't know his voice…."
John 10:1-18

* * *

This message from the Master as recorded in John 10 grew out of the religious leaders' decision to excommunicate the man who had been born blind. They were false shepherds who truly did not care for him. So Jesus transitioned from talking about the relationship of light and darkness to the relationship of the shepherd and the sheep.

In first century Judaism, this would have been a familiar and relatable illustration. A sheepfold was an enclosure made of rocks, with an opening for the "gate". The "gate" was most often a shepherd or a "porter" – lying across the opening. It would not have been unusual for several flocks to be gathered together in the same sheepfold overnight. One of the shepherds or the porter would have been the "gate", or the "gatekeeper". He knew each shepherd who had placed a flock in the sheepfold. He wouldn't let anyone else into the sheepfold. If someone was trying to rob the sheep, the thief would have to climb over the wall. But even if they got in, they wouldn't be able to get the sheep to follow. In the morning, the shepherd would come to the gate and call out his own flock. The sheep of that respective flock would respond because they knew their shepherd's voice.

It's universally known that sheep are not very smart. They will die of starvation or dehydration with food and water all around them, if no one leads them to eat or drink. They will walk off a cliff and fall to certain death, if no one stops them. But before we hasten to be too harsh in our assessment, let's be mindful that they are smart enough to recognize the voice of their shepherd... and to do what he says. And that's a lot smarter than most of us! But i digress.

Though the people to whom Jesus was speaking understood the elements of His illustration, they did not understand what He meant by it. So He patiently explained it to them.

I AM the Gate (verses 7-10). The only way in and out of the sheepfold is through the gate. Those who trust Him enter into His flock and His sheepfold, and have the privilege of going "in and out" and finding pasture. As the Gate, He delivers sinners from bondage and leads them into freedom.

Those who "came before" Him (vs. 8) are like the religious leaders of the day that had just "kicked" the man born blind out of the fold. They were not true gatekeepers. They did not have the best interest of the sheep at heart. They did not love the sheep, nor did they have the approval of the Father. They exploited the sheep and abused them for their own purpose. They were only interested in providing for and protecting themselves. And behind these false gatekeepers was the "thief" (vs. 10), which is Satan.

We must be discerning of gatekeepers today. Not all who portray themselves to be shepherds are true to the Father's calling and purpose. Be watchful and discerning of who is at the gate.

. . .

I AM the Good Shepherd (verses 11-18). Jesus willingly sacrificed Himself for His sheep. As a matter of fact, as the "Lamb of God" (John 1:29, 36), He willingly took on the form of a sheep. He came down and took on flesh so that He could identify with us. It was only as a Sheep without blemish that He could be the sacrifice for our sin. And it was only as a Sheep following the Father that He could show us how to follow Him. As a sheep, He was the Son of Man, reflecting His humanity. But as the Good Shepherd, He reflected His deity as the Son of God. He is not merely a hireling who watches over the sheep only because He is paid to do so. When there is danger, the hireling will run, but the true shepherd will stay to protect and care for the flock. He will willingly lay down His own life for His sheep.

He is our Good Shepherd because He knows each one of His sheep individually. He knows our nature. He knows our needs. He knows our quirks and our short-comings. He knows our fears. He knows our secret thoughts. And He knows us better than anyone else – including ourselves. As He called each of His disciples, He already knew them before they had first met Him. On their initial meeting, He changed Simon's name to "Peter", because He already knew that on this "rock" He would build His church. He had already seen Nathanael under the fig tree before they ever met. He knew what was in the heart of Judas Iscariot as He called him to be His disciple. He knew each and every one of their hearts. Just as He knows each and every one of ours.

He is our Good Shepherd because His sheep know His voice. Because He knows us intimately, He speaks to us as no other can. He speaks in a voice that no other can imitate or replicate. He speaks the truth that we need to hear – not necessarily always what we "want" to hear. He speaks His truth that is absolute, perfect and unchanging. He speaks truth that is sharper than any two-edged sword. And He speaks it "when" we need to hear it. His sheep may not always want to hear His voice, but we know His voice. And as His sheep spend more and more time with Him, we know Him more intimately. And as we follow Him more closely, we grow to love and trust Him more and more. He has "our best" in His heart. He knows better than we do what "our best" is, and He is able to bring it about.

He is our Good Shepherd because He follows the Father. He follows Him obediently..., perfectly..., lovingly. The true Shepherd was sent by the Father. The true Shepherd sent by the Father loves the sheep perfectly and cares for them meticulously. The Father bears witness to the true Shepherd.

And because our Good Shepherd follows the Father, His sheep can follow Him with confidence..., with hope..., and with assurance. Because as another shepherd wrote:

The Lord is my Shepherd;
I have all that I need.
He lets me rest in green meadows;
He leads me beside peaceful streams.
He renews my strength.
He guides me along right paths,
bringing honor to His name.
Even when I walk
through the darkest valley,
I will not be afraid,
for You are close beside me.
Your rod and Your staff
protect and comfort me.
You prepare a feast for me
in the presence of my enemies.
You honor me by anointing my head with oil.
My cup overflows with blessings.
Surely Your goodness and unfailing love will pursue me
all the days of my life,
and I will live in the house of the Lord
forever.
Psalm 23

* * *

47

THE GOOD NEIGHBOR

The man wanted to justify his actions, so he asked Jesus, "And who is my neighbor?" Jesus replied with a story: "A Jewish man was traveling from Jerusalem down to Jericho, and he was attacked by bandits. They stripped him of his clothes, beat him up, and left him half dead beside the road. "By chance a priest came along. But when he saw the man lying there, he crossed to the other side of the road and passed him by. A Temple assistant walked over and looked at him lying there, but he also passed by on the other side. "Then a despised Samaritan came along, and when he saw the man, he felt compassion for him. Going over to him, the Samaritan soothed his wounds with olive oil and wine and bandaged them. Then he put the man on his own donkey and took him to an inn, where he took care of him. The next day he handed the innkeeper two silver coins, telling him, 'Take care of this man. If his bill runs higher than this, I'll pay you the next time I'm here.' "Now which of these three would you say was a neighbor to the man who was attacked by bandits?" Jesus asked. The man replied, "The one who showed him mercy." Then Jesus said, "Yes, now go and do the same."
Luke 10:29-37

* * *

Jesus wasn't responding to a sincere seeker. He was responding to an "expert" in religious law who was attempting to test Jesus. There was no good motivation in the original question. But our Good Shepherd is able to take even what the enemy intends for his evil purpose and turn it for good. A question that was intended to trip up Jesus was masterfully turned into one of the greatest lessons for you and me as we continue our journey walking with the Master.

. . .

Jesus never said that this story was a parable. It could well be the report of an actual occurrence. It could well be an actual occurrence in the life of one or more of the people that Jesus was addressing at the time. In that day, a story that made the Jews look bad and the Samaritans look good at best would have put off the Jews from hearing the truth Jesus was communicating. At worst, it would have been dangerous. Thus, it was very risky to tell a story like this hypothetically. But don't forget, Jesus knew everything about everyone who was within the sound of His voice. The same Jesus, who had written in the dirt the secret sins of the religious leaders who had brought forth the woman caught in adultery, was able to use actual events in the lives of some of these to teach a truth. Perhaps it was an experience straight out of the life of the "expert". Perhaps it is an experience straight out of one of our lives!

A few years ago, i had the opportunity to visit this treacherous path between Jerusalem and Jericho. From a topography standpoint, the route isn't much better today. It's a narrow, winding path through some rocky and barren landscape. Back in the first century, it apparently was also a "high crime" area that neither the Roman soldiers nor the Jewish leaders cared enough to police.

The first people to come upon this Jewish man who had been robbed, beaten and left for dead were a Jewish priest and a Levite. The priest had been serving God at the temple all week, and he was anxious to get home. He had put in enough time ministering to others for one week. Surely there was someone else who could take care of this poor fellow. (i'm ashamed to admit that i can relate to him.) Also, perhaps the robbers were hiding out just waiting for the next person to stop. He didn't want to take that risk. Anyway, the man was not a member of his synagogue. So he left it for the next person coming along to help him. Then the Levite did exactly what the priest did – nothing! Warren Wiersbe writes, *"Such is the power of the bad example of a religious man."*

The fact that the "hero" is a Samaritan made the point of the account so much more poignant to the Jews. It would have been one thing if a Jew had stopped to help a Samaritan, but a Samaritan stopped to help a Jew that two Jews had already passed by. The Samaritan was showing love to someone who hated him. He was risking his own life and spending his own money. And he wasn't seeking any credit or honor for what he was doing. Instead, he felt compassion and *"showed him mercy."*. There was no earthly reason for him to do what he did – giving of his time and his resources – without expecting anything in return.

The "expert" had wanted to have an intellectual discussion of *"who is my neighbor"*. Jesus forced him to consider one in need. How easily do we talk about abstract ideals and never personally provide any practical help? Getting involved personally will require getting your hands dirty. It will require allowing yourself to be inconvenienced. And there's a good possibility that your effort won't be appreciated. The "expert" wanted to make the issue philosophical; Jesus made it practical!

A year or so ago, my son and daughter-in-law took a now 12-year old young man into their hearts – and in many respects, into their home. This young man happens to be a different race and skin tone from my son and his wife. Though he lives with his grandmother, mother and siblings, he has been in great need of a godly male influence. A few weeks ago, as LaVonne and i were visiting with Justin and Amanda, we had the opportunity to see this lived out up close and personal. We witnessed a selflessness and genuine love on the part of our kids that made us deeply proud of them – and personally challenged. They're living life with this young man – warts and all! "Personal space" is "sacrificed". Schedules are rearranged. But the dividends are huge! The love that is being shared – and the example of Christ's love that is being shown – is making Kingdom impact in all of their lives… and rippling out to others from there.

Ministering to the Jewish man on the side of the road cost the Samaritan two silver coins and some time, but not helping cost the two Jewish religious leaders much more. It cost them the opportunity to invest the time and resources with which God had entrusted them. It cost them the opportunity to be better men and caring neighbors. They could have been a good influence in a bad world, and yet they chose to be a bad influence. The Samaritan's deed of mercy has inspired sacrificial ministry across centuries… and across the world.

As you walk with the Master, don't ever think that your efforts in ministry are wasted. Do so as unto the Father, and He'll make sure that no act of loving service in the Master's Name is ever wasted. *"Love the LORD your God with all your heart, all your soul, all your strength and all your mind.* ***And love your neighbor as yourself'*** (Luke 10:27). And as Jesus said, *"**now go and do the same.**"*

* * *

48

A QUESTION OF "OR" OR "AND"

As Jesus and the disciples continued on their way to Jerusalem, they came to a certain village where a woman named Martha welcomed Him into her home. Her sister, Mary, sat at the Lord's feet, listening to what He taught. But Martha was distracted by the big dinner she was preparing. She came to Jesus and said, "Lord, doesn't it seem unfair to You that my sister just sits here while I do all the work? Tell her to come and help me." But the Lord said to her, "My dear Martha, you are worried and upset over all these details! There is only one thing worth being concerned about. Mary has discovered it, and it will not be taken away from her."

Luke 10:38-42

* * *

We were created to worship our Creator. After Jesus returns, we will spend eternity together with *"a vast crowd, too great to count, from every nation and tribe and people and language, standing in front of the throne"* (Revelation 7:9-11) worshiping God. King David, who the LORD declared to be a man after His own heart (1 Samuel 13:14), wrote that God is *"enthroned in the praises"* (Psalm 22:3) of His people. He desires to be worshipped. He deserves our worship. He created us for worship.

But He also created us for work. In Genesis we read, *"The LORD God placed the man in the Garden of Eden to tend and care for it"* (Genesis 2:15). And don't lose sight that this occurred before man fell in sin. He created us to be fruitful. He created us to subdue all of creation. He created us in

His image with skill, and strength, and abilities. He created us to work… for His glory.

On this particular day, Jesus had arrived in Bethany. He came to the home of two sisters, Martha and Mary, and their brother, Lazarus (not mentioned in this passage). This is the first time chronologically that we meet this family in Scripture. But we know that a deep friendship existed between them and Jesus – either beginning on this particular day, or having begun sometime prior to this. From the moment Jesus arrives, we see Martha as a "worker-bee", taking care of all of the arrangements for their guests. Martha is the elder sister, and unquestionably has the gift of hospitality. She is busily at work making sure that everything is just right. It is very probable that until Jesus arrived, Mary was working right alongside of her sister – attending to their home and preparing for their guests' arrival. (By the way – don't forget that Jesus traveled with an entourage which included more than the twelve apostles. The gathering in the upper room after His ascension was 120 believers. Many of those folks had followed Jesus as He traveled throughout the three years of His ministry. So this was no small gathering… and hosting them was no small effort!)

But, when Jesus arrived, Mary immediately placed herself at His feet, listening to His every word. We see Mary in Scripture three times – here in Luke 10, John 11:32 and John 12:3 – and on all three occasions, Mary is at the feet of Jesus.

Mary and Martha are frequently contrasted as examples of a choice that each of us need to make. Will we be a worker-bee like Martha, OR will we be a worshipper like Mary? But i don't believe that is what Jesus is saying through this passage. i don't believe it is an "either/or" contrast of work and worship, but rather a "both/and". He created us for both. They are not independent from one another; in many respects they are mutually dependent. We worship Jesus as we bring all of who we are, including our work. And when we work, as unto the Lord, we are expressing worship.

At some point Martha became overwhelmed with all she was doing, and all that still needed to be done. Be mindful – she wanted the experience of her honored Guest to be the best it could possibly be. In many respects, it was an expression of worship for her. BUT, she had become frustrated and upset. She needed help – but, additionally, she wanted recognition for her efforts and wanted her Guest to know why she wasn't sitting at His feet. Her focus had turned from honoring her Guest to seeking honor for herself. We can make that mistake in our work… but we can also make that mistake in our worship. In recent weeks, we have attended worship services at a variety of churches. And in a number of those services, we have felt as if we were being ushered into the throne room in worship of God; but in others, we have felt that we were witnessing a performance that drew more attention to itself. i don't say this critically of the churches we have visited; i say this as a reminder that we can be wrongly focused in our worship, just as we can be in our work.

Jesus responded to Martha by saying, *"My dear Martha, … there is only one thing worth being concerned about. Mary has discovered it, and it will not be taken away from her."* Mary was demonstrating the truth that **what we do *with* Christ is far more important than what we do *for* Christ**! And she wasn't demonstrating that truth by her physical posture there at His feet; she was demonstrating it through the condition of her heart – focused on the Savior, not frustrated – attuned to the Savior, not upset – and abiding with the Savior, not distracted.

As we walk with the Master, each of us needs to set aside time each day to sit at His feet – to spend time with Him in His Word and allow Him to speak to us that which He has for us for that day. We need to take that time to talk with Him through prayer – praising Him, confessing our sins, thanking Him and seeking His direction and intercession. But we also need to set aside the time for work – to spend time doing those things for which He has equipped us and set before us – AND continue to be with Him throughout that portion of your day as well. Don't leave Him sitting at the "quiet time chair", abide with Him every minute – in worship AND in work. That is the one thing worth being concerned about!

* * *

49

A LESSON IN PRAYER

Once Jesus was in a certain place praying. As He finished, one of His disciples came to Him and said, "Lord, teach us to pray, just as John taught his disciples."
Jesus said, "This is how you should pray:
"Father, may Your name be kept holy.
May Your Kingdom come soon.
Give us each day the food we need,
and forgive us our sins,
as we forgive those who sin against us.
And don't let us yield to temptation."
Luke 11:1-4

* * *

There is a question among Biblical scholars as to chronologically when this discussion took place between this disciple and Jesus. Matthew records it earlier in Christ's ministry, immediately following the sermon on the mount. Luke chose to insert it here as we draw closer to the end of His earthly ministry. It's not so important as to when it took place, but rather that it took place.

John the Baptist had apparently taught his disciples to pray. The apostles Andrew and John, and most likely a few others, had been taught by John the Baptist. John obviously had been a man of prayer. He had modeled a life of prayer, unlike anything they had witnessed among their rabbis. They had witnessed a genuineness and intimacy in his prayer life with the

Father that had prompted them to seek his teaching in prayer. But there was something they saw and heard in Jesus as He prayed, that prompted them to want even more.

Jesus had been off by Himself praying to the Father, as He always did. They were having another Father-Son conversation about what was on Their hearts. The Father and Son had ***always*** talked to one another – and i do mean ALWAYS. There had ***never*** been a time that they didn't speak with each other. Their conversation in prayer was personal and intimate. They talked about everything. There was nothing too insignificant, and there was nothing "out of bounds". It was a conversation that never came to an end; it would only momentarily pause. It demonstrated an intimacy of relationship between two Persons that was beyond anything that the disciples had ever witnessed or experienced. And i believe the more the disciples heard Jesus talking with the Father, the more they desired to have that kind of relationship. Remember, at this juncture, they were still not at the place of TRULY understanding Who Jesus was – but they saw – and heard – the intimacy that He had with the Father. And their souls hungered for it.

It is important to note that this disciple did not ask Jesus to teach them ***how*** to pray. He – and they – were not asking about the logistics or mechanics of prayer – they wanted to pray like Jesus prayed.

i do not believe that Jesus ever intended His response to become a "model" prayer that followers would "mindlessly" repeat. Jesus Himself said, *"When you pray, don't babble on and on as the Gentiles do. They think their prayers are answered merely by repeating their words again and again"* (Matthew 7:7). He was explaining the intimacy of the conversation. First, never lose sight of Who the Father is. He is the Sovereign and Almighty God. He is our Father and Creator of all things. He is holy and worthy of all worship. He is NOT one of the boys! He doesn't exist to be at our "beck and call". He exists to be worshipped.

Second, the Father has a mission which is all about His Kingdom and His glory. Everything and everyone somehow is a part of that mission. If God works all things together for our good (if we love Him and are called according to His purpose) and His glory (Romans 8:28), then every circumstance and every person somehow is a part of His greater purpose. Therefore there is nothing we are experiencing and no one we will encounter that is not somehow a part of His purpose and His mission. Pray that His Kingdom will come soon – that His purpose will be accomplished – and that pain and suffering and death will be no more.

Third, trust Him for His provision of every aspect of our lives – for the food we eat, the air we breathe, the time that is needed, and so forth – all for the accomplishment of His work in and through our lives. It is all His. He provides it all. He is our Creator... our good, good Father… our Benefactor. We don't have anything that has not come from Him. But He desires to be asked by His children. If we as a sinful people desire to be asked by our children, and in turn desire to give them good gifts, how much more does our Heavenly Father! And let us not forget to thank Him! i once heard someone ask, "what if you woke up today with only the things you thanked God for yesterday?"

Fourth, seek His forgiveness for your sins. Jesus never had to do this… but He knew our nature, and He knew that we will need to seek forgiveness every day until we are in glory. Sin separates us from a holy God. Let us not allow anything to remain in our lives unconfessed and unforgiven that would hamper the intimacy of our relationship with Him. Newsflash – He knows our sins. We're not hiding anything from Him by not confessing them and seeking His forgiveness. We're just further punishing ourselves by allowing ourselves to be robbed of the intimacy with the Father.

Fifth, don't harbor ill-will toward anyone. Bitterness and anger toward others is a consuming disease that destroys from within. They may have not sought forgiveness. They may not have come to a place of repentance. But regardless, we must forgive them and ask God to remove any bitterness, or anger or unforgiveness that we are holding on to. None of us have the capacity to forgive like that, apart from the Father. Only He can enable us to do that.

Lastly, Jesus said that we are to ask the Father to keep us from yielding to temptation. He doesn't say keep us from temptation. We live in a fallen world. We have a fallen nature. Even Jesus, who did not have a fallen nature, was tempted. He faced all the temptations we do, *"yet He did not sin"* (Hebrews 4:15). We must continue to ask the Father to keep us from yielding.

. . .

Jesus also told the disciples, *"When you pray. Don't be like the hypocrites who love to pray publicly… where everyone can see them.… … Go away by yourself, shut the door behind you and pray to your Father in private"* (Matthew 7:5-6). Do not seek to be told by others that you are a great pray-er, and conversely, don't shrink from prayer because you don't think you are eloquent enough. Prayer is personal; it's between you and the Father. It's a private conversation with the One who loves you the most and desires His absolute best for you. And He knows what our best is… He knows how to bring it about… and He is able to do so. And in so doing, He will bring Himself glory!

How's your prayer life? Is there anyone asking you to teach them to pray? Allow the Master to lead you and teach you to pray.

* * *

50

THE RELIGIOUS FRATERNITY

As Jesus was speaking, one of the Pharisees invited Him home for a meal. So He went in and took His place at the table. His host was amazed to see that He sat down to eat without first performing the hand-washing ceremony required by Jewish custom. Then the Lord said to him, "You Pharisees are so careful to clean the outside of the cup and the dish, but inside you are filthy — full of greed and wickedness! Fools! Didn't God make the inside as well as the outside? So clean the inside by giving gifts to the poor, and you will be clean all over. "What sorrow awaits you Pharisees!

For you are careful to tithe even the tiniest income from your herb gardens, but you ignore justice and the love of God.

... For you love to sit in the seats of honor in the synagogues and receive respectful greetings as you walk in the marketplaces.

... For you are like hidden graves in a field. People walk over them without knowing the corruption they are stepping on."

... What sorrow also awaits you experts in religious law! For you crush people with unbearable religious demands, and you never lift a finger to ease the burden.

... For you build monuments for the prophets your own ancestors killed long ago. But in fact, you stand as witnesses who agree with what your ancestors did. They killed the prophets, and you join in their crime by building the monuments!

... For you remove the key to knowledge from the people. You don't enter the Kingdom yourselves, and you prevent others from entering."

As Jesus was leaving, the teachers of religious law and the Pharisees became hostile and tried to provoke Him with many questions. They wanted to trap Him into saying something they could use against Him.

Luke 11:37-53

* * *

In the third century, Rabbi Simlai taught that there were 613 mitzvah (precepts and commandments) recorded in the Torah. 365 of them were negative commands to abstain from certain acts. Interestingly, that was one for each day of the year (excluding leap years). 248 were positive commandments which outlined acts to be performed. It was said that the number 248 coincided with the number of bones and main organs in the human body. In addition, the Talmud is the repository of the Oral Torah. It outlines an exhaustive code of conduct to be practiced as it relates to a wide variety of rituals, worship practices, God-man and interpersonal relationships. It includes laws and customs that bore the weight of Law related to dietary practices, Sabbath and festival observance, marital relations, agricultural practice, and civil claims and damages. The Pharisees and their scribes prided themselves on being the keepers of all of these laws, commands, tenets and rules. They studied for their lifetimes to know and understand even the most minute details. They were considered to be the most expert and accurate expositors of Jewish Law. As such, they were the primary teachers and enforcers of the Law. They were the judge, jury and executioner of Jewish Law. The Law controlled every aspect of the life of a Jew. And in many ways, the Pharisees and their scribes "controlled" the Law.

The Pharisees were at various times a political party, a social movement and a school of thought in Israel. The apostle Paul was a Pharisee prior to his encounter with the Master on the road to Damascus. The Jewish historian Josephus is thought to have been a Pharisee. Just before the fall of the Temple in 70 A.D., it is estimated that there were approximately 6,000 Pharisees. They claimed Mosaic authority for their interpretation of Jewish Laws.

In the first century, there were two primary leadership groups within Judaism – the Pharisees and the Sadducees. The two actively opposed one another due to disagreements of belief, philosophy and politics. The Sadducees accepted and integrated Greek philosophy into their beliefs, they followed only the written Torah and rejected the Oral Torah teachings that came to comprise the Talmud, and they rejected any existence of life after death. When the establishment of Roman rule became apparent, the Sadducees resisted Roman rule, but the Pharisees – perhaps more politically savvy – actively supported their new rulers.

. . .

It was an elite group. In many respects, the Pharisees maintained social order – but always in a way that kept their authority and control intact. Their religious practice had become an end to itself. They had long ago moved from following Jehovah God to following a collection of rules and tenets. Their beliefs and practice no longer centered around relationship, but rather on customs and traditions. They were focused on their religious practice and not on treating people with justice and love. They sacrificed their relationship with God for a list of rules.

The Pharisee that hosted Jesus for a meal in this passage did not do so in order to learn from Jesus or truly get to know Him. This man had hosted the Master, so he might find a reason to accuse Jesus. Everything that Jesus was teaching threatened the Pharisees' way of life. His teaching threatened their authority and control. He was threatening their "status quo".

Our love for God and our concern for people must set the tone for our lives. In an attempt to trap Jesus, an expert in religious law once asked Him: *"Teacher, which is the most important commandment in the law of Moses? Jesus replied, "'You must love the LORD your God with all your heart, all your soul, and all your mind.' This is the first and greatest commandment. A second is equally important: 'Love your neighbor as yourself.' The entire law and all the demands of the prophets are based on these two commandments"* (Matthew 22:36-40). And in that one statement, Jesus took all of the 613 commands and their countless rules and traditions that were being taught and enforced by the Pharisees and set them aside. He was saying: get your heart right about loving God and caring for others, then all of the rest will fall in line and no longer be "religious camouflage" for your selfishness.

Woe unto you… for you are careful to tithe … but you
ignore justice and the love of God.
Woe unto you… for you love to sit in the seats of honor…
{and seek your own honor}.
Woe unto you… for you are like hidden graves in a field…
{covering up corruption}.
Woe unto you… for you crush people with unbearable
religious demands….
Woe unto you… for you build monuments for the
prophets… {but reject their prophecy}.
Woe unto you… for you remove the key to knowledge from

> the people… {preventing yourselves and others from entering the Kingdom}.

Jesus rebuked them for leading the Jewish people away from worshipping the Father into a religious fraternity of rules and regulations. There are two possible outcomes to a rebuke from Jesus – repentance or hostile disobedience. The Pharisees chose the latter and became even more determined to destroy Jesus. Isn't it interesting that Luke closes this passage by saying, as Jesus was leaving, *"they wanted to trap Him into saying something they could use against Him"*? Because they knew that every accusation He had just made was truth – and they could not refute it.

Here is the challenge for us as we walk with the Master. Are we walking with Him as if we are a part of some elite fraternity (or sorority)? Have we turned to religion, or have we turned to Jesus? Are we seeking Him and following Him with our whole heart, or are we following Him because of what's in it for us? Are we seeking our way and wearing our "religious camouflage"? Or by His grace are we following Him, having denied ourselves and taken up the cross He has placed before us to follow Him? The only fraternity of which i want to be a part is the fraternity of those who are following Jesus!

* * *

51

THE GREATER TRAGEDY

About this time Jesus was informed that Pilate had murdered some people from Galilee as they were offering sacrifices at the Temple. "Do you think those Galileans were worse sinners than all the other people from Galilee?" Jesus asked. "Is that why they suffered? Not at all! And you will perish, too, unless you repent of your sins and turn to God. And what about the eighteen people who died when the tower in Siloam fell on them? Were they the worst sinners in Jerusalem? No, and I tell you again that unless you repent, you will perish, too." Then Jesus told this story: "A man planted a fig tree in his garden and came again and again to see if there was any fruit on it, but he was always disappointed. Finally, he said to his gardener, 'I've waited three years, and there hasn't been a single fig! Cut it down. It's just taking up space in the garden.' "The gardener answered, 'Sir, give it one more chance. Leave it another year, and I'll give it special attention and plenty of fertilizer. If we get figs next year, fine. If not, then you can cut it down.'"

Luke 13:1-9

* * *

Scripture does not tell us why Pilate had some of the Galilean people killed as they were offering sacrifices in the Temple. There is an incident recorded in Jewish history, that dates to just before Jesus began His ministry, that may shed some light on Pilate's motivation. Pilate had decided to build an aqueduct from the Pools of Solomon to the city of Jerusalem. To pay for it, he demanded money from the temple treasury. The Jewish people were outraged that money that had been dedicated to God would be used for such a purpose. They sent a delegation to Pilate to demand their money back. Pilate sent soldiers into the crowd dressed as common people and, at his signal, they killed the people who were demanding the money. Whatever triggered the incident, Pilate used his power in tragic ways to keep the people of Israel in line as subjects of Rome, and these Galileans had been killed as his most recent examples.

Jesus speaks of another incident where eighteen people died in an accident when a tower in Siloam fell on them. Again, this incident is mentioned nowhere else in Scripture, nor recorded in Jewish history. But both of these are examples of the question, "why do bad things happen to good people?" Why does tragedy occur at the hands of a cruel despot? Why do lives perish in the wake of an accident? Are these people worse sinners? And is God meting out His punishment upon them?

There are three factors at play here in the question that is being asked of Jesus. First, be mindful that the religious leaders are looking for ways to catch Jesus in a trap. What better trap than to have Him make some disparaging remark about the Roman Prefect? And His remark would dutifully be carried back to Pilate, for appropriate discipline to be dispensed! Be mindful of this dark motivation behind most of the questions being asked of Jesus.

But the second factor here is that the view of God the Father had been grossly distorted by a religious belief system of rules and laws. God has been denigrated to the point that His perceived sole purpose is to demand obedience and dispense punishment when it is not given. And it was being modeled before their eyes by discompassionate religious leaders who did not walk in holiness and righteousness, and meted out their own version of cruel punishment.

The third factor is a product of the second. If they saw the Father as one whose sole purpose is to pass judgment and dispense divine punishment, then wouldn't the people be correct in judging for themselves that those who were killed had to be "worse sinners"?

Their belief was that human tragedy – whether it be in the form of human violence or natural disaster – must be divine punishment. And that it was very appropriate for them to believe that one who was experiencing tragedy was in fact guilty of some great sin and therefore had fallen under the punishment of God. By the way, that's exactly what Job's "friends" had said to him. And that same question – and that same line of thinking – is still being used today!

Jesus immediately turned their questions and their false beliefs to a moment to call for their repentance. Because the eternal issue was not the tragedies of which they spoke; the greater tragedy is that — unless they repented of their sin and turned to Jesus for forgiveness – each one would perish for eternity. The question was not, "Why did these people die?" but, "What right do we have to live?" None of us are sinless!

Jesus then used the story of a barren fig tree to illustrate His point. The Father is gracious and long-suffering toward each and every one of us – as our Creator having planted us in His "garden". He has made the way for each of us to repent, follow Him and bear fruit (Matthew 3:7-10). He has had every right to cut us down, but in His mercy, He has spared us. Yet, we cannot presume upon the kindness and long-suffering of the Father, for the day of judgment will come. Not one of us knows when our last day on this side of eternity will be.

Jesus doesn't supply a conclusion for the parable. Did the tree bear fruit? Was the tree spared or cut down? We have no way to know about the tree. But we can answer as far as our own lives are concerned!

We live in a day when we hear of disasters and tragedies that have occurred every day. It can be pretty overwhelming to hear the constant flow of news reports. But the fact of the matter is – unless Jesus returns first – the probability of each and every one of us dying is still one-out-of-one. The greatest tragedy will be if, when that day arrives, we have not repented of our sin and received the free gift of eternal life that we can only have in Jesus.

So, as you finish this chapter, that's my question to you. If you haven't yet done so, you can do so right now. And if you have, there are many who have yet to hear. *"If we get figs next year, fine. If not, then you can cut it down."* Don't let that happen to your family member, your neighbor, your co-worker or that one who has even yet to hear the name of Jesus. Because that would be the greater tragedy!

52

COUNT THE COST

A large crowd was following Jesus. He turned around and said to them, "If you want to be My disciple, you must, by comparison, hate everyone else—your father and mother, wife and children, brothers and sisters—yes, even your own life. Otherwise, you cannot be My disciple. And if you do not carry your own cross and follow Me, you cannot be My disciple. "But don't begin until you count the cost. For who would begin construction of a building without first calculating the cost to see if there is enough money to finish it? Otherwise, you might complete only the foundation before running out of money, and then everyone would laugh at you. They would say, 'There's the person who started that building and couldn't afford to finish it!' "Or what king would go to war against another king without first sitting down with his counselors to discuss whether his army of 10,000 could defeat the 20,000 soldiers marching against him? And if he can't, he will send a delegation to discuss terms of peace while the enemy is still far away. So you cannot become My disciple without giving up everything you own. "Salt is good for seasoning. But if it loses its flavor, how do you make it salty again? Flavorless salt is good neither for the soil nor for the manure pile. It is thrown away. Anyone with ears to hear should listen and understand!"

Luke 14:25-35

* * *

"A large crowd was following Jesus." That often was the case. The crowd was following to see what they could get from Jesus. There wasn't any cost to follow Jesus as a part of the crowd. If you were part of the crowd, you could come and go as you liked. The crowd was made up of the inquisitive, the skeptical, the fickle and the adversarial. They had either witnessed a miracle performed by Jesus, or heard about one. Some of them had heard that Jesus fed the hungry, and they wanted food. Some were sick or deformed, and they wanted to be healed. They either wanted to experience a miracle, or witness one firsthand. A few thought that He was preparing to overthrow Rome and establish a new kingdom. They were motivated out of need, curiosity, or, in the case of His adversaries, a desire to find fault with Him.

Today, we would often be excited to hear about large crowds gathering for an event, or to see and hear a speaker. We would tend to think – the larger the crowd, the more successful the event. But Jesus knew better; He knew what was in their hearts (John 2:24). He knew that, though a large crowd was following, few were actually followers. He knew that the crowd that was here today could very easily be gone tomorrow. So He did something that was very "anti-seeker-sensitive". He turned to them and began to teach a message designed to deliberately thin out the ranks. He made it clear that He is more interested in "quality" than "quantity". LaVonne and i recently visited a church that has placed a high value on small group discipleship. The mission statement for their small groups is *"more time with fewer people leads to greater Kingdom impact."* That is exactly what we see Jesus modeling here in Luke 14 and throughout the Gospels.

Jesus repeatedly makes a distinction between salvation and discipleship. Warren Wiersbe writes, *"salvation means coming to the cross and trusting Jesus, whereas discipleship means carrying the cross and following Jesus."* As we already saw in chapter 27, Jesus makes it clear that our relationship with Him must take priority over any other relationship we have, including our spouse and our family. And the reality is that if we keep our relationship with Him rightly-oriented, we will be in the place to have the best relationship we could possibly have with our spouse and/or our family.

And then He goes on to say, *"if you do not carry your own cross and follow Me, you cannot be My disciple."* Let's be mindful of the context for those to whom Jesus was speaking. The "cross" in that day was used as an instrument of capital punishment. Death on a cross was intended to be particularly slow, painful, humiliating and public. In many cases, the condemned were forced to carry their cross to the place of execution. So this was a symbol of death – death to self. It is not a decision that is made lightly. Death on a cross is not something you do and then change your mind! Death on the cross is not just for the emotion of the moment; it is forever.

And those dying on a cross didn't get to choose their instrument of execution. It was placed on them by the authority under whom they were being executed.

If we truly will die to self and carry our own cross, it will be a "slow" death in that it will last a lifetime. It's not a "one-and-done" decision; it's a continuous choice for the rest of our lives. It will be a "painful and humbling" death. Jesus will bring us face-to-face with our own sinful, flesh nature. We will need to face that wretched sinner that we are – apart from Him. Most of us have perfected a mask that we wear on the outside to cover the ugliness of our sin on the inside. But as we die to self, that mask is stripped away so that Jesus can do His transforming work of chipping away everything in our lives that does not conform to His image. And that chipping can be painful. It can be humbling.

And as He is doing that work, it will be "public". There is no such thing as an "undercover" follower of Jesus. If i have denied myself and am carrying my own cross, it will be conspicuous to those around me. The conspicuousness will come from the fact that my sinful flesh cannot walk in that way – only Jesus can. And if i am truly carrying my cross, i'm not the one who will be seen – it will be Jesus! Because – we don't choose the cross we are to carry, He does. The one under whose authority we are, chooses the cross. The cross He chooses for us to carry is His will, not ours. The path we walk is His path, not ours. We're following Him, not ourselves.

Thus Jesus said, there is a cost to be counted. There is a cost we must count. It is the "cost" we have just described. The cost is surrendering our own will to His – with no strings attached – and no ability to reclaim our will. It is a complete and total surrender.

But i can't help but wonder – when Jesus says *"first calculating the cost"* – if He is referring to Himself, and not us. He is the Builder – building His Church and His Kingdom. He is the King – establishing His Kingdom. He is the Master Chef – creating His masterpiece. All to fulfill His purpose and bring glory to His Name. He knows exactly what is needed. We are saved – only because He laid down His life. He paid the ultimate cost with His shed blood. And as the Builder, the King and the Chef, He knows exactly what it will take to fulfill His work through His disciples. He knows the cross that we each must carry. He knows what it will entail.

And He has uniquely crafted the cross that He has for each one of us to carry. It is uniquely fit for our specific section of the building. It is uniquely positioned for our assigned place on the battlefield. And it is uniquely flavored for our portion in the recipe. All because He has counted and determined the cost.

As you walk with the Master, answer this important question that Jesus is asking. Are you simply a part of the crowd that is following Jesus? Or, have you come to that place that you have denied yourself, taken up the cross He has for you, and counted the cost to follow Him? Not as a part of the crowd, but as a part of His handiwork designed and used for His purpose (2 Timothy 2:21). If not, step away from the crowd and follow Him today. Whatever the cost, He is worth it!

* * *

53

LOST AND FOUND

Tax collectors and other notorious sinners often came to listen to Jesus teach. This made the Pharisees and teachers of religious law complain that He was associating with such sinful people — even eating with them! So Jesus told them this story: "If a man has a hundred sheep and one of them gets lost, what will he do?" "...Or suppose a woman has ten silver coins and loses one. Won't she light a lamp and sweep the entire house and search carefully until she finds it?" ...To illustrate the point further, Jesus told them this story: "A man had two sons. The younger son told his father, 'I want my share of your estate now before you die.' So his father agreed to divide his wealth between his sons. A few days later this younger son packed all his belongings and moved to a distant land, and there he wasted all his money in wild living. ...So he returned home to his father. And while he was still a long way off, his father saw him coming. Filled with love and compassion, he ran to his son, embraced him, and kissed him. His son said to him, 'Father, I have sinned against both heaven and you, and I am no longer worthy of being called your son.' But his father said to the servants, 'Quick! Bring the finest robe in the house and put it on him. Get a ring for his finger and sandals for his feet. And kill the calf we have been fattening. We must celebrate with a feast, for this son of mine was dead and has now returned to life. He was lost, but now he is found....'"

Luke 15:1-31

* * *

The Pharisees and their scribes had established a hierarchy of sin – dividing "acceptable" sins from those that proper Jewish society would have deemed to be "unacceptable". They would have identified "notorious sinners" as people who led conspicuously immoral lives and/or engaged in highly questionable occupations. But it also would have included people with certain diseases or disabilities that were perceived to be a sign of some great sin. This group would have been physically and morally unapproachable by these religious leaders. Tax collectors were generally hated and despised by their fellow countrymen. Though referred to separately in this passage, they would have also been considered to be a part of this larger group. No "respectable" Jew would have had anything to do with this collection of "notorious sinners". The result was that the Pharisees viewed this group as being "beyond saving" and themselves as not being in the need of saving. Sadly, the Pharisees never saw themselves as being among the lost.

Before we go any further, let's camp on this point for a moment. This idea of "acceptable" sins is not unique to the scribes and Pharisees. I believe that we in the church today function under a similar system of ranking sin. For example, if we were asked about the sins of murder, sexual immorality, stealing or drunkenness, we would tend to agree that these egregious sins are "unacceptable". But what about the sins of gossip, creating strife, covetousness or gluttony? We might tend to view these less egregious sins as "more acceptable". I would agree that they are definitely more prevalent – even within the church – but that doesn't make them more acceptable! Please don't misunderstand me, i do believe that Scripture teaches that there are sins that are worse in the eyes of God than others (1 John 5:16-17). However, Scripture also teaches that the "wages" of ALL sin is death (Romans 6:23), and ALL of us have sinned and fallen short (Romans 3:23). My point is that all of us are sinners in need of a Savior! The Pharisees were taking a position that the tax collectors and "notorious sinners" did not deserve the attention of Jesus – and how could anyone who was righteous associate with them! i, for one, am grateful that Jesus came to seek and save sinners! For i am one!

One more side road worthy to mention: It's interesting to note that sinners were drawn to Jesus. Not because He catered to them, or compromised on truth, but because He genuinely cared for them, and welcomed them. Whereas the Pharisees repelled them. How are we viewed by our world today? Do our words and actions reflect those of Jesus or those of the Pharisees?

. . .

Jesus spoke these three parables in response to the accusations being made by the Pharisees and their scribes. He was clearly communicating the message of salvation: God welcomes and forgives repentant sinners. God is seeking and searching just as the shepherd seeks out the lost sheep and the woman searches for the lost coin. But there is also our part in salvation. The lost son willingly repented and returned to his father.

The fact that the shepherd goes out to seek one lost sheep and the woman searches for her one lost coin is a reflection of the truth that our Lord *"does not want anyone to be destroyed, but wants everyone to repent"* (2 Peter 3:9). He seeks and searches for every last one! And the heavens rejoice *"when even one sinner repents"* (Luke 15:10).

In the parable of the lost son, we see two beautiful pictures: one of repentance, and the other of acceptance. The rebellious son comes to the end of himself – and realizes how far he has fallen. He knows that his selfish way has led to failure and destruction. He has exhausted everything that the world has to offer and has been left empty and broken – lying in a pig sty. He literally has hit bottom and knows that there is only one choice. He can continue to languish in his filth or he can seek his father's forgiveness. Having gone as far as he can on the path away from his father, he makes a 180-degree turn back toward his father. That's the picture of repentance:

- coming face-to-face with the reality of our sin,
- lamenting over our sin and its effects on ourselves, on others and on God,
- confessing it to ourselves, to those we have wronged, and to God,
- acknowledging that we are powerless over our sin and cannot change ourselves, and
- making a 180-degree turn toward God.

As we turn toward God, He is there to meet us and accept us with arms out-stretched wide to receive us, to forgive us and to restore us into right relationship with Him as His child. Picture the son's rags being exchanged for a fine robe, his once filthy feet now being cradled in his father's sandals, and the signet ring on his finger showing that he has been restored. Then he enters into a banquet announcing to the world and celebrating his return. What a gift! Jesus is extending that very same gift of forgiveness and restoration to "notorious sinners" like me… and you.

With none too sinful to receive it, as long as we are not too hard-hearted or proud to accept it!

As we walk with the Master, we have a life-changing message to share – a message of grace, of forgiveness, and of restoration and acceptance. The lost are waiting to be found!

* * *

54

THE DISHONEST MANAGER

Jesus told this story to his disciples: "There was a certain rich man who had a manager handling his affairs. One day a report came that the manager was wasting his employer's money. So the employer called him in and said, 'What's this I hear about you? Get your report in order, because you are going to be fired.' "The manager thought to himself, 'Now what? My boss has fired me. I don't have the strength to dig ditches, and I'm too proud to beg. Ah, I know how to ensure that I'll have plenty of friends who will give me a home when I am fired.' "So he invited each person who owed money to his employer to come and discuss the situation. He asked the first one, 'How much do you owe him?' The man replied, 'I owe him 800 gallons of olive oil.' So the manager told him, 'Take the bill and quickly change it to 400 gallons.' 'And how much do you owe my employer?' he asked the next man. 'I owe him 1,000 bushels of wheat,' was the reply. 'Here,' the manager said, 'take the bill and change it to 800 bushels.' "The rich man had to admire the dishonest rascal for being so shrewd. And it is true that the children of this world are more shrewd in dealing with the world around them than are the children of the light. Here's the lesson: Use your worldly resources to benefit others and make friends. Then, when your possessions are gone, they will welcome you to an eternal home. "If you are faithful in little things, you will be faithful in large ones. But if you are dishonest in little things, you won't be honest with greater responsibilities. And if you are untrustworthy about worldly wealth, who will trust you with the true riches of heaven? And if you are not faithful with other people's things, why should you be trusted with things of your own? "No one can serve two masters. For you will hate one and love the other; you will be devoted to one and despise the other. You cannot serve God and be enslaved to money."

Luke 16:1-13

* * *

So let me get this straight – is Jesus commending this manager to His disciples for his dishonesty? It sounds like He is affirming his self-protective actions. But that can't be right! What is Jesus teaching the disciples – and us – through this story? (By the way, Jesus never says this is a parable. This may be a true story. Regardless, Jesus has something He wants us to learn through it.)

The manager was hired by a rich man to manage the rich man's financial affairs. All of the resources are owned by the rich man. The manager is a steward of that which has been entrusted to him. He is not the owner of the resources! And he is accountable to the owner.

John Piper writes, *"the possession of money… is a test run for eternity. Can you pass the test of faithfulness with your money? Do you use it as a means of proving the worth of God and the joy you have in supporting His cause? Or does the way you use it prove that what you really enjoy is things, not God?"*

Earlier in the Gospel of Luke, we see Jesus teaching His disciples about money and possessions. He told them, *"Seek the Kingdom of God above all else, and He will give you everything you need…. Sell your possessions and give to those in need. This will store up treasure for you in heaven! And the purses of heaven never get old or develop holes. Your treasure will be safe; no thief can steal it and no moth can destroy it. Wherever your treasure is, there the desires of your heart will also be"* (Luke 12:31, 33-34).

Jesus is not commending the manager for his dishonesty, but He is pointing out that the same principle that this man is counterfeiting for personal gain, done in God's way produces Kingdom gain. The manager is generously – and shrewdly – giving away his master's resources to win favor with those who could provide him with a place to live after his job comes to an end. He is storing up treasure in a way that will bring future benefit – in this case, for himself. If God is not our Master, then we will become servants of money, just like this man – and money is a terrible master! But if God is our Master, then money will be our servant.

As followers of the Master, we are, in fact, to be just as generous and just as shrewd – but not for personal gain – rather for Kingdom gain. We are to give away – generously and wisely – the resources that our Master has entrusted to us so that the Kingdom is extended, the gospel is advanced, and needs are met.

Warren Wiersbe writes:

> *"The thief says, 'What's yours is mine – I'll take it!'*
> *The selfish man says, 'What's mine is mine – I'll keep it!'*
> *The follower of Jesus says, 'What's mine is a gift from God – I'll share it!'"*

We are stewards of that with which the Master has entrusted us – including the gospel, for His Kingdom purpose. It is the purpose for which He still gives us breath. If our salvation was merely about ourselves, we would be in heaven right now. But we continue to walk with Him on this side of heaven because there is more that He still wants to accomplish in and through our lives. He is building His Kingdom and we are following Him as a part of that work – giving of the time, talent and treasure that He has provided us – so that the lost can hear and respond to the Good News..., and so that believers can be disciples who disciple others... who disciple others. And as we do so, Jesus says we are storing up treasure for ourselves in heaven – in essence, the infinite joy of being a child of God. The big difference between the dishonest manager and us – if we are being true to our Master – is that we don't give of our time, talent and treasures to "get". We give so that <u>others</u> might "get".

One last reminder as you walk with the Master: *"When you give..."* – not "if" you give – *"don't let your left hand know what your right hand is doing. Give your gifts"* – of time, talent and treasure – *"in private, and your Father, who sees everything, will reward you"* (Matthew 6:3-4).

* * *

55

A TALE OF TWO MEN

Jesus said, "There was a certain rich man who was splendidly clothed in purple and fine linen and who lived each day in luxury. At his gate lay a poor man named Lazarus who was covered with sores. As Lazarus lay there longing for scraps from the rich man's table, the dogs would come and lick his open sores. "Finally, the poor man died and was carried by the angels to sit beside Abraham at the heavenly banquet. The rich man also died and was buried, and he went to the place of the dead. There, in torment, he saw Abraham in the far distance with Lazarus at his side. "The rich man shouted, 'Father Abraham, have some pity! Send Lazarus over here to dip the tip of his finger in water and cool my tongue. I am in anguish in these flames.' "But Abraham said to him, 'Son, remember that during your lifetime you had everything you wanted, and Lazarus had nothing. So now he is here being comforted, and you are in anguish. And besides, there is a great chasm separating us. No one can cross over to you from here, and no one can cross over to us from there.' "Then the rich man said, 'Please, Father Abraham, at least send him to my father's home. For I have five brothers, and I want him to warn them, so they don't end up in this place of torment.' "But Abraham said, 'Moses and the prophets have warned them. Your brothers can read what they wrote.' "The rich man replied, 'No, Father Abraham! But if someone is sent to them from the dead, then they will repent of their sins and turn to God.' "But Abraham said, 'If they won't listen to Moses and the prophets, they won't be persuaded even if someone rises from the dead.'"

Luke 16:19-31

* * *

The Pharisees had just overheard Jesus telling the story of the dishonest manager (chapter 54) to His disciples. Luke records in verse 14 that the Pharisees scoffed at Jesus because they *"dearly loved their money."* Jesus responded by telling this story. Again, He does not indicate that this is a parable. This could very well be a true account – and perhaps, one or both of the men in the story were known by one or more of the Pharisees. Whether they knew the rich man or not, they could relate, because in many respects, Jesus was describing some or all of the men who were listening to Him.

Jesus never told the rich man's name. The Pharisees were left to insert the name of any individual they knew who best met his description – including their own name. The man was rich and famous. He lived in luxury, and was splendidly clothed. He was a man of position, accustomed to being served and pampered, and used to getting his way. He was a man of power – a product of his great wealth. He was a man that very few – if any – would refuse. He ate and drank only the finest, and invited those with whom he chose to surround himself to attend his opulent banquets. He didn't have a care in this world. And he gave no regard for those who did.

Lazarus (which means "God is my help") was a poor beggar and outcast, covered in open sores. Each day he would lay at the rich man's gate hoping that someone would throw a few scraps his way. But the only attention he got was from the dogs who came to lick his sores.

One day the rich man died. A great funeral was organized on his behalf. It was the grandest that money could buy. It was filled with grand accolades about his goodness, and probably his generosity. But it was a stark contrast to the torment that awaited him, as he left his body behind and stepped into the other side of death.

Lazarus also died. No funeral was organized. No accolades were spoken. His body was simply taken to the Valley of Gehenna and burned with the refuse of the city. Lazarus didn't look back as he stepped from this life into eternity and was carried by angels to a heavenly banquet table and seated beside Abraham. He, who had been the poor beggar, had now become the truly rich man.

. . .

Death is the great leveler. For the man who had been rich on earth had now become the tormented beggar in death. His torment was not the result of his riches; it was the result of how he had lived his life and thereby used his riches. He had lived a life of selfish ambition, focused on no one and nothing except himself. He hadn't sought to honor God or walk with God, unless by outward appearance, it was to his advantage. He had never once ministered to or comforted the least of these. He had never used any of his wealth to assist the poor and needy, including Lazarus who laid at his gate. And he cried out to Father Abraham for pity and a mere drop of water, but there was none to be gained. His choice had been made on this side of eternity, and now couldn't be undone.

It appears that the man did develop some degree of compassion because he asked that Lazarus return from the dead to tell his brothers about the torment that awaited them if they didn't repent of their sins and turn to God (verse 30). *"But Abraham said, 'If they won't listen to Moses and the prophets, they won't be persuaded even if someone rises from the dead'"* (verse 31).

On several occasions, i have had the difficult responsibility of preaching at funerals of people who died without having a saving relationship with Jesus. And in most of those instances, i did not know the individual before they died. It is difficult to speak comfort to surviving family members and friends when you know that their deceased loved one is now experiencing the very torment that this man describes. But i learned to take a cue from this man. i would confess that though i did not know the individual in life, i could confidently assure them of what he or she would want them to know in death. One of the saddest conversations is the one with a loved one who has come to that realization that their friend or family member is not in heaven but is now permanently separated from God. It is a moment without hope – the hope of being reunited with them at the throne of God. But the reality is that the deceased loved one would no longer want anyone to follow them in their footsteps. Their message from the grave is "turn to Jesus"!

Alas, most of the Pharisees, if not all, maintained hardened hearts and never received this truth from the very One who now holds *"the keys of death and the grave"* (Revelation 1:18). They rejected the very One who did exactly what the rich man asked (verses 27-28) – He returned from the grave – and in so doing, made the way for us to live forever with Him – if we will repent and turn to Him.

. . .

i am mindful that "Good News" is only good news if it is received – and accepted – **in time**. The rich man now knows the Good News, but it's no longer good news for him. And there are still many who have yet to hear. Pray that the Lord will soften their hearts to receive His Good News. Pray that those who have been given the Good News will go out and share it. And then, go and do likewise. Because we have been sent by Jesus to do just that. "*As the Father has sent Me, so I am sending you*" (John 20:21).

* * *

56

SIX LESSONS TO LIVE BY

One day Jesus said to His disciples, "There will always be temptations to sin, but what sorrow awaits the person who does the tempting! It would be better to be thrown into the sea with a millstone hung around your neck than to cause one of these little ones to fall into sin. So watch yourselves! "If another believer sins, rebuke that person; then if there is repentance, forgive. Even if that person wrongs you seven times a day and each time turns again and asks forgiveness, you must forgive." The apostles said to the Lord, "Show us how to increase our faith." The Lord answered, "If you had faith even as small as a mustard seed, you could say to this mulberry tree, 'May you be uprooted and be planted in the sea,' and it would obey you! "When a servant comes in from plowing or taking care of sheep, does his master say, 'Come in and eat with me'? No, he says, 'Prepare my meal, put on your apron, and serve me while I eat. Then you can eat later.' And does the master thank the servant for doing what he was told to do? Of course not. In the same way, when you obey Me you should say, 'We are unworthy servants who have simply done our duty.'"

Luke 17:1-10

* * *

Jesus and the disciples were making His last journey toward Jerusalem. The disciples would soon be ministering to others in His place. As they walked, Jesus was preparing His disciples for the time that He would no longer be with them. And these are six important lessons for each of us, as we walk with the Master.

. . .

"There will always be temptations to sin." We are all sinners living in a sinful world. We are walking with a Master who Himself was tempted. But take heart, we have a High Priest who *"understands our weaknesses, for He faced all of the same testings we do, yet He did not sin"* (Hebrews 4:15). As we saw in chapter 7 of this book, Satan threw everything he had in his arsenal against Jesus. He attempted to tempt Him physically (through hunger), soulishly (through a short-cut to "achieve the goal") and spiritually (in an attempt to rob the Father of the worship due Him). And Satan's attempts didn't stop in the wilderness; they continued to the cross. So He has equipped us with all we need to resist temptation.

Our Master has given us His Word (to show us the truth of every situation), His Spirit (to guide us and empower us in the way we should go) and Himself as our High Priest (to continually intercede on our behalf). Be mindful, God is not the author of temptation (James 1:13). Temptation comes from our flesh nature, from the sinful world in which we live, and from the author of lies himself. But take courage that the victory has already been won, *"because the Spirit who lives in you is greater than the spirit who lives in the world"* (1 John 4:4). *"So humble yourselves before God. Resist the devil, and he will flee from you"* (James 4:7). Submission to the Father was the path that Jesus always walked in – including his temptation in the wilderness (Matthew 4:1-11) – and it is the path that He would have us walk in to defeat the enemy and his temptations.

"But a greater sorrow awaits those who cause a little one to sin. *So watch yourselves!"* We must take heed not to cause others to stumble. By "little ones", Jesus is not only referring to children, He is also referring to new believers who are young in their faith. As John writes, we must live in the light and not cause others to stumble (1 John 2:10). Therefore, we must choose to abstain from even those things that are "lawful" (1 Corinthians 10:23-24) so as not to cause others to stumble in their walk. We don't choose to abstain in order to lead a righteous life and be accepted by God. We are accepted through the costly grace of God; therefore we choose to honor Him by abstaining from anything that could potentially bring dishonor to Him by causing another to stumble or by failing to build up my neighbor.

"If another believer sins, rebuke that person so there can be repentance and forgiveness." The operative underlying word in this admonition is love. The Pharisees were experts at rebuking in condemnation. That's not what Jesus was talking about. The motivation for going to a brother or sister

must be the love of Christ (Ephesians 4:15). Our aim is not to embarrass or hurt the offender. Rather, it is borne out of a heart to help them be freed from any bondage in sin and experience the fullness of joy in their walk with Christ. It is not legalistic retribution; it is compassionate "CPR". A loving rebuke using the Word of God that leads to true repentance will result in a cleansing forgiveness for all involved. And it will lead to the restoration of relationships with one another – and with the Father.

"If someone wrongs you... *and asks forgiveness, you must forgive.*" Even if the offender doesn't repent and seek forgiveness, we must forgive. i can just imagine Jesus turning to James and John, the Sons of Thunder, and saying "no calling down fire from heaven to burn them up" (Luke 9:54)! Jesus was telling the disciples what Paul would later say, "love *keeps no record of being wronged*" (1 Corinthians 13:5). Forgiveness is not a cheap exchange of words. True forgiveness involves some degree of pain. Someone has been hurt and there is a price to pay for the healing of the wound. Warren Wiersbe writes, *"Love motivates us to forgive, but faith activates that forgiveness...."* Which then brings us to the lesson about faith.

"It's not the size of your faith; it's the object of your faith." Timothy Keller writes, *"It is not the strength of your faith but the object of your faith.... Strong faith in a weak branch is fatally inferior to weak faith in a strong branch."* The psalmist said the same thing another way: *"Commit your way to the LORD; trust in Him, and He will do it"* (Psalm 37:5 NASB). He will give us the faith to forgive..., the faith to follow..., and the faith to finish. It will be a faith to do the difficult (verses 1-3), to do the impossible (verses 4-6) and to do the menial (verses 7-10).

"A faithful servant shouldn't expect a special reward for doing what the Master has told him to do." We are servants of the Master by His grace. We don't deserve to be servants. We don't obey to merit favor; we obey because we have been favored. Our obedience doesn't seek its own way; it is an expression of our love for Him (1 Corinthians 13:5). Serving Him isn't our duty; it's our delight.

As we walk with the Master, we will need to hold onto these lessons. i'm not sure that any of us truly "master" them completely on this side of glory. But i am grateful that our Master is there to lovingly remind us and enable us until we do.

57

HE HAD TO CALL HIM BY NAME

A man named Lazarus was sick. He lived in Bethany with his sisters, Mary and Martha.... So the two sisters sent a message to Jesus telling Him, "Lord, your dear friend is very sick." But when Jesus heard about it He said, "Lazarus's sickness will not end in death. No, it happened for the glory of God so that the Son of God will receive glory from this." So although Jesus loved Martha, Mary, and Lazarus, He stayed where He was for the next two days. Finally, He said to His disciples, "Let's go back to Judea." ... When Jesus arrived at Bethany, He was told that Lazarus had already been in his grave for four days. ...Martha said to Jesus, "Lord, if only You had been here, my brother would not have died. But even now I know that God will give You whatever You ask." ...Jesus told her, "I am the resurrection and the life. Anyone who believes in Me will live, even after dying. Everyone who lives in Me and believes in Me will never ever die. Do you believe this, Martha?" ... When Mary arrived and saw Jesus, she fell at His feet and said, "Lord, if only You had been here, my brother would not have died." When Jesus saw her weeping and saw the other people wailing with her, a deep anger welled up within Him, and He was deeply troubled. "Where have you put him?" he asked them. "Roll the stone aside," Jesus told them.... Then Jesus looked up to heaven and said, "Father, thank You for hearing Me. You always hear Me, but I said it out loud for the sake of all these people standing here, so that they will believe You sent Me." Then Jesus shouted, "Lazarus, come out!" And the dead man came out, his hands and feet bound in graveclothes, his face wrapped in a headcloth. Jesus told them, "Unwrap him and let him go!" Many of the people who were with Mary believed in Jesus when they saw this happen. But some went to the Pharisees and told them what Jesus had done.... "This man certainly performs many miraculous signs. If we allow Him to go on like this, soon everyone will believe in Him. Then the Roman army will come and

destroy both our Temple and our nation." So from that time on, the Jewish leaders began to plot Jesus' death....
John 11:1-57

* * *

As we saw earlier in chapter 48, Lazarus, Mary and Martha had become dear friends of Jesus. Only John records this particular event, but it was without question one of the greatest miracles that Jesus performed. Though He had raised others from the dead, He had not yet raised anyone from the grave – and Lazarus had been in the grave for four days! It was a miracle that could not be ignored by the religious leaders. It was the miracle that aroused the most response – from His followers... and His enemies. But, don't let me get ahead of myself. And forgive me – this passage has a lot for us to hear – so this chapter is slightly longer than the others.

There are a number of "key players" in this account. Let's look at them:

The Messenger. Jesus was in the town of Bethabara (approximately 20 miles from Bethany). It would have taken a messenger a day to carry the message to Jesus from Bethany. Then Jesus and the disciples remained in Bethabara for two more days. On the fourth day, Jesus and the disciples traveled to Bethany. That means that Lazarus died soon after the messenger left to bring the message to Jesus, and he was already in the grave by the time Jesus received the message. Jesus knew that – and He knew that the additional delay in His departure for Bethany would only serve to bring greater glory to the Father and the Son. This needs to serve as a reminder to us that **the Master's timing is absolutely perfect!** His delays are purposeful. If you are experiencing a delay in an answer from the Master, trust that He sees the big picture – and we don't. Trust His timing.

The Disciples. Those who should have known Jesus the best, still often knew Him the least. Imagine their quandary. First is the news that Jesus' close friend is very sick. Couldn't Jesus have prevented him from being sick? Shouldn't a close friend like Lazarus have special privileges, like being immune from disease? Now that Jesus had received the news, why wouldn't He heal Lazarus from a distance, just like He did the Roman officer's servant (chapter 23)? Secondly, the disciples – and Jesus – are well aware that the religious leaders are plotting against Him and a return trip back into Judea would be very risky for Jesus. This is another consideration for Him to heal Lazarus from a distance. But Jesus appears to cast that concern aside and resolves to go to Bethany over the objections of His disciples. Thirdly, the puzzlement of the disciples is only further compounded when Jesus announces to them that Lazarus is dead. Why risk this trip to see a dead man? And when Thomas declares, *"Let's go, too – and die with Jesus"* (verse 16), it is an expression of resignation – that "nothing good is going to come from this". Little did he know!

Regrettably, we as 21st century followers of Jesus often respond just like those 1st century disciples. We expect that as followers of Jesus that we should have special privileges. There is an oft-quoted statement by Corrie ten Boom that *"the safest place is in the center of God's will"*. But we distort the meaning when we think we deserve and are assured of protection from any harm. As a matter-of-fact, nothing could be further from the truth, and Corrie ten Boom herself demonstrated through her life and her actions that she understood the risk and the dangers of walking with Christ. But she could be confident that He was walking with her in each and every step. Lazarus wasn't immune to death or disease as a follower – or as a dear friend; he, however, could be confident that Jesus would work all of it for the glory of God. And incidentally, if you are a follower of Jesus, you too are His dear friend (John 15:15).

The Sisters. As i search Scripture, i cannot find one incident where anyone died in the physical presence of Jesus. It may have occurred. He may have been there when his earthly father, Joseph, died. But again, there's nothing recorded in Scripture. Thus, Martha's first statement to Jesus upon His arrival was one of confident faith based upon what she had witnessed – *"Lord, if only You had been here, my brother would not have died"* (verse 21). But the second part of her statement was also very telling in light of all she had witnessed – *"But even now I know that God will give You whatever You ask"* (verse 22). But even given that faithful statement, Martha did not believe that Jesus could raise her brother from the dead in the present time. She knew his body would rise again "at the last day" like "everyone else" but even this dear friend of Jesus could not even imagine that He could raise Lazarus this very day. And Mary, the one who we always see at the Master's feet – even on this occasion – expressed the same beliefs as her sister. Though she, too, loved the Master with all of her heart – her faith was limited.

We read that *"a deep anger welled up within Him, and He was deeply troubled"* (verse 33). Jesus wasn't angry at Mary, or Martha, or His disciples, or the crowd..., He was angry at Satan and the ravages of sin and death in the world He had created. He was angry at the enemy for sowing the lies of fear and hopelessness. And He wept over the fact that the One who is *"the Resurrection and the Life"* was standing right there in their midst, and they could not see Him because the enemy had blinded them with his lies.

How often are we blinded from seeing the reality of Who Jesus is, the promise He has given and His ability to bring it about? How often have we allowed the enemy and his lies to limit our view of Who Jesus is? He is the only Way. He is the only Truth. And His word is Life (John 14:6). His only limitation is in our minds and hearts because we have allowed ourselves to be deceived by Satan's lies. The only thing standing between the spoken promise of God and our realization of that promise is a faith that we have allowed the enemy to limit (Matthew 17:20). Trust His Word. Trust His promise. Trust Him!

The Crowd. The crowd was watching this. They were taking it all in. The questions they were asking among themselves were not very different from those of the disciples, or Martha, or Mary. That needs to be a reminder to us of the influence our actions and our words have on those around us. As followers of Jesus, He has entrusted us with relationships that He intends to use to draw others to Himself. But our words and actions can often be the greatest barrier that prevents others from seeing Jesus for Who He truly is. Jesus drew the crowd into the moment. He asked the crowd to show Him where the body was buried – not because He didn't know – but because He wanted them to be drawn in closer to what was about to occur. He asked them to *"roll the stone aside"*. Again, not because He couldn't remove it, but they needed to witness what was about to occur, up close and personal. They heard Him call out to His Father in heaven. Not because He and the Father hadn't already spoken, but because they needed to hear it. All of this, so that they might witness a miracle to the glory of God. And as we see in verse 45, many believed in Jesus as a result of what they witnessed.

Lazarus. *"Then Jesus shouted, 'Lazarus, come out!'"* (verse 43). i have already mentioned this in chapter 24, but it is worthy to repeat again here. Jesus called out "Lazarus" by name because, otherwise, there would have been a parade of every dead body within the sound of His voice coming out of their graves. Because when He returns, a shout from Him will cause those who are dead to rise (1 Thessalonians 4:16). On this particular day, only Lazarus was to come forth.

On the morning that my mother went to be with the Lord several years ago, her caregiver, Jackie, arrived at her apartment as usual. She found Mother attempting to get out of bed, despite the hospital rails on her bed designed to help prevent her from doing so. Jackie gently and lovingly helped her lay back down and placed Mother's head on the pillow. She drew in her last breath here and her next in glory. i can't help but think, when she was trying to get out of bed, that Jesus was beckoning her to come to Him – and her body was trying to tag along. Praise God that at that moment she stepped out of her tired, worn out body and stepped into her heavenly body. The healing we had been praying for was now complete, and she was at that moment standing before Jesus in all of His majesty and all of His glory.

That's how i envision Lazarus. He heard the Master's voice and He arose. Now there is an important difference between these two accounts. In the case of my mother, Jesus was inviting her to leave her corrupted body and this fallen world and enter into His heavenly paradise. In the case of Lazarus, Jesus was beckoning him to return to a corrupted body and a fallen world. And he would one day need to experience physical death for the second time. And yet, he obeyed the Master. He stepped back into those binding graveclothes and "came out"! i truly believe that it was Lazarus who demonstrated the greatest faith that day! Though there is no record of anything that Lazarus ever said, this single act qualifies him to be one of the greatest men of faith in Scripture.

The Religious Leaders. Though many did believe in Jesus as a result of what they witnessed (verse 45), from that day forward *"the Jewish leaders began to plot Jesus' death"* (verse 53). They had determined that *"if we allow Him to go on like this, soon everyone will believe in Him. Then the Roman army will come and destroy* ***our*** *Temple and* ***our*** *nation"* (verse 48). They knew – rightly so – that Jesus was about to change the status quo! Though they didn't have eyes to see – He was about to defeat death – and make the way for us to have everlasting life. That which truly is the greatest gift that has ever been given, was seen by them as a threat to their position, their power and their very existence. They had become co-conspirators with Satan.

. . .

i am sad to say that there are still many co-conspirators with Satan today – most grievously, even within the church. There are those who are threatened by change in the status quo resulting from a fresh movement of the Spirit of Christ – a movement to follow Jesus for the sake of His mission and His glory, whatever the cost. They are threatened by loss of position, power, perceived standing in the community and tradition. Satan is still a liar and a deceiver. And these co-conspirators are blinded by the same selfish ambition that motivated the Pharisees. But the good news is that, though the co-conspirators may believe that *they* are in control, there is only One who is truly in control. The Pharisees' actions did not determine that Jesus would die on a cross, the Father did. It was His plan of redemption from the beginning of time. God used even the depravity of the human heart to fulfill His purpose at Calvary. And He continues to do so today.

So, as you walk with the Master, rest in the reality that the One who told Peter to "come" and step out of the boat, is the same One who told Lazarus to "come forth", and is the same one who has told you and me to "follow Me". Trust Him! Follow Him! Do not let the deceiver diminish your faith. Your Master is able! He *"is able, through His mighty power at work within us, to accomplish infinitely more than we might ask or think"* (Ephesians 3:20) – all for His glory!

* * *

58

TEN LEPERS LEAPT

As Jesus continued on toward Jerusalem, He reached the border between Galilee and Samaria. As He entered a village there, ten men with leprosy stood at a distance, crying out, "Jesus, Master, have mercy on us!" He looked at them and said, "Go show yourselves to the priests." And as they went, they were cleansed of their leprosy. One of them, when he saw that he was healed, came back to Jesus, shouting, "Praise God!" He fell to the ground at Jesus' feet, thanking Him for what He had done. This man was a Samaritan. Jesus asked, "Didn't I heal ten men? Where are the other nine? Has no one returned to give glory to God except this foreigner?" And Jesus said to the man, "Stand up and go. Your faith has healed you."

Luke 17:11-19

* * *

After Lazarus was raised from the dead, Jesus continued on His journey to Jerusalem. But the journey was not a straight line. When He left Bethany, He traveled northwest to the village of Ephraim, near the wilderness (John 11:54). From there, He traveled further north to the border of Samaria and Galilee (verse 11). Remember, the steps of the Son were ordered by the Father. Every move along the path was according to the Father's divine purpose. *"The LORD directs the steps of the godly. He delights in every detail of their lives"* (Psalm 37:23). Every detail and every encounter was a part of the Father's eternal plan. That was true for Jesus. It's true for us. Often as we are walking with the Master, we see Him lead us in an unexpected direction. Our map says we should travel "west", but He leads us to turn to the "north". From our perspective, it doesn't make any sense. But from His, it makes perfect sense. It's all a part of His plan. Trust Him in the direction. Trust His purpose. He's leading you right where you need to be... even if you can't see it yet.

On this particular day, the Father led the Son to an encounter with ten men. These men probably all came from different backgrounds. We know that at least one of them was a Samaritan. But more than likely, not all of them were. The village was a border town. So probably some of the men were Galilean. It's possible there was even a Judean in their midst. They were a group of different cultures, different beliefs, different races. They were brought together by one common circumstance. They all had leprosy, and the disease was no respecter of culture, belief, race or position. They were considered outcasts. They were unclean. So they stayed "at a distance" from the village, and they weren't permitted to have any contact with anyone in the village. If they attempted to do so, they would be stoned to death. If anyone else attempted to have contact with them, they would have also been deemed to now be unclean and would be banished from the village. Thus, this assembly of ten very different men was destined to a life of isolation, disease and death – all brought on by one common malady. i can't help but be mindful that each one of us is just like those lepers. We come from different cultures, beliefs, races and social classes, but we, too, are bound by a common malady – sin. Because of it we are isolated and separated from all that our Creator intended for us. And it is a condition that leads to death. But gratefully, the very same Jesus is able to heal us – and save us – if we will but cry out to Him.

i am a little bit of a germaphobe, but i am also a hand-shaker. If i am meeting you, i will reach out my hand as an expression of trust, respect, openness and friendliness. It is my way of greeting you. But i am also aware that handshakes are some of the best carriers of germs and disease. And i know that no matter how clean my hand may be, i do not transfer cleanness to your hand if we shake. Rather, what transfers is any uncleanness that exists on one or both of our hands. Simply put, cleanness does not transfer by touch, but uncleanness does. And that of course was the principle regarding any contact with these lepers.

In the midst of their hopeless condition, they saw Jesus. They immediately recognized Him and knew that He had the power to heal them. There was not a moment of hesitation as they cried out, "*Jesus, Master, have mercy on us!* (verse 13). They didn't have to spend time thinking about whether they should ask Him, or how they should ask Him – they cried out from their hearts. They didn't need to be convinced of their need to cry out (pray). Unfortunately many of us are languishing in a condition or situation that Jesus desires to remedy, and yet, we refuse to cry out. James wrote, *"… you don't have what you want because you don't ask God for it"* (James 4:3). **These men were not hesitant to ask!** And that is the first important lesson for each one of us!

Notice Jesus' response – *"Go show yourselves to the priests."* It's very similar to what He said to the servants at the wedding feast at Cana. He told them to *"dip some out, and take it to the master of ceremonies"* (John 2:8). He never said that He had transformed the water into wine. He never told these lepers that they were healed. As i said in chapter 8, i don't believe the water was transformed until the servants drew out the water in obedience to Jesus. And Luke writes the lepers were not cleansed until they turned and began to make their way toward the priests (verse 14). In both instances, if the servants and the ten men had not exercised faith there would not have been any change – the master of ceremonies would have gotten a mouthful of water, and the ten men would have remained lepers. All ten of these men demonstrated faith, and they were healed. **They obeyed with total abandonment.** That is the second important lesson for each one of us.

All of these men were men of faith, but all of them – except one – lacked one thing. Therein is the third important lesson for us. **Only one returned to the feet of Jesus giving Him thanks.** And yes, it was the Samaritan – the one least likely to thank a Jewish Rabbi. The other nine had also received the gift of healing, but they had failed to thank the Giver. But before we judge them too harshly, how often do we do the exact same thing? How often are we quick to pray, but slow to praise? How much of our time in prayer is spent in thanksgiving to the Father for all that He has done and all that He has provided, as compared to our list of needs and requests? And how many of us – like these nine – have stopped short of receiving all that the Master wants to do in, through and for us, due to our spirit of thanklessness? Ten were healed physically, but only one left that day with his sins forgiven.

Ten lepers leapt, but only one gave thanks.
Ten lepers were healed, but only one was cleansed.
Ten lepers encountered Jesus, but only one followed Him.

As you walk with the Master, be sure to be like the one.

* * *

59

A LESSON IN ENDURANCE

One day Jesus told His disciples a story to show that they should always pray and never give up. "There was a judge in a certain city," He said, "who neither feared God nor cared about people. A widow of that city came to him repeatedly, saying, 'Give me justice in this dispute with my enemy.' The judge ignored her for a while, but finally he said to himself, 'I don't fear God or care about people, but this woman is driving me crazy. I'm going to see that she gets justice, because she is wearing me out with her constant requests!'" Then the Lord said, "Learn a lesson from this unjust judge. Even he rendered a just decision in the end. So don't you think God will surely give justice to His chosen people who cry out to Him day and night? Will He keep putting them off? I tell you, He will grant justice to them quickly! But when the Son of Man returns, how many will He find on the earth who have faith?"

Luke 18:1-8

* * *

Jesus often used stories or "parables" to reinforce the truth He was teaching the disciples throughout their walk with the Master. He used the stories – sometimes fictional, and sometimes true – to illustrate divine truth. Sometimes the stories used points of comparison to illustrate truth, and sometimes He used contrast. If we view the widow as a comparison to God's people and the judge as a comparison to God, we will miss important truth in this parable. Jesus is not teaching that if we just persist in prayer, the Father will finally capitulate to our request. The widow and the judge are contrasts to who we are in Christ and who the

Father is. And the lesson to be learned is not one of mere persistence, but rather the faith to endure.

The widow was a stranger to the judge – they had no prior relationship and she was totally unknown to him. In the first century, women had little standing before the law. Therefore, they were not welcome to come into the "courtroom" before a judge. And in this woman's circumstance, she had no husband to stand for her – or with her – in court. Neither does she appear to have a friend to advocate on her behalf. So she had no relationship and no means of representation. Also, proceedings in the court were determined by the judge, and not by the law. So there was no precedent and no promise on which she could stand. Lastly, bribery was common practice in keeping the "wheels of justice" properly "greased". As a poor woman, she did not have the resources to get the attention or concern that her dispute warranted. As a result of all of this, she had absolutely no standing before this judge – even if her cause was just and right.

In contrast, the judge to whom we bring our petition is our Heavenly Father (Luke 11:13). We are His children and He cares for His children. He has given us open and easy access into His presence – at any time – to get the help that we need (Ephesians 3:12). Our Lord and Savior is our Advocate and our High Priest (Hebrews 4:14-16). Because of Him we can come boldly to the throne of our gracious God. He has given us His Word on which we can stand. We don't stand before Him in poverty; we come before Him adorned in the riches He has made available to us (Philippians 4:19).

But not only is the widow a contrast, so is the judge. Our Heavenly Father is not anything like this judge. We do not need to argue with Him or bribe Him with our promises for Him to answer our prayers. He does not ignore our requests like this judge. He is attentive to our every cry, concerned about our every need, and ready to answer when we call. He doesn't respond to our needs because He has grown weary of us; He responds to bring glory to His Name.

Why then do we sometimes see delays in answers to prayer when Jesus has said that *"He will grant justice to them quickly"*? We must be mindful that with God "timing" is more important than "time". We live in a "bubble" of finite space and time. Therefore, we think in those terms. We establish and perceive "deadlines" consistent with that understanding. But an eternal, infinite Creator of time and space is not limited to those boundaries. Rather, He is working all things together in His timing according to His purpose for His glory – and yes, our ultimate good (Romans 8:28). He alone knows all of the details and all of the moving parts. He alone knows how best for the answer to unfold. And He alone knows the best timing to accomplish His purpose. As the prophet Isaiah wrote, *"I AM the LORD; in its time I will hasten it"* (Isaiah 60:22 ESV).

The Father *wants* to act on our behalf. **It's not a question of whether He will act; it's a question of whether we will pray.** Jesus said we *"should always pray and never give up"* (verse 1). Paul wrote that we are to *"never stop praying"* (1 Thessalonians 5:17).

Jesus closes out this teaching with the question – *"But when the Son of Man returns, how many will He find on the earth who have faith?"* Or put another way – When Jesus returns, will He find that His followers have kept praying, or that we have lost heart and given up? John Piper writes, *"If we lose heart and drift away from prayer, then the Son of Man will not find faith in us when He returns."* You see, prayer is not simply about our needs. Prayer is the means that the Father gave us by which He stokes our faith in Him. Through prayer He brings our will into alignment with His will. Prayer is the shovel. Faith is the furnace. The grace of God is the fuel. For it is by God's grace we have been saved through faith (Ephesians 2:8), and it is by His grace we have His answer through faith. And it all begins…, continues…, and endures – until He returns – through prayer.

As you walk with the Master, remember this lesson – pray without ceasing – and endure to the end!

* * *

60

YOU LACK ONLY ONE THING

As Jesus was starting out on His way to Jerusalem, a man came running up to Him, knelt down, and asked, "Good Teacher, what must I do to inherit eternal life?" "Why do you call Me good?" Jesus asked. "Only God is truly good. But to answer your question, you know the commandments: 'You must not murder. You must not commit adultery. You must not steal. You must not testify falsely. You must not cheat anyone. Honor your father and mother.'" "Teacher," the man replied, "I've obeyed all these commandments since I was young." Looking at the man, Jesus felt genuine love for him. "There is still one thing you haven't done," He told him. "Go and sell all your possessions and give the money to the poor, and you will have treasure in heaven. Then come, follow Me." At this the man's face fell, and he went away sad, for he had many possessions.

Mark 10:17-22

* * *

Throughout our time together on this walk with the Master, we have seen many people following Jesus. Most have followed Him from a distance seeking what was in it for them – a miracle, a meal, even money and prestige. A smaller number have followed Him closely and intimately because they believe, and they have surrendered their life to Him. Many that have followed from a distance have turned away – rejecting His statements that He came from heaven, and that He is the son of God – rejecting Him. Some have rejected because He threatens their power and position. Some have actually come to the very feet of Jesus. And in each of those instances, their lives have forever been changed. They have been healed.

Their sins have been forgiven. They have experienced the love and the touch of the Master. Only one ever knelt at His feet and walked away feeling worse than when he had come to Him. And that brings us to this encounter.

As Jesus continued His journey to Jerusalem and the cross, a man came running up to Him. This encounter is not only recorded by Mark, but also by Matthew (19:16-22) and Luke (18:18-23). Matthew tells us that he was a young man. Luke tells us that he was a religious leader, in a position of authority. All three writers tell us that he was very rich and had many possessions. From all outward appearances, he had everything going for him. Mark tells us that as he approached Jesus, he knelt down. Unlike most of the religious leaders who questioned Jesus, this young man does not evidence that he had a deceptive purpose. He doesn't show any sign that he is trying to "trap" Jesus with his question. In many respects, he comes seeking Jesus in an attitude similar to Nicodemus. He is a student of the Law – very possibly a teacher himself. Along the way, through what he has heard or witnessed firsthand, he respects Jesus as a Teacher – as one who teaches with authority. And he comes with a sincere question – "what must I do (or what good deed must I do) to inherit eternal life?"

In all three accounts, he addresses Jesus as "Good Teacher". For the young man, it is a title of respect. It is probably a title he has used at other times in his past to address mentors and teachers that he greatly respected. All three accounts record the same answer from Jesus: "*Why do you call Me good? Only God is truly good. But to answer your question, you know the commandments….*" Jesus' first statement ("*Why do you call Me good? Only God is truly good.*") is NOT a side comment before He gives the man His answer ("*But to answer your question, you know the commandments….*"). His first statement, in any respects, IS the answer.

Note the commandments that Jesus specifically lists in His answer to the young man:

- You must not murder,
- You must not commit adultery,
- You must not steal,
- You must not testify falsely,
- You must not cheat anyone, and
- Honor your father and mother.

And the young man replied that he had obeyed all of these commandments since his youth. He had the view – just like so many today – that he could do something to merit eternal life. But if we compare this list to the complete list of the ten commandments (Exodus 20:1-17), we see that these are the fifth through tenth commandments. This grouping speaks to how we relate to others around us. But the first four commandments speak to how we relate to God. In a few days from this point, after Jesus' triumphal entry into Jerusalem, another religious leader (in an attempt to trap Him) will ask Jesus what the most important commandment is. Jesus will say, *"You must love the LORD your God with all your heart, all your soul, and all your mind"* (Matthew 22:36-37). When Jesus said to this rich young man that "only God is truly good", He was pointing him back to this very first commandment – that eternal life is the result of our relationship with God and not what we have done (or not done) for others.

And the true test of this young man's relationship with God was to be seen in how he responded to Jesus' statement: *"Go and sell all your possessions and give the money to the poor, and you will have treasure in heaven. Then come, follow Me."* The issue was not the young man's riches; the issue was that he valued his riches over a relationship with God. And he did not see himself as a condemned sinner before a holy God. He thought his superficial good works would merit favor with God.

And that is where many of us stumble. We value riches, or possessions, or position, or other relationships over a relationship with God. John, in his Gospel writes, that *"God so loved the world…"* (John 3:16). Mark tells us here, that *"Jesus felt genuine love for him."* The Father and the Son have first loved us. *"We love Him, because He first loved us"* (1 John 4:19).

But when we refuse to love Him with our whole heart, soul and mind – when we refuse to surrender everything else in our lives to Him – we walk away sad – we walk away empty – we walk away incomplete and unfulfilled – just like this rich young ruler. No matter what else he possessed, there was a void in his life that would never be filled apart from one thing – a loving relationship with his heavenly Father. Jesus didn't plead with him. He spoke the truth in love. Then it was up to the young man to decide.

• • •

And that is true for each one of us. No matter what else we possess, there is a void in our lives that will never be filled apart from one thing – a loving relationship with our heavenly Father. Jesus won't plead with us either. He has spoken His truth to us in love. And it is up to each of us to decide.

* * *

61

HE CLIMBED A TREE

Jesus entered Jericho and made His way through the town. There was a man there named Zacchaeus. He was the chief tax collector in the region, and he had become very rich. He tried to get a look at Jesus, but he was too short to see over the crowd. So he ran ahead and climbed a sycamore fig tree beside the road, for Jesus was going to pass that way. When Jesus came by, He looked up at Zacchaeus and called him by name. "Zacchaeus!" He said. "Quick, come down! I must be a guest in your home today." Zacchaeus quickly climbed down and took Jesus to his house in great excitement and joy. But the people were displeased. "He has gone to be the guest of a notorious sinner," they grumbled. Meanwhile, Zacchaeus stood before the Lord and said, "I will give half my wealth to the poor, Lord, and if I have cheated people on their taxes, I will give them back four times as much!" Jesus responded, "Salvation has come to this home today, for this man has shown himself to be a true son of Abraham. For the Son of Man came to seek and save those who are lost."

Luke 19:1-10

* * *

As Jesus continued on His journey to Jerusalem, He entered into Jericho. In that day, Jericho was a winter resort for Jerusalem aristocracy, complete with a hippodrome stadium for horse and chariot racing, and numerous aqueducts to irrigate the rich vegetation. It was the site of one of Herod's palaces and considered to be a beautiful "city of palms". John Wesley wrote that during this time period, *"about twelve thousand priests and Levites dwelt there, who all attended the service of the temple."* So it was a thriving city, frequented by the "rich and the famous".

Just like we've seen throughout our walk with the Master – nothing with Jesus is by chance – nothing is random. Jesus didn't come to Jericho to see the rich and famous, He came for the express purpose of transforming the lives of a blind beggar along the side of a road (Luke 18:35-43) and one slightly-statured tax collector.

Zacchaeus was the chief tax collector in this prosperous town. As we've already seen in chapters 18 and 53, tax collectors committed to pay to Rome each year a stated amount of tribute taxes for their specific region. They then made their living extorting far and above that amount from the local citizenry in order to pay Rome and line their own pockets with riches. A tax collector could walk up to a man on the street and tax him for what he was carrying – and much more. If he went to collect taxes from a widow who could not pay, he would evict her from her home. They were hated and despised by their neighbors, but they were protected by the Roman soldiers. As chief tax collector, Zacchaeus was responsible for the whole region of Jericho. Thus he also collected a portion from the tax collectors who were under his charge – and his title and responsibility enabled him to enjoy an even larger portion of the spoils earned on the backs of the local citizens. As a result, he was viewed with disdain by everyone in the region. It doesn't appear that Zacchaeus was distressed by the feelings of his neighbors – and it appears he was quite content with the status quo – until he had a personal encounter with Jesus!

Zacchaeus, like everyone else, had heard about Jesus. And he saw and heard the commotion as Jesus walked through the town. Little did he know, that he was the very one that Jesus had come to see. Being vertically challenged, he climbed a sycamore tree to get a better view of Jesus. Imagine his excitement, when Jesus looked up at him and said, "*Quick, come down! I must be a guest in your home today.*" Jesus hadn't come to stop at the mayor's house, or the chief Pharisee, or Herod himself; Jesus had come to see a deceitful tax collector!

At some point between verses 7 and 8, Zacchaeus surrendered his life to Jesus. We don't know what their conversation was. But we do know that salvation had come to Zacchaeus (verse 9) and he would never be the same. He was one of those people who got saved – and never got over it! As he repented of his sin and received forgiveness from his Lord, he knew without anyone having to tell him that he needed to make public restitution for his sin. He knew that where he had cheated others, he must give back to them according to the Mosaic Law (Exodus 22:1).

Imagine the reaction when Zacchaeus began to return fourfold that which he had taken from his neighbors. They had heard about Jesus performing miracles, but they had never imagined that He could change the heart of a "crook" like Zacchaeus! The sad thing is, i fear that though most of them rejoiced at the unexpected financial windfall they received, most, if not all, of them were too blind to see the real miracle that Jesus could bring about in each of their lives as well.

Zacchaeus is a great picture that you can't stay where you are – and how you are – and follow the Master. He could no longer cheat and extort. He now had a heart to give – and not take. And there weren't too many opportunities to do that as a tax collector! A change in his heart necessitated a change in his entire life. Jesus had come to Zacchaeus *"to seek and save"* him. And on that day, Zacchaeus began his own walk with the Master. Scripture doesn't tell us what happened with him from there. But i like to think that after he made restitution, he left Jericho and caught up with Jesus along the way and followed Him… to Calvary… and for the rest of his days. i look forward to meeting that vertically-challenged man one day in heaven. And something tells me that though he may have been slight of stature physically, he became a giant of a man in the Kingdom of God.

As we come to the last chapter of this book, that is my prayer for you. God has ordered our steps to walk this leg of our respective journeys with the Master together. We have no idea where He will lead from here. But He has much in store – all for the sake of His Kingdom – and all for the glory of His Name – no matter how much time remains.

He is the Potter, and He will continue His work to mold and shape us
more into His image
(Isaiah 64:8).
He is *"the Son of Man {who} came to seek and save those who are lost"* and He
will continue
to work through us for His purpose until all have heard
(Ephesians 3:20-21).
He is the Son of the Living God, and to Him all majesty is due
(Jude 1:25).

He is the Master, and what He begins He will complete… until the day of
His return
(Philippians 1:6).

So *"now may the God of peace make you holy in every way, and may your whole spirit and soul and body be kept blameless until that day when our Lord Jesus Christ comes again. {He} who calls you, is faithful;
He will do this"*
(1 Thessalonians 5:23-24)

as you continue your walk with the Master!

* * *

BOOK FIVE

TAKING UP THE CROSS

LESSONS LEARNED IN THE WILDERNESS

TAKING UP THE CROSS

KENNETH A. WINTER

SCRIPTURE REFERENCE AND DAY OF THE WEEK LISTING BY CHAPTER

* * *

Palm Sunday

1 Everyone Loves Him! (Matthew 21:1-11)

Monday

2 Created To Bear Fruit (Mark 11:12-14)
3 Cleansing The Temple (Matthew 21:12-16)

Tuesday

4 The Withered Fig Tree (Mark 11:20-26)
5 Who Gave You The Right? (Mark 11:27-33)
6 Which Son Truly Obeyed (Matthew 21:28-32)
7 The Wicked Farmers (Mark 12:1-12)
8 The Marriage Feast (Matthew 22:1-14)
9 Give To God What Belongs To Him (Luke 20:20-26)
10 One Bride For Seven Brothers (Matthew 22:23-33)
11 The Most Important Commandment (Mark 12:28-34)
12 Whose Son Is He? (Matthew 22:41-46)
13 It's Not The Seat That Makes The Man (Matthew 23:1-12)
14 The Eight Woes (Matthew 23:13-36)
15 The Widow's Treasure (Mark 12:41-44)
16 What About The Temple? (Mark 13:1-4)
17 The Parousia (Matthew 24:3-8)
18 In The Coming Days (Mark 13:9-13)
19 Perilous Times (Matthew 24:15-28)

20 Then He Will Come! (Matthew 24:29-31)
21 One Will Be Taken, One Will Be Left (Matthew 24:32-41)
22 Let's Be Ready (Matthew 24:42 – 25:13)
23 Let's Talk About The Talents (Matthew 25:14-30)
24 Sheep And Goats (Matthew 25:31-46)

Wednesday

25 The Master Teaches While The Teachers Conspire (Luke 21:37 – 22:2)

Earlier in the week (Saturday Night)

26 Wherever The Gospel Is Preached (Matthew 26:6-13)

Wednesday, continued

27 The Traitor's Consent (Luke 22:3-6)

Maundy Thursday

28 Just As He Had Told Them (Luke 22:7-13)
29 The Hour Has Come (Luke 22:14)
30 You Will Never Wash My Feet (John 13:3-17)
31 The Passover Supper (Luke 22:15-20)
32 A Betrayal And A Denial Foretold (John 13:21-38)
33 Who Is Greatest? (Luke 22:24-30)
34 A New Commandment (John 13:33-35)
35 A Word Of Comfort (John 14:1-6)
36 A Word Of Oneness (John 14:7-15)
37 The Helper Is Coming (John 14:16-31)
38 A Walk Through A Vineyard (John 15:1-8)
39 He Calls Us Friends (John 15:9-25)
40 The Sorrow Won't Last (John 16:16-22)
41 Our Lord's Prayer (John 16:23-27; 17:1-26)
42 Don't Let Temptation Overpower You (Luke 22:39-46)
43 A Betrayal, An Arrest And A Healing (Luke 22:47-53)

Good Friday

44 Who Was Standing Before The High Priest? (John 18:12-14, 19-24)
45 The Rooster Crowed (John 18:15-18, 25-27)
46 A Traitor's Remorse (Matthew 27:1-10)
47 The Prefect's Part (Luke 23:1-7)
48 A King's Mockery (Luke 23:8-12)
49 A Criminal's Release (Luke 23:13-25)
50 They Aren't The Only Ones Who Mocked Jesus (Mark 15:16-20)
51 He Took Up The Cross (Mark 15:21)
52 A Place Called Golgotha (John 19:17-27)

53 It Is Finished! Or Is It? (John 19:28-30)
54 Laid In A Tomb (Luke 23:50-56)

Resurrection Sunday

55 They Came To Anoint Him (Mark 16:1-8)
56 Now It's Finished! (John 20:1-10)
57 Their Eyes Were Opened (Luke 24:13-35)
58 Peace Be With You (John 20:19-29)

The days thereafter, leading up to His ascension

59 Cast The Net (John 21:1-14)
60 Feed My Sheep (John 21:15-17)
61 Our Times Are In His Hands (John 21:18-23)

* * *

PREFACE

Then He said to the crowd, "If any of you wants to be My follower, you must give up your own way, take up your cross daily, and follow Me."
Luke 9:23

* * *

As we reviewed in chapter 36 of *Walking With The Master,* the disciples thought that they were getting ready to step into positions of power. For those in the crowd who were beginning to see Jesus as the Messiah, they thought they would soon be out from underneath the rule of Rome and would be their own masters. But to their surprise, Jesus said (paraphrased), "if you want to follow Me, you must give up your right to be your own master, and you must take up an instrument of death." That was not the message they were expecting! And Jesus went on to say (paraphrased), "if you try to keep your life, you'll lose it. *But if you give up your life for My sake, you will save it."* The people were thinking about what the Messiah was going to do for them, and instead, Jesus told them that they must die to themselves.

Jesus lived in a day when religious leaders taught one thing, but lived another. (Regrettably, that is too often true today.) But Jesus not only lived out what He taught, He made the way for <u>us</u> to be able to live it out. Otherwise, we would have been doomed to fail. Only One could live up to what He taught – and that was Jesus Himself. So, it is only through the power of His Holy Spirit living within us that we can possibly live it out.

Remember, Jesus was not telling them how they could be "saved" from the penalty of sin. Salvation is not a work that we do. There is absolutely nothing we can do to earn salvation. It is the free gift of God extended by His grace and received by us purely through faith in Him. Jesus is talking about the result of our salvation, not the cause of it. We must first be saved in order to have His Spirit living within us. And we must have His Spirit living within us in order to truly be His follower.

Now, if we don't desire to follow Him, then we need to question whether we truly have surrendered our lives to Him as our Savior. Salvation and followship are two sides of the same coin. We can't separate them. Though the way we often live out our lives would indicate that we think we can.

In the sixty-one chapters of this fifth book of the ***Lessons Learned In The Wilderness*** series, we're going to look at what it means to take up the cross – the cross He has chosen for us – and follow Him. And the backdrop for our time will be the last forty-seven days of His earthly ministry, picking up at the triumphal entry into Jerusalem and continuing to the day He ascended into heaven. Jesus knew from before the beginning of time that the day would come when He would literally carry His cross to that hill on Golgotha. He knew that His work of salvation could not be completed without the cross. It would require death – a death that once and for all would conquer sin, death and the grave. And the cross would not only be the instrument through which that would be accomplished, but it would also forever be a reminder of that completed work. That's why it was fitting for Him to tell us that if we are going to follow Him, we must take up our cross – that instrument that is also the reminder of His work – our salvation.

i don't believe there was ever a moment that Jesus was not mindful of the cross that was before Him. He often talked about the fact that His time had not yet come. He knew that the work of the cross was before Him. It was the defining moment of God's eternal plan. It was the primary reason that the Father sent the Son. It was the way that the Father ultimately brought glory to His Name through the redemption of a lost world unto Himself.

And in many respects, the same is true for us. Our salvation is not God's end game for our lives. It's not just about ourselves – though too often we act like it is. In many respects, our salvation is a starting point. He has reconciled us unto Himself and then given us an opportunity to be a part of His eternal plan. As followers of Jesus, He has called us to be ambassadors of Christ, ministers of the gospel, and missionaries of His redemptive work, all for His purpose and His glory. And He has equipped us and empowered us to be a part of His plan by placing His Holy Spirit within us.

So, He reminds us that first, we must give up our own way. Our lives cannot be about our comfort and our personal preferences. Life cannot be about "what's in it for me". i must surrender my soulish ambition. i must relinquish control of my life and surrender it to Him. i must be about His agenda and His purpose – whatever it is – and wherever it is. My only choice will be whether i follow Him or not. If i choose to follow Him, i don't get to choose where, what, when or how. If He leads me to go halfway around the world, or halfway across the room, i don't get to say "no". He is in control.

Secondly, He tells us that we are to take up the cross that He has set before us. That cross will look different for each of us. In John 21:21, after Jesus had told Peter what was in store for him, Peter asked, *"What about him, Lord?"* (Peter was referring to John.) Jesus responded by saying, *"What is that to you? As for you, follow Me"* (John 21:22). The Father has a unique role for each of us. He has equipped and placed us uniquely. He has shaped the cross we are to take up. We don't get to shape it. We are simply to take it up – splinters and all.

Thirdly, He reminds us that taking up the cross is a daily – and a continuous – act. It is not a "one and done". It is an act of surrender and obedience that continues every moment and every day until we are in heaven with Him. We are never too young or too old, or too busy. We are never retired or otherwise engaged. We are never "between jobs". It is "job one"! We are followers of Jesus – each day, every day.

Lastly, He makes sure we understand that we are to follow Him. We are not to go out and do our own thing, or make our own path. He is the One who goes before us, not the other way around. The great news about that is that we don't need to figure it all out – we just follow Him. i have often said that i look forward to meeting Enoch one day in heaven. We read in Genesis 5 and Hebrews 11 that Enoch walked with God. Enoch never had to figure out which way to turn. All he had to do was keep his eyes on God. And as he did, one day the Lord took him home. i want to have that kind of intimate walk with the Lord. One moment walking with Him here, and the next walking with Him in heaven. And since i don't know when that moment will be, i don't want to be off doing my own thing when that moment arrives. i want to be following Him.

Over the next sixty-one chapters, we will see through the Gospels what "taking up the cross" looked like in the life of Jesus and what He has determined it will look like in our lives. He doesn't promise that there won't be a cost – there will be. And He doesn't promise that it will be easy – it won't be. But it is the journey He has set before us – a journey that will further His purpose in and through our lives – and a journey that will lead to His glory.

My prayer is that this book encourages you along the way!

* * *

1

EVERYONE LOVES HIM!

As Jesus and the disciples approached Jerusalem, they came to the town of Bethphage on the Mount of Olives. Jesus sent two of them on ahead. "Go into the village over there," He said. "As soon as you enter it, you will see a donkey tied there, with its colt beside it. Untie them and bring them to Me. If anyone asks what you are doing, just say, 'The Lord needs them,' and he will immediately let you take them." This took place to fulfill the prophecy that said, "Tell the people of Jerusalem, 'Look, your King is coming to you. He is humble…,
riding on a donkey's colt.'" The two disciples did as Jesus commanded. They brought the donkey and the colt to Him and threw their garments over the colt, and He sat on it. Most of the crowd spread their garments on the road ahead of Him, and others cut branches from the trees and spread them on the road. Jesus was in the center of the procession, and the people all around Him were shouting, "Praise God for the Son of David! Blessings on the One who comes in the name of the Lord! Praise God in highest heaven!" The entire city of Jerusalem was in an uproar as He entered. "Who is this?" they asked. And the crowds replied, "It's Jesus, the prophet from Nazareth in Galilee."

Matthew 21:1-11

* * *

It's the first day of the week, and everyone loves Jesus! Well, maybe not everyone. But, at this moment, you would think everyone does, by the way that the crowd is acting. There were probably two million people in and around Jerusalem for the celebration of Passover that year. The celebration always brought pilgrims to Jerusalem. But the crowd was unusually large that day. The people had seen that Jesus always came to

Jerusalem for the religious festivals. They knew that Passover would be no exception. Thus, large numbers had come that year for the express purpose of seeing Jesus. Many had traveled down from Galilee, having witnessed the miracles He performed there. His fame and notoriety had spread throughout Judea as well, particularly after He raised Lazarus from the dead (John 12:17-18). The people wanted to see Jesus perform more miracles.

But most of them were blinded to the truth of who Jesus really was. They were blinded by the teachings of their religious leaders. Instead of pointing the people to the truth of the Word, they had pointed the people to their man-made traditions (Luke 11:52). The leaders had never been interested in the truth. They merely sought to protect their own self-interests of position, power and prestige. And the people themselves were also blinded by their own selfish desires – desiring only what Jesus could do for them.

Those very desires are what prompted them to cry out, "Hosanna!" This Hebrew word means "Save Now!" They were quoting from Psalm 118:25-26: *"Please, Lord, please save us. Please, Lord, please give us success. Bless the one who comes in the name of the Lord. We bless you from the house of the Lord."* But their emphasis was on save us! Give us success! Do for us! And they lavished Him with praise, welcoming the Miracle Worker into their midst, expecting to be rewarded by His miracles.

Jesus had planned for this day – from before the beginning of time. This was the only time in the ministry of Jesus that He planned and promoted a public demonstration. Up until then, He had deliberately avoided public scenes. But now, the defining moment of time and space had arrived. Up until now, each time that Jesus had entered Jerusalem, He had done so unobtrusively through the "sheep gate". But on this day, He entered conspicuously as King through the "Golden Gate" (aka the "Eastern Gate"). (It is worthy to note that when He returns, He will again enter Jerusalem from the east. Though men have now sealed up the current eastern gate and made it humanly impassable, one day all of those man-made "barricades" will fall away, and the gates will open to our returning King!)

Jesus had not only planned this day from eternity past, He had also planned for it the previous time He was in Jerusalem. He had made arrangements for a donkey and its colt to be available. The keeper of the animals was to expect two of His disciples, and have everything ready for them. Everything was to be as the prophet Zechariah had recorded: *Rejoice, O people of Zion! Shout in triumph, O people of Jerusalem!* ***Look, your King is coming to you.*** *He is righteous and victorious,* ***yet He is humble..., riding on a donkey's colt.*** (Zechariah 9:9).

And yet, Zechariah was writing simultaneously about two different occurrences when Jesus would enter into Jerusalem. The portion of the verse that i have emboldened relates to this entry into Jerusalem as we see quoted above in Matthew 21. On that day, the crowd was not witnessing the arrival of their victorious, judging King. The triumph had not yet occurred. It was still a few days away. They were welcoming the arrival of their saving King. A donkey's colt was the royal animal of Jewish monarchs. It symbolized Jesus' station as King. But it was also a symbol of peace – the peace and the salvation that He was bringing to all people. It was a picture of Jesus, the humble Savior and Servant. He was presenting Himself as King, approaching His cross – not as a victim – but as the coming Victor.

(Bear in mind, Zechariah is also giving us a glimpse of Jesus' triumphal entry on the day still yet to come when He returns. The underlined portion of that verse speaks to the day He will return in triumph and victory – a day that is rapidly drawing near!)

On what we now call "Palm Sunday", His time had arrived. The "spontaneous" demonstration of praise and accolades from the people frightened the leaders and left them to conclude if they did not destroy Jesus now, they would be destroyed. Jesus was forcing the religious leaders to act now, in the time and way He had chosen. Don't lose sight of the fact that He was in complete control of what was about to unfold. No, everyone did not love Jesus, but by this act of obedience to the Father, the Father and the Son both demonstrated their love for everyone.

Jesus knew what was in the minds and hearts of everyone in the crowd, and each one of the religious leaders. He knew that the shouts of praise today would turn into shouts to crucify Him in just a matter of days. He was no more disillusioned or distracted by the shouts of praise than He would be by the shouts that He be crucified. That's the lesson for us to grasp. If we are following Jesus, there will be days that we are experiencing the adulation and praise and "love" from the crowd. Those are the days that are easier to experience – but don't be deceived by them. Because, if we truly are following Jesus in obedience, we will encounter days when many of that same crowd turn against us. If they did it to Jesus, why should we expect anything different?

But don't lose sight that regardless of how the crowd acted, Jesus loved them. He loved them from the back of a donkey's colt, and He loved them from the vantage point of His cross. As you take up the cross and follow Him, ask Him to give you that same love for the crowd around you, no matter what your vantage point is today. That kind of love doesn't exist within us apart from Him. But ask Him to position your heart so that He can love them through you.

* * *

2

CREATED TO BEAR FRUIT

The next morning as they were leaving Bethany, Jesus was hungry. He noticed a fig tree in full leaf a little way off, so He went over to see if He could find any figs. But there were only leaves because it was too early in the season for fruit. Then Jesus said to the tree, "May no one ever eat your fruit again!" And the disciples heard Him say it.
Mark 11:12-14

* * *

It's the second day of the week. Jesus and His disciples are returning to Bethany each evening. More than likely, they are lodging with Lazarus, Martha and Mary, then each morning they are returning to Jerusalem. En route, Jesus was hungry. Apparently, Martha hadn't fed them breakfast that morning. He saw a fig tree beside the road, and it was in *"full leaf"*. Both Matthew and Mark tell us that Jesus *"went over to see if He could find any figs"*.

Let's stop and consider that a moment. Jesus knew whether or not that tree had figs on it long before He went over to see it. Our God is all-knowing. Jesus Himself had taught, *"What is the price of five sparrows — two copper coins? Yet God does not forget a single one of them"* (Luke 12:6). There isn't a detail that escapes His view or His knowledge. Just as Jesus knew everything about each of the men that accompanied Him – the one who would betray Him, the one who would deny Him, the one who would doubt Him – He knew there was no fruit on that fig tree. Some of the Pharisees had already discovered that Jesus knew the sins that they had committed in the shadows, even though they had thought no one else knew (see *Walking With The Master,* chapter 43). He knows all things past, present and future. So, if He was hungry, why was He walking over to a fig tree that He already knew was barren? And secondly, Jesus had turned a little boy's lunch into a feast for thousands. If He was hungry, why didn't He just turn some of the leaves into fruit? Something tells me that there is a whole lot more to this than what meets the eye!

One other fact about fig trees before we move on: in that part of the world, fig trees produce leaves in March/ April, then bear mature fruit twice each year – the first at the beginning of June, and the second from August through October. Since this event would have taken place during the March/ April timeframe, Mark rightly records that *"it was too early in the season for fruit."* But, during this time of year as fig trees were becoming fully-leafed, they would produce a crop of small knobs, called "taqsh" (pronounced "tuhk-wAAsh"). In essence, they are a forerunner to the mature figs and drop off the tree before the "real" fruit is formed. Most often, the taqsh were left to fall off the tree, but on occasion they would be eaten by hungry peasants. If, however, there are no "taqsh", it is an indication that there will be no figs. So, it was evident to Jesus that the absence of taqsh meant that there would be no figs when the time came.

Thus, the example of the fig tree proved to be a lesson to be learned. The tree gave the outward appearance that it was healthy and growing. It was pleasing to the eye, and all indications were that in its time, it would produce a bountiful harvest. But Jesus knew, and on closer inspection showed the disciples, that the tree was not healthy. God created the tree with one purpose – His purpose – to bear fruit. He didn't create it to be a fruitless tree. And though harvest time had not yet arrived, it was obvious by the condition of the tree that it would be fruitless.

In a parallel passage, Luke writes that as Jesus *"came closer to Jerusalem and saw the city ahead, He began to weep."* He knew that *"It is too late, and peace {was} hidden from {their} eyes. Before long your enemies… will crush you into the ground… because you did not recognize it when God visited you"* (Luke 19:41-44). The Father had created and called His people, Israel, to bear fruit to His glory – to bear witness to His Majesty and to worship Him through their very lives. And yet, they had rejected Him. They had turned their focus upon themselves to the point that they no longer even recognized Him – when He stood in their presence. Though the destruction of Jerusalem had not yet taken place, all of the signs were already present. It was obvious that the nation – God's people – would be fruitless. But the lesson did not stop with them.

In just a few days from then as we see recorded in John 15, Jesus would teach the disciples that each one of them was to be a branch – attached to Him, grafted into the Vine. Their purpose as a branch would be to bear fruit – fruit that brings glory to the Father, fruit that remains, and fruit that multiplies. He would remind them that a branch cannot bear fruit on its own. It can only bear fruit when it is attached in a healthy way to the vine. We will look at the John 15 passage further in chapter 36, but for now suffice it to say that the life and sustenance for the fruit to be borne can only come from the vine. The branch's role is but to remain grafted into the vine in order for it to be used to bear fruit. If the branch pulls away from the vine it will become fruitless.

That picture of the branch and the vine is a picture of how we are to walk with Jesus. He said, *"Yes, I am the Vine; you are the branches. Those who remain in Me, and I in them, will produce much fruit. For apart from Me you can do nothing"* (John 15:5). We were created – and we have been redeemed – in order to be used by our Master to bear fruit. We don't produce the fruit; He does! But in His sovereignty, He has chosen to use us as the branches through whom He produces His fruit. We are to be prepared in season and out of season (2 Timothy 4:2) to bear fruit – whether it is March/April, June, August thru October – or any moment of any day. That is true for us as individual followers of our Master, and that is true for us as local bodies of believers.

Regrettably, too many of us as followers, and too many of us as local churches, look like that fig tree. On the outside we present with a full crop of leaves, seemingly healthy and growing. But our Master knows all too well that our lives are fruitless and not producing a harvest.

Jesus has called us to turn from ourselves, take up the cross and follow Him – that includes being branches that remain in Him – healthy branches that are usable by Him to bear His fruit. So, what does the Master see in your life? Are you a healthy growing branch with leaves and taqsh or mature fruit? Or are you a branch that appears to be healthy but is really barren? Allow Him to make you into that usable branch today – *"ready for the Master to use you for every good work"* (2 Timothy 2:21).

* * *

3

CLEANSING THE TEMPLE

Jesus entered the Temple and began to drive out all the people buying and selling animals for sacrifice. He knocked over the tables of the money changers and the chairs of those selling doves. He said to them, "The Scriptures declare, 'My Temple will be called a house of prayer,' but you have turned it into a den of thieves!" The blind and the lame came to Him in the Temple, and He healed them. The leading priests and the teachers of religious law saw these wonderful miracles and heard even the children in the Temple shouting, "Praise God for the Son of David." But the leaders were indignant. They asked Jesus, "Do you hear what these children are saying?"

"Yes," Jesus replied. "Haven't you ever read the Scriptures? For they say, 'You have taught children and infants to give You praise.'"

Matthew 21:12-16

* * *

It's still the second day of the week. Yesterday, Jesus entered the city as King. Today, He enters as High Priest to cleanse His temple.

This was the second time that Jesus cleansed the temple in Jerusalem. The first time was at the beginning of His earthly ministry, as we see recorded in John 2:13-22. That time, Jesus made a whip from some ropes and chased them all out of the temple. Unfortunately, He didn't chase them far enough and they had slithered back inside.

. . .

Now three years later, nothing had changed. The outer court of the Gentiles had again become a marketplace where visiting Jews could exchange their money for temple currency and purchase animals to be sacrificed. The practice had originally been borne out of convenience for the travelers from out of town, but it had denigrated into a VERY profitable business. The outer court had originally been intended to be a place where "non-believers" could enter and learn about the one true God of Israel. But its use as a market had transformed the space from one being used for a missionary purpose to one now being used for a mercenary purpose.

Every Israelite, rich or poor, who had reached the age of twenty was required to pay a temple tax of one-half shekel into the temple treasury. This tax was to be paid using a Hebrew half shekel. At Passover, all adult males who wished to worship at the temple would bring his "offering". Since foreign money with any foreign image was considered to be "corrupt and unclean", the money changers would sell "temple coinage" at a very high rate of exchange and add an additional charge for their services. The judges, who inspected the offerings that were brought by the pilgrims, were quick to detect any blemish in the non-temple coinage, which further increased the exchange trade.

The dealers charged exorbitant prices, but no one could oppose them. They profited from the wealthy by providing four-legged animals for sacrifice, and they profited from the poor by selling them doves. It had become the ultimate "convenience store". The former high priest, Annas, was the manager of the enterprise, assisted by his sons, and they operated under the protection of the current high priest, his son-in law, Caiaphas. Their motivation was greed and extortion. It had truly become a "den of thieves". They were using their religion to cover up their sin. As we mentioned earlier, two million people were in Jerusalem that week to celebrate Passover. Do not lose sight that this had become BIG business!

Jesus was not the first to be sent by the Father to rebuke the religious leaders and the people of Israel for this practice of turning the temple into a marketplace. Over six hundred years earlier, God had sent the prophet Jeremiah to deliver the same rebuke. *"Don't you yourselves admit that this Temple, which bears My name, has become a den of thieves? Surely, I see all the evil going on there. I, the Lord, have spoken!"* (Jeremiah 7:11) The leaders had rejected that word from God just as they had rejected the first rebuke from Jesus.

. . .

Jesus repeats the words of the prophet Isaiah, *"My Temple will be called a house of prayer for all nations"* (Isaiah 56:7). It is to be a place where prayer bears evidence of dependence upon God and reliance on His Word. As He demonstrated in the healing of the blind and the lame, His Temple was to be a place where people were welcomed and received the help that they needed. It was to be a place where God's power was evident in the transformation of lives. And as evidenced by the children, as they gave praise, it was to be a place where God was praised and belief in God was displayed. Jesus reminded them of the Scripture – *"You have taught children and infants to tell of Your strength ("to give You praise"* – Greek version*), silencing Your enemies and all who oppose You"* (Psalm 8:2). Not only had the temple become as fruitless as the fig tree; it had become a stumbling block to true seekers desiring to worship the one true God.

And we read that the leaders were indignant and plotted even more fervently how to kill Jesus. They could think of nothing else, *"because all the people hung on every word He said"* (Luke 19:48). He threatened their financial enterprise. He threatened their power over the people. He threatened their position of leadership. There was nothing godly within them. Their hearts were as cold as stone. They could think of nothing else, but how they would rid themselves of Jesus. That which had been building for three years in their hearts had now escalated to the point of action. They would not be dissuaded. They were afraid of Him. They needed to act now! Little did they know that they did not control the timing, the Father did.

If we would take up the cross, there are many lessons for us in the cleansing of the temple – in our own lives, and in the local church bodies of which we are a part. First – the abomination that the marketplace practices became began with a simple and subtle compromise. It was a means to make it easier for foreigners to participate in worship. Those who had begun the practice probably did so to enhance worship, never intending to hamper it. It is a reminder to us to guard every facet of our worship and not compromise or redirect our focus from the One we worship, no matter how seemingly inconsequential our redirect might be. Second – our lives and our local body are to bear evidence of our dependence upon God and our reliance on His Word. We are to be welcomers and helpers of all who God brings across our path. His presence and His power are to be conspicuously evident in our lives, in our praise, our beliefs and our actions. Third – we must never lose sight that we have been called to be ambassadors of the gospel to all nations – through our prayer and through our actions.

The apostle Paul wrote, *"Don't you realize that all of you together are the temple of God and that the Spirit of God lives in you?"* (1 Corinthians 3:16). The lesson of the cleansing of the temple is much like the lesson of the barren fig tree. We have been called to be fruit bearers. Let's be certain that we have allowed the Master to cleanse our temple, so that we are fit for His purpose and His glory.

* * *

4

THE WITHERED FIG TREE

The next morning as they passed by the fig tree He had cursed, the disciples noticed it had withered from the roots up. Peter remembered what Jesus had said to the tree on the previous day and exclaimed, "Look, Rabbi! The fig tree you cursed has withered and died!" Then Jesus said to the disciples, "Have faith in God. I tell you the truth, you can say to this mountain, 'May you be lifted up and thrown into the sea', and it will happen. But you must really believe it will happen and have no doubt in your heart. I tell you, you can pray for anything, and if you believe that you've received it, it will be yours. But when you are praying, first forgive anyone you are holding a grudge against, so that your Father in heaven will forgive your sins, too."

Mark 11:20-26

* * *

It's now the third day of the week. For the third day in a row, Jesus and the disciples are headed back to Jerusalem after overnighting in Bethany. As they walk, they pass a dead fig tree. The disciples notice that the tree has withered from the roots up. It has withered due to a complete lack of water and nutrients. And Peter is the one who remembers that the Master had cursed this tree the day before. In one day, a tree that was full of leaves and had given the outward appearance of health and growth had now shriveled and died. A process that should have taken weeks, or maybe months, had occurred overnight. Not only was it seemingly cut-off from its source of water at its roots, but also all of the moisture that had existed within the tree had immediately dried up.

. . .

In chapter 2, we looked at the fact that a tree that had been created to be fruitful had been found by Jesus to be fruitless. Now, immediately after Peter points out the dead tree, Jesus begins to teach the disciples about faith. Though it seems like an abrupt change of subject, it's not!

Remember, Jesus was using this tree as a practical illustration of the spiritual health of the people of Israel. But He was also using it to teach His disciples – then and now – what it means to truly follow Him and abide in Him. If we follow and abide in Him, we will be His disciples indeed (John 15:5), and He will bear fruit through our lives. His Living Water will flow through us (John 7:38-39) and we will reflect His Light (John 8:12). Our fruitfulness is not based upon our effort, it is based upon our abiding. Without His Living Water flowing and His Light reflecting through us, we are a dead branch – withered – just like that fig tree. Fruitfulness is not intended for our glory, it is for His. In a few days from now, Jesus will tell them, *"if you remain in Me and My words remain in you, you may ask for anything you want, and it will be granted! When you produce much fruit, you are My true disciples. This brings great glory to My Father"* (John 15:7-8).

Jesus now turns the conversation from fruit to faith, because fruit will not occur apart from faith. We must live in an attitude of total dependence on Him – acting and asking in alignment with His Word. When Jesus speaks His Word, and His Word "remains" in us, it requires a response on our part – and that response is either faith or faithlessness. We can't remain in a neutral place. That would be like the servant in the parable of the talents who buried his talent. He took no action – which was faithlessness.

And Jesus is telling the disciples here, that if a mountain – otherwise known as some significant, immovable impediment – is standing between us and what God has told us to do, we must step out in faith, trusting and asking God to move the mountain. The prophet Zechariah wrote of Zerubbabel when he was chosen to lead the Jews back to Jerusalem, *"Nothing, not even a mighty mountain, will stand in Zerubbabel's way; it will become a level plain before him!* (Zechariah 4:7a). Why couldn't a mighty mountain stand in his way? Because he was walking in obedience to God on His mission. Nothing could stand in His way! No mountain can stand in our way, if we are walking in obedience to God's Word and His will. So, we must be certain that we are praying in response to a word from God and in alignment with the will of God (1 John 5:14-15). If that is so, we will see God take those mountains and "throw them into the sea"! Let's be clear – Jesus is not saying that, if we pray hard enough and long enough, and really believe, God is obligated to answer our prayer no matter what we ask. That is not faith in God; that's faith in our feelings. True faith must be rooted in God's Word – it is our response to His truth.

Then Jesus went on to talk about forgiveness. We are to walk – not only in the word of God, according to the will of God, but also – abiding in the love of God (John 15:7-14). If the branch is to abide in the Vine, there can't be anything standing between ourselves and God, or ourselves and another person. If we hold a grudge, or fail to forgive, we are sinning and inhibiting our abiding relationship with the Vine. So, Jesus says, before you pray, make sure you are not holding unforgiveness in your heart. Forgive that individual, and where possible make amends. But let me hasten to add that our forgiveness does not obligate God to act, it simply unblocks the pathway.

Earlier, i mentioned the parable of the talents. We will look at it in detail in chapter 22. But if you recall, the master in the parable takes the talents he had left with that faithless servant and gives them to one of the faithful servants (Matthew 25:28). Once judgement is declared by the master, the faithless servant is left with nothing. It wasn't gradual; it was immediate.

Through a simple fig tree, Jesus taught His disciples about fruitfulness, faithfulness and forgiveness. If we would take up the cross and follow Jesus, we too must heed the lesson of the withered fig tree.

How long does it take for a fruitless fig tree to wither after the Master has judged it and found it to be barren? It's immediate. And the same is true of us!

* * *

5

WHO GAVE YOU THE RIGHT?

Again they entered Jerusalem. As Jesus was walking through the Temple area, the leading priests, the teachers of religious law, and the elders came up to Him. They demanded, "By what authority are You doing all these things? Who gave You the right to do them?" "I'll tell you by what authority I do these things if you answer one question," Jesus replied. "Did John's authority to baptize come from heaven, or was it merely human? Answer Me!" They talked it over among themselves. "If we say it was from heaven, He will ask why we didn't believe John. But do we dare say it was merely human?" For they were afraid of what the people would do, because everyone believed that John was a prophet. So they finally replied, "We don't know." And Jesus responded, "Then I won't tell you by what authority I do these things."

Mark 11:27-33

* * *

This is the day after Jesus has cleared out the temple. The leading priests, teachers and elders are all still stinging from His rebukes the day before. They are indignant and combative. They are out for Jesus' blood. Up until yesterday, they had been fearful of what Jesus was doing. Up until then, they had viewed Him as one who was challenging their authority. But yesterday, He had completely undermined their authority. He had shut down their financial enterprise. He had taken action that demonstrated a flagrant disregard for their position. And their fear turned into unadulterated hatred of Him. Now they were singularly focused on His destruction. They were now on His trail, like bloodhounds of hate.

. . .

A sticking point for them had always been that Jesus didn't respect their official authority as the leaders of their religion. He had never once come to them seeking their approval to do anything that He did. They had never delegated Him any authority. And He had been running roughshod over them for far too long. Of all of the things that Jesus had said and done, that was His major offense to them. So, it's no wonder that, as He returned to the temple that morning, their first question – or should i say their first accusation – is a challenge to His authority. ***"Who gave You the right to do what You are doing?"***

Jesus did not demean Himself by directly answering their question. He knew their motive. He knew that they did not desire to follow Him. They now sought to crucify Him. They were not seeking truth. They were looking for evidence to use to destroy Him. Jesus never rebutted sincere questions from sincere seekers. He always gave genuine answers to sincere inquiries. But there was nothing sincere about what these men were asking. It was just a part of their plot. Instead, Jesus very deftly countered their question with another question, and in so doing, exposed their hypocrisy and their hard-heartedness.

Why did Jesus ask them about John the Baptist? Because He was the forerunner that the Father had sent to speak His truth to His people. Remember, there had been silence for over 400 years. God had not spoken to His people during that time – until He sent John to prepare the way for His Son. And the truth that John spoke, the religious leaders rejected. There is a principle here that we need to grab onto. **God will not teach us new truth if we have rejected the truth that He has already given us**. The leaders would never accept the truth of Jesus because they had rejected God's truth through John. Bear in mind, if they had received God's message through John, they would have submitted to the authority of Jesus and the accounts of the Gospels would have looked VERY different. But God knew how they would respond – long before He sent John!

Now the Pharisees had another dilemma. How should they respond to Jesus' question? They weren't considering "what is true?" or "what is right?" but rather, "what is safe?". The Pharisees knew, whichever way they answered Jesus, the crowd would turn on them, and their authority, position and prestige would be totally lost. So, they refused to answer by pleading ignorance.

. . .

In an environment of ever-increasing political correctness, that has become an operative strategy in our day and time as well. Too often, we are compromising "what is true" and "what is right" in favor of "what is safe". How often are we following the way of the Pharisee instead of following the way of our Master?

God has given us His Word, His gospel and His truth. We have a choice. Do we accept it, or do we reject it? And if we accept it, we cannot compromise it for what is "safe". His truth is what sets sinners free (John 8:31-32). Compromised truth is no longer truth. It has become a lie. That was true with the Pharisees, and it's just as true today.

Jesus said, *"I have been given all authority in heaven and on earth. Therefore, go and make disciples of all the nations.... Teach these new disciples to obey all the commands I have given you"* (Matthew 28:18-20). Jesus, of course, never required any authority from the religious leaders. He had been given all authority from the Father. The Father gave Jesus the right! It was His "birthright" as the eternal Son of God. And as His followers, we have "the right" as children of God. We have the right – and the mandate – to go and make disciples of all peoples. We cannot step back. We must press forward under His authority – under His right. And we must proclaim His truth boldly and rightly – which, my friends, will probably not be "safely". After all, He called us to take up the cross and follow Him – and there wasn't anything safe about His journey.

* * *

6

WHICH SON TRULY OBEYED?

"But what do you think about this? A man with two sons told the older boy, 'Son, go out and work in the vineyard today.' The son answered, 'No, I won't go,' but later he changed his mind and went anyway. Then the father told the other son, 'You go,' and he said, 'Yes, sir, I will.' But he didn't go. "Which of the two obeyed his father? They replied, "The first." Then Jesus explained His meaning: "I tell you the truth, corrupt tax collectors and prostitutes will get into the Kingdom of God before you do. For John the Baptist came and showed you the right way to live, but you didn't believe him, while tax collectors and prostitutes did. And even when you saw this happening, you refused to believe him and repent of your sins."

Matthew 21:28-32

* * *

It's still the third day of the week. Jesus had arrived in the temple to teach, and immediately the priests and elders came to confront Him. As we saw in chapter 5, Jesus has just responded to their demand to tell them by whose authority He does what He does, by asking them from whom John the Baptist's authority came. Because of their rejection of John and the message of God's truth that he delivered, combined with their realization that if they now denounced John then the people would rise up against them, they had refused to answer Jesus' question. Before the religious leaders can scatter to avoid any further light being shone on their sin, Jesus immediately confronts them with a trilogy of parables. Here is the first of the three:

A man with two sons told the older boy, 'Son, go out and work in the vineyard today.' The son answered, 'No, I won't go,' but later he changed his mind and went anyway. Then the father told the other son, 'You go,' and he said, 'Yes, sir, I will.' But he didn't go. "Which of the two obeyed his father?

As Jesus later explains, the first son represents the tax collectors and prostitutes – those who the religious leaders would deem unworthy. That first son initially rejects his father and refuses to go out into the vineyard. But later in the day, he changes his mind. He repents and, in so doing, makes a 180 degree turn and does what the father told him to do. The second son tells the father that he will work in the vineyard, but, in fact, does not do so. He represents the religious leaders, who on the outside want everyone to believe that they are obedient sons of God, whereas in reality they have rebelled against Him and rejected His word. Jesus left no doubt with the priests and elders as to who was who in the parable. Although the religious leaders answered rightly as to which son truly obeyed the father, they took even greater offense from Jesus' remarks instead of being convicted of their sin.

This parable is as relevant today as it was the day Jesus taught it. There are still many who want to give an outward appearance of godliness. Like the religious leaders that Jesus is confronting, they know the jargon. They know the rituals. They know how to act. They are active in church. They may possibly be leaders in the church. But in all reality, there has been no transformation in their lives. The apostle Paul cautioned Timothy that in the last days, the numbers of these people within the church would be on the increase. He said, *"They will act religious, but they will reject the power that could make them godly. Stay away from people like that"* (2 Timothy 3:5).

Paul described that transformation clearly to the church in Corinth when he wrote, *"So we have stopped evaluating others from a human point of view. At one time we thought of Christ merely from a human point of view. How differently we know Him now! This means that anyone who belongs to Christ has become a new person. The old life is gone; a new life has begun!"* (2 Corinthians 5:16-17).

A number of years ago, we moved from Southeast Florida to Central Virginia. We tell folks that we moved "south" to Virginia. Even though geographically we didn't, culturally we did. For the first time in our lives, we lived in the "proper south". We quickly observed that unlike South Florida, there is more of a pretense of religion in the "proper south". We observed churches on most every corner. But we quickly began to recognize that there were many who "acted religious" but had truly never experienced "new life".

As i write this, i am reminded of two dear friends who, when i first met them, didn't know one another. Their names are Mike and Bill. i met them both within a matter of days after they had surrendered their respective lives to Christ. They were both middle-aged and had lived their younger lives apart from a relationship with Jesus. Both of them had the scars to prove it. They hadn't learned the religious jargon yet. They were both as new in their faith as you can possibly be. But though they didn't know all of the right words, there was an aura about them that reflected a changed life – a life that reflected Christ. There wasn't anything contrived. There was a genuine, authentic and transparent transformation. And i am grateful to be able to tell you, over twenty years later, that genuine and authentic walk with Christ has not dimmed. These guys had been transformed by Christ into "new persons", scars and all!

i pray that has been your experience. i pray that, like the "first son" in Jesus' parable, you have repented of your sin, surrendered your life to Christ and been transformed by the power of the gospel – scars and all! The first son may have come "late", but gratefully he came.

The last days that Paul references in 2 Timothy 3 have never been closer than they are right now. These cannot be days for religious pretense and jargon. *"For God says, 'At just the right time, I heard you. On the day of salvation, I helped you." Indeed, the "right time" is now. Today is the day of salvation'"* (2 Corinthians 6:2).

The religious leaders walked away from Jesus offended, bitter and hardhearted. They had a religion of exterior decorations, with nothing real inside. Don't make that same mistake! Jesus didn't come to redecorate your life; He came to make it new! If you would take up the cross and follow Him, first make sure that your life has been made new. Then head on out into the vineyard. The Father is waiting for you.

* * *

7

THE WICKED FARMERS

Then Jesus began teaching them with stories: "A man planted a vineyard. He built a wall around it, dug a pit for pressing out the grape juice, and built a lookout tower. Then he leased the vineyard to tenant farmers and moved to another country. At the time of the grape harvest, he sent one of his servants to collect his share of the crop. But the farmers grabbed the servant, beat him up, and sent him back empty-handed. The owner then sent another servant, but they insulted him and beat him over the head. The next servant he sent was killed. Others he sent were either beaten or killed, until there was only one left — his son whom he loved dearly. The owner finally sent him, thinking, 'Surely they will respect my son.' But the tenant farmers said to one another, 'Here comes the heir to this estate. Let's kill him and get the estate for ourselves!' So they grabbed him and murdered him and threw his body out of the vineyard. What do you suppose the owner of the vineyard will do?" Jesus asked. "I'll tell you — he will come and kill those farmers and lease the vineyard to others. Didn't you ever read this in the Scriptures?

'The stone that the builders rejected has now become the cornerstone.
This is the Lord's doing, and it is wonderful to see.'"

The religious leaders wanted to arrest Jesus because they realized He was telling the story against them — they were the wicked farmers. But they were afraid of the crowd, so they left Him and went away.
Mark 12:1-12

* * *

Once more, Jesus confronted the religious leaders, before they could scatter away, using the second parable of the trilogy with imagery that was very clear to them. The prophet Isaiah had described the vineyard as the nation of Israel (Isaiah 5:1-7). God had planted His people. He had led them out of bondage. He had made them a mighty nation, holy unto Himself. He had provided for them. He had protected them. He had "cultivated" them. Their whole purpose for existence was to worship Him, and to be a people through whom He made His Name known and brought glory to Himself. The religious leaders were blind to a lot of things, but they were not blind to that! So as Jesus told this story, there was no mistaking who and what He was talking about. Jesus was speaking to the religious leaders in the most pointed and direct parable of His ministry.

The owner and planter of the vineyard is the Father. The vineyard is supposed to bear the fruit of worship and obedience. The servants He sends are the prophets. The wicked tenant farmers are the religious leaders. Obviously, the son whom the Father "loved dearly" is Jesus. Their plan to kill Jesus so that they can "maintain control" is clearly exposed. Jesus has again shined His light on their darkness and their sinful plans. Jesus then asks the leaders, *"What do you suppose the owner of the vineyard will do?"* Matthew in his account records, *"The religious leaders replied, 'He will put the wicked men to a horrible death and lease the vineyard to others who will give him his share of the crop after each harvest'"* (Matthew 21:41). In so replying, they condemned themselves.

With every fiber of their being raging inside them, they wanted to extinguish the light and arrest Him right then. But they feared how the crowd might react, so they looked for a way to hastily slither away. But before they could get away, Jesus continued by telling them the judgement they would experience. That judgement was in fact fulfilled in 70 A.D. when Titus, then a Roman military commander, besieged and captured Jerusalem, destroying the city and burning and destroying the Temple. The people were killed, or enslaved and taken to Rome.

As Jesus concluded the parable, He quoted the Messianic Psalm 118:22-23 – *"The stone that the builders rejected has now become the cornerstone. This is the Lord's doing, and it is wonderful to see."* In so doing, He again brought judgement on the Pharisees, because they were the "builders" who had rejected Jesus, their promised Messiah. To them, He had become a stumbling block, threatening their plans and their selfish ambitions. And their rejection was manifested in His coming crucifixion. But Jesus very clearly told them that there was nothing they could do to Him that had not been permitted by the Father. The Pharisees may have plotted to kill Jesus, but it was all a part of the Father's plan of redemption. As the prophet Isaiah wrote, *"Therefore, this is what the Sovereign Lord says: 'Look! I am placing a foundation stone in Jerusalem, a firm and tested stone. It is a precious cornerstone that is safe to build on. Whoever believes need never be shaken'"* (Isaiah 28:16). Jesus is the Cornerstone – the One through whom the Father has reconciled His creation back to Himself, through His crucifixion and His resurrection. He is the One – and only One – on whom the true temple can be built. Jesus, in essence, was saying to the religious leaders the same thing Joseph had said to his brothers: *"you meant evil against me, but God meant it for good in order to bring about this present result, to preserve many people alive"* (Genesis 50:20 NASB).

Several weeks later, after Pentecost, the apostles Peter and John were standing before these very leaders. And they recalled what Jesus had said on this day in the temple, as they too bore witness:

"Then Peter, filled with the Holy Spirit, said to them, 'Rulers and elders of our people, are we being questioned today because we've done a good deed for a crippled man? Do you want to know how he was healed? Let me clearly state to all of you and to all the people of Israel that he was healed by the powerful name of Jesus Christ the Nazarene, the man you crucified but whom God raised from the dead. For Jesus is the one referred to in the Scriptures, where it says,
'The stone that you builders rejected
has now become the cornerstone.'
There is salvation in no one else! God has given no other name under heaven by which we must be saved"
(Acts 4:8-12).

This parable was a condemnation of the religious leaders, and it stands as a condemnation of anyone who would deny Jesus as the Messiah, the Son of the Living God. But if we are to take up the cross and follow Him, we can take it up with the confidence and assurance that He is our Cornerstone, our One Foundation, by Whom we are saved and by Whom all must be saved. The religious leaders were the wicked farmers that slithered away, but we must be His faithful followers that boldly proclaim that Good News from the rooftops!

* * *

8

THE MARRIAGE FEAST

Jesus also told them other parables. He said, "The Kingdom of Heaven can be illustrated by the story of a king who prepared a great wedding feast for his son. When the banquet was ready, he sent his servants to notify those who were invited. But they all refused to come! "So he sent other servants to tell them, 'The feast has been prepared. The bulls and fattened cattle have been killed, and everything is ready. Come to the banquet!' But the guests he had invited ignored them and went their own way, one to his farm, another to his business. Others seized his messengers and insulted them and killed them. "The king was furious, and he sent out his army to destroy the murderers and burn their town. And he said to his servants, 'The wedding feast is ready, and the guests I invited aren't worthy of the honor. Now go out to the street corners and invite everyone you see.' So the servants brought in everyone they could find, good and bad alike, and the banquet hall was filled with guests. "But when the king came in to meet the guests, he noticed a man who wasn't wearing the proper clothes for a wedding. 'Friend,' he asked, 'how is it that you are here without wedding clothes?' But the man had no reply. Then the king said to his aides, 'Bind his hands and feet and throw him into the outer darkness, where there will be weeping and gnashing of teeth.' For many are called, but few are chosen."

Matthew 22:1-14

* * *

Just before the religious leaders scattered, Jesus had one more indictment for them through this third parable of the trilogy. In the first parable (chapter 6), He indicted them for failing to be obedient sons. In the second (chapter 7), He called them out for their attempts to commandeer the Kingdom for their own selfish ends, persecuting and killing God's messengers, the prophets, and even His Son. In this third of the three, Jesus rebuked them for throwing away the honor and privilege of their covenant relationship with God, thereby dishonoring the Almighty and the Son.

The main character of this parable is the king, representing God the Father. His son represents Jesus the Messiah. Although He is not an active character in the parable itself, He is central to its meaning, serving as the reason for the wedding banquet. The feast represented the future union of the bridegroom (Jesus) with His bride (the church). Participation in this celebration presupposes that he/she has placed his/her faith in Jesus and become a part of His people (His church). The invitation to the feast was an invitation to salvation and it was an invitation to enjoy the king's blessing – the "food" of the feast, as well as the honor of being invited.

As in the second parable, the king sent two groups of servants as messengers. The first group went out to those who had been invited to the banquet to tell them to come. The invitees, representing Israel, God's chosen people (and its leaders in particular), knew they were supposed to attend the celebration – they had already been invited. The messengers (the prophets) informed them that it was time to attend. However, the invitees refused to accept the invitation. But this invitation was truly a command. To disregard this invitation was not an option; rejection went beyond discourtesy to the point of rebellious disobedience. Israel had not been invited but *commanded* to pay the price and reap the blessing of Kingdom citizenship. And yet they rejected his invitation and, in so doing, rejected the king.

But the king was patient, even in the face of such discourtesy, to send a second group of messengers to the people. This group conveyed the Lord's patient pleading with His rebellious people over the centuries through His prophets, as well as John the Baptist, and would continue through the apostles. The message they carried to the people was, "I have gone to a lot of trouble and great expense to prepare this banquet. Dinner is on the table. It is a magnificent feast! Only the best has been prepared. Come celebrate with us!" Participation in the feast, in honor of the king's son, was both a responsibility and a privilege. The king was appealing, "Come honor my son and enjoy the honor of my blessing."

. . .

This second group of messengers received two responses – apathy and aggression. Some people invited to the wedding feast thought they had more important things to do. They chose to ignore the messengers and tend to their fields and businesses – the everyday pursuits that had taken possession of their hearts. But others responded like the tenants in the second parable, mistreating and killing the messengers. The one significant difference between the action of these invited wedding guests and that of the tenants in the second parable was that the wedding guests had no motive for mistreating and killing the king's servants. The murder of the messengers and the message of rejection to the king and his son were irrational, since the king intended only good by his invitation.

God's offer of a covenant relationship with Israel carried a price for those who accepted it, but the blessing and honor that the Kingdom citizen received would far outweigh the cost of discipleship. God offered redemption, forgiveness, salvation, and reward. Those who rejected God's grace were displaying blindness to the point of insanity. They returned a curse for God's blessing.

Because of their perverted attitude, the king sent a third messenger, his army. They would serve as messengers of judgment for the irrational rebellion of these unwilling wedding guests. The armies destroyed the murderers and burned their cities. This signified God's judgment of those who reject His covenant relationship.

Meanwhile, the celebration was waiting; the son was yet to be honored. So the king sent out his messengers again – but to a different set of invitees this time. The original invitees did not deserve to come. Their self-absorption and irrationality had displaced their loyalty to the king and his son. The new guests were those who would be honored by such an invitation. These were the riff-raff, the outcasts of society, that the messengers would find along the byways, including every possible prostitute and tax collector.

The messengers went out into the streets and invited all the people they could find, both good and bad. Whereas those who should have been "good" (Israel, God's chosen people) had shown themselves to be evil, the king treated all who were evil as though they were good. The impartiality of the king represented the impartial grace of God, inviting all people of all nations into the Kingdom. By extension, we can identify the king's servants or messengers now to include the apostles, the New Testament believers, and us, if we are faithful to be ambassadors of His Good News.

It was as shocking then, as it is now, that God accepts the worst of sinners unconditionally. As long as a sinner shows a willingness to accept God's grace by faith, God will transform him or her into a Kingdom citizen. With such a group of people, the king filled his wedding hall. It was a blend of good and evil, Jew and Gentile, slave and free, wealthy and poor. Truly, the Lord will fill His Kingdom with all peoples from all nations. He will reject those who refuse His invitation into honor and privilege, replacing them with true worshipers – those restored from sin by His grace.

At this point, Jesus clarified exactly who could take part in His celebration of faith. After the guests had gathered in the wedding hall, the king inspected them and discovered a man not dressed properly. In that day, wedding clothes (sometimes supplied by the host) were not a particular style of garment. But they were to be the cleanest and best clothes each person had to wear. This man was displaying disrespect by wearing less than the best available to him. The king addressed the man as "friend", implying that he was open to an explanation. But when questioned, the man had no answer. He was guilty of failure to honor the king's son in a proper manner. The proper garment represents the righteousness of Christ provided through His death. To refuse it is to refuse Christ's sacrifice. To refuse Christ is to refuse life. The invitation has gone out to everyone, but only those wearing the righteousness of Christ can enter into the marriage feast. There is an open invitation to the wedding feast, but there is a dress code.

There will be many shocked church attenders when the Lord returns, who think that they have responded to the Lord's invitation to come to the banquet of heaven, but in fact have never really, with their hearts, surrendered their lives to enter into His presence. They walked in the door of the church, but they never opened the door of their heart to Him. With their lips they honor Him, but their hearts are far away. It's as though they were never even there. When the Master says, "Change your clothes," they adjust their collars or shine their shoes, or tidy up their shirts or pants, but they won't take off those cherished habits. They won't strip away their selfish ambition, or the love of money, or the addiction to pornography, or whatever else has control of their lives. They want the hope of heaven, but they won't dress for heaven. They won't change their clothes. And Jesus says in the end on the graduation day, "Bind him hand and foot and cast him into outer darkness. He never really enrolled with his heart. It was all a show."

This disrespectful man was recognized as ill-prepared as every imposter will be. At the king's command, he was bound and thrown into the darkness. This represents exclusion and separation from the celebration in the Kingdom of light and truth. The weeping and gnashing of teeth indicates eternal extreme pain and sorrow.

Jesus' closing statement had a proverbial tone. Note that He did not say that *all* men and women are called. But *many* are invited. God has issued to a wide audience His invitation (command) to join with Him in covenant relationship. But few are chosen. Not everyone who is invited will be among the chosen. The adjective *chosen* suggests that the "decision" is not totally in our hands, but it is a response to God's sovereign election. In particular, the unbelieving religious leaders were among those called but not chosen.

The parable's basic lessons are clear. The king issued a gracious invitation to people he wished to view as friends. They rejected the invitation. Their rejection sparked a severe judgment from the king. Their rejection caused the king to extend the invitation even further to anyone who would come. Their refusal served to open the gates wide. But though the gates were thrown wide open, those actually chosen were limited by specific criteria – the righteousness of Christ.

We are invited guests. There is a seat at the celebration with our name on it if we have surrendered our life to Christ. But we have also been called to be the messengers extending the king's invitation to those who have not yet heard it. The gates are open wide – whomsoever will may come. But many have yet to hear that they have been invited. There is no substitute for the true gospel – the Good News. There is only one way by which we can be saved. But as we have previously said – it's only Good News if it gets there in time!

* * *

9

GIVE TO GOD WHAT BELONGS TO HIM

Watching for their opportunity, the leaders sent spies pretending to be honest men. They tried to get Jesus to say something that could be reported to the Roman governor, so he would arrest Jesus. "Teacher," they said, "we know that You speak and teach what is right and are not influenced by what others think. You teach the way of God truthfully. Now tell us — is it right for us to pay taxes to Caesar or not?" He saw through their trickery and said, "Show Me a Roman coin. Whose picture and title are stamped on it?" "Caesar's," they replied. "Well then," He said, "give to Caesar what belongs to Caesar, and give to God what belongs to God." So they failed to trap Him by what He said in front of the people. Instead, they were amazed by His answer, and they became silent.

Luke 20:20-26

* * *

The religious leaders withdrew from the courtyard in the temple to escape the light that Jesus was shining on them and their sinful motives. They sequestered themselves behind closed doors – and away from piercing eyes – so that they could discuss their dark plans to kill Jesus safely away from the light. They needed to catch Jesus saying something that would be so egregious that the Roman authorities would permit His crucifixion. So the logical first attempt was to trap Him in making a statement against Roman authority. And who better to pose the question than supporters of King Herod (Herodians)?

Though the Pharisees and the Herodians were enemies of one another,

Jesus was their common enemy. The Herodians saw Jesus as a threat to Roman rule. Without Roman support, King Herod would be unable to retain the power and position that Roman soldiers guaranteed him. Without Herod, the Herodians would lose whatever benefits and advantages they enjoyed as loyal supporters of King Herod. Though the Pharisees resented Rome, they had learned how to survive (and profit) within the rule of their Roman oppressors. And though they viewed Herod and his Edomite supporters as interlopers, Jesus was now a much bigger threat to their continued profit and power over the people. Believing the principle that "the enemy of my enemy is my friend", the Pharisees and the Herodians formed an alliance to entrap Jesus.

The Herodians began their questioning by flattering Jesus in an attempt to disarm Him. *"Teacher, we know that You speak and teach what is right and are not influenced by what others think. You teach the way of God truthfully."* Jesus knew their hearts. He knew the evil motivation behind their question. He wasn't drawn in by their feeble attempt to manipulate Him through flattery. We, however, would be wise to remember that one of the most common ploys of Satan is to begin his attempts of manipulation through flattery or half-truths. Though we rarely will have the clear understanding that Jesus had of the true motivation behind questions that are being asked of us, be wary of questions that are preceded by veiled flattery.

Next came their big question. *"Is it right for us to pay taxes to Caesar or not?"* i think it was difficult for them to mask the smug smiles that were in their hearts after they asked their question. They were confident that they had just trapped Jesus. There was no good way for Him to answer that question. All they needed to do now was to wait for Him to answer the question in one way or the other, and He would no longer be a problem. The people of Israel were an occupied nation required to pay taxes to their Roman oppressors. Every tax payment was another expression of the Roman boot pressing down on the necks of the people. If Jesus spoke in favor of paying the tax, the Jews would rise up against Him. If Jesus opposed the tax, He would be in trouble with Rome. Regardless, the Herodians had Jesus right where they wanted Him.

At that moment, Jesus had a choice. He could call out the Herodians and the Pharisees for their evil intent and their hypocrisy and refuse to answer them. Or He could use this moment as an opportunity to silence His enemies and teach the people an important truth.

. . .

Either Jesus didn't have a coin in His pocket, or He wanted to reinforce that the Kingdom of God was about so much more than money. So, Jesus asked His questioners to produce a coin. In so doing, they illustrated that they possessed the coins, and, in their use of them, showed that they deemed them to have value. As they did, He asked, *"Whose picture and title are stamped on it?"* By the simple fact that the coins bore the image of Caesar, they were acknowledging and accepting His authority. At that point, Jesus differentiated between that which belongs to Caesar and that which belongs to God, and in so doing, taught them – and us – several important truths.

If we would honor God, we must honor and obey the rulers whom God has placed, or allowed to be placed, in authority over us. Paul would later write. *"Everyone must submit to governing authorities. For all authority comes from God, and those in positions of authority have been placed there by God.... So you must submit to them, not only to avoid punishment, but also to keep a clear conscience.... Give to everyone what you owe them: Pay your taxes and government fees to those who collect them, and give respect and honor to those who are in authority"* (Romans 13:1-7). (By the way, bear in mind that Nero, the persecutor of Christians, was the Roman emperor when Paul wrote these words.) As followers of Christ, we have dual citizenship. Though heaven is our home, we must respect our earthly authority, by obeying the laws – unless they are in direct violation of God's law (Acts 5:29). We must pay our rightful taxes, being above reproach in how we do so. In this answer, Jesus was clearly teaching that taxes were merely the citizen's responsibility to pay back for services performed. And we must pray for all of those who are in authority – whether we agree with them or not – and whether they are acting in a godly way or not. In honoring earthy authority, we are honoring God.

An important, quick side road: Respecting and honoring those in authority does not mean that we blindly and silently accept injustice and sinful actions. We have been called to be salt and light. We are to be voices for what is right, what is God-honoring, and that which aligns with the truth of His Word. We are not to sit silently by as injustice is being perpetrated by governmental authority. BUT, we must challenge and work to change it in a way that is God-honoring and is respectful of positions of authority. We are living in a day and time when godless actions are being confronted in ungodly ways by people who profess to be God's people. We would be wise to pay heed to the words of Jesus and the apostle Paul!

. . .

Second, we must honor and obey God. He is our creator. He has stamped each one of us with His image. All that we have – and all that we are – is from Him. Our honor to Him is not through simple coinage; our honor to Him is through the submission of the totality of our lives in worship of Him. This is the primary truth Jesus was teaching that day. The religious leaders wanted to elevate the issue of money and taxes to entrap Jesus because they failed to live out this important truth. Honoring and obeying include surrender and submission to the Father, His Son and His Spirit. We are most like the Pharisees and the Herodians when we elevate issues of money over being wholly submitted and surrendered to our Lord.

If we would take up the cross and follow Jesus, yes, we must give to "Caesar what belongs to him", but more importantly, we must give to God all that belongs to Him – our very lives!

* * *

10

ONE BRIDE FOR SEVEN BROTHERS

That same day, Jesus was approached by some Sadducees — religious leaders who say there is no resurrection from the dead. They posed this question: "Teacher, Moses said, 'If a man dies without children, his brother should marry the widow and have a child who will carry on the brother's name.' Well, suppose there were seven brothers. The oldest one married and then died without children, so his brother married the widow. But the second brother also died, and the third brother married her. This continued with all seven of them. Last of all, the woman also died. So tell us, whose wife will she be in the resurrection? For all seven were married to her." Jesus replied, "Your mistake is that you don't know the Scriptures, and you don't know the power of God. For when the dead rise, they will neither marry nor be given in marriage. In this respect they will be like the angels in heaven. "But now, as to whether there will be a resurrection of the dead —haven't you ever read about this in the Scriptures? Long after Abraham, Isaac, and Jacob had died, God said, 'I am the God of Abraham, the God of Isaac, and the God of Jacob.' So He is the God of the living, not the dead." When the crowds heard Him, they were astounded at His teaching.

Matthew 22:23-33

* * *

The Herodians had their time at bat, and Jesus struck them out! So now it's the Sadducees time at bat. Hopefully you are seeing that none of these questions are being asked of Jesus "by chance" or at random. These questions are all being orchestrated from behind the scenes with one clear purpose in mind.

. . .

Though the Pharisees and Sadducees both made up the ruling body called the Sanhedrin, the groups were deeply divided over doctrinal beliefs. The Pharisees accepted the authority of the five Books of Moses (known as the Torah), as well as the oral teachings of laws, commands and traditions handed down over the years (known as the Talmud). The Sadducees, however, did not accept the authority of the Talmud, or any of the wisdom or prophetic books. The Pharisees believed in the resurrection of the dead, but the Sadducees did not believe in angels, the spirit world or the resurrection of the dead (Acts 23:8). As you can imagine, the two groups often debated their differences to no satisfactory conclusion. i am of the belief that this question being posed to Jesus is one that the two groups had debated ad nauseam. But today the two groups had come to at least one point of agreement – to pose the question to Jesus. Finally, unbeknownst to them, they brought the question to the only One who could answer them with complete authority!

i have entitled this chapter "One Bride For Seven Brothers". i'm playing off the title of a 1954 American musical film entitled "Seven Brides For Seven Brothers". Set in the mid-1800's, it is the story of *"Adam, a back-woodsman, who is the eldest of seven brothers, and goes to town to get a wife. He convinces Milly to marry him that same day. When they return to his backwoods home, she discovers he has six brothers - all living in his cabin"* (Source: IMDb). She is only married to one, but she finds she is having to care for seven – all at the same time. And the story goes from there. In this question being posed to Jesus, there is only one bride, and her husband has died. According to the Jewish law of "levirate" marriage (levirate meaning "a husband's brother"), *"if two brothers are living together on the same property and one of them dies without a son, his widow may not be married to anyone from outside the family. Instead, her husband's brother should marry her…"* (Deuteronomy 25:5). The purpose of the custom was to preserve a man's name if he should die without a male heir. (Incidentally, levirate marriage is still practiced today in parts of the world.) Apparently in the scenario being posed to Jesus, each of the remaining six brothers, after having fulfilled his responsibility to the Law by taking her to be his wife, dies. Thus, she has been married to each of the seven. This premise was, in fact, one of the reasons that Sadducees refused to believe in the resurrection.

Though the Pharisees believed in the resurrection of the dead, their understanding was errant. They believed that the afterlife was merely an extension of the present. They believed that whatever relationships, whatever physical defects or deformities, whatever scars, even to the point that whatever clothes you had on when you died, is exactly what you'd be like in the next life. Their false thinking assisted in the false thinking of the Sadducees. Thus, the idea that a woman could have multiple husbands was inconceivable. Therefore, as their logic played out, the resurrection of the dead was inconceivable.

And how does Jesus respond? He doesn't pull any punches! He says, *"Your mistake is that you don't know the Scriptures, and you don't know the power of God."* These were probably two areas on which the Sadducees prided themselves as being the authority – knowing the Scriptures and knowing the power of God. And Jesus challenged them right at the heart of their pride. To quote John MacArthur, Jesus in essence is saying, *"Had you known the Scriptures you would have known God promises resurrection. Had you known the power of God you would have known that God can raise people in a state where that's not going to be an issue. If you knew the power of God, you would know that He wouldn't recreate people with the same problems as here. He's not limited to that, as if God has spent all His creative power on the way we are and can't improve on it? If you knew the power of God and if you knew the Scriptures, you wouldn't be so spaced-out in your thinking."* Jesus tells them with authority that there will be no marriage in heaven. There will be no death. There will be no childbirth. It will no longer be necessary to bear children to replace those that die. Sex, marriage, reproduction, childbirth, all that is for this life only, not the next life. God's creation of life will be complete. God is raising up worshipers in this life that will worship Him for eternity in the next life. We, too, can become disoriented – just like the Pharisees and the Sadducees – when we view the next life as a mere extension of this one.

We can also become disoriented when we think of life on this side of glory as our primary life. The reality is that life on this side is preparation for eternity; the other side is eternity. As Jesus said, *"Long after Abraham, Isaac, and Jacob had died, God said to Moses, 'I am the God of Abraham, the God of Isaac, and the God of Jacob.' So He is the God of the living, not the dead. You have made a serious error"* (Mark 12:26b-27).

And when Jesus concluded, you could have heard a pin drop. The crowd was astounded by His teaching and the authority with which He spoke. And the Sadducees were silenced. As Luke writes, *"No one dared to ask Him any more questions"* (Luke 20:40).

There are still questions even in our minds. Though Scripture and Jesus are clear about the fact of the resurrection and the work that Christ has completed to "prepare a place for us" (John 14:2), there are still questions we have that won't be answered until we are there. There is a great cloud of witnesses who have gone before us who now understand. And, if we are followers of our Lord Jesus Christ, we, too, will one day join them either at the time of our death – or upon His return – whichever occurs first.

As we take up the cross and follow our Master, let us be careful to not make a serious error. There is but one bride – the Church – and one day soon, we are going to meet our Groom – our Lord and Savior, Jesus Christ!

* * *

11

THE MOST IMPORTANT COMMANDMENT

One of the teachers of religious law was standing there listening to the debate. He realized that Jesus had answered well, so he asked, "Of all the commandments, which is the most important?" Jesus replied, "The most important commandment is this: 'Listen, O Israel! The Lord our God is the one and only Lord. And you must love the Lord your God with all your heart, all your soul, all your mind, and all your strength.' The second is equally important: 'Love your neighbor as yourself.' No other commandment is greater than these." The teacher of religious law replied, "Well said, Teacher. You have spoken the truth by saying that there is only one God and no other. And I know it is important to love Him with all my heart and all my understanding and all my strength, and to love my neighbor as myself. This is more important than to offer all of the burnt offerings and sacrifices required in the law." Realizing how much the man understood, Jesus said to him, "You are not far from the Kingdom of God." And after that, no one dared to ask Him any more questions.

Mark 12:28-34

* * *

Some of the greatest teaching from Jesus was in response to questions that were intended to trap Him. As we look at this encounter, it's still the second day of the week. The Sanhedrin has put forth the Herodians and the Sadducees, both of whom have failed miserably in trapping Jesus. So they sent out a lawyer – an expert in religious law.

As we saw in chapter 50 of ***Walking With The Master,*** the scribes (the lawyers) had determined that the Jews were obligated to obey 613 mitzvah (precepts and commandments) recorded in the Torah. 365 of them were negative commands to abstain from certain acts. Interestingly, that was one for each day of the year (excluding leap years). 248 were positive commandments which outlined acts to be performed. It was said that the number 248 coincided with the number of bones and main organs in the human body. And that was just in the Torah! That didn't include the exhaustive code of conduct to be practiced as it related to rituals, worship practices, God-man and interpersonal relationships that made up the Talmud. That was a lot of which to keep track! No wonder they needed a team of lawyers to keep a close eye! One of the favorite pastimes of the scribes was discussing which of these divine commandments was the greatest. These men, who were considered to be the greatest religious minds in the land, had spent countless hours in debate over the answer to that question, and had never come to a resolution. So, at the behest of the Sanhedrin in their "game" of "let's trap Jesus", one of them poses the question to Jesus, *"Of all the commandments, which is the most important?"*

Bear in mind, the scribes had debated this ad nauseam. But Jesus never blinked an eye or hesitated for even a moment. He immediately – and authoritatively – replied, quoting the confession of faith that pious Jews recited each morning and evening, called "The Shema", from Deuteronomy 6:4-5:

> *"Listen, O Israel! The Lord is our God, the Lord alone. And you must love the Lord your God with all your heart, all your soul, and all your strength."*

And He followed it up by quoting Leviticus 19:18:

> *"… love your neighbor as yourself…."*

The teachings of the religious leaders of the day had little to do with love. Their teaching stressed duty, obligation and rules. Even though they would regularly quote "The Shema", it was by rote and in word only. Very little was said or taught about love, let alone lived out. But Jesus made love the most important thing. He was teaching that love for God and love for our neighbor was the purpose of the Law and the fulfillment of the Law. He was revealing to them the truth that Paul would later write:

"Owe nothing to anyone—except for your obligation to love one another. If you love your neighbor, you will fulfill the requirements of God's law. For the commandments say, 'You must not commit adultery. You must not murder. You must not steal. You must not covet.' These—and other such commandments—are summed up in this one commandment: 'Love your neighbor as yourself.' Love does no wrong to others, so love fulfills the requirements of God's law" (Romans 13:8-10).

Warren Wiersbe says it well when he writes that Jesus was telling them that *"if we love God, we will experience His love within and will express that love to others. We do not live by rules, but by relationships – a loving relationship {with} God that enables us to have a loving relationship with others."* Again, i believe you could have heard a pin drop. The crowd – and the scribe – had never heard that truth expressed. Time and again, they had debated the Law and missed the very point of it! As Jesus' answer began to sink in, we see a moment of transparency and authenticity. The scribe, who had intended to trap Jesus, now sincerely commended Him. Imagine the Pharisees' anger as they heard their representative commending Jesus and confessing the very truth that Jesus had just spoken. The Word of God had just spoken to the man's heart and he was beginning to understand. Further Scripture came to his mind:

"You do not desire a sacrifice, or I would offer one. You do not want a burnt offering. The sacrifice You desire is a broken spirit. You will not reject a broken and repentant heart, O God" (Psalm 51:16-17).

"What can we bring to the Lord? Should we bring Him burnt offerings? Should we bow before God Most High with offerings of yearling calves? Should we offer Him thousands of rams and ten thousand rivers of olive oil? Should we sacrifice our firstborn children to pay for our sins? No, O people, the Lord has told you what is good, and this is what He requires of you: to do what is right, to love mercy, and to walk humbly with your God" (Micah 6:6-8).

So what did Jesus mean when He said to the scribe, *"You are not far from the Kingdom of God"*? i believe He was affirming the scribe as he was now facing truth honestly. The scribe was now testing his beliefs against the Word of God and not against the teachings of men. There hadn't yet been a complete change of heart, but the man had made a quantum leap in his journey toward the Kingdom of God. i pray that he made it the rest of the way. And if so, i look forward to meeting him one day in heaven. Because if i do, i believe his testimony will be very similar to that of the man who once was physically blind – *"I once was blind, but now I see"* (John 9:25).

Three up! Three down! Jesus had pitched a no-hitter. The Sanhedrin didn't have anyone else to put before Jesus that day. But as we know, they weren't done trying.

As we've seen, in every instance, Jesus responded with truth. As you take up the cross to follow Him, remember that, no matter who you face in your journey today, lies and deceit cannot survive in the light of truth. And the core of that truth is *"love the Lord your God with all your heart, all your soul, all your mind, and all your strength."* And *"love your neighbor as yourself!"* Live out that truth – and add words where appropriate!

* * *

12

WHOSE SON IS HE?

Then, surrounded by the Pharisees, Jesus asked them a question: "What do you think about the Messiah? Whose son is He?" They replied, "He is the son of David." Jesus responded, "Then why does David, speaking under the inspiration of the Spirit, call the Messiah 'my Lord'? For David said, 'The Lord said to my Lord, Sit in the place of honor at my right hand until I humble Your enemies beneath Your feet.' Since David called the Messiah 'my Lord,' how can the Messiah be his son?" No one could answer Him. And after that, no one dared to ask Him any more questions.

Matthew 22:41-46

* * *

In the preceding chapters, we have looked at how the Sanhedrin sent their ambassadors to ask questions of Jesus that they thought would trap Him. These were questions that they frequently debated among themselves, never able to come to agreement. In each instance, Jesus had responded with the absolute truth. The crowd had been amazed by His teaching. The religious leaders, having been shut down in each of their attempts, dared not ask any more questions of Jesus.

Now, Jesus has a question for them. Unlike the questions they asked of Jesus, His question to them was one in which all of them could agree upon the answer – at least initially. *"Whose son is the Messiah?"* All of them – the Pharisees, the Sadducees, the Herodians and the scribes – could confidently answer, *"He is the son of David."* They presumed that Jesus was asking them a theological question – just as they had asked Him. And this one was in their "wheel house". They knew the answer to this. They knew the promises of God through the prophets, including Jeremiah, who wrote:

"The day will come, says the Lord, when I will do for Israel and Judah all the good things I have promised them. In those days and at that time I will raise up a righteous descendant from King David's line. He will do what is just and right throughout the land. In that day Judah will be saved, and Jerusalem will live in safety. And this will be its name: 'The Lord Is Our Righteousness.' For this is what the Lord says: David will have a descendant sitting on the throne of Israel forever. And there will always be Levitical priests to offer burnt offerings and grain offerings and sacrifices to Me"
(Jeremiah 33:14-17).

But for Jesus, this was not a theological question, this was a personal question, on par with when He asked His disciples, *"Who do you say that I am?"* (Matthew 16:15). So Jesus followed up with a second question, *"Why does David, speaking under the inspiration of the Spirit, call the Messiah 'my Lord'?"* He was quoting David, from Psalm 110:1:

"The LORD said to my Lord, "Sit in the place of honor at My right hand until I humble Your enemies, making them a footstool under Your feet."

Every one of these religious leaders knew that this passage referred to the Messiah, and they knew that only the Messiah could sit at the right hand of the Lord God Jehovah. Not a one of them could question the authority or the accuracy of the text. Which led Jesus to ask His third question: *"Since David called the Messiah 'my Lord,' how can the Messiah be his son?"* How can the Messiah be both David's Son and David's Lord? Not one of the religious leaders dared to consider the possibility of the Messiah being both. Like the other theological issues we have looked at, the leaders had debated this truth but never come to agreement. One picture of the Messiah in the Old Testament had been as the Son of Man (Jeremiah 33), another as the Son of God (Psalm 110). Another picture had shown Him to be a Suffering Servant (Isaiah 53). Still others showed Him to be a Reigning Monarch (Zechariah 9). Were there to be two Messiahs? How could God's Servant suffer and die? Peter would later write, *"This salvation was something even the prophets wanted to know more about when they prophesied about this gracious salvation prepared for you. They wondered what time or situation the Spirit of Christ within them was talking about when He told them in advance about Christ's suffering and His great glory afterward"* (1 Peter 1:10-11).

The fact of the matter is that the Answer was standing right before them, but their eyes – and hearts – were blind to the truth. Because the only answer is that as God, the Messiah is David's Lord and, as man, He is David's Son. The Messiah is both the Son of God AND the Son of Man. He could not be one or the other, He must be both. The crowds had already declared Jesus to be the Messiah. They had shouted it throughout the city as Jesus entered two days before. In so doing, they were unknowingly declaring His deity, as well as His humanity. But the leaders refused to consider that possibility. It was a question whose answer could only be given with praise. But their response was silence. Two days earlier, as He entered Jerusalem, some of the Pharisees had told Him to rebuke the crowd for declaring Him to be the Messiah. Jesus had responded, *"I tell you, if these were silent, the very stones would cry out"* (Luke 19:40). i believe as the Pharisees stood there now in silence, the stones were crying out – but regrettably their ears were deafened to hear them. The Pharisees didn't have the courage to question Him further, nor did they have the courage to face the truth and act on it. And in so doing, they condemned themselves to eternal damnation.

In the 4th century, Augustine wrote the confession, *"Christ is both David's Son and David's Lord: David's Lord always, David's Son in time. David's Lord, born of the substance of his Father; David's Son, born of the Virgin Mary, conceived by the Holy Spirit. Let us hold fast both."*

Every one of us have stood, or are standing, at the crossroad of that life or death decision. It is not a theological question; it's a personal question. Before we can ever take up the cross to follow Jesus, we must answer the question of Whose Son He is. The religious leaders were so blinded by tradition, selfish ambition, and pride that they would not see the truth and act on it. Will we stand silent with them, or stand boldly and join Augustine in confessing who Jesus is – and be saved?

* * *

13

IT'S NOT THE SEAT THAT MAKES THE MAN

Then Jesus said to the crowds and to His disciples, "The teachers of religious law and the Pharisees are the official interpreters of the law of Moses. So practice and obey whatever they tell you, but don't follow their example. For they don't practice what they teach. They crush people with unbearable religious demands and never lift a finger to ease the burden. "Everything they do is for show. On their arms they wear extra wide prayer boxes with Scripture verses inside, and they wear robes with extra-long tassels. And they love to sit at the head table at banquets and in the seats of honor in the synagogues. They love to receive respectful greetings as they walk in the marketplaces, and to be called 'Rabbi'. "Don't let anyone call you 'Rabbi,' for you have only one teacher, and all of you are equal as brothers and sisters. And don't address anyone here on earth as 'Father,' for only God in heaven is your Father. And don't let anyone call you 'Teacher,' for you have only one teacher, the Messiah. The greatest among you must be a servant. But those who exalt themselves will be humbled, and those who humble themselves will be exalted."

Matthew 23:1-12

* * *

Before we delve into this passage, just a few reminders about the Pharisees, so that we have some context. The role of the Pharisees did not exist prior to the middle of the 2nd Century BC. The Hellenistic rule of Judea and the surrounding area was overthrown through the Maccabean Revolt of 165 BC. Soon after, a new monarchy was formed which established priests as the political, as well as religious, authority. The Pharisee (or "separatist") party emerged as a sect of scribes and sages from within the larger group. The Pharisees were considered the most expert and accurate expositors of Jewish law. In contrast to the Sadducees, who came from the more wealthy and elite strata of Jewish society, the Pharisees were more eclectic and popular with the common people. In addition to the written Scriptures, the Pharisees were the preservers and promoters of the oral law and traditions. Pharisaic Judaism is considered by many to be the progenitor of Rabbinic Judaism which influences all mainstream forms of Judaism today. Though the Pharisees were initially more welcoming to Roman rule because they believed it would enable the more Hellenistic influence of the Sadducees on Judaism to be diminished, the tide turned at the end of the 1st Century BC. Thus, in the time period of the Gospels, the Sadducees were more politically aligned with Rome, and controlled the Temple and the financial enterprise of Judaism, whereby the Pharisees controlled the synagogues and enjoyed more of the favor of the common Jews. In Jesus' day, there would have been approximately 6,000 Pharisees. They were seen as, and set themselves up to be, the authorities of the Law and the religious rulers over the people. They enjoyed a followship by the people. That is until John the Baptist, and then Jesus, arrived on the scene and began to call them out.

Now, it is important to remember that not all Pharisees were identical in their beliefs. Though the majority had come to the place of seeing Jesus as a threat to their position and power, there were some in their midst who were drawn to the teachings of Jesus – Nicodemus, Joseph of Arimathea, the unnamed Pharisee in Mark 12:33-34 that we looked at in chapter 11, and possibly Gamaliel (Acts 5:34), to name a few.

In this passage, we see our Lord's last public message, and it is a scathing denunciation of the false religion created by the Pharisees that paraded under the guise of truth. Bear in mind that given the popularity of the Pharisees, many of the people in the crowd would have been aghast at Jesus' remarks as He called them out for sitting in seats for which they were not worthy.

First, they had placed themselves in the seat of Moses (vs. 2), as interpreters and arbitrators of the Law. They were not given that authority by God through Scripture. Therefore they had no God-given right to interpret or establish Law. Anything that they taught that was outside of Scripture was without foundation. The authority was Scripture and not their position. Jesus told the people that they were to obey the Word of God that the Pharisees taught, but not their traditions and man-made rules.

. . .

What's more, Jesus said, they were not practicing and obeying Scripture themselves. They were teaching one way, and living another. Jesus denounced their hypocrisy (vs. 3), both for their outward actions and their inner hearts (vs. 4). They were practicing a religion of rules and not a life of loving, honoring and following the Father. It was a religion that placed crushing demands and burdens on the people, but never reflected the love of God. Jesus taught that His yoke is easy to bear, and His burden is light (Matthew 11:30). The Pharisees had been teaching the absolute opposite and placing unreasonable burdens on the people.

Second, they had placed themselves in the seat of honor (vs. 6). They sought to draw attention to themselves. They loved the recognition, the respect, the prestige and the honor of their position. This meant using religious ornaments to call attention to their piety. They sought the accolades of man and to be served by all around them. No wonder the disciples had been confused when they saw Jesus get up from His seat to wash their feet. Jesus had come to seek and to serve. The religious leaders, whose teachings they had grown up under, had come to be served and be honored. They lived for the pomp and the circumstance, and the adulation of the crowd. Whereas Jesus had taught, "Do not sit in the seat of honor" (Luke 14:8). There is a quote from Albert Einstein that in many ways communicates what Jesus was saying: *"Try not to become a man of success, but rather try to become a man of value."*

Third, they had placed themselves in the seat of God (vs. 9). The Pharisees prided themselves on their titles. They loved to receive the greeting of Rabbi (or teacher), or even to be addressed as Father. And Jesus told them clearly that there is but one Father, and one Teacher. And the Teacher was standing before them.

Jesus closed this portion of His message by saying, *"The greatest among you must be a servant. But those who exalt themselves will be humbled, and those who humble themselves will be exalted."* In essence He was saying, your worth does not lie in the place you sit. Servants don't sit – they serve. Servants don't exalt themselves – they serve in humility. Servants will not be exalted in heaven because of where they sat – they will be exalted in heaven for Who they served.

. . .

As you and i take up the cross, there is much in this word from Jesus that applies to us, just as it did to the Pharisees. When we serve, are we seeking the applause of men or the applause of heaven? Are we seeking earthly rewards or heavenly rewards? Are we seeking rewards at all? Or are we simply following our Savior, serving as He does, as we serve Him? Don't look for the seat in the front row, look for the towel and the basin in the corner. Because it's definitely not about the seat!

* * *

14

THE EIGHT WOES

… Woe to you, scribes and Pharisees, hypocrites, because you shut off the kingdom of heaven from people; for you do not enter in yourselves, nor do you allow those who are entering to go in.
Woe to you… because you devour widows' houses, and for a pretense you make long prayers; therefore you will receive greater condemnation.
Woe to you… because you travel around on sea and land to make one proselyte; and when he becomes one, you make him twice as much a son of hell as yourselves.
Woe to you… who say, 'Whoever swears by the temple, that is nothing; but whoever swears by the gold of the temple is obligated.'
…Woe to you… for you tithe mint and dill and cummin, and have neglected the weightier provisions of the law: justice and mercy and faithfulness; but these are the things you should have done without neglecting the others. You blind guides, who strain out a gnat and swallow a camel!
Woe to you… for you clean the outside of the cup and of the dish, but inside they are full of robbery and self-indulgence.
Woe to you… for you are like whitewashed tombs which on the outside appear beautiful, but inside they are full of dead men's bones and all uncleanness.
Woe to you… for you build the tombs of the prophets and adorn the monuments of the righteous, and say, 'If we had been living in the days of our fathers, we would not have been partners with them in shedding the blood of the prophets….'
Matthew 23:13-36 (NASB)

* * *

When we think of Jesus, we most often think of Him as our Loving Savior. He and the Father loved us so much that Jesus came to this earth to pay the penalty for our sin. *"There is no greater love than to lay down one's life for one's friends"* (John 15:13). Jesus was not only pronouncing His love for us; He was calling us His friends. We also often think of Jesus as the Gentle Servant, who lived humbly and served selflessly. But we water down the gospel when we fail to recognize Him as the Righteous Judge. Though we see Him most often in the Gospels as the Loving Savior, we see Him upon His return in the Book of Revelation as the Righteous Judge. And just as He, as our Savior, has extended His salvation to each and every one of us – each and every one of us will stand before Him as our Judge.

On that day in the temple, three days before He would be crucified, He stood as Judge over the scribes and Pharisees rendering His verdict and His pronouncement over them. Do not think for a moment that Jesus had allowed His emotion to get the better of Him. This was not like you or i might do – allowing our anger to seize control of our tongue and spew venom upon those who have hurt us. He was speaking out of an anger that was godly and a judgement that was righteous. Let us be mindful, on that day when we stand before Him as Judge, there are three things that we never want to hear Jesus say to us!

The <u>first</u> is, **we never want Jesus to call us hypocrites**. Throughout this pronouncement, Jesus repeatedly referred to the scribes and Pharisees as hypocrites, who taught and said one thing, but lived another.

- Through their false leadership and false teaching, they prevented others from making their way to heaven. Instead of teaching truth, they taught lies that the people accepted as truth. And though each of us are responsible for our own decisions, these men carried an even greater weight because of their part in keeping the people blinded to the Truth.
- Though they made great pretense through lengthy and showy prayers that they were servants of God, they failed to demonstrate any compassion for those around them, and actually took advantage of them, including the widows, for their own selfish greed.
- Though they made great show of teaching others the Law, they were converting others to their man-made beliefs and not leading them to become followers of the Almighty God. They

were promulgating a religion and not introducing anyone into a personal relationship with God.

- The Pharisees had contrived a system whereby people would make oaths in the temple by swearing on gold or objects of value. Thereby those elements became "dedicated to God" and could not be used for anything else. It enabled the Pharisees to build rich treasure chests for personal gain but still appear to be pious in their practice.
- The Pharisees majored on the minors. They had rules for every minute area of life. But they would totally ignore the most important things – loving God and loving their neighbor. As an example, Jesus was not denouncing the practice of tithing, He was correcting them that they were not to tithe out of obligation to a set of rules, they were to tithe as an expression of love, thanksgiving and worship to a loving Heavenly Father Who entrusts us with everything we possess.
- The Pharisees were more concerned about their outward appearance than the spiritual condition of their hearts. They sought the praise of men, and were therefore most concerned about what could be seen on the outside. But God, who could see on the inside, saw their greedy and self-indulgent hearts.
- Jesus used the example of the tombs related to ceremonial cleansing to illustrate the same truth. The Pharisees placed all of their attention on the outside appearance and totally ignored the death and decay of their hearts.
- Finally, throughout much of their history, the religious leaders had rejected the prophets of God, and, in many instances, they had been complicit in their murder or persecution. Three contemporary examples to this group would be their treatment of John the Baptist and, in the days ahead, of Jesus Himself, followed by His apostles and other believers. They were guilty of building monuments to the very prophets they had murdered. And though these Pharisees in most instances had not had a personal hand in their murder, their hearts reflected the same attitudes.

The second is, **you never want Jesus to address you by saying, *"woe to you!"*** "Woe" is a word of judgement. It signifies that impending condemnation, doom, and wrath await you. Whatever reward the Pharisees enjoyed in this life was but momentary. What awaited them was an eternity of damnation separated from God. Their "outward" appearances and feeble attempts to earn God's forgiveness through their works was all for naught. Jesus knew their hearts and He knew the judgement that awaited them.

i can't finish this chapter without including a third statement that you never want to hear Jesus say to you. Though He did not speak these words on this day to the scribes and Pharisees, they were included in His Sermon on the Mount. And again, though He did not speak them here, the scribes and Pharisees would have said to you that they were spokespersons for God to the people. So it is fitting to include this statement here as well. **You never want to hear Jesus say to you, *"I never knew you; depart from Me"*** (Matthew 7:23 – NKJ).

As you take up your cross and follow Jesus, remember that the only outcome of playing at religion is "woe". The Pharisees rejected the Savior and rejected the salvation that can only come through Him. Jesus is the only way. Our salvation is from Him and through Him. Our walk with Him is empowered by Him. He is not fixated on our outer appearance. He sees our heart. And if our heart is truly where it needs to be – cleansed of our sin, seeking Him, loving Him and obeying Him – then the outside is going to look just the way it should – like Jesus!

* * *

15

THE WIDOW'S TREASURE

Jesus sat down near the collection box in the Temple and watched as the crowds dropped in their money. Many rich people put in large amounts. Then a poor widow came and dropped in two small coins. Jesus called His disciples to Him and said, "I tell you the truth, this poor widow has given more than all the others who are making contributions. For they gave a tiny part of their surplus, but she, poor as she is, has given everything she had to live on."
Mark 12:41-44

* * *

It is fitting that after Jesus spent the day shining His light on the hypocrisy of the Pharisees, He concluded His day by illuminating the genuineness of a widow's faith. Jesus did something that would be very inappropriate for you or me to do. He sat down near the collection box and watched as the people placed their offerings in the box. He watched how and what the people gave. But He really wasn't watching how much each person gave. He was watching how much each one kept for themselves. And, by the way, He still does!

Compared to the overall budget for the upkeep and operation of the temple, two small coins would seem to be inconsequential. But in God's economy, she gave more than all the others combined. Her gift did not represent the least; it represented the most – her very all. She kept nothing for herself but gave it all to Him. And that, too, is an important distinction, she was not giving to the temple, or a cause, or a budget, she was giving to God. Many others had given generously, but she gave out of her full devotion to God. Many others had given what the law required, but she gave as a debtor of grace, knowing that all that she had belonged to God. She knew that she wasn't an owner, she was simply a steward of what had been entrusted to her. So, as she gave, she was merely returning to the Owner that which He already owned.

Jesus commended the woman for giving in the way that Paul commended the churches in Macedonia to the church in Corinth:

> *"… They gave not only what they could afford, but far more. And they did it of their own free will. …Their first action was to give themselves to the Lord and to us, just as God wanted them to do. …You know the generous grace of our Lord Jesus Christ. Though He was rich, yet for your sakes He became poor, so that by His poverty He could make you rich. …Whatever you give is acceptable if you give it eagerly. And give according to what you have, not what you don't have"* (2 Corinthians 8:3-12).

There is so much for us as 21st century followers of Jesus to learn from this "poor widow" about the way we are to give of our finances – but also, of our lives.

1. Do we give in order to receive the approval of others, or do we give to honor God? Jesus observed that many who gave did so in a way to bring attention to themselves, in order for them to garner the esteem of the crowd. Earlier in His ministry, Jesus had taught, *"When you give…, don't do as the hypocrites do – blowing trumpets in the synagogues and streets to call attention to their acts of charity! I tell you the truth, they have received all the reward they will ever get"* (Matthew 6:2). Paul would later write to the church in Galatia, *"Obviously, I'm not trying to win the approval of people, but of God. If pleasing people were my goal, I would not be Christ's servant"* (Galatians 1:10).
2. Do we give in order to receive the appreciation and thanks of others, or do we give as an expression of our thanksgiving and appreciation to God? Too often we give expecting to be thanked in return. The fact of the matter is that our giving is to be an expression of our thanksgiving to God. When Zacchaeus gave half of his possessions to the poor (Luke 19:8), it was out of a grateful heart to Jesus for his salvation. He did not give to receive thanks; he gave to express his thanks to God.

3. Do we give in order to receive back, or do we give in order to "pay it forward" and extend the grace that has been extended to us? Granted we can't outgive God as we give sacrificially. He promises that if we give with our whole heart, with an open palm and not a tightened fist, that we will receive back *"in full – pressed down, shaken together to make room for more, running over, and poured into [our] lap"* (Luke 6:38). We have already received more than we could ever repay – we have received His free gift of eternal life.
4. Do we give out of joy, or do we give out of duty? *"Take delight in the Lord, and He will give you your heart's desires"* (Psalm 37:4) Yes, He has commanded us to delight in Him, but that is because He delights in every detail of our lives (Psalm 37:23). And He does not want us to give reluctantly or merely out of duty, but joyously. *"...don't give reluctantly or in response to pressure. 'For God loves a person who gives cheerfully'"* (2 Corinthians 9:7).
5. Do we give out of our contentment in Christ, or do we give out of obligation? Paul wrote, *"... I have learned how to be content with whatever I have. I know how to live on almost nothing or with everything. I have learned the secret of living in every situation, whether it is with a full stomach or empty, with plenty or little"* (Philippians 4:11-12). We must learn how to not only live out of contentment, but also, to give out of contentment.
6. Do we give out of faith, or do we determine what we give out of our plenty? The writer of Hebrews wrote, *"...it is impossible to please God without faith"* (Hebrews 11:6). And that also is true in both the way we live, as well as the way we give. The widow gave all that she had by faith, knowing that her provision came from God.

Whose approval are you seeking? Winston Churchill once said, *"We make a living by what we get, but we make a life by what we give."* As you take up the cross, Jesus is leading – but He is also watching. He is watching to see if we have learned from this "poor widow". She, too, stands as a part of that great cloud of witnesses. They all are watching to see if we will give everything. After all, He loves us so much that He gave everything for us, and He has given everything to us. How can we give any less?

* * *

16

WHAT ABOUT THE TEMPLE?

As Jesus was leaving the Temple that day, one of His disciples said, "Teacher, look at these magnificent buildings! Look at the impressive stones in the walls." Jesus replied, "Yes, look at these great buildings. But they will be completely demolished. Not one stone will be left on top of another!" Later, Jesus sat on the Mount of Olives across the valley from the Temple. Peter, James, John, and Andrew came to Him privately and asked Him, "Tell us, when will all this happen? What sign will show us that these things are about to be fulfilled?"
Mark 13:1-4

* * *

It's the end of the third day of the week. It has been a long day for Jesus that started with the withered fig tree, continued through the various ploys of the religious leaders to trap Him which culminated in His rebuke of the leaders, then was followed by the beautiful contrast of the faithful widow. Jesus and the disciples were now leaving the Temple and heading to the Mount of Olives to spend the night.

Let's add some context for the moment. It's halfway between His triumphal entry and His crucifixion. Jesus is as aware of what will occur over the next few days as He is of what has occurred during the last few. He sees, not only what is behind, but also, what lies ahead – over the course of the next week – and over the millennia that will follow. Imagine if you will that it is September 10, 2001, and you are standing at the top of one of the towers of the World Trade Center. You are looking out at the panoramic view of New York City and admiring the impressiveness of this architectural marvel. In your wildest imagination, you cannot possibly conceive that the place you are standing right then will no longer exist within less than twenty-four hours. Now, imagine Jesus is standing there right beside you. He too can see the physical marvel before your eyes, but He is able to see the destruction that will take place the next morning.

The first Temple (originally built by King Solomon) was destroyed by the Babylonians in 586 B.C. The second Temple was built as a modest structure in 516 B.C. by Jewish exiles who had returned to Jerusalem from Babylon under the leadership of the appointed governor Zerubbabel. During the reign of King Herod the Great in the 1st Century B.C., the Temple was refurbished and transformed into a compound of magnificent structures. Work would have been completed on or about the time of Jesus' birth and the birth of many of His disciples. Thus, for them, because of its complete refurbishing, it was a "modern" structure.

Each of them had been to the Temple many times before in their lifetimes, so the sight was not a new one. But, in an effort to decompress from the many tensions of the day, they turned their conversation to reflect on the "impressive" and "magnificent" buildings that made up the Temple compound. And as they did, Jesus replied, *"Yes, look at these great buildings. But they will be completely demolished. Not one stone will be left on top of another!"* This was not merely conjecture on the part of Jesus, nor was it solely a prophetic word. The patriarchs and prophets of the Old Testament had prophesied about events that would take place in the future. They had prophesied about the Messiah by faith. They had not seen the Messiah. They only knew of the promise of the Messiah. But this wasn't like that. As Jesus spoke, He literally could see the destruction of the Temple. Jesus saw this event, as well as the other future events we will look at in the next few chapters. These were not speculations or possible outcomes. These were actual events that He could see. We now know that the second Temple was destroyed by the Romans in 70 A.D., within less than fifty years from when this conversation took place. And in a matter of days, the True Temple, where the glory of God resides, would be crucified. "It" would be rebuilt in three days' time as Jesus arose from the dead as He had also prophesied (John 2:19). Imagine the shock and dismay of Jesus' disciples when they heard that the physical Temple would be destroyed. And bear in mind, they still were not clear on all that what was about to occur within the next few days.

• • •

This begins what is often referred to as the "Olivet Discourse" (because it took place on the Mount of Olives) in which Jesus unfolds the eschatological (meaning "end things") events which will end this age. This discourse is recorded in Matthew 24, Mark 13 and Luke 21. Again, we will look at the discourse over the coming chapters. Mark (bear in mind his source would have been Peter) is the only Gospel in which we see that this was a "private" conversation that Peter, James, John and Andrew had with Jesus. Matthew infers it, and Mark's Gospel would have been Luke's source.

It is very significant that this conversation unfolded on the Mount of Olives, for three reasons. The first reason was very personal to Jesus. It was because this was the place to which Jesus often retreated when He was in Jerusalem in order to spend One-on-One time with the Father. It was the place that They would have long conversations in prayer. The second was somewhat pragmatic. It was the place where Judas would betray Him in two nights' time. The Father had ordained that Jesus would be arrested and led away from the Mount of Olives. The first three days of this time in Jerusalem, Jesus and the disciples had overnighted in Bethany. But now He switched to the Mount of Olives, so He could clearly establish a nightly pattern – a pattern that Judas would use to lead the posse that would arrest Him. Jesus was not only using this time to teach about the end of the world, He was using it to further order the steps of His last days leading to His crucifixion. And this second reason ties very clearly with the third, which is prophetic. The Mount is just to the east of Jerusalem. It is just outside the gates of the city. And when Jesus returns to establish His Kingdom, *"His feet will stand on the Mount of Olives"* (Zechariah 14:4). The place of His intimate times with the Father, the place of His betrayal and arrest, and the place of His return are all right there at the Mount of Olives.

And on that coming day, the new Temple – the everlasting Temple – will be established. The second Temple, for all of its magnificence, will pale in comparison.

On that day the sources of light will no longer shine, yet there will be continuous day! Only the Lord knows how this could happen. There will be no normal day and night, for at evening time it will still be light.
On that day life-giving waters will flow out from Jerusalem, half toward the Dead Sea and half toward the Mediterranean, flowing continuously in both summer and winter. And the Lord will be King over all the earth.

On that day there will be one Lord – His name alone will be worshiped.
(Zechariah 14:6-9)

And what a great day that will be! And as that day approaches, take up the cross and follow Him!

* * *

17

THE PAROUSIA

Later, Jesus sat on the Mount of Olives. His disciples came to Him privately and said, "Tell us, when will all this happen? What sign will signal Your return and the end of the world?" Jesus told them, "Don't let anyone mislead you, for many will come in My name, claiming, 'I am the Messiah.' They will deceive many. And you will hear of wars and threats of wars, but don't panic. Yes, these things must take place, but the end won't follow immediately. Nation will go to war against nation, and kingdom against kingdom. There will be famines and earthquakes in many parts of the world. But all this is only the first of the birth pains, with more to come.

Matthew 24:3-8

* * *

The Greek word "Parousia" (pronounced pair-oo-see-ah) is a noun that means "a coming" or "a presence."[1] Most commonly in the New Testament, the word refers to the coming return of our Lord Jesus Christ. And on the evening of this passage, Jesus sat with Peter, James, John and Andrew on the Mount of Olives and answered their questions about the Parousia.

As we saw in chapter 16, as they were walking to the Mount, Jesus had declared to the disciples that the Temple would be completely demolished. That prompted these disciples to ask three questions:

1. When will all this happen?
2. What sign will signal Your return?
3. What sign will signal the end of the world?

Jesus didn't respond to their questions to satisfy idle curiosity or merely to resolve any confusion they had about end-times prophecy. And we must be careful of our motivation as well. There are many students of the Word that relish the study of biblical prophecy as an intellectual pursuit or in an effort to predict the actual arrival of our Lord's return. Jesus, in fact, was equipping them so they would not be deceived by false teaching or drawn away from following Him in His mission. He was equipping them – as He is equipping us – to be people of Issachar – who understand the times and know what to do (1 Chronicles 12:32).

Jesus actually answered their questions in reverse order by explaining the events that will lead up to what He later described in this passage as a time of tribulation. *"For then there will be a great tribulation, such as has not occurred since the beginning of the world until now, nor ever will"* (Matthew 24:21 NASB). He describes these initial events as *"the first of the birth pains"*. The analogy of "birth pains" references back to the prophecy of Isaiah:

"Scream in terror, for the day of the Lord has arrived – the time for the Almighty to destroy. Every arm is paralyzed with fear. Every heart melts and people are terrified. Pangs of anguish grip them, like those of a woman in labor. They look helplessly at one another, their faces aflame with fear. For see, the day of the Lord is coming – the terrible day of His fury and fierce anger. The land will be made desolate, and all the sinners destroyed with it. The heavens will be black above them; the stars will give no light. The sun will be dark when it rises, and the moon will provide no light"
(Isaiah 13:6-10).

The first of these "birth pains" or "pangs of anguish" are:

1. *"Many will come in My name, claiming, 'I am the Messiah.' They will deceive many."* i searched on the web for "Messiah claimants" and was over-

whelmed by the length of the list. When Jesus said "many" will come, it was no exaggeration. Here are just a few of the names[2]:

- Simon Magus – a Samaritan born soon after Christ ascended in the early 1st century, who called himself the "Standing One".
- Ann Lee (1736-1784) – a central figure to the Shakers – who considered herself to be Christ's female counterpart.
- Victor Manuel Gomez Rodriguez, who later changed his name to Samael Aun Weor – born in Colombia in 1917 and declared himself to be Messiah in 1972
- Sun Myong Moon (1920 – 2012) – founder of the Unification Church who declared himself to be the second coming of Christ to fulfill Jesus' unfinished mission.

The list goes on ad nauseam, and, as Jesus warned, each of these deceived many to follow them. The Apostle John writes in The Revelation (6:1-8) about the four seals that will be broken in the last days, the first of which is the Antichrist, the final world dictator who will declare himself to be the Messiah and will lead the nations away.

In addition to this list of false Messiahs is an unending list of false teachers teaching false doctrine, who also have deceived many. We need to be watchful. We need to be discerning of Truth. And we need to be bold to proclaim Truth and denounce false teaching.

2. *"You will hear of wars and threats of wars…. Nation will go to war against nation, and kingdom against kingdom."* Wars by themselves do not announce the end of the age. Throughout history there have been wars. Even the enforced peace of the Roman Empire in the early 1st Century disintegrated into national conflicts. The second of the seals that John writes about (Revelation 6:3-4) is the unleashing of war and slaughter. There will be increased incidents of war.

3. *"There will be famines and earthquakes in many parts of the world."* We already are seeing increased incidents of natural disasters – earthquakes, tsunamis, tornadoes, floods – that have caused countless deaths and destruction. We see increased famine resulting from those disasters, as well as from military conflicts, and ineffective use of natural resources. It is estimated that 815 million of the 7.6 billion people in the world today

are suffering from chronic undernourishment, and 9.1 million people currently die of hunger every year.[3] The third of the seals (Revelation 6:5-6) will be increased famine.

One side road while we are on this subject. Our Master has clearly called us, as we will again see in chapter 24 (Matthew 25:35), to minister to those in need around us – and specifically the basic needs of hunger, thirst, clothing, etc. Let's not be just observers of our times, let's be active in ministering to the needs of our times. There are ways that each and every one of us can be involved in meeting those needs locally – in our own communities – and globally – into the impoverished regions of the world. One of the organizations that i have seen God use first-hand to work effectively in helping to meet these needs outside of the US is Baptist Global Response (gobgr.org). i have found that in many instances they have been the first responders to needs when they occur.

4. There will be *"more to come."* The fourth of the seals (Revelation 6:7-8) will be ever-increasing death resulting from war, disaster and famine.

And Jesus said that these are but the beginning "pangs of anguish" that will "signal the end of the world".

One further side road before we close this chapter: Jesus did not address the rapture of His church in this discourse. We will look at the rapture further in the last book of this series. But it is the belief of many students of the Word who are followers of Jesus, that believers in the present age of the church will be raptured by Christ and taken to heaven before the Tribulation begins. Then at the close of the Tribulation, they will return to earth with Him. i agree with that interpretation – but i'll reserve further discussion for a later chapter.

In the meantime, we have been called to take up the cross in these days. There has never been a generation closer to the end of the age than we are. We have been called to be alert (Matthew 24:42) and we have been called to be faithful servants carrying out the Master's business (Matthew 24:45-47) and being about His mission (Matthew 28:19-20). The Parousia is drawing near. Let's not be found asleep or distracted at the post (Matthew 24:48-51)!

[1] gotquestions.org
[2] Wikipedia.org
[3] WorldHunger.org

* * *

18

IN THE COMING DAYS

"When these things begin to happen, watch out! You will be handed over to the local councils and beaten in the synagogues. You will stand trial before governors and kings because you are My followers. But this will be your opportunity to tell them about Me. For the Good News must first be preached to all nations. But when you are arrested and stand trial, don't worry in advance about what to say. Just say what God tells you at that time, for it is not you who will be speaking, but the Holy Spirit. A brother will betray his brother to death, a father will betray his own child, and children will rebel against their parents and cause them to be killed. And everyone will hate you because you are My followers. But the one who endures to the end will be saved.

Mark 13:9-13

* * *

Jesus continues to answer the questions we looked at in the last chapter that Peter, James, John and Andrew have posed to Him there on the Mount of Olives. As a reminder, it is the end of the third day of the week, two nights before He is to be arrested and betrayed. He is still unpacking what will lead up to the end of the age and signal His return.

Before we look at these next "signs" for which He instructs them to watch, let's talk about "time". The persecution that He says will occur actually began with the apostles in just a few short weeks after this very conversation. In many respects, the coming of the end of the age began right then, early in the 1st Century. The penultimate event of history is the crucifixion, burial and resurrection of Jesus. In God's plan:

- First, He created the heavens and the earth in order to raise up and gather worshipers unto Himself, through whom He would ascribe glory to His Name. But we immediately separated ourselves from our Creator through our sin and disqualified ourselves from being able to worship a Holy God, so…
- Secondly, He unfolded His redemptive plan to reconcile His sinful creation back to Himself through the death, burial and resurrection of His Son, which leads us to the final part of the plan…
- Thirdly, through the power of His Holy Spirit, now working in and through the followers of His Son, He multiplies that multitude of worshipers from every language, people, tongue and tribe, culminating in that final day when He gathers us all together before His throne (the end of the age).

So truly, the final days began after Christ completed His redemptive work and returned to the right hand of the Father, thereby enabling the Holy Spirit to be sent to earth to be about His work. The period between the first to the second part of the plan was approximately 4,000 years, and now the Holy Spirit has been about His work for the last 2,100 years since Jesus had this conversation with His disciples. There is no question we are in those final days. Only God knows how long they will continue. *"But you must not forget this one thing, dear friends: A day is like a thousand years to the Lord, and a thousand years is like a day"* (2 Peter 3:8). So, it should not come as a surprise to us that the disciples began to experience some of the very occurrences that Jesus described as being signs of the last days. Nor should it surprise us that we are.

Jesus taught that His followers would experience persecution, and that we would experience it "officially" and "personally". Believers will stand before local councils, governors and leaders and be beaten, persecuted, imprisoned and even executed for their faith in Christ. It began with Peter and John being arrested in Acts 4, and it continued with all of the apostles and many of the 1st Century followers being martyred or persecuted. And it has continued throughout history to this day. Today, it is estimated that there are 215 million Christians that are experiencing high levels of persecution in the "fifty most difficult countries in which to be a Christian"[1].

And that persecution is not confined to "official" authorities. It continues and is often even more severely inflicted "personally" by family members and neighbors.

God has used a good friend, Nik Ripken, to open my eyes to the ever-growing reality of persecution around the globe. Nik writes[2],

"Christians who live in nations where persecution is not a normal occurrence often cringe in horror upon hearing reports that their brothers and sisters around the globe are experiencing the atrocities of suffering and death for their faith in (and their witness of) Jesus Christ.... Admittedly, we cannot fully comprehend all of God's purposes in allowing Christ's followers to be persecuted. Only those purposes which are clearly articulated in Scripture may be known to us, and they are few in number. The book of Acts records the fact that the early believers left Jerusalem and scattered to other key cities as a result of intense persecution (Acts 11:19). Here, one may conclude that God purposed to use persecution to spread and multiply the Church. Persecution serves to test and strengthen one's faith (Romans 5:3-4; James 1:3, 1 Peter 1:6-7, 4:12). There is a mysterious purpose in persecution and suffering related to bringing about the Kingdom of God (2 Thessalonians 1:4-5). Scripture tells us that Jesus was "perfected" as the author of salvation and in His obedience through suffering (Hebrews 2:10, 5:8-10). This principle has limited but valid application to God's purposes for suffering in the lives of Christian leaders. And, finally, one of God's purposes in affliction and suffering is to equip His servants with the ability to comfort and sustain others who endure similar afflictions (2 Corinthians 1:3-11)."

Jesus said, *"everyone will hate you because you are My followers."* If they hated and crucified Him, why would we expect anything different? We cannot expect the world to treat us any differently than it treated Jesus. And as the end of the age draws near, this will only increase.

Jesus went on to teach, *"For the Good News must first be preached to all nations."* In the first century, the Apostles and other followers of Christ scattered to the nations to proclaim the Good News to all that had not heard. Today, men and women are still scattering to the nations, having been sent out to continue that mission. Currently 4.3 billion people live in areas where less than 2% of their population are followers of Jesus, and 932 million of those live in areas where there are no known believers or churches to provide a witness.[3] We are to be witnesses in these last days.

We must go, we must send, and we must undergird those who have been sent.

Lastly, in this passage, Jesus told them that His followers must endure to the end. Enduring faith is not the product of our profession of faith. Our profession of faith opened the door for the Holy Spirit to enter into our lives and indwell us. Enduring faith is then the product of God's Spirit at work within us and through us. John Piper said it well – *"'We must' becomes 'we will' because 'God will'."* And the Apostles wrote these truths to those new followers of Jesus in the early church to encourage them that "God will":

"He is able to keep you from stumbling and to present you blameless before the presence of His glory"
(Jude 1:24).
"He who began a good work in you will bring it to completion at the day of Jesus Christ"
(Philippians 1:6).
"{Christ} will sustain you to the end.... God is faithful, through whom you were called into fellowship with His Son"
(1 Corinthians 1:8-9).
"The Lord will bring me safely to His heavenly kingdom"
(2 Timothy 4:18).

And those words are as true for us today as they were for them. As we take up the cross to follow Jesus – no matter what wilderness we may be walking through – we must continue to be like those people of Issachar (who we looked at in the last chapter), understanding our times, walking in the mission of our Master and enduring to the end – no matter how many days there are yet to come.

[1] OpenDoorsUSA.org
[2] NikRipken.com
[3] Global Status of Evangelical Christianity, IMB, published 3/1/2018

* * *

19

PERILOUS TIMES

"Therefore, when you see the abomination of desolation which was spoken of through Daniel the prophet, standing in the holy place (let the reader understand), then those who are in Judea must flee to the mountains. Whoever is on the housetop must not go down to get the things out that are in his house. Whoever is in the field must not turn back to get his cloak. But woe to those who are pregnant and to those who are nursing babies in those days! But pray that your flight will not be in the winter, or on a Sabbath. For then there will be a great tribulation, such as has not occurred since the beginning of the world until now, nor ever will. Unless those days had been cut short, no life would have been saved; but for the sake of the elect those days will be cut short. Then if anyone says to you, 'Behold, here is the Christ,' or 'There He is,' do not believe him. For false Christs and false prophets will arise and will show great signs and wonders, so as to mislead, if possible, even the elect. Behold, I have told you in advance. So, if they say to you, 'Behold, He is in the wilderness,' do not go out, or, 'Behold, He is in the inner rooms,' do not believe them. For just as the lightning comes from the east and flashes even to the west, so will the coming of the Son of Man be. Wherever the corpse is, there the vultures will gather."

Matthew 24:15-28

* * *

Jesus continues to answer the three questions that His disciples have asked Him about the end of the age:

1. When will all this happen?
2. What sign will signal Your return?

3. What sign will signal the end of the world?

In revealing these truths to the apostles and, through them, to us, Jesus is providing us with knowledge that should lead to an understanding and fear regarding the coming judgement of God. There should be a terror that grips the human heart when it contemplates God's judgment on sin. The apocalyptic revelations are a warning to all mankind about the end result of sin and that we had better be prepared for the Lord's return. It is a warning to the non-Christian to repent or they will suffer God's judgment, and it is a warning to us as followers of Christ to live our lives in a worthy manner.

As He talks through the events, He now comes to the most perilous of times that are triggered by what He and the prophets call "the abomination of desolation". As Matthew notes, Daniel recorded this coming event as follows:

> *"The ruler will make a treaty with the people for a period of one set of seven, but after half this time, he will put an end to the sacrifices and offerings. And as a climax to all his terrible deeds, he will set up a sacrilegious object that causes desecration, until the fate decreed for this defiler is finally poured out on him" (Daniel 9:27).*

The event will occur halfway through the seven year period of the Great Tribulation that will immediately precede Christ's return. At the beginning of that period, a man portraying himself to be a man of peace (the anti-Christ) will rise to a position of power across the entire world. His arrival and the resulting abominations are being restrained until their proper time by the Spirit of God. But in His time, He will remove His hand of restraint. During the first half of the anti-Christ's seven-year reign, he will establish a treaty of global peace and will blindly be accepted by most. But halfway through, his true nature will be revealed. He will set himself up to be worshipped and destruction will be poured out across the earth. Paul writes:

> ... on that day "*... a great rebellion against God {will arise} and the man of lawlessness [will be} revealed — the one who brings destruction. He will exalt*

himself and defy everything that people call god and every object of worship. He will even sit in the temple of God, claiming that he himself is God. ...And you know what is holding him back, for he can be revealed only when his time comes. For this lawlessness is already at work secretly, and it will remain secret until the One who is holding it back steps out of the way"
(2 Thessalonians 2:3-7).

The "abomination of desolation" will herald a time of danger for those who live in Judea that will occur so quickly that as soon as one hears of it, they should flee immediately without stopping to make any preparation. The ramifications will be global as the world enters into a time period of three and a half years of unprecedented destruction and desolation, so severe that it *'has not occurred since the beginning of the world until now, nor ever will."*

Daniel wrote, *"Wise leaders will give instruction to many, but these teachers will die by fire and sword, or they will be jailed and robbed. During these persecutions, little help will arrive, and many who join them will not be sincere. And some of the wise will fall victim to persecution. In this way, they will be refined and cleansed and made pure until the time of the end, for the appointed time is still to come. The king will do as he pleases, exalting himself and claiming to be greater than every god, even blaspheming the God of gods. He will succeed, but only until the time of wrath is completed. For what has been determined will surely take place. He will have no respect for the gods of his ancestors, or for the god loved by women, or for any other god, for he will boast that he is greater than them all. Instead of these, he will worship the god of fortresses—a god his ancestors never knew—and lavish on him gold, silver, precious stones, and expensive gifts. Claiming this foreign god's help, he will attack the strongest fortresses. He will honor those who submit to him, appointing them to positions of authority and dividing the land among them as their reward"*
(Daniel 11:33-39).

And this false Christ and his *"false prophets will arise and will show great signs and wonders, so as to mislead, if possible, even the elect."* But Jesus warns for His elect not to be deceived by signs and wonders, for they are but counterfeit imitations of God's power. When Jesus returns, there will be no question that it is Him! At the appropriate time, according to the Father's timetable, He will return in all majesty and power. *"For just as the lightning comes from the east and flashes even to the west, so will the coming of the Son of Man be."*

But before He returns, *"all the rulers and their armies {will gather} to a place with the Hebrew name Armageddon"* (Revelation 16:16). And the awful carnage that results from this battle will result in a massive field of death that Jesus depicts when He says, *"Wherever the corpse is, there the vultures will gather."* In the next chapter of this book, we will look at His pronouncement of His glorious return.

At this point, let me stop and take a moment to talk about why i have included this chapter, as well as the three that preceded it, to walk through Jesus' teaching of the end times. You might be asking, "what does that have to do with my wilderness journey?" Or, "what does that have to do with my taking up the cross and following Him?" The reality is that it has everything to do with both questions. We follow a Living Savior who will be returning! We may still be here to be raptured with the church just prior to these "end of the ages" events, or we may have already stepped into eternity before those events unfold. But first, we need to live and follow Him with full anticipation and expectation of His soon return. This is not hypothetical, futuristic prophecy that doesn't apply to us. Jesus is talking about the day we live in. The wilderness we are walking in is surrounded by the world events that are rapidly unfolding toward that day of His return. Let's not become so myopic with our own wilderness journey that we miss the bigger picture.

And second, let's not miss the bigger purpose! Sin destroys. The enemy deceives. We live in a world that is in a free fall toward death and destruction. God will return to judge His creation for our sin. And the verdict is eternal damnation. BUT Jesus saves. And we as His followers have that message of salvation. The very circumstances that each one of us are walking in today is but a platform through which He will make His message known and bring glory to Himself. That's why we follow! And that's why He wants us to know. Yes, perilous times lie ahead… but the cross and the empty grave lie behind. Let's be faithful to carry the cross, proclaiming the good news of the empty grave so that others can escape those perilous times in the days ahead.

* * *

20

THEN HE WILL COME!

"But immediately after the tribulation of those days the sun will be darkened, and the moon will not give its light, and the stars will fall from the sky, and the powers of the heavens will be shaken. And then the sign of the Son of Man will appear in the sky, and then all the tribes of the earth will mourn, and they will see the Son of Man coming on the clouds of the sky with power and great glory. And He will send forth His angels with a great trumpet and they will gather together His elect from the four winds, from one end of the sky to the other."
Matthew 24:29-31

* * *

Throughout the last three chapters, we have been looking at Jesus' response to the three questions that His disciples have asked Him about the end of the age:

1. When will all this happen?
2. What sign will signal Your return?
3. What sign will signal the end of the world?

As we have seen, He started His answers by responding to the third question. We have looked at the events that He tells us will signal the end of the age (the world). Now He comes to the answers to the first two questions.

. . .

What will signal His return and when will it occur? Immediately following the Battle of Armageddon (Revelation 16:16), the earth will be plunged into utter darkness! The sun will cease to shine. The moon will have no light to reflect, and the stars will fall and be snuffed out. Jesus is quoting from Ezekiel 32:7:

I will veil the heavens and darken the stars.
I will cover the sun with a cloud, and the moon will not give you its light.
I will darken the bright stars overhead and cover your land in darkness.
I, the Sovereign Lord, have spoken!

The earth will be as a darkened void – just as it was before God commanded there to be light. The darkness will be so pervasive that one will not be able to see their hand right in front of their eyes. It will be a demonstration of God's might and power – but also, a demonstration of what this world looks like absent His presence. Apart from His light, we are surrounded by darkness, covered with darkness and lost in our darkness. Without light there can be no morning, and there can be no joy (Psalm 30:5). Without light, there can be no life. Without light, there can be no hope.

Jesus said that in the midst of that absolute darkness the sign of His return will appear in the sky. He doesn't tell us how long the darkness will last. He doesn't tell us what that sign will be. Theologians have debated and conjectured what it might be. i believe it will be Him shining forth as the Light of the World. It will be a light that radiates from Him and overpowers the darkness in every corner of the earth. We already know that there is no need for artificial light in heaven because the Shekinah "*glory of God illuminates the city, and the Lamb is its light*" (Revelation 21:23). He will shine upon all of the earth as bright as the noonday sun. No darkness will be permitted to hide from His light. "*… all the tribes of the earth will mourn*" because Christ's return will finalize their defeat. The power that Satan and the principalities of this world have been permitted to exercise will now be bound – bound by Christ's might, His power and His light! To quote Paul Maxwell from his article on the *Desiring God* blog:

"The tribes of the earth — the captains of industry, the earthly-minded, the self-livers, the others-blamers, the indulgent, the wolves, the servant-abusing — they will mourn, because the Great Shepherd has come to gather His elect, to name the

faithful, to harvest His fruit. He brings great joy to the weary who have spent their lives for others in His name.... {There will be} a global mourning among those who have recklessly cast aside the free offer of Christ's grace in this life. And the unseen faithful and generous servants will finally rest."

The nations will walk in His Light and will bring their honor and glory to Him (Revelation 21:24, 26). As we saw in Matthew 24:14 (in chapter 18) – *"This gospel of the kingdom shall be preached in the whole world as a testimony to all the nations, and then the end will come."* Peoples from every language, tribe and nation will be gathered from the four corners of the world – *"from one end of the sky to the other"* – drawn to His light, drawn to His presence and drawn to His feet – where every knee will bow and every tongue will declare that Jesus Christ is Lord, to the glory of God the Father (Philippians 2:10-11).

So, as we take up the cross to follow Him, let's not lose sight of "the end" – the return of our Lord, receiving all the worship, praise, honor and glory that is due Him. In the midst of the darkness and trials of our journey, as we follow Him, let's not lose sight of the reality that His Light will prevail. Every speck of darkness will be eradicated. Every shadow will be removed. Though the enemy may appear to have the upper hand right now, he is a defeated foe. When Jesus "appears in the sky", it's all over! The psalmist David said it best:

Fret not yourself because of evildoers; be not envious of wrongdoers!
For they will soon fade like the grass and wither like the green herb.
Trust in the LORD, and do good; dwell in the land and befriend faithfulness.
Delight yourself in the LORD, and He will give you the desires of your heart.
Commit your way to the LORD; trust in Him, and He will act.
He will bring forth your righteousness as the light, and your justice as the noonday.
(Psalm 37:1-6 ESV)

In the meantime, let's dwell in the land, cultivating faithfulness, staying true to Him and His mission. Let's remain steadfast in making disciples of all peoples – those within our current traffic patterns – and those within the traffic patterns where He is sending us to engage. For that day is drawing near!

* * *

21

ONE WILL BE TAKEN, ONE WILL BE LEFT

"Now learn the parable from the fig tree: when its branch has already become tender and puts forth its leaves, you know that summer is near; so you too, when you see all these things, recognize that He is near, right at the door. Truly I say to you, this generation will not pass away until all these things take place. Heaven and earth will pass away, but My words will not pass away. But of that day and hour no one knows, not even the angels of heaven, nor the Son, but the Father alone. For the coming of the Son of Man will be just like the days of Noah. For as in those days before the flood they were eating and drinking, marrying and giving in marriage, until the day that Noah entered the ark, and they did not understand until the flood came and took them all away; so will the coming of the Son of Man be. Then there will be two men in the field; one will be taken and one will be left. Two women will be grinding at the mill; one will be taken and one will be left."
Matthew 24:32-41

* * *

As a reminder, Jesus is only two days away from His arrest and subsequent execution. His days on this earth, including those after His resurrection, are drawing to a close. Though His disciples do not know – nor are they able to comprehend – all that is about to occur, they can sense His time with them is coming to an end. And those who have walked with Him the closest want to know when He's coming back. In many respects, they are already longing for His return. In response to their questions, Jesus is describing His second coming to earth – when He will return as Judge.

. . .

When the branch on the fig tree begins to put forth its leaves, you know that spring has dawned, and summer is near. You know that the fruit of the season will arrive in its time, not far behind. You know the time is coming. And so it is with the return of the Master. The unmistakable signs of the times will herald His return. But the days of this age (or the days of *"this generation"*) will not pass, and the day of His return will not occur, until all of the events that He has described have taken place. It's interesting that Jesus says that even He as the Son of Man does not know the exact moment. That day and hour is known by *"the Father alone"*. That should be a reminder to us that we are not to spend our time watching for the signs of His return and obsessing on the "when", we are to be good stewards of the time He has given us now and invest our lives in being about His mission. Because, as He goes on to say, the only thing that endures will be His word – His gospel. Even heaven and earth will pass away. John writes, *"Then I saw a new heaven and a new earth, for the old heaven and the old earth had disappeared"* (Revelation 21:1).

No, we don't know the day and the hour. And there's a reason for that! The Lord wants every generation to live in expectancy, every generation to live in preparedness. We don't know what generation it's going to come upon. But when it comes, it's going to come in catastrophic proportion, and it's going to come rapidly. We don't know what generation that will be, and even the generation that it comes upon will not know the exact moment. Thus, Christians dating back to the very 1st century church have always lived in the eagerness of the coming of Christ.

Jesus compared these coming days to the days of Noah. In that day, the people lived as though God did not exist. They had rejected the word of God and did not believe that God would judge them. On the day that the rains began to fall and the flood waters began to rise, they were going about their lives as usual, without any thought of, or regard for, God. Luke includes a reference to the people of Sodom, just prior to their destruction (Luke 17:28-29), and then goes on to say, *"Yes, it will be 'business as usual' right up to the hour when the Son of Man returns"* (Luke 17:30).

But at that given moment, enough will have been enough! John also writes, *"Then another angel came from the Temple and shouted to the One sitting on the cloud* {referring to Jesus}, *'Swing the sickle, for the time of harvest has come; the crop on earth is ripe.' So the one sitting on the cloud swung His sickle over the earth, and the whole earth was harvested"* (Revelation 14:15-16). Using the imagery in this verse, the seed is planted, the grain grows to its full ripeness, and then it is harvested. The Lord has patiently waited for the final ripening of evil. He has waited for the full ripening of sin. And God is not going to return to judge this world until the harvest is ripe, and sin has run its course. He will not return until all the ungodliness has been revealed. That includes the evil of evil that is still unrevealed – as hard as it is to imagine that there is any more evil that has not yet been revealed. But when that evil has been revealed and sin has run its full, rampant course, then the sickle will be "swung" and the harvest will be ready. So, the Father is patiently waiting to allow sin to run its reckless course, to spend itself, to ripen to the point where it will be fully, finally, and forever harvested.

i believe the other reason the Lord is patiently waiting is to allow for the gathering of His church. He is waiting to gather all the saints whose names are written in the Lamb's book of life. Paul writes in his epistle to the Romans, *"… this will last only until the full number… comes to Christ"* (Romans 11:25). God is waiting to gather all of those from every language, people, tribe and nation who will throughout eternity give Him glory, give Him praise, give Him honor, give Him adoration and serve Him. He is gathering worshipers for His eternal heaven to praise and glorify His Name.

Then at that moment, *"One will be taken, and one will be left."* Somewhere along the line, the church began to believe that Jesus was talking here about His return to rapture His bride. The idea has been taught that one will be taken to join Jesus in the clouds and one will be left on this earth to endure the tribulation. But remember, Jesus is making this statement AFTER He has described the days of the tribulation. As we will discuss in the next book as we study the epistles, the rapture of the church will have already occurred before the tribulation takes place. He is describing now His awaited return, marking the end of the tribulation. These folks who are being taken are not being raptured, they're being "taken" into judgement, and will not be entering into the millennial kingdom (the one thousand years of Christ's reign that will follow His return). The ones who remain will be those who have come to faith during the tribulation period.

Imagine that moment as men and women, young and old, are "taken" into eternal separation from God. And the moment before, they stood with one who apparently was a follower of Jesus (because he or she remained). Imagine the loss that follower will experience as that family member, or coworker, or friend is taken. Yes, there will be great joy in the return of our Lord, but there will also be great sorrow for those who will no longer have an opportunity to follow Jesus.

As we take up the cross to follow Jesus, let's not be distracted by the things that will pass away. Let's be about His mission so that "less are taken", and "more are left".

* * *

22

LET'S BE READY

"Therefore, be on the alert, for you do not know which day your Lord is coming. But be sure of this, that if the head of the house had known at what time of the night the thief was coming, he would have been on the alert and would not have allowed his house to be broken into. For this reason, you also must be ready; for the Son of Man is coming at an hour when you do not think He will. Who then is the faithful and sensible slave whom his master put in charge of his household to give them their food at the proper time? Blessed is that slave whom his master finds so doing when he comes. Truly I say to you that he will put him in charge of all his possessions. But if that evil slave says in his heart, 'My master is not coming for a long time,' and begins to beat his fellow slaves and eat and drink with drunkards; the master of that slave will come on a day when he does not expect him and at an hour which he does not know, and will cut him in pieces and assign him a place with the hypocrites; in that place there will be weeping and gnashing of teeth.

Then the kingdom of heaven will be comparable to ten virgins, who took their lamps and went out to meet the bridegroom. Five of them were foolish, and five were prudent. For when the foolish took their lamps, they took no oil with them, but the prudent took oil in flasks along with their lamps. Now while the bridegroom was delaying, they all got drowsy and began to sleep. But at midnight there was a shout, 'Behold, the bridegroom! Come out to meet him.' Then all those virgins rose and trimmed their lamps. The foolish said to the prudent, 'Give us some of your oil, for our lamps are going out.' But the prudent answered, 'No, there will not be enough for us and you too; go instead to the dealers and buy some for yourselves.' And while they were going away to make the purchase, the bridegroom came, and those who were ready went in with him to the wedding feast; and the door was shut. Later the other virgins also came, saying, 'Lord,

lord, open up for us.' But he answered, 'Truly I say to you, I do not know you.' Be on the alert then, for you do not know the day nor the hour."
Matthew 24:42 – 25:13

* * *

Jesus begins this particular passage with the admonition to "be on the alert" and He ends with the exact same words. There are at least four "audiences" to whom Jesus was speaking those words. First, He was responding to questions from His disciples – He was speaking to them. Second, Jesus' earthly ministry was primarily to the Jewish people – He was speaking to the Jews. Third, He was speaking to those who would follow Him before the Tribulation – those who have already gone to be with Him in heaven or those who will be raptured by Him prior to the Tribulation. By the way, as His people, we will escape the Tribulation, but He never promised that we will escape tribulation. Fourth, He was speaking to His followers who will come to faith in Him during the Tribulation (after the rapture, but prior to His return).

For those of us in that third category – those of us following Him today – we live in a place between the already and the not yet. We look back to the cross, where Jesus bore our sins, and we look forward to His second coming. We live in the last days, but not yet in the last of the last days. We live with a sense of what is already true and what is yet to come to pass. We live with the excitement, thrill, and joy of looking for the coming of our Lord Jesus Christ.

Peter said it this way, *"Blessed be the God and Father of our Lord Jesus Christ, who according to His great mercy has caused us to be born again to a living hope through the resurrection of Jesus Christ from the dead to obtain an inheritance which is imperishable and undefiled and will not fade away, reserved in heaven for you, who are protected by the power of God through faith for a salvation ready to be revealed in the last time"* (1 Peter 1:3-5 NASB). We live in that "not yet" place of living hope! We are clothed in His righteousness, but we are not yet like Him in all ways. And our hearts are filled with anticipation for the day we will see Him. Those who are not His followers should look to that day when they will see Him with great fear and trembling. Paul wrote, *"Knowing therefore the terror of the Lord, we persuade men..."* (2 Corinthians 5:11). To think of the coming of our Master is either to think in hope and anticipation of His glory, or to think in fear and dread of His eternal judgement. So, we look to His return – for those of us who know the

Savior, with a living hope, and for those who do not, with fear and dread.

For us, "being on the alert" means we are to carry the cross with the awareness that one day we will stand in His presence to give an account. We do not know the day or the hour. And as He said, He will come even *"when you do not think He will"*. We must live and walk in the ready.

Blessed is the servant (or slave) that is walking in the ready and is about his master's business. Every one of us – believer and non-believer alike – have been given gifts to carry out our Creator's purpose. Every single person in the world has been given life, breath, privilege – all granted to us by God as a stewardship, for which we will be accountable. And hell will be populated not only by Satan and his angels, but by people who with unrepentant hearts wasted that privilege and who embezzled the gifts that God intended for His purpose. The servant's task is to serve the Master and those He has placed before us. And the day of accountability is coming soon!

Lastly, Jesus relates the parable of the ten virgins to teach us the suddenness and the unexpectedness of His return. It should call us to readiness, preparedness and alertness so that we are not caught in an unexpected moment unprepared for His coming. Let's be mindful that the first time Jesus came, the world was not ready. They should have been. The prophets had marked out very clearly the signs for which the world should be watching. They said there would be a forerunner. There was. They identified him as a voice crying in the wilderness. That's exactly who John the Baptist was. They said the Messiah would be born in Bethlehem, He was; born of a virgin, He was; born of the line of David, He was. They said He would come to Galilee, He did. They said He would have great power, He had it. But the world still was not prepared and not ready. John writes, *"He came into the very world He created, but the world didn't recognize him. He came to His own people, and even they rejected Him"* (John 1:10-11).

Now, the lesson of the parable is very simple. It is not complex. The parable is meant to teach us that Jesus is coming. That He is coming to judge sinners and to reward the righteous. That He is coming in a sudden and unexpected moment and everyone should be prepared. And afterward, there will be no second chance. People may knock all they want, but the door will be shut. The day of opportunity will have come and gone forever.

The church has known for over 2,000 years that Christ is returning for His bride, and yet, many of us have become lethargic and derelict in our responsibility. Among too many of us, there is no longer an excited anticipation for the soon-return of our Lord and Savior. As a result, there is little effective witness being given that the Lord is returning.

The Master has called us to "be on the alert". We have no idea how much time remains – before we are with Him in heaven, or before He returns. Let us carry the cross that He has placed before us in a way that honors Him, that brings glory to Him and furthers His mission!

* * *

23

LET'S TALK ABOUT THE TALENTS

"Again, the Kingdom of Heaven can be illustrated by the story of a man going on a long trip. He called together his servants and entrusted his money to them while he was gone. He gave five bags of silver to one, two bags of silver to another, and one bag of silver to the last — dividing it in proportion to their abilities. He then left on his trip. The servant who received the five bags of silver began to invest the money and earned five more. The servant with two bags of silver also went to work and earned two more. But the servant who received the one bag of silver dug a hole in the ground and hid the master's money. After a long time, their master returned from his trip and called them to give an account of how they had used his money. The servant to whom he had entrusted the five bags of silver came forward with five more and said, 'Master, you gave me five bags of silver to invest, and I have earned five more.' The master was full of praise. 'Well done, my good and faithful servant. You have been faithful in handling this small amount, so now I will give you many more responsibilities. Let's celebrate together!' The servant who had received the two bags of silver came forward and said, 'Master, you gave me two bags of silver to invest, and I have earned two more.' The master said, 'Well done, my good and faithful servant. You have been faithful in handling this small amount, so now I will give you many more responsibilities. Let's celebrate together!' Then the servant with the one bag of silver came and said, 'Master, I knew you were a harsh man, harvesting crops you didn't plant and gathering crops you didn't cultivate. I was afraid I would lose your money, so I hid it in the earth. Look, here is your money back.' But the master replied, 'You wicked and lazy servant! If you knew I harvested crops I didn't plant and gathered crops I didn't cultivate, why didn't you deposit my money in the bank? At least I could have gotten some interest on it.' Then he ordered, 'Take the money from this servant, and give it to the one with the ten

bags of silver. To those who use well what they are given, even more will be given, and they will have an abundance. But from those who do nothing, even what little they have will be taken away. Now throw this useless servant into outer darkness, where there will be weeping and gnashing of teeth.'"
Matthew 25:14-30

* * *

The master did not apportion his talents equally to his servants. He gave more to some and less to others. But he entrusted them all. He was the determiner of what and how much would be given to each. He was a wise master. He knew their abilities. In many ways, he knew them better than they knew themselves. He knew that too much could overwhelm, and too little would undertax their ability. Thus, he entrusted each proportionate with their ability. And then he left – for a long time.

There were several risks that the master took in what he did. First, he entrusted others with a portion of his wealth. Jesus did not say whether it was all of his wealth or only a portion, but regardless, the master was putting at least a portion of his kingdom "at risk" by investing in his servants. He determined that his work and his kingdom would be best furthered through his servants. He didn't have to make that choice. He could have grown his kingdom in any way he chose – and as a successful master, he probably could have done so in an even more effective way. But he chose to grow his kingdom through his servants.

Second, since he entrusted each servant with differing amounts, he risked creating envy and/or pride between the servants, Those who received more could become prideful over the ones who received less, and those who received less could become envious of those who received more. The servants would not have fully comprehended the master's thinking or his plan as he divided the talents in the way that he did. Thus, his allocation could have created enmity among the servants, and the kingdom work could be hampered by any strife that ensued.

Third, the master was gone a long time. Without his physical presence, the servants were free to make their own choices. Would they be diligent today in the task the master had given them, or would they find more pleasurable or satisfying ways to expend their time? The servants knew there would be a reckoning, but as time passed, the temptation would become greater to focus on the pleasures of today and allow tomorrow to take care of itself. Perhaps doubt could even begin to creep in that the master wasn't really coming back.

Fourth, for one of the servants, fear of the master created a paralysis that led to faithlessness. This servant "bought the lie" that said, "what difference can my meager talent make?" He convinced himself that the other servants could do so much better and so much more, so he followed his fear and his faithless "self-talk" and buried his talent. [Forgive a quick side road: This kind of fear and self-talk is prevalent in Kingdom work today. You've heard the adage that 20% of the people do 80% of the work. Though this principle may not be the sole factor, it is definitely a contributing factor. God's people have belittled the talent with which the Master has entrusted them, have buried it and are not using it for the Kingdom. Thus, the work and mission of the Kingdom goes undermanned and under-funded in the midst of the plentiful resources the Master has provided.]

One day, probably when they least expected it, the master returned, and the day of accountability had arrived.

The faithful servants honored their master and wanted to please him by wisely investing the talents with which he had entrusted them. Though each returned a different amount, they were rewarded equally. It is a reminder that God is a rewarder of faithfulness. His reward is not proportionate to the quantity of our talents, it is proportionate to the faithfulness of our use of the talents. They began as servants, and they were promoted to rulers. They were faithful in the few, and the master entrusted them with much more, increasing their capacity for greater service and responsibility. They had labored and toiled, and now they entered into their reward.

The unfaithful servant disobeyed and dishonored his master by doing nothing. He robbed his master of that which was due him. His one talent could have brought an increase of another talent, bringing honor to his Master. But instead, he allowed his fear of failing to keep him from trying to succeed. His fear paralyzed him from acting, and he buried his talent. As a result, even that which he had was lost. He lost his opportunity to serve – not for trying and failing, but for failing to try. He gained no praise or reward from his master. He experienced a loss of intimacy with the one who had trusted him. That's outer darkness! It could be that he looked at his talent as too meager to be of any use, as compared to the amounts received by the other two. It is a reminder to us to never disparage the amount that the Master has given us. We have been appointed as a steward of the Master, and He will take whatever He has entrusted us with and multiply it for His glory, if we will be faithful stewards.

What will the Master say to us upon His return? Will we have labored faithfully and stewarded wisely? Paul wrote, "*...it is required of stewards that they be found faithful*" (1 Corinthians 4:2 ESV). The measure of our faithfulness will not be in the eyes of men, but rather, in the eyes of our Master. He knows what He has entrusted us with. He knows what constitutes the cross He has called us to carry. May He find us faithful with what He has entrusted us – faithful to the end. And on that day, may we hear Him say, "Well done My good and faithful servant. Enter into the joy of your Master!"

* * *

24

SHEEP AND GOATS

"But when the Son of Man comes in His glory, and all the angels with Him, then He will sit upon His glorious throne. All the nations will be gathered in His presence, and He will separate the people as a shepherd separates the sheep from the goats. He will place the sheep at His right hand and the goats at His left. Then the King will say to those on His right, 'Come, you who are blessed by My Father, inherit the Kingdom prepared for you from the creation of the world. For I was hungry, and you fed Me. I was thirsty, and you gave Me a drink. I was a stranger, and you invited Me into your home. I was naked, and you gave Me clothing. I was sick, and you cared for Me. I was in prison, and you visited Me.' Then these righteous ones will reply, 'Lord, when did we ever see You hungry and feed You? Or thirsty and give You something to drink? Or a stranger and show You hospitality? Or naked and give You clothing? When did we ever see You sick or in prison and visit You?' And the King will say, 'I tell you the truth, when you did it to one of the least of these My brothers and sisters, you were doing it to Me!' Then the King will turn to those on the left and say, 'Away with you, you cursed ones, into the eternal fire prepared for the devil and his demons. For I was hungry, and you didn't feed Me. I was thirsty, and you didn't give Me a drink. I was a stranger, and you didn't invite Me into your home. I was naked, and you didn't give Me clothing. I was sick and in prison, and you didn't visit Me.' Then they will reply, 'Lord, when did we ever see You hungry or thirsty or a stranger or naked or sick or in prison, and not help You?' And He will answer, 'I tell you the truth, when you refused to help the least of these My brothers and sisters, you were refusing to help Me.' And they will go away into eternal punishment, but the righteous will go into eternal life."

Matthew 25:31-46

* * *

When the Son of Man first came, He came in all humility to a modest stable. He was announced by a choir of angels, and laid in a feeding trough. But when He returns – He will return in all of His glory – accompanied no longer by a choir of angels, but by the entire angelic host. He will return – not as a baby – but as the Conquering King of Kings reigning on His glorious throne. When He first came, He was ignored by most, including those who knew the prophesies and should have been watching for Him. But this time when He returns, no one will miss His return – and it will be marked by awe and dread.

When the Son of Man returns, He will gather the "ethnos" – those who are alive from every language, tribe, people and nation. Every one will stand before His presence – those who followed, those who rejected, those who rejoice in His return, and those who now stand in fear – those who *"will go away into eternal punishment"* and those who *"will go into eternal life"*.

As the Good Shepherd, *"He will separate the people as a shepherd separates the sheep from the goats"*. In the first century, it would have been very common for a shepherd to be leading a flock which included both sheep and goats. The shepherds would divide them for feeding and for resting. They would move them together and then separate them. That was necessary because sheep and goats do not feed or rest well together. Sheep are for the most part docile, gentle, easily led and easily scared. Goats, on the other hand, are unruly, rambunctious, almost fearless and they create all kinds of problems for the sheep. Thus, the shepherd needed to separate them.

"He will place the sheep at His right hand and the goats at His left." Be mindful that the right hand is the hand of blessing, the hand of honor, and the hand of inheritance. When Jacob was asked by his son Joseph to bless his grandsons, Ephraim and Manasseh, he was very careful to make sure that his right hand was placed on the grandson that was to be blessed as the child of inheritance. If you remember, he crossed his hands in order to be sure that he placed his right hand on Ephraim (Genesis 49:8-20). And that's what you have here. The sheep represent the followers of Christ, those who are entering into the inheritance, and they are placed on the right hand.

. . .

As the King of kings, He says *"to those on His right, 'Come, you who are blessed by My Father, inherit the Kingdom prepared for you from the creation of the world."* We need to understand the importance of what Jesus is saying here. If we miss this, we could walk away thinking that the "sheep" enter into eternal life because of their good works. But nothing could be further from the truth! Jesus is saying that the sheep – the saints – are entering into the Kingdom because the Father has determined to bless them because they are a part of His family through their relationship with Christ, by grace through faith. Just as Jacob's grandsons were blessed by virtue of their relationship to their father, Jacob's son, we who are followers of Jesus are blessed by virtue of our relationship to the Father's Son. Further when He says, *"inherit the Kingdom prepared for you"*, He is emphasizing that salvation by faith is what brings us into the inheritance. The Kingdom was prepared for those who are followers of Christ. Our inheritance is not because of our works. Our works are evidence of our faith. What we do evidences what we are and Whose we are.

Jesus specifically mentioned six types of mercy ministry: those who hunger, those who are thirsty, those who are in need of hospitality, those who need clothing, those who are sick, and those who are imprisoned. We are to show mercy to Christians because we see Christ in them, and we are to show mercy to unbelievers because we want to see Christ in them. We help suffering believers because they bear the name of Christ. And we help suffering unbelievers in the hope that they will come to bear the name of Christ. The Kingdom is for people who minister to others in the name of Christ in that way – who meet a need...whatever that need might be. And in the first century culture that's what the needs were. People were hungry and had no food, they could be thirsty and need a drink. They could be strangers without a place to stay, ill clothed and needing proper clothing, sick and needing someone to come and attend to their sickness, or in prison and needing someone to come and visit them to find out why they were there and work to get them out. That's what they needed in that day. And those needs still exist in our day. But so do other needs, other hurts, other problems, and other anxieties. And Jesus is saying to us that we are to demonstrate to Him that we are people of the Kingdom chosen by the Father with the mandate to meet those needs. In fact, He says if you've done that, you've done it to Me. The Kingdom is for people who do that for Christ, reflecting genuine salvation.

As the Judge, Jesus turns to the "goats", those who are not His followers, and says, *"Away with you, you cursed ones, into the eternal fire prepared for the devil and his demons."* He says, "you never demonstrated the love of God which is the mark of the manifestation of My presence. You never revealed a changed life. You never showed love for your neighbor." He's not talking about the milk of human kindness and compassion, He's talking about the love of Christ. And if the love of Christ is not within me, i have none to give. Paul was writing to the believers in the church in Galatia, *"So then, as we have opportunity, let us do good to everyone..."* (Galatians 6:10).

And note that Jesus says that those cast away are sent *"into the eternal fire prepared for the devil and his demons."* Hell was created for Satan and his demons; it was not created for people. It was never God's desire that people should enter into hell. That outcome is solely the result of rejection of the free gift of salvation which has been extended by God's grace. And the lack of compassion and mercy that He is rebuking in this passage is a reflection of the lack of Christ's presence in their lives.

But many will cry out, "Now wait a minute. We prophesied in Your name. We cast out demons in Your name. We've done many wonderful works in Your name. Are You telling us, You don't know us?" (Matthew 7:22). And there are going to be lots of folks in that line saying, "Look at all the greatness, look at all the grandeur, look at all the splendor, look at all the wonders we did in Your name." But Jesus will say, "I don't know you."

Remember, it's not just about what we have done. He is talking about sins of omission, as well as sins of commission. Not doing good is the moral equivalent of doing evil. That was the case with the third servant who got one talent. It wasn't what he did, it was what he didn't do. The servant wasn't immoral, he just did nothing. He buried the talent and paid no attention to it. That is what caused him to be into outer darkness. Also, the five virgins weren't vile, they were just negligent. People will be cast into hell for what they didn't do. And what they didn't do was believe in the Lord Jesus Christ. It is the absence of righteousness. It is the absence of the love of God that comes through faith in Christ. It is the absence of those kinds of deeds that demonstrate righteousness and demonstrate God's love. It is the presence of the sin of unbelief, and the absence of faith. And the result is an eternity cast away and separated from God.

• • •

As we take up the cross and follow Jesus, let's be a people who are watchful for the opportunities the Master gives us to meet a need – to share a cup of cold water in His Name – to be a reflection of His love and His gospel, not only in word, but also in deed. That's why He has left us here with an assignment – an assignment to be His sheep – not goats!

* * *

25

THE MASTER TEACHES WHILE THE TEACHERS CONSPIRE

Every day Jesus went to the Temple to teach, and each evening He returned to spend the night on the Mount of Olives. The crowds gathered at the Temple early each morning to hear Him.

The Festival of Unleavened Bread, which is also called Passover, was approaching. The leading priests and teachers of religious law were plotting how to kill Jesus, but they were afraid of the people's reaction.

Luke 21:37 – 22:2

* * *

Jesus was back in the Temple teaching. The crowds were surrounding Him, hoping to catch a glimpse of another miracle, or hear Him speak truth with authority to the religious leaders, or to teach the Scriptures in a way they had never heard before. And the religious leaders watched Him from the shadows.

The Feasts of Passover (also known as the Festival of Unleavened Bread, which occurs in the March/April timeframe), Pentecost (also known as the Festival of Harvest, which occurs in the May/June timeframe) and Tabernacles (also known as the Festival of Shelters, which occurs in the September/October timeframe) were the three most important feasts for the Jews (Leviticus 23). According to the Law handed down through Moses, all Jewish males were expected to go to Jerusalem to appear before the Lord for these three "pilgrimage" feasts (Deuteronomy 16:16).

. . .

As we saw in a previous chapter, it is estimated that 2 million people made their pilgrimage to Jerusalem for Passover that particular year. Many had in fact come to see and hear Jesus, more than to observe the Passover. The crowd was excited to see Him. Large crowds gathered in Jerusalem always caused the Roman leaders to be anxious of possible uprisings, and this record "excited" crowd made them more so. Passover commemorates God's deliverance of the people of Israel from the bondage of Egypt. So there were strong political overtones to this particular festival that potentially made it an ideal time for a "would-be messiah" to attempt to overthrow Rome. That's why the Roman Governor Pontius Pilate and King Herod were both in Jerusalem that week, instead of in their mansions in Caesarea and Tiberius, respectively. They were in Jerusalem to help keep the peace.

You will recall that the very first Passover was in fact the night of the tenth plague that God brought upon Egypt due to Pharaoh's refusal to let His people go. On that fateful night, God had told the Israelites to sacrifice a spotless lamb, and stain the top and sides of their doorframes with its blood (Exodus 12:21-22). No one was to leave their home until morning. Then the Lord sent an angel of death to pass through the land and to strike down any firstborn son who was not in a home with blood on the doorframe. He would "pass over" the households that had blood on the doorframe (Exodus 12:23). The blood of the lamb is what saved the Israelites from death. It was not the Israelites' ancestry or good standing as God's people that saved them, it was the blood of the lamb. And through the blood of the lamb, God enabled the Israelites to be delivered from the bondage of slavery.

As the Jews prepared to commemorate their deliverance through the blood of a lamb, the Lamb of God sat there in their midst teaching from the Scripture. The people were blind to who He was, and unaware of what He was about to do. Don't forget, the cross did not "happen" to Jesus. The cross was an appointment for Jesus, not an accident. The cross had been determined even before time began. And there was Jesus, fully aware of what was about to unfold – calmly, clearly and courageously teaching the people the Truth of God.

The religious leaders had long seen Jesus as a threat to their power and had debated what should be done about Him. The people were blinded to who Jesus was to a great extent because their religious leaders refused to see Jesus for who He was. It wasn't so much that their eyes were blind as it was that their hearts were hardened. And His demonstration in the Temple a few days earlier was the "final straw" – He had now cast aspersion on their lucrative financial enterprise. They had already determined that He needed to die, the question was how they could pull it off. The crowds loved Jesus. More and more were coming to Him. Jesus was a threat, but if they inflamed the crowd by seizing Him, the tide would turn against them and they would be stripped of their power and their control. The religious leaders knew that they could not apprehend Jesus in the Temple in the midst of the crowds. So they withdrew to the house of Caiaphas, the high priest (Matthew 26:3-4), to ponder, debate and discuss their options among themselves. Surely there was a way to rid themselves of Jesus!

i am mindful that some of these very men in their younger days were more than likely among the leading priests and teachers that King Herod the Great had consulted to ascertain the birthplace of the Messiah (Matthew 2:4-5) thirty or so years earlier. Even then, though they were able to provide information for the wise men to locate Jesus, they were disinterested themselves from trying to locate Him. They showed no signs of a heart seeking after the promised Messiah. As a matter of fact, through the information they provided, they had assisted Herod in his attempt to kill the Messiah by having all the little boys under two years of age who lived in and around Bethlehem killed. And i am pretty confident that they had connected those dots somewhere along the line – between that baby boy born in Bethlehem and this same Jesus. Somehow, they had failed the first time. They were determined not to fail again!

What a contrast – the swirling hatred in their hearts as they connived and conspired to kill Jesus – and the calmness, gentleness and steadfastness of Jesus as He prepared to be crucified. It brings to mind the contrast between the fruit of the flesh and the fruit of the Spirit that Paul wrote about:

"When you follow the desires of your sinful nature, the results are very clear: sexual immorality, impurity, lustful pleasures, idolatry, sorcery, hostility, quarreling, jealousy, outbursts of anger, selfish ambition, dissension, division, envy, drunkenness, wild parties, and other sins like these. Let me tell you again, as I have before, that anyone living that sort of life will not inherit the Kingdom of God.
But the Holy Spirit produces this kind of fruit in our lives: love, joy, peace, patience, kindness, goodness, faithfulness, gentleness, and self-control. There is no law against these things!"

(Galatians 5:19-23).

The irony is that, as the religious leaders prepared to celebrate the holiest festival of their religious lives, they paid great attention to cleansing their homes but never gave a thought to cleansing their hearts. In the midst of a commemoration of the saving of firstborn sons, they were conspiring to kill a firstborn Son. And the very meal they were preparing to eat pointed to the very One they were preparing to kill.

As you take up the cross, walk in the fruit of His Spirit, walk in the steadfastness of His mission and keep your eyes on Him. Don't be concerned about what the enemy may be conspiring, rather, keep your ears and your heart attuned to what He is saying to you and what He is teaching you. He knows the plans He has for you.

* * *

26

WHEREVER THE GOSPEL IS PREACHED

Meanwhile, Jesus was in Bethany at the home of Simon, a man who had previously had leprosy. While He was eating, a woman came in with a beautiful alabaster jar of expensive perfume and poured it over His head. The disciples were indignant when they saw this. "What a waste!" they said. "It could have been sold for a high price and the money given to the poor." But Jesus, aware of this, replied, "Why criticize this woman for doing such a good thing to Me? You will always have the poor among you, but you will not always have Me. She has poured this perfume on Me to prepare My body for burial. I tell you the truth, wherever the Good News is preached throughout the world, this woman's deed will be remembered and discussed."

Matthew 26:6-13

* * *

Earlier in the week, while Jesus and His disciples were still spending their evenings in Bethany, Jesus was at the home of Simon. Simon previously had leprosy, and it is highly probable that he was healed by Jesus. It was through that miracle of healing that they probably became friends. In fact, he could have been the leper that Jesus healed as recorded in Matthew 8:1-4. This account in Matthew 26, combined with the parallel accounts in Mark 14:1-9 and John 12:1-8, would tend to indicate that Simon's home was also the home of Lazarus, Martha and Mary, which would tend to imply that Simon – the former leper – whom Jesus healed – is the one who John called Lazarus, the one who Jesus raised from the dead – John 11). That being true would mean that in many respects,

Simon/Lazarus had twice been dead to his sisters. The first time they were separated from him by leprosy. Lepers were forced to live in isolation away from everyone else in a "sentence" of death. And the second time, he had truly been dead and in the grave for four days.

So, on this night, Jesus and His disciples were hosted for dinner by the family – Simon/Lazarus (the host, reclining at the table – John 12:2), Martha (serving, as always – John 12:2), and Mary (again coming to the feet of Jesus – John 12:3). While Jesus, His disciples and His host were eating, Mary *"came in with a beautiful alabaster jar of expensive perfume and poured it over His head."* Then she proceeded to anoint *"Jesus' feet with it, wiping His feet with her hair"*, and *"the house was filled with the fragrance"* (John 12:3). If i am correct about Simon and Lazarus being the same person, i want you to think about the thanksgiving that was overflowing in the hearts of that family. They had a deep love for Jesus, and He had a deep love for them. He called them His "friends". Simon/Lazarus was expressing his thanksgiving by hosting and supping with his "Friend", enjoying intimate conversation and fellowship. Martha was expressing her thanksgiving through her love language – serving, and doing so with excellence.

Then, in walked Mary – expressing her thanksgiving, her love and her worship – by anointing Jesus' head and feet with expensive perfume. She was taking the same care that would typically have been reserved for a deceased loved one in preparation for burial. Only Jesus knew that, in fact, that was what Mary was doing. Not another person in that room – including Mary – knew that in just a matter of days Jesus' body would be buried in a tomb. Even when Jesus made that statement to the disciples, they did not yet understand. And here was Mary presenting worship to her Lord in the best way she knew how, overflowing with love and adoration. Later the apostle John would describe the vision of what worship will look like in heaven in the Book of Revelation. I would venture that this expression of worship by Mary was the closest he saw on this side of heaven to that heavenly vision.

And yet, in the midst of pure, authentic worship, the naysayers came out – criticizing her excess and her impropriety. Though their criticisms were couched in a "godly", "we-care-about-the-poor" way; they were actually godless. When Judas said – *"What a waste; it could have been sold for a high price and the money given to the poor"* – he was really revealing the condition of his cold heart. He revealed a heart that was unable to express true worship. On a quick side road – over the years, i have frequently heard church members expressing criticism of the way others worship – whether it be through the style of their music, expressions through the raising of hands, or the like. Regrettably, most often, the criticism has been more of a commentary of the critic's lack of heart for authentic worship. Mary was worshiping authentically with her whole heart.

Unfortunately, a number of the disciples were taken in by Judas' false piety and echoed his concerns. This needs to be a reminder to us to be discerning in all things before we lend our support. Take the question to Jesus first, before you join in. Listen to what He has to say about the matter, before you cast any aspersion. In this instance, they would have clearly heard Jesus calling out Judas for his errant thinking. As a matter of fact, Jesus went on to declare that little else from that evening would be remembered, but "*wherever the Good News is preached throughout the world, this woman's deed will be remembered and discussed.*"

Matthew has actually backtracked in his chronology to include this event at this point in his Gospel account. And i have inserted it out of order as well. The event actually occurred before Jesus' triumphal entry into Jerusalem. But Matthew inserted it here. At the same time, he is describing how the religious leaders are plotting how to execute Jesus. They fear a bad reaction from the crowd even more than they fear Jesus. So, they are having difficulty in coming up with an answer. What they needed was someone from within His inner circle that could help them with their plan.

On that night at the home of Simon/Lazarus, Judas became that man. Don't misunderstand me, Jesus had always known that Judas would betray him – but the Father's timing was just days away. This event and the rebuke from Jesus were all it took in Judas' heart to set his betrayal in motion. Even this pure expression of worship would be used by the Father to accomplish His plan of redemption.

As you take up the cross, remember these three lessons from the dinner that night:

- worship your Lord authentically, with a pure heart like Mary,

- take every word of criticism before the Lord to discern what is pure and what is true, before you act on it, and
- trust the Father with every detail. Nothing occurs in isolation – He is working all things together for His glory and our good!

Take it from the woman whose deed will be remembered wherever the Good News is preached!

* * *

27

THE TRAITOR'S CONSENT

Then Satan entered into Judas Iscariot, who was one of the twelve disciples, and he went to the leading priests and captains of the Temple guard to discuss the best way to betray Jesus to them. They were delighted, and they promised to give him money. So he agreed and began looking for an opportunity to betray Jesus, so they could arrest Him when the crowds weren't around.

Luke 22:3-6

* * *

Don't lose sight of the fact that Judas didn't set out on his journey to follow Jesus with betrayal on his mind. He followed Jesus because he truly believed that Jesus was the promised Messiah. He "believed" in Jesus. He was an "early adopter" and supporter, and he wanted to get in on the "ground floor" of Jesus' eventual rise to power. It is important to understand, at the outset, that Judas never envisioned that he would betray Jesus. Rather, Judas envisioned that he would be a part of His trusted circle – maybe not as close as Peter, James and John, but certainly close behind. After all, he was the keeper of the treasury for Jesus and the disciples. Judas believed that Jesus had seen his financial skills and abilities, and valued him as a member of His leadership team when the day arrived for His reign as King. Judas "trusted" that Jesus would enable him to be successful and achieve his desires of life – position, possessions and power. Therefore, in the short-term, he was willing to sacrifice all of those things. He was willing to wander the Judean wilderness with Jesus with the rest of the disciples. From his perspective, it was a good investment that would pay off in the end.

. . .

But as time went on and Judas witnessed one miracle after another, he was becoming impatient for the day that Jesus would declare Himself. At first, his impatience was subtle and subdued, but that night that Jesus allowed Mary to waste that expensive perfume and pour it over his head and feet, he couldn't contain his exasperation. If Jesus was going to rise to power, He needed to be more discerning in the best ways to utilize financial resources. He needed to call upon His trusty advisors – like Judas – to give Him counsel. He couldn't just leave it up to the riff-raff to make their own decisions. Those funds could have been invested much more wisely – and Judas could probably have done so in a way that also enabled him to derive some amount of personal gain for himself as well. But that would never happen if Jesus was going to allow things to occur in such an "unconstrained" way.

What's more, Jesus entered into Jerusalem with the people shouting His accolades in every corner of the city. This was the largest crowd that had ever been in Jerusalem at one time. Many, if not most, of them had come to see Jesus. If there was ever a time for Jesus to declare Himself, this was it! And yet, Jesus was showing no sign that He was moving in that direction, and Judas became more and more frustrated. At that moment, blinded by his own selfish ambition, he decided to take things into his own hands. Over the prior years, his ambition had been just the foothold that Satan needed to occupy Judas' thoughts, but his decision to "take things into his own hands" opened the door for Satan to take full control. And let's not forget – Satan is a crafty liar! We can only imagine the convincing "self-talk" that Satan was speaking into his ear to encourage him in his folly.

Judas had witnessed the failed attempts of the religious leaders to entrap Jesus. Time and again, he had seen Jesus outsmart them, out-maneuver them, and outwit them at every turn. The religious leaders were just the pawns that he required for his plan to force Jesus to show His hand. The leaders wanted to arrest Jesus, so if Judas could help them do that, Jesus would have to declare His authority and establish His Kingdom. That would be the game-changer – Jesus would be declared King – and Judas would finally achieve all that he had been working toward. And this was the time. This was the week! So off he went to find his "unlikely" allies, to convince them to go along with his plan.

. . .

As Jesus would later declare, *"Why didn't you arrest me in the Temple? I was there every day"* (Luke 22:53). But the religious leaders were afraid of the reaction of the crowd. They knew that they could not take action in the light. They knew that whatever they did, it had to be done clandestinely and in the cover of darkness. (Just a quick reminder for you and me: Satan never works in the light. Darkness is his greatest ally! As a matter of fact, Jesus said the night He was arrested, *"This is your moment, the time when the power of darkness reigns"* (Luke 22:53b).) So imagine the delight of the religious leaders when one of Jesus' own disciples approached them to discuss the best way for Jesus to be arrested. These unwitting allies all savored their own craftiness.

To seal the deal, the religious leaders agreed to pay Judas thirty pieces of silver. Lest we think Judas betrayed Jesus for the money, let's be clear. Thirty pieces of silver was NOT a lot of money. Hebrew culture did not place a high value on slaves – and in that day, the value of a slave was thirty pieces of silver (Exodus 21:32). Judas was too ambitious to have betrayed Jesus for such a paltry sum. And the religious leaders were too self-aggrandizing to stoop to paying a high bounty for One they disdained so greatly. The thirty pieces of silver was much like the "ten dollars and other good and valuable consideration" used in legal agreements today. It merely implied that both parties had entered into an agreement that was mutually advantageous. And the religious leaders and Judas saw this agreement as "mutually advantageous". So the promise was sealed – and all that remained was to now watch and wait for the right time.

But again, there is great irony even in that presumptuous statement – because the religious leaders and Judas NEVER controlled the timing. The timing always was in the Father's hands – and the religious leaders' and Judas' traitorous agreement was always a part of His all-knowing plan. So, you ask, did God cause Judas to betray Jesus? Did the Father place it in the hearts of the religious leaders to conspire against His own Son? The answer to both questions is a resounding "NO"! But God knew what was in their hearts. And He knew what was in the heart of Satan and his feeble attempt to destroy the Son. And He permitted them all to exercise their own free will in order to fulfill His redemptive plan. Please forgive my repetition in saying this, but the cross did not "happen to" Jesus. He and the Father love us so much that He was a willing participant. It was the Father's plan. The plan didn't hinge on Judas' choice to betray Jesus. The Father and the Son knew it was in his heart long before he did.

. . .

As you take up the cross, make sure you have emptied your heart of any selfish ambition. Because the cross He would have you carry – and anything and everything you may encounter by taking it – is not about you – it's all about God's redemptive and perfect plan for His glory!

* * *

28

JUST AS HE HAD TOLD THEM

Now the Festival of Unleavened Bread arrived, when the Passover lamb is sacrificed. Jesus sent Peter and John ahead and said, "Go and prepare the Passover meal, so we can eat it together." "Where do you want us to prepare it?" they asked Him. He replied, "As soon as you enter Jerusalem, a man carrying a pitcher of water will meet you. Follow him. At the house he enters, say to the owner, 'The Teacher asks: Where is the guest room where I can eat the Passover meal with My disciples?' He will take you upstairs to a large room that is already set up. That is where you should prepare our meal." They went off to the city and found everything just as Jesus had said, and they prepared the Passover meal there.

Luke 22:7-13

* * *

It was the fifth day of the week – Thursday – the 14th day of Nissan on the Hebrew calendar. The Passover Festival began at dusk with the Passover meal and continued for seven days, as it still does. In preparation for the festival, all leavening (or Chametz) was removed from the households of the Jews. Leaven symbolized corruption, or sin, thus, for the seven days of Passover, Jews were to only eat unleavened bread (Exodus 12:15). Often any Chametz remaining in the household the day before Passover was removed and destroyed by burning. That morning in Jerusalem the pungent odor of burning Chametz would have permeated the air in and around the city. Every household was completing their preparations.

. . .

The preparations were so important to Jesus that He sent His two most trusted disciples – Peter (the one upon whom He would build His church – Matthew 16:18) and John (the one to whom He would entrust the care of His mother – John 19:26-27). Notice that when Jesus instructed them to go and prepare the meal, they wisely asked Him for His specific instruction. Both of these men would have known what preparations were required under the Law. Both of them had traveled to Jerusalem many times before for the observance of Passover. Both of these men were leaders. It would have been very easy for them to receive instruction from Jesus to "go" and then head off to do what they believed would be the right thing to do. How often do we attempt to go off and do God's work in our way? How often do we fail to ask the Lord the "how" question? How often do we make our own plan and ask Jesus to bless it instead of asking Him His plan so we can join Him in His activity? Gratefully, Peter and John asked. And Jesus had all the details already worked out. i wonder how much time and energy Peter and John would have needlessly spent if they had failed to ask. As you take up the cross that Jesus has called you to carry, don't forget to continue to ask Him the "how" question. Peter may have had his shortcomings as the day progressed, but he started the day well by wisely asking Jesus "how".

Just as Jesus had arranged for the donkey and its colt to be available for His entry into the city at the beginning of the week, it appears that Jesus had made prior arrangements for the Passover meal. Apparently, the last time He was in Jerusalem for the Feast of Dedication in the winter (John 10:22), He had taken time to make these arrangements. Remember, the record crowd in Jerusalem would have made it very difficult to find a room in the city – but Jesus had already taken care of that detail. He had left nothing out of His planning, as reflected by the detailed instructions that He gave Peter and John. As they entered Jerusalem:

1. There would be a man waiting to meet them.
2. He would know who they were (in a crowd of two million no less!).
3. He would be carrying a pitcher of water so that he could be identified by them.
4. They were to follow him.
5. As he entered the house, they were to follow him in and speak to the owner.
6. They were to ask on behalf of the "Teacher" where the room was that they would be using for the meal.

7. The owner would take them to the room that had been reserved and was of sufficient size for all of them to gather.
8. It was there that Peter and John were to make preparations for the meal so that everything would be ready when Jesus and the other disciples arrived.

Bear in mind that Jesus knew He would be betrayed and arrested that night. He knew it that morning when He gave Peter and John these instructions, and He knew it back in the fall when He made these arrangements. He wasn't distracted by what was about to occur. To the contrary, His planning and preparation was complete to the most "minor" detail – because nothing in God's providential plan is minor! Don't lose sight that our God is God over all the details. There is nothing in our path – or in our lives – that escapes His notice – or that escapes His foreknowledge.

Imagine if you knew exactly what the stock market was going to do tomorrow. You could buy or sell today and tomorrow in a way that would maximize your financial gain because it would all be mapped out for you. You would know the exact time and manner to execute your strategy – and there would be no guessing involved – no matter how informed the guessing might be. Well, we serve a God and follow a Master who knows exactly what tomorrow holds – and His designs are much greater than anything that will happen in the stock market! He has a perfect plan and path for us – including the most minor detail, if we will but ask, heed and follow His plan!

The meal typically was conducted in a family home or, as pilgrims gathered in Jerusalem, in a room set aside for that purpose with a gathering of family members or friends. There would have been a table large enough for Jesus and His disciples to gather around. There would be pillows for everyone to be seated on the floor in a reclining position. The menu would have included an unleavened flatbread called "matzo", bitter herbs called "maror", dipping bowls of salt water, and red wine to drink (symbolizing the lamb's shed blood). The Gospel accounts do not reference other elements that may have also become a part of a Passover meal, so i will not include them here. It is however very possible that other elements were a part of their meal that night. Peter and John were charged with the responsibility to make sure that everything was in place, and they found everything as Jesus told them it would be.

. . .

The same Lord who directed the angel of death to "pass over" the homes whose door posts were stained with the blood of the lamb, and who directed the people through Moses to observe the Passover each year was now going to lead His disciples through one last remembrance. And the Lamb of God made certain that every detail was in place – just as He had told them.

As you take up the cross to follow Him, everything will be ready – every detail that is needed will be in place – to accomplish His plan and purpose. Trust Him and heed His word – just as He has told you.

* * *

29

THE HOUR HAS COME

When the hour had come, He reclined at the table, and the apostles with Him.
Luke 22:14 (NASB)

* * *

God's timing is perfect. He is eternal. He is not constrained by such things as time or space. He created it all. Time is as much His creation as we are. He can turn it backward, as we see recorded in 2 Kings 20:9-11. He could have just as easily turned it forward, as we see in the same passage. He can make time stand still, as we see recorded in Joshua 10:12-13. He does everything according to His own timing. He chose to create heaven and earth, and all of its inhabitants within six days. He put the rotation of the earth, the sun and the moon in motion to create through each rotation a day in time. He determined that each orbit of the earth around the sun would equate to one year with four seasons. He created time, as He did all of His creation, for His purpose and to bring Him glory. And nothing and no one can frustrate His plan, His purpose, or His timing.

God created man, and from him woman, to worship Him. He created them as man and woman in order to procreate and multiply into a multitude of people who would worship Him. And He knew, even before creating that first man and woman, and choosing to give them a free will, that they would sin against Him. Therefore He also knew before He created them – and before He created time – that He would need to make a way for His creation to be redeemed. As a result, everything – including time – was created by Him with His plan in mind.

The apostle Paul writes, *"But when the fullness of the time came, God sent forth His Son..."* (Galatians 4:4 NASB). The "fullness of time" means the timing was as it should be. There are many who have tried to answer the question as to why Jesus came to earth as a baby at the moment He did. Some have pointed to the unification of the world under Roman rule. Prior to the Romans, the Greeks had set the stage with a common trade language. Others have pointed to the growing existence of even pagan worship that emphasized the need for blood sacrifice. But the problem with all of that is that it is man's feeble attempt to understand God's wisdom. The reality is that only God knows the reason for why that time was His perfect time for the Son to be born, and it was! God ordered every millisecond leading up to it, and He ordered every moment from His birth to this moment in the upper room. Repeatedly throughout the Gospels, we have seen the religious leaders making feeble attempts to arrest Jesus or stone Him, and He just disappeared before their eyes. And what was the reason that Jesus continued to give? His hour had not yet come (John 7:30). And, by the way, God has ordered every millisecond leading up to Jesus' return as well. And as Jesus said, *"no one knows the day or hour when these things will happen, not even the angels in heaven or the Son Himself. Only the Father knows"* (Matthew 24:36). But on that night in the upper room at the beginning of Passover, the hour had come.

Hold onto this truth about time and timing. We have a tendency to grow impatient as we "wait" on God for answers to our prayers. We like to place deadlines on God – those we deem to be real based upon influences outside of our control, as well as deadlines that we sometimes contrive to "test" God. Remember He controls the timing – and He knows His purpose for His "seeming" delay. He will accomplish His purpose in His time. Here is what God Himself has said, as recorded by the prophet Isaiah:

"I am God, and there is none like me. Only I can tell you the future before it even happens. Everything I plan will come to pass, for I do whatever I wish" (Isaiah 46:9-10).

And He will do so according to His perfect timing!

Jesus was reclining at the table. This was the moment of peace and calm before the storm. It is very similar to the night Jesus was sleeping in the boat in the midst of the storm. Jesus knew all that was about to unfold, and yet there He reclined. You and i would have been at the very least anxious, if not outright panicked. But as the Son of God, He knew that nothing was about to occur that was not in accordance with the Father's plan. And as the Son of Man, He knew that the next almost-twenty-four-hours were going to require tremendous physical strength and endurance. So He availed Himself to the rest that the Father now provided.

Grasp this truth! In the midst of your journey, as you take up the cross, there will be moments of rest in the midst of, or in preparation for, great activity. Don't rest when you are to be active, and don't be active when you are to be resting. But avail yourself to the time of rest that the Father has provided. Unlike Jesus, we don't know what is ahead – but the Father does – and He is providing this time to renew your strength to endure.

That brings us to what i believe is the most important truth of this particular verse. His apostles were there surrounding Him. He was in their midst. They were enjoying the intimacy of His presence. At the most critical twenty-four-hour period in human history – and most likely heavenly history – Jesus was right there with His own. And He was preparing to pour into them, nurture them and encourage them. He knew of what they had need. He knew that the very foundation of their belief in Him was about to be shaken. He knew the tragedy and despair they would experience. But He also knew the victory they would witness and experience on the other side of their pain. So He was going to spend every moment He possibly could with them to enable them to walk through the hours ahead.

We need to take confidence in the reality that no matter what lies ahead, the Master is right there with us. And He will not leave us or forsake us – not ever! He knows the victory on the other side of the pain. i don't know what the hour may be for you, or for me. It will look different for each one of us. But i do know that as we follow Him, an hour will come when we are to enter into something in our path that He has permitted for His purpose and His glory. In that hour, trust Him in the timing, rest in the intimacy of His presence and know that He is walking with you every step of the way!

* * *

30

YOU WILL NEVER EVER WASH MY FEET

Jesus knew that the Father had given Him authority over everything and that He had come from God and would return to God. So He got up from the table, took off His robe, wrapped a towel around His waist, and poured water into a basin. Then He began to wash the disciples' feet, drying them with the towel He had around Him. When Jesus came to Simon Peter, Peter said to Him, "Lord, are You going to wash my feet?" Jesus replied, "You don't understand now what I am doing, but someday you will." "No," Peter protested, "You will never ever wash my feet!" Jesus replied, "Unless I wash you, you won't belong to Me." Simon Peter exclaimed, "Then wash my hands and head as well, Lord, not just my feet!" Jesus replied, "A person who has bathed all over does not need to wash, except for the feet, to be entirely clean. And you disciples are clean, but not all of you." For Jesus knew who would betray Him. That is what He meant when He said, "Not all of you are clean." After washing their feet, He put on His robe again and sat down and asked, "Do you understand what I was doing? You call Me 'Teacher' and 'Lord,' and you are right, because that's what I am. And since I, your Lord and Teacher, have washed your feet, you ought to wash each other's feet. I have given you an example to follow. Do as I have done to you. I tell you the truth, slaves are not greater than their master. Nor is the messenger more important than the one who sends the message. Now that you know these things, God will bless you for doing them.

John 13:3-17

* * *

There is absolutely no one who has ever walked on this earth who has had more authority, more majesty and more adoration due Him than Jesus Christ. Every ruler who has ever lived, the most wealthy, the most powerful, and the most famous all fall short of His glory and His authority. The Father had sent Him, and He would return to the Father.

i grew up in Palm Beach County, Florida. It has been said that the island of Palm Beach is home to ten percent of America's wealth. It is the island of the rich and famous. Our current U. S. President has a home there. Whenever he is in town, traffic is rerouted on land, sea and air. i would not even venture to guess how many people are in his entourage and service to make sure his every need is met, and every comfort is provided. i don't say that critically of the President, nor do i disparage in any way the other residents of the town and the way they are served. i mention them solely as a point of comparison. Jesus, who has authority over every one of them – and every one of us – and is worthy of all praise, all worship, all respect, and all reverence, got up from the table, took off His robe and wrapped a towel around His waist like a servant. There are a very few of us who would ever do that – and none of us are the King of Kings.

But this wasn't the first or the last time that our Lord gave no regard to His divine privilege. The apostle Paul writes:

"Though He was God, He did not think of equality with God as something to cling to. Instead, He gave up His divine privileges; He took the humble position of a slave and was born as a human being. When He appeared in human form, He humbled himself in obedience to God and died a criminal's death on a cross" (Philippians 2:6-8).

Then Jesus kneeled before each of His disciples, washed their dirty feet, and dried them with the towel He was wearing around His waist. Let that picture sink in! His humility. His selflessness. And He is the Almighty God. Now – think about whose feet He is washing. One of the men will vehemently deny that he even knows Him before the night is out. One of them will doubt that He could possibly have resurrected from the grave, in just a few short days. And if that's not enough, one of them will betray Him and provide the means for Him to be arrested that very night. And all of those who remain, except one, will scatter when He is arrested and will not follow Him to the cross. There is not a lot that is praiseworthy about these men over the next few days. These are Jesus' closest friends – and all but one will abandon Him. And yet, Jesus, who knew everything that would transpire, and knew everything about them, washed their feet.

Scripture only records how Peter reacted. We don't know what the others said or did, if anything. I can't help but wonder what was going through the mind of Judas as Jesus was washing his feet. Or Thomas, the skeptic. Or John, the beloved. (It's interesting to me that John did not include any personal commentary about the experience.)

But we do know what Peter did. "All or nothing Peter" never hesitates to be the first one to speak up (until later that night) and he is always the one jumping in with both feet. When he sees what Jesus is about to do to him, he protests – *"You will never ever wash my feet!"* Peter probably had the clearest understanding of who Jesus was (which made his denial later that night even more devastating for him). So, to him, to have the Son of God abase Himself to such a degree would have been so inappropriate. Rather, he was probably thinking, *"Lord, I need to wash Your feet. And I'm embarrassed that I didn't even think of it!"* But then when Jesus tells him, *"Unless I wash you, you won't belong to Me"*, in true Peter-form He says, "Then Lord, wash all of me!"

After Jesus had washed all of their feet, He put His robe back on and returned to His place reclining at the table. As their Almighty God, He washed their feet. As their Lord and Teacher, He used the experience to teach them an important Kingdom principle. He is the Master; they – and we – are the slaves. He is the King; they – and we – are the messengers. As He has done, we are to do likewise. If He served, we are to serve. If He abased Himself for the sake of the Kingdom, we are to abase ourselves for the sake of the Kingdom. If He gave all for us, we are to give all for Him.

i would expect that if Jesus walked up to any one of us right now and knelt down to wash our feet, our response may be very similar to Peter – "Oh no Jesus, You will never ever wash my feet." But would that response be driven, like Peter, by our understanding of His Majesty, or would it be driven by our unwillingness to wash the feet of others. Who has the Master placed before you to wash their feet? It may be literal, or it may be to minister to a difficult need. As He has done, we are to do likewise. And just like Jesus told the disciples that night, *"Now that you know these things, you must do them. And the Father will bless you for doing them."* But allow me to add a caution. Don't do them in order to receive a blessing. Do them because our Master and Teacher did. Do them because our Almighty God did. Do them because it is Him who we take up the cross to follow!

* * *

31

THE PASSOVER SUPPER

Jesus said, "I have been very eager to eat this Passover meal with you before My suffering begins. For I tell you now that I won't eat this meal again until its meaning is fulfilled in the Kingdom of God." Then He took a cup of wine and gave thanks to God for it. Then He said, "Take this and share it among yourselves. For I will not drink wine again until the Kingdom of God has come." He took some bread and gave thanks to God for it. Then He broke it in pieces and gave it to the disciples, saying, "This is My body, which is given for you. Do this in remembrance of Me." After supper He took another cup of wine and said, "This cup is the new covenant between God and His people—an agreement confirmed with My blood, which is poured out as a sacrifice for you."
Luke 22:15-20

* * *

Luke records that Jesus was "very eager" to eat this Passover meal with His disciples. But Luke doesn't record whether or not the disciples were "eager" to eat this meal with Jesus. Obviously, Jesus had a perspective that the disciples did not. Jesus knew the suffering He was about to endure. He knew that the very meaning of the meal did not only look back to "that night" in Egypt when the angel of death "passed over" and the covenant that God had made with His chosen people, but from this moment on, the meal of remembrance would now be looking forward to the fulfillment of God's Kingdom under the new covenant.

What were the disciples thinking as they gathered around that table?

Were some of them caught up in the tradition of the Passover meal without much thought about its deeper meaning? Were they going through the motions on "autopilot" as they walked through the very familiar components of the meal? Were some of them still processing what Jesus had just done in washing their feet? Were they so preoccupied with their thoughts that they really weren't considering the deeper meaning of what Jesus was telling them at the moment? Or were some – specifically Judas Iscariot – thinking only about what he was about to do – and considering how he might inconspicuously slip out of the room?

The Passover meal incorporated significant traditional elements, reflecting God's covenant with His chosen people, and we have no reason to believe that Jesus would not have incorporated them into their evening:

- First, the supper would have begun with a prayer of thanksgiving for God's deliverance through the Exodus from Egypt and the heritage He had given to His chosen people.
- Next, they would have eaten raw vegetables dipped in salt water, as a reminder of the tears of gratitude shed by their enslaved ancestors.
- Then they would have broken bread – the "matzah" – an unleavened bread symbolizing the haste and urgency with which the people exited from Egypt (not having the time to allow the bread to rise).
- They would have eaten "maror" – the bitter herb – as a reminder of the bitterness of the slavery endured by their ancestors.
- They would have reclined at the table during the meal as a reminder that they were a free people, and no longer standing as servants or slaves in bondage.
- They would have eaten roasted meat, probably roast lamb, as a reminder of the lamb that was sacrificed for their deliverance.
- Throughout the evening four cups of wine would have been passed, each cup traditionally representing the specific promises of God in Exodus 6:6-8 under the old covenant, which were respectively:
- I will free you from slavery (the first cup at the start of the meal),
- I will redeem you (the second cup during the meal),
- I will be your God and you will be My people (the third cup of redemption after the meal), and
- I will bring you into the land I have promised (the final cup at the conclusion of the meal).

But on that night Jesus unveiled the new covenant between God and all people.

First, Jesus shared that He would *"not drink wine again until the Kingdom of God has come."* Under the old covenant, the lamb was shed for the deliverance of God's chosen people. But under the new covenant, Jesus as the Passover Lamb was to be slain to ransom people from every language, tribe and nation. When He says, "the Kingdom of God has come", He is speaking of that time upon His return when the multitudes of all peoples are reached and gathered, and His Kingdom is established.

Second, He presented the bread as His body which would be given freely – not taken – and broken as the ransom for all people. The Father had sent Him as the Lamb of God to be offered as the once and for all sacrifice for the forgiveness of sin.

Third, as He presented the final cup, He said, *"This cup is the new covenant between God and His people—an agreement confirmed with My blood, which is poured out as a sacrifice for you."* In essence that new covenant, as opposed to the old covenant above, is:

Through My blood which is poured out, I make the way so that

- All people can be freed from the slavery of sin,
- All people can be redeemed from the consequence of sin,
- All people can be restored into a relationship with their God and they will be His people, and
- All people can enter into the Kingdom of God.

And in so doing, Jesus instituted His Supper of Remembrance that we might gather to remember what He has done and the covenant He has made through the breaking of His body and the shedding of His blood. The apostle Paul would later write:

"On the night when He was betrayed, the Lord Jesus took some bread and gave thanks to God for it. Then He broke it in pieces and said, "This is My body, which is given for you. Do this in remembrance of Me." In the same way, He took the

cup of wine after supper, saying, "This cup is the new covenant between God and His people — an agreement confirmed with My blood. Do this in remembrance of Me as often as you drink it." For every time you eat this bread and drink this cup, you are announcing the Lord's death until He comes again"
(1 Corinthians 11:23-26).

As we gather to do so, we are to do so in remembrance of Him. So, as you take up the cross to follow Him, what are you thinking about as you gather around that table? Are you possibly distracted like the disciples were? Are you caught up in the tradition of the Lord's Supper without giving much thought to its meaning? Are you going through the motions on "autopilot" as you partake of the elements of the Supper? Are you preoccupied with thoughts on other matters, and not considering the meaning of what Jesus has done? Or, like Judas Iscariot, are you thinking about other things you need to do? Do not ever allow your observance of the Lord's Supper to become routine or perfunctory. We have an advantage that the disciples did not have that night. The disciples did not know what was about to unfold, but we do know the price that Jesus paid. Remember the covenant that was made between the Almighty God and you through the broken body and shed blood of our Savior. Do so in remembrance of Him!

* * *

32

A BETRAYAL AND A DENIAL FORETOLD

Now Jesus was deeply troubled, and He exclaimed, "I tell you the truth, one of you will betray Me!" The disciples looked at each other, wondering whom He could mean. The disciple Jesus loved was sitting next to Jesus at the table. Simon Peter motioned to him to ask, "Who's He talking about?" So that disciple leaned over to Jesus and asked, "Lord, who is it?" Jesus responded, "It is the one to whom I give the bread I dip in the bowl." And when He had dipped it, He gave it to Judas, son of Simon Iscariot. When Judas had eaten the bread, Satan entered into him. Then Jesus told him, "Hurry and do what you're going to do." None of the others at the table knew what Jesus meant. Since Judas was their treasurer, some thought Jesus was telling him to go and pay for the food or to give some money to the poor. So Judas left at once, going out into the night. As soon as Judas left the room, Jesus said, "The time has come for the Son of Man to enter into His glory, and God will be glorified because of Him. And since God receives glory because of the Son, He will give His own glory to the Son, and He will do so at once. Dear children, I will be with you only a little longer. And as I told the Jewish leaders, you will search for Me, but you can't come where I am going. So now I am giving you a new commandment: Love each other. Just as I have loved you, you should love each other. Your love for one another will prove to the world that you are My disciples." Simon Peter asked, "Lord, where are you going?" And Jesus replied, "You can't go with Me now, but you will follow Me later." "But why can't I come now, Lord?" he asked. "I'm ready to die for you." Jesus answered, "Die for Me? I tell you the truth, Peter — before the rooster crows tomorrow morning, you will deny three times that you even know Me."

John 13:21-38

* * *

As we have said multiple times, the events unfolding that night were not happening "to" Jesus. This plan of redemption had been set forth by the Father before the beginning of time. Jesus had always known what was going to occur. Jesus knew when He called Judas Iscariot to follow Him, that he would betray Him. For there to be a cross, there needed to be an arrest. For there to be an arrest, there needed to be a betrayal. For there to be a betrayal, there needed to be a betrayer. Judas did not betray Jesus because God put it in his heart. Satan put it in his heart. But God knew Satan would do it, and God knew Judas would make that choice.

But for all of that foreknowledge, Judas' action still caused Jesus to be deeply troubled. i don't believe, at that moment, that He was troubled about the betrayal; i believe He was troubled about Judas. Jesus loved Judas. Jesus had walked together with all of His disciples for over three years. They had walked together intimately. They laughed together. They cried together. Jesus poured His life into each of those men – even Judas. Yes, He knew that Judas was about to betray Him. But He also knew that, soon after, Judas would hang himself. And most importantly, He knew that Judas would spend eternity in the torment of hell. As Peter would later write, the Lord *"does not want anyone to be destroyed, but wants everyone to repent"* (2 Peter 3:9). "Everyone" includes Judas. In spite of what Judas was preparing to do, Jesus never "gave up" on him, or stopped loving him. That was Judas' choice, not Jesus' choice. Jesus extended His love, even when it was not returned. As we take up the cross, we are to do the same.

Four other observations regarding this passage: First, notice that Jesus treated Judas as the guest of honor. It would have been the custom for the host of a special feast to take a piece of bread, dip it in sauce and present it to the guest of honor. Jesus was not giving the piece of bread to Judas solely to signify to John who the traitor was. He was extending honor and grace to Judas even up to the last moment. Jesus extended His grace, even when it was not returned. As we take up the cross, we are to do the same.

Second, by turning away from his Lord, Judas opened his heart to Satan. It is a reminder to each of us that there is no place of neutrality. If we do not turn to Jesus, we are, in fact, turning to Satan. There is no middle ground. Just ask Judas. As we take up the cross, let's make sure that our heart remains turned toward Jesus.

. . .

Third, when Jesus declared to the disciples that one of them would betray Him, John records that *"the disciples looked at each other, wondering whom He could mean."* But what is telling is that apparently only Peter and John took the initiative to ask Jesus who the traitor was. That would indicate that each one thought it might be the other, or each one thought it might be himself. But apparently, except for John and perhaps Peter, no one suspected Judas when he got up to leave. So, each of the other disciples apparently believed that any one of them was capable of betraying their Lord, including himself. That needs to be a sobering reminder to each one of us. Those who at that time had the most intimate relationship with the Savior did not see themselves as being incapable of betraying Him. Before we rush to passing judgement on Judas, we too need to take a thorough examination of our own hearts, lest we fall into the same pit. Each and every one of us is capable of betraying our Savior by our word, our action or our inaction. Don't think that you're beyond betraying Jesus. It has been said that we are all one step away from stupid! And stupid is a character issue; it is not a knowledge issue. It is only by His grace and by the power of His Holy Spirit that we can possibly remain faithful to the end. Don't take that for granted. The disciples knew they were vulnerable, and so are we. As we take up the cross, let's make sure that we walk circumspectly.

And lastly, at the end of this passage, we have a very practical example of this same truth. Jesus tells Peter that he will deny Him before the night is out. This comes on the heels of Peter declaring that He will follow Jesus anywhere – even to death. Peter believed he was incapable of such a thing. After all, he is Peter, the one on whom Jesus said He would build His church. He's Peter, the leader of the other disciples. He's Peter, the first to boldly declare Jesus to be the Christ, the Son of the Living God. He's Peter, one of Jesus' most intimate followers and friends. And he's Peter, the one who before the sun rises would do exactly what Jesus told him – he would betray his Lord.

Take heart that we have a resource that the disciples did not have that night. If you are a follower of Christ, His Holy Spirit lives within you to empower you to walk according to His Spirit, evidencing His character – His love, His grace and His righteousness. As you take up the cross, make sure you stay close to Jesus, filled with His Spirit.

* * *

33

WHO IS GREATEST?

Then they began to argue among themselves about who would be the greatest among them. Jesus told them, "In this world the kings and great men lord it over their people, yet they are called 'friends of the people.' But among you it will be different. Those who are the greatest among you should take the lowest rank, and the leader should be like a servant. Who is more important, the one who sits at the table or the one who serves? The one who sits at the table, of course. But not here! For I am among you as one who serves. You have stayed with Me in My time of trial. And just as My Father has granted Me a Kingdom, I now grant you the right to eat and drink at My table in My Kingdom. And you will sit on thrones, judging the twelve tribes of Israel."

Luke 22:24-30

* * *

Jesus had just washed their feet. He had just declared that one of them was going to betray Him. And yet, all the disciples could seemingly think about was their position in the Kingdom. This wasn't the first time. It had occurred several times before (Mark 9:33-37 and Luke 9:46-48). Even the mother of James and John had asked the question to Jesus (Matthew 20:20-28). But no matter how many times Jesus answered them, they kept coming back to the same question.

Now bear in mind, they had all given up their homes and their careers to follow Jesus. By this time, they truly believed Jesus was the Messiah, and that He would come into His Kingdom. And they wanted to know –

"what's in it for me?" We have served faithfully. Aren't we assured positions of honor in the Kingdom?

Perhaps the discussion arose as they were discussing which disciple was going to betray Jesus. Or perhaps it arose as they discussed the seating arrangements around the table. Jesus had just given Judas the piece of bread dipped in sauce that was befitting the guest of honor. Then Jesus had apparently sent him off on an important mission. Perhaps Judas would have the greatest position in the Kingdom. Whatever prompted the discussion, it ensued.

There actually is an appropriate context for this discussion that Jesus would bring them back to toward the end of this passage. But the way the discussion started was just flat out soulish! It was framed in the way the world would look at position, instead of a Kingdom point of view. Jesus again brought them back to the reality that in the Kingdom, *"those who are the greatest among you should take the lowest rank, and the leader should be like a servant."* Notice that He said, *"like a servant"*. That indicates that we are not just to serve, but we are to serve in the posture of humility of a servant and with the selflessness of a servant. Instead of the greatest being "the big man" sitting in the seat of honor, it is the servant humbly serving all those in the room. Jesus was again totally redefining "greatness". He wasn't telling them not to be great – or – that they wouldn't have positions of greatness in the Kingdom, He was redefining what that meant!

In the day of the apostles, as well as in our day (because it has not changed), greatness is defined by position, power, influence, wealth and recognition. It is an elevation of self. It is an "all about me" focus and goal. It's the game of Monopoly, and whoever has the most wealth at the end of the game wins. But Jesus was telling them that self, or selfish ambition, is the enemy of servanthood. It is the exact opposite of greatness in the Kingdom.

Jesus said, *"I am among you as one who serves."* He is our model. He who deserved the greatest that the world possibly could have offered, served. He who was worthy of all accolades and honor was a servant of all. He who was worthy of all comfort and adoration, endured trials and aspersions for the sake of the gospel, and served. He who endured loneliness and being misunderstood – all for the sake of the gospel – served. He who gave even His own life for us – and for the sake of the gospel – served. He who is the greatest in the Kingdom is the Servant of all, and he or she who would be honored in the Kingdom must likewise be a servant of all.

It's interesting that Jesus did not rebuke them regarding the question of position in the Kingdom. He only rebuked them for their worldly perspective. In spite of their weaknesses and failures, Jesus extended grace and affirmed them for having stayed with Him until the end (though they didn't realize the "end" had come). Jesus knew that He was entrusting these remaining eleven disciples with the "keys of the Kingdom". He was entrusting them with His mandate and commission to make disciples of all peoples. They were to be bridges through whom His Holy Spirit would work to draw all peoples unto Himself. They had a significant role in the Kingdom. And just as the master had entrusted his servants with talents to invest for the sake of the master's business, Jesus was entrusting these men with "talents" to be invested for the sake of the Kingdom. He assured them here that – just like the returning master had said to his faithful servants – if they were faithful with what He entrusted to them, they would receive positions of honor in the Kingdom. As a matter of fact, He told the apostles that they would *"eat and drink at My table in My Kingdom. And you will sit on thrones, judging the twelve tribes of Israel."*

We, too, have been entrusted with the "keys of the Kingdom". We, too, have been commissioned to make disciples of all peoples. We are to be His ambassadors of reconciliation (2 Corinthians 5:20) – the bridges through whom His Holy Spirit works, as He draws peoples unto Himself. And when Jesus returns there will be an accounting that we will need to make to Him, of what we have done with that which He has entrusted us.

Let me hasten to add at this point, lest there be any confusion, we are not earning our "place" in heaven. Our place in heaven has been extended to us through the grace of God, sealed by the shed blood of the Son of God, and has been received by faith through the forgiveness of God. There is nothing we can do to merit or earn our place in heaven, We do however "earn" our "position" in heaven. We will be rewarded for faithful stewardship of the time, talent and treasures with which God has entrusted us for His Kingdom purpose. Our motivation is not the "position" we will receive. Our motivation is out of love for our Master, and a God-given desire to honor Him and obey Him. It is our expression of worship unto Him. And yes, just like the master in the parable, He will reward His faithful servants.

. . .

So, the question for us as we take up the cross and follow Jesus is not, "Who will be the greatest in the Kingdom?" The question for us in this hour must be, "How can i be the greatest He has called me to be for His Kingdom?" Oswald Chambers put it another way – "How can I be My Utmost For His Highest?" And that will only occur if we follow Him as faithful servants of the Servant.

* * *

34

A NEW COMMANDMENT

Dear children, I will be with you only a little longer. And as I told the Jewish leaders, you will search for Me, but you can't come where I am going. So now I am giving you a new commandment: Love each other. Just as I have loved you, you should love each other. Your love for one another will prove to the world that you are My disciples."
John 13:33-35

* * *

As we will see over the next eight chapters of this book, God used John in his Gospel to reveal in detail all of what Jesus taught His disciples that night just before He was betrayed (John 13 – 16). Remember, the Gospel of John is not primarily a chronological account of Jesus' life and ministry here on earth. The focus of the Gospel of John is the deity of Christ and the glory of God as revealed through the Son. So, he takes his time to walk us through the rich teachings of Jesus on the very last night He was with His disciples before He went to the cross. The teachings of that night fall into the category of "last words", those truths He wanted His disciples to remember if they forgot everything else. So, pull up close, and let's not miss a word. Jesus said, "I am going…" and *"you can't come where I am going"* – at least for now. *"So now I am giving you a new commandment…."*

"…Love each other." They had already heard Jesus say, earlier in the week, that the greatest commandment is to *"love the Lord your God with all your*

heart, all your soul, and all your mind", and the second greatest is to *"love your neighbor as yourself"* (Matthew 22:37-39). Now He says that He is giving them a new commandment to *"love each other."* Love God. Love Your neighbor. Love each other. Why did Jesus feel it was important to add that third statement? Isn't loving each other a part of loving your neighbor? Earlier in His ministry, His mother Mary and His half-brothers had come looking for Jesus, and He said, looking at His disciples gathered around Him, *"whoever does the will of God, he is My brother and sister and mother"* (Mark 3:35 NASB). Jesus was communicating that His followers were not only family to Him, but also to one another. So that when He said, "love God, love your neighbor and love each other", He was saying, "yes, love your neighbor, and make sure you don't leave out loving your family of brothers and sisters in Me." Jesus knew that sometimes we can be more loving and giving to our neighbors around us than we are to our immediate family beside us. He knew that sometimes we can be loving neighbors and still be a feuding family. Sometimes we can be more forgiving of others than we can be of immediate family members – whether it be our nuclear family or our family in Christ. i will confess that some of my greatest disappointments and some of my greatest hurts have occurred at the hands of church family members. Too often new church plants are a result of church splits instead of good mission strategy. And those splits have most often occurred within church families that forgot – or failed to – love each other.

Tertullian was a theologian in the early church (A.D. 155 – A.D. 240). He wrote that the Roman government was disturbed by the early church. So, they sent spies to infiltrate and observe worship gatherings. They came back to their Roman leaders with a report that was something like this: "These Christians are very strange people. They speak of One by the name of Jesus, who is absent, but who they expect to return soon. And my, look at how they love one another, and are ready to die for each other." Jesus said, *"There is no greater love than to lay down one's life for one's friends"* (John 15:13). And the early church took Him seriously. We are to love each other!

"...Like I have loved you." The apostle Paul writes, *"Love is patient and kind. Love is not jealous or boastful or proud or rude. It does not demand its own way. It is not irritable, and it keeps no record of being wronged. It does not rejoice about injustice but rejoices whenever the truth wins out. Love never gives up, never loses faith, is always hopeful, and endures through every circumstance"* (1 Corinthians 13:4-7). Paul was writing to a church. He was describing the love of Christ – and the love that they – and we – are to have for one

another. It is a love that is selfless. It is a love that is unconditional. It is a love that doesn't give up.

And, it is a love that "*...proves that you are My disciples.*" It's interesting that Jesus didn't say that it would be their doctrine that proved that they were His disciples. He didn't even say it would be their service or their mission that distinguished them as being His disciples – though in reality, love for one another will in fact drive our service and our mission. He didn't say it would be the eloquence of their speech. He didn't say it would be the orderliness or beauty of their worship experiences. He said it would be their – our – love for one another. So, we have got to ask the question: Do we love each other in a way that proves we are followers and disciples of Jesus? The "proof" is in our love – or lack thereof. As those not within the body of Christ encounter us, are they overwhelmed, like those Roman spies were, by our love for one another? Or do they witness division, criticism, gossip or enmity?

Why was Jesus giving a "new commandment"? Because He was birthing something new. He was birthing His church. He was instructing the apostles who would be the first shepherds of His church. He was instructing those to whom He was giving the assignment to go forth and make disciples. But before He talked about how they were to do that, He told them that they had to love each other. Before He told them to baptize new believers, He told them that they had to love each other. Before He went to the cross and expressed His ultimate love for them – and for us – He told them to follow His lead and love each other. Before they – or us – could take up the cross and follow Him, there must be a love – His love – for one another.

i am convinced that if we truly would be followers of Jesus and be people who take up the cross and follow Him, then everything He is calling us to be and to do can be encapsulated in these simple truths:

Love God. Love our neighbors. Love each other.

* * *

35

A WORD OF COMFORT

"Don't let your hearts be troubled. Trust in God, and trust also in Me. There is more than enough room in My Father's home. If this were not so, would I have told you that I am going to prepare a place for you? When everything is ready, I will come and get you, so that you will always be with Me where I am. And you know the way to where I am going." "No, we don't know, Lord," Thomas said. "We have no idea where You are going, so how can we know the way?" Jesus told him, "I am the way, the truth, and the life. No one can come to the Father except through Me."

John 14:1-6

* * *

Jesus and the disciples were still in that upper room. He had just told them He must leave them, and that they could not come with Him – at least for now. Remember, they had no idea what was going to happen later that night. There was still a part of them that was waiting for Jesus to declare Himself as the Messiah and establish His Kingdom. A few minutes earlier, He had told them that one of them was going to betray Him and now He has said that He's going away. To put it mildly, they were troubled. They couldn't understand what was happening. None of this looked anything like the way they thought their time with Jesus would end. They had been thinking about positions in the Kingdom – and now Jesus was telling them that He was leaving. Do you hear their confusion and anxiety?

. . .

Thus, Jesus spoke words of comfort and encouragement to them. *"Don't let your hearts be troubled. Trust in God, and trust also in Me."* Jesus was saying, "You know Me. You know Me better than anyone else knows Me. You know I am trustworthy. You know that the Father sent Me. And you know You can trust Him as well. So, whatever happens, don't be troubled. The Father and I have this. And We are worthy of your trust!"

"Besides, where I am going there is more than enough room for each one of you. I am going to make the way for your arrival. I am going to make preparations for you. If I don't go, you won't be able to follow. But if I go, then, after everything is ready, I will be able to come and get you when the time is right. Then, from then on, we will always be together. You will be where I am. I will be where you are. We will never again be separated. And you know where that is. It's the Father's house. And you know the way!" Jesus was speaking words of assurance. He was speaking truth that they could hold onto in the midst of tumultuous times.

This passage is often quoted during funeral services. The loss of a loved one is a tumultuous time. We're grieving the loss of one who has gone. We are experiencing sorrow, knowing we will not see them again on this side of eternity. We miss them. We ache for them. The certainty that their life brought to ours is gone. We can no longer call upon him or her for advice, for counsel, for encouragement, or for comfort. Our life has just been turned upside down. And in the midst of all that hurt, upheaval and uncertainty, we need an anchor. We need a truth we can hold onto. We need someone or something that we can hold onto with complete confidence and trust. So it was at that moment with the disciples.

At that point, Thomas spoke up. He may have been the one speaking, but i would venture that his question was also on the minds of others in that room. Remember, they were troubled and uncertain. They were seeking certainty. They were seeking truth they could understand, and truth they could hold on to. And i am so glad he asked. Because he asked, we know the answer!

Thomas said, "Lord, we really don't know where You are going. We have no idea! We've never been there. We've never seen it. (Remember, Thomas was one who needed to see in order to believe!) So how can we possibly know the way?

. . .

Jesus, in essence, replied, "Thomas, you know the way. You know the way because you know Me – and I am the way! Whatever confusion you experience, whatever trouble you encounter, whatever sorrow or pain you are walking through – I am the way! My way leads through all the mess, all the pain and all the confusion. My way leads to the Father's house. My way leads to the place where there is no pain and there is no suffering. My way leads to that place where we will forever and always be together."

"Thomas, I am THE Way. I am not a way; I am the only way. Don't be duped into trying another way, or make the mistake of trying to follow your own way. I am the only way. Only My way leads to the Father's house. Other ways may seem right in your own human thinking, but those ways will take you where you don't want to go. Like you said, you've never seen the Father's house. But I have! You don't know the way there. But I do! And I'm the only one that does. Trust Me, Thomas – and all – I am THE WAY!"

"And Thomas, I am THE TRUTH! I am not a truth. My word is absolute. My word is without error. My truth does not change based upon season or whim. It is not situational. It is not relative. It is absolute! You will never know the truth of any situation, or trial, or circumstance until you hear from Me. I existed before the beginning of time. My truth has been the same from before the beginning, and will remain beyond the end of time. My truth is ageless. My truth is matchless. And my truth is beyond reproach. If you need an answer, I am the One to ask. I am the only One to ask! Trust Me, Thomas – and all – I am THE TRUTH!"

"Lastly, Thomas, I am THE LIFE! In Me, through Me and by Me have all things been created. All life comes from Me. Tomorrow on a cross and in three days from now when I step forth out of that tomb, I will carry the keys to death and hell. I will have conquered death once and for all. I am the Creator of life and the Defeater of death. Through Me – and Me alone – you can experience life – abundant life – life to the max! Only through Me can you escape the chains of sin and death. Only through Me can you experience unfettered life. I am the only One who can make that promise. Trust Me, Thomas – and all – I am THE LIFE!"

"And no one comes to the Father except through Me!" I and the Father are one. If you have seen Me, you have seen the Father. For this is how the

Father loved the world, He gave His one and only Son, so that everyone who believes in Him will not perish but have eternal life." There is no plan "B". I am the only way to the Father.

"Trust Me, Thomas – and all – as you take up the cross to follow Me, I alone am the Way. I alone am the Truth. I alone am the Life. Follow Me."

* * *

36

A WORD OF ONENESS

"If you had really known Me, you would know who My Father is. From now on, you do know Him and have seen Him!" Philip said, "Lord, show us the Father, and we will be satisfied." Jesus replied, "Have I been with you all this time, Philip, and yet you still don't know who I am? Anyone who has seen Me has seen the Father! So why are you asking Me to show Him to you? Don't you believe that I am in the Father and the Father is in Me? The words I speak are not My own, but My Father who lives in Me does His work through Me. Just believe that I am in the Father and the Father is in Me. Or at least believe because of the work you have seen Me do. I tell you the truth, anyone who believes in Me will do the same works I have done, and even greater works, because I am going to be with the Father. You can ask for anything in My name, and I will do it, so that the Son can bring glory to the Father. Yes, ask Me for anything in My name, and I will do it! If you love Me, obey My commandments."

John 14:7-15

* * *

Don't lose sight of the fact that the focus of John's Gospel is that we would see, discover and know Jesus as the Son of the Living God. John desired that we see Jesus in the fullness of His glory as God incarnate. Jesus' desire for His disciples – and for us – is that each of us would see the glory of the Father and come to know the Father through Him. He's just told the disciples that He is going to His Father's house to make a way for them – and us – to join Him. So, He seizes this moment to remind them that if they REALLY know Him, they know the Father.

. . .

Throughout the Gospels, Philip was bringing people to Jesus. As soon as Jesus had found him (John 1:43), he had immediately gone off to find Nathanael and bring him to Jesus (John 1:45). And he had been bringing people ever since, including the Greek pilgrims who were seeking Jesus earlier that week (John 12:20-22). So, Philip responds to Jesus with a heartfelt desire and ambition to see the Father. He says, "Lord, you don't need to take us to Him. We KNOW that You are His Son. Simply show Him to us, so we can get a glimpse of Him like Moses did, and we will be satisfied." Just like the Greeks had said to him, "We would see Jesus", he is now saying to Jesus, "We would see the Father!" And just like the Greeks knew that Philip could help them to see Jesus, Philip knew that Jesus was able to show him the Father.

Can you think of a greater desire than "we would see the Father"? Each of us have worthy goals, but can you think of a higher goal than the desire to see the glory of God! i don't believe that Jesus' response to him was one of consternation. i believe He was now patiently helping Philip – and that entire group – truly begin to understand that, in seeing Jesus, they had seen the Father.

The Merriam-Webster dictionary defines "oneness" as being "the quality or state or fact of being one: such as singleness, integrity, wholeness, harmony, sameness, identity, unity and union." Jesus would have Philip and all the disciples – and us – know that He and the Father are One – in every aspect of that definition of oneness. Jesus would have us all know that He and the Father are One in appearance. "If you've seen Me, you've seen the Father." "Everything that I am, and everything that I do is a reflection of the Father."

"*The words I speak are not My own.*" The Father and the Son can never say anything that is contrary to one another. The Son only speaks the words of the Father. And that Word endures. It is true. It is honest. It is certain. It is without error. The very Word of the Father became flesh in the Person of His Son (John 1:14) and that very Word is unfailing love and faithfulness. If we have heard the Son, we have heard the Father.

"*My Father who lives in Me does His work through Me.*" Every miracle and every action, including Christ's crucifixion and resurrection, were according to the Father's plan and the Father's timetable. Each act and action were a work of the Father through the Son, and a work of the Son in the Father – for the two of Them are One – in appearance, in word, and in work.

But then Jesus went on to say, *"anyone who believes in Me will do the same works I have done, and even greater works."* Those who believe in the Son are one with Him. When He says, "believes", He's not talking about mere mental assent. He's not simply describing some intellectual exercise; He is talking about a belief that involves our whole heart, soul and mind. It is a surrendering of our life to Him in the way that the apostle Paul describes as:

"I have been crucified with Christ; and it is no longer I who live, but Christ lives in me; and the life which I now live in the flesh I live by faith in the Son of God, who loved me and gave Himself up for me"
(Galatians 2:20 NASB).

We are one with Him in the work. We are no longer focused in our work, rather, we are focused in joining Him in His work – responding to His activity and His invitation. In so doing, we are able to see Him accomplishing *"even greater works"*, because it is the work of His Holy Spirit in us and through us. Again, as Paul writes:

"The Spirit of God, who raised Jesus from the dead, lives in you. And just as God raised Christ Jesus from the dead, He will give life to your mortal bodies by this same Spirit living within you"
(Romans 8:11).

And we are one with Him in bringing glory to the Father through prayer. He said, *"You can ask for anything in My name, and I will do it, so that the Son can bring glory to the Father. Yes, ask Me for anything in My name, and I will do it!"* Even if we don't know what to pray, His Holy Spirit within us will guide us in prayer:

"...the Holy Spirit helps us in our weakness. For example, we don't know what God wants us to pray for. But the Holy Spirit prays for us with groanings that cannot be expressed in words. And the Father who knows all hearts knows what the Spirit is saying, for the Spirit pleads for us believers in harmony with God's own will"
(Romans 8:26-27).

We are joined together with Him in prayer as one – His Holy Spirit within us and the Son of God sitting on the right hand of the Father interceding for us.

And lastly, we are one with Him in love through obedience. Jesus said, "*If you love Me, obey My commandments.*" As we saw in the last chapter, the world around us will know we are His disciples by the love we have for each other. And the world will also know we are His disciples because we obey Him. Don't misunderstand – we're not His because we obey Him, rather, we obey Him because we are His. Our obedience is simply an expression of love – it's not an expression of law. Our son's wife refers to us as her mother and father – in love – not, in law. It is a reminder to all of us that our bond comes through love, not through law. Thus, it is with Jesus. We are one with Him through our obedience because it expresses our love for Him – in light of the fact that He first loved us – with a love that included the cross.

That night in the upper room, Jesus wanted them to fully understand His oneness with the Father, and their oneness with Him. And today, at this moment, as we take up the cross and follow Him, He would have us fully understand as well.

* * *

37

THE HELPER IS COMING

"And I will ask the Father, and He will give you another Advocate, who will never leave you. He is the Holy Spirit, who leads into all truth. The world cannot receive Him, because it isn't looking for Him and doesn't recognize Him. But you know Him, because He lives with you now and later will be in you. No, I will not abandon you as orphans.... When the Father sends the Advocate as My representative — that is, the Holy Spirit — He will teach you everything and will remind you of everything I have told you. I am leaving you with a gift — peace of mind and heart. And the peace I give is a gift the world cannot give. So don't be troubled or afraid. Remember what I told you: I am going away, but I will come back to you again.... Come, let's be going."

John 14:16-31

* * *

Throughout the Gospels, we see the weakness and foibles of the disciples. We see them cry out in fear even when Jesus is in their midst. We see them doubt Jesus. We see them deny Jesus. We see them scatter in fear. We see them easily distracted from the mission of Jesus. We see them argue with one another. We see petty rivalries break out between them. We see them blinded by their own emotion. We see them make bone-headed mistakes. They are really a lot like us, aren't they? But the thing that we need to remember is that throughout the time of the Gospels – until Acts 2:4 – they were not equipped in the way that we are (if we are followers of Jesus). Oh sure, they walked with Jesus. They knew Him intimately. They were eye-witnesses to the miracles He performed. They heard His teaching first hand – and what's more, He would often further explain His teachings privately to them. And yet, they were lacking one very important gift. Though the Holy Spirit had been at work in the world, He was not in them. They had the benefit of the teaching of Jesus, and the application of Jesus, but they did not have the benefit of the empowerment of the Holy Spirit dwelling within them.

i have often thought that, though the Sermon on the Mount (Matthew 5 – 7) was the greatest and most beautiful sermon ever preached, apart from the salvation of Jesus and the empowerment of the Holy Spirit, it is the greatest indictment against us all. Because, apart from His saving grace and the filling of His Spirit, there is no way we can walk in the truths of that message. We don't have it within us. And neither did the disciples… until the Day of Pentecost!

But, on this night, in the upper room, before they left to go to the Garden of Gethsemane on the Mount of Olives, Jesus made them a promise. He told them that, though He was going away, the Father would send another – an Advocate (NLT) – a Comforter (KJV) – a Helper (NASB) – a Counselor (HCSB) – the Holy Spirit (CEV). And once He came to dwell within them, He would never leave them. Jesus needed to leave them to sit at the right hand of the Father. But until He returns, the Father would send One who would not go away. He would be with them and in them – and with us and in us – 24/7. His role was – and is – to lead them – and us – in all truth. The Spirit of God would have the capacity to speak to them – and us – through the Word of God with such clarity and accuracy that they – and we – would know the Truth of God. His role was – and is – to be a guide in all truth.

Jesus said, *"The world cannot receive Him, because it isn't looking for Him and doesn't recognize Him."* The world cannot receive Him because first they must believe in Jesus Christ as Savior and Lord. Until that occurs, the world isn't even looking for Him, because He can only be seen through spiritual eyes. And it doesn't recognize Him because He can only be seen and worshiped in spirit and truth. The Holy Spirit is the Teacher to lead us and guide us into truth. Without Him, the Bible is a book of history and a book of facts. Without Him, we will stutter and trip and fall just like the disciples even did that night.

And Jesus assured them that they would know Him, *"because He lives with you now and later will be in you."* The Spirit could not be in them then, because Jesus needed to return to the Father before His Spirit could come to dwell within them. It is through the indwelling of the Spirit of Christ that the character of Christ – the fruit of the Spirit of Christ – love, joy, peace, patience, kindness, goodness, faithfulness, gentleness, self-control (Galatians 5:22-23) – can be made manifest within us and through us. It is the indwelling Spirit of Christ who takes the Word of God to thoroughly prepare and equip us for every good work (2 Timothy 3:16-17).

Jesus promised that He would not *"abandon* {them} *as orphans"* – without comfort, without help, without an advocate. They would not be left to their own devices or their own defenses. They would not be left with the task that Jesus was giving them without the Resource required to carry it out. They would not be left to find their own way. They would not be left powerless against Satan and the ways of the world. The Father would send the Advocate as the Son's Representative. And He will teach them – and us – all things, reminding them – and us – of all things that Jesus has taught.

Then Jesus gave them the gift of peace. By peace, He meant so much more than just the absence of war or distress. He meant wholeness, completeness, joy, contentment. In the world, peace is something that is hoped for or worked for, but for the follower of Christ, peace is a gift of God received by faith. In the world, peace is enjoyed in the absence of trouble, but in the life of a follower of Christ, peace is experienced in spite of trouble. It is the peace that Jesus modeled as He slept in the boat in the midst of the storm. It is the peace that He modeled even that night in the upper room knowing He would be arrested, beaten and crucified all within the next 18 – 24 hours. He then reminded them that, though He was going away, He would come back again. But now it was time for them to be going.

That same reminder is given to us. Jesus has given us that gift of peace – peace that is not dependent on our circumstances, but peace that can overshadow our circumstances and give us comfort and hope. Peace that can even sleep in the midst of a storm. And He gave it not only as a promise, He sealed the promise by sending His Spirit. Jesus is coming back! But in the meantime, as you take up the cross, walk in the fullness of His Spirit. He still has more for you to do. And until He returns, walk in His perfect peace. *"Come, let's be going."*

* * *

38

A WALK THROUGH A VINEYARD

"I am the true grapevine, and My Father is the gardener. He cuts off every branch of Mine that doesn't produce fruit, and He prunes the branches that do bear fruit so they will produce even more. You have already been pruned and purified by the message I have given you. Remain in Me, and I will remain in you. For a branch cannot produce fruit if it is severed from the vine, and you cannot be fruitful unless you remain in Me. Yes, I am the vine; you are the branches. Those who remain in Me, and I in them, will produce much fruit. For apart from Me you can do nothing. Anyone who does not remain in Me is thrown away like a useless branch and withers. Such branches are gathered into a pile to be burned. But if you remain in Me and My words remain in you, you may ask for anything you want, and it will be granted! When you produce much fruit, you are My true disciples. This brings great glory to My Father."
John 15:1-8

* * *

Jesus and the disciples were now headed from the upper room to the Garden of Gethsemane. More than likely, they were walking through a vineyard in the Kidron Valley. It would have been a full moon, so they would have been able to clearly see all that was around them. So, Jesus used the vineyard as an illustration of a foundational truth.

As i write this, i am reminded of a trek that i and a few friends made through a city in China. Some of the members of our group were from the US, and some lived in that city. Our Chinese friends were giving us a guided tour of some of their favorite sites. Along the way, we stopped at an art shop that had beautiful, colorful sketches hanging on the walls. And most of the sketches included a wise saying that was also penned on the canvas. We came upon one that was a beautiful drawing of a grapevine with clusters of grapes. i asked one of our friends to translate the words that were inscribed beside the drawing. She read, *"I am the Vine, you are the branches; he who abides in Me and I in him, bears much fruit, but without Me you can do nothing."* She was speaking the exact same words that Jesus said to His disciples in that vineyard that night. She was reading this important truth – the essence of what Jesus wanted His disciples to remember in the hours, days and years to follow. He wanted them to remember who He was, who they were and what their purpose was.

A number of us in the group had heard that verse before. But some of our friends were reading that verse for the very first time. They wanted to know where the saying came from and who said it. Having never read it before, or seen a Bible, or studied about Jesus, they proceeded to tell the rest of us that this saying was about a relationship between two people – one was the vine and the other was the branch. They perceived that the branch's purpose was in the vine and that apart from the vine, the branch was incapable of doing anything! Our friends clearly understood the truth of what Jesus was saying – the very first time they ever heard it! The owner of the shop had been quietly listening in the background. Having heard our friends' comments, she pulled out her Bible, and together we had the opportunity to show our friends where the saying was written. Later, having given each of our friends a Bible, we encouraged them to read more about Jesus – who He is and what He has said. But, as i said, folks, they got it – the first time – they understood this simple truth that Jesus is the Vine, and as His followers, we are the branches. All our friends needed to know now was, who this Jesus is.

That night in the vineyard, the disciples knew who Jesus was. You and i know who Jesus is. The question is, do we truly understand the truth He was sharing? Like our Chinese friends said, it is all about a relationship between two people – each one of us, in a relationship with the Person of Jesus Christ. He is the VINE. It is in Him and through Him that all we need for life and nourishment flows. It is through Him that we have life – life that is abundant and fruitful. We are the BRANCHES. Jesus has made the way for us to be grafted into His Vine – by accepting Him and trusting Him to be our Savior and LORD. The branch apart from the vine is dead, and so are we if we are apart from Him. Our branch is drying up and decaying. But through Jesus' death, burial and resurrection, He made the way for us to have life – to be grafted into the Vine and, through Him, to have everlasting, abundant life.

And Jesus, right at the beginning, told His disciples that this was the Father's plan. The Father is the VINEDRESSER. He sent the Vine, He prepared the way for the branches to be grafted and He even selected the branches – so that through the branches, the Vine could produce fruit. Fruit that remains – inner fruit and outward fruit. Fruit that is full and sweet. And the Vinedresser tenderly cares for His branches so that they produce the fullest crop possible. When the branches fall into the dirt, the Vinedresser doesn't throw them away or abandon them. He lifts them up and cleans them off and helps them to flourish again so that they can bear fruit. So it is with you and i. God didn't graft us onto the Vine so that we might grow and become beautiful branches. He grafted us onto the Vine so that through us He can bear fruit. And the Vinedresser lovingly does in our lives all that He needs to do to maximize the crop.

As we understand our relationship (as the branch) to Jesus (the Vine) and to the Father (the Vinedresser), there are three principles that our LORD would teach us regarding the work He is doing through all of our lives, in order to bear fruit that is full and sweet.

First, if your life consistently bears no fruit, God will intervene to discipline you. Branches that are covered in dirt won't bear fruit. Air and light can't get in. The branch sags. No fruit develops. Our sin is just like that dirt. It prevents the Light of God's Word from shining in and through our lives. It keeps us from getting the nourishment we need. It causes our lives to "sag". But, because God loves us and desires His best for us, and desires to cleanse us and free us from sin so that we can live a more abundant life for His glory, He disciplines us. Not to punish us, but to move us from barrenness toward fruitfulness. Allow God's discipline to train you and cleanse you; not only to escape sin but also to grow you in maturity. Allow Him through His discipline to take you not just from minus ten to zero but from minus ten to plus ten. Don't resist His discipline; respond to it – and in so doing allow Him to take you to a new level of fruitfulness.

Second, if your life bears some fruit, God will intervene to prune you so that you bear more fruit. The Father's strategy for coaxing a greater harvest out of His branches is not the one we would prefer. His plan is to prune, which means to thin, to reduce or to cut-off. The Vinedresser's secret for more ... is less. In the process of pruning, He will cut away immature commitments and lesser priorities to make room for more growth. The vinedresser removes the growth that is preventing the sun from reaching into the area where fruit should form. So it is with the Father. He will prune away the areas of our lives that are preventing the S-O-N from reaching in and producing fruit.

We so easily get caught up in appearances – how we look and what we have. We're more concerned with how we as branches look. But the branch's purpose isn't to look good, or even feel good. The branch's purpose is to bear fruit. Our Father, the Vinedresser, will prune away anything that is keeping us from bearing more fruit. Pruning is about our values and our personal identity. When Jesus told His friends what it would cost to follow Him, many turned back. Yet the impact of those who didn't turn back is still shaking the world. His artful pruning is not just "taking away"; He is faithfully "making room" to add strength, productivity and spiritual power in our lives, so that through our lives, He can shake the world.

Lastly, God does not want us to do more for Him, He wants us to be more with Him. He is inviting us to abide more deeply in Him. Abiding isn't a suggestion, it's a command! Abiding doesn't come naturally, it's a choice and an action that we must take. It means placing our complete trust and faith in Him. It means seeking, longing for, thirsting for, waiting for, seeing, knowing, loving, hearing and responding to ... His Person. Abiding is the connection to the Vine. It is the place through which all of the life nutrients flow and the fruit is produced. The amount of fruit isn't dependent on the size of the branch, it is dependent on the size of the connection – and what flows from the vine through the branch as a result of the connection. And the harvest that results brings great joy – and great glory – to the Vinedresser.

Yes, our Chinese friends were right on target. It comes down to a relationship with a person – the Person of the Vine – Jesus! As you take up the cross, don't only FOLLOW Him, make sure you ABIDE in Him.

* * *

39

HE CALLS US FRIENDS

"I have loved you even as the Father has loved Me. Remain in My love. When you obey My commandments, you remain in My love, just as I obey My Father's commandments and remain in His love. I have told you these things so that you will be filled with My joy. Yes, your joy will overflow! This is My commandment: Love each other in the same way I have loved you. There is no greater love than to lay down one's life for one's friends. You are My friends if you do what I command. I no longer call you slaves, because a master doesn't confide in his slaves. Now you are My friends, since I have told you everything the Father told Me. You didn't choose Me. I chose you. I appointed you to go and produce lasting fruit, so that the Father will give you whatever you ask for, using My name.... If the world hates you, remember that it hated Me first. The world would love you as one of its own if you belonged to it, but you are no longer part of the world. I chose you to come out of the world, so it hates you. Do you remember what I told you? 'A slave is not greater than the master.' Since they persecuted Me, naturally they will persecute you.... They will do all this to you because of Me, for they have rejected the One who sent Me. They would not be guilty if I had not come and spoken to them. But now they have no excuse for their sin. Anyone who hates Me also hates My Father. If I hadn't done such miraculous signs among them that no one else could do, they would not be guilty. But as it is, they have seen everything I did, yet they still hate Me and My Father. This fulfills what is written in their Scriptures: 'They hated Me without cause.'"

John 15:9-25

* * *

Jesus and the disciples were still en route to the Garden of Gethsemane. As they walked, Jesus declared to them that they were His friends. Yes, He was still their Master, but they were no longer slaves. They were His friends.

When God was setting in motion His plan to raise up a chosen people through whom He would bring glory to His Name, He sought out a friend. And that friend was Abraham (2 Chronicles 20:7; Isaiah 41:8; James 2:23). God chose Abraham and appointed him (Genesis 12:1). He wasn't God's friend on his own merits. Abraham was a liar and a deceiver (Genesis 12:18-19; Genesis 20:2). He was a sinner, chosen solely by God's grace. But God confided in him and told him His plan (Genesis 12:2-3). God chose to save Abraham's nephew Lot, and his family, simply because His friend Abraham asked Him to do so (Genesis 18:22-33). God chose a friend through whom He would bless "all the families of the earth" (Genesis 12:3).

God was now preparing to do a new work. He was preparing to enter into a new covenant through which all the peoples of the earth would be blessed. It would not be a covenant of Law sealed through the shed blood of sacrificial lambs, it would be a covenant of Grace sealed through the shed blood of the Sacrificial Lamb – His one and only Son. Thus, God had again chosen friends through whom He would carry out this new work. These were friends with whom He had confided. These were friends who He had chosen – one by one. These were friends into whom He had poured His life. These were friends for whom He was about to die. These were friends to whom He had just promised to send a Helper.

Abraham did not choose to be God's friend; God chose Abraham. The disciples did not choose to be Jesus' friends; Jesus chose them. He appointed them to go and produce fruit. He appointed them to go and make disciples. He appointed them to go and spread the Good News.

Did you ever wonder why God needed a chosen people to declare His glory to the nations? Why did He need Abraham to be the friend through whom He raised up a chosen people? He is God. He could have chosen a much more efficient way to make His Name known and declare His glory to the nations. But for some reason He chose to use a people who became more known for their grumbling, complaining and stiff-necked ways than for their faithfulness to God. There were some bright lights in the bunch –

Moses, Joseph, David, Daniel, Isaiah, Hosea – but even these men had times in their lives when they fell short of the glory of God. And yet, that was the Father's plan. They were the people through whom He would send His Son.

But Jesus had now come. So why did God still need a people – a new people, if you will – to declare His gospel to the nations? Why did He need this "ragtag" bunch of uneducated men to be His friends to further His plan? Jesus could have returned from the grave, declared Himself the Messiah, immediately established His Kingdom on earth and reigned from then forevermore. He could have presented His majesty and declared His truth far more effectively and eloquently than this fraternity of fishermen, tax collectors and sinners. Well, at least they had spent three years under His teaching. Therefore, they had some qualification for Him to call them "friends".

But His pronouncement of them as friends didn't stop with those eleven men. Notice He prefaced His statement by saying, *"You are My friends if you do what I command."* Then He went on to say, *"This is My commandment: Love each other in the same way I have loved you."* That means that if we do what He has commanded, we, too, are His friends. If we love each other in the same way He has loved us, we are His friends. As we abide in His Word, He has told us *"everything the Father told {Him}"*, and therefore He calls us friends – not by our choosing, but by His. And as His friends, He has chosen us to be a people through whom He makes His Name known. We are His friends for His purpose. He is building His Kingdom according to His design, and He has chosen us to be a part of that work as His friends.

Jesus went on to tell the apostles two important truths that they needed to know if they were going to continue as His friends – and those truths apply to us as His friends as well. First, He said, *"I appointed you to go and produce lasting fruit, so that the Father will give you whatever you ask for, using My name."* As we continue in the Master's mission of producing fruit, we must be fully reliant on the Father – just as Jesus was. Therefore, if we would be about His task in His way, we must continually be bringing the work before Him. We must know what the Father would have us do. In order to know, we must continually be asking Him. And Jesus has promised that whatever we ask according to His will, in His Name, the Father will grant. We can walk confidently knowing that, just as the Father ordered the steps of the Son, He will order our steps, and He will provide everything that is needed to accomplish His plan and His activity to bear fruit. As a "friend" of Jesus, the Father will provide us with all that is needed, so we can walk with a bold confidence.

The second truth, however, is not quite as reassuring. He promised that if we follow Him as His friends the world will hate us. The world hated Jesus, so it only makes sense that the world will hate us as well. The world rejected Jesus and hated Him "without cause". Jesus said, *"The world would love you as one of its own if you belonged to it, but you are no longer part of the world. I chose you to come out of the world, so it hates you. Do you remember what I told you? 'A slave is not greater than the master.' Since they persecuted Me, naturally they will persecute you…."* No one wants to be hated. But the reality is that if we are not being hated by the world, the world is not seeing us as friends and followers of Jesus. If they hated the Master, they will hate His followers. But let's be careful to make sure that if we are experiencing the hatred of the world, it is because we are faithfully following Jesus and NOT just being obnoxious sinners. i fear that too much of the "hatred" being directed toward Christians today is not due to our "Christlikeness", but rather due to our sinful worldliness. Let's make sure we know the difference.

One last point before we close this chapter. Though Abraham, Moses and David were all referred to by God as being His friends, they never referred to God as their Friend. He is Jehovah God. He is our Savior, our Lord and our Master. He isn't – and never will be – one of the boys. Though He sees us as His friends, it is not a reciprocal friendship. The same John who reclined next to Jesus that night in the upper room (John 13:23) would in later years fall at His feet as a dead man (Revelation 1:17) when he saw Him in His glory. Let's be careful that we do not allow our position in Christ as His friends to blind us to the majesty of Who He is and the reverence that is due Him.

Yes, as you take up the cross, remember, He has called you friend!

* * *

40

THE SORROW WON'T LAST

"In a little while you won't see Me anymore. But a little while after that, you will see Me again." Some of the disciples asked each other, "What does He mean when He says, 'In a little while you won't see Me, but then you will see Me,' and 'I am going to the Father'? And what does He mean by 'a little while'? We don't understand." Jesus realized they wanted to ask Him about it, so He said, "Are you asking yourselves what I meant? I said in a little while you won't see Me, but a little while after that you will see Me again. I tell you the truth, you will weep and mourn over what is going to happen to Me, but the world will rejoice. You will grieve, but your grief will suddenly turn to wonderful joy. It will be like a woman suffering the pains of labor. When her child is born, her anguish gives way to joy because she has brought a new baby into the world. So you have sorrow now, but I will see you again; then you will rejoice, and no one can rob you of that joy."

John 16:16-22

* * *

Jesus continued to speak words of encouragement and truth to His disciples as they walked from the upper room to the Garden to pray. Already that night, Jesus had used the traditional observance of Passover to teach His disciples new truth. And His teaching did not cease when they left the upper room, it continued throughout their journey. Allow me to make a quick observation before we get into the passage. Notice that Jesus does not waste a moment or a motion. Nothing with Jesus is perfunctory. No moment of traditional "religious" reflection passes without Jesus using it in our lives to open our eyes and hearts to

His truth. No journey we take is solely about the journey. Jesus uses every moment of the journey to reveal His truth about Himself and about ourselves. His reflections along the way are not purposed to scold us or defeat us. His words to us throughout the journey are intended to lead us to a greater understanding of Him, as He draws us closer to Him. Jesus knew what was ahead for His disciples. He continued to use this time to prepare them. He knows what is ahead for us, and He is using this time in our respective journeys with Him to prepare us.

i wonder how attentive the disciples were to all Jesus was saying. Were they even listening? Remember, they didn't know what was about to happen, so they didn't realize that these were some of His last words to them. They were tired – it had been a long day – and a long week. They were anxious – not because they had an idea of what was ahead, but because Jesus' words to them were portending times of uncertainty. As a result, their anxiety was distracting them from hearing all of what Jesus had to say. Since they didn't know what was about to occur, they didn't have context for what He was saying. We experience those same challenges as we take up the cross to follow Jesus. We can become tired – or anxious – or lack understanding because we don't know what's ahead. In the midst of the journey, hold onto the truth that Jesus is always preparing us for what lies in our road ahead. He knows exactly what we will have need of. So, lean into Him. Listen attentively and – if you are able – journal what Jesus tells you through His Word. That simple act of journaling will help you remember His promise – His truth – when the time comes.

Jesus was teaching them important truths about joy and sorrow. He knew that, in just a few hours, He would be arrested and the disciples would scatter in fear. He knew He would be crucified the next day and they would grieve over His death and be fearful about their own lives. He wanted them to know that *"in a little while you won't see Me anymore. But a little while after that, you will see Me again."* Though He would die, and His enemies would rejoice in thinking that they had been victorious, He, in three days' time, would rise again and return as the Victor. He wanted them to hold to His promise even when everything looked dark. He wanted them to remember that the journey would not end in death, it would end in resurrection. Thus, they could be confident that though they might sorrow for a season, "joy would come in the morning" (Psalm 30:5).

But Jesus' promise was not only regarding His three days in the tomb.

This promise looked to the days that would pass before He returned to establish His Kingdom on earth. Those days too would pass, just like His days in the tomb. In the meantime, the Father would send His Spirit to indwell, to comfort, to encourage and equip as they – and we – walk through those days. But, though they – and we – would experience sorrow – and for some, hatred, ridicule and persecution – those days too would come to an end – and they would end in joy. Just as He promised to rise again from the grave, He promised to return again, and they – and we – must walk in the joy of His promise. Though we look back on His resurrection from the tomb with sight as a historical fact, we too look forward to His return with the same eyes of faith as the disciples who He was encouraging that night.

But His promise of joy in the midst of sorrow went even further. He likened the pain that we will endure throughout these days until He returns – or until we are with Him – as those of *"a woman suffering the pains of labor. When her child is born, her anguish gives way to joy because she has brought a new baby into the world."* Pain is a part of the process. It can't be avoided. But the pain will not endure indefinitely. It will be transformed into joy. Jesus was not minimizing pain, suffering or sorrow. He acknowledged its reality. But He was assuring them – and us – that it will not last. It will endure – perhaps for a season – but then it will be gone. Our pain will not be replaced by joy, it will be transformed into joy! And when it is, that joy will remain for eternity. Pain and sorrow are real – but they are finite. They will end. But the joy that comes "in the morning" will endure.

If you are a follower of Jesus and are walking through sorrow, or have tears in your eyes, be assured that this is not the end. He has promised joy – joy that will endure for eternity! In that day, our joy in His presence will exceed and overshadow any sorrow we may have experienced in our lives on this side. Remember, we may have sorrow now, *"but I will see you again; then you will rejoice, and no one can rob you of that joy."*

* * *

41

OUR LORD'S PRAYER

"At that time, you won't need to ask Me for anything. I tell you the truth, you will ask the Father directly, and He will grant your request because you use My name. You haven't done this before. Ask, using My name, and you will receive, and you will have abundant joy.... I'm not saying I will ask the Father on your behalf, for the Father Himself loves you dearly because you love Me and believe that I came from God."

After saying all these things, Jesus looked up to heaven and said, "Father, the hour has come. Glorify your Son so He can give glory back to you.... My prayer is not for the world, but for those You have given Me, because they belong to You. ... Now protect them by the power of Your name so that they will be united just as We are.... Now I am coming to You. I told them many things while I was with them in this world so they would be filled with My joy.... I'm not asking You to take them out of the world, but to keep them safe from the evil one.... Make them holy by Your truth; teach them Your word, which is truth.... I am praying not only for these disciples but also for all who will ever believe in Me through their message. I pray that they will all be one, just as You and I are one—as You are in Me, Father, and I am in You. And may they be in Us so that the world will believe You sent Me.... Father, I want these whom You have given Me to be with Me where I am.... I have revealed You to them, and I will continue to do so. Then Your love for Me will be in them, and I will be in them."

Selected verses from John 16:23-27
and John 17:1-26

* * *

As Jesus and the disciples concluded their final steps to the Garden of Gethsemane, Jesus gave them one more word of instruction on how they were to pray. The instruction He gave them is very familiar to us – many of us have been hearing it for most of our lives. But for the disciples, it was unfamiliar. It was a "new way" to pray – prayer that would lead to joy, prayer that would be offered in power, and prayer that would reveal God's glory.

Jesus told them that they should always direct their prayer to the Father. He told them that they would not need to ask Him (Jesus) for anything; rather, they should make all of their requests to the Father. And the Father, who loves them – and us – because of our love for the Son, will answer those requests. It is worthy to repeat that Jesus emphasized that they were not to pray to Him, expecting Him to pass their requests on to the Father. He clearly told them – and us – to pray to the Father – in Jesus' Name (that was the "new part"). Praying in Jesus' Name doesn't mean a simple tag at the end of our prayer. It means we are asking and walking according to the will of the Son. He had just taught them that their love for the Son would be expressed through their abiding in Him and their obedience to Him. John would later go on to write, "*And we are confident that He* (the Father) *hears us whenever we ask for anything that pleases Him* (the Son). *And since we know He* (the Father) *hears us when we make our requests, we also know that He* (the Father) *will give us what we ask for*" (1 John 5:14-15). And as we pray to the Father, Jesus will be interceding on our behalf. Paul wrote to the believers in Rome: "*Christ Jesus is He who died, yes, rather who was raised, who is at the right hand of God, who also intercedes for us*" (Romans 8:34 NASB). Therefore, as His disciples – both those then and we now – abide in Him and obey Him, we can boldly and confidently approach the Father's throne, knowing the access that we are granted to Him through the Son, and knowing that the Son is interceding on our behalf. We have the "inside track" through prayer, because of the Son, to the Father!

And Jesus' intercession on our behalf began that night in the Garden. As Jesus now arrived at the Garden, He transitioned from speaking with His disciples to speaking with His Father. This is not the passage in Scripture that is typically entitled "The Lord's Prayer", as i have entitled this chapter. Rather, we looked at that passage (Luke 11:1-4) as we explored the lesson that Jesus gave His disciples in prayer in chapter 49 of ***Walking With The Master***. And though Mark records that Peter, James and John fell asleep while Jesus was praying (Mark 14:32-42), apparently John was alert for enough of the time that He was able to hear a portion of our

Lord's prayer to the Father. And, as a result, He was able to share it with us here.

First, Jesus acknowledged that the hour had come – the hour for which the Father had sent Him to earth. Jesus prayed that the Father would glorify the Son through all that was about to transpire so that the Father, in turn, would be glorified through the Son. Jesus never sought glory for Himself alone. He and the Father are One. The Father was revealed through the Son, and the Father was glorified through the Son. Remember, Jesus is 100% God and 100% man. He prayed that the Father would glorify Him as the Son of God, so that He (Jesus) would endure to the end and glorify the Father as the Son of Man. He knew all that He was about to bear on our behalf and in obedience to the Father. Jesus was about to go to battle with sin and death – two powerful foes. Satan was amassing all of the resources he could muster in an attempt to defeat Jesus. In the heavenly realm, Jesus was embarking on the greatest spiritual battle that ever was. And He asked His Father to glorify Him, so that sin and death would be defeated, and the Father would be glorified.

Second, Jesus prayed for His disciples. He prayed for their protection. He prayed for their unity – for their oneness together in Christ. He prayed that they would be filled with joy. He prayed that they would be delivered from the attempts of the evil one to attack them. He prayed that they would be set apart and sanctified in all truth. He prayed that as they went out in obedience to His command as His ambassadors, that they would not only go out in His Name, but also, that they would be clothed in His righteousness and His holiness. Jesus saw all that laid in their paths ahead – in the immediate days – but also, in the weeks, months and years ahead. He prayed that they would run the race with endurance and finish well.

Third, Jesus prayed for *"all who will ever believe in Me through their message."* If you are a follower of Jesus, He prayed for you! He prayed for our oneness in Him. He prayed that the Son and the Father would be revealed through our lives – not only through our words, but also through our actions. He prayed that our lives would be characterized to the world around us through our love for one another, and the Father's love expressed through us to the world around us. In so praying, He was praying that our lives would never be reflective of bigotry, hatred, uncaringness or selfish ambition. He prayed that our very thoughts, attitudes, words and actions would radiate the Father's love.

. . .

He prayed that we would walk in fellowship with Him – that we would "be with Him". And that fellowship is not only for the hereafter, it is for the here and now. He was praying that we wouldn't walk according to a set of rules and regulations, like the religious leaders of His day. Rather, He prayed we would walk each and every moment in intimate fellowship and relationship with Him – not only in our prayer closets – but throughout every moment of our everyday lives.

And He prayed that we would behold His glory – the glory as the Only Begotten of the Father. We would see His glory as the Baby in the manger – as the Feeder of the five thousand – as the Savior on the cross – as the Risen Lord emerging from the tomb – and as the Coming King who will return to judge the earth. We would see His glory as the King of Kings and the Lord of Lords.

Long before we knew Him, He knew us. Long before we chose Him, He chose us. Long before we began to follow Him, He interceded for us. And He still does! As you take up the cross to follow Him, walk in the boldness and the confidence – and the love – that He prays for us.

* * *

42

DON'T LET TEMPTATION OVERPOWER YOU

Then, accompanied by the disciples, Jesus left the upstairs room and went as usual to the Mount of Olives. There He told them, "Pray that you will not give in to temptation." He walked away, about a stone's throw, and knelt down and prayed, "Father, if You are willing, please take this cup of suffering away from Me. Yet I want Your will to be done, not Mine." Then an angel from heaven appeared and strengthened Him. He prayed more fervently, and He was in such agony of spirit that His sweat fell to the ground like great drops of blood. At last He stood up again and returned to the disciples, only to find them asleep, exhausted from grief. "Why are you sleeping?" He asked them. "Get up and pray, so that you will not give in to temptation."

Luke 22:39-46

* * *

Before Jesus withdrew to a place where He could spend time with the Father in prayer there in the Garden of Gethsemane on the Mount Olives, He instructed His disciples to *"pray that you will not give in to temptation"*. He left eight of His disciples in one place in the Garden, then Peter, James and John (Mark 14:32-33) in another, as He then went just a stone's throw away to pray to the Father.

As we saw in the last chapter, Jesus used this time to pray for Himself, His disciples, and all of those who would follow Him in the future. He prayed that each one of us would not give in to temptation, and He instructed His disciples to join with Him in that prayer. Matthew in his account of these events (Matthew 26:36-46) records that three times Jesus returned to the disciples and found them sleeping. It was late. It had been a long day. It had been a very long week. The disciples were exhausted. They were grieving over the foreboding words that Jesus had spoken to them that night. And they had no grasp of what was taking place that night in the Garden.

Take a moment in the hush of Gethsemane and listen. Hear the sobbing of Jesus' soul. Hear the falling drops of His blood. There in the Garden at the base of an olive tree, just a few yards away, kneeling low in agonizing prayer, is the Savior praying for you and for me as He prepares to take on our humanity and our sin.

You see, the battle of Calvary was actually being fought right there in Gethsemane, and the victory of Calvary was won that night in Gethsemane. Jesus knew that His time in the hands of His accusers and persecutors would be momentary in the scope of eternity and limited in the hands of the Father. He wasn't agonizing over the humiliation and abuse, or the shame and pain of the cross. He also knew full well that He would rise from the grave, and death would be defeated. He wasn't agonizing over death.

His agony came from the reality that He knew that He would be made sin for us. He, who knew no sin, would carry the full weight of our depraved, despicable and decadent sin. Every immoral, self-serving, evil, disobedient act and action that had ever been committed and would ever be committed was being placed on Him. We cannot imagine the weight of that burden, nor the cost of our sin. And the result of sin is separation from God. For all time and eternity, Jesus had never been separated from the Father. And now in this selfless act, not only was He carrying the weight of our sin, He was also bearing the agony of a time that He would be separated from the Father. Remember, He and the Father are One. When He most needed the connection with the Father, He would be separated from Him. Separation from the Father was the great agony of the cross. It wasn't the physical pain over which Jesus agonized; it was that deep spiritual pain.

And it wasn't the physical pain that Satan was tempting Him to avoid either; it was that spiritual pain. You remember that Satan had been defeated in his attempts to tempt Jesus after those forty days in the wilderness as recorded in Matthew 4:1-11 (***Walking With The Master,*** *chapter* 7). But on this night, he returned, in a "last ditch" effort to tempt Jesus once and for all. The tempter came to once again offer Jesus the crown without the cross. We will never really know or fully comprehend the full weight of Jesus' pain. We will never know or understand the full weight of that temptation or the agony that He endured. We will never fully understand the bitterness of that cup of suffering. There is a rare physical phenomenon known as "hematidrosis", in which, under great emotional stress, the tiny blood vessels rupture in the sweat glands and produce a mixture of blood and sweat. Such was the agony – and the temptation – that our Savior endured.

Then just as the angels ministered to Jesus after Satan tempted Him in the desert, they also came to minister to Him after Satan tempted Him in the Garden. The angels could not die for our sins, but they could strengthen our Savior as He courageously accepted the cup of suffering. The famous Scottish pastor and writer, Dr. George Morrison, said, *"Every life has its Gethsemane, and every Gethsemane has its angel."*

Remember, Jesus was not only praying to the Father about what He would endure over the next twenty-four hours. He was not only praying that the Father would glorify the Son so that the Father would be glorified through the Son. He was also praying for His disciples. He knew they would be tempted – to scatter – to deny Him – to hide in fear. He knew that their worlds would be turned upside down – and they would feel as if they had no place to turn and no one to whom they could turn. He knew they were entering into the most difficult days of their lives. And He agonized for them. He desired that they would pray to the Father that they would not give in to temptation. He had just promised them that if they prayed according to His will that the Father would hear and answer their prayer. But instead of praying, they slept. Three times He told them, and three times they responded by sleeping. So, when the enemy came, they were unprepared. As a result, they scattered. They denied Him (at least we know Peter did). They hid in fear.

As we take up the cross, there are two truths we need to hold onto out of this passage. The first is the depth of our Father's and our Savior's love for us and the magnitude of the agony that He endured for our salvation, even knowing that multitudes would reject His free gift and would never embrace His saving love. The second is our need to pray that we not give in to temptation. Temptation remains at our doors – in different forms. As Jesus taught us to pray to the Father, "don't let us yield to temptation, but rescue us from the evil one" (Matthew 6:13). The Father is ready, waiting and able to answer that prayer. He has angels standing by to minister to our needs. All Jesus has told us to do is ask! Let's not be found sleeping.

* * *

43

A BETRAYAL, AN ARREST, AND A HEALING

But even as Jesus said this, a crowd approached, led by Judas, one of the twelve disciples. Judas walked over to Jesus to greet Him with a kiss. But Jesus said, "Judas, would you betray the Son of Man with a kiss?" When the other disciples saw what was about to happen, they exclaimed, "Lord, should we fight? We brought the swords!" And one of them struck at the high priest's slave, slashing off his right ear. But Jesus said, "No more of this." And He touched the man's ear and healed him. Then Jesus spoke to the leading priests, the captains of the Temple guard, and the elders who had come for Him. "Am I some dangerous revolutionary," He asked, "that you come with swords and clubs to arrest Me? Why didn't you arrest Me in the Temple? I was there every day. But this is your moment, the time when the power of darkness reigns."

Luke 22:47-53

* * *

The hour had come. Even while Jesus was still speaking to His disciples, the crowd approached. John tells us that Judas came with a Roman cohort of six hundred men (John 18:3), plus the leading priests and elders from the Temple, as well as the captains of the Temple guard (Luke 22:52). They came with their lanterns, torches and weapons. Humanly speaking, it would have been a very overwhelming sight for Jesus and the eleven disciples. Why such a large crowd to arrest Jesus? Did they fear He would run away or hide in the Garden? If you have visited the Garden and that portion of the Mount of Olives, you know that that portion of land is not very large. Even in the dark, it would have been very difficult for anyone to hide in the terrain. Did they expect Jesus to resist arrest? Did they fear He would perform a miracle and again slip from their grasp? Remember, their previous attempts had been unsuccessful, and the religious leaders were not going to take any chances. What they didn't realize was that their previous attempts had not been in alignment with the Father's timing – but this was His time. Remember, Jesus had intentionally established a "routine pattern" that week. He had been spending each night on the Mount of Olives since Tuesday so that Judas would know exactly where He and the remaining disciples would be.

Why did Judas need to identify Jesus for the soldiers? Again, the religious leaders were taking every precaution. Don't lose sight of the fact that as the Son of Man, Jesus took on an appearance of those that He came to live among. Recall that on the Mount of Transfiguration (Matthew 17:1-9), Jesus took on a very different appearance as the Son of God. And when John sees Him as the Son of God in Revelation (1:17), he falls at His feet as dead. As the Son of God, Jesus clearly stands out above the crowd. But when He first came – to pay the penalty for our sins – He took on our appearance, that of a humble servant. In their "craftiness", the religious leaders – and Judas – didn't want the Roman soldiers to make a mistake and arrest the wrong man.

Why did Judas "greet" Jesus with a kiss? It was customary for disciples to greet their teachers with a loving and respectful kiss. However, this kiss was anything but loving and respectful, it was the basest kind of hypocrisy and treachery. That's what betrayal is. The writer of Proverbs says it well: "*You can trust a friend who corrects you, but kisses from an enemy are nothing but lies*" (Proverbs 27:6 CEV).

But let's also look at the disciples' response. Earlier in the Gospels, when Jesus sent out His disciples to proclaim the Good News, He had instructed them not to take anything with them, even though they would be "lambs among wolves" (Luke 10:3-4). He was teaching them that the Father would provide all the resources that were needed, and they had seen Him faithfully do so. But on this night, they would have resources in hand, and they would have the choice to make as to which resources they would depend upon – those of the Father or those of the world.

Luke records that when Jesus and the disciples were leaving the upper room earlier that night, He had told them, "'*take your money and a traveler's bag. And if you don't have a sword, sell your cloak and buy one! For the time has come for this prophecy about Me to be fulfilled: 'He was counted among the rebels.' Yes, everything written about Me by the prophets will come true.' 'Look, Lord,' they replied, 'we have two swords among us.' 'That's enough,' He said"* (Luke 22:36-38). Just as Isaiah had prophesied in Isaiah 53:12, Jesus would be counted among the rebels. And that night, Jesus knew that His disciples would respond to the ways of the world by acting like the world – just like we often do. He knew they would attempt to enter into battle using the weapons of the world, and then when that failed, they would flee. So, two swords were more than enough to prove the point. Apparently, one of those swords was in Peter's possession.

The saying, "never bring a knife to a gun fight", means that one should bring the appropriate weapon for the fight. The battle that night in the Garden was a spiritual battle. Peter chose the wrong weapon – a sword made of metal. He should have chosen the right sword – the Word of God (Ephesians 6:17). And not only did Peter choose the wrong weapon, he also failed to look to his Master. He asked, *"Lord, should we fight?"* But instead of waiting to hear from the One who was able to calm the storm, He just plowed ahead to do what He thought was right in his own eyes. Peter was backing up the boastful words he had uttered in the Upper Room (Luke 22:33) and on the way to the Garden (Matthew 26:33-35). Peter had been sleeping when he should have been praying, talking when he should have been listening, and boasting when he should have been fearing. (How often have we done that?) And now, his impetuous actions led to his cutting off the right ear of Malchus, a servant to the high priest (John 18:10, 26). Let that be a reminder to us that most often our impetuous ways will lead to further hurt and destruction. Peter was right to ask Jesus the question – but he should have waited for the answer!

How did Jesus respond? When faced with actions of malice, Jesus responded with grace. He showed grace to Peter by rebuking his sin and repairing the harm that he had done. He showed grace to Malchus by healing his ear. He showed grace to the mob by willingly yielding Himself to them. And He showed grace to us by submitting to each step of the journey to Calvary.

This was the Master's last miraculous act before the cross. He could have summoned twelve legions of angels to protect Himself and His disciples (Matthew 26:53). But instead, He chose to inconspicuously heal the ear of an obscure servant. It is very probable with all that was taking place that the only ones who knew that Malchus was injured were Malchus, Peter and Jesus. And yet, in the midst of all of the turmoil, Jesus never withheld His healing grace.

Then Jesus rebuked the priests, the captains and the elders for waiting for the cover of darkness. They thought the darkness gave them advantage. But the reality was that nothing – not even evil – would be able to do anything that the Father was not permitting them to do. The Father's redemptive purpose would not be thwarted – even by the evil intent that these men displayed. That is an important lesson for us to hold onto. If the power of darkness is reigning, it is only because the Light of the world has permitted it for His greater redemptive purpose. The world will betray you. Evil will endeavor to bind you. But the Master's grace and purpose will prevail. Trust Him! Look to Him! And wait for His answer. It will come!

* * *

44

WHO WAS STANDING BEFORE THE HIGH PRIEST?

So the soldiers, their commanding officer, and the Temple guards arrested Jesus and tied Him up. First, they took Him to Annas, since he was the father-in-law of Caiaphas, the high priest at that time. Caiaphas was the one who had told the other Jewish leaders, "It's better that one man should die for the people...." Inside, the high priest began asking Jesus about His followers and what He had been teaching them. Jesus replied, "Everyone knows what I teach. I have preached regularly in the synagogues and the Temple, where the people gather. I have not spoken in secret. Why are you asking Me this question? Ask those who heard Me. They know what I said." Then one of the Temple guards standing nearby slapped Jesus across the face. "Is that the way to answer the high priest?" he demanded. Jesus replied, "If I said anything wrong, you must prove it. But if I'm speaking the truth, why are you beating Me?" Then Annas bound Jesus and sent Him to Caiaphas, the high priest.

John 18:12-14, 19-24

* * *

They arrested the Almighty Son of God! They tied up the Creator of the universe using materials He had created! Can you think of anything more preposterous? They thought they had authority over Him! Can you think of anything more presumptuous? Can you think of anything more absurd than placing God on trial? But can you think of anything more amazing than the fact that He willingly allowed Himself to be subjected to this humiliation – for me – and for you?

. . .

John is the only Gospel writer that includes this detail that after they arrested Jesus in the Garden, they first took Him to the home of Annas. Annas was not the current high priest. He was the father-in-law of the current high priest, Caiaphas. He had been the high priest prior to his son-in-law. But he currently did not hold that position. Therefore, he had no legal standing under Mosaic Law in this proceeding. And yet, his home was the first place the guards and soldiers brought Jesus. Why would they have brought Jesus here, and not taken Him directly before Caiaphas?

You will recall that in chapter 3 we looked at Jesus' cleansing of the temple. That had only occurred three days before this. And you may recall that we discussed the fact that Annas was the overseer of all of the financial enterprises that were profiting from the buying and selling taking place within the Temple. Annas saw Jesus' actions as a direct attack on himself, his position, his authority and on his financial livelihood. Though Annas by no means acted alone, he was without question one of, if not the leader of, the principal plotters behind the arrest and crucifixion of Jesus. I believe his purpose for having Jesus brought to him first was two-fold. First, i believe in his arrogance, he wanted Jesus to know that he – Annas – was in charge, and that though Jesus may have been in control the day He cleansed the Temple, today was Annas' day. And he had the arrogance to think he was now getting the last word. Second, Annas is considered, even in secular history, to have been crafty and clever. As one of the main architects of this plot to have Jesus crucified, he doubtless believed that he was the best qualified to "catch" Jesus in saying something that could be used against Him in the planned trial.

John also carefully inserted the notation that it was Caiaphas who had said, *"It's better that one man should die for the people...."*. Caiaphas made that statement after Jesus had raised Lazarus from the dead (John 11:50). And in doing so, he was saying that Jesus must die so that the Romans would not take away the privileges of the Jewish nation – and particularly the privileges of its religious leaders. John inserted this statement as a reminder that the religious leaders had already predetermined that Jesus was to die – and that the trial that was about to unfold was nothing but a mockery – a diabolical plot – conceived in the minds of the likes of Annas and Caiaphas, and birthed from the heart of Satan. And Caiaphas and Annas were truly very likeminded. They both believed that Jesus' death would lead to their salvation. But the salvation they were seeking was the salvation of their power, their positions and their profits. These were the "high priests" who stood before Jesus!

. . .

It's amazing to me that Annas had the audacity to ask Jesus to tell him what He had been teaching. Jesus had been speaking publicly for over three years and had repeatedly taught in the very Temple where Annas oversaw his enterprise. As we've already said, Annas was looking for Jesus to say something that could be used against him in the trial. But Annas could have done that while Jesus was speaking in the Temple. It is possible that Annas had never taken the time to listen to Jesus personally. Perhaps he had relied on the accounts of other religious leaders and couldn't be bothered to listen to Jesus himself. Listening would have interfered with his Temple enterprise. He wouldn't permit truth to stand in the way of his personal religious business.

In chapter 25, we looked at the fact that some of the older religious leaders in this day would have, in their younger days, likely been some of the leading priests and teachers that King Herod the Great had consulted to ascertain the birthplace of the Messiah (Matthew 2:4-5) thirty or so years earlier. Annas most definitely would have been one of them. They – and he – showed no signs of a heart seeking after the promised Messiah. As a matter of fact, through the information they provided, they had assisted Herod in his attempt to kill the Messiah by having all the little boys under two years of age who lived in and around Bethlehem killed. Again, i am pretty confident that Annas had connected those dots somewhere along the line – between that baby boy born in Bethlehem and this same Jesus. Somehow, they had failed the first time. He was determined not to fail again!

Bear in mind that everything that was now being done to Jesus was illegal under Mosaic law:

1. Annas was no longer the high priest. He had no legal authority to detain or question Jesus.
2. There was no witness of Jesus having done anything that violated the Law. And the Law required that there be witnesses before an arrest took place.
3. No trial was ever to begin at night. (They had arrested Jesus under the cover of darkness to avoid the watchful eyes of the crowds.)
4. No trial was ever to begin and end on the same day.
5. No prisoner was ever to be struck in any way unless proven guilty.

But to me, the greatest irony of this passage is the reality that truly there is only one High Priest in this account, and His Name is Jesus. He alone is the High Priest (Hebrews 4:14). And as He was brought before each one that night, beginning with Annas, the reality is that they were standing before Him – indicted by their own sin. Caiaphas and Annas (the "high priests") sought to sacrifice Jesus' life for their own selfish salvation. But Jesus – the true High Priest – had come to offer Himself as <u>the</u> Sacrifice for many (Matthew 20:28) – through whom many would be saved.

This plot may have been hatched in the minds of Annas and Caiaphas (the high priests), and been birthed from the heart of the deceiver (Satan), but it was allowed to unfold only because it was permitted by the Father. It was the Father's redemptive plan and it required no one less than the High Priest Himself, the Son of the Living God.

As we take up the cross to follow Jesus, we, too, will encounter attempts to falsely accuse and decry the works of God. Follow the lead of the One who has stood in that place – and through it all brought glory to the Father. Because He is your High Priest and His work, His will and His Word will prevail!

* * *

45

THE ROOSTER CROWED

Simon Peter followed Jesus, as did another of the disciples. That other disciple was acquainted with the high priest, so he was allowed to enter the high priest's courtyard with Jesus. Peter had to stay outside the gate. Then the disciple who knew the high priest spoke to the woman watching at the gate, and she let Peter in. The woman asked Peter, "You're not one of that man's disciples, are you?" "No," he said, "I am not." Because it was cold, the household servants and the guards had made a charcoal fire. They stood around it, warming themselves, and Peter stood with them, warming himself.... Meanwhile, as Simon Peter was standing by the fire warming himself, they asked him again, "You're not one of His disciples, are you?" He denied it, saying, "No, I am not." But one of the household slaves of the high priest, a relative of the man whose ear Peter had cut off, asked, "Didn't I see you out there in the olive grove with Jesus?" Again, Peter denied it. And immediately a rooster crowed.

John 18:15-18, 25-27

* * *

When John writes, *"another of the disciples"* and *"that other disciple"*, he is, as you know, referring to himself. We have previously looked at the fact that John was apparently well-known in the circles of the religious leaders. You will recall that it was probably John that orchestrated the conversation that took place between Nicodemus and Jesus (John 3), and he was the only disciple present when the conversation took place. And here we see that he has no difficulty entering the high priest's courtyard, nor does the servant watching at the gate question his request to grant Peter access through the gate. It is quite possible that John's family had position and influence in the community. That being the case, we have no idea why his brother, James, hadn't joined he and Peter, but apparently, he had chosen to scatter with the other disciples. Perhaps, as the eldest son, he had gone to alert their mother, who was also a part of the entourage that followed Jesus. Regardless, John was able to provide Peter with access.

John, because of his standing, was able to gain access nearer to where the questioning of Jesus was taking place. It doesn't appear that anyone confronted him about being a disciple of Jesus, though the leaders most assuredly would have known that to be the case. It could have been because of his position in their society, but, more likely, i would venture that at that moment the religious leaders were more focused on their plans regarding Jesus than they were on His followers. So, it appears that no one confronted John.

But that was not the case with Peter. Instead of standing with the "high and mighty" of society, Peter was warming his hands with the household servants and guards around the fire. He had no position, and they had no pretense. The first questioner was the servant woman to whom John had made his request to allow Peter to enter. Again, she, like the others there, knew John was a disciple of Jesus. Other translations, include the word "too" or "also" in her question, evidencing her understanding about John. And since Peter hadn't entered further into the courtyard with John, but had stayed with the servants, there was an opportunity for her to question him further. Bear in mind she wasn't one of the accusers, she was merely an inquisitive servant. i personally think she was using the question more as a conversation starter than as leveling an accusatory challenge. It's quite possible she just wanted to know more about this Jesus that she had heard of, or perhaps seen, and who better to ask than one of His disciples? But rather than seeing it as an opportunity to tell her about Jesus, in the midst of the chaos and confusion over all that was taking place, he denied that he was a follower.

But remember, Peter was the "de facto" leader of the other disciples. He was always conspicuously seen with Jesus when He was teaching or performing miracles. So, others of the servants and guards had to have seen him with Jesus in days past. As they talked among themselves, they became certain that he was one of the disciples. So, again someone asked him. Like before, it wasn't accusatory; it was an honest inquiry. But again, the disciple who always spoke out boldly when others stood silent was tongue-tied by fear.

The third question to Peter came from a slightly different perspective. This was a relative of Malchus, the servant whose ear Peter had cut off, but Jesus had healed. This relative was apparently in the crowd when they arrested Jesus, so this question was asked with a different motivation. Possibly this person was preparing to accuse Peter of cutting off Malchus' ear. Or, more than likely, the story of how Jesus had healed his ear was now being repeated among the servants, and this servant wanted to hear more about it from someone who was standing right there. Regardless, it was another opportunity for Peter to bear witness to the grace and mercy of Jesus. But instead, He adamantly denied even knowing Jesus! Three opportunities to bear witness – all refused and denied.

Therein is the reminder to each one of us. As we take up the cross and follow Jesus, He will grant us many opportunities to bear witness about Him and His gospel of grace and mercy. Prayerfully, we will be walking in a way that distinguishes us as one of His followers. As a result, He will grant us with occasions to respond to the same type of questions that were being directed to Peter. How will we respond? Will we seize the moment and the opportunity to bear witness and bring glory to God, or will we become tongue-tied by fear or anxiety and avoid the conversation? Yes, Peter denied Jesus, but, when we fail to seize the opportunity to bear witness, so do we.

Earlier that night, Peter had boastfully declared to Jesus that he was willing to die with Him (Luke 22:33), to which Jesus replied that Peter would deny Him three times before the rooster crowed the very next morning (Luke 22:34). i am certain that Peter neither believed nor received what Jesus said to him. At the moment of Jesus' statement, he could not conceive that he would ever deny Jesus.

But now, the rooster crowed. Peter remembered Jesus' words. And Matthew, Mark and Luke record Peter's personal testimony that *"he left the courtyard, weeping bitterly"* (Luke 22:62).

What's that i hear? Is it the rooster crowing? Have we been faithful to the

Master's call to make disciples and bear witness of His gospel? If so, continue to ask for His grace and mercy to stay the course in His mission. If not, allow the tears of repentance to flow and His Spirit to fill you with the boldness to share His truth. Because the rooster didn't just crow for Peter, it crows for us as well.

* * *

46

A TRAITOR'S REMORSE

Very early in the morning the leading priests and the elders of the people met again to lay plans for putting Jesus to death. Then they bound Him, led Him away, and took Him to Pilate, the Roman governor. When Judas, who had betrayed Him, realized that Jesus had been condemned to die, he was filled with remorse. So, he took the thirty pieces of silver back to the leading priests and the elders. "I have sinned," he declared, "for I have betrayed an innocent man." "What do we care?" they retorted. "That's your problem." Then Judas threw the silver coins down in the Temple and went out and hanged himself. The leading priests picked up the coins. "It wouldn't be right to put this money in the Temple treasury," they said, "since it was payment for murder." After some discussion they finally decided to buy the potter's field, and they made it into a cemetery for foreigners. That is why the field is still called the Field of Blood. This fulfilled the prophecy of Jeremiah that says,
"They took the thirty pieces of silver— the price at which he was valued by the people of Israel, and purchased the potter's field, as the Lord directed."
Matthew 27:1-10

* * *

Apparently, John and Peter weren't the only disciples of Jesus at the home of Caiaphas that early morning. While Peter had been with the servants denying Jesus, Judas Iscariot had been standing near the religious leaders continuing in his betrayal of Jesus. He was standing close and watching carefully. He fully expected Jesus at any moment to say "enough!" and declare Himself the Messiah and establish His authority over everyone in the room. This was the moment for which Judas had been waiting. His three years of following Jesus were now going to pay off. These religious leaders who had treated Judas with disdain were about to have the tables turned. Jesus was about to establish His Kingdom. Judas was about to step into his position of authority. And these religious leaders were moments away from having their authority stripped away. Judas was certain of how this was all going to end. Surely Jesus would be appreciative of how Judas had helped prompt the moment. And perhaps that had been Jesus' plan all along. Judas would have plenty of opportunity to talk through this with Jesus once He declared Himself. That's how blinded Judas had become by his own sin.

Then Caiaphas, Annas, and the entire high council said to Jesus, *"Tell us, are You the Messiah?" But He replied, "If I tell you, you won't believe Me. And if I ask you a question, you won't answer. But from now on the Son of Man will be seated in the place of power at God's right hand." They all shouted, "So, are You claiming to be the Son of God?" And He replied, "You say that I am." "Why do we need other witnesses?" they said. "We ourselves heard Him say it"* (Luke 22:67-71). Judas couldn't believe his ears. Jesus was not taking control of the situation (or so Judas thought). Instead of declaring Himself, Jesus was allowing Himself to be bound, and the religious leaders were taking Him to Pilate to be crucified. And Jesus was going willingly. Judas became filled with confusion, which quickly turned to the realization that Jesus had been condemned to die. And he – Judas – had been the one who betrayed Jesus. At that moment, the scales that had blinded him from seeing his own treachery and deceit fell from his eyes. He realized that he had been complicit in the plot to murder Jesus – the Messiah. Matthew records that he became filled with remorse. Regrettably, he did not become filled with repentance. Repentance would have led to forgiveness of his sin. Repentance would have led to restoration of his relationship with Christ, and through Christ with the Father. But instead he fell short and stopped with remorse. The Oxford Dictionary defines remorse as "deep regret or guilt for a wrong committed". It is a guilt and regret that is inconsolable. Remorse can become so great that one "drowns" in their guilt, shame and regret. Remorse left unattended leads to death. Repentance, on the other hand, though it begins with a sincere regret or remorse is, in fact, a turning point – a turning to God for forgiveness, receiving His forgiveness and walking according to His righteousness. Repentance leads to life – a life that is free of the bondage of remorse.

But Judas never made that turn. He verbalized his sin to the religious leaders, but he never sought the forgiveness of God. And if we had any question about the heart condition of the religious leaders, their response of *"What do we care? That's your problem"* leaves no doubt that they were anything but men of God. Thus, Judas' remorse led to death – physically. He immediately went out and hung himself. But his remorse also led to death – eternally. Having never repented and sought forgiveness, he died eternally separated from God.

So, let's wrap this chapter up with two closing points. First, could Judas have been forgiven by God? He betrayed the Son of God. You can't get any worse than that! But the fact of the matter is that even Judas could have been forgiven by God. That man whose name is now synonymous with betrayal could have experienced the forgiveness of the Heavenly Father and – even the One he betrayed – Jesus. Scripture tells us *"if we confess our sins to Him, He is faithful and just to forgive us our sins and to cleanse us from all wickedness"* (1 John 1:9). All wickedness. Even Judas' wickedness.

Earlier this week, i met a man by the name of Leon. Leon has spent 38 years in prison for doing some very evil things. But in the midst of that time in prison, God brought someone across his path who shared the gospel with him. He told Leon about repentance and God's merciful forgiveness extended by His grace through the shed blood of His Son. And Leon repented, asked God to forgive Him, and surrendered His life to Christ. Since then the Lord has used Leon to share that Good News with many men – young and old – who are on that same path he was on. God is using Leon as an ambassador of His gospel and His grace. God can forgive a repentant sinner like Leon. God can forgive a repentant sinner like Ken. God would have forgiven a repentant sinner like Judas – if he would have only repented and sought the forgiveness of God.

That leads me to the second point. As you take up the cross and follow Jesus, He will bring people across your path who are drowning in their remorse. They feel shame, guilt and regret for what they have done, but they are content to just wallow in their remorse. They prefer to medicate their remorse with everything and anything that lessens the pain, but they stop short of the only remedy. Years ago, i had the blessing to know Dr. Henry Brandt, a renowned Christian psychologist. Dr. Brandt wrote a book that was originally entitled, "When You're Tired Of Treating The Symptoms And You're Ready For A Cure, Give Me A Call"[1]. (You can imagine the challenge of fitting that title on the book cover!) But there's a lot of truth in that statement. When you stop short at remorse, you just want to treat the symptoms. Only repentance leads to the cure. We have the cure – it is the Good News of the gospel. Let's be faithful to share it widely – because there are too many "Judases" lost in their remorse.

[1] Re-released as "The Heart of the Problem: How to Stop Coping and Find the Cure for Your Struggles" by Dr. Henry Brandt and Dr. Kerry L. Skinner (2015)

* * *

47

THE PREFECT'S PART

Then the entire council took Jesus to Pilate, the Roman governor. They began to state their case: "This man has been leading our people astray by telling them not to pay their taxes to the Roman government and by claiming He is the Messiah, a king." So Pilate asked Him, "Are You the king of the Jews?" Jesus replied, "You have said it." Pilate turned to the leading priests and to the crowd and said, "I find nothing wrong with this Man!" Then they became insistent. "But He is causing riots by His teaching wherever He goes—all over Judea, from Galilee to Jerusalem!" "Oh, is He a Galilean?" Pilate asked. When they said that He was, Pilate sent Him to Herod Antipas, because Galilee was under Herod's jurisdiction, and Herod happened to be in Jerusalem at the time.
Luke 23:1-7

* * *

After the death of the Roman client King Herod the Great, the Herodian kingdom was divided into three parts, each ruled by one of his three sons. His son Herod Archelaus was subsequently deemed incompetent by the Roman emperor Augustus and a succession of prefects was put in place to govern that province. Prefects were military men who would typically only govern a portion of larger provinces. Pontius Pilate was the fifth prefect (or governor) of the Roman province of Judea. Herod the Great's other two sons – Herod Antipas and Philip – were still in power at the time of this account. Herod Antipas ruled over the provinces of Galilee and Perea, and Philip ruled over the territories north and east of the Jordan River. In essence, Pilate, Philip and Herod

Antipas were equals in their accountability before Rome, and were careful to honor one another's authority.

As we already discussed in chapter 25, large crowds gathered in Jerusalem always caused the Roman rulers to be anxious about possible uprisings, and the record crowd gathered for this Passover made them even more so. Accordingly, Pilate and Herod Antipas were already both in Jerusalem that week to help keep the peace, instead of at their mansions in Caesarea and Tiberius, respectively.

Both rulers were familiar with the ministry of Jesus. They were well aware of His growing popularity among the people. Pilate, being a military leader with the responsibility of keeping peace and order, had kept track of Jesus' movements and actions through his centurions and soldiers. You will recall that Herod Antipas had executed John the Baptist. He, too, kept close tabs on Jesus' movements. Galilee had become Jesus' home and where He had spent the majority of His time during the three years of His ministry. They both were aware of the growing crowds that followed Him. But neither ruler appeared to be concerned that Jesus was a threat to their rule. We have no record that Jesus ever visited either of the cities in which these men lived. Let's be clear, if either of these rulers thought Jesus was a threat to Roman rule, they would have immediately arrested Him long before this.

The religious leaders made three claims about Jesus to Pilate:

1. He was telling the people not to pay their taxes.
2. He was claiming to be king, in a plan to overthrow Roman rule.
3. He was inciting the people to riot.

As we know, all of these claims were false. And Pilate knew all of these claims were false. As i've already said, if he had thought for a moment that any of these claims were true, he would have long before arrested Jesus. He knew the real motivation of these religious leaders. He knew they were threatened by His popularity. He saw this as a religious dispute.

Pilate didn't much care for the religious leaders. He knew their disdain for his religious beliefs, and he held theirs in equal regard. As prefect, his primary role was to keep law and order utilizing a small auxiliary force of approximately 3,000 locally recruited soldiers, to collect the imperial taxes due Rome and oversee limited judicial functions. Beyond that, the local municipal council – the Sanhedrin – under the leadership of the high priest – Caiaphas – was to attend to all other administrative matters. Pilate clearly saw this as an administrative matter, and did not want to get drawn into one of their religious debates. He could find no reason for Jesus to even be brought before him, let alone find any guilt in Jesus.

But he also could not permit an uprising of the people under his watch. The crowd had amassed to about two million people. The soldiers at his disposal could not contain that crowd if a riot broke out. Obviously, the religious leaders were not going to take "no" for an answer, and the crowd that was with them was beginning to become animated. As he continued to look for a way to keep himself out of a matter that he did not believe was his to adjudicate and, at the same time, not incite this crowd that could easily be stirred, he was presented with an opportunity. Since Jesus was a Galilean, this was Herod's problem! He welcomed the opportunity to "pass the buck" – at least for the moment.

So, what was the prefect's part in all of this? To answer that, we need to remember that Jesus was never the victim of human decisions. He wasn't the victim of the corrupt disciple who betrayed Him. He wasn't the victim of the corrupt high priests who orchestrated His arrest. He wasn't the victim of the Sanhedrin who condemned Him. Nor was He the victim of Herod or Pilate, who ultimately had Him executed. He was God's chosen Lamb in His redemptive plan. God had determined before the beginning of time that He would die as the atonement for our sin. But nonetheless, each of these corrupt and tragic characters do play a very particular role in the murder of the Son of God. They cannot escape their personal responsibility.

The better way to put it is to say that none of them really determined the destiny of Jesus. But what they did with Jesus determined their own destiny. None of them really condemned Jesus, but each of them condemned himself. In reality, it wasn't Jesus that was on trial. It was them who were on trial, and they all damned themselves.

There is a defining moment in everyone's life. Everyone ultimately has to decide what they will do with Jesus. You can't "pass the buck". You can't "wash your hands of it". Even no decision is a decision. God had a plan, but Pilate had a choice. God knew the choice Pilate would make, but He didn't cause Pilate to make it. *"The Lord is not slow about His promise, as some count slowness, but is patient toward you, not wishing for any to perish but for all to come to repentance"* (2 Peter 3:9). He is not wishing for any to perish – Judas, Annas, Caiaphas, Herod, Pilate, Ken, or you – but wants all to come to repentance.

The prefect's part was not to condemn an innocent Man; his part was to follow Jesus. He chose the wrong part. Many of you know that my life verse is from the apostle Paul's admonition to the Colossian church: *"So we tell others about Christ, warning everyone and teaching everyone with all the wisdom God has given us. We want to present them to God, perfect in their relationship to Christ. That's why I work and struggle so hard, depending on Christ's mighty power that works within me"* (Colossians 1:28-29). If we would take up the cross and follow Jesus, we are to warn and teach everyone – that includes the Judases, the Annases, the Caiaphases, the Herods and the Pilates – everyone. Let us be faithful to do "our part", trusting the Holy Spirit to prompt them to do "their part".

* * *

48

A KING'S MOCKERY

Herod was delighted at the opportunity to see Jesus, because he had heard about Him and had been hoping for a long time to see Him perform a miracle. He asked Jesus question after question, but Jesus refused to answer. Meanwhile, the leading priests and the teachers of religious law stood there shouting their accusations. Then Herod and his soldiers began mocking and ridiculing Jesus. Finally, they put a royal robe on Him and sent Him back to Pilate. (Herod and Pilate, who had been enemies before, became friends that day.)
Luke 23:8-12

* * *

Herod Antipas would have been a young man of 17 or 18 years of age when Jesus was born. He would have been an understudy of his father, King Herod the Great, when the wise men arrived from the east seeking the birthplace of The King (Matthew 2:1-8). He would have witnessed how his father directed the wise men, and how he responded when the wise men failed to return with news of the "baby's" location (Matthew 2:16-18).

Over thirty years had passed since that time, and Herod the Great had long been dead. Herod Antipas, now as ruler over Galilee and Perea, began to hear about the ministry and miracles being performed by Jesus in Galilee. It would be interesting to know if Herod ever connected the Baby who the wise men sought with the Miracle Worker who he was now hearing about. Luke writes, "*When Herod Antipas, the ruler of Galilee, heard about everything Jesus was doing, he was puzzled. Some were saying that John the Baptist had been raised from the dead. Others thought Jesus was Elijah or one of the other prophets risen from the dead. 'I beheaded John,' Herod said, 'so who is this man about whom I hear such stories?' And he kept trying to see Him"* (Luke 9:7-9). John the Baptist had not performed any miracles, but Herod allowed for that possibility if he had, in fact, been raised from the dead. Having had John beheaded, Herod's conscience was no doubt convicting him. Had God sent John back from the dead to judge him? Herod wanted to see Jesus, but his pride would never permit him to travel into the countryside to seek Him out. And Jesus did not make it a point to mingle with the "high and mighty" of society. As i mentioned in the last chapter, there is no record that Jesus ever visited the city of Tiberius, where Herod's palace was situated. Therefore, their paths did not cross.

One year earlier, while Jesus was in Perea, the religious leaders had wanted to get Him back into Judea where they could watch Him more closely and entrap Him. So, the Pharisees attempted to frighten Jesus back to Judea. As Luke writes, *"At that time some Pharisees said to Him, 'Get away from here if you want to live! Herod Antipas wants to kill You!' Jesus replied, 'Go tell that fox that I will keep on casting out demons and healing people today and tomorrow; and the third day I will accomplish My purpose. Yes, today, tomorrow, and the next day I must proceed on My way. For it wouldn't do for a prophet of God to be killed except in Jerusalem!'"* (Luke 13:31-33). There is no record that Herod was truly seeking to kill Jesus. That was an attempted ploy by the Pharisees. However, Jesus rightly knew that Herod was a fox. [A quick word of context: In that day, Jews did not perceive foxes to be crafty or clever, rather they viewed them as being inferior vermin. Great men were "lions"; lesser men were "foxes". Brilliant men were "lions"; inept men were "foxes".] Herod had demonstrated his baseness as a leader in divorcing his first wife, in lusting after his step-daughter and in having John the Baptist beheaded. In referring to Herod as a fox, not only was He declaring that Herod held no true power over Him, but He was also belittling the Pharisees for their feeble threat.

Now, several weeks later, in the Father's timing, Jesus is brought before Herod, and he is "delighted" at the opportunity to finally see Jesus perform a miracle. Obviously, Herod does not view Jesus as a threat – as his father had once viewed Jesus when He was a baby. Herod viewed Jesus more as a curiosity – a performer. That should give us great insight into both his political and spiritual worldviews. Thus, he begins to ask a series of questions, intended to elicit a miraculous act from Jesus. But to his consternation, Jesus remains silent. Jesus is not there to "perform" for

Herod. Neither is He there to "prove" Himself to Herod. Herod does not seek truth, he seeks entertainment. Allow me to pause on that important truth. Jesus never came to provide entertainment to a curious crowd; He came to provide truth to – and make the way for – honest seekers. We would do well to remember that the gospel is never to be viewed as entertainment, with our focus being on the creativity or skillful execution of our presentation. The gospel is uncompromising in truth and is to be rightly communicated in word and in action.

The priests and teachers, who had earlier been unsuccessful in manipulating Jesus with their idle threats, now turned their attention to manipulating Herod with their false accusations. And Herod – being a fox, instead of a lion – was as easily swayed by them as he had been by his wife, Herodias (Mark 6:17). Instead of truly seeking truth, or attempting to stand on truth, Herod was more concerned with the public opinion being expressed by the priests and teachers. Thus, the fox was easily swayed to join in the mockery and ridicule of the one True King in the room – the Lion of Judah. In an attempt to gain even more approval from the religious leaders, it was probably Herod's idea to have one of his old robes placed on Jesus as a mockery.

But, having been the executor of John the Baptist, "the fox" determined that he would not be responsible for this Man's death, so he craftily defers the matter back to Pilate. Since the leaders in Judea were seeking the death of Jesus in Judea, he deferred the matter to the prefect of Judea. In that action, Herod created a stronger alliance – and gained political capital – with not only the religious leaders, but also with Pilate. It is worthy to note, however, that any capital gained through the mockery of truth is short-lived. Within just a few short years, Herod's favor waned, and he was removed from power by Rome and exiled to Gaul. The adage is true that "he who doesn't stand for something, will fall for anything" – and such was the life of Herod Antipas, the fox.

They mocked Jesus and, in doing so, they mocked Truth and Righteousness. Mockery is defined as "contemptuous language or behavior directed at a particular person or thing"[1]. Scripture tells us that "the king's heart is in the hand of the LORD" (Proverbs 21:1), and so is the heart of those who walk as spiritual leaders among the flock. In mocking Jesus, they were mocking the very authority under whom they were placed in their positions of leadership. They were making a mockery of God's law and the divine authority over them. In their effort to make a mockery of Jesus, they truly made a mockery of themselves and, in doing so, sealed their eternal fate. They would have been wise to heed the truth that was later penned by the apostle Paul: "*Don't be misled — you cannot mock the justice of God. You will always harvest what you plant. Those who live only to satisfy their own sinful nature will harvest decay and death from that sinful nature. But those who live to please the Spirit will harvest everlasting life from the Spirit*" (Galatians 6:7-8).

Any attempt by a king to mock the King will always result in the king himself being mocked – by death and decay. And that truth holds true for those who aren't kings. So, as we take up the cross to follow our King, let us take care to do so in a way that brings Him honor – and that nothing in our thoughts, attitudes or actions makes a mockery of Him, His Word or His mission.

[1] Oxford English Dictionary

* * *

49

A CRIMINAL'S RELEASE

Then Pilate called together the leading priests and other religious leaders, along with the people, and he announced his verdict. "You brought this man to me, accusing Him of leading a revolt. I have examined Him thoroughly on this point in your presence and find Him innocent. Herod came to the same conclusion and sent Him back to us. Nothing this man has done calls for the death penalty. So, I will have Him flogged, and then I will release Him." Then a mighty roar rose from the crowd, and with one voice they shouted, "Kill Him, and release Barabbas to us!" (Barabbas was in prison for taking part in an insurrection in Jerusalem against the government, and for murder.) Pilate argued with them, because he wanted to release Jesus. But they kept shouting, "Crucify Him! Crucify Him!" For the third time he demanded, "Why? What crime has He committed? I have found no reason to sentence Him to death. So, I will have Him flogged, and then I will release Him." But the mob shouted louder and louder, demanding that Jesus be crucified, and their voices prevailed. So, Pilate sentenced Jesus to die as they demanded. As they had requested, he released Barabbas, the man in prison for insurrection and murder. But he turned Jesus over to them to do as they wished.

Luke 23:13-25

* * *

Pilate was trying to escape making a decision about Jesus – but he could not. He had already announced for a second time that he did not find Jesus guilty of any of the charges the religious leaders had made against Him. Pilate knew that Herod had also not been able to find fault with Jesus. Herod had avoided making a pronouncement by simply mocking Him, putting a robe on Him and sending Him back to Pilate. But

Pilate, try as he might, could not avoid making a decision – and he knew that the fair and just decision was very different from the politically-correct decision being sought by those before him. Pilate knew that a Jewish uprising under his watch would bring a hasty conclusion to his political and military career. He was not prepared to sacrifice his own well-being for this Jew. However, he knew that this Jew was innocent of every charge being made against Him.

The reality is that it was Pilate who was on trial, not Jesus. Jesus was not trying to escape from the decision, but Pilate was. He sought an easy escape. The decision between the release of Barabbas versus Jesus should have been a "no-brainer". A prevailing custom called for the prefect to commute one prisoner's death sentence at Passover. Barabbas was a thief (John 18:40), a murderer and an insurrectionist. Pilate knew that the religious leaders' motivation for seeking the execution of Jesus was their envy of His standing with the ever-growing multitude. But he underestimated the depths to which religion can sink when it goes wrong. To Pilate's surprise, the chief priests and elders were successful in persuading the crowd who stood in front of Pilate to ask for the release of Barabbas. But bear in mind, the Pharisees had put together a crowd of "ringers". The crowd was not representative of the general populace gathered in the city for Passover. This crowd was made up of the religious leaders of the nation. This crowd – or jury, if you will – was by no means impartial or representative of the crowd that had shouted "Hosanna" when Jesus entered Jerusalem a few short days prior. This crowd was made up of the very people who felt threatened by Jesus' ministry. Imagine a judge asking a biased crowd for their decision as to what should be done with a man on trial! He knew Jesus was innocent, and yet, he feared that a riot was about to break out.

He carefully questioned Jesus, and even trembled at His answers. But even the Truth of the Word would not make a difference in his decision. The question came down to what was right versus his own selfish ambition, and his selfish ambition won out. He chose being popular over being right. He chose expediency over character, and compromise over what was just. There is at least one moment in everyone's life where they must stand up for what is right. This was Pilate's moment, and he failed miserably.

Imagine being Barabbas. He had been found guilty by a legal tribunal and had been condemned to death. There was never any question as to his guilt – in the minds of his condemners or in his own mind. He knew that he deserved his sentence of death. He knew that at any moment the Roman soldiers would be coming to take him from his prison cell to the hill of execution outside the city walls to be crucified on a cross. There would be no appeal. There would be no mercy. His sentence had been issued and his fate was sealed. Off in the distance, he heard the crowd shouting his name. It began as a dull roar, but the shouts quickly increased in volume. Then he heard them repeatedly shouting, "Crucify him!" The crowd was obviously shouting for his blood. The time of his execution had arrived. The soldiers arrived at his cell and led him out still bound. But to his surprise, instead of being led to Golgotha under the weight of a cross, he was led to stand before Pilate. There was another Man, also bound, standing there as well. Then the unimaginable took place. The man clothed in unrighteousness who deserved to be crucified for his transgressions was set free, and the Man clothed in righteousness – the One without sin – was undeservedly condemned by Pilate to be crucified. The criminal was released, and the Savior was condemned.

Keep the faces of Pilate and Barabbas both in your mind's eye. They are familiar faces – not only from this Gospel account – but also, they are the faces of many people that we encounter every day. They are the "Pilates" who refuse to make a decision about Jesus. They can find no fault with Him, but they are easily swayed by the crowd. It's not politically correct to decide in favor of Jesus, so the "Pilates" either make no decision, or give into the peer pressure of the crowd. But alas, they are the ones who are condemned to death – condemned by their rejection. And yes, there are also the "Barabbases" – and i am one. Their offenses and unrighteousness have rightly condemned them to death. But, undeservedly, Jesus has paid the price in their stead. Jesus has paid the price for their release.

Don't lose sight of Who the judge was on that day. This was the Father's plan. Jesus was the Judge and the Savior. Pilate was the sinner who rejected Jesus. And let there be no doubt that though it was the Father's plan, Pilate made his own choice. Barabbas was the sinner set free through the crucifixion of Jesus. (Let me hastily add that there is absolutely no indication in Scripture that Barabbas believed in Jesus. So, i am not making a claim that he was saved for eternity that day. However, the events of that day are a great picture of Christ's substitutionary death on the cross for our sins and, in that sense, Barabbas is a picture of those of us who have been set free through the sacrificial death of our Savior.)

• • •

One other picture that begins there in Pilate's court and continues to Calvary is that of Jesus freely and willingly taking up the cross that day. There was no one in that crowd, and there has been no one since that day, that merited His action. There was no one then, and no one since, who merited release or favor. As we take up the cross to follow our Savior, we will encounter many who do not merit our favor or our grace. Don't forget that neither do we, and Jesus extended it anyway. Go, and do likewise.

* * *

50

THEY AREN'T THE ONLY ONES WHO MOCKED JESUS

The soldiers took Jesus into the courtyard of the governor's headquarters (called the Praetorium) and called out the entire regiment. They dressed Him in a purple robe, and they wove thorn branches into a crown and put it on His head. Then they saluted Him and taunted, "Hail! King of the Jews!" And they struck Him on the head with a reed stick, spit on Him, and dropped to their knees in mock worship. When they were finally tired of mocking Him, they took off the purple robe and put His own clothes on Him again. Then they led Him away to be crucified.

Mark 15:16-20

* * *

We live in a world that is a mere shadow of what our Creator intended for it to be. The consequence of sin is so pervasive that it casts its pallor across every facet of our lives. Daily we are bombarded with news reports of acts of brutality perpetrated by one person upon another without any degree of shame or guilt. It has become so common place to the point that our senses have almost become numb to the daily reports. But often something occurs that is so egregious – or so close to home – that we cry out asking why a loving God would ever permit such a thing. Surely if there is a God in heaven, He would not permit these atrocities to occur.

Prior to making his final judgement, Pilate had Jesus scourged in the hopes that would satisfy the blood thirst of the religious leaders and the crowd they had incited to ask for crucifixion. Though he knew that Jesus was without guilt, he still permitted Him to go through the brutality of a Roman scourging. The Roman scourge was a short whip made of two or three leather thongs or ropes connected to a handle. The thongs were knotted with pieces of metal or bones at various intervals, with a hook at the end. The scourge was intended to quickly remove the flesh from the body of the victim stopping just short of death. The Romans were masters of this cruel form of punishment. And this torturous act was Pilate's attempt to free this innocent Man! Such was the state of our Lord when Pilate acquiesced to the religious leaders and turned Jesus over to the soldiers to be crucified.

As we saw in chapter 47, the entire military force under Pilate's command was 3,000 men for all of Judea. They were organized into ten cohorts of 300. One of those cohorts would have been based at the Praetorium. The soldiers were the brute force presence used by Rome to maintain law and order over its subjects. Though many had been locally recruited, they were a constant reminder to the Jewish people of their oppressive Roman ruler. Thus, they were viewed with disdain and disrespect by the Jews. But because they were not Roman citizens, they were also looked down upon by their Roman leaders. The rank and file soldiers were not selected for their good character; they were selected for their sadistic brutality and fighting ability. Most of the time, they were forced to control their growing hatred for the Jewish people and the frustration they felt by not being able to physically express that hatred. It was to this group that Pilate released Jesus – and there were no constraints on their actions, except that they had to deliver him to Golgotha for crucifixion.

We cannot fully comprehend the unbridled brutality, torture and humiliation that was unleashed on Jesus by these 300 men as they sought to satisfy their sadistic appetites. One writer describes a "game" that the Roman soldiers often "played" called "hot hand". The soldiers would each hold up a fist in the face of their victim. Then they would blindfold him, and each soldier would hit him in the face. They would beat their victim until his face was unrecognizable. Then they would remove the blindfold, and the victim was to identify which fist had not hit him. The prisoner was never able to identify the right one, and even if he did, the soldiers wouldn't admit it. So, the blindfold would be put back on him, and the "game" would continue. In the case of Jesus, even the mockery of the robe placed on His shredded flesh and the crown of thorns pressed into His brow were intended to subject Jesus to more brutality and torture.

. . .

But in the midst of it all, our Savior quietly suffered and did not speak out or fight back. By a single command, He could have surrounded Himself with a multitude of angels to protect Himself from the suffering. By a simple thought, He could have reduced the soldiers to a pillar of salt. By a single word, He could have said, "Enough!" and brought it all to an end. But He did not. He allowed Himself to suffer the fullness of the depravity of His fallen creation on our behalf, according to the Father's plan. It was a lesson that Mark's readers would need to learn as they soon faced some of the very same persecution themselves:

"For God called you to do good, even if it means suffering, just as Christ suffered for you. He is your example, and you must follow in His steps. He never sinned, nor ever deceived anyone. He did not retaliate when He was insulted, nor threaten revenge when He suffered. He left His case in the hands of God, who always judges fairly"
(1 Peter 2:21-23).

But even beyond the physical suffering, Jesus allowed Himself to be subjected to the humiliation and ridicule of being spat upon and taunted in mock worship, until they tired of mocking Him. Then after that morning of inhumane suffering, they led Him away to be crucified.

Again, surely if there is a God in heaven, He would not permit these atrocities to occur – even to His Own Son. And yet, He did. He wasn't the author of the brutality. We, as a fallen creation, don't need any help in being brutal. Our sin has fully equipped us for that task. But He permitted it because He had a purpose beyond what anyone could imagine. The religious leaders who thought they were victorious couldn't comprehend it. The Roman soldiers with their insatiable and unconscionable thirst for brutality were blind to it. Even His followers who hid in fear were unable to understand it. It was a dark day, and it was going to get even darker. But our God has told us, *"My thoughts are nothing like your thoughts," says the LORD. "And my ways are far beyond anything you could imagine"* (Isaiah 55:8). Paul would soon write to a group of believers who were being persecuted in Rome, *"And we know that God causes everything to work together for the good of those who love God and are called according to His purpose for them"* (Romans 8:28). And if God causes "everything" to work together, then that includes the brutality that was extended to His Son… to the Roman believers to whom Paul was writing… and to you and me.

Every action that the Roman soldiers perpetrated upon Jesus was an act of mockery in the face of a Holy God. Every deed of brutality, every word of disrespect, and every unrepentant action was an affront and an offense. And the brutality and the mockery did not end with the Roman soldiers. It has continued through the ages – even to this day. There continue to be governments, religious leaders and even family members who brutalize and mock Jesus through their actions and words inflicted upon brothers and sisters around this globe today who are being persecuted for their faith in Christ. And, in an even more pervasive way, through mockery that continues to be inflicted in ever increasing subtle ways of disregard and dishonor directed toward Jesus.

But one day, that will all stop. One day, our Lord will say, "Enough!" And on that day, He will return – not as a Suffering Savior, but as the King of Kings. Until that day, continue to take up the cross and follow Him, *"even if it means suffering, just as Christ suffered for you."*

* * *

51

HE TOOK UP THE CROSS

A passerby named Simon, who was from Cyrene, was coming in from the countryside just then, and the soldiers forced him to carry Jesus' cross. (Simon was the father of Alexander and Rufus.)
Mark 15:21

* * *

According to Roman law, one who was found guilty and condemned to death was required to carry his cross, or at least the cross beam, to the place of his crucifixion. Jesus left the Praetorium bearing His cross, but along the way the Roman soldiers conscripted Simon the Cyrene to carry Jesus' cross.

Let's ponder the question as to why someone was needed to carry His cross. The obvious explanation is the one that we immediately presume to be correct, and the one we see depicted in dramatizations of His crucifixion. That being, that physically, Jesus could no longer walk under the weight of the cross. Jesus would have been 33 years of age. He had spent most of His life as a carpenter and therefore would have had a muscular physique. Throughout the three-plus years of His ministry, He walked all over the countryside. And earlier that week, He had physically driven the moneychangers out of the Temple. Jesus had been in excellent physical condition. But after the brutal scourging and beatings that Jesus received at the hands of the Roman soldiers that morning, as the Son of Man, He would have been at near-death physically. But don't lose sight that He is also the Son of God. He could have easily called upon supernatural strength to shoulder that cross. Luke records in his Gospel (Luke 23:32) that the two criminals were also led out with Him to be executed. They, too, would have been scourged and beaten that morning, and yet, there is no mention of anyone else carrying their crosses. Though i don't in any way minimize the physical effects of the scourging and the beatings that He bore for my sins – and yours, i do wonder if, according to the Father's plan, there weren't at least two other reasons for someone else to carry His cross.

The first of the two has to do with the reason that Roman law required the cross to be carried. It was to be carried by one who was guilty. Jesus wasn't guilty of anything. Jesus lived a righteous, sinless life. Even the pagan Pilate could not find any guilt in Jesus. Jesus wasn't being crucified because He was guilty. The Father had ordained that the Son would be crucified to bear the iniquity of our sin. It was not for Jesus to carry that cross – it was for a sinner to do so.

At that moment – just the right moment – the Father led Simon the Cyrene to arrive at that place along the way to Golgotha. Simon was a Hellenistic Jew coming to Jerusalem for the observance of Passover. Cyrene was situated in modern-day Libya, on the northern coast of Africa. Settled by the Greeks in 630 B.C. and later infused with a significant Jewish population, Cyrene was the capital of the Roman district of Cyrenaica at the time of Jesus' crucifixion. By then, Cyrene was home to a large number of Greek-speaking, or Hellenistic, Jews. It was possibly some of his Cyrenian "brothers" who had approached Philip earlier in the week (John 12:20-21) about meeting Jesus. Unbeknownst to Simon, the Father had planned for his life to be transformed that day – and the impetus would be that the Roman soldiers would force him to carry Jesus' cross.

i would imagine that Simon's immediate reaction was resentment. Of all of the people on the road at that moment, why were the soldiers singling him out to carry the cross for this Man? Since Simon was just arriving in the city, i don't believe that he immediately knew that this was Jesus who was being led to be crucified. i do believe, that like the other Greeks i mentioned, he had heard of Jesus, but i don't believe that when the soldiers first pulled him out of the crowd that he knew who this Man was. And the soldiers didn't give him a choice. They commanded him to do so, and to refuse would have been fatal for him. So, get this picture in your mind. Jesus is ahead being led by the soldiers to His death, and there was Simon, following Jesus, carrying the cross. As they continued along the path, Simon would have heard the shouts from the crowd. He would have heard the grief-stricken cries of the women trailing behind (Luke 23:27). And at some point, he realized who this Man was. He heard Jesus turn to the women and say, *"Daughters of Jerusalem, don't weep for Me, but weep for yourselves and for your children"* (Luke 23:28). Jesus then bore witness to what would occur in the end times. Even as He was being led to His death, this Man, Jesus, was speaking as One in authority. Perhaps it was at that moment that Simon believed. Perhaps it was later as he stood to watch at the foot of the cross. Perhaps it was later after he heard that Jesus had risen from the tomb. But at some point, Simon believed in Jesus. Mark is the only Gospel account that records the names of his two sons – Alexander and Rufus. It would appear that Mark is mentioning these two men as familiar names to the church. Remember, Mark was with the apostle Paul in Rome. He would have been a discipler of the believers there in Rome. And Paul references a believer by the name of Rufus in his letter to the church in Rome (Romans 16:13). Very possibly the Rufus that he mentions is Simon's son. He also references the mother of Rufus, so it would appear that the whole family had become followers of Jesus.

You will recall that earlier in His ministry, as recorded in Luke 9:23, Jesus had told those in the crowd, *"If anyone would come after Me, let him deny himself and take up his cross daily and follow Me"* (ESV). Simon gives us a picture of that. Though he didn't at first choose to follow Jesus, at some point he appears to have made that choice. And here, on this day, he is carrying the cross of Jesus and following Him all the way to Calvary. The Father had a path for Simon to follow – and He led him to follow Jesus. The Father had a cross for him to carry – and it was the cross on which our Savior shed His blood for the forgiveness of your sin, and mine.

And today, the Father has a path for us – a path to follow Jesus. And He has a cross for us to carry – a cross that the Father will use as a part of His redemptive plan for His glory. The Roman soldiers gave the task to Simon out of disdain for him and contempt for Jesus, but the Father orchestrated the plan out of His perfect will for Simon and His love for His Son. No matter the cross you are carrying, or the one who has placed it onto your shoulders, the Father has orchestrated it – out of His perfect will for you and His love for His Son. Take up the cross and follow Him!

* * *

52

A PLACE CALLED GOLGOTHA

...He went to the place called Place of the Skull (in Hebrew, Golgotha). There they nailed Him to the cross. Two others were crucified with Him, one on either side, with Jesus between them. And Pilate posted a sign on the cross that read, "Jesus of Nazareth, the King of the Jews." The place where Jesus was crucified was near the city, and the sign was written in Hebrew, Latin, and Greek, so that many people could read it. Then the leading priests objected and said to Pilate, "Change it from 'The King of the Jews' to 'He said, I am King of the Jews.'" Pilate replied, "No, what I have written, I have written." When the soldiers had crucified Jesus, they divided His clothes among the four of them. They also took His robe, but it was seamless, woven in one piece from top to bottom. So, they said, "Rather than tearing it apart, let's throw dice for it." This fulfilled the Scripture that says, "They divided My garments among themselves and threw dice for My clothing." So that is what they did. Standing near the cross were Jesus' mother, and His mother's sister, Mary (the wife of Clopas), and Mary Magdalene. When Jesus saw His mother standing there beside the disciple He loved, He said to her, "Dear woman, here is your son." And He said to this disciple, "Here is your mother." And from then on, this disciple took her into his home.

John 19:17-27

* * *

Golgotha would have been outside the city wall, but near the city. The Romans conducted their executions by crucifixion near a road with high visibility (in this case, leading into Jerusalem). It was a part of the death penalty that the victim would die in the most conspicuous and humiliating way possible. It also reinforced the ironclad rule of Roman law and served as a further deterrent to those who may be considering breaking the law. It was common for the victim's crime to be written on a sign that was hung on the cross – also as a further deterrent. The sign would be written in the three main languages of that region in order to ensure that the maximum number of people were able to read it. It was written in Hebrew, the language of religion. It was written in Latin, the language of law and order. And it was written in Greek, the language of culture and education. In so doing, the Romans were unknowingly proclaiming some of the first written words of the gospel message in ways that people from many tongues and tribes could understand.

Notice the attempt of the religious leaders to have the sign changed. People have been attempting to change the message of the gospel ever since. But, also, notice Pilate's defiance to their request as his feeble attempt to exercise his power despite the way he had allowed them to manipulate him. Accordingly, in an attempt to counteract the message of the sign, *"the leading priests, the teachers of religious law, and the elders mocked Jesus"* by standing nearby and scoffing, *"…so He is the King of Israel, is He? Let Him come down from the cross right now, and we will believe in Him!"* (Matthew 27:41-42). i don't know about you, but as i read those words, other similar words come to mind – *"Then the devil took Him to the holy city, Jerusalem, to the highest point of the Temple, and said, 'If you are the Son of God, jump off!'"* (Matthew 4:5-6). Even in those last moments, the religious leaders were being the conduit of the voice of Satan, as he continued to make every attempt to mock Jesus and tempt Him to step down from the very purpose for which the Father had sent Him.

The soldiers overseeing a crucifixion were permitted to confiscate and share whatever personal belongings their victims had. In this case, all that Jesus possessed was a pair of sandals, a girdle, an outer robe, a head covering and a tunic (which was seamless). Apparently, each of the soldiers took one of the first four items of clothing and they then gambled for the seamless tunic (in fulfillment of Psalm 22:18). i am mindful that we live in a culture that is preoccupied with accumulating "things". But our Savior – who owns the cattle on a thousand hills (Psalm 50:10) – died without possessing one single item. i am not advocating that we are all to take a vow of poverty, but i am mindful that if we are to take up the cross and follow our Savior, He did not walk the way of accumulating possessions. As a matter of fact, He told the rich young man to sell all that He had (Matthew 19:21). Let's make sure that we have our priorities in the right order.

. . .

Jesus, as the Son of Man, was saying goodbye to His mother Mary, because He would rise again as the glorified Christ. He was honoring and completing His responsibility as the firstborn son of His earthly mother. First, He was assuring her salvation. Mary needed to come to faith in Christ just as every believer. Jesus was dying on the cross for the sins of the entire world – and that included Mary. He was making the way for her to be saved. She, then, had to believe, accept and follow Him. Second, through His resurrection, He was clearing her name forever. Her reputation that had suffered the injustice of gossip and innuendo for over thirty-three years would at last be vindicated. Third, as her firstborn son, He was making sure that she would be cared for the remainder of her earthly days. And in order to do so, He turned to His disciple John, whom He loved as a brother.

It is interesting to remember that Mary had other sons – James, Joseph, Jude and Simon (Mark 6:3) as well as daughters. We know that at least James and Jude went on to be followers of Jesus, if not all of His earthly family members. James, as the next oldest son, would have culturally been expected to be given the responsibility by Jesus to care for his widowed mother. We don't know all of the reasons that Jesus did not follow that cultural norm – but here are two things we do know. First, James and the other brothers had not yet believed in Jesus at the time of His crucifixion. They did not believe in Jesus until after His resurrection. Therefore, they were not like-minded, and He could not entrust His mother to anyone who was not. Second, Scripture makes no mention of His brothers being present at His crucifixion. Given the detailed account of who was there, it is reasonable to assume that they were not at the foot of the cross. Also, given the Passover celebration, they, in fact, would have been in Jerusalem, but they obviously chose to not follow Him to the cross. Remember, at that point they had believed that He could be the Messiah, but they did not believe Him to be the Son of God. So, they either stayed away from the cross due to fear of retribution upon His family members, or due to their unbelief since He had failed to declare Himself and establish His Kingdom, or due to their personal embarrassment over the way He had now sullied the family's reputation. So, as His dying request, He entrusted His mother to John's care. (As a footnote, all indications are that John remained in Jerusalem for many years following Christ's resurrection in order to care for Mary, and he did not leave the city until she had died.)

. . .

All of this occurred – and more – as our Savior hung on the cross. There are details about His crucifixion that the Gospel writers do not include. The Father Himself caused a veil of darkness to fall across the whole land (Luke 23:44) while His Son hung on that cross. There was a transaction that took place that day between the Father and the Son. It was a transaction for the sins of the world – which is beyond anything that we can comprehend. The only thing we can do is accept by faith the forgiveness that was appropriated only through the death of Jesus on that cross. Only through His death is the veil of darkness pierced. Only through His death are we enabled to walk in His holy light.

That day on Golgotha must have seemed like a triumph to Satan. He had bruised the heel of the woman's seed as foretold in Genesis 3. It must have seemed like a victory to the religious leaders. The threat to their position and power had been eliminated forever. And to a watching world, it must have seemed like a brutal murder – to many, an injustice. But to the Father, it was the only way His creation would ever be able to cross the sinful divide back to Him.

* * *

53

IT IS FINISHED! OR IS IT?

Jesus knew that His mission was now finished, and to fulfill Scripture He said, "I am thirsty." A jar of sour wine was sitting there, so they soaked a sponge in it, put it on a hyssop branch, and held it up to His lips. When Jesus had tasted it, He said, "It is finished!" Then He bowed His head and gave up His spirit.
John 19:28-30

* * *

Let's not lose sight of the fact that our Savior is as much man as if He was not God at all, and as much God as if He was not man at all. He is both fully divine and fully human. There was never a time when Jesus became God. He has always been God. But Jesus has not always been man. He became man through His incarnational birth in the manger. As the ancient theologian Gregory of Naziansen put it, "Remaining what He was, He became what He was not." The writer of Hebrews writes, "*it was necessary for Him to be made in every respect like us, His brothers and sisters, so that He could be our merciful and faithful High Priest before God. Then He could offer a sacrifice that would take away the sins of the people. Since He Himself has gone through suffering and testing, He is able to help us when we are being tested*" (Hebrews 2:17-18). He became man so that He could die for our sins – so that He could be that unblemished sacrifice. He had to be human in order to pay the penalty for humans. But, as this passage tells us, He didn't cease being human after His crucifixion. He continues as the Son of Man to be a merciful and faithful High Priest. His humanity enables Him to more fully sympathize with us and identify with us. In that moment on the cross when He died, He paid the price once and for all as the sacrifice for the forgiveness of sin. His mission as the perfect Lamb of God was now finished.

His sufferings were now behind Him. He had refused to drink the pain-deadening wine that was always offered to those about to be crucified (Matthew 27:34). Bear in mind, the Roman soldiers did not offer that narcotic out of compassion, they offered it so that the amount of time that a victim suffered the humiliation and brutality of the cross would be lengthened. The excruciating pain accelerated the onset of death. Deadening the pain slowed it down. This would partially explain why the criminals being crucified on either side of Jesus that day were still alive after Jesus died (John 19:31-33). The criminals probably accepted the wine offered by the soldiers. But our Lord was accomplishing so much more on that cross, and He knew that His mind needed to be clear. Thus, He endured the intense excruciating physical pain to its fullest.

There was also a suffering and pain that was far greater than the physical pain that Christ endured. During the three hours of darkness from noon until 3:00PM (Matthew 27:45-49), Jesus felt the full wrath of God, as He carried the full burden of sin, and He experienced complete separation from the Father for the first and only time in His existence. Remember, sin separates us from a Holy God. Jesus was carrying the full burden of sin. That sin separated Him from His Father. We will never fully comprehend the pain and suffering He endured that was caused by that separation and isolation. But He endured that suffering because the Father so loves the world that He sent the Son, and the Son so loves the Father that He endured to the end.

After the sufferings leading up to the cross, and His sufferings on the cross, Jesus was "spent". His physical body was dehydrated and depleted of any moisture. He was parched. He was only able to whisper the words, *"I am thirsty."* One of the soldiers took pity on Jesus and moistened His lips with the cheap sour wine that the soldiers were drinking. We tend to picture that Jesus was hanging many feet up in the air, but the reality is that Jesus' feet were no more than three to four feet off the ground. So, the soldier put the soaked sponge on the end of a branch and reached up and held it to His lips. Even the Messianic prophecy of Psalm 69:21 – *"... they offer me sour wine to satisfy my thirst"* – was fulfilled. That bit of moisture didn't quench Jesus' thirst, but it was all He needed to speak out His last words in triumph, *"It is finished!"*

• • •

Our Lord's sufferings were finished. The prophecies foretelling His incarnation and death were now all fulfilled, including the twenty-eight specifically related to His crucifixion. The sacrifice for our sin was now complete. It was finished! As He bowed His head and gave up His Spirit, *"...the curtain in the sanctuary of the Temple was torn in two, from top to bottom. The earth shook, rocks split apart, and tombs opened"* (Matthew 27:51-52). The earth quaked and the Roman officer, overseeing the crucifixion, declared, *"This Man truly was the Son of God!"* (Matthew 27:54).

Yes, it was finished! Our redemption was made complete. Jesus had met the righteous demands of the holy law. He had paid our sin debt in full. Jesus had completed the work that the Father had given Him to do (John 17:4).

But His work did not stop there. Through His death, *"He entered once for all into the holy places, not by means of the blood of goats and calves but by means of His own blood, thus securing an eternal redemption"* (Hebrews 9:12 ESV). Through His death, He seized the keys of death and the grave (Revelation 1:18). Through His death, He set free the captives of death and the grave (Luke 4:18). Through His death, He set the standard for how we as His followers should live sacrificially (John 15:13). Through His death, He set the stage for the greatest miracle that was to follow (Mark 16:6).

From the day of His incarnational birth to the day of His death on the cross, Jesus was on a mission given to Him by the Father. Even at a young age, He knew that He must be about His Father's business (Luke 2:49). In His last days leading up to the cross, Jesus resolutely set out for Jerusalem (Luke 9:51). Without His death on the cross, there is no mission. Without His shed blood, there is no redemptive work. It is only through His death on the cross that the mission is able to continue. And continue it does. Christ's pain and suffering, and death on the cross is finished, but the mission continues. That's why He has called us to take up the cross and follow Him in being about the Father's mission. It is finished! But the work continues....

* * *

54

LAID IN A TOMB

Now there was a good and righteous man named Joseph. He was a member of the Jewish high council, but he had not agreed with the decision and actions of the other religious leaders. He was from the town of Arimathea in Judea, and he was waiting for the Kingdom of God to come. He went to Pilate and asked for Jesus' body. Then he took the body down from the cross and wrapped it in a long sheet of linen cloth and laid it in a new tomb that had been carved out of rock. This was done late on Friday afternoon, the day of preparation, as the Sabbath was about to begin. As His body was taken away, the women from Galilee followed and saw the tomb where His body was placed. Then they went home and prepared spices and ointments to anoint His body. But by the time they were finished the Sabbath had begun, so they rested as required by the law.

Luke 23:50-56

* * *

Customarily it would have been the responsibility of Jesus' family and friends to arrange for His burial. But remember that this had all unfolded in less than twenty-four hours. No one ever expected Jesus to die that day, so no burial arrangements had been made. Most of His family and close followers had scattered out of fear, and those who remained were just barely coping with what was taking place. They had all traveled to Jerusalem from Galilee and they had very little in the way of money. So, they had nothing at their disposal with which to bury Jesus' body. Luke records that the few family and friends who were there were standing at a distance watching after Jesus died (Luke 23:49). They were experiencing overwhelming grief. Burial may have not yet even crossed their minds. Even if it did, they had no resources. And Sabbath was rapidly approaching. The bodies of the victims of crucifixion were usually left to be eaten by birds or wild animals, or thrown like worthless garbage into the dump and burned. But that would not be the case for the Son of God – His Father had a plan.

Not all of the religious leaders had sought the crucifixion of Jesus. There were at least two voices of reason present when the high council deliberated. Though their voices did not carry the day, they appear to have spoken out (John 7:50-51). One was Nicodemus, from Galilee, and the other was Joseph, from the town of Arimathea in the province of Judea.

Joseph's decision to go to Pilate and request the body of Jesus would not have been popular with Caiaphas, Annas and most of the members of the high council. Though he had apparently argued against their plan to arrest Jesus and have Him sentenced to death, those words of rebellion against the authority of the high council leadership were at least restricted to behind closed doors. But now, this action to go to Pilate was an outward expression of his dissention and would have been considered to be an outright act of betrayal of his Sanhedrin brothers. This action would have been political suicide for Joseph, jeopardizing his position on the Sanhedrin, his influence in the community, and his personal wealth. It would have taken great courage and strength of character for him to go to Pilate to arrange for a suitable burial for the body of Jesus.

The apostle John writes that Nicodemus also assisted in the burial. He brought embalming ointment to assist Joseph in the preparation of Jesus' body for burial (John 19:39-40). But even his action was not done as publicly as that of Joseph. Joseph apparently paid for the linen cloth and provided the newly hewn tomb. The two men needed to act quickly so that Jesus' body could be laid in the tomb before the beginning of Sabbath at dusk. They were resolved to act in a way contrary to the actions of the high council, but they would not violate the laws of Sabbath. You and i would do well to follow the example of these two men. They stepped out boldly and followed Him to His death. We don't follow Him to His death. We serve a risen Savior. Are we as prepared to follow Him no matter the cost?

But let's back up a moment to where Jesus declared, *"It is finished!"* At that moment, Luke records that He also said, *"Father, I entrust My spirit into Your hands"* (Luke 23:46). Remember, Jesus was as much man as if He was not God at all. That means that at that moment of Jesus' death, His soul and spirit departed from His body – which is the exact same thing that will occur to you and me at the moment of our deaths, if Jesus does not return before then. Joseph and Nicodemus did not lay Jesus in the tomb. He had already departed. They were just laying His dead body in the tomb. Peter tells us that Jesus was very busy while His body was laying in that tomb. In 1 Peter 3:19, we read that Jesus' spirit entered into Hades and proclaimed His victory over Satan and his hosts to the evil spirits that Jesus' half-brother Jude describes in Jude 1:6. And Paul writes in Ephesians 4:8, in fulfillment of the prophecy in Psalm 68:18 – *"You ascended on high, leading a host of captives in Your train…"* (ESV) – that Jesus gathered all the redeemed who had been awaiting His redemption and took them from paradise to their permanent dwelling in heaven. That train into heaven would have included Abraham, David, Joshua, Daniel, the beggar Lazarus, and all those who had been previously justified by faith. Folks, those were some great, "gettin' up" days in the spirit world for those for whom faith had now become sight (2 Corinthians 5:7).

Meanwhile, on the earth, no one, even those closest to Jesus, could fully grasp all that had happened, let alone what was taking place at that moment, or what was about to take place. In the spiritual realm, there was great rejoicing among the saints and great sorrow among the demons. Whereas on earth, there was great rejoicing among the enemies of Jesus, and great sorrow among His family and followers. Though He had foretold that He would rise again, not one of His family or followers seemed to be watching by faith with hopeful anticipation. Interestingly enough, the only ones who seemingly remembered His promise were the religious leaders who petitioned Pilate to post guards at the tomb. And they didn't believe He would rise from the dead, but they were fearful that His followers would remove His body and make that claim (Matthew 27:62-66).

How often do we get caught up in our grief and pain, and lose sight of our Lord's promises? How often do we get so focused on all of the swirling activity around us, and lose sight that the One who has promised is able – and faithful – to accomplish all that He promised He would? How often do we lose sight that even death and the grave can't defeat Him? You might be walking through a period of time right now in your journey that feels just like it did for Mary, for John, for Mary Magdalene, for Peter. All you see and all you feel is pain. The grief and despair are overwhelming. It feels like Jesus is laying in the tomb and there is no hope. Don't believe that lie! Don't even try and figure it all out. You can't! But i'm here to tell you – Jesus isn't laying in that tomb. He is at work on your behalf! And in His time, you will rise out of that circumstance and pain. Trust Him – He who promised is able – and faithful – "*...to do far more abundantly beyond all that we ask or think, according to the power that works within us*" (Ephesians 3:20 NASB).

It's not over!

* * *

55

THEY CAME TO ANOINT HIM

Saturday evening, when the Sabbath ended, Mary Magdalene, Mary the mother of James, and Salome went out and purchased burial spices so they could anoint Jesus' body. Very early on Sunday morning, just at sunrise, they went to the tomb. On the way they were asking each other, "Who will roll away the stone for us from the entrance to the tomb?" But as they arrived, they looked up and saw that the stone, which was very large, had already been rolled aside. When they entered the tomb, they saw a young man clothed in a white robe sitting on the right side. The women were shocked, but the angel said, "Don't be alarmed. You are looking for Jesus of Nazareth, who was crucified. He isn't here! He is risen from the dead! Look, this is where they laid His body. Now go and tell His disciples, including Peter, that Jesus is going ahead of you to Galilee. You will see Him there, just as He told you before He died." The women fled from the tomb, trembling and bewildered, and they said nothing to anyone because they were too frightened.

Mark 16:1-8

* * *

Throughout His earthly ministry, there were a number of women who traveled with Jesus and His disciples. Some were members of His extended family or those of His disciples, such as Salome (the mother of James and John, and the wife of Zebedee) and Mary (the mother of James the Less, and the wife of Clopas). Some of the women had been healed by Jesus, or were those from whom He had cast out evil spirits, including Mary Magdalene (Luke 8:2) and Joanna (the wife of Chuza, the household manager of Herod Antipas – Luke 8:3). These, and many others, *"were contributing from their own resources to support Jesus and His disciples"* (Luke 8:3). Mark lists Mary Magdalene, Mary (the mother of James) and Salome as coming to the tomb that morning. Luke indicates that Joanna was also there. (As a footnote: Luke is the only Gospel writer that includes Joanna, not only at the tomb, but also at other parts of his account. He is also the only Gospel writer that includes details of what occurred in the court when Jesus was brought before Herod Antipas. Given the role of Joanna's husband, she was probably one of Luke's eyewitnesses.) Luke also says that there were other women, so there was at least one other unnamed woman in the group (Luke 24:10).

These women were unable to make the needed preparations for the burial of Jesus' body before sunset on Friday. They just didn't have enough time between the time He died and the time that sunset occurred. Joseph of Arimathea and Nicodemus had been able to make quick arrangements but, before the women realized what was happening, the sun was setting, and Sabbath was beginning. But i hope you see the sovereign hand of God in their delay. The Father's plan was perfect. He had ordained for Joseph and Nicodemus to bury His Son's body, but He had a different assignment for the women. He didn't need for them to be at the tomb when Jesus' body was placed. They were to arrive at the tomb for a totally different purpose!

They apparently were able to prepare some of the spices and ointments on Friday, just before the Sabbath (Luke 23:56). They were then able to purchase those that they still needed and make their final arrangements after dark on Saturday night. But they would need sunlight to do what they needed to do, so they waited until Sunday at sunrise. As the women were walking to the tomb, they realized that the stone would be too heavy for them to roll away in order to gain entry. Remember, this plan was unfolding quickly. They hadn't been able to think through all of the details. Fortunately, the Father had been planning the details for eternity, and He had not forgotten anything!

At this point, let's synchronize the chronology of this account with those in Matthew 28, Luke 24 and John 20. As the women approached the tomb, they saw that the large stone had been rolled away from the entrance. Apparently, Mary Magdalene left the other women to go and alert Peter and John. Meanwhile, the other women entered the tomb and encountered the angels who declared to them that Jesus had risen from the dead. i am not sure what the Greek word is – but apparently the women "freaked out!" They fled from the tomb, trembling and bewildered. Remember, Jesus had tried to prepare them. He had told them He would rise again. But even these, His closest followers, couldn't quite believe it. They had all been there when Jesus called Lazarus to come out of the tomb, but they weren't expecting Jesus to call Himself out of the tomb. Let's be honest – would you have expected it?

Now remember, the night of Jesus' arrest, the disciples had all scattered – except John and Peter. John and Peter had stayed in Jerusalem – they had gone to Caiaphas' home. The rest of the group took off – and probably went to Bethany (where they had been spending the night earlier in the week). Mary Magdalene apparently headed into the city to find Peter and John. The other women apparently headed toward Bethany, where they had probably been staying as well. Mary Magdalene found Peter and John and told them that the stone had been rolled away from the tomb. She was certain that the religious leaders had taken Jesus' body. So, all three of them headed back to the tomb.

We'll pick up on this narrative in the next chapter but, before we do, let's remember what has taken place. Jesus has completed the work that He had to do while His soul and spirit were absent from His physical body. He has completed the work of redemption and He has set the captives free! Jesus had told the Pharisees that He would give them the sign of the prophet Jonah (Matthew 16:4) – He would arise on the third day. He had also told them that if they destroyed "this temple" – His body – He would, in three days, raise it up (John 2:19). He had completed the work that the Father had for Him to do within the timeframe that the Father had set for it to be accomplished. And the Father's timing is perfect!

What has the Father promised you that He will accomplish in and through your life? What has He revealed as a promise from His Word that you are holding by faith, but have not yet experienced by sight? Allow the experience of these women to be a reminder that what He promises, He will accomplish. And He will accomplish it in His timeframe! He won't be late – but He also won't be early. His timing is perfect. And it will probably occur when we are focusing elsewhere on a task that is before us. The women came to anoint the body of Jesus, never expecting that He had risen. Most often His answer will come at a time and in a way that we least expect it. (Incidentally, so will His return. That's why He has told us to stay alert! – 1 Thessalonians 5:6)

. . .

Hold this truth in the light of His resurrection – what He begins, He completes (Philippians 1:6), and what He promises, He fulfills. As Moses said, *"God is not a man, so He does not lie. He is not human, so He does not change His mind. Has He ever spoken and failed to act? Has He ever promised and not carried it through?"* (Numbers 23:19). No, He hasn't! And the empty tomb is proof! Trust Him!

* * *

56

NOW IT'S FINISHED!

Early on Sunday morning, while it was still dark, Mary Magdalene came to the tomb and found that the stone had been rolled away from the entrance. She ran and found Simon Peter and the other disciple, the one whom Jesus loved. She said, "They have taken the Lord's body out of the tomb, and we don't know where they have put Him!" Peter and the other disciple started out for the tomb. They were both running, but the other disciple outran Peter and reached the tomb first. He stooped and looked in and saw the linen wrappings lying there, but he didn't go in. Then Simon Peter arrived and went inside. He also noticed the linen wrappings lying there, while the cloth that had covered Jesus' head was folded up and lying apart from the other wrappings. Then the disciple who had reached the tomb first also went in, and he saw and believed— for until then they still hadn't understood the Scriptures that said Jesus must rise from the dead. Then they went home.

John 20:1-10

* * *

Mary Magdalene was the one from whom Jesus cast out seven demons (Luke 8:2). Some scholars also believe that she was the woman who knelt at the feet of Jesus and anointed His feet with perfume and her tears, wiping them off with her hair (Luke 7:38). She was someone that we all need to aspire to be – someone who was saved by Jesus, and never got over it! She was eternally grateful to her Lord for His salvation.

. . .

John is the "other disciple", "the one whom Jesus loved". Throughout his Gospel account, he always refers to himself in that manner, but any of His disciples could have used that title for themselves. As a matter of fact, each of us should think of ourselves in that way. John wrote, *"We love Him, because He first loved us"* (1 John 4:19 KJV). Each of us is one whom Jesus loves.

John is also a *"friend who sticks closer than a brother"* (Proverbs 18:24). John "stuck" with Peter when Peter desperately needed a friend. Peter ached because of his denial of Jesus. His remorse was overwhelming. But gratefully, he didn't stop with remorse like Judas had. He was repentant for his sin. And he truly sought forgiveness. It would have been easy for John to "write Peter off" in light of his denial of Christ. Too often Christians are known for doing just that – writing off those who have fallen. But John chose to love Peter. He had heeded Jesus' words in the upper room to *"love each other"* (John 13:34). And the Lord used John in His healing work to cleanse and repair Peter's heart.

It is ironic that the religious leaders were concerned about the disciples stealing Jesus' body, and that Mary's first thought was that the religious leaders had taken His body. That thought just added to her grief. So, she let John and Peter run on ahead back to the tomb. She wasn't in any hurry to see an empty tomb. Her thoughts were now even more consumed by her grief.

Peter and John weren't truly expecting the resurrection of Jesus any more than Mary Magdalene was. They probably thought that she had made a mistake in what she saw. Perhaps, she had gone to the wrong tomb. They weren't running to the tomb expecting to find Jesus alive. They were expecting to uncover Mary's error and find His body.

John apparently was the faster runner. He got to the tomb before Peter did (remember Peter was also the older of the two). But John stopped at the doorway looking in. Uninhibited Peter charged past John right into the tomb. There they both saw the linen wrappings neatly rolled up. It was at that moment that John writes, *"he saw and believed"* (John 20:8). John couldn't yet prove that Jesus was risen, but He believed it with all his heart. He believed that Jesus had risen according to the Scriptures, and he believed once and for all that Jesus truly was God in the flesh. The two of them then departed to return to where they had been staying.

This time they didn't run. They walked, pondering all that they had just seen.

About that time, Mary Magdalene arrived back at the tomb. She remained outside weeping. Then *"as she wept, she stooped and looked into the tomb"* for the first time. She saw two angels who asked her why she was weeping. *"They* (the religious leaders) *have taken away my Lord, and I do not know where they have laid Him."* She then turned and saw Jesus standing there. But due to her grief, she did not recognize Him. Thinking He was the gardener she again sought an answer from Him as to where His body was laid. At that moment, Jesus spoke her name and she knew! Having seen Jesus, she believed! And off she went to deliver the good news and His instructions to Peter and John (John 20:11-18).

In the meantime, Jesus appeared to the other women (Mary - the wife of Clopas, Salome, Joanna, and at least one other) who had been at the tomb earlier as they were running to find the other disciples (Matthew 28:8-9). Imagine their reaction. They had not expected to encounter the living Lord Jesus; they had expected to anoint His body. If they were terrified when they saw the angels, can you just imagine how they felt when they saw Jesus? And Jesus said to them, *"Don't be afraid!"* (Matthew 28:10).

The eyes of the "one whom Jesus loved" were opened to the reality of who Jesus was by faith. The woman who had never gotten over what Jesus had done for her, as well as the other women who had been at the tomb, encountered the truth of who Jesus was by sight. Peter and the others continued to contemplate all of these things based upon what these witnesses were telling them. But the day wasn't over! Faith would become sight for many more.

In some respects, as followers of Jesus who are taking up the cross and following Him, we are in the same place as these men and women. We have heard the reports of the witnesses. He has given us His Word. His work on the cross is finished and the tomb is empty! If the work had stopped at the cross, we, as His followers, would be the most pitiable – and the most sorrowful. Because we would be following a dead savior. And a dead savior isn't really a savior at all. He would have set us up to fail. He would have set a standard that we by no means could reach, and He would have failed to make a way whereby we can be saved. As we go through the pain, suffering and death of this life, we would be doing so without hope. But the tomb IS empty. Jesus arose from the dead! Today, we accept that fact and receive that assurance according to the reports of the many witnesses and the authority of Scripture. Like John, our eyes have been opened to that reality by faith. And "the day" isn't over – soon that faith will become sight! We have that hope because we follow a Living Savior who rose from the grave. Salvation in Him is complete. It truly has been finished!

* * *

57

THEIR EYES WERE OPENED

That same day, two of Jesus' followers were walking to the village of Emmaus, seven miles from Jerusalem. As they walked along, they were talking about everything that had happened. As they talked and discussed these things, Jesus Himself suddenly came and began walking with them. But God kept them from recognizing Him. He asked them, "What are you discussing so intently as you walk along?" They stopped short, sadness written across their faces. Then one of them, Clopas, replied, "You must be the only person in Jerusalem who hasn't heard about all the things that have happened there the last few days." "What things?" Jesus asked. "The things that happened to Jesus, the Man from Nazareth," they said. "He was a prophet who did powerful miracles, and He was a mighty teacher in the eyes of God and all the people. But our leading priests and other religious leaders handed Him over to be condemned to death, and they crucified Him. We had hoped He was the Messiah who had come to rescue Israel. This all happened three days ago. "Then some women from our group of His followers were at His tomb early this morning, and they came back with an amazing report. They said His body was missing, and they had seen angels who told them Jesus is alive! Some of our men ran out to see, and sure enough, His body was gone, just as the women had said." ...Then Jesus took them through the writings of Moses and all the prophets, explaining from all the Scriptures the things concerning Himself. ...As they sat down to eat, He took the bread and blessed it. Then He broke it and gave it to them. Suddenly, their eyes were opened, and they recognized Him. And at that moment He disappeared! They said to each other, "Didn't our hearts burn within us as He talked with us on the road and explained the Scriptures to us?" And within the hour they were on their way back to Jerusalem. There they found the eleven disciples and the others who had gathered with them, who said, "The Lord has really risen! He appeared to Peter."

Luke 24:13-35

* * *

Emmaus was a small village seven miles northwest of Jerusalem. Clopas and his companion were downhearted as they made the journey from Jerusalem to Emmaus. Before they left Jerusalem, Clopas' wife (Mary) had told them that, when she and some of the other women had gone to the tomb to anoint Jesus' body that morning, the tomb was empty. (This encounter between Clopas and his wife had apparently taken place before his wife and the other women had personally encountered Jesus along the way.) They had given an amazing report that they had seen angels who said that Jesus was alive. But the women had been somewhat hysterical, so it was difficult to discern what they really had seen or heard. The two men had learned that Peter and John had also been to the tomb, and that, in fact, Jesus' body was gone. But the question still remained – where was the body of Jesus?

Clopas and his traveling companion had both been followers of Jesus. As a matter of fact, Clopas' son (James the Less) was one of Jesus' disciples. After Clopas and his wife (Mary) had spoken, she had headed off with the other women to tell their son and the other disciples what they had seen and heard. But Clopas and his fellow traveler didn't know what to make of it all. They believed Jesus to be a prophet of God who did powerful miracles. And, without question, He was the mightiest teacher they had ever heard. They had believed that He was the Messiah who had come to rescue Israel. But then the leading priests and other religious leaders had handed Him over to be condemned to death, and He had been crucified. Now all their hopes that He was the Messiah had been dashed. His death made no sense. They had faithfully followed Him for three years. What were they to do now? Had they been wrong?

As they walked along, discussing these things, Jesus joined them – though they did not recognize Him. He was a stranger to them. Bear in mind, they weren't looking for Him either. They thought He was dead and gone. They were blinded to who He was by their grief and their doubts. As they continued together, this Stranger graciously began to explain the prophecies regarding the Messiah to them, one by one, with great clarity. When they arrived in Emmaus, they prevailed upon the Stranger to join them for a meal. And as Jesus took the bread and broke it – just as He had many times before as they ate together – their eyes were opened – and they saw Him! Luke writes that *"at that moment He disappeared!"* Within the hour they were on their way back to Jerusalem to tell the others what they had seen and heard.

At some other time that day, after Jesus appeared to Mary Magdalene outside the tomb, He also appeared to Peter. It occurred sometime after Peter and John had visited the empty tomb. And it occurred when he and John were apart from one another. John had believed by faith that Jesus had risen when he saw the empty tomb. Peter hadn't known what to believe. And his belief had been further clouded by his remorse over his denial of Jesus.

It is noteworthy that we do not know any of the details surrounding Jesus' appearance to Peter. We only know that it occurred. Luke and Paul bear witness to their face-to-face meeting (Luke 24:34 and 1 Corinthians 15:5), but the content of their encounter was kept private. There was something that needed to be reconciled between the two of them. It apparently was a two-part conversation. John shares the second part in John 21:15-17. It was a chiding and a word of correction, and we will look at that portion in chapter 60 of this book. But the first part of that conversation was a personal and private transaction of healing that took place between Peter and His Lord. Jesus knew that before correction could take place, healing needed to occur. And that healing needed to occur before Jesus and Peter were together with the other disciples. He knows that in our lives as well. He knows when He needs to rebuke us. He knows when He needs to correct us. And He also knows when He needs to heal us. He knows the "what", the "how" and the "when". And He will take the same care with us that He took with Peter. It's called grace. It's called mercy. It's called love. And we would do well to show that grace, mercy and love to one another.

Jesus knew what Clopas and his companion needed. They needed to have their eyes opened. And He knew what Peter needed. He needed to be forgiven and have his heart healed. And our risen Savior knows of what we have need. May God give us the eyes, the ears and the hearts to receive it.

* * *

58

PEACE BE WITH YOU

That Sunday evening the disciples were meeting behind locked doors because they were afraid of the Jewish leaders. Suddenly, Jesus was standing there among them! "Peace be with you," He said. As He spoke, He showed them the wounds in His hands and His side. They were filled with joy when they saw the Lord! Again, He said, "Peace be with you. As the Father has sent Me, so I am sending you." Then He breathed on them and said, "Receive the Holy Spirit. If you forgive anyone's sins, they are forgiven. If you do not forgive them, they are not forgiven." One of the twelve disciples, Thomas (nicknamed the Twin), was not with the others when Jesus came. They told him, "We have seen the Lord!" But he replied, "I won't believe it unless I see the nail wounds in His hands, put my fingers into them, and place my hand into the wound in His side." Eight days later the disciples were together again, and this time Thomas was with them. The doors were locked; but suddenly, as before, Jesus was standing among them. "Peace be with you," He said. Then He said to Thomas, "Put your finger here, and look at My hands. Put your hand into the wound in My side. Don't be faithless any longer. Believe!" "My Lord and my God!" Thomas exclaimed. Then Jesus told him, "You believe because you have seen Me. Blessed are those who believe without seeing Me."

John 20:19-29

* * *

This is the first time that all of Jesus' disciples are back together since the night of His arrest, with the exception of Judas Iscariot (the betrayer, who is no longer counted among their group, and has himself already committed suicide) and Thomas (the doubter, whose absence from this gathering is a curiosity). They had secretly gathered, and the door to the room was locked. The room was abuzz with the reports. Mary Magdalene had told the group about how Jesus had spoken to her as she stood outside the tomb. John shared how he and Peter had witnessed the empty tomb, and his belief that Jesus truly was the Son of the Living God. Mary, Joanna and Salome relayed their encounter with the angels in the tomb, and then how Jesus had appeared to them on their way to report to the disciples. Then Peter told them that Jesus was alive and had appeared to him earlier in the day. Finally, Clopas and his companion had just returned from Emmaus and were telling *"their story of how Jesus had appeared to them as they were walking along the road"* (Luke 24:35). Luke records that right as they were telling about their encounter with Jesus, He suddenly appeared in the room (Luke 24:36).

The disciples' heads were spinning. They kept hearing these reports from brothers and sisters that they respected, but this was all still hard to believe. How could this possibly be true? Jesus had been subjected to unspeakable brutality and had died on the cross. They had witnessed it, albeit from a distance after they scattered. Could this be a part of the religious leaders' plot to not only murder Jesus, but to defame His teachings and His miracles? Was this all a part of the plan to now draw out His close followers and arrest them as well? At that moment, there was still more fear than faith present in that room.

Then all of a sudden – Jesus appeared – out of nowhere! And the door was locked! i would venture to say that these guys were ready to jump out of their skins! And if we had been there, we would have been ready to do the same. They thought they were seeing a ghost (Luke 24:37). So, it is no wonder that the first words out of Jesus' mouth were *"Peace be with you!"* Be at peace, the One – the only One – who can make sense of it all is now in the room! Jesus calmed their fears and gave them assurance. He ate a piece of broiled fish to assure them that He wasn't a ghost (Luke 24:42-43). He showed them the wounds in His hands, His feet and His side to prove to them that He who was dead was now alive. The work that the Father had given Him to do was now complete. Gradually the disciples' fear and anxiety turned to peace and joy! Allow me to conjecture that, at some point, Jesus' and Peter's eyes knowingly locked for a moment as they saw the rest of the disciples gradually and finally coming to that place of peace. Peter had experienced that same emotional roller coaster earlier that day – and i am certain that his was to an even greater degree.

. . .

Then for a second time, Jesus said to them, *"Peace be with you"*. But this time it wasn't a word of peace for them, it was a word of peace that they were now to go forth and share with a world that desperately needed peace. As the Father had sent Him, He was now sending them (and us)!

Again, we aren't given any explanation as to why Thomas was not in the room that night. John is the only Gospel writer who gives us that report. Surely, Thomas didn't have a more pressing appointment. But later when he did join the other disciples, he refused to accept their testimony. He held to the conviction that since he wasn't there to see it, it must not be true. Thus, he became "Doubting Thomas" – to this day defined as "a skeptic who refuses to believe without direct personal experience." His skepticism and faithlessness robbed him of joy for eight long days before Jesus again appeared in their midst and stood among them, this time including Thomas. Jesus again declared, *"Peace be with you"*, but this time He added a rebuke to Thomas with a truth that we too would do well to embrace – don't believe simply because you see; believe because of Who I am and what I have said" (paraphrase John 20:29).

It would do us well to repeat and rehearse the truths that the disciples learned and experienced on those two occasions:

1. No matter our situation or circumstance, we will always find peace in the presence of our Savior. As the apostle Paul wrote to the church, *"Don't worry about anything; instead, pray about everything. Tell God what you need and thank Him for all He has done. Then you will experience God's peace, which exceeds anything we can understand. His peace will guard your hearts and minds as you live in Christ Jesus"* (Philippians 4:6-7).

2. We have not heard the full truth about any situation until we have heard from Jesus. As you cast your doubts and fear on Him, trust Him for the answers that you need to know – not necessarily all the answers you want to have, but all the answers you need to know. Some of those answers will not come until we are in His presence. But in the meantime, He has promised that *"You are truly My disciples if you remain faithful to My teachings. And you will know the truth, and the truth will set you free"* (John 8:31-32).

3. The peace He gives us – His gospel – is not just for us. He has entrusted

it to us to share it with others. As Jesus said that night, *"As the Father has sent Me, so I am sending you."*

4. Don't believe simply because you see; believe because of Who Jesus is and what He has said.

Peace be with you! "*...Because you belong to Christ Jesus, God will bless you with peace that no one can completely understand. And this peace will control the way you think and feel*" (Philippians 4:7 CEV).

* * *

59

CAST THE NET

Later, Jesus appeared again to the disciples beside the Sea of Galilee. This is how it happened. Several of the disciples were there — Simon Peter, Thomas (nicknamed the Twin), Nathanael from Cana in Galilee, the sons of Zebedee, and two other disciples. Simon Peter said, "I'm going fishing." "We'll come, too," they all said. So, they went out in the boat, but they caught nothing all night. At dawn Jesus was standing on the beach, but the disciples couldn't see who He was. He called out, "Fellows, have you caught any fish?" "No," they replied. Then He said, "Throw out your net on the right-hand side of the boat, and you'll get some!" So, they did, and they couldn't haul in the net because there were so many fish in it. Then the disciple Jesus loved said to Peter, "It's the Lord!" When Simon Peter heard that it was the Lord, he put on his tunic (for he had stripped for work), jumped into the water, and headed to shore. The others stayed with the boat and pulled the loaded net to the shore, for they were only about a hundred yards from shore. When they got there, they found breakfast waiting for them—fish cooking over a charcoal fire, and some bread. "Bring some of the fish you've just caught," Jesus said. So, Simon Peter went aboard and dragged the net to the shore. There were 153 large fish, and yet the net hadn't torn. "Now come and have some breakfast!" Jesus said. None of the disciples dared to ask Him, "Who are You?" They knew it was the Lord. Then Jesus served them the bread and the fish. This was the third time Jesus had appeared to His disciples since He had been raised from the dead.

John 21:1-14

* * *

As we begin this chapter, let's be mindful that this account comes from the Gospel of John. John is the only Gospel writer who includes the incidents described in this twenty-first chapter of His account. John basically concludes His Gospel account at the end of John chapter 20 (John 20:30-31), but then he adds chapter 21 as an epilogue. We would do well to ask "why?" Let's also remember that John's Gospel account is a first-hand account, unlike the other three Gospels. Matthew witnessed much of what He wrote, but His Gospel includes many details that he heard about from others, including Jesus' birth, childhood and more. Mark and Luke both wrote their Gospels exclusively using details provided by others. But John was an eyewitness to most every detail included in his Gospel beginning with John 1:15. From that point forward, very little is second hand. The first fourteen verses of the Gospel of John are his introduction, comprising his summary of the most important truth that he wants his readers to glean from his account – that being that Jesus Christ is the Son of God – a conclusion that he personally did not fully come to until he stepped into the empty tomb (John 20:8). He states it right up front in his Gospel because he wants his readers to hear every detail in that light. And just look at all of the details in John 21:1-14. So, let's look at why John included his epilogue.

During the forty days between His resurrection and His ascension, Jesus appeared and disappeared at will. This is the third time He has appeared to His disciples. Though He had a physical body, it was a resurrected body. He was able to come and go as He pleased – at one moment He was there with His disciples, at another He was with His Father in heaven. Jesus was preparing His disciples for the time that He would no longer be with them continually in bodily form. He was preparing them for the coming of the Spirit and their future ministry assignments. The disciples never knew when He would appear, so they had to remain alert. (Incidentally, we would do well to heed that lesson ourselves!)

After His resurrection, Jesus instructed the disciples to meet Him in Galilee (Matthew 28:7 and Mark 16:7), which is why they were gathered there that day. They apparently had been waiting for a while. Peter, not being one to sit around and wait, decided that he wasn't going to miss a good opportunity to go fishing. He enlisted the other fishermen in the group to join him – Thomas, Nathanael, the brothers James and John, and two others (probably Andrew and Philip). These were the seven who had been fishermen when Jesus first called them to follow Him – and it was "still in their blood". Apparently, Matthew, Simon the Zealot, James the Less and Thaddeus were the landlubbers and went off to do something else that night – perhaps sleep (it was nighttime). Hopefully, they showed up on the shore at dawn and didn't miss the very special breakfast! (One other side road: note that Thomas was in the boat with the others. i am convinced that he had determined to never again be the one absent from the group when Jesus showed up!)

The events on the boat that night should sound very familiar. Over two years earlier, Peter, Andrew, James and John had been fishing all night and they hadn't caught anything (Luke 5:1-11). Jesus instructed them to go out where it was deeper and cast their nets one more time. You will recall that their nets were so full they began to tear. It was then that Jesus had told them to follow Him. They had followed, and not looked back. And oh, what a two-plus-years journey it had been!

Well this morning, they also had been fishing all night without success. It was now dawn and they were probably getting ready to return to shore. Jesus was standing on the shore. The sun was just coming up, and they were a distance out in the sea, so they couldn't see that it was Jesus. He told them to throw out their net on the right-hand side and they would "get some". Remember, they didn't know it was Jesus – but something told them they needed to cast the net one more time. And just like that time two-plus years earlier, there were so many fish they couldn't haul in the net. As a matter of fact, John includes the detail that they caught 153 large fish. And this time, the net hadn't torn. That familiar memory is all it took to prompt John to say, *"It's the Lord!"* He knew His Lord's ways – and though he couldn't recognize His form and he hadn't recognized His voice, he knew it was Him! And this time, Jesus didn't need to tell Peter to come – hearing from John that it was their Lord, he jumped in the water and headed for Jesus.

This is the last miracle that Jesus performed as a part of His earthly ministry before He ascended to the Father – nets full of fish. It's reminiscent of His first miracle that day in Cana – water pots full of wine. Jesus never did anything halfway. He still doesn't! When Jesus shows up there is abundance – perhaps not always in fish or wine, but in abundant life, abundant joy and abundant mercy. Jesus was preparing to send out His disciples as His ambassadors to be about His mission in the spreading of His gospel and the making of His disciples who would in turn make other disciples. Two-plus years ago, He had called them to follow Him bodily, now He was preparing to tell them to continue to follow Him – though not bodily, but by His Spirit. Jesus' call to us has not been to follow Him bodily; but His call to us has been the same as that morning beside the sea – to follow Him by His Spirit. And one day, when He returns, we'll follow Him in His resurrected body with our resurrected bodies. And oh, by the way – i don't want to miss that "breakfast" – and neither do you!

One other note, along those lines – notice that Jesus already had breakfast prepared, but it wasn't complete until they added some of their catch. There was fruit of their labor by faith that had yet to be added before breakfast was ready. There is fruit of the labor that He has called us to that, by faith, has yet to be added to the "pot" before He returns and calls us to sit down with Him for the marriage supper of the Lamb (Revelation 19:6-9). He's already preparing it, but He is at work in and through our lives to produce fruit that is yet to be added. Cast the net on the right-hand side. There are still fish to be drawn in! There are still many yet to hear!

* * *

60

FEED MY SHEEP

After breakfast Jesus asked Simon Peter, "Simon, son of John, do you love Me more than these?" "Yes, Lord," Peter replied, "you know I love You." "Then feed My lambs," Jesus told him. Jesus repeated the question: "Simon, son of John, do you love Me?" "Yes, Lord," Peter said, "you know I love You." "Then take care of My sheep," Jesus said. A third time He asked him, "Simon, son of John, do you love Me?" Peter was hurt that Jesus asked the question a third time. He said, "Lord, You know everything. You know that I love You." Jesus said, "Then feed My sheep."

John 21:15-17

* * *

In the last chapter, we looked at one of the reasons as to why John had included this epilogue in his Gospel account. The second reason was that there was an unfinished piece of business that we, as readers, needed to know and understand.

On their first meeting, John tells us that Jesus had renamed Simon, the son of John. He was henceforth to be called "Peter", the rock (John 1:42). Jesus had later said that *"... upon this rock I will build My church, and all the powers of hell will not conquer it"* (Matthew 16:18). Jesus was preparing to build His church and He was giving these disciples – and others who they would disciple – the assignment to disciple and lead this new church. Principal among those to whom He was giving that assignment was

Simon Peter, the rock… but also, the one who had denied Him. As we already looked at in chapter 57, on the day of His resurrection, Jesus appeared to Peter. It was a personal and a private time of healing and forgiveness for Peter. Peter had sinned against His Lord, and that sin had created a separation between him and Jesus. But gratefully, Jesus' shed blood on the cross covered that sin – as well as so much more. So there needed to be that moment when Peter confessed his sin, sought forgiveness and received it from Jesus. i am certain that Jesus took Peter in His arms as Peter confessed his sin and wept in the embrace of His Lord and His Savior. Jesus already knew his sin. Peter's confession was not for Jesus' sake, it was for Peter's sake. At that moment, Peter was forgiven, and his relationship was reconciled with Jesus. He no longer needed to walk in grief and shame. He had been forgiven. And He had been set free. Jesus was not only faithful to come to Peter like that, He has faithfully come to each and every one of us, on more than one occasion, when we have sinned against Him and sought His forgiveness. Peter knew, as well as anyone, that, *"If we claim we have no sin, we are only fooling ourselves and not living in the truth. But if we confess our sins to Him, He is faithful and just to forgive us our sins and to cleanse us from all wickedness"* (1 John 1:8-9). That confession and the seeking of Christ's forgiveness is a deeply personal matter between us and our Lord. It's not for show. It's not for the crowd. It's between us and Jesus, just like it was between Peter and Jesus. Because Peter had been forgiven, he could boldly declare to the disciples that night in the locked room before Jesus appeared that Jesus was alive! Peter could wholeheartedly, without any degree of guilt or shame, welcome Him into the room that night. He could, without any hesitation, jump into the water and make a beeline for Jesus that morning at the shore. He was forgiven. He had been set free of his sin.

But – there is a public side to our sin – just as there was to Peter's. Peter's denial of Jesus had become well known among the followers. Therefore, Peter's confession and forgiveness needed to be as equally well known. Also, Peter was in a position of leadership within the newly forming church. Thus, He had accountability as a leader. (Incidentally, that is why John had to include it in his Gospel account. It needed to be clear that Peter had confessed his sin and had been forgiven. Otherwise, the church would have been off to a very shaky start.)

One other point, before we look at that conversation between Peter and Jesus. Note that public confession, where it is needed, must follow that time of personal confession and forgiveness, not the other way around.

Public confession bears witness to authentic and sincere confession that has already taken place. It must never be "a show".

Jesus asked, "Peter, *do you love Me more than these?*" Do you love Me above all others? Do you love me in a way that causes your love for everyone else to pale in comparison? (Matthew 10:37). Peter was not expecting Jesus to ask him that question. So, his initial response was along the lines of "of course, I love you, Jesus. How could you think otherwise?" But when Jesus asked him a second time, his response was in greater earnest, wanting to leave no doubt of his love for Jesus. Then, when Jesus asked him a third time, he was greatly hurt. He may have at that point realized that Jesus was asking that question once for each of the three times Peter had denied Jesus. If he in fact made that connection, this third asking of the question hit him the hardest. Had Jesus not truly forgiven him? Peter responded, *"Lord, You know everything. You know that I love You."* Peter wanted to be clear with his answer that he loved Jesus with all of his heart, soul and mind (Matthew 22:37). Why did Jesus ask three times? Peter needed to confess his love for Jesus – and he needed to confess it, not in a perfunctory way, but rather, with his whole heart. And the disciples needed to hear Peter confess his love in that way. There was to be no doubt in anyone's mind as to Peter's love for his Lord.

Then, in response to each of Peter's answers, Jesus replied – "feed My lambs," "take care of My sheep," and "feed My sheep." Jesus was publicly restoring Peter to his apostleship and leadership. He was reminding this fisherman – and the other disciples who were surrounding them – that He was calling them to be shepherds caring for the sheep, protecting the sheep and nurturing the sheep. In fact, they were to be under-shepherds, walking in obedience to Him, under His authority and His leadership as the Good Shepherd (John 10:11), the Great Shepherd (Hebrews 13:20-21), and the Chief Shepherd (1 Peter 5:4). And as an under-shepherd, the most important thing they must do is love Jesus with their whole heart, soul and mind.

Though within the church there is a distinct role and calling as pastor to be the undershepherd of the flock, each one of us to some degree are shepherds. We have all been instructed to make disciples – to be disciples who disciple others. As a discipler we are in fact shepherding – we are caring for those who we are discipling, we are nurturing them, and we are helping to feed them. We, too, would be wise to remember that the most important thing any undershepherd must do is love our Lord with our whole heart, soul and mind.

As Jesus said, *"do you love Me?" "Then feed My sheep."*

* * *

61

OUR TIMES ARE IN HIS HANDS

"I tell you the truth, when you were young, you were able to do as you liked; you dressed yourself and went wherever you wanted to go. But when you are old, you will stretch out your hands, and others will dress you and take you where you don't want to go." Jesus said this to let him know by what kind of death he would glorify God. Then Jesus told him, "Follow Me." Peter turned around and saw behind them the disciple Jesus loved — the one who had leaned over to Jesus during supper and asked, "Lord, who will betray You?" Peter asked Jesus, "What about him, Lord?" Jesus replied, "If I want him to remain alive until I return, what is that to you? As for you, follow Me." So, the rumor spread among the community of believers that this disciple wouldn't die. But that isn't what Jesus said at all. He only said, "If I want him to remain alive until I return, what is that to you?"

John 21:18-23

* * *

Peter had just been restored by Jesus to walk in the way that the Lord was placing before him. He had confessed his undying love for his Savior. And Jesus had just explained that Peter would follow Jesus to his death – a death on the cross. At that point, Jesus said, *"Follow Me."* It wasn't the first time that Jesus had told him to follow Him – and it wouldn't be the last. Jesus would remind him – and encourage him – to follow Him every day until his journey on this earth was completed. This moment may have been the last that Jesus stood in front of Peter physically and told him to "Follow Me", but He would continue to do so through His Spirit. Peter's journey with Jesus was not ending there on the shore of the Sea of Galilee, nor would it end a few days later at the Mount of Olives (Acts 1:1-11) when Jesus ascended into heaven one last time. His journey with Jesus would continue throughout eternity – for a finite period on this side of glory – and for an infinite period on the other side of glory.

Jesus had given Peter, the other disciples and each and every one of us who are His followers an assignment that each one of us is to be about on this side of glory. The assignment was/is to *"tell people about* {Him} *everywhere – in Jerusalem, throughout Judea, in Samaria, and to the ends of the earth"* (Acts 1:8). The assignment to tell was to be accomplished with our actions, as well as with our words – and with our very lives. He said we were/are to be His witnesses, making *"disciples of all the nations, baptizing them in the name of the Father and the Son and the Holy Spirit"* (Matthew 28:19). And Jesus said that the Father had given Him all authority (Matthew 28:18), and that He would send His Holy Spirit to indwell, equip and empower each of His followers to carry out His assignment (Acts 1:8). That is the purpose for which He left Peter and His disciples to continue the work when He ascended into heaven. And that is the purpose for which He has left each of us here after we have entered into a saving relationship with Him. Our lives are not about us, our circumstances and our situations; our lives are about Him, His gospel and His glory. Too often, we become so focused on the former that we lose sight that our purpose is in the latter.

Right after Jesus told Peter how he would die, and that he was to follow Him, Peter turned around and saw John. As he did, he asked Jesus, *"What about him, Lord?"* (referring to John). That question is an example of how easily we can become distracted. Jesus rebuked Peter and reminded him that his job was to follow, not to be focused on the paths of other believers. The writer of Hebrews records that we are to keep *"our eyes on Jesus, on whom our faith depends from start to finish"* (Hebrews 12:2). To be distracted by ourselves, our circumstances or other Christians is to be disobedient to Jesus. And that disobedience will cause us to miss the perfect will of God. We are to keep our eyes of faith on Him – and on Him alone.

Throughout our walk through the Gospels, we have repeatedly seen the way that the Father ordered His Son's steps according to His perfect timing. Not one encounter was "per chance". Not one moment was wasted. Not one circumstance was unexpected by the Father. The Father had known it all from before the beginning of time. And He had ordered the steps of His Son to fulfill His perfect redemptive plan.

The Father not only ordered the steps of His Son, He has ordered the steps of His Son's followers. He ordered Peter's steps in the work He had prepared for him in the furtherance of His gospel. Peter was the first to preach the Good News on the day of Pentecost when 3,000 believed and were baptized. He was the first to proclaim the gospel to the Gentiles. He suffered persecution, imprisonment, beatings and crucifixion – all for the sake of the gospel (Acts 5:41). John fulfilled his assignment to care for Mary, the mother of Jesus, and then went on to be the leader of the church of Ephesus, was persecuted in Rome by being cast into boiling oil, and then was exiled on the island of Patmos. The paths of each of the disciples were very different. John's brother – James – was the first disciple to be martyred, and John was the last one of that original group to die.

Each of their paths was unique, just as ours are. As we walk in the steps that the Lord has set before each one of us, we will experience very different circumstances. Some will experience extreme persecution. Some will experience severe health challenges. Some will experience painful losses. Some will experience abundant blessing. Some will experience abundant loss.

Whatever the path is that He has set before us, as we take up the cross to follow Jesus, we would do well to remember the words of our Savior to Peter – *"As for you, follow Me."* Our times are in His hands. Our circumstances are in His hands. Our very lives are in His hands. And He has permitted it all. He has ordered our steps through it all. Heed the words of the prophet Isaiah – *"Forget the former things; do not dwell on the past"* – {or even the present!} *"See, I am doing a new thing! Now it springs up; do you not perceive it? I am making a way in the wilderness and streams in the wasteland"* (Isaiah 43:18-19 NIV). Our God is in control – and He who began the good work, *"will continue His work until it is finally finished on the day when Christ Jesus returns"* (Philippians 1:6).

Take up the cross that He has placed before you – and follow Him!

* * *

BOOK SIX

UNTIL HE RETURNS

LESSONS LEARNED IN THE WILDERNESS

UNTIL HE RETURNS

KENNETH A. WINTER

CHAPTER SCRIPTURE LISTING

* * *

Chapter 1 *He Will Return* (Acts 1:9-11)
Chapter 2 *Waiting Is Not Inactivity* (Acts 1:12-14)
Chapter 3 *Why All This Concern?* (Acts 1:15-26)
Chapter 4 *The Helper Comes* (Acts 2:1-8)
Chapter 5 *Let The Nations Be Glad* (Acts 2:9-12)
Chapter 6 *A Drink At Joel's Place* (Acts 2:13-21)
Chapter 7 *A Prearranged Plan* (Acts 2:22-36)
Chapter 8 *What Should We Do?* (Acts 2:37-41)
Chapter 9 *Fully Devoted Followers* (Acts 2:42-47)
Chapter 10 *He Jumped Up* (Acts 3:1-11)
Chapter 11 *In Whose Name Do You Do This?* (Acts 4:1-7)
Chapter 12 *We Must Obey God Rather Than Men* (Acts 4:8-22)
Chapter 13 *Praying For Boldness* (Acts 4:23-31)
Chapter 14 *They Gave It All* (Acts 4:32-37)
Chapter 15 *Pride Comes Before A Fall* (Acts 5:1-11)
Chapter 16 *A Miraculous Escape* (Acts 5:12-28)
Chapter 17 *If It Is Of God, You Will Not Stop It* (Acts 5:29-42)
Chapter 18 *Chosen To Serve* (Acts 6:1-7)
Chapter 19 *Grace-full* (Acts 6:8-15)
Chapter 20 *Keep Gazing Upward* (Acts 7:51-60)
Chapter 21 *The Power Of God Isn't For Sale* (Acts 8:9-24)
Chapter 22 *A Divine Appointment* (Acts 8:26-40)
Chapter 23 *A Damascus Road Encounter* (Acts 9:1-9)
Chapter 24 *The Courage Of Ananias* (Acts 9:10-19)

* * *

PREFACE

* * *

In my first book I told you, Theophilus, about everything Jesus began to do and teach until the day He was taken up to heaven after giving His chosen apostles further instructions through the Holy Spirit. During the forty days after He suffered and died, He appeared to the apostles from time to time, and He proved to them in many ways that He was actually alive. And He talked to them about the Kingdom of God. Once when He was eating with them, He commanded them, "Do not leave Jerusalem until the Father sends you the gift He promised, as I told you before. John baptized with water, but in just a few days you will be baptized with the Holy Spirit." So when the apostles were with Jesus, they kept asking Him, "Lord, has the time come for You to free Israel and restore our kingdom?" He replied, "The Father alone has the authority to set those dates and times, and they are not for you to know. But you will receive power when the Holy Spirit comes upon you. And you will be My witnesses, telling people about Me everywhere – in Jerusalem, throughout Judea, in Samaria, and to the ends of the earth."

Acts 1:1-8

* * *

In ancient times the Phoenicians, the Carthaginians and the Romans aided by the beliefs of Greek mythology believed that Hercules had set two pillars in place to serve as a warning. We now know those pillars to be the Rock of Gibraltar to the north and debatably either the Monte Hacho in Ceuta or the Jebel Musa in Morocco to the south. These two "pillars" flank the entrance to the Strait of Gibraltar. The narrow strait connects the Atlantic Ocean with the Mediterranean Sea and separates southern Europe from northern Africa. The "pillars" were said to have been put in place to designate the edge of the world. The ancients believed that the world was flat and that sailing vessels would fall off the edge of the world if they sailed beyond the horizon. Therefore, the pillars were deemed to mark a boundary beyond which no man should go. As such a warning was inscribed on the rocks – "NON PLUS ULTRA" – meaning "nothing more beyond". These words carried the urgent warning to all that would attempt to pass by them – NOTHING MORE BEYOND. The warning was believed to be truth and remained in place until Christopher Columbus discovered the New World at the end of the 15th century. Following that discovery, King Charles V of Spain had the negative word "NON" expunged in order to change the inscriptions from being a warning of nothing more beyond to a reminder that there was MORE BEYOND. The now-modified inscription further served as a reminder of the King's mission to extend the spread of Christianity into the newly discovered lands. Thus it became even more than a reminder; it became a challenge.

The physician Luke is faithful to record here in the first chapter of Acts, the final words Jesus spoke to His disciples as He stood before them on the mount just before He ascended into heaven. It is interesting to note that even during the days after His resurrection, the disciples were still expecting Jesus as the Messiah to *"free Israel and restore our kingdom"* right then. They still had not yet realized that there was still more to be done. They couldn't see past their immediate circumstances and grasp the Father's bigger purpose and plan. Jesus' resurrection was not the end of the road; rather, it was a brand new beginning. And that new beginning would be signaled by His departure to join the Father and the arrival of the Holy Spirit. It would be marked by His instructions to them – and to each of us who are His followers.

His instructions in many respects could be defined as "more beyond". Jesus had already told His disciples the night before He was arrested that He was *"going to prepare a place for* {His followers}", and *"when everything is ready"* He would return for His followers (John 14:2-3). There was "more beyond" – there was the place that He was going to prepare. But also, there was "more beyond" – He would return. And further, there was "more beyond" – there was work to be done until He returns. He told them that the Father has set the date and time for His return; it is not for us to know. They were not – and we are not – to be fixated on the date and time; rather, they – and we – are to be faithful in the work.

In many respects, it is the ultimate wilderness journey. We have no idea all the twists and turns that lie in the path ahead, any more than those disciples did. But in the Father's timing, we will arrive at the end of that wilderness journey. In the Father's ultimate wisdom, sovereignty and grace He sent His Holy Spirit to guide, enable, equip and comfort them – and us – for all that is in store in the journey beyond. And He has given us clear instruction as to what we are to be about – *"you will be My witnesses, telling people about Me everywhere—in Jerusalem, throughout Judea, in Samaria, and to the ends of the earth."* We are to let the world know that there is MORE BEYOND. Our lives, our actions and our words are to bear that inscription... until He returns. We are to be bearers of that inscription and that message until He returns – across the street in Jerusalem, down the road in Judea, outside of our comfort zone in Samaria, and to every corner at the very ends of the earth. Because the reality is for those who do not have a personal relationship with Christ, there is NO MORE BEYOND. Apart from a saving relationship with Him, our sin will destine us for an eternity separated from Him – not in eternal life, but in eternal death. Sin is in fact that negative word "NON". But through Christ's death, burial and resurrection He made the way for that negative word "NON" caused by our sin to be expunged – and in exchange He gave us more beyond – eternal and abundant life that He has gone ahead to prepare for us. Life we can only have through Him if we will but receive it. Jesus' words to each of us are MORE BEYOND – they are LIFE – abundant life here and eternal life beyond. Life that He laid down His own life to give us.

No matter where you are in your journey until He returns, there is more beyond. The cover of this book is a depiction of that Rock of Gibraltar and the ocean and the lands that extend beyond. It is also a depiction of that mount from which Jesus ascended on the day He gave them – and us – His instructions. In this book we will look at how the men and women who were there on the mount that day, as well as others that would join them, continued in that journey beyond. Let us learn from them. Let us be challenged and encouraged by them. And let us be faithful to join them in living out that message of MORE BEYOND, until He returns.

* * *

1

HE WILL RETURN

After saying this, He was taken up into a cloud while they were watching, and they could no longer see Him. As they strained to see Him rising into heaven, two white-robed men suddenly stood among them. "Men of Galilee," they said, "why are you standing here staring into heaven? Jesus has been taken from you into heaven, but someday He will return from heaven in the same way you saw Him go!"
Acts 1:9-11

* * *

During the forty days that followed Jesus' resurrection, He appeared to individuals or small groupings of His disciples on multiple occasions, but He joined with the apostles as a group at least four times. Luke records that *"He appeared to the apostles from time to time"* (Acts 1:3), so it could have been many more times than four, but Scripture records four specific appearances. The first was the night of His resurrection in the locked upper room. The second was eight days later as they were together in a room. This time Thomas was with them. The third was along the shore of the Sea of Galilee. And the fourth was this day in Acts 1 on the Mount of Olives when He ascended into heaven. The first two of these four times, He suddenly appeared in their midst and then disappeared. On the third time, He suddenly appeared on the shore preparing breakfast while Peter and six of the other disciples were out on the sea in a boat fishing. At the conclusion of that time He again disappeared. To the extent that anyone can ever become "accustomed" to having someone appear and disappear out of and into thin air, the apostles probably became less surprised by Jesus' successive sudden appearances and departures. They came to realize that He could appear before them at any time.

On this particular day, He appeared to them at some other undisclosed place and then "led them" (Luke 24:50) to the Mount of Olives. Either as they walked or upon their arrival, He told them *"now I will send the Holy Spirit, just as My Father promised. But stay here in the city until the Holy Spirit comes and fills you with power from heaven"* (Luke 24:49). The disciples knew that this time was different from the other times He had disappeared. This time He was leaving. And though they had never known when He would appear or disappear, this time had a feeling of greater permanence. He was going to another place (the Father's house) and He would stay there until the work was completed. Jesus had already explained to the disciples on multiple occasions that He needed to return to His Father in heaven. He needed to return in order to "prepare a place" in His Father's home for all of His followers (John 14:2). He would be preparing that place by accomplishing His purposes in and through His bride – the Church. He needed to return so that He could send His Holy Spirit to empower and enable His followers in all things (John 14:16-17). And He needed to return to make intercession on their/our behalf to the Father as their/our interceding High Priest (John 14:12-14). His followers knew that the day of His departure had arrived.

In addition to the apostles, there was a larger group that also made up His closest followers. In total there were about one hundred twenty believers (Acts 1:15) who walked with Jesus to the mount that day to "see Him off". i would venture that they were sad. They didn't know when they would see Him again, and they would miss Him. i would also venture they were frightened. For the last three years, many of His followers had been with Him most every day. He was always there to turn to with a question. He was the Teacher. He was the Miracle Worker. And though He had sent seventy-two of them out on their own on the one occasion (Luke 10:1-24), they still returned to Jesus when their assignment was completed. They knew He had told them that He would send His Holy Spirit as a Helper and a Guide, but they had not yet experienced the presence of the Holy Spirit – they had experienced the presence of Jesus. Thus, with hearts of sadness and uncertainty, they gathered around Jesus to say farewell.

You may have a similar tradition to my wife and me. Whenever family and guests are departing from our home, we go outside and stand at the end of the driveway or on our front porch to wave goodbye and see them off until they are out of sight. That's what His followers were doing that day.

As they stood there, He didn't disappear as He had done on several occasions. Rather, He was *"taken up into a cloud"*. Thirty-three years earlier Jesus had arrived on this earth humbly, as He was wrapped in swaddling clothes and laid in an animal's feeding trough. But today as He began to ascend into the Father's presence in heaven, He was wrapped in the Shekinah glory cloud. You may recall that was the cloud – the cloud of God's presence and glory – that led the Israelites through the wilderness (Exodus 13:21-22)[1]. And it was that cloud that filled the tabernacle with the "awesome glory of the Lord" (Exodus 30:34-38)[2]. Jesus was enveloped by the glory of God, because Jesus is the reflection of God's glory (Isaiah 60:1-3). The disciples had always been witnessing the glory of God whenever they looked upon Jesus, but as they looked upon the ascending Jesus, they saw Him "clothed" in the glory of God.

Jesus didn't "vanish" as He had on the other occasions; rather, He ascended until they could no longer see Him. Having grown up in Southeast Florida, i can remember standing outside on clear days watching the launch of the various spacecraft. We would stand there straining to see the spacecraft as it grew smaller and smaller, and the vapor trail began to disappear. We would stare until there was nothing more to see. That's what the disciples were doing that day – they were straining to get the last glimpse they could possibly get of Jesus.

Luke records that suddenly two "white-robed men" were standing there with them. Remember, it wasn't just a handful of people; there were over one hundred people. Two people can slip into a crowd that size and not be immediately noticed, but these guys were apparently pretty easy to spot. Luke is careful to write that they were "men"; he doesn't say "angels". Luke had very specifically said that "angels" announced Jesus' birth to the shepherds (Luke 2:8-15)[3]. The appearance of angels frightened the shepherds, but Luke does not record that the group was frightened by the appearance of these two men. Dwight L. Moody contended that the two men were Moses and Elijah, who would have been familiar faces to at least Peter, James and John from the day they accompanied Jesus to the Mount of Transfiguration (Luke 9:30-31)[4]. But regardless of who they were, they were heavenly messengers who the Father had sent to assure, encourage and challenge those who were staring off into heaven. The message was clear: *"someday He will return from heaven in the same way you saw Him go!"*

He will return in the same way – enveloped in the glory of God. He will not return this time as a humble baby in a stable, He will return as the King of Kings and Lord of Lords. He will return to establish His Kingdom once and for all. And He will return to the exact same place. The prophet Zechariah writes, *"On that day His feet will stand on the Mount of Olives, east of Jerusalem"* (Zechariah 14:4).

When will He return? "Someday." And i would add – that day continues to draw closer! The Father has determined the day, and as Jesus told His disciples just before He ascended, *"The Father alone has the authority to set those dates and times, and they are not for you to know"* (Acts 1:7). We don't know the "when", but we know the "how". He will return in the exact same way as they saw Him go. And we know the "where". He will return to the exact same place from which they saw Him depart. And we know the "why". He will return to judge His creation and establish His Kingdom. Therefore, in the meantime, we must be about His purpose and His mission – until that day – the day He returns.

Wherever we are in our journey – whatever circumstance we are walking through today – the Master has given us a purpose. He has given us a mission. He will return. Let's be found faithful in His mission until that day!

---

1. *The Journey Begins,* Ch. 12
2. *The Journey Begins,* Ch. 61
3. *Walking With The Master,* Ch. 2
4. *Walking With The Master,* Ch. 37

2

WAITING IS NOT INACTIVITY

Then they returned to Jerusalem from the mount called Olivet, which is near Jerusalem, a Sabbath day's journey away. And when they had entered, they went up to the upper room, where they were staying, Peter and John and James and Andrew, Philip and Thomas, Bartholomew and Matthew, James the son of Alphaeus and Simon the Zealot and Judas the son of James. All these with one accord were devoting themselves to prayer, together with the women and Mary the mother of Jesus, and his brothers.
Acts 1:12-14 (ESV)

* * *

Jesus ascension into heaven occurred on the Sabbath. We know it was the Sabbath because Luke records that the group, who was gathered on the mount when He ascended, traveled a Sabbath day's journey back to the upper room in Jerusalem. He would have had no reason to explain the distance if it had not occurred on the Sabbath. i think it's worthy to note that our Lord's incarnational and redemptive ministry on earth is concluded on the day of Sabbath rest, just as was the case of His initial work of creation. The first time He made all things new, He concluded the work with the Sabbath. This time He had made the way for all things to be made new. The Sabbath, or in our case the Lord's Day, is to be a reminder and an indication that when God finished His work, He rested, but it is also a reminder to us that what He begins, He completes. In both instances the Sabbath was the exclamation point at the end of the work. Luke further adds that the group *"returned to Jerusalem filled with great joy"* (Luke 24:52). Though the group would have been saddened to see Him go, they were joyful because they knew that He would return.

Let's look at who all was there. The group was made up of the eleven remaining apostles, Mary (the mother of Jesus), the half-brothers of Jesus (Mary's other sons) , the women that had traveled with Him, and other men totaling about 120 believers. It was quite a diverse group. We know that at least seven of them were fishermen (Peter, Andrew, John, James, Philip, Bartholomew and Thomas). There was one who had fought against Rome (Simon the zealot) and one who had worked for Rome (Matthew the tax collector). A case can be made that James the son of Alphaeus and Judas the son of James may have been carpenters. The other women with Mary (the mother of Jesus) would have included Mary Magdalene (the first person to whom Jesus appeared after His resurrection), Salome (the mother of James and John), Mary (the mother of James the son of Alphaeus), and Joanna (the wife of King Herod's household manager). Four of the group were Jesus' half-brothers – James, Joseph, Jude and Simon – who had most recently become followers of Jesus. Though they had known Him their entire lives, they had only come to believe on Him as the Son of God since His resurrection. Prior to His resurrection, they would have been like some church attenders today. They grew up hearing the stories about Jesus, but they had yet to truly believe on Him. But once they believed, they believed with their whole hearts. For example, we know that James would become one of the elders of the first church in Jerusalem, and would write the Epistle of James, and Jude would become an ambassador of the gospel and write the Epistle of Jude.

It is very probable that some of the others counted among that group would have been Lazarus (the one who Jesus raised from the dead) and his two sisters, Martha and Mary. It probably included Joseph of Arimathea and Nicodemus, both of whom had been Pharisees that came to be followers of Jesus. After they had received permission from Pontius Pilate to bury the body of Jesus, they would have been ostracized by the High Council of religious leaders. And many more would have been in their number.

Though each one had a unique story of how they came to follow Jesus, Luke records that they were united in one accord. There is no question that they were united in their love for Jesus. But their unity had to go beyond that. Jesus had commissioned them for His purpose to make disciples of all people. In order to do that they couldn't only be united in their love for Him, they had to be united in their love for one another. It would have been easy for them to become divided. John could have stood before the other apostles and proudly declared that he was the only one that stood at the cross with Jesus. Peter could have been denounced for his denial of Jesus. Mary Magdalene could have established her importance by reminding everyone that Jesus had appeared to her first after His resurrection. Thomas could have been marginalized for His skepticism about Jesus' resurrection. His half-brothers could have been belittled for their failure to follow Jesus before His resurrection. Mary, the sister of Lazarus, could have proudly declared that Jesus had promised that wherever the gospel was preached her actions would be remembered (Matthew 26:13). They could have all gotten into another discussion about who would be the greatest in the Kingdom! But they knew that just before He had been arrested, Jesus had told them to love one another (John 13:34-35). They could not solely love Jesus and have faith in Jesus, they needed to love one another and have faith in one another.

They returned to the upper room – the place where Jesus had washed their feet before His arrest, and the place He had appeared to them on the night of His resurrection. In both instances they would have been surprised – the first time by His unexpected arrest and crucifixion that soon followed – and the second by His unexpected appearance and resurrection. Now they were gathering again without clearly knowing what was going to happen. All they knew this time was that they were to go and wait – wait for the Holy Spirit to come upon them. That had never happened before. They had no idea what that would mean or what that would look like. But Jesus had promised. So out of their love for Him and for one another they went together to that upper room to wait.

But they didn't just stay in the upper room. Luke records that they also spent time in the Temple, praising God (Luke 24:53). i don't know about you, but i think that was pretty gutsy. The religious leaders who had Jesus arrested and crucified were still in charge. In some respects, these followers of Jesus were "marked" men and women. The disciples had scattered and fled the night of Jesus' arrest for fear of what would happen to them. Most of them had stayed away from Golgotha on the day Jesus was crucified for the same reason. But now they were boldly entering the Temple to praise and worship God while they were waiting. And the Holy Spirit had not yet come upon them. They weren't emboldened by the power of the Holy Spirit. They were emboldened by their love and faith in Jesus and encouraged by their love for one another.

They knew that waiting was not inactivity. It required obedience – obedience to the Master and His commands. Obedience is not inactive; it is proactive. Even obedience in waiting requires a conscious decision and action to stay the course and not pursue a different course. When Jesus fasted in the wilderness for forty days, Satan attempted to tempt Jesus into taking a path other than what the Father had set forth for Him. But Jesus never deviated. He never gave up on being obedient to the Father. Obedience is often difficult. It often requires a great deal of faith in order to persevere, even when common sense may say otherwise. For example, those disciples had been told to go and make disciples. To some it would have made a whole lot more sense to invest their time in developing a plan and a strategy. They could have had maps prepared and displayed on the walls that designated each person's responsibilities.

i am currently in the midst of doing something that i believe God has told me to do. I am walking by faith in obedience to what i believe He has said. i am in that "waiting room". And it is taking a whole lot more work and activity to remain in this "waiting room" than it would take to step out of the room and pursue my own way. There is nothing inactive about obedience.

Waiting requires oneness – oneness with the Master, but also oneness with one another. As we've already seen, the believers that were waiting had a lot that they could have allowed to divide them, but they worked at remaining one. There were some pretty strong personalities among them, and potentially some pretty strong opinions. But they knew that they needed to remain united in their love, their faith and their obedience.

Their waiting involved prayer – diligently seeking the Father and trusting that the Son was interceding on their behalf. Their waiting involved worship – worshipping the One who is sovereign and worthy of all worship. And their waiting involved anticipation – trusting that the One who had promised will be faithful to accomplish that which He has promised in ways that are *"infinitely more than we might ask or think"* (Ephesians 3:20).

. . .

In your wilderness journey today, you may be waiting in your own upper room. And you are finding that waiting is very hard work! It is by no means inactivity. It requires obedience, faithfulness, oneness, prayer, worship and anticipation. Trust the One who has told you to wait in that upper room. He is faithful! Just ask the one hundred and twenty!

* * *

3

WHY ALL THIS CONCERN?

During this time, when about one hundred twenty believers were together in one place, Peter stood up and addressed them. "Brothers," he said, "the Scriptures had to be fulfilled concerning Judas, who guided those who arrested Jesus. This was predicted long ago by the Holy Spirit, speaking through King David… in the book of Psalms, where it says, 'Let his home become desolate, with no one living in it.' It also says, 'Let someone else take his position.' So now we must choose a replacement for Judas from among the men who were with us the entire time we were traveling with the Lord Jesus – from the time He was baptized by John until the day He was taken from us. Whoever is chosen will join us as a witness of Jesus' resurrection." So they nominated two men: Joseph called Barsabbas (also known as Justus) and Matthias. Then they all prayed, "O Lord, You know every heart. Show us which of these men You have chosen as an apostle to replace Judas in this ministry, for he has deserted us and gone where he belongs." Then they cast lots, and Matthias was selected to become an apostle with the other eleven.
Acts 1:15-26

* * *

Ten days passed between Jesus' ascension and the arrival of His promised Holy Spirit. Scripture tells us generally that His followers spent that time gathered in the upper room and in the Temple praying, praising and worshiping God. But in the midst of that period of time, Luke records two specific incidents: the specifics of how Judas Iscariot died and how Matthias was selected to replace Judas as the twelfth apostle. We know that there are details that the Holy Spirit led the writers of Scripture not to include. And we know that everything that was included was for a purpose: "*All Scripture is inspired by God and profitable for teaching, for reproof, for correction, for training in righteousness*" (2 Timothy 3:16 NASB). Therefore, i think it is reasonable to ask why these two specific details were inserted in the midst of this time of waiting. As a matter of fact, i think it is also reasonable to ask how these details are applicable to us in our respective journeys.

Peter gives us the key to the answer right up front when he tells us that what the Holy Spirit predicted long ago had to be fulfilled.

The first prophecy that Peter referenced was in regard to Judas. He reminded the other disciples that King David recorded, "*Let his home become desolate, with no one living in it*" (Psalm 69:25), meaning that his evil deed would cause his name to become reprehensible for posterity and his final resting place would become contemptible.

In the first century A.D., the name Judas was a name synonymous with honor, and therefore a very popular name (two of the twelve disciples were named Judas). The name was given in recognition of Judas Maccabaeus, one of the great generals in Jewish history. He and his followers defeated the Syrian armies in 165 BC, restored the religious rites and rededicated the Temple in Jerusalem. Simon Iscariot would have named his son Judas in the hope that he would be a man of honor in the tradition of Judas Maccabaeus. But, as Judas' treachery became notorious, that was no longer the case. Today If you look up the name Judas in the dictionary, you will find "*one who betrays another under the guise of friendship; a deceiver or traitor*"[1]. As a result, the name "Judas" was no longer a popular choice among parents determining the name for their bouncing baby boys. Judas' name became reprehensible as a result of his treachery as foretold by the prophecy.[2]

Both Matthew and Luke give us an account of Judas' death. When Judas fully realized the consequences of his betrayal of Jesus – the condemnation of Jesus to die and the damnation of his own soul for his part in the deed – he took the thirty pieces of silver and threw them at the feet of the leading priests and elders. The priests themselves considered the money as "payment for murder" (Matthew 27:6). Matthew records that right after Judas threw down the coins, he "went out and hanged himself" (Matthew 27:5). Luke, the physician, adds that the hanging rope broke causing Judas' body to fall headfirst to the ground causing his body to split open, spilling out his intestines. It was a gruesome death brought about by his gruesome treachery. Because that land was defiled by his suicide, the priests decided to use the coins to purchase the land to be used as a graveyard for foreigners and the "dregs" of society. As the news of Judas' death spread, the field became known as "the field of blood". When Luke writes that *"Judas had bought a field with the money he received for his treachery"* (Acts 1:18), he also is saying that the payment for Judas' treachery bought the field. His treachery and the use of the ransom to purchase just such a burial site was in fulfillment of the prophecy recorded by Zechariah – *"So they counted out for my wages thirty pieces of silver. And the Lord said to me, "Throw it to the potter" – this magnificent sum at which they valued me! So I took the thirty coins and threw them to the potter in the Temple of the Lord"* (Zechariah 11:12-13). Judas' final abode – his burial place -- became contemptible as a result of his treachery as foretold in the prophecy.

The second prophecy that Peter referenced is in regard to choosing a replacement for Judas. He reminded the apostles – and us – that King David recorded, *"Let someone else take his position"* (Psalm 109:8). The night Jesus was arrested, the apostles were engaged in another discussion about which of them would be the greatest in the Kingdom. After having corrected their thinking from being rulers to being servants, Jesus told them that upon His return each of them would *"sit on thrones, judging the twelve tribes of Israel"* (Luke 22:30). Even though Jesus had only ascended to heaven a few days before, the apostles always believed and acted in a way that was consistent with their belief that His return was imminent. Therefore, they saw the selection of a twelfth apostle to replace Judas as an urgent need, so that they might be prepared for His return.

Though the Holy Spirit had not yet been sent to empower them, they still had the Word of God and prayer. Jesus had on multiple occasions made it clear that Peter was to be their leader (Matthew 16:19, Luke 22:31-32, John 21:15-17). When Peter referenced the prophecies of King David, he was not doing so on his own, he was being led by the Spirit of God, even though he was not yet indwelt by the Holy Spirit. Thus Peter responded to the leading of the Word and the Holy Spirit to fill that vacant position. Through their process, the Lord subsequently led them to select Matthias.

Now, let's come back to our original question: why all this concern with how Judas died, the field his blood-money bought, and the way he got replaced as an apostle?

. . .

First, and most importantly, what the Holy Spirit says, will be fulfilled, no matter how long it takes. Prophecy was fulfilled – even through those who rebelled against God. No matter what people may choose to do, God's promises in His Word are invincible, irrefutable and indomitable. Even when you are being betrayed His purpose will not fail. Even when you see godless action taking place around you and to you, He ultimately prevails. God has no need to panic. Not even Judas or Satan could undermine or escape the all-encompassing invincibility of God's purpose. No one and no thing can!

Second, the importance of the memory of Jesus that Matthias preserved when he replaced Judas corresponds to the importance of God's written Word in our lives. It was important that whoever replaced Judas was someone who had been a follower of Jesus the entire time from His baptism to His ascension. It was important that they had heard and witnessed Jesus' teaching and miracles firsthand. The Holy Spirit was soon to arrive to indwell those believers – and specifically the apostles. It was important that they not only be filled by His Spirit, but they also needed to be rooted in His Word (His teaching). They did not have benefit of the New Testament. They would be the writers and messengers of those truths. It was imperative that they be firsthand witnesses.

The same principle holds true for us. We too must not only be filled with the Holy Spirit; we must also be rooted in His Word. At the timeframe of this passage in the upper room, the Holy Spirit had not yet come to indwell them and the New Testament had not yet been written. But today we have both! John Piper writes, *"…if our roots are not sunk deep into the words and deeds of Jesus (preserved for us by the apostles), then it is certain that our branches will not reach very high into the sky of God's power."*

One other point that is worthy to note: this is the last time that you ever see believers casting lots to discern God's will. Remember, at this moment in time, they were not indwelt by the Holy Spirit. Once the Holy Spirit came to live within them, He led them and guided them in all truth. Jesus had told His disciples the night of His betrayal, *"When the Spirit of truth comes, He will guide you into all truth. He will not speak on His own but will tell you what He has heard. He will tell you about the future"* (John 16:13). He guides us today. We do not need to cast lots; we only need to listen to His voice and follow His leading.

• • •

The words spoken and the actions they took that night in the upper room two thousand years ago do concern us! They point us to His unfailing Word. They point us to His unchanging character. And they point us to the invincible outcome of His purpose! All of which we must hold onto – until He returns!

---

1. Merriam-Webster Dictionary
2. *Walking With The Master*, Ch. 19

4

THE HELPER COMES

On the day of Pentecost all the believers were meeting together in one place. Suddenly, there was a sound from heaven like the roaring of a mighty windstorm, and it filled the house where they were sitting. Then, what looked like flames or tongues of fire appeared and settled on each of them. And everyone present was filled with the Holy Spirit and began speaking in other languages, as the Holy Spirit gave them this ability. At that time there were devout Jews from every nation living in Jerusalem. When they heard the loud noise, everyone came running, and they were bewildered to hear their own languages being spoken by the believers. They were completely amazed. "How can this be?" they exclaimed. "These people are all from Galilee, and yet we hear them speaking in our own native languages!

Acts 2:1-8

* * *

A few years ago my wife and i had the rare privilege of spending ten days in the heart of Jerusalem for a personal spiritual retreat. We stayed in an apartment on the second floor of a home that had been transformed into a prayer center. Though it was late June/ early July, the temperature was moderate and we kept our windows open to enjoy the refreshing light breeze that was present most of the time. Throughout our time there – and since – we couldn't help but think about the disciples as they waited in their upper room for ten days in light of the experience we were having in our upper room. Here are some thoughts i captured in my journal as our time was drawing to an end:

. . .

"Today i sit in an upper room in Jerusalem. It is not 'the' upper room where the apostles gathered; but for me personally it is 'my' upper room because it is a place where the Lord has permitted me to wait before Him, to hear His voice, to experience His presence and to be renewed with a fresh filling of His Spirit. Though i know that He is able to do those things in my life wherever i am – whenever i am willing to be still before Him – it is an added blessing to do so here in Jerusalem where the Lord Himself says that He will make His home among His people (Joel 3:21). i hear the joy of children laughing and playing in the near distance mixed with the sounds of gentle breezes and the chirping of birds. i envision – as best i can – what that day will be like when our Lord returns to make His home among His people.

"We are here at the Lord's invitation – not only to spend this time with Him, but also to do so in this place. He made the way for us to be able to do so. Otherwise we could not be here. As clearly as He instructed the apostles to wait for Him, He instructed us to come to this place.

"Truly the Lord has enabled us to be still in this place, and know that He is God. There have not been any flames or tongues of fire – and i have not been given the ability to speak in other languages – or even to improve my proficiency in the English language . And yet, i have some small sense of what the apostles felt on that day – having experienced the rush of wind and been visited by and indwelt by His Spirit.

"i know that i was indwelt by His Spirit many years ago at the moment of my salvation, but He has allowed me over these past several days to experience a fresh renewing of my spirit and a fresh filling of His presence. i know that i cannot tarry here – any more than those select disciples were able to tarry in His presence on the Mount of Transfiguration (Matthew 17). The time will soon arrive for us to come "down from the mountain" or (if you will permit) from our 'upper room'. Life awaits at the base of the mountain – the day-to-day demands of life, the many opportunities of ministry, and the activities that i can allow to so easily distract me. But i know that just as He has allowed us to be in this upper room with Him, He allows us to walk down the mountain and into the day-to-day with Him, enabled, guided and empowered by His Holy Spirit.

"Yes, i know that this is one of those mountaintop experiences – and i know that i cannot live on the mountaintop even though i would like to. But it does cause me to yearn even more for His return – that day when He returns to make His home among His people."

. . .

That is the closest i will ever come to knowing how the disciples felt as they awaited the arrival of the promised Helper. And then the "*sound from heaven like the roaring of a mighty windstorm... filled the house*". The Helper had come! He filled them to the point that they overflowed. His filling was conspicuous. People came running because they knew there was a difference in these followers. They looked different. They spoke differently. They were ignited by the Holy Spirit. And the people knew the difference wasn't of the disciples' own making. They were "just Galileans" after all!

That same Holy Spirit dwells within us if we have become followers of Jesus. Is the world around us seeing a difference as well? Is it seeing a group of people who look different, talk differently and reflect the Person of Jesus? And if we name the Name of Jesus, we don't need to wait in an upper room for the Helper to come. He entered into our lives at the moment of our salvation.

As i write this chapter, i just received an email from The Barna Group. Barna is an evangelical research group based out of Ventura, California. Based upon their polling, they shared the following facts today:

- One-quarter of practicing Christians says there is a person who they cannot forgive.
- Almost half of practicing Christians say mercy doesn't influence their thoughts or actions or they haven't thought about whether it does.
- Christians grapple with whether certain people deserve compassion or forgiveness, and they are not all that different from non-Christians when it comes to embodying merciful attitudes and actions.

Their conclusion was that the Church is struggling to embody mercy today. Our struggle is because we have relegated the Helper to the back row of our lives instead of the driver's seat. Jesus sent His Holy Spirit to enable and empower us to embody Him, His love and His mercy. If our lives don't reflect His presence or His power it is because we have quenched the igniting of His Holy Spirit. Even the early church struggled. The apostle Paul wrote to the church in Thessalonica: "*Do not stifle the*

Holy Spirit" (1 Thessalonians 5:19) and to the church in Ephesus: *"Be filled with the Spirit"* (Ephesians 5:18). We would do well to heed his counsel.

The Helper has come! We are no longer awaiting His arrival. He has come like the roaring of a mighty windstorm. Jesus, ignite Your Spirit within us. Fill us to overflowing. So that the world might see You – Your Person and Your power – for the glory of Your Name!

* * *

5

LET THE NATIONS BE GLAD

Here we are—Parthians, Medes, Elamites, people from Mesopotamia, Judea, Cappadocia, Pontus, the province of Asia, Phrygia, Pamphylia, Egypt, and the areas of Libya around Cyrene, visitors from Rome (both Jews and converts to Judaism), Cretans, and Arabs. And we all hear these people speaking in our own languages about the wonderful things God has done!" They stood there amazed and perplexed. "What can this mean?" they asked each other.
Acts 2:9-12

* * *

It is telling that the very first thing that happened after the Holy Spirit arrived was that the people of the fifteen different language groups from three continents that were gathered in Jerusalem heard the disciples praising God in their own language – simultaneously. The disciples were not yet preaching the Good News; they were praising God for what He had just done. Theologians have debated for almost two thousand years as to whether the disciples were divinely and instantaneously enabled to speak in those different languages or if the people's ears were simultaneously attuned by the Holy Spirit to hear in their own language. Or was it a combination of both? Regardless, it was quite a feat! And the fact that it was the first evidence of the Holy Spirit's presence reinforces His principle purpose – to draw all people to worship God and bring glory to His Name.

You may recall that over twenty-three hundred years earlier, God had pronounced judgement on the people at the Tower of Babel by confusing their language (Genesis 11:1-9). In building their tower, they were attempting a feat in rebellion against God in order to bring glory to themselves. God is jealous for His glory and He will not share it, so He confounded their plan by confounding their language. The judgement of differing languages caused the people to scatter and each group to go their own way. But on Pentecost, when the Holy Spirit came, He united them around the praises being offered to Him. For the first time in over twenty-three hundred years they were able to simultaneously hear the same praises to God in their own heart language. At that moment – just like in heaven to come – language was no longer a divider to worship.

Throughout the Book of Acts – and for that matter, throughout Scripture – we see the followers of Christ on mission to make His Name known – just as Jesus told us to be just before He ascended into heaven. But the Holy Spirit's first act was not about mission, it was about worship. He began with the reminder, as John Piper writes in his book *"Let the Nations Be Glad"*, that *"Missions is not the ultimate goal of the Church. Worship is. Missions exists because worship doesn't.*

"Worship is ultimate, not missions, because God is ultimate, not man. When this age is over, and the countless millions of the redeemed fall on their faces before the throne of God, missions will be no more. It is a temporary necessity. But worship abides forever.

"Worship, therefore, is the fuel and goal of missions. It's the goal of missions because in missions we simply aim to bring the nations into the white hot enjoyment of God's glory. The goal of missions is the gladness of the peoples in the greatness of God. 'The Lord reigns; let the earth rejoice; let the many coastlands be glad!' (Psalm 97:1 ESV). *'Let the peoples praise Thee, O God; let all the peoples praise Thee! Let the nations be glad and sing for joy!'* (Psalm 67:3-4 NASB).

"But worship is also the fuel of missions. Passion for God in worship precedes the offer of God in preaching. You can't commend what you don't cherish. Missionaries will never call out, 'Let the nations be glad!' who cannot say from the heart, 'I rejoice in the Lord...I will be glad and exult in Thee, I will sing praise to Thy name, O Most High' (Psalm 104:34; 9:2 ESV). *Missions begins and ends in worship.*

. . .

"If the pursuit of God's glory is not ordered above the pursuit of man's good in the affections of the heart and the priorities of the church, man will not be well-served and God will not be duly-honored. I am not pleading for a diminishing of missions but for a magnifying of God. When the flame of worship burns with the heat of God's true worth, the light of missions will shine to the darkest peoples on earth."

Apparently the sound of the wind drew the people to the place where the disciples were gathered, but it was their praise and worship of God that captured the attention of the people. The Holy Spirit was "the sound of the wind". It is He that drew the people. And that's as true today as it was then. Jesus said, *"No one can come to Me unless the Father who sent Me draws them to Me..."* (John 6:44). And the Father "draws" through His Holy Spirit. Once drawn, the people encountered God through the praise and worship that was being offered up to Him. Why? Because God inhabits the praises of His people! (Psalm 22:3)

Several years ago, on a different visit to Jerusalem than the one i referenced in the last chapter, i was with a group as we visited the Church of St. Anne, erected near the site of the Pool of Bethesda. We were not the only people inside the church admiring the beautiful early twelfth century architecture. There was a large number of people, obviously from a wide variety of countries. We heard many languages being spoken. The acoustics in the chapel were absolutely amazing. At some point, someone began to sing the hymn, "How Great Thou Art" in another language. Very quickly everyone in the church joined in singing that familiar song in their own respective language. We didn't know one another's languages, but we all knew the words and the meaning in our own language. The difference of our languages quickly got lost in the blending of our voices – and our hearts – in praise. We went on to sing two other hymns together. i can't remember which hymns they were, but i remember thinking that this is what heaven is going to be like – people from every language, people, tribe and nation gathering around the throne praising God in one voice. And we all knew that God was inhabiting our praises. It wasn't the place; it was the praise. None of us wanted to leave. You could see the reluctance on everyone's face. But soon we did. Since then, I have had other similar experiences, but that one reigns supreme in my memory. Even as i write this, the memory of that day reawakens the anticipation of what it will be like when we are all gathered together around His throne.

The disciples and the people experienced a taste that day. The Holy Spirit drew the people together. Together they heard and understood the praises being lifted up to Him. And God inhabited that praise and worship. And the nations were glad.

That same Holy Spirit dwells within us if we are followers of Jesus. He is still at work to draw all people to worship God. What do they hear when they are drawn in our direction? Are they hearing praise? Let's not lose sight – that's why He left us here… and that's why He sent His Holy Spirit… until He returns.

* * *

6

A DRINK AT JOEL'S PLACE

But others in the crowd ridiculed them, saying, "They're just drunk, that's all!" Then Peter stepped forward with the eleven other apostles and shouted to the crowd, "Listen carefully, all of you, fellow Jews and residents of Jerusalem! Make no mistake about this. These people are not drunk, as some of you are assuming. Nine o'clock in the morning is much too early for that. No, what you see was predicted long ago by the prophet Joel:
'In the last days,' God says, 'I will pour out My Spirit upon all people. Your sons and daughters will prophesy. Your young men will see visions, and your old men will dream dreams. In those days I will pour out My Spirit even on My servants – men and women alike – and they will prophesy. And I will cause wonders in the heavens above and signs on the earth below – blood and fire and clouds of smoke. The sun will become dark, and the moon will turn blood red before that great and glorious day of the Lord arrives. But everyone who calls on the name of the Lord will be saved.'
Acts 2:13-21 (referring to Joel 2:28-32)

* * *

On the day of Pentecost, the Holy Spirit came to call out a body of believers to form the church – those through whom God has chosen to work to fulfill His purpose. The day before Pentecost there was no church. The day after Pentecost there was a church. This was "Day Zero".

It is important for us to understand the context for the day that God sent

His Holy Spirit – not only for the Jewish people of the day, but also for us. Pentecost is a Greek name. The Jews called it the Festival of the Harvest. It was one of the three annual festivals that the Jews were to observe as established by God through Moses on Mount Sinai right after God had given the ten commandments (Exodus 23:14-16). The first of the three festivals was the Festival of Unleavened Bread (the Passover), remembering God's deliverance of the people from their bondage in Egypt. The second was this festival called the Festival of Harvest, celebrating the first fruits of the harvest season. The third was the Festival of the Final Harvest (or the Ingathering), celebrating the end of the harvest season. All of these were established by God for the people to acknowledge Him – His deliverance, His goodness and His provision.

From a Kingdom perspective these three festivals coincide with significant events not only for His people who were under the Law, but for those of us who are the recipients of His grace. As we see throughout the Gospels, and as we explored in *Taking Up The Cross*, in His infinite grace, God arranged for the crucifixion and resurrection of the Son to coincide with the Festival of Unleavened Bread (the Passover). As a result, that event no longer only looks back to the salvation of the firstborn of the Israelites through the sacrifice and shedding of a lamb's blood, it now serves as a reminder of the sacrifice and shed blood of the Son through whom deliverance from the bondage of sin is now available to all. With the arrival of His Holy Spirit on the Day of Pentecost (the Festival of the Harvest), God was signifying that the harvest of the fruit of salvation had now begun. He was pouring out His Spirit as the signal and the conduit of the last days – the days of harvest in which the fruit of salvation will be brought in to the Kingdom. But more on that in a moment. For the follower of Christ, the third festival, the Festival of the Final Harvest, points to the day that Jesus will return for the completion of the harvest season.

Most everyone within the sound of Peter's voice was a lifelong Orthodox Jew or a proselyte, having gathered in Jerusalem for the Festival of the Harvest. They were drawn to investigate the sound of the rush of winds and the sound of the multiple languages being spoken. Seeing the Galileans at the center of all of the uproar, some had tried to explain away what was taking place by saying that the disciples were drunk. But all of the disciples were practicing Jews. They had been seen and witnessed in the Temple for the prior week (and even longer counting their time in the Temple with Jesus). Orthodox Jews did not eat or drink before nine o'clock in the morning on the Sabbath or on a holy day like Pentecost, nor did they usually drink wine except with meals. So when Peter initially stepped forward to speak to the crowd and refute the allegation of drunkenness, he was reminding everyone that the accusation was ludicrous and a violation of the Law. i can't help but wonder if Paul had this reaction in mind when he admonished the believers in Ephesus, "*And do not get drunk with wine, for that is debauchery, but be filled with the Spirit*" (Ephesians 5:18 ESV). Strong drink may bring a temporary exhilaration, but the Spirit gives a deep satisfaction and a lasting joy. We are vessels of the Holy Spirit. He – and He alone – should be seen to be at work in and through our lives.

But coming back to the moment, Peter immediately pointed them to the prophecy of the last days as recorded by the prophet Joel in their Scriptures. Joel was writing that the day of the Lord's return would be heralded by the pouring out of the Spirit of God. This should not seem strange or contrary. They were witnessing the fulfillment of the beginnings of that prophecy. The day was coming when all of this would be fulfilled, but on this day they were seeing a glimpse of it. As the people looked and stared at a group of Galileans, they would have been incredulous. The announcement that the Holy Spirit who Joel was writing about was now being poured out upon these Galileans would have been incredible to the Jews, because they thought God's Spirit was only given to a few select people (Numbers 11:28-29). But here were one hundred twenty of the followers of Jesus – men and women – enjoying the blessing of the same Holy Spirit that had empowered Moses, David and the prophets. The last days had dawned with the arrival of Jesus – and they would come to a climax with His return. The arrival of the Holy Spirit affirmed that they had entered into the first days of the harvest – the last days as foretold by the prophets.

Joel says that one feature of the last days will be the outpouring of the Holy Spirit on people of every kind – men and women, young and old, high and low. God's people will be clothed with power; they will receive power. And the main effect of this power seems to be bold, prophetic speech. Believers of all kinds are going to be so gripped by the Spirit of God that they see the greatness of Jesus and the purpose of Jesus with extraordinary clarity and speak it with extraordinary boldness. The people were seeing that take place before their eyes – from Galileans no less.

But though Joel's prophecy pointed to a period of time that began on that day of Pentecost, it also is a prophecy that points to the return of Christ. That means that we are in the midst of those days – until He returns. There is a promise that in the last days the Spirit will be poured out on all flesh – all the nations will be reached. The true church of Christ will be awakened and revived and sent with extraordinary passion and zeal and prophetic power, and – right in the midst of terrorism and war and persecution and natural disasters – the flaming end-time church of Christ will finish the Great Commission, and welcome the King. God's promise through the giving of His Spirit is to empower His people again and again through the extraordinary filling of His Spirit until the witness to His name has reached all the peoples – to the end of the earth.

i have entitled this chapter *"A Drink At Joel's Place"*. i was inspired to do so by a book of that same title written by my childhood pastor, Dr. Jess C. Moody. The book is a collection of essays that struggle with the question as to why the world in which we live is no longer drawn to the church in the way that the crowds were drawn to the disciples on the Day of Pentecost – "Day Zero". Moody writes, *"We are the church. The name church implies God. God means miracle. If we say we are the church and we cannot come up with a miracle, the world thinks we are phony. Maybe they are correct. If the only success they see in our lives or our churches is that which can be explained in terms of organization and management – that is, something the world could do with the same expenditure of effort and technique, they will one day repudiate us."* Dr. Moody wrote that statement over fifty years ago. The day that the world *"will one day repudiate us"* is no longer in the future; the day has long since passed.

Dr. John Piper writes that, as the last days grow closer to their end, *"the love of many will grow cold. Yes, there will be apostasy on a large scale. Yes, people will simply forsake the faith when the world turns up the heat. But in the midst of all that unbelief and coldness and treachery, Jesus says that the gospel will be preached through the whole world as a testimony to all the nations. In the face of all that persecution and in the midst of all that deadness, the true church of God is going to have extraordinary power, extraordinary zeal, extraordinary passion and love for Jesus."*

Piper concludes that thought by asking the question, *"What is it like to live as Christians in a time when the power of the Kingdom has already arrived but not in its fullness, and a time when the end of this age is almost over, but not yet fully over?* Regrettably, i think we all know what it is like. Because we are that generation. The Holy Spirit of God dwells within us, but we see none of His power. The apostle Paul wrote a very clear self-diagnostic for us to apply: *"When you follow the desires of your sinful nature, the results are very clear: sexual immorality, impurity, lustful pleasures, idolatry, sorcery, hostility, quarreling, jealousy, outbursts of anger, selfish ambition, dissension, division, envy, drunkenness, wild parties, and other sins like* these" (Galatians 5:19-21). Then he went on to say, *"But the Holy Spirit produces this kind of fruit in our lives: love, joy, peace, patience, kindness, goodness, faithfulness, gentleness, and self-control"* (Galatians 5:22-23). The world does not see the latter, because we have chosen to walk in the former. Gratefully, Paul went on to write the prescription that will make the difference: "{nail} *the passions and desires of* {our} *sinful nature to His cross and* {crucify} *them there. Since we are living by the Spirit, let us follow the Spirit's leading in every part of our lives"* (Galatians 5:24-25).

Those are worthy words to heed as we continue our respective journeys in the wilderness. He has placed our feet on this path for His purpose – a purpose that will only be accomplished through the fullness of the power of His Holy Spirit. Let us follow the Spirit's leading in every part of our lives and be filled with His Spirit… until He returns.

* * *

7

A PREARRANGED PLAN

"People of Israel, listen! God publicly endorsed Jesus the Nazarene by doing powerful miracles, wonders, and signs through Him, as you well know. But God knew what would happen, and His prearranged plan was carried out when Jesus was betrayed. With the help of lawless Gentiles, you nailed Him to a cross and killed Him. But God released Him from the horrors of death and raised Him back to life, for death could not keep Him in its grip.... God raised Jesus from the dead, and we are all witnesses of this. Now He is exalted to the place of highest honor in heaven, at God's right hand. And the Father, as He had promised, gave Him the Holy Spirit to pour out upon us, just as you see and hear today. For David himself never ascended into heaven, yet he said,
'The Lord said to my Lord, "Sit in the place of honor at My right hand until I humble Your enemies, making them a footstool under Your feet.' So let everyone in Israel know for certain that God has made this Jesus, whom you crucified, to be both Lord and Messiah!"
Acts 2:22-36 (quoting Psalm 110:1)

* * *

Throughout the book, *Taking Up The Cross,* we looked at the truth that Jesus was never a victim of the religious leaders, or the Roman rulers, or the crowd, or even Judas Iscariot – because Jesus was never a victim. Jesus was always the Victor! The cross was never an infliction upon the Son, it was an instrument of the Father. Jesus was not crucified because of the religious leaders' treachery, the Roman rulers' impotence, the crowd's endorsement or Judas Iscariot's betrayal, though all are accountable before God for their own actions. If those individuals had the ability or the power over God to do anything contrary to His divine purpose, then He wouldn't be very divine! If the Sovereign, Almighty God can be defeated or manipulated by any of His creation then He is neither sovereign nor almighty. As a matter of fact, He would no longer be God if His creation had power over its Creator. As Peter said, *"God knew what would happen, and His prearranged plan was carried out"* (Acts 2:23).

Many of those to whom Peter was speaking would have been in Jerusalem the day that Jesus was crucified. Some of them may have been in the group that cried, *"Crucify Him! Crucify Him!"* But most of them were probably not a part of the group that had called for His crucifixion, and yet Peter says, *"**you** nailed Him to a cross and killed Him"* (Acts 2:23). i would venture that with that statement he got everyone's attention. He could say it because everybody in that crowd was involved in the crime against Jesus that brought Him to His death. The essence of the crime against Jesus was not the ending of His physical life. The essence of the crime against Jesus was the rejection of the Father in Jesus' life. In essence, their acceptance or rejection of Jesus would be a referendum on their acceptance or rejection of the Father. They could not profess to follow the Father and reject the One He had sent and endorsed. So Peter recounted all of the ways that the Father had endorsed His Son for the accomplishment of His purpose through His prearranged plan.

Jesus was handed over to be crucified on the grounds of blasphemy. He claimed to be the Son of God (Luke 22:70-71). He claimed that the Father was endorsing Him as Messiah (Luke 22:67-69). But the Jewish rulers rejected this role of the Heavenly Father in Jesus' life. They called Jesus a blasphemer. Therefore, if a person rejects the true role of the Father in the life of Jesus, that person votes for the charge of blasphemy. And to cast your vote on the side of blasphemy – to reject the Father's endorsement of Jesus – is to say in your heart, *"Crucify Him! Crucify Him!"* That was true then, and it is just as true now.

When Jesus performed a miracle, a wonder or a sign, it was the Father's endorsement – *"This is My beloved Son with whom I am well pleased, hear Him!"* (Luke 9:35) Peter declared that it was the Father who did the " . . . *signs through Him, as you well know."* He was "publicly endorsed" by the Father and, don't miss this, Peter emphasized that the Father Himself did the miracles through Jesus. It was the power of the Father working in and through the Son to heal the sick and still the storm and cast out demons and raise the dead. While He was on the earth, the Father gave Jesus as the Son of Man the fullest endorsement any "human" ever had. He gave him His Spirit "without limit" (John 3:34).

The Father further endorsed Jesus by planning His death for the sins of His people. The Father planned the suffering and death of Jesus so that forgiveness of sins could be preached to all the nations (Isaiah 53). The difference between the Father's plan to crucify Jesus and Pilate's plan to crucify Jesus was that Pilate was dismissing and rejecting Jesus as a mere pretender, whereas the Father was honoring His Son as the Servant of the Lord and the Savior of the world. The Father planned the death of Jesus not to disown Him or dishonor Him or reject Him, but to glorify Him as the perfect, flawless Lamb of God, who takes away the sin of the world. The Father's plan for Jesus to die was not an indictment like the plan of the Jewish leaders, but rather, an endorsement of His infinite worth so that He could save the Jew and the Gentile alike.

The Father endorsed Jesus by raising Him from the dead. Peter says "{you} *killed Him. But God released Him… and raised Him*" (Acts 2:23-24.) You voted "no" against Jesus. But the Father voted "YES" for Jesus. You denounced Him, but the Father endorsed Him. You killed Him, but the Father raised Him. Peter fully intended for the crowd to feel the clash between their rejection of Jesus and the Father's acceptance of Jesus; their defamation of Jesus and the Father's affirmation of Jesus. What matters here ultimately is not that they killed a Man, but that their words and actions bore witness to the fact that they are against God.

Now this is a shocking and stunning thing for people to hear and extremely hard to admit. These are religious people that Peter is addressing. They are moral people. They are worshiping people. They are people who know hundreds of verses in God's Word by heart. And he is telling them that their minds are totally at odds with God. They claim to know God. They claim to love God and worship God and follow God. And Peter says that they are diametrically opposed to God. They are "anti-God".

The test of whether we are "anti-God" or not is not whether we say we believe in God, or whether we say we know God, or love God, or serve God. The test is whether we embrace God the Father's endorsement of Jesus. If we say we know God but reject the Father's endorsement of Jesus as the worker of miracles; if we say that we know God but reject the Father's endorsement of Jesus as **the** Passover sacrifice that takes away sin; if we say we know God and reject the Father's endorsement of Jesus by raising Him from the dead, then we don't really know God. In fact we are against God. We are "anti-God".

This is what cut those listening to Peter to the heart. They saw that in their zeal "for" God they had been against God. We need to understand this today! Because in our "live-and-let-live" pluralistic society hardly anyone would dare say to another person, "You claim to know God, but in fact you are "anti-God"; you are against God." Why? Because you do not embrace God the Father's endorsement of Jesus. Jesus is the test of all true knowledge of God. Are we with the Father in His endorsement of Jesus by raising Him from the dead, or are we against Him?

The Father endorsed Jesus by seating Him on His right hand and putting all His enemies under His feet. Peter quotes the prophecy of King David who foresaw that God the Father would exalt the risen Messiah to His right hand and give Him a place of rule and supremacy over every other person and power in the universe. This endorsement of Jesus exposes the ultimate horror of rejecting Him. In rejecting Jesus, not only have they rejected the One who the Father declared to be Messiah by raising Him from the dead; they have also rejected the One whom the Father declared to be the Lord of the universe by exalting Him to His right hand.

Lastly, the Father endorsed Jesus as the only One worthy to receive the Holy Spirit and pour Him out in full portion upon sinners who repent. The Father has given Jesus the privilege of pouring out the Holy Spirit and clothing His people with the Spirit's power from on high (Luke 24:49).

What is at stake here and at every point in this message that Peter was bringing to the crowd is God the Father. The Father endorsed Jesus as the Worker of miracles on the earth. The Father endorsed Jesus as the perfect Sacrifice for sins. The Father endorsed Jesus as the risen Messiah. The Father endorsed Jesus by exalting Him to be Lord of the universe. To reject Jesus is to repudiate the Father! To vote "no" on Jesus is to oppose God the Father. That's the issue. And that is what pierced their hearts! (Acts 2:37)

. . .

The question before the crowd back then is the same question before all people today. Do you join God the Father in His affirmation of Jesus, or do you stand against Him in the life of Jesus? The Father had a prearranged plan – a plan that could only be accomplished through His Son. And the Father has a plan for our lives – a plan that can only be accomplished through the Son that He sent in order for that plan to be fulfilled. Join with the Father in His affirmation of His Son, and follow His Son in the journey of your life… trusting Him to fulfill His plan for His glory… until He returns.

* * *

8

WHAT SHOULD WE DO?

Peter's words pierced their hearts, and they said to him and to the other apostles, "Brothers, what should we do?" Peter replied, "Each of you must repent of your sins and turn to God, and be baptized in the name of Jesus Christ for the forgiveness of your sins. Then you will receive the gift of the Holy Spirit. This promise is to you, to your children, and to those far away – all who have been called by the Lord our God." Then Peter continued preaching for a long time, strongly urging all his listeners, "Save yourselves from this crooked generation!" Those who believed what Peter said were baptized and added to the church that day – about 3,000 in all.

Acts 2:37-41

* * *

With this chapter, i'm going to make a transition. Throughout the first five books of the ***Lessons Learned In The Wilderness*** series and throughout the first few chapters of this book, i have endeavored to share truth in a way that it is applicable to you, the reader, whether you are already a follower of Christ, or you have not yet come to that place. My prayer has been that if you do not have a saving relationship with Christ that the Spirit of God would use the Truth of His Word as shared through these books in drawing you into a personal relationship with Him. That is exactly what we see occurring in the lives of the three thousand new believers recorded in these verses. The Spirit of God used the Word of God to lead the three thousand to repentance and faith. If you have not yet come to that place, i beseech you that there will never be a better time to repent of your sins and turn to God than right now. Put this book down, go before God in prayer and receive forgiveness for your sins without any further delay. Heed the instructions that the apostle Peter gave to those who were standing before him. You are one of the very people to whom he was referring – as are we all – when he said, *"this promise is… to those far away"*. He was talking about us in this generation and all the generations to follow! How we turn to Christ has not changed in two thousand years, and it will not change until He returns! So, if you have not done so, i pray even now that you will do so today!

From here on, in this chapter and for the remainder of this book, i am going to be writing as if you already are a follower of Christ. We're going to look at the instruction from the Word for believers and followers of Jesus. i'm going to transition from "what must we do" *to be saved,* to "what must we do" *as one who is already saved.*

We begin these verses with the statement that *"Peter's words pierced their hearts"*. Allow me to make a few clarifications. The listeners were convicted of their sin. The Spirit of God used the Word of God to bring conviction to their hearts. Only the Spirit of God can do that. Conviction is not brought about by eloquence of speech or the charisma of the messenger, rather through a working of the Holy Spirit. And the words that were spoken were not Peter's words! Peter knew that! Luke, the writer of this account, knew that! Peter was simply the mouthpiece. He was the conduit. The Spirit of God was speaking through Peter. Don't read this as if this fisherman had special training to deliver this message. Though he was the first to speak that day, it appears that the crowd asked the question of all the apostles which opens up the possibility that all of them may have spoken at some time that day. But even as it relates to all twelve, the only gifting they had was the presence of the Spirit of God. The Spirit was given to equip all of those who repent and believe, not just those twelve, or your pastor, or your small group leader. He was given to equip and empower you.

And again, the words that the Spirit of God spoke through Peter – and the others – was the Word of God. *"For the Word of God is alive and powerful. It is sharper than the sharpest two-edged sword, cutting between soul and spirit, between joint and marrow. It exposes our innermost thoughts and desires"* (Hebrews 4:12). It's the Word of God – that two-edged sword – that *"pierced their hearts"*. The message was not about what Peter thought; it was about what the Word of God says. The Word brought conviction that caused them to repent and turn from their religion and turn to Christ.

Repentance means i am no longer walking in the way that i was. i have turned and am now walking toward God and with God by His grace. It's a change of heart – from a heart filled with sin to a heart that has been made new by Christ.

He next told them that once they had repented, they must be baptized. Baptism is not part of repentance; it follows repentance as a testimony of the forgiveness we have received. Put another way: we are not baptized in order to be saved; we are baptized because we have been saved. A clear example that baptism is not a part of salvation, but, rather, an obedient act that follows salvation, is the new believers that came to faith in the home of Cornelius. Luke records that they had received the Holy Spirit before they were baptized (Acts 10:44-48).

Again, **baptism is an act of obedience**. Jesus said we are to be baptized (Matthew 28:19). But it must **follow** repentance, otherwise all we did was get wet! **It is an act of proof.** It is an outward expression of the sincerity of our repentance and faith. **It is an act of identification**. Through baptism we are publicly identifying with our Savior and Messiah – bringing glory to Him, just as He did when He was baptized by John the Baptist (Matthew 3:15). **It is an act of witness**. Baptism by immersion reflects exactly what has occurred in our life. As we are lowered into the water we demonstrate that our sin nature has been put to death with Christ on the cross, and as we are raised back up out of the water, we demonstrate the new life in which we walk with the resurrected Christ.

Three thousand new believers were baptized on that day. Did you ever wonder how they were able to baptize that many people in one day? In that day, as Jews prepared to bring their sacrifices into the Temple, they first needed to go through a purification ritual in a bath called a "mikveh". Thus far, archaeologists have uncovered two hundred of those mikveh pools in and around Jerusalem, of which fifty are located on the southern side of the Temple Mount. Peter and the other apostles preached to the crowd on the southern side of the Temple. In His sovereignty, the Father had already arranged for pools to be in place for those baptisms long before anyone else knew they would be needed!

Lastly, Peter told the crowd that following their repentance they would receive the gift of the Holy Spirit. The apostles had waited in an upper room for eight days to receive the gift of the Holy Spirit, but that would no longer be the case. From that day forward the gift of the Holy Spirit would immediately be given at the point of repentance. And how much of the Holy Spirit would they receive? Remember, the Holy Spirit is a Person. He's not an "it". You don't receive a portion of a Person; you receive all or nothing. And Peter said, *"you will receive the gift of the Holy Spirit"* – that's the whole Person. The same Holy Spirit who empowered Peter to speak on that day indwells every believer – whether they have been saved for one second or one hundred years.

As you walk through your personal life journey, even in the midst of a wilderness, God will bring people across your path that His Holy Spirit is convicting of sin and drawing to Himself. He will bring people across your path who are asking, "What should we do?" The answer to that question hasn't changed in two thousand years. *"This promise is to you, to your children, and to those far away…."* Until He returns, we have been entrusted with that promise – not to keep – but to share!

* * *

9

FULLY DEVOTED FOLLOWERS

All the believers devoted themselves to the apostles' teaching, and to fellowship, and to sharing in meals (including the Lord's Supper), and to prayer. A deep sense of awe came over them all, and the apostles performed many miraculous signs and wonders. And all the believers met together in one place and shared everything they had. They sold their property and possessions and shared the money with those in need. They worshiped together at the Temple each day, met in homes for the Lord's Supper, and shared their meals with great joy and generosity – all the while praising God and enjoying the goodwill of all the people. And each day the Lord added to their fellowship those who were being saved.

Acts 2:42-47

* * *

Three thousand believed, repented and were baptized. They comprised the first church – "The First Church of Jerusalem". And the Lord added to their fellowship daily. Let's take a few minutes and look back at that first church.

All the believers devoted themselves.... The word "devoted" means *"given over to"*, *"ardently enthusiastic and loyal"*, and *"placing the needs of the object of your devotion over your own"*. We often refer to sports fans as being devoted. One of my nephews attended the University of Georgia and became a loyal Georgia Bulldog. As a matter of fact, during his undergrad days, he became so ardently enthusiastic at football games that he painted his bare upper torso red, put on a red wig, sported a letter on his chest and became affectionately known as "W", as together with eleven other fans, they spelled out "GEORGIA DAWGS" in the bleachers. That could probably be described as a number of things , one of them being "devoted". There are degrees of devotion as illustrated by my nephew. But as we see in these verses, these believers were fully devoted. There wasn't anything "halfway" in their belief or their actions.

They were fully devoted to their Lord. They repented and surrendered their life to Christ and never looked back. In our day we often give the appearance that we "added" Christ to our lives. We keep on doing many of the things we were doing before we "got saved". Those around us may – or may not – see a difference that Christ has made in our lives. But those three thousand… were radically transformed. They knew that apart from the saving work of Christ all they had was a religion that made little or no difference in their lives. They knew that apart from Christ they were dead in their sin. They knew that His Spirit and His Word had "pierced their hearts" and there was no going back. Their devotion to Jesus led them to become fully devoted to His Word. Remember, at that point, there was no New Testament. It hadn't been written yet. The apostles' teaching was the spoken word of Jesus' teachings that would become our New Testament. Together with the Old Testament, the two would subsequently become the full and complete Word of God, as we know it now. They were fully devoted to God's Word – every word! And one of the teachings from Jesus' words was that they were to love one another. They took Jesus' words seriously when He had said, *"Your love for one another will prove to the world that you are My disciples"* (John 13:35). That word from Jesus meant that if they were going to be fully devoted to Him and His Word, they also needed to be fully devoted to one another.

Their devotion led to awe. Their belief and repentance was not a "one and done conversion". Rather they became a day-in, day-out community of believers – learning, applying and witnessing the fruit of Jesus' teachings in their own lives, as well as in one another's lives. They saw the power of God working through signs and wonders. The miracles and the life transformation they witnessed never became routine; rather, their awe led to increased faith… which led to greater awe… which led to even greater faith…. There was a sense of wonder and awe – and godly fear – at the stark reality of what they saw and heard.

Their awe led to selflessness. When Jesus became Lord of their lives, they were no longer the central figure in their own lives. Selfish ambition was abandoned to be replaced by sacrificial generosity. They began to understand that everything they possessed was from God. And none of their possessions were truly theirs; they were but stewards of the gifts with which God had entrusted them. When they began to see themselves as stewards they realized that the gifts that God had given them were not for self-expression or self-fulfillment, but to fill what was lacking in someone else by meeting genuine needs. They realized that even the grace that God had extended to each one of them was not meant to end with them, but was to be extended to someone else (1 Peter 4:10). Apart from selfless and sacrificial compassion, grace would merely end up in storage, not in action. It was never our Lord's intention that we fill our barns with His grace, rather, that His grace and His gifts be poured out to others (Luke 12:16–21).

Their devotion to one another and their growing selflessness bonded them in such a way that if one was in need, the others did not feel they had the right to live on in prosperity without giving up something to meet the need. Thus, they sold their possessions and used the money to meet the needs of the poor in the church.

Their selflessness led to contagious joy. Their love for one another was expressed joyfully, not grudgingly. i mentioned this in *Taking Up The Cross* but it is worthy of repeating. Tertullian was a theologian in the early church (A.D. 155 – A.D. 240). He wrote that the Roman government was disturbed by the early church. So they sent spies to infiltrate and observe worship gatherings. They came back to their Roman leaders with a report that went something like this: "These Christians are very strange people. They speak of One by the name of Jesus, who is absent, but who they expect to return soon. And my, look at how they love one another, and are ready to die for each other." Jesus said, "*There is no greater love than to lay down one's life for one's friends*" (John 15:13). And the early church took Him seriously.[1] Their love – and their joy – were contagious!

We would do well to look within our own local fellowships. If our faith community is committed, but not compelling to anyone, we should be asking serious questions about what we're committed to. Are we known for our joy and our love, or are we known solely for what we're against? John Piper writes, "*Churches are dying today because they are not doing anything which the world should look at and say: 'There is evidence that God is real and that He is glorious.' Many churches have forgotten why they exist –*

namely, to meet needs in the name of Jesus so that people will be moved to give God glory (Matthew 5:16). *And when a church forgets that it exists for others and for God, it becomes in-grown and self-satisfied, and can go on year after year like a social club with a religious veneer. But its life is ebbing away, and people are no longer saying: 'Look at all their good deeds and the humble spirit of love in which they are done; their God must be a glorious God of encouragement.'"*

Let's recap what we see in "The First Church of Jerusalem":

- They were devoted to the teaching of Jesus as told to them by the apostles (which we have in the New Testament).
- They experienced wonders and signs (which they had the faith to see).
- They lived in a state of wonder and awe as they saw day-in and day-out the stark reality of God's presence and power in healings, deliverances and the changed lives of people that the Lord was adding to the church.
- They shared their possessions freely with the needy, as though they didn't even own them.
- They spent time together worshiping as a body in the Temple.
- They spent time together fellowshipping and ministering in small groups in their homes almost every day.
- And when they gathered together with each other, they met with God. They prayed and they praised.

What caused all of this to occur? What was the driving force that made those believers free from the enslavement of their possessions, eager to meet needs, filled with gladness and generosity, and distinguished by their praise and prayer when they came together day after day? It was that joyful, trembling sense of awe that you don't trifle with God or His Word. Regrettably that is not our experience today. In our day, for most people, including most professing Christians, God is an idea to talk about, or an inference from an argument, or a family tradition to be preserved. Only for a very few is God a stark, fearsome, stunning, awesome, shocking present REALITY. He is seen as being tame.., distant.., out of touch.., and silent. Where are the churches of whom Luke could say today, "devotion, awe, wonder, selflessness, trembling – is upon every soul"? The absence of those characteristics has a direct effect on the way we seek God, the way we seek His Word, the way we accumulate possessions for ourselves, the way we ignore the needy, the way we trivialize fellowship, and the way we play more than we pray.

. . .

It is time that we prayed for an outpouring of the Holy Spirit in an extraordinary way. It is time that we prayed that the Spirit of God would pierce our hearts with the Word of God and a holy, joyful awe would come upon the church, and people, not things, would become precious beyond words. Pray that we would again become fully devoted followers of our Lord, His Word and one another... until He returns.

---

1. *Taking Up The Cross,* Ch. 34

10

HE JUMPED UP

Peter and John went to the Temple one afternoon to take part in the three o'clock prayer service. As they approached the Temple, a man lame from birth was being carried in. Each day he was put beside the Temple gate, the one called the Beautiful Gate, so he could beg from the people going into the Temple. When he saw Peter and John about to enter, he asked them for some money. Peter and John looked at him intently, and Peter said, "Look at us!" The lame man looked at them eagerly, expecting some money. But Peter said, "I don't have any silver or gold for you. But I'll give you what I have. In the name of Jesus Christ the Nazarene, get up and walk!" Then Peter took the lame man by the right hand and helped him up. And as he did, the man's feet and ankles were instantly healed and strengthened. He jumped up, stood on his feet, and began to walk! Then, walking, leaping, and praising God, he went into the Temple with them. All the people saw him walking and heard him praising God. When they realized he was the lame beggar they had seen so often at the Beautiful Gate, they were absolutely astounded! They all rushed out in amazement to Solomon's Colonnade, where the man was holding tightly to Peter and John.

Acts 3:1-11

* * *

For a moment, imagine you have miraculously been transported back to this period of time in Jerusalem. Imagine you have been in the city for about a year beginning with the days leading up to the Passover until this day. Until that moment, you had never heard of Jesus. The day you arrived in Jerusalem, you stood in the midst of a crowd as Jesus proceeded along the streets in the midst of the throng riding on the colt of a donkey. Those standing around you were laying down palm branches ahead of His path as they shouted, *"Hosanna!"* You turned to one of the people beside you and asked who this was riding the colt and why everyone was extending such honor to Him. The person looked at you in amazement that you had no idea who this Man was. He explained that this was Jesus of Nazareth. He was a Miracle Worker. He had made the blind to see, the deaf to hear and the lame to walk. He had even raised a man from the dead who had been in the grave for four days. Some say He is the Messiah who will lead Israel to throw off the oppressive rule of Rome and lead it to again become a great nation. This person wasn't certain about that claim, but there was no question that God's Spirit was with Him.

After Jesus passed by where you were standing, you fell in behind Him with the rest of the crowd to see what He was going to do. Jesus' journey ended at the Temple where He dismounted. He then entered the Outer Court and quietly walked around, looking, but not saying anything. He then made His way through the Beautiful Gate into the hall of prayer. There were a number of people begging at the gate. Some were lame. Some were blind. Each had been brought by family members or friends in the hopes that their friend or loved one would receive charity – or possibly a miracle of healing. Jesus looked on the people with compassion. He didn't ignore them, but He didn't stop to heal them. He continued on into the Temple and spent time in prayer. He and His disciples then quietly left.

The next day was Monday, and while you were at the Temple, Jesus returned. There was no large crowd or procession that day. But as He entered the Temple this time, He overturned the merchants' tables and stalls and drove them out into the Stoa (the area designated for merchants outside the Temple). A great commotion ensued and you saw that those who were begging by the Beautiful Gate obviously feared that they would be overrun by the people as they fled the Temple. Gratefully no one was harmed, but it caused the beggars to be wary in the days ahead.

The following day was Tuesday. Jesus again returned. This time, He remained in the Court of the Women for the entire day. A crowd continuously gathered around Him as He taught. Some of those who normally sat by the Beautiful Gate were brought to Jesus by family or friends, and He healed them! Those who remained at the Gate mourned the fact that they could not make their own way to Jesus. Perhaps their family or friends would help bring them to Jesus when He returned the next day. But Jesus didn't return the next day. As a matter of fact, Jesus never returned to the Temple. The religious leaders had Him crucified on Friday. The following Monday there was talk at the Temple that Jesus had risen from the dead. The religious leaders all said that was a lie. They said that His disciples had moved His body to make people think He was alive. But others, in hushed tones, talked about how Jesus had said He would rise from the dead after three days.

Seven weeks later, there was another commotion in Jerusalem. A sound like a roaring wind had been heard coming from an upper room in the heart of the city. Soon those who had been followers of Jesus began to praise God in languages other than their own, and all the visitors were able to hear the praise in their own language. You even heard it in your language! Several of Jesus' disciples gathered a crowd on the southern steps leading into the Temple and began to preach that Jesus was alive. And as they taught from the Scriptures, three thousand people became believers and were baptized. In the weeks and months that followed, growing numbers of these disciples of Jesus would come to the Temple to pray.

Today, about a year after Jesus was last in the Temple, two of the disciples that you had seen with Him – Peter and John – arrived to take part in the three o'clock prayer service. As they approached the Temple, a lame man was carried in. You recognized the lame man. He had been placed by the gate each day. He was there that day when Jesus had healed those who had been brought to Him. He had looked for Jesus every day after that, until He heard He was crucified. His hope had been crucified with Jesus. As Peter and John passed by him, he asked them for money. But he asked everyone for money – some would give, and others would look the other way.

Peter and John stopped, looked at him intently and said, *"Look at us!"* The lame man turned and looked at them *eagerly.* Peter said to him, *"I don't have any silver or gold for you."* The man's heart sank. *"But I'll give you what I have. In the name of Jesus Christ the Nazarene, get up and walk!"* The lame man didn't really know who these two were, but he knew who Jesus was! And he knew Jesus had healed the lame! Peter reached out and took the man's right hand, and immediately he jumped up! He stood, he walked, he leapt and he praised God! He knew he had been healed by Jesus! Jesus had been his hope. Jesus was his hope. Jesus had healed him.

. . .

Peter and John thought back to a conversation they had once had with Jesus. One of the disciples had asked Him, *"why was this man born blind?"* (John 9:2) Jesus had replied, *"This happened so the power of God could be seen in him"* (John 9:3) The same was true of this man who was born lame. But he had not been born lame so that others would see the power of God displayed through Jesus while He was in the Temple; he had been born lame that the people would see that same power of God displayed through the followers of Jesus! Everyone knew who this man was. Everyone knew he had been born lame. Everyone knew that he had just been healed. And everyone rushed to see Peter and John.

The prophet Isaiah wrote, *"And when He comes* (referring to Jesus), *He will open the eyes of the blind and unplug the ears of the deaf. The lame will leap like a deer, and those who cannot speak will sing for joy!"* (Isaiah 35:6) Jesus made the blind to see, the deaf to hear, the lame to walk and the dumb to speak. And Jesus said, *"Anyone who believes in Me will do the same works I have done, and even greater works, because I am going to be with the Father"* (John 14:12). And because Jesus was going to be with the Father, He had sent the Spirit that would empower and enable them to do the works that Jesus had done. Notice that Peter did not say, "in the name of Peter, get up and walk". He said, "in the name of Jesus". This man was made to walk to bring glory to the Son and to the Father – not to bring glory to Peter.

So it begs the question, if God could use Peter and John in that way, could He also use us? There are some who would say that the gifts of miracles and signs was limited to the apostles. To me, that contradicts what Jesus said up above in John 14:12, when He said, *"anyone who believes in Me…."* i also believe that in days past and in our current day there are charlatans that claim to have the gifts of miracles and signs who are attempting to bring glory – and profit – to themselves. Jesus taught that whatever He does will always be done in a way that brings glory to God and not the person. So here's the thing. The same Holy Spirit that entered into Peter and John and the other disciples gathered in that upper room, entered into the three thousand who believed later that day – and entered into you on the day you repented and believed. Does that mean God's Spirit will work through you in bringing about a miracle or a healing? i believe that it means He could, if He chooses to do so. God still works in miraculous ways. He is doing so every day – all around the world. It may appear to be less obvious in western culture – but perhaps that is more a reflection of the condition of our belief and our faith than it is of Him. But if each of us is honest, we will admit that we have seen God do the miraculous in our midst as well. i do, however, believe it is more conspicuous in other cultures around the world because their hearts haven't grown cold and their faith is more like that of a child. Peter and John knew that the Spirit of God within them was able to heal that man. They knew it as surely as they knew anything.

But also remember, it was the Father's perfect timing – that He had ordered from before the beginning of time. Jesus could have easily healed this man on one of His visits to the Temple – but that wasn't the Father's plan. It certainly didn't mean that Jesus was unable. It meant the Father had a different plan!

What's the take-away for us? Peter and John were not only empowered by the Spirit of God, they were guided by the Spirit of God. They were watchful and responsive to His activity. The Father initiated the activity, not them. We must walk each moment of each day with that kind of awareness and watchfulness. Then – like Mary told the servants in Cana – ""Do whatever He tells you" (John 2:5 NLT). Trust that He will equip you and empower you to accomplish what He has directed you to do. Trust that He will turn the water into wine. Trust that He will make the lame to walk. Trust that He will speak through you the words that He would have you say. If we do, we will see Him do what only He can to cause others to "jump up" and give Him the praise and the glory!

* * *

11

IN WHOSE NAME DO YOU DO THIS?

While Peter and John were speaking to the people, they were confronted by the priests, the captain of the Temple guard, and some of the Sadducees. These leaders were very disturbed that Peter and John were teaching the people that through Jesus there is a resurrection of the dead. They arrested them and, since it was already evening, put them in jail until morning. But many of the people who heard their message believed it, so the number of men who believed now totaled about 5,000. The next day the council of all the rulers and elders and teachers of religious law met in Jerusalem. Annas the high priest was there, along with Caiaphas, John, Alexander, and other relatives of the high priest. They brought in the two disciples and demanded, "By what power, or in whose name, have you done this?"

Acts 4:1-7

* * *

It started with the testimony of one man who was faithful to give praise to God for what He had done. Often that's how God begins a work of salvation. It happened through the woman at the well in Sychar. It happened through the faithfulness of one young boy who gave his sack lunch to Jesus. It happened through Lazarus when he walked out of that tomb. Seeing and hearing that the man born lame was now walking, leaping and praising God, the people in the Temple were *"absolutely astounded"* (Acts 3:10) and they *"rushed out in amazement"* to where the man was *"holding tightly"* (Acts 3:11) to Peter and John. *"Peter saw his opportunity and addressed the crowd"* (Acts 3:12). He wasted no time in asking the crowd two questions to get their focus on the right Person:

"what is so surprising about this?" and *"why stare at us as though we made this man walk by our own power or godliness?"*

It would have been easy for the group to get carried away talking about the miracle and totally miss the Miracle Worker. i am mindful that sometimes we get carried away as we share our own personal stories of how we came to believe in Jesus. We spend a good bit of our time talking about our days before we walked with Christ, then another bit about what our lives are now like since following Christ, but little to no time talking about the Miracle Worker through whom our lives have been changed. Peter immediately shifted the conversation from the miracle to the Miracle Worker.

And he quickly turned their attention away from John and himself. It can be easy to fall into the trap of pride and false modesty when God has worked through us. We start to feel good about what "we've" done or what "we've" said, and we allow the conversation to linger on about how great a Christian we are for God to use us in such a great way. A good friend, mentor and former leader, Dr. Tom Elliff, tells the story that he knew God was preparing to lead him to leave the church, where he pastored for twenty years to enter into a new chapter of ministry, when people started to refer to it as "Brother Tom's church". Our God is jealous for His glory (Isaiah 42:8) and He will share it with no other. Peter was careful to not allow any of that glory to be misdirected to him. He immediately redirected the focus – and we would be wise to heed his example.

"For it is the God of … all our ancestors who has brought glory to His servant Jesus by doing this. This is the same Jesus whom you handed over and rejected before Pilate, despite Pilate's decision to release Him. You rejected this holy, righteous One and instead demanded the release of a murderer. You killed the Author of life, but God raised Him from the dead. And we are witnesses of this fact! Through faith in the name of Jesus, this man was healed – and you know how crippled he was before" (Acts 3:13-16).

Peter knew that these men had rejected the teachings of Jesus. Approximately one year earlier He had stood in that very Temple and taught and healed. Many of them (if not all of them) had heard Him firsthand. They had been eye witnesses of some of the miracles He performed. And yet they had rejected Him and His teaching. They had been complicit in His execution, either overtly or covertly through their silence. Some of them may have been in the crowd in Pilate's courtyard who had cried out, *"Crucify Him!"* Many of them were those to whom Jesus was referring when, from the cross, He said, *"Father, forgive them, for they know not what they do"* (Luke 23:34). And the Father answered His Son's prayer and extended His grace and mercy to them.

"Friends, I realize that what you and your leaders did to Jesus was done in ignorance. But God was fulfilling what all the prophets had foretold about the Messiah – that He must suffer these things. Now repent of your sins and turn to God, so that your sins may be wiped away" (Acts 3:17-19). And hundreds of those gathered there on Solomon's Colonnade believed and repented, and received God's forgiveness that day. Some of the group were probably Pharisees. Some of the group could have been a part of the Sanhedrin. But all of that group became followers of Jesus!

Be mindful that where the Spirit of God is at work, Satan will show up to oppose the work and attempt to silence the witness. That was true that day, just as it is today. The same men that had plotted to have Jesus crucified were not going to sit silently by and allow this work of God to continue. In a very short while they had seen five thousand of their people turn from religion to Jesus. The power base of the religious leaders was again being threatened. If they permitted this to occur much longer they would be left without a people to rule – and they were jealous for their own positions and power! They sent out some of the priests and Sadducees, together with the Temple guard, to arrest Peter and John, and keep them from speaking any further.

The next morning the high council had Peter and John brought before them. They demanded to know, *"By what power, or in whose name, have you done this?"* Now that was just flat out silly! They knew "in whose name" the lame man had been healed. They knew "in whose name" the message of repentance had been preached. And they knew "in whose name" Peter and John stood before them. Remember, Caiaphas and Annas, and probably the rest of the clan, knew John and knew that he was a disciple of Jesus. They knew he stood at the foot of the cross. And they knew of Peter. They had probably heard about Peter's denial. They probably felt reasonably confident that Peter would cave-in under their interrogation. After all, he had denied Jesus three times in their homes in response to the questions of mere servants. Surely Peter would be so intimidated by Annas himself that he would again deny Jesus and this "movement" would be squelched.

. . .

From a worldly perspective, it wasn't a bad plan. The council's only problem was that they weren't expecting the power and the presence of the Holy Spirit. Luke reminds us that Peter *"was filled with the Holy Spirit"* (Acts 4:8). Annas wasn't intimidating a vulnerable fisherman, he was preparing to debate the Spirit of the Almighty God! Talk about showing up unprepared! Annas was ill-equipped to have that conversation. But bear in mind, so was Peter, apart from the presence, power and filling of the Holy Spirit.

The Holy Spirit was the principal actor in all of this. Peter and John were simply supporting cast members. The Holy Spirit had made the lame man to walk. The Holy Spirit had convicted the hearts of those who believed that day. The Holy Spirit had boldly spoken the Word of God through Peter. And it was the Holy Spirit who would now take on these religious leaders. Peter and John's role in all of this was to walk according to His guidance, emptied of their own selves and filled with His Spirit. If they had attempted to do any of this on their own, they would have failed miserably – and nothing of eternal Kingdom impact would have occurred. But because everything that was done, was done in the Name above all names – the Name of Jesus – and was done under the power of His Holy Spirit, a body was healed, lives were transformed and God was glorified.

We would do well to remember that until He returns. Because at the Name of Jesus *every* knee will bow (Philippians 2:10).

* * *

12

WE MUST OBEY GOD RATHER THAN MEN

Then Peter, filled with the Holy Spirit, said to them, "Rulers and elders of our people, are we being questioned today because we've done a good deed for a crippled man? Do you want to know how he was healed? Let me clearly state to all of you and to all the people of Israel that he was healed by the powerful name of Jesus Christ the Nazarene, the Man you crucified but whom God raised from the dead....The members of the council were amazed when they saw the boldness of Peter and John, for they could see that they were ordinary men with no special training in the Scriptures. They also recognized them as men who had been with Jesus. But since they could see the man who had been healed standing right there among them, there was nothing the council could say. So they ordered Peter and John out of the council chamber and conferred among themselves. "What should we do with these men?" they asked each other. "We can't deny that they have performed a miraculous sign, and everybody in Jerusalem knows about it. But to keep them from spreading their propaganda any further, we must warn them not to speak to anyone in Jesus' name again." So they called the apostles back in and commanded them never again to speak or teach in the name of Jesus. But Peter and John replied, "Do you think God wants us to obey you rather than Him? We cannot stop telling about everything we have seen and heard." The council then threatened them further, but they finally let them go because they didn't know how to punish them without starting a riot. For everyone was praising God for this miraculous sign – the healing of a man who had been lame for more than forty years.

Acts 4:8-22

* * *

Peter and John had just been brought before the high council. Luke tells us that Peter was filled with the Holy Spirit. The Holy Spirit had already entered into Peter's life on the Day of Pentecost. He didn't need to reenter. But rather Peter did need to be filled. Being indwelt by the Spirit of God is a one-time act. For Peter, it was at Pentecost. For you and me, it was when we believed, repented and received Christ as our Savior. But being filled with the Spirit of God is a continuing decision on our part. It is an ongoing decision about who will be in control of our lives.

Peter had consciously decided that the Spirit of God would be in control – and not Peter. As followers of Christ, we, too, must continually make that choice. Who sits in the "driver's seat" of our life? Am i the one who is steering and accelerating or braking – or have i turned those controls over to the Spirit of God? In some respects, walking with Christ would be so much easier if we didn't have the choice -- if somehow our flesh nature had been removed altogether at salvation. But though our flesh nature has been redeemed at salvation, it is still with us. The Holy Spirit is doing an ongoing work of sanctifying our flesh nature – but that nature will be with us until the day we stand face-to-face before Jesus. Until then we must continually crucify our flesh nature. That's what Jesus was talking about when He said, *"If anyone would come after Me, let him deny himself and take up his cross daily and follow Me"* (Luke 9:23 ESV). The decision to deny self and take up the cross is continual. Peter is a great picture in Scripture of what we look like when the flesh nature is in control versus the Spirit of God. When Peter's flesh nature was in control, He looked at Jesus and proudly boasted that he would follow Jesus to the death. Then he proceeded to deny His Lord three times out of fear over the simple questions of a few powerless servants. The result of his flesh nature being in control was denial of his Lord and deep personal shame. But in this passage, we see just the opposite! The flesh nature has been denied – or crucified – and the Spirit of God is fully in control. We would do well to learn from Peter's example.

Being filled with the Spirit, Peter could speak with confidence and courage in the presence of people who otherwise may have intimidated him with their position and power. The Spirit of God empowered him by giving him the strength and the power. The Spirit of God enabled him by giving him the words to speak. The Spirit of God emboldened him with the confidence and boldness to be unwavering in the speaking of truth. The very fact that Peter was not intimidated amazed the religious leaders. He spoke with an authority unlike anything he had heretofore demonstrated. It was the authority they had only witnessed from two others before this – Jesus and John the Baptist. The religious leaders knew that Peter and John were disciples of Jesus – and their boldness and actions confirmed it. Jesus had told His disciples that *"a disciple is not above his teacher, but everyone when he is fully trained will be like his teacher"* Luke 6:40 ESV). Their words and their actions affirmed that they were disciples of Jesus. Boldness and clarity come when we spend time with Him, speak His truth, and are led by His Spirit. Do our words and actions affirm that we are disciples of Jesus?

It would be nice to believe that if we are filled with the Spirit of God then those around us will rightly respond to the truth we are speaking. But that's not the case. The religious leaders rejected truth when Jesus spoke it to them, and they rejected the truth that the Spirit of God spoke through Peter. As a matter of fact, their hearts were so hardened to the truth that they attempted to discredit the undeniable truth of the healing of the lame man. The religious leaders were not seeking truth; they were seeking a way to avoid the truth. Their lack of acceptance was never a problem of the mind; but a problem of the heart and will. Those who benefit – or perceive themselves to benefit – from wrong-doing and wrong-thinking will usually turn a deaf ear and a blind eye to contrary evidence of what is right and what is true. The mind selectively sees and perceives reality in order to justify what the heart desires. And as the prophet Jeremiah wrote, *"The human heart is the most deceitful of all things, and desperately wicked"* (Jeremiah 17:9).

Peter and John knew that their calling wasn't to win an argument; their calling was to stand up and bear witness. We would do well to heed that lesson. Both groups had to choose between what was popular, safe or right? Peter and John knew that standing up for the truth of the gospel was right, though it was not the safe or popular choice with the religious leaders. The Spirit of God will always lead us to stand for what is right over what is popular or what is safe. Our flesh nature, however, will always choose what is safe or self-satisfying over what is true. The high council had no difficulty rejecting the truth, but they feared the backlash from the crowd if they attempted to deny the miracle. Thus they sought a way to reject the truth but remain politically correct.

Often one of the great obstacles to our speaking out about God's truth is that we think we have to win. Or we think we have to operate with the assumptions of secular leaders. But Peter shows us that this is not what we have to do. Our calling is not to win or to borrow the assumptions of the world. Our calling is to stand up and tell it like it is in the eyes of God. Peter defined it clearly – *"Do you think God wants us to obey you rather than Him?"*

Then Peter says, "*We cannot stop telling about everything we have seen and heard.*" He is a witness. As one who is filled with the Spirit, he stands up and tells it like he sees it. Let the chips fall where they will. Don't worry if the public doesn't even agree with you. Your job is not to win. Your job is to walk in the Spirit of God, proclaiming His truth and acting according to His works, no matter how the world may respond. We must obey God rather than men – and the only way we will do that is if we are filled with His Spirit. As the apostle Paul wrote, *"So I say, walk by the Spirit"* (Galatians 5:16 NIV)… until He returns.

* * *

13

PRAYING FOR BOLDNESS

As soon as they were freed, Peter and John returned to the other believers and told them what the leading priests and elders had said. When they heard the report, all the believers lifted their voices together in prayer to God: "O Sovereign Lord, Creator of heaven and earth, the sea, and everything in them – You spoke long ago by the Holy Spirit through our ancestor David, Your servant, saying, 'Why were the nations so angry? Why did they waste their time with futile plans? The kings of the earth prepared for battle; the rulers gathered together against the Lord and against His Messiah.' In fact, this has happened here in this very city! For Herod Antipas, Pontius Pilate the governor, the Gentiles, and the people of Israel were all united against Jesus, Your Holy Servant, whom You anointed. But everything they did was determined beforehand according to Your will. And now, O Lord, hear their threats, and give us, Your servants, great boldness in preaching Your word. Stretch out Your hand with healing power; may miraculous signs and wonders be done through the name of Your Holy Servant Jesus." After this prayer, the meeting place shook, and they were all filled with the Holy Spirit. Then they preached the word of God with boldness.

Acts 4:23-31 (quoting Psalm 2:1-2)

* * *

Peter and John had just returned from their time before the high council. They had been threatened to *"never again speak or teach in the Name of Jesus"* (Acts 4:18). How did they and the other believers respond? By confessing the awesomeness of God in prayer. The greatest concentration of spiritual power in that day and in Jerusalem was in that prayer gathering. Perhaps it was the greatest concentration of any time or any place. There was no doubt. There was no hesitance. There was no fear. There was no question. There was no division. The Spirit of God united them and they lifted their voices TOGETHER. The people were of one heart and one mind, and God was pleased to answer their requests.

Their prayer was founded on the Word of God as recorded by David in Psalm 2:1-2. In His Word, God speaks to us and tells us what He plans to do. In prayer, we speak to Him and make ourselves available to Him for His will to be accomplished through us. They were not telling God what to do; they were asking Him to do His will in them and through them. They were not asking for their will to move heaven; they were asking for God's will to be done on earth. They did not pray for their circumstances to be changed, or for their enemies to be put out of office. Rather, they asked God to empower them and embolden them to make the best use of their circumstances in order to accomplish what He had already determined. This was a demonstration of their faith that God has a plan, His plan is perfect, and His plan will prevail. They did not ask God for a way of escape from the path that was before them; they asked Him to enable them to walk in the path according to His purpose. Phillips Brooks, the minister who wrote the lyrics to *"O Little Town of Bethlehem"*, also wrote, *"Do not pray for easy lives. Pray to be stronger men and women. Do not pray for tasks equal to your powers. Pray for powers equal to your tasks."* They did not pray for the persecution to cease; they prayed for courage and boldness to endure in the midst of persecution.

Each of us walk through difficult circumstances at times and for seasons of our lives. You may be walking through one right now. As i write this, a member of my family is walking through a difficult and challenging time. It is an attack from the enemy. God is not the author of the circumstance. He is not the author of deceit, or illness, or hardship. But He is the *"Sovereign Lord, Creator of heaven and earth, the sea, and everything in them."* We would do well to follow the example of those gathered in prayer that day – not praying according to our will, but according to His; not praying for escape, but praying for His Spirit to enable us, empower us and embolden us through it.

The early church acknowledged that the leaders of their day – *"Herod Antipas, Pontius Pilate the governor, the other Gentiles in positions of authority, and the religious leaders of Israel were all united against Jesus."* Their evil actions had all led to the crucifixion of Jesus. Yet all of their evil intentions had been used by the Father to accomplish His perfect plan – the resurrection of His Son and His victory over death. Therefore, the church had no need to fear! Their "enemies" were already defeated foes. But wisely, they also knew that they could not allow their faith in God's divine sovereignty to become an excuse for them not to take responsibility for the action He was calling them to take. Again, the words of St. Augustine are a wise reminder, *"Pray as though everything depends upon God, and work as though everything depends upon you."*

The believers did not ask for protection; they asked for power. They did not ask for the destruction of their enemies; they asked for boldness and power to preach the Word and heal the sick. They did not ask that their own agenda or their own needs be furthered; rather, that the Name of the Father and the Son be exalted.

God's answer was to shake the place where they were meeting, and again fill them with His Spirit. He filled them to overflowing – and the result of the filling was that *"they preached the word of God with boldness."* And it didn't stop there. It also further deepened their unity (Acts 4:32) and their desire to sacrifice and share with one another (Acts 4:34).

Phillips Brooks also wrote, *"nothing lies beyond the reach of prayer except that which lies outside the will of God."* That early church prayed according to God's will and He answered in mighty power. About thirty years later, James (the half-brother of Jesus, who did not become a follower until after Jesus arose from the dead) would write this reminder to the early church, *"You do not have because you do not ask. You ask and do not receive, because you ask with wrong motives, so that you may spend it on your pleasures"* (James 4:2-3 NASB). The same God who answered the prayers of those early believers is waiting to respond to those same prayers today… and every day… until He returns.

* * *

14

THEY GAVE IT ALL

All the believers were united in heart and mind. And they felt that what they owned was not their own, so they shared everything they had. The apostles testified powerfully to the resurrection of the Lord Jesus, and God's great blessing was upon them all. There were no needy people among them, because those who owned land or houses would sell them and bring the money to the apostles to give to those in need. For instance, there was Joseph, the one the apostles nicknamed Barnabas (which means "Son of Encouragement"). He was from the tribe of Levi and came from the island of Cyprus. He sold a field he owned and brought the money to the apostles.

Acts 4:32-37

* * *

They felt that what they owned was not their own. The hearts of the believers had disconnected from their "stuff" and "connected" with the Spirit of God. They no longer felt entitled. They now felt blessed. They were no longer possessed by their belongings. That which they had was now seen as a means with which to minister to others. Luke writes that the believers were *united in heart and mind.* They were no longer united with their personal possessions. They were united with one another. They were united in Christ. They were "believers"! They not only believed in Jesus for their salvation; they believed in Him and trusted Him for all that they needed. Their satisfaction and worth no longer came from what they possessed; their complete satisfaction was in God through Christ.

. . .

Today as twenty-first century believers, we read that passage and immediately want to issue disclaimers. "Surely God does not intend for us to give away all that we have!" That statement in and of itself is a reflection of the condition of our hearts, our trust and our belief. The passage doesn't tell us that they all sold their possessions all at once. It says that they shared everything they had so that no need went unmet. Needs were met as they arose through the provision that God placed within the body of believers. The issue was ownership. They didn't all immediately sell everything that they had; rather, they immediately surrendered the "deed" to all that they had to the One who had provided it. Through that transaction of "surrender", they were acknowledging that they were no longer the owners. Their possessions were no longer theirs to keep – or even to give. That decision lied solely with the Owner. The possessions were His to use as He saw fit.

There are many today who want to debate whether or not we are to tithe ten percent of our income to God through His local storehouse – the church. We see the tithe established in the Old Testament as early as Genesis 14 as a starting point for giving to the Lord. Additionally, we see a multitude of offerings that were to be given over and above the tithe. The debate today surrounds whether those commands that were given to God's people under the Law still apply to those of us who are now under grace. i have heard many who profess to be followers of Christ use "grace" as a justification that we are no longer to give ten percent because we are no longer under the Law. They are using "grace" to justify their refusal to honor God with the provisions He has given. This passage in Acts 4 clearly demonstrates that we are no longer to return ten percent of what God has provided back to Him; rather, we are to return ONE HUNDRED percent. He does not own one-tenth of what we have. Grace shows us that He owns all that we have! If we are giving a tithe of our income through the local church – that's only the beginning point – not a point of debate.

These early believers knew that giving had nothing to do with percentages or amounts; it had everything to do with their hearts. About two years prior to this, many of them had been eye witnesses to Jesus' sacrifice for them on the cross. Their hearts were tightened in their relationship with Jesus and one another, and loosened in their relationship to "things". Faith in Christ creates a bond of love with people, and cuts the bond of love with possessions. We are to be freed from the love of things and firm in our love for others. Over the years, i have heard pastors and teachers (myself included) talk about "giving sacrificially". But, in light of this passage, i think we get that wrong. i can only sacrifice something i own. If i no longer own it, it is no longer mine to sacrifice. i have "abandoned" all that i am and all that i have to the Master. i no longer have any rights or say over its disposition. i am simply the caretaker for the Owner, carrying out His directive, trusting that as i do He will also provide for my needs.

Joseph, or as we better know him – Barnabas, is a great picture of abandonment. As a Levite, Barnabas would have been far from being affluent. Barnabas' act of selling a field and bringing the proceeds to the apostles was tantamount to the widow who gave the mite. He wasn't giving from his plenty; he was basically giving all that he had. Because he had surrendered it to God long before any money was ever received from a buyer! But Barnabas' abandonment was not only seen in the property that was sold, it was seen through his other actions as well. Later in Acts we see that Barnabas was abandoned to His Lord in his willingness and obedience to reach out to a new convert by the name of Saul when all the rest of the believers in Jerusalem were afraid of him (Acts 9:26-27). Through his abandonment, God led Barnabas, a Jew, to leave his home in Cypress to go to Antioch and co-shepherd the new Gentile church (Acts 11:22). From there, Barnabas and Paul were led by the Spirit of God to preach the gospel to Gentiles throughout modern-day Turkey, Syria and Cypress (Acts 13-14). But it all began with a demonstrated freedom *from* the love of "stuff" and an overwhelming love *for* Jesus.

They gave it all – not at the point that they sold their property – they gave it all before that. They gave it all when they surrendered their lives to Jesus. The sale of property, the giving of all that they owned, was merely evidence of their surrender and abandonment. Like Barnabas or the widow who only had the mite, it doesn't matter how much or how little you have. The question before every one of us is – have we given it ALL? What are we continuing to hold onto tightly? What are we refusing to let go of? The old saying is still true – "Jesus is not Lord at all, if He is not Lord over all"! Surrender your all to Him today – all that you are and all that you have. Then, when He directs you to give or to go, it will all already be His!

* * *

15

PRIDE COMES BEFORE A FALL

But there was a certain man named Ananias who, with his wife, Sapphira, sold some property. He brought part of the money to the apostles, claiming it was the full amount. With his wife's consent, he kept the rest. Then Peter said, "Ananias, why have you let Satan fill your heart? You lied to the Holy Spirit, and you kept some of the money for yourself. The property was yours to sell or not sell, as you wished. And after selling it, the money was also yours to give away. How could you do a thing like this? You weren't lying to us but to God!" As soon as Ananias heard these words, he fell to the floor and died. Everyone who heard about it was terrified. Then some young men got up, wrapped him in a sheet, and took him out and buried him. About three hours later his wife came in, not knowing what had happened. Peter asked her, "Was this the price you and your husband received for your land?"

"Yes," she replied, "that was the price." And Peter said, "How could the two of you even think of conspiring to test the Spirit of the Lord like this? The young men who buried your husband are just outside the door, and they will carry you out, too." Instantly, she fell to the floor and died. When the young men came in and saw that she was dead, they carried her out and buried her beside her husband. Great fear gripped the entire church and everyone else who heard what had happened.

Acts 5:1-11

* * *

Barnabas had just selflessly and humbly given quite a sum of money to the church. Since the church shared all things, the believers were all aware and were probably talking about his generosity. More than likely, his gift was drawing more attention to him than he would have liked. He was mature enough in his walk with Christ to realize that no glory should come to him. God had entrusted the parcel of land to him as provision for the body. God had directed him to sell the land and surrender the proceeds to the church for the ministry of the body. There was nothing glorious about that act as it related to Barnabas – all glory belonged to God. But others wanted to ascribe glory to Barnabas, and still others were envious of that glory. Envy and pride are as old as the days of the Garden of Eden. And that nature still exists within us, even as believers, if we fail to surrender it to Jesus and ask Him to take it captive. That's true today, and that was true among the believers of the early church. Though Barnabas had surrendered that nature and refused to be "puffed-up" by the recognition he received, there were others within the body that sought that recognition for themselves. After all, why shouldn't their generosity be rewarded? (Can't you just hear the serpent whispering in their ear?)

Ananias and his wife, Sapphira, were two of those early believers. They also owned property. We're not told whether God led them to sell the property, or whether they chose to do so on their own. But either way, they sold it. They chose to keep part of the money, and give the remainder to the church. Again, we don't know what, if any, God had directed them to give. If God directed them to sell the property, He would have also directed them as to what portion they should give. It may or may not have been all of the proceeds. At issue here is not the amount that they gave. The issue is that they lied. And they apparently lied in order to garner the recognition that they had seen Barnabas receive. Otherwise there was no reason to claim that their gift was the full amount of the proceeds they had received.

Ironically, the name Ananias means "God is gracious" which is a testimony to His grace and mercy. But God is also holy. When Ananias and Sapphira lied, they not only did so to the believers in the church, they lied to God. There was a purity in that initial church. That's not to say that the early believers did not sin. We can be certain that they did; they were frail sinners just like you and me. But what made this sin of Ananias and Sapphira so repulsive to the Lord was their introduction of hypocrisy and deceit into His newly formed church, through their feeble attempt to glorify their own names. God Himself has told us, "*...I, the Lord your God, am a jealous God...*" (Exodus 20:5). He is jealous for His glory and He will not share it. *"I am the LORD; that is My name! I will not give My glory to anyone else..."* (Isaiah 42:8).

Lest there be any confusion, Peter didn't do anything that caused Ananias to "fall to the floor and die". God did! God dealt with the sin of Ananias and Sapphira swiftly and severely. Too often, we presume upon God's grace without regard to the fact that He is holy and just. He does not "wink" at our sin. The forgiveness of our sin cost Him the agony and sacrifice of His only Son on the cross. He paid dearly for our sin because of His grace. And He will not allow His grace to be trivialized by our wanton disregard for His holiness. We would do well to join with those believers who, when Ananias fell to the ground, were "terrified" before God. They realized that God was not "one of the boys" to be disregarded, lied to or defamed.

Even in its infancy, Satan was attempting to defeat the church. He was fresh on the heels of the reality that he was impotent to defeat Jesus. Satan's best efforts had been defeated at the empty tomb. So now he turned his attention to Jesus' bride – the church. Satan knew that his best opportunity to defeat Jesus was through the church, and that defeat will not come from outside the church, it will come from within the church. He knows how to lie to and deceive church members – even sincere followers of Jesus. He used the soulish ambition of Ananias and Sapphira to get them to do his bidding, and he convinced them that no one would ever be the wiser. He used the same tactic in the Garden with Eve, and he still uses it today. We would do well to remember the admonition from Paul to *"put on all of God's armor so that you will be able to stand firm against all strategies of the devil"* (Ephesians 6:11). Because as Peter wrote, *"...your great enemy, the devil... prowls around like a roaring lion, looking for someone to devour"* (1 Peter 5:8). Satan lied to and through Ananias and Sapphira, and the lie led to their deaths.

But at the root of their sin was pride. The writer of Proverbs tells us, *"pride comes before destruction, and an arrogant spirit before a fall"* (Proverbs 18:18 CSB). It was pride that transformed Lucifer into Satan (Isaiah 14:12-15). It was pride that led to Adam and Eve's sin (Genesis 3:4-6). And it was pride that led Ananias and Sapphira to attempt to deceive the Holy Spirit.

The early church saw God enter into their midst through His Holy Spirit in "great power", extending His "great grace". Then, in this moment, they were moved by "great fear". As we continue in our journey until He returns, we would do well to remember the words of the writer of Hebrews: *"Therefore, since we are receiving a Kingdom which cannot be shaken, let us have grace, by which we may serve God acceptably with reverence and godly fear. For our God is a consuming fire"* (Hebrews 12:28-29 NKJ).

* * *

16

A MIRACULOUS ESCAPE

The apostles were performing many miraculous signs and wonders among the people. And all the believers were meeting regularly at the Temple in the area known as Solomon's Colonnade. But no one else dared to join them, even though all the people had high regard for them. Yet more and more people believed and were brought to the Lord – crowds of both men and women. As a result of the apostles' work, sick people were brought out into the streets on beds and mats so that Peter's shadow might fall across some of them as he went by. Crowds came from the villages around Jerusalem, bringing their sick and those possessed by evil spirits, and they were all healed. The high priest and his officials, who were Sadducees, were filled with jealousy. They arrested the apostles and put them in the public jail. But an angel of the Lord came at night, opened the gates of the jail, and brought them out. Then he told them, "Go to the Temple and give the people this message of life!" So at daybreak the apostles entered the Temple, as they were told, and immediately began teaching. When the high priest and his officials arrived, they convened the high council – the full assembly of the elders of Israel. Then they sent for the apostles to be brought from the jail for trial. But when the Temple guards went to the jail, the men were gone. So they returned to the council and reported, "The jail was securely locked, with the guards standing outside, but when we opened the gates, no one was there!" When the captain of the Temple guard and the leading priests heard this, they were perplexed, wondering where it would all end. Then someone arrived with startling news: "The men you put in jail are standing in the Temple, teaching the people!" The captain went with his Temple guards and arrested the apostles, but without violence, for they were afraid the people would stone them. Then they brought the apostles before the high council, where the high priest confronted them. "We gave you strict orders never again to teach in this Man's name!" he said. "Instead, you

have filled all Jerusalem with your teaching about Him, and you want to make us responsible for His death!"
Acts 5:12-28

* * *

God was at work in a new way! Many of those who were alive had been born during the latter part of the four hundred years of silence between the last prophet of the Old Testament – Malachi – and the arrival of John the Baptist. During those years the people had not heard a fresh word from God. Then God Himself showed up on the scene in the form of Jesus and the religious leaders rejected Him and crucified Him. When they should have been hungry to hear afresh from God, they had become quite content with their traditions and their own religious practices. They had settled into a very comfortable rut and were dedicated to maintaining their status quo. They thought their problems were over when they crucified Jesus. They thought they would be returning to "the good old days" of tradition and no longer having their leadership challenged.

But now, two years later, these followers of the very Jesus whom they had crucified were still on the scene performing miracles that even went beyond what Jesus had done (John 14:12). They boldly proclaimed that Jesus had risen from the dead. They preached a truth that was alive about a Living Savior that didn't square with the religious leaders' dead traditions. The apostles were disregarding the warnings from the religious leaders to stop teaching about Jesus. They were refuting the doctrine of the Sadducees by openly teaching that Christ had risen from the dead. And the people were being drawn to the apostles by their teaching and through the miracles they performed. The streets were abuzz with excitement. The sick were being healed simply by the shadow of an apostle passing over them. No one had ever seen anything like this. Caiaphas and the other religious leaders were again envious and saw their positions being threatened. They wanted the miracles to stop. They wanted the sick to remain sick. They wanted the dead to remain dead. They wanted this emerging living faith to be silenced and dead tradition to again become the order of the day. They wanted these uneducated, ordinary Galileans to know their place and leave the teaching to the educated, ordained, and "approved" professionals.

But those "ordinary" apostles, now filled with the Holy Spirit, could not be silent. They could not be disobedient to their Lord's direction to make His Name known among people everywhere, beginning right there in

Jerusalem. Their mandate was to go and tell, and they could do no less. They were prepared to risk everything so that the Good News could be proclaimed through the power of the Holy Spirit. The religious leaders, who were preoccupied with protecting themselves and their way of life, could not understand these uneducated men who were willing to risk it all.

The Sadducees failed to understand that the obedience of the apostles was, in itself, the evidence and sign that the Holy Spirit had been given. Their radical obedience came from the power of the Holy Spirit. They filled Jerusalem with their teaching because, in the face of great danger, they obeyed God and not man. They obeyed God and not man because they had received the power of the Holy Spirit. They could not be silenced, regardless of the threat of persecution. Hugh Latimer, martyred for his faith in 1555, once said, "*Whenever you see persecution, there is more than a probability that truth is on the persecuted side.*" The apostles were on the side of truth and by the power of the Holy Spirit, they could not be silenced.

Just as Jesus promised (Acts 1:8), the Holy Spirit came upon the disciples with unusual fullness, and the result was supernatural power leading to courageous, life-giving witness. And that power was not merely the quiet power of preaching that looked natural, it was supernatural. It was life-changing. It was manifestly supernatural – tongues of fire, the sound of wind (Acts 2:2–3), a shaking building (Acts 4:31), and remarkable healings and deliverance (Acts 5:16). The result was that "*more and more people believed and were brought to the Lord.*" Acts 1:8 was unfolding: the Spirit came upon the church in an unusual way; extraordinary power was manifested; and life-giving testimony was bringing people into the Kingdom.

Power is a very dangerous thing – both for those who have it, and for those who don't, but wish they did. The danger if you have it is pride, and the danger if you don't is jealousy. And both are based on bad mistakes. Pride is based on the mistake of believing that the power is ours, or that we in our own strength fulfilled the conditions to get it. But in fact the power is God's, and if we fulfilled any conditions to get it – like faith or prayer or purity – it was not us, but the grace of God in us (1 Corinthians 15:1). On the other hand, jealousy is not just the passion to have the power that someone else has. In itself, there may be nothing wrong with that – to want God's power in your life that you see in the life of another. Jealousy goes beyond that desire and becomes the anger and the resentment that someone else has it and you don't. Jealousy doesn't just want you to have what another has; it wants them to not have it.

The root of jealousy is three-fold. First, it is "lovelessness" (1 Corinthians 13:4). If you love another person, you will rejoice if God gives them power, even if He doesn't give it to you. Second, it is faithlessness. If you have faith in the sovereign grace of God to give power according to His own divine wisdom, then you will praise Him for the times and ways of His outpouring, and not question Him or resent His choices. God knows what He is doing, and He is wise and good in giving the Spirit in power wherever He pleases. Faith may cry for it to come; but faith also does not criticize God for when and where it comes. Third, it is "truthlessness". The Sadducees would have said, "there is no resurrection. The reason we are angry that these Christians are doing works of power is that they are deceiving the people to believe what is not true. There is no resurrection and they are leading the people astray." Jesus had given His disciples the antidote for "truthlessness" when He taught them, *"You are truly My disciples if you remain faithful to My teachings. And you will know the truth, and the truth will set you free"* (John 8:31-32). The religious leaders had rejected Truth and embraced their lies.

Their jealousy turned to rage which led to persecution – in this case, imprisonment. But in this instance, God used their imprisonment as another demonstration of His power. Before we look at their escape, let's be mindful that God does not promise that He will make a way of escape from every instance of persecution. As a matter of fact, He told His disciples that they would be imprisoned, betrayed and many would be killed (Luke 21:12-16). But He has promised that He will never leave us or forsake us (Hebrews 13:5). Stephen was stoned to death even though he was filled with the Spirit and spoke with power (Acts 7:58). The apostle James was later killed by Herod (Acts 12:1). An angel of God came again and again for Paul and for Peter. But there were many times when God did not stop the beatings and lashings, or the stoning, or the shipwrecks. And there was one last time when He did not stop their instruments of death. In those instances, no angel came to rescue them, but the Holy Spirit walked with them every step of their way.

But on this day, God sent an angel to lead the apostles in the way of miraculous escape. The miraculous spiritual power of God is precious because it is God's and it comes – or does not come – according to His sovereign plan. It is a precious thing for such great power to be in the hands of an all-wise, loving God. It is God's power and not ours. It is in God's control and not ours. It comes – or does not come – according to God's perfect plan. Upon rescuing the apostles from prison, the angel of the Lord told them to return to the very place where they had been arrested. He told them to: *"Go to the Temple and give the people this message of LIFE!"* When escape and deliverance come to us and we are freed and empowered to serve others, the purpose of our deliverance will be that we **give** LIFE. And when deliverance does not come and we are left in our suffering, the purpose will be that we might **live** LIFE. If we are delivered from distress by the power of God, His purpose is that we be ambassadors of life to other people – true life, eternal life, the forgiveness of sins and a personal relationship with the ever-living God. It is a precious thing to be empowered to give life to others.

But if you are not delivered, if the angel does not come to open the door, what then? Well, then the time may have come to simply **live** LIFE. There may be nobody else to whom you are to give it. Your days of giving may be over. They will be over for each of us sooner or later. But this too is precious: When God withholds delivering power, He gives us the grace and strength to endure. Be mindful that *"in all these things we are more than conquerors through Him who loved us"* (Romans 8:37 ESV).

As we end this chapter, be mindful of these closing thoughts. The apostles did not resist arrest. Filled and empowered by the Spirit of God, they trusted Him completely. They knew that they need not take anything into their own hands. They simply needed to follow Him, trust Him and obey Him. They could trust Him for the outcome. As a result, the more the Sadducees tried to stop the miracles, the more their actions only multiplied the miracles. God's purpose would be accomplished.. His Name would be made known. By their own admission the Sadducees bore witness that Jerusalem was filled with the teaching about Jesus, and the accusers (the religious leaders) had now become the accused (Acts 5:28) – all through the obedience of uneducated men walking in the power of the Holy Spirit.

So, with our eyes open to the price and the preciousness of the power of the Holy Spirt, let us also *"give the people this message of life"* either by "giving" it or "living" it… until He returns… as His Spirit rests upon us.

* * *

17

IF IT IS OF GOD, YOU WILL NOT STOP IT

But Peter and the apostles replied, "We must obey God rather than any human authority. The God of our ancestors raised Jesus from the dead after you killed Him by hanging Him on a cross. Then God put Him in the place of honor at His right hand as Prince and Savior. He did this so the people of Israel would repent of their sins and be forgiven. We are witnesses of these things and so is the Holy Spirit, who is given by God to those who obey Him." When they heard this, the high council was furious and decided to kill them. But one member, a Pharisee named Gamaliel, who was an expert in religious law and respected by all the people, stood up and ordered that the men be sent outside the council chamber for a while. Then he said to his colleagues, "Men of Israel, take care what you are planning to do to these men! Some time ago there was that fellow Theudas, who pretended to be someone great. About 400 others joined him, but he was killed, and all his followers went their various ways. The whole movement came to nothing. After him, at the time of the census, there was Judas of Galilee. He got people to follow him, but he was killed, too, and all his followers were scattered. So my advice is, leave these men alone. Let them go. If they are planning and doing these things merely on their own, it will soon be overthrown. But if it is from God, you will not be able to overthrow them. You may even find yourselves fighting against God!" The others accepted his advice. They called in the apostles and had them flogged. Then they ordered them never again to speak in the name of Jesus, and they let them go. The apostles left the high council rejoicing that God had counted them worthy to suffer disgrace for the name of Jesus. And every day, in the Temple and from house to house, they continued to teach and preach this message: "Jesus is the Messiah."

Acts 5:29-42

* * *

There are two powerful statements in this exchange between the apostles and the high council. The first was made by Peter. "We must obey God" – not your god – not the one you have created in your own image – rather, we must obey the God of our ancestors – the One and only true God. He is the God who raised Jesus from the dead – after you in your jealousy and hatred had Him crucified. You rejected the One through whom God chose to bring repentance and forgiveness to His people – the One who now sits on His right hand as Prince and Savior. And in so doing, you have rejected God. Though you sit in seats of religious authority, you have chosen not to place yourself under God's authority – and we must obey Him rather than you. His Spirit bears witness to His truth and His authority, but you have not been given His Spirit because you have rejected Him.

As we can imagine, the high council became furious and decided to kill the apostles. After all, they had killed one Galilean, why not eradicate the movement by killing a few more?

The second statement was made by Gamaliel. He appears to have been a voice of reason. His voice appears to have been one that carried weight with Caiaphas, Annas and the others on the high council. Remember that only two years earlier this same council had met to discuss and plot the killing of Jesus. It is reasonable to presume that if Gamaliel was present for this discussion about the apostles, he was present at the discussions about Jesus. The absence of his name in conjunction with those earlier discussions would tend to indicate that he supported the popular view of the council to crucify Jesus. So, who was Gamaliel and why did he speak up here when he apparently had not done so two years earlier?

Gamaliel was considered to be one of the greatest teachers of the Law in all the annals of Judaism. When the apostle Paul was defending his pedigree in Jewish Law, he cited Gamaliel as being his teacher because the name obviously carried great weight and respect (Acts 22:3). Gamaliel was a Pharisee and, in the Talmud, he bears the titles of "*Nasi*" meaning "prince", and "*Rabban*" meaning "our master". Some believe that he was the president of the Great Sanhedrin in Jerusalem. Regardless, he held great authority and influence within the council.

. . .

Gamaliel used two examples in his statement to dissuade the other members of the high council from choosing to execute the apostles. The first was Theudas. Apparently Theudas was a zealot who lived at the dawn of the first century A.D. He gathered a following of about four hundred men who joined him in an attempted insurrection. His attempted revolt ended in his death, which in turn resulted in his now-leaderless followers scattering and going their separate ways. As a result, the whole movement fell apart. His second example was Judas of Galilee, who was also a leader of a group of zealots. It was a similar situation. In 6 A.D. he got a number of people to follow him in an attempted raid on a Roman armory. Their attempt also failed, and he, too, was killed. The result was that all of his followers also scattered.

Both of the events that Gamaliel referenced occurred twenty to thirty years earlier, which means they had occurred long before Jesus was brought before the high council as well. But Gamaliel apparently did not choose to make the same argument at Jesus' "trial" that he was making now at the apostles' "trial". That would indicate that he believed that the work of Jesus would stop with His death. Gamaliel believed that Jesus' followers would scatter. Remember, the devoted followers of Jesus at the time of His crucifixion were only about one hundred twenty men and women. Though thousands flocked to Jesus to witness and experience His miracles, only one hundred twenty really followed Him to the end. In Gamaliel's mind at the time of Jesus' crucifixion, Jesus had less followers than Theudas or Judas of Galilee. He didn't make the argument before the council then because he believed the movement would fail with Jesus' death.

But two things happened! First, Jesus did not stay dead! Though Gamaliel probably never saw the resurrected Jesus himself, he was witnessing the boldness of His followers who were now unwaveringly proclaiming His resurrection. These uneducated fisherman were speaking with a boldness and an authority unlike he had ever witnessed – and his spirit was bearing witness to the fact that they were speaking truth. Jesus was the Son of the Living God! No matter what he and the other religious leaders had tried to do, Jesus had been victorious. The shedding of Jesus' blood had not stopped the movement; it had fueled the movement! Second, there was no denying that tens of thousands of people had since become followers of Jesus – three thousand on just one day! And some of those had been Pharisees! There was a movement taking place that could not be denied, and Gamaliel's eyes were becoming opened to the truth. The Holy Spirit was at work in His life. And the pivotal point for him was this: *"If they are planning and doing these things merely on their own, it will soon be overthrown. But if it is from God, you will not be able to overthrow them. You may even find yourselves fighting against God!"* Gamaliel had already come to the conclusion that he and the other members of the high council were *"fighting against God!"* His argument and authority swayed the decision of the other council members and they decided to "accept his advice".

Biblical historians, including Josephus, tell us that Gamaliel subsequently became a follower of Jesus. Whether it occurred before his remarks to the high council or after, we can see the evidence of the Holy Spirit at work in his life. In that light, i want us to see the sovereignty of God through all of this. First, it was always the Father's plan that His Son would be crucified on the cross. Remember Jesus was not a victim; He was – and is – the Victor. Gamaliel remained blinded to these very arguments at Jesus' trial because it served the Father's purpose for him to be so. Second, it was the Father's plan that this Jewish rabbi be a part of His plan to preserve the lives of the apostles in the early days of the formation of His church. It was God's timing for Gamaliel's eyes to be opened to truth and, in the Father's sovereignty, He had ordered his steps to stand in that place with the authority and respect he commanded for just such a time. Third, God was also already at work in and through Gamaliel to help equip a young man by the name of Saul, who would by all accounts become the greatest Christian missionary who has ever lived.

So here's the takeaway for us… until He returns. "If it is of God, it will not be overthrown. You may even find yourselves fighting against God!" His plan will not be thwarted. His purpose will prevail. Trust Him. Follow Him. No matter the circumstance. No matter who stands before you. The apostles rejoiced that God had counted them worthy. Even if you are flogged, don't lose sight that our God is sovereign. He was then, and He always will be.

* * *

18

CHOSEN TO SERVE

But as the believers rapidly multiplied, there were rumblings of discontent. The Greek-speaking believers complained about the Hebrew-speaking believers, saying that their widows were being discriminated against in the daily distribution of food. So the Twelve called a meeting of all the believers. They said, "We apostles should spend our time teaching the word of God, not running a food program. And so, brothers, select seven men who are well respected and are full of the Spirit and wisdom. We will give them this responsibility. Then we apostles can spend our time in prayer and teaching the word." Everyone liked this idea, and they chose the following: Stephen (a man full of faith and the Holy Spirit), Philip, Procorus, Nicanor, Timon, Parmenas, and Nicolas of Antioch (an earlier convert to the Jewish faith). These seven were presented to the apostles, who prayed for them as they laid their hands on them. So God's message continued to spread. The number of believers greatly increased in Jerusalem, and many of the Jewish priests were converted, too.

Acts 6:1-7

* * *

The church was experiencing amazing growth. In three years, it is estimated that the church had grown to twenty-five thousand men and women. It was a supernatural movement, but it was not pure. The apostles were casting nets into the sea of the world as fishers of men empowered by the Holy Spirit. Not all of the "fish" who were drawn in were Spirit-filled believers. They all had been gripped by the power of God, but they were not all truly born again. They were all touched by the Spirit of God, but not all were transformed. They were all excited about the supernatural power they were witnessing, but not all had truly been crucified in their flesh. They were all caught up in the movement, but not all had experienced true brokenness for sin or passion for holiness. There were the likes of the deceitful Ananias and Sapphira in the Jerusalem movement (Acts 5:1-11), the power-hungry magician Simon in the Samaritan movement (Acts 8:13-24), the fearful, retreating John Mark in the missionary band (Acts 13:13; 15:38), the doctrinally confused Apollos in the Asian movement (Acts 18:24-28), the professing Christians in Ephesus who for some time concealed their black magic (Acts 19:18), and so on. None of that should come as a shock to us. The same is true today.

As we've already said, Satan was never able to defeat Jesus, so he turned his attention on trying to defeat His bride – the Church. Satan was not going to sit idly by while a movement of God was taking place. He began his effort by stirring up rumblings of discontent within the body, which then grew into complaints and accusations of discrimination. The apostles were doing absolutely everything. Everybody turned to them for everything, and they realized that they could no longer handle the demands at the level that was needed. The demands were not being adequately met. And the apostles knew that they could not neglect the Word of God in order to meet them.

The conflict came to a head between the Hellenists (the Greek-speaking Jews) and the Hebrews (the Hebrew- or Aramaic-speaking Jews), and the failure of the church to properly nurture the Greek-speaking widows. It was a two-fold threat to the movement of the gospel. First, the system the emerging church had developed (Acts 4:34) to take care of the needs within the body was not working for the Hellenist group. If that failure to properly care for the Hellenist widows continued, the church would fail in loving and caring for one another, the glory of Christ would be diminished in the eyes of the world, and the movement of the gospel could experience a serious reversal. The second threat to the movement would be if the apostles left their primary calling to the ministry of the Word in order to serve those needs. The felt needs would be met but the advance of the gospel would suffer. The "best" was being threatened by the "good", not something "bad". And that is usually the case.

The Spirit of God led the apostles to respond immediately so that Satan could not use the issue to gain a foothold in the growing church. He led the apostles to respond in a way that brought unity rather than further division within the church. The apostles instructed the church to appoint seven Hellenistic leaders (their Greek names tell us their ethnicity), who were trustworthy and full of the Spirit and wisdom, to take care of the need. They delegated the responsibility, enabling the apostles to keep on devoting themselves to the ministry of the Word and prayer. The widows were cared for and the ministry of the Word of God was not forsaken. Both were utterly crucial. Either threat could have undermined the church and ended its amazing growth. The issue was resolved by utilizing the full diversity of gifts and abilities that God had already placed within the church.

Everyone agreed with the solution, and seven men were chosen as the precursors of those who would soon become known as deacons. It is interesting to note that six of the seven men were subsequently used by God in the spread of the gospel throughout Jerusalem, Samaria and the uttermost parts. The exception was Nicolas of Antioch, who later demonstrated that his understanding of the gospel was more syncretistic, being caught up in the fusion of religious beliefs instead of truly entering into a relationship with Jesus Christ. Of the six who became passionate evangelists, all but Philip were subsequently martyred for their faith, the first of whom being Stephen, as we will see in the next two chapters of this book.

The result of the selection of these seven men was that *"God's message continued to spread. The number of believers greatly increased in Jerusalem...."* Attention to the Word of God and the mission of God was not forsaken or diminished. They did not become so inwardly focused that they forsook the mission of Christ, but they also remained faithful to the ministry to the saints. The outcome was a new breakthrough in evangelistic power. Now, even priests, who had been heretofore hostile to the gospel (Acts 4:1), were responding to the Word of God and obeying the faith. It is estimated that there were eight thousand priests attached to the Temple in Jerusalem – and now "many" of them were responding. The church had been tested. She had passed the test by nurturing the widows and guarding the Word. And God honored this triumph with new power and fruitfulness.

So, what is the application for us today? First, let us be mindful of our priorities as followers of Jesus. We must never lose sight that we have been charged by our Lord to be His witnesses – to make disciples. It is easy for us to allow other activities to consume our attentions and our energies. We must be as passionate as the apostles to stay rightly focused. But second, we must never lose sight of the ministry opportunities that

God places before the body. The same Holy Spirit who placed within the early church seven men who were uniquely equipped to carry out their specific ministry function has also equipped the body today to carry out His ministry purposes. We must remain watchful and obedient to His direction. God has uniquely equipped us for His purpose and He has chosen us for His service. God raised up those seven men, including Nicolas, for that hour. We must pray that there are no obstacles – inside our lives or inside the church – that will hinder the work of the Spirit of God through the Word of God in our lives and in our churches, and that the same power that brought thousands into the church in the Book of Acts will do the same today – until He returns – throughout our Jerusalem and around the world.

* * *

19

GRACE-FULL

Stephen, a man full of God's grace and power, performed amazing miracles and signs among the people. But one day some men from the Synagogue of Freed Slaves, as it was called, started to debate with him. They were Jews from Cyrene, Alexandria, Cilicia, and the province of Asia. None of them could stand against the wisdom and the Spirit with which Stephen spoke. So they persuaded some men to lie about Stephen, saying, "We heard him blaspheme Moses, and even God." This roused the people, the elders, and the teachers of religious law. So they arrested Stephen and brought him before the high council. The lying witnesses said, "This man is always speaking against the holy Temple and against the law of Moses. We have heard him say that this Jesus of Nazareth will destroy the Temple and change the customs Moses handed down to us." At this point everyone in the high council stared at Stephen, because his face became as bright as an angel's.

Acts 6:8-15

* * *

Earlier Luke described Stephen as *"a man full of faith and the Holy Spirit"* (Acts 6:5), and now he describes him as *"a man full of God's grace and power"*. The former description is the cause and the latter is the effect. Stephen was *"a man full of God's grace and power"* because he was *"a man full of faith and the Holy Spirit"*. To be full of grace, which means God's favor, is the result of being full of faith. There are several expressions of grace, but all of them come as a result of faith. The apostle Paul wrote, *"For by grace you have been saved through faith"* (Ephesians 2:8 ESV). So there's grace that comes in the form of salvation and it comes by faith. Paul also wrote that he pleaded to the Lord to remove his thorn in the flesh, and in response *"He said to me, 'My grace is sufficient for you, for My power is made perfect in weakness.' Therefore,* [Paul went on to say], *I will boast all the more gladly of my weaknesses, so that the power of Christ may rest upon me"* (2 Corinthians 12:9 ESV). There's grace that overcomes, and is made perfect in weakness. And it too comes by faith. And there is grace that comes in the midst of persecution that also comes through faith. *"But even if you should suffer for righteousness' sake, you will be blessed"* (1 Peter 3:14 ESV). And finally, there is the grace of extending loving kindness toward others that comes by faith. Paul wrote that *"He might display the surpassing riches of His grace, demonstrated by His loving kindness to us in Christ Jesus"* (Ephesians 2:7). i believe this may be the kind of grace that Luke bears witness to within Stephen's life. He was full of grace toward others.

That, in fact, is part of the reason that the church chose him to be one of the men responsible for helping the Hellenist widows. But, the greatest example came as he stood before the high council at the end of Acts chapter 7. They had been stoning him, the rocks were smashing against his head and shattering his body, and yet, he looked up to heaven and cried out with a loud voice, *"Lord, don't charge them with this sin!"* (Acts 7:60) That is nothing short of graciousness and loving kindness. That is bestowing favor upon those who attack you – even kill you. How in the world could he possibly do that? How could he be so forgiving? Because he believed that God was sovereign, even over persecution and death. He wasn't busy trying to protect himself. He was willing to die if God wanted him to do so. Only by faith could he so completely trust God's grace in such a way that loving kindness was being expressed even at the point of his death.

But also, he was a man full of God's power. Because he was full of the Holy Spirit. If you're full of the Holy Spirit then you are full of God's power! Jesus promised, just before He ascended to sit at the right hand of the Father, *"you will receive power when the Holy Spirit comes upon you"* (Acts 1:8). When we are right in our hearts toward God and obedient to His Spirit, He will then be gracious toward us and express His power on our behalf. We will never know grace toward others and experience the power of God working in and through us until we are filled with His Spirit. It is a simple spiritual principle! Luke records that Stephen *"performed amazing miracles and signs among the people"* (Acts 6:8). The power of God and the grace of God were exhibited in his life because he believed God and obeyed the Spirit, and the same is true for us.

. . .

Be mindful that Stephen came to faith in Christ as a Hellenist (Greek-speaking) Jew. Those that began to debate with him were also Hellenist Jews. They came from Cyrene (northern Africa), Alexandria (Egypt), Cilicia (on the southern coast of Asia Minor), and other parts of Asia. They represented the people of other languages and ethnicities that were assembled in Jerusalem as proselytes of Judaism. They were some of the very ones who had heard the apostles speaking in their own languages on the Day of Pentecost, but even then had rejected the truth. It is very likely that one of those who was debating him was Saul of Tarsus in Cilicia (Acts 21:39), who of course would later become the apostle Paul. Stephen in many respects was a precursor to the ministry of the apostle Paul. He was sharing the gospel with people who were from the Gentile nations – the very places where Paul would take the gospel. He confronted those congregations of Jews with the truth and countered the opposition of their Jewish bigotry. He was treated with insults and violence and subsequently stoned, just like Paul would one day be. So, in a very real sense, the mantle of Stephen fell upon Saul of Tarsus that day. But Saul, one of Stephen's bitterest opponents, had no idea that it was taking place.

Since none of the Hellenist Jews were able to stand against the wisdom and power of the Holy Spirit, the only tact available to them was false witness and deceit. Those were the same weapons they had employed against Jesus. They were unable to refute the truth and power of His word so they turned to lies and false accusations. Let's not lose sight that Stephen was brought before the same high council that had tried and "convicted" Jesus, four years earlier, and had tried and released the apostles, slightly more than two years earlier.

It is interesting to note that as the high council stared at Stephen, his face began to become *"as bright as an angel's."* Only one other man in history has been described in that way, and that man is Moses (Exodus 34:29-30). The council was accusing Stephen of blaspheming Moses, and God's response was to bear witness by allowing his face to reflect the glory of God, just as He had done through His servant Moses. In essence, God was saying, "This man is not against Moses! He is like Moses – he is My faithful servant! His face even reflects My glory – just like Moses!"

As we see in Acts 8:1, Stephen's life and ministry marked the climax of the church's witness to the Jews. From here the gospel would push out to the rest of Judea, Samaria and the ends of the earth through the scattering of the newly formed church. As we will see in the next chapter, Stephen was not a victim; rather, God accomplished His victory though his life. The victory was that the gospel was being preached with grace and power to the Jews, and now God was preparing to send that good news out to the rest of the world through other men and women who were full of faith and the Holy Spirit. The evidence of their anointing and filling would be just like Stephen's. Their lives would reflect the grace and power of the Holy Spirit's presence.

The same is true today. If we are filled with the Holy Spirit, walking with Him by faith, our lives will be "grace-full". Our faces may not become as bright as an angel's, but our lives will bear witness through the fullness of grace and the power of His presence… until He returns.

* * *

20

KEEP GAZING UPWARD

"You stubborn people! You are heathen at heart and deaf to the truth. Must you forever resist the Holy Spirit? That's what your ancestors did, and so do you! Name one prophet your ancestors didn't persecute! They even killed the ones who predicted the coming of the Righteous One – the Messiah whom you betrayed and murdered. You deliberately disobeyed God's law, even though you received it from the hands of angels." The Jewish leaders were infuriated by Stephen's accusation, and they shook their fists at him in rage. But Stephen, full of the Holy Spirit, gazed steadily into heaven and saw the glory of God, and he saw Jesus standing in the place of honor at God's right hand. And he told them, "Look, I see the heavens opened and the Son of Man standing in the place of honor at God's right hand!" Then they put their hands over their ears and began shouting. They rushed at him and dragged him out of the city and began to stone him. His accusers took off their coats and laid them at the feet of a young man named Saul. As they stoned him, Stephen prayed, "Lord Jesus, receive my spirit." He fell to his knees, shouting, "Lord, don't charge them with this sin!" And with that, he died.

Acts 7:51-60

* * *

Let's not get the idea that being full of grace means that we do not stand for and declare the truth. i think too often today we have bought into the lie of a false grace that declares "live and let live". We have become confused into thinking that if we are standing up for truth, we are being judgmental and "grace-less". As Stephen's life shows us, nothing could be further from the truth!

. . .

Throughout the preceding fifty verses of this chapter in Acts 7, Stephen recounts the promises and the pursuit of God from the time of Abraham through the prophets as He was at work to raise up a people through whom He would bring glory to His Name. But now Stephen confronts them with the reality that they rejected the truth from every prophet that God sent to them, including Moses – whom they were now accusing him of blaspheming – and Jesus – whom this very group had murdered. He confronted the high council with the reality that they had disobeyed the very Word of God that through their position they were charged to honor and guard. They had so compromised the truth that they had crucified the very One who was the personification of God's grace and truth (John 1:14). Instead of seeking and worshiping their Creator, they had created a god in their own image that they now served. Their god was their tradition, their position and their misguided power. And they had become so blinded by the god they created that they didn't recognize the Glory of God when He stood before them. Stephen was by no means preaching a message of "live and let live", he was confronting them with the truth of God's Word.

And, no, it wasn't popular. The Jewish leaders were infuriated. They literally shook their fists at him in rage. If it had occurred today, they would have accused him of being intolerant. But Stephen, because he was full of the Holy Spirit, did not divert his gaze to their rage or back down from his mission. He kept gazing upward toward heaven with His eyes on the glory of God and his faith directed toward the Son of God. And he told them exactly what he was seeing. He chose to go right on speaking the truth when he knew that it would cost him his life. He chose to die rather than not speak the Word of God empowered by the Spirit of God. He chose to honor the One, rather than the crowd. The Jewish leaders killed him in their feeble attempt to silence the truth. They saw it as so threatening that it was better to kill a good man than to let this truth be spread. They had thought when they murdered Jesus that they were squashing the truth. And they had been wrong! Now, they were making the same mistake. They thought that by stoning Stephen they would silence the truth.

As we saw in chapter 17 of this book, when they had earlier considered the fate of the apostles, they had been halted in their murderous intent by the wisdom of Gamaliel. No such wisdom was going to dissuade them today. They were blinded by their rage – because God in His sovereignty permitted them to be blinded. Does that mean that He loved the apostles more than He loved Stephen? Of course not! That would be like saying He loved the apostles more than Jesus because He let His Only Son die. God had a purpose in Christ's death (and subsequent resurrection) – our redemption. He had a purpose in the apostles escaping death that day – the establishment of His church. And He had a purpose in Stephen's death – the advancement of His mission.

You see, in the religious leaders' attempt to silence the truth, they had underestimated God's plan. Stephen was to be the catalyst that triggered an explosive growth of the church. It was his martyrdom that scattered the believers to the ends of the earth (Acts 8:1).

Allow me to take a side road here. Stephen was also important because of who he was and the very character of his life. He is great proof that the effect of a follower's life has nothing to do with the length of it, and the effect of a follower's ministry has nothing to do with how long it lasts – or how many that follower is able to personally lead to Christ. Stephen's ministry was short. He never had opportunity to preach to the multitudes that many others did. He was the first martyr for the Christian faith. Yet, his life – and death – was the catalyst that caused the church to move out in the next step of Christ's commission to reach Judea, Samaria and the ends of the earth with the gospel. Stephen was the trigger that God used to "shoot" the church out into the world.

And one who would subsequently become the greatest missionary of the gospel who has ever lived – a man named Saul – stood there and kept watch over the coats of the accusers. As Stephen kept his gaze turned upward toward heaven, Saul kept his gaze turned downward toward the coats on the ground. We now know that in a short while (Acts 9), God would turn Saul's gaze upward as well – and, as a result, use him as His chosen instrument to take the Good News *"to the Gentiles and to kings, as well as to the people of Israel"* (Acts 9:15).

But on this day – the day of Stephen's death – Stephen kept gazing upward full of grace and truth, as Saul kept gazing downward while truth was being denied and silenced. So the question for us, as we stand in our respective crowd is – are we gazing upward speaking truth or gazing downward in silence? This may be the very moment that God has ordained for His grace and truth to be proclaimed and revealed through the power of His Holy Spirit. Let's be careful to keep our eyes gazing in the right direction as we speak up with words of grace and truth… until He returns.

* * *

21

THE POWER OF GOD ISN'T FOR SALE

A man named Simon had been a sorcerer there for many years, amazing the people of Samaria and claiming to be someone great. Everyone, from the least to the greatest, often spoke of him as "the Great One – the Power of God." They listened closely to him because for a long time he had astounded them with his magic. But now the people believed Philip's message of Good News concerning the Kingdom of God and the name of Jesus Christ. As a result, many men and women were baptized. Then Simon himself believed and was baptized. He began following Philip wherever he went, and he was amazed by the signs and great miracles Philip performed. When the apostles in Jerusalem heard that the people of Samaria had accepted God's message, they sent Peter and John there. As soon as they arrived, they prayed for these new believers to receive the Holy Spirit. The Holy Spirit had not yet come upon any of them, for they had only been baptized in the name of the Lord Jesus. Then Peter and John laid their hands upon these believers, and they received the Holy Spirit. When Simon saw that the Spirit was given when the apostles laid their hands on people, he offered them money to buy this power. "Let me have this power, too," he exclaimed, "so that when I lay my hands on people, they will receive the Holy Spirit!" But Peter replied, "May your money be destroyed with you for thinking God's gift can be bought! You can have no part in this, for your heart is not right with God. Repent of your wickedness and pray to the Lord. Perhaps He will forgive your evil thoughts, for I can see that you are full of bitter jealousy and are held captive by sin." "Pray to the Lord for me," Simon exclaimed, "that these terrible things you've said won't happen to me!"

Acts 8:9-24

* * *

It was now about four years since the Holy Spirit had been given to the Jews. *"A great wave of persecution"* had now begun on the day that Stephen was killed (Acts 8:1). It swept over the church, and many of the believers, except the apostles, scattered throughout Judea and Samaria. The church did not cease to exist in Jerusalem; rather, as it scattered elsewhere, it still continued to grow. Thus, the apostles remained in Jerusalem for a season to shepherd that still growing church through her infancy, despite the threats that were specifically made against them by the religious leaders and the persecution that was now being directed toward the believers. It is very possible that the initial persecution was primarily being directed toward the Hellenistic Jewish believers, as was the case with Stephen.

Philip, the second of the seven Hellenistic Jewish leaders who were selected to minister to the widows, was directed by God to go to Samaria. Jesus had at one time prohibited the apostles from going there (Matthew 10:5-6). But now, the Lord was inviting Philip to enter into the labor that He had begun through His encounter with the woman at the well (John 4). Philip was not only to declare God's Word, but he was also to demonstrate God's power through miracles.

Sadly, wherever God sows His true believers, Satan will eventually sow his counterfeits. It was as true in the first century church as it is today. It was true in the ministry of John the Baptist (Matthew 3:7) and Paul (Acts 13:6; 2 Corinthians 11:1-4, 13-15), and it was even true in the ministry of Jesus (Matthew 23:15, 33; John 8:44). The enemy seeks to devour, and if he is unsuccessful at that, he will turn his attention to deceive. Satan's instrument in this case was a sorcerer by the name of Simon. The people were amazed by the "things" that Simon did, and, as a result, they believed the "things" he said. Training in the identification of counterfeit currency always begins with studying the real thing. Recognizing counterfeit faith is best identified in the same way. Genuine truth and works will always align with God's Word and glorify Him. The enemy's counterfeit actions and lies will always bring attention to self. Simon relished in being called *"the great one"* by the crowd.

When Simon witnessed the miracles performed by Philip, he did not demonstrate a faith in the Word of God; rather, he placed his faith in the miracles themselves. His belief was like many of the people who witnessed the miracles of Jesus, but refused to acknowledge His Word. Simon's "belief and baptism" were not the result of true repentance; they were part of his attempt to manipulate and deceive in order to gain favor and power. i can relate to that. There was a time that i was going through the motions of belief. My motivation was more to win the heart of the woman i was pursuing, than to pursue Jesus as my Lord and Savior.

Let's take a momentary side road. Simon had truly not repented and believed, but there were many who had – and they were baptized by Philip. Luke tells us that they had not yet received the Holy Spirit (Acts 8:15-16) even though they had trusted in Christ. Paul, writing to the church in Ephesus, tells us, "*... when you believed in Christ, He identified you as His own by giving you the Holy Spirit, whom He promised long ago. The Spirit is God's guarantee that He will give us the inheritance He promised and that He has purchased us to be His own people...*" (Ephesians 1:13-14). So, if God gives us the Holy Spirit when we believe in Christ (like Paul says), why didn't the Samaritans receive the Holy Spirit immediately upon believing in Christ (like Luke says)? It would seem to be a contradiction – and that's the reason for this side road.

In these beginning days of the church (Acts chapters 1 through 10), we see God working in ways that were unique to that time period. The two elements we need to understand are these. First, before Jesus ascended, He told His disciples that they would receive power and then they would tell the Good News in Jerusalem, Judea, Samaria and the ends of the earth (Acts 1:8). There was an initial order to the spread of the Gospel that applied at the start, but no longer applies today – first to Jerusalem, then to Judea and Samaria, followed by the ends of the earth.

Second, Jesus told Peter, in the presence of His other apostles, "*And I tell you, you are Peter, and on this rock I will build My church, and the gates of hell shall not prevail against it. I will give you the keys of the Kingdom of heaven, and whatever you bind on earth shall be bound in heaven, and whatever you loose on earth shall be loosed in heaven*" (Matthew 16:18-19 ESV). Jesus very specifically gave the "keys to the Kingdom" to Peter. He gave Peter the unique privilege of opening the door (loosing on earth and in heaven) the releasing of the Holy Spirit. Peter was the one who preached on the Day of Pentecost and the door was opened to the Jews in Jerusalem and Judea. We see here that Peter (and John) laid their hands on these new believers and the door was opened to the Samaritans. Later in Acts 10, we see that God used Peter to open the door to the Gentiles (the ends of the earth). Once the doors were opened, they no longer need to be reopened. And the truth that Paul wrote to the Ephesians applies to us today. We are immediately identified and indwelt by the Holy Spirit at the point of our salvation.

Let's come back to Simon. There is a word in the English language today – "simony" – which means "the buying or selling of something spiritual."[1] Its origins are in this very passage. Peter confronted Simon for his sin in thinking he could buy the power and presence of the Holy Spirit. That still exists today. People attempt to gain positional or spiritual favor from God and/or recognition from man through "good works" or through the giving of financial gifts as a "quid pro quo". As i mentioned earlier, i attempted to impress and receive favor through my disingenuous actions. Within the church, we may want to appear to others to be "more spiritual" than we truly are in order to gain favor or position, and that fake façade most often quickly falls away and reveals our true hypocrisy.

Regrettably, there is no indication that Simon ever truly repented. Oh, he was "sorry", and he asked Peter to pray that he would escape the judgement of God, but he stopped short of turning from his own way and turning to Christ. He sought power and recognition, but never sought the Savior.

There are those walking through a wilderness journey today who attempt to spiritualize their circumstances in an effort to "buy" sympathy or recognition. They believe God owes them something, or the church owes them something. Their focus is on themselves and what they can "get" through the journey – not on the promises and faithfulness of God even in the midst of the trials and the hardships. An attitude surfaces that God "owes" me – based upon what i have done or what has happened to me. i sometimes see that attitude being expressed through comments on my blog posts. But here's the reality – just as it was for Simon – the power of God is not for sale! It's not earned. It's not deserved. We can only witness and experience the power of God working in us and through us when our hearts are turned and surrendered to Him – and even then, only for His purpose and glory. The power of God isn't about us – it's all about Him. And it's not for sale!

---

1. Encyclopedia Britannica

22

A DIVINE APPOINTMENT

As for Philip, an angel of the Lord said to him, "Go south down the desert road that runs from Jerusalem to Gaza." So he started out, and he met the treasurer of Ethiopia, a eunuch of great authority under the Kandake, the queen of Ethiopia. The eunuch had gone to Jerusalem to worship, and he was now returning. Seated in his carriage, he was reading aloud from the book of the prophet Isaiah. The Holy Spirit said to Philip, "Go over and walk along beside the carriage." Philip ran over and heard the man reading from the prophet Isaiah. Philip asked, "Do you understand what you are reading?" The man replied, "How can I, unless someone instructs me?" And he urged Philip to come up into the carriage and sit with him.... So beginning with this same Scripture, Philip told him the Good News about Jesus. As they rode along, they came to some water, and the eunuch said, "Look! There's some water! Why can't I be baptized?" He ordered the carriage to stop, and they went down into the water, and Philip baptized him. When they came up out of the water, the Spirit of the Lord snatched Philip away. The eunuch never saw him again but went on his way rejoicing. Meanwhile, Philip found himself farther north at the town of Azotus. He preached the Good News there and in every town along the way until he came to Caesarea.

Acts 8:26-40

* * *

Philip was in the midst of a great spiritual awakening that was spreading throughout Samaria. God was using him in a great way, and many were repenting of their sins and believing in Jesus, when an angel of the Lord told him, *"Go south down the desert road that runs from Jerusalem to Gaza."* God was directing him to leave a work among the multitudes to go to a desolate place. That doesn't necessarily align with a successful career path from a human perspective – even if you're a pastor. Whenever we hear a pastor announce that God has called him to go elsewhere, it is rarely to a "smaller" church. And such a move would be even more puzzling, if we are serving in a place where the power and the presence of the Spirit of God is mightily at work, and many are coming to faith and the church is growing. But such was the case with Philip.

We aren't told whether or not he had a conversation with God as to the wisdom of such a move. However, with all we do know about Philip and his walk with God, i tend to think that he immediately set out on the journey to Gaza without ever questioning God. He was in Samaria because God had placed him there. The work that was occurring in Samaria was a work of the Holy Spirit of God, and not of Philip. i don't believe that Philip ever got confused about that. i don't believe he ever tried to take any credit, or saw himself as being instrumental in any way. He was a man full of faith and full of the Holy Spirit – led by, empowered by and used by God for His purpose. Therefore, it didn't matter whether the assignment was in Samaria, Gaza or Azotus. All that mattered was that he was in the place where God would have him.

During my years of serving with the International Mission Board of the Southern Baptist Convention, i had the blessing and privilege of meeting thousands of men and women who, in response to God's call, were leaving successful careers in the U.S. – in a myriad of vocations – business, education, healthcare, agriculture, etc., as well as church ministry – to go to a remote part of the world, where there were few, if any, other believers. They were going in obedience to God in order to share the Good News of Christ with a people group who, most often, had never heard the Name of Jesus. From a human perspective, it was rarely a "step up". But i rejoiced, as i heard the testimonies of these men and women, because these men and women knew that following Jesus wherever He leads is ALWAYS a step up!

Philip, like the men and women i've mentioned, had no idea who he would encounter. All he knew was that God told him to go – and God's direction is never haphazard. We constantly saw Jesus model obedience to the Father in His journeys – sometimes traveling long distances to see just one person, and sometimes to engage a multitude. But the numbers never mattered. It was all about the Father's plan – and the divine appointment that He was orchestrating. In this case with Philip, the divine appointment was with an Ethiopian eunuch – the Secretary of the Treasury for the Queen of Ethiopia.

A few years ago, almost to the day as i write this, i was blessed to travel throughout the country of Ethiopia with a group of pastors from the U.S. i was leading the group and coordinating our schedule. As i look back i can clearly see the Father's hand in assembling that group of men. Our group was comprised of a Korean pastor, a Hispanic pastor, a Chinese pastor, two African American pastors, a white pastor of Italian descent and me. Most of us did not know one another prior to traveling together. We were traveling to spend time with men and women that God was using to spread the gospel throughout Ethiopia and other parts of Central Africa. Our goal was to encourage these workers, as well as to see where God might be leading these pastors to lead their churches to join with Him in the work He was doing among the people in that part of the world. Each of these men also held (and continue to hold) positions of significant leadership in influencing other pastors and churches in doing the same. As a result, we were given an opportunity to see the work in many places within a short window of ten days. We were constantly on the move – riding on every form of transportation imaginable.

On one of the days we were flying through one of the smaller airports in the country. We had spent the day with a team of eight people who were being used by God in a great movement of the gospel among a nomadic people. We were scheduled to depart on a flight at 5:00 P.M. to go to another city to meet up with another team. There was only one plane at the airport when we arrived – the one we were scheduled to take. As it turned out, it was experiencing mechanical failure. The airline representatives continued to tell us that they were working on the problem as day became night, and night kept getting later. i became acutely aware that we hadn't allowed for this much of a delay in our schedule, and we would be forced to cancel some of the visits we had planned. As i was working through the adjustments to our schedule, i began to observe something take place that had been totally unplanned – by us!

The majority of people in the waiting room were native to the country and only spoke their native language of Amharic. None of us knew Amharic, but we were grateful that the airline representatives also knew English. As we sat there, we noticed that there was a Chinese man who was obviously injured, traveling with a companion. It turned out that he had sustained a work injury earlier that afternoon, and was on this flight to get to a hospital in our destination city in order to receive needed medical care. They only spoke Mandarin Chinese. The Chinese pastor with us was able to communicate with them as to what was happening with our delays and was able to assist them with interim care, all the while sharing the gospel in word and deed as the night progressed. Also in the waiting area was a young Korean woman who was traveling alone and was obviously distraught over the delay. The Korean pastor began to minister to her to calm her fears, and in so doing was also able to share the gospel. The Lord provided one of our pastors with the opportunity to minister to a young Amharic man who spoke English. As it turned out, he was a believer who was struggling over a decision that he needed to make regarding the direction of his life. The night before God had told him, through a dream, that He would bring someone across his path who would provide him with words of wisdom regarding his decision. The pastor who was with us was able to point him to the Word of God and challenge him in his walk with God. And on it went with all of our team, each one experiencing the hand of God orchestrating divine appointments. We finally departed on a replacement plane at 10:00 AM the next morning. We hadn't gotten much sleep, and we all felt a little gamey – but we also knew that we had been right where the Father had intended for us to be. And just like Philip, when our assignment was completed, He "snatched us away" on our plane and we found ourselves headed to His next assignment for us.

As we read about Philip in the Book of Acts, his divine appointment with the Ethiopian wasn't the exception, it was the norm. Because Philip walked in obedience as the Father directed him – wherever, whenever, and however. The Spirit of God went before him to prepare the way, to order his steps and empower him for the work. As followers of Jesus, divine appointments should be the norm for us as well, and not the exception. Whatever your journey looks like today, God has a purpose and a plan in the midst of it. It may be right where you are, or He may interrupt you and lead you somewhere else. It probably won't happen when you expect it or the way you expect it, but it will happen if you follow the Spirit's lead. He has arranged for those divine appointments throughout the path ahead. And He will continue to do so… until He returns.

* * *

23

A DAMASCUS ROAD ENCOUNTER

Meanwhile, Saul was uttering threats with every breath and was eager to kill the Lord's followers. So he went to the high priest. He requested letters addressed to the synagogues in Damascus, asking for their cooperation in the arrest of any followers of the Way he found there. He wanted to bring them – both men and women – back to Jerusalem in chains. As he was approaching Damascus on this mission, a light from heaven suddenly shone down around him. He fell to the ground and heard a voice saying to him, "Saul! Saul! Why are you persecuting me?" "Who are you, lord?" Saul asked. And the voice replied, "I am Jesus, the One you are persecuting! Now get up and go into the city, and you will be told what you must do." The men with Saul stood speechless, for they heard the sound of someone's voice but saw no one! Saul picked himself up off the ground, but when he opened his eyes he was blind. So his companions led him by the hand to Damascus. He remained there blind for three days and did not eat or drink.

Acts 9:1-9

* * *

Saul set out on a journey that day. It was a journey of his own choosing. He was on a mission – his own mission. No one sent him. He had to solicit letters of endorsement to provide to the synagogues in Damascus so that he could obtain their cooperation. No one gave him those letters. He had to solicit them. There are two possible reasons for his actions. One possibility is that he had become so caught up in the rhetoric of the religious leaders that he truly had developed a deep-seated hatred for these followers of Jesus. He had guarded the cloaks while the others had stoned Stephen. Since that day he had begun to make a name for himself as a persecutor of Christ followers there in Jerusalem. He had become a part of the threat that prompted the believers to scatter. As he saw it, the believers were a threat to the very fiber of the established religious community, and he saw this as a holy war to eliminate their influence. As such, he was willing to go fight battles that even the religious leaders themselves had no interest in fighting. They were content to be rid of the many believers who had fled from Jerusalem; Saul was not.

A second possibility was his own selfish ambition. Saul apparently was a good student and a quick learner. He was probably a graduate of the university in Tarsus – the greatest Greek university of the day. He was a student of Gamaliel, considered by most to be the greatest Hebrew scholar of the day. He obviously aspired to become an influential religious leader himself, perhaps even the high priest. This ambitious young man saw this journey as a way to prove himself to the religious leaders and garner their support so that he might more quickly rise in the ranks of leadership. Thus, either his hatred or his ambition – or both – created an eagerness in his heart to "kill the Lord's followers". He was on a mission to kill them. Let there be no confusion – Saul was not pursuing God. He was declaring war on God. And yet, God in His sovereignty, in His mercy, and by His grace was Himself pursuing Saul – not for his defeat, but for his transformation.

As he approached Damascus at midday, suddenly he saw a bright light from heaven that caused even the sun to pale. He could not stand in its presence and immediately he fell to the ground. As he did, he heard the voice of the Lord Jesus speaking to him. Though his companions heard the sound of someone's voice, they could not distinguish what Jesus was saying, and they were not blinded by the light. Without Saul having any awareness, the Father had ordered his steps that day to have an encounter with the Living Lord Jesus. None of his companions shared in that encounter – it was a personal encounter between Jesus and Saul. It was not a gradual encounter; it was sudden and momentary. In a brief moment Saul knew four things.

First, he now knew firsthand that Jesus was alive. Saul may have possibly been in the crowd the day Jesus was crucified five years earlier. He had refused to accept the testimony from the believers about the resurrection of Jesus. His disbelief had been central in his persecution of the believers. But now he knew that Jesus was alive.

. . .

Therefore, second, he knew that he had been wrong. He had denied Jesus and been a part of murdering innocent Christians. He was immediately overcome by his sin. There was no hiding his sin in this light. There was no denying his sin. Jesus had just totally illuminated all the darkness of his sin. He had no choice other than to repent – which was no small thing for this self-righteous Pharisee. Saul's encounter on that road, in some ways, is similar to the encounter that Isaiah describes in Isaiah 6, and John describes in Revelation 1. Each of them fell at the feet of Christ when they encountered His holiness and His righteousness. Each of them were overwhelmed by their own sinfulness. Each of them could do nothing but confess their sin and repent. Saul knew he was a sinner in need of a Savior and lying there in the dirt, he surrendered his life to Christ.

Third, he knew that everything about his life had to change – his mission, his pursuits, his ambition and his values. He knew everything had just changed. He could no longer chase after anything in his life that he had been pursuing – everything had been made different. He no longer sought the approval of others (the religious leaders); He sought the approval of only One (Jesus). He could no longer do anything he had been doing – all of his so-called good works and attempts at legalistic self-righteousness were all as filthy rags. He could no longer walk in those rags. He must now walk in the righteousness of Christ. His circle of friends (albeit probably a small circle) would have to change. The very ones that to this moment he had been persecuting would now become his circle of friends. He was a new person – the old had passed away (2 Corinthians 5:17).

Fourth, not only had his life just been transformed, but so had his purpose. This Hebrew of the Hebrews would become the apostle to the Gentiles. This one who had made it his life focus to scatter and persecute the sheep would now be a shepherd. This enforcer of the law would now be a proclaimer of grace. He had now been transformed into a vessel of honor to be used by the Master (2 Timothy 2:20-21).

Saul had set out on his journey to arrest others, but instead, Jesus arrested him. He had set out in a religious pursuit, but instead, he had gained the righteousness of Christ -- all because of the grace, mercy and sovereign purpose of God! His had been a journey totally contrary to God's purpose, but now God had transformed the purpose to align with His sovereign plan.

. . .

And the same is true for us. Your journey through your wilderness may have begun out of your own selfish desires or ambition. Or it may have been driven by your rebellion against God. Or it may have begun as a result of someone else's rebellion. Or it may have arisen due to a circumstance that you had no control over. The journey may in fact be a path in a relationship or a decision that will result in you being led away from God – and the best that He desires for you. The fact of the matter is that whatever prompted the journey, God can – and will – use the journey for you to have a fresh encounter with Him and to experience the transformation that He intends for your life. It was a personal journey that day for Saul – hopefully his traveling companions were transformed on another day. It's a personal journey for you as well. He is going with you – every step of the way. And He will continue to do so… until He returns.

* * *

24

THE COURAGE OF ANANIAS

Now there was a believer in Damascus named Ananias. The Lord spoke to him in a vision, calling, "Ananias!"
"Yes, Lord!" he replied. The Lord said, "Go over to Straight Street, to the house of Judas. When you get there, ask for a man from Tarsus named Saul. He is praying to Me right now. I have shown him a vision of a man named Ananias coming in and laying hands on him so he can see again." "But Lord," exclaimed Ananias, "I've heard many people talk about the terrible things this man has done to the believers in Jerusalem! And he is authorized by the leading priests to arrest everyone who calls upon Your name." But the Lord said, "Go, for Saul is My chosen instrument to take My message to the Gentiles and to kings, as well as to the people of Israel. And I will show him how much he must suffer for My name's sake." So Ananias went and found Saul. He laid his hands on him and said, "Brother Saul, the Lord Jesus, who appeared to you on the road, has sent me so that you might regain your sight and be filled with the Holy Spirit." Instantly something like scales fell from Saul's eyes, and he regained his sight. Then he got up and was baptized. Afterward he ate some food and regained his strength. Saul stayed with the believers in Damascus for a few days.
Acts 9:10-19

* * *

On April 21, 1855, God prompted a Sunday School teacher in Boston by the name of Edward Kimball to visit a young man who was attending his Sunday School class. The young man wasn't attending the class willingly. His uncle had made it a condition of his employment as a shoe salesman. The boy would only get the job if he attended the class.

Edward Kimball's visit took place at the shoe store where the young man worked. Here is Kimball's account of the visit: "*When I was nearly there I began to wonder whether I ought to go in just then during business hours. I thought my call might embarrass the boy, and that when I went away the other clerks would ask who I was, and taunt him with my efforts in trying to make him a good boy. In the meantime I had passed the store, and, discovering this, I determined to make a dash for it, and have it over at once. I found him in the back part of the building wrapping up shoes. I went up to him at once, and putting my hand on his shoulder, I made what I felt afterwards was a very weak plea for Christ. I don't know just what words I used. I simply told him of Christ's love for him, and the love Christ wanted in return. That was all there was. It seemed the young man was just ready for the light that then broke upon him.*"[1] Dwight L. Moody, a shoe salesman, surrendered his life to Christ that day. God went on to use D. L. Moody as an evangelist, publisher, pastor and the founder of the Moody Bible Institute to have far-reaching impact for the Kingdom that continues to this day. And God used a humble, unknown servant who had to work up the courage to go talk to Moody to set his feet on the right path. The same could also be said of another humble, otherwise unknown, servant of God by the name of Ananias.

Ananias was a follower of Jesus living in Damascus. We don't know how Ananias came to faith in Jesus. It may have been through the ministry of Jesus Himself, or through the ministry of the seventy-two that Jesus sent out. Possibly, he was one of those who were gathered in Jerusalem on the Day of Pentecost, or soon thereafter. He apparently was one of the more mature believers, and was recognized as a respected and trusted leader of the believers there in Damascus. He, together with the other believers in Damascus, were very familiar with the persecution that the believers were experiencing in Jerusalem. Word had also apparently already reached them that Saul was coming to Damascus to persecute and arrest the believers there. Ananias was very familiar with Saul's terrible reputation when God directed him to go to Saul. It is reasonable to imagine that Ananias and the other believers were terrified as they awaited Saul and his cohort, for they knew their lives might be lost for the sake of Christ. They were awaiting his arrival to the city with great dread.

Note what Ananias did. He made a point to tell God all about Saul, as if God wasn't fully aware! "*I've heard many people talk about the terrible things this man has done to the believers in Jerusalem! And he is authorized by the leading priests to arrest everyone who calls upon Your name.*" As if to say, "God, You must not know all the facts about this man. Otherwise, surely You wouldn't be sending me to him!" Ananias showed his fear and anxiety here. He did not yet have unwavering trust in God. As a matter of fact, he reminds me of me! i suspect i would have said the same thing to God – just in case He had somehow forgotten or overlooked some of the details. After all, this guy was dangerous! Didn't God know that? Over the years, i have had some honest conversations with men and women who sensed God's call to carry the gospel to some pretty difficult places. They have shared some of the conversations that they have had with God. "Um…God…don't You know that country is closed to missionaries? Don't You know that Your people are persecuted in that nation? Don't You know what could happen to me, or to my family, if we go there, God?"

But God knows all about those people, just like He knew all about Saul. He told Ananias *"Go, for Saul is My chosen instrument to take My message to the Gentiles and to kings, as well as to the people of Israel. And I will show him how much he must suffer for My name's sake.""* God knew exactly who Saul was and gave Ananias the assurance that He was still in control. As a matter of fact, providence dictated that He would use this man to do incredible things for His kingdom. Saul, the chief of sinners, the persecutor of the church, was to be God's chosen means of bringing the gospel to great and small, Jew and Gentile alike.

Ananias was obedient. He appeared before Saul and had the great honor of laying his hands on this broken man in the name of the Holy Spirit. At that moment, the scales fell from Saul's eyes and he regained his sight. As a testimony to his new found faith in Christ, he was baptized, probably by the hand of Ananias himself. We then read that *"Saul stayed with the believers in Damascus for a few days."* Whether at that point Saul was the student or the teacher, we do not know. Perhaps he sat and learned at the feet of Ananias.

At this point, Ananias disappears from Luke's account and we do not hear any more about him. His role in the drama of Acts was brief, yet very significant. We see a man who wavered when he heard God's voice, yet despite his initial hesitation, he was faithful and obedient. While at first he thought he might have to correct God, in the end he submitted himself and his very life to God's call. God then used this man to further His purposes in launching the career of one of the most influential apostles. Ananias' small act of obedience, just like Edward Kimball's, led to a great harvest for the Kingdom.

• • •

And this is the lesson of Ananias for us to learn. There will be times when God will direct us through His Word in ways that seem contrary to our own reasoning. We do not know – and may never know – the full significance of what God intends. Let's not forget that our perspective is finite and limited. God's perspective is infinite, taking in all of history in a single glance. We need to trust Him, His Word, and His voice; trusting that He will never lead us astray. It will take courage – just like it did for Ananias and Edward Kimball. Courage that can only come through the confidence that we do not go alone; His Holy Spirit, who is within us, will go before us, will go with us and will empower us... every step of the way... until He returns.

---

1. from *Twice-Born Men: True Conversion Records of 100 Well-Known Men in All Ranks of Life* compiled by Hy Pickering

25

A HIDDEN JOURNEY IN THE WILDERNESS

Saul stayed with the believers in Damascus for a few days. And immediately he began preaching about Jesus in the synagogues, saying, "He is indeed the Son of God!" All who heard him were amazed. "Isn't this the same man who caused such devastation among Jesus' followers in Jerusalem?" they asked. "And didn't he come here to arrest them and take them in chains to the leading priests?" Saul's preaching became more and more powerful, and the Jews in Damascus couldn't refute his proofs that Jesus was indeed the Messiah. After a while some of the Jews plotted together to kill him. They were watching for him day and night at the city gate so they could murder him, but Saul was told about their plot. So during the night, some of the other believers lowered him in a large basket through an opening in the city wall. When Saul arrived in Jerusalem, he tried to meet with the believers, but they were all afraid of him.

Acts 9:19-26

* * *

Luke writes that Saul stayed with the believers in Damascus for a few days following the day that Ananias laid his hands upon him, and he regained his sight. Luke also tells us that Saul arrived in Jerusalem after the believers in Damascus lowered him through an opening in the city wall. There is an important part of the narrative that the Holy Spirit chose to tell us through Saul himself, and not through Luke. Saul tells us that *"it was not until three years later that I finally went to Jerusalem…"* (Galatians 1:18). That means that three years transpired between verse 19 and verse 26. Saul also writes *"I went away into Arabia and later returned to the city of Damascus"* (Galatians 1:17). That means that somewhere between verse 21 and verse 23 Saul was in Arabia and then returned to Damascus. We don't know if that was for the full three years, but it was apparently for a long portion of it. So what was he doing and why did Luke leave a three year gap in his narrative?

Apparently, Saul only remained in Damascus initially for a matter of days – long enough for his sight and strength to be regained (Acts 9:18-19). During those initial days, Saul was already boldly proclaiming that Jesus, the One whose followers he had been persecuting, was in fact the Son of God. He did not delay in bearing witness to the grace and mercy of God. His witness was immediate – and the Jews, both believers and non-believers alike, were amazed by the conspicuous transformation in his life. But after a few days, the Lord led Saul on a wilderness journey into Arabia so that He might prepare and equip Saul for the work He had chosen for him to do. Though Saul had been an ardent student of the Word under the teaching of the religious scholars, there was much that needed to be clarified before he could effectively minister as an apostle. And if Saul was going to be His apostle to carry the Good News to the Gentiles, he needed to be taught firsthand by Jesus. Remember, the apostles did not have benefit of the written New Testament as we do – they were the writers of that New Testament under the direction of the Holy Spirit. And they were writing what they had seen and heard from Jesus. It's interesting to note that the duration of this time in Arabia is approximately three years, similar to the amount of time that Jesus spent discipling His other apostles.

Though the Holy Spirit did not lead the writers of the New Testament to tell us many of the details about Saul's time in Arabia, we know that it pleased God "*to reveal His Son to me so that I would proclaim the Good News about Jesus to the Gentiles. When this happened, I did not rush out to consult with any human being. Nor did I go up to Jerusalem to consult with those who were apostles before I was. Instead, I went away into Arabia…*" (Galatians 1:16-17). And throughout his time in Arabia, Jesus was his Teacher. Saul explained, "*I received my message from no human source, and no one taught me. Instead, I received it by direct revelation from Jesus Christ*" (Galatians 1:12). Later, Saul (now the apostle Paul) wrote to the believers in Corinth, "*I have traveled on many long journeys. I have faced danger from rivers and from robbers. I have faced danger from my own people, the Jews, as well as from the Gentiles. I have faced danger in the cities, in the deserts, and on the seas. And I have faced danger from men who claim to be believers but are not. I have worked hard and long, enduring many sleepless nights. I have been hungry and thirsty and have often gone without food. I have shivered in the cold, without enough clothing to keep me warm"* (2 Corinthians 11:26-27) Some of these details refer to his missionary journeys, but some, such as the flooding rivers, the danger of robbers, the danger in the deserts, the cold and the lack of food may very well refer to the three years in Arabia. As Jesus led Saul on his wilderness journey with Him, it is very likely that it included time at Mount Sinai (Galatians 4:25). It is also most likely that Jesus led Saul to evangelize as he journeyed through the wilderness of Arabia. Jesus often sent out His apostles to preach and perform miracles throughout His earthly ministry It would be reasonable to believe He followed a similar pattern with Saul. Thus, Saul was already a "marked man" when he returned to Damascus.

Saul is a reminder to each of us that often Jesus will take us on a wilderness journey with Him in order to prepare us and equip us for the task that He is placing before us. There are things that He can only teach us when we are one-on-One with Him in the deserts, or the floods, or the difficulties of a wilderness journey. He alone determines how long the journey will take and where it will lead. Though He is using the time in the wilderness to prepare us for what He has in store after the wilderness, He also has work for us right there in the midst of the wilderness! Through the preparation and the work, He is teaching us truths we can only learn directly from Him. Though Saul was already a bold witness before Jesus led him out into the wilderness of Arabia, he returned to Damascus as a vessel prepared and ready to be used by the Master for every good work (2 Timothy 2:21).

Also, as we have already seen, there is not much recorded in Scripture about this journey. That should serve as a reminder to us that often the wilderness journey that God leads us in, or permits us to travel, is one that is personal and private. It is an intimate journey between our Lord and us. That's not to say that we don't bear witness and bring glory to God as Saul did. But it is to say that our Lord knows us, and knows our frame, better than we know ourselves. He knows just what we need. Allow Him to draw you close in the journey. Allow Him to remove the dross from your life and refine you to be that vessel that is prepared and useful to Him.

Prior to that initial day on the road to Damascus, Saul's personal ambition had been all wrapped up in what people thought about him. He had built that ambition over a lifetime. He wanted the early Christians to fear him for his ferocity. He wanted the Jews to admire him for his piety. He wanted the Jewish leaders to respect him for his fervency. He wanted God to accept him for his solemnity. But all of that changed. Some of it changed instantly at the moment of his salvation, but some of it changed through a work of sanctification, as he journeyed with Jesus through the wilderness of Arabia. By his own admission, Saul ceased being a "people pleaser". He wrote, *"No, I am trying to please God. If I was still trying to please people, I would not be Christ's servant"* (Galatians 1:10). He realized that he stood before an audience of One – the One who had chosen him, called him, extended His undeserved mercy to him (Galatians 1:15), and led him through a wilderness to prepare him. He knew that his relationship with Christ was not because of His efforts. He knew that his "righteous" deeds were but filthy rags (Isaiah 64:6).

When Saul returned to Damascus, his preaching was so powerful that the Jews could not refute him. It wasn't ferocity, or piety or fervency that they saw. His power and authority came from the fact that, like Peter and the other disciples, he had been with Jesus (Acts 4:13).

Yes, his Lord made a way of escape through the city wall of Damascus, but perhaps even more importantly He allowed him to walk with Him through the trials and challenges of a wilderness journey – all so that the Father's mission and purpose would be fulfilled. And that same God will also lead you and i through each and every step of our way… until He returns.

* * *

26

AN OPENING IN THE WALL

After a while some of the Jews plotted together to kill him. They were watching for him day and night at the city gate so they could murder him, but Saul was told about their plot. So during the night, some of the other believers lowered him in a large basket through an opening in the city wall.
Acts 9:23-25

* * *

When Saul returned to Damascus, the Jews soon plotted together to kill him. The "hunter", Saul, had now become the hunted. Having been an ardent persecutor of Christians, he was fully aware of all of the means that were at his "hunters'" disposal. He may have actually trained some of these Jews in the best way to capture the Christians. He could anticipate the details of the next steps in the playbook of the plot against him. He had written the playbook! Saul was a brilliant man. He probably had "plays" in his playbook that these men had never thought of. It would have been very easy for him to be overconfident in his own knowledge and his own ability to thwart the plans of those who were plotting against him. He easily could have determined to rely on his own ability to overcome the problem himself.

Jesus had appeared to Saul personally on the road to Damascus. He had just returned from almost three years in the Arabian wilderness being led in a one-on-One journey with the Son of God. He was on a first name basis with the Creator of the universe. He could have begun to believe that he was invincible – kind of like a spiritual "Iron Man". He could have developed a spiritual arrogance that nothing or no one could defeat him by virtue of his spiritual position.

Do i hear you saying that either or both of those positions would have been silly for him to take? Well, i mention them both because they are positions that we, as believers, have been known to take. When we encounter a difficulty or a challenge in life, too often our first instinct is to fight it off in our own ability or make our own plans. It may be a health issue, a financial setback, a personal attack, or even a spiritual attack – and our first recourse is to try and overcome it "our way". We're not going to "bother" God with it. We can deal with it on our own. Our wit, wisdom and strength will get us through.

Or perhaps, we take the "super-Christian" approach of "name it and claim it". We believe that since we are a child of God, nothing can overtake us or overcome us because we have special privileges. And if something does overcome us, we blame God because it must be His fault, because as His child we are supposed to be exempt from life's difficulties. As a result, we do nothing, believing we will miraculously escape our problems. But Saul himself (later as Paul) counted it a privilege to suffer for the sake of Christ. As a matter of fact, he says *"everyone who wants to live a godly life in Christ Jesus will suffer persecution"* (2 Timothy 3:12).

And as the writer of the letter to the Roman believers, Paul wrote the truth that Jesus had taught him: *"The Holy Spirit helps us in our weakness. For example, we don't know what God wants us to pray for. But the Holy Spirit prays for us with groanings that cannot be expressed in words. And the Father who knows all hearts knows what the Spirit is saying, for the Spirit pleads for us believers in harmony with God's own will. And we know that God causes everything to work together for the good of those who love God and are called according to His purpose for them"* (Romans 8:26-28). The apostle John did likewise when he wrote, *"And we are confident that He hears us whenever we ask for anything that pleases Him. And since we know He hears us when we make our requests, we also know that He will give us what we ask for"* (1 John 5:14-15). And Jesus Himself said, *"But if you remain in Me and My words remain in you, you may ask for anything you want, and it will be granted!"* (John 15:7). In all three instances, the Lord tells us that if we ask according to His Word and His will, we can walk assuredly in His answer. Years ago, i heard Dr. Charles Stanley say, *"If God tells you to run your head through a brick wall, you start running and trust Him to make a hole in that wall."* The key is what God has said – and once we know what He has said, trusting Him to make the way to bring it about.

Jesus had said that Saul was His chosen instrument to take His *"message to the Gentiles and to kings, as well as to the people of Israel"* (Acts 9:15). Saul could walk confidently knowing that as long as he continued in obedience according to the Lord's will that nothing could defeat him until that work was accomplished. And God would make a "hole" even where it otherwise seemed impossible. In Saul's situation, God made an opening in the city wall for him to escape.

As i write this, i am running head-first toward a wall. God has given me a clear promise through His Word. In recent weeks, He has been affirming His promise almost every day through His Word and in so many other ways. In my own strength and according to my own ability, it is an impossible task. i am not running toward the wall because i think it is a good idea. In my own wisdom, i think it is a terrible idea. But my wife and i believe with all our hearts that it is what God has told us to do. And He has promised that in His perfect timing and in His perfect way, He will bring it about. So the question before us is – do we trust Him at His word? And if so, are we willing to charge ahead according to His word? Do we trust that when we arrive at the wall He will make the opening? It won't happen through my own ability. It won't happen simply because i am His child. It will only happen if we are walking by faith, trusting Him at His word.

That's what Saul did. And God made an opening in the wall. The result was that the Good News was preached to the nations. God's work was accomplished in His way according to His word and for His glory. That was true two thousand years ago in Damascus, and it's true today. And it will continue to be true… until He returns.

* * *

27

WHOSE BARNABAS ARE YOU?

When Saul arrived in Jerusalem, he tried to meet with the believers, but they were all afraid of him. They did not believe he had truly become a believer! Then Barnabas brought him to the apostles and told them how Saul had seen the Lord on the way to Damascus and how the Lord had spoken to Saul. He also told them that Saul had preached boldly in the name of Jesus in Damascus. So Saul stayed with the apostles and went all around Jerusalem with them, preaching boldly in the name of the Lord. He debated with some Greek-speaking Jews, but they tried to murder him. When the believers heard about this, they took him down to Caesarea and sent him away to Tarsus, his hometown. The church then had peace throughout Judea, Galilee, and Samaria, and it became stronger as the believers lived in the fear of the Lord. And with the encouragement of the Holy Spirit, it also grew in numbers.

Acts 9:26-31

* * *

When Saul arrived in Jerusalem the believers were afraid of him. They thought his witness was a deception in order to entrap them. They had known him before he had left Jerusalem. And they knew that he had left Jerusalem in order to persecute the believers in Damascus. They knew what he was capable of. The believers, including the apostles, questioned whether he was even a believer. But on top of that, he was calling himself an apostle. What right did he have to call himself an apostle? He hadn't walked with Jesus – or so they thought. So they would not accept him into their fellowship.

. . .

That is, until Barnabas took action. Luke tells us that Barnabas *"was a good man, full of the Holy Spirit and strong in faith"* (Acts 11:24). We have already seen that he was selfless and generous as he sold his property and gave all of the proceeds to the church (Acts 4:36-37). Barnabas was very quickly seen within the newly-developing church as a leader – but this "son of encouragement" was more than that – he was a leader-maker. He was willing to take a risk for the sake of the Kingdom. He was willing to take the risk and sell his property, and he was willing to take the risk and reach out to Saul. He was willing to put his riches and his reputation at stake for the cause of Christ. He not only reached out to Saul; he put his arm around him and drew him close.

If you have read my other books in this series, you have heard me speak of a man by the name of Bryan Evans, who was a Barnabas in my life for a number of years. God brought Bryan into my life to be a part of the journey that led to my salvation in Christ. Bryan reached out to me as a friend and a discipler. Initially, because of the place where i was walking, i saw him as somewhat extreme in his relationship with Christ, but i never questioned the genuineness of his faith. When, as a new believer, i was seeking God's direction for my life, he volunteered to meet with me each morning before the crack of dawn to pray together. As i followed the Lord's leading to enter into pastoral ministry, Bryan was there to pray for me and encourage me every step along the way. When, as a pastor, i needed someone to lead through some challenging projects, he was there to stand in the gap with me and lead. i rarely saw Bryan when he wasn't surrounded by several men in whom he was pouring his life. Bryan, like Barnabas, was a leader-maker – and though time and distance now separate us, i'm sure he still is!

Barnabas convinced Peter and James (the half-brother of Jesus) to meet with Saul. Saul tells us in Galatians 1:18 that he did not meet with any of the other apostles at that time. But over the next fifteen days, he told Peter, James – and Barnabas – about the work that God had done in his life over the prior three years from the moment of his salvation until the current time. In particular, he told them about the time that he had spent following Jesus in the wilderness of Arabia. Bear in mind, there is no indication that Jesus appeared to him bodily, or in any way other than how he appeared to him on the Road to Damascus. However, Jesus discipled Saul – in whatever way He chose to do so – in the truths that He had taught the other apostles and in the truths that a newly forming church needed to know. By the conclusion of Saul's time with Peter and James, they were convinced in the veracity of his testimony and the genuineness of his transformation, as well as his apostleship.

Saul accompanied some of the leaders of the Jerusalem church – at least, Peter, James and Barnabas – as they went all around the city, *preaching boldly in the name of the Lord.* As they preached, many of the Jews recognized Saul. In particular the Hellenistic Jews – those who had engineered the trial and death of Stephen – recognized him as one who had been one of them. They began to debate with Saul, and he may have sensed a need to take up the witness of Stephen, in whose death he had been complicit. The Jews soon began to make attempts to murder him, but God had other plans for Saul. He tells us through Luke, *"I was praying in the Temple and fell into a trance. I saw a vision of Jesus saying to me, 'Hurry! Leave Jerusalem, for the people here won't accept your testimony about Me.' 'But Lord,' I argued, 'they certainly know that in every synagogue I imprisoned and beat those who believed in You. And I was in complete agreement when your witness Stephen was killed. I stood by and kept the coats they took off when they stoned him.' But the Lord said to me, 'Go, for I will send you far away to the Gentiles!'"* (Acts 22:17-21).

Knowing the threat against Saul, the believers aided him in making his way to Caesarea so that he could travel to his hometown of Tarsus – probably to tell his family and hometown friends about Jesus. Though Scripture is silent on the point, i would conjecture that Barnabas was right there with him every step of the way. He was with Saul when the Jews were debating with him, and he was there accompanying Saul to Caesarea. Barnabas didn't "make leaders" from a distance. He was there with him – with his arm around him – walking with him through "thick and thin". Such was the son of encouragement!

We'll pick back up with Saul in chapter 32 of this book, after a seven year period of time will have passed, but in the meantime Tarsus became his "base of ministry" as he began to carry the gospel to the Gentiles. He evangelized in the regions of Syria and Cilicia (Galatians 1:21), planting churches as he went (Acts 15:41). Also it is very likely that some of the trials that he writes about in 2 Corinthians 11:24-36 occurred during this period, including at least a half dozen beatings at the hands of the Jews, as well as the Romans (at the urging of the Jews). He apparently was shipwrecked twice during that period. Those seven years were anything but a "cakewalk". Through those years, the gospel was being preached and the

Kingdom advanced among the Gentiles long before he and Barnabas were reunited in Tarsus (Acts 11:25).

Though Barnabas and Saul were apart for those seven years, God had used Barnabas to encourage and help strengthen Saul in his faith. He had introduced him to the apostles, enabling Saul to go out with the endorsement of the Jerusalem church. He had been the friend and companion that Saul needed in that season – and he would be again. A "Barnabas" may not walk with us permanently, but his/her efforts on our behalf will always have lasting impact. Everyone needs at least one Barnabas in our lives. Thankfully, often God brings more than one. And He, in turn, gives us opportunity to be a Barnabas in others' lives. Be that Barnabas that God has equipped you to be, and called you to be. Step up boldly and courageously as He brings that one across your path, being that friend and that encourager that *"sticks closer than a brother"* or a sister (Proverbs 18:24). God has so ordered your journey to prepare you as a Barnabas, and to bring that one across your path who is in need of a Barnabas. Don't miss the invitation!

The seven years that followed, while Saul was in Tarsus, Syria and Cilicia, may have been a time of "peace" in Jerusalem, Judea and Samaria, but it wasn't a season of complacency. The church grew and strengthened. God raised up new workmen to continue the work. Barnabas was there to encourage those new workmen. God is still raising up new workmen today – workmen for you to encourage – and He will continue to do so… until He returns.

* * *

28

IT IS WHAT IT IS, OR IS IT?

Meanwhile, Peter traveled from place to place, and he came down to visit the believers in the town of Lydda. There he met a man named Aeneas, who had been paralyzed and bedridden for eight years. Peter said to him, "Aeneas, Jesus Christ heals you! Get up, and roll up your sleeping mat!" And he was healed instantly. Then the whole population of Lydda and Sharon saw Aeneas walking around, and they turned to the Lord. There was a believer in Joppa named Tabitha (which in Greek is Dorcas). She was always doing kind things for others and helping the poor. About this time she became ill and died. Her body was washed for burial and laid in an upstairs room. But the believers had heard that Peter was nearby at Lydda, so they sent two men to beg him, "Please come as soon as possible!" So Peter returned with them; and as soon as he arrived, they took him to the upstairs room. The room was filled with widows who were weeping and showing him the coats and other clothes Dorcas had made for them. But Peter asked them all to leave the room; then he knelt and prayed. Turning to the body he said, "Get up, Tabitha." And she opened her eyes! When she saw Peter, she sat up! He gave her his hand and helped her up. Then he called in the widows and all the believers, and he presented her to them alive. The news spread through the whole town, and many believed in the Lord.

Acts 9:32-42

* * *

Over the last fifty years, the idiom "it is what it is" has sprung forth from the fatalists in our midst who firmly believe that we are victims -- victims of our circumstances, our situations, our upbringing, our medical condition, etc. It communicates that we have resigned ourselves to the belief that our situation is immutable, and nothing or no one can change it. It is used to convey a sense of resignation, helplessness and hopelessness. "That's just the way I am." "That's just the way my spouse is." "That's just the way my kids are." "That's just how people like me are treated." "That's just the way the system works." "It's always been this way, and it will never change."

This journey with Peter is a reminder that we will never know the truth of any situation until we have heard from Jesus. In His world, the only thing that is immutable is that sin separates us from a Holy God. And He Himself made the way – the only way -- whereby we might overcome that immutable truth. He is not dead; He's alive. He is not distant. He is not silent. He is not weak. His arm has not grown short. He is mighty and He is able to save – spiritually, physically, and emotionally. Throughout His earthly ministry, Jesus healed. He raised the dead. He stilled storms. He met physical needs. He was the King of the reality that it is NOT what it is, if Jesus says it isn't. And as Peter shows us – He still is! What He began to do through His earthly ministry, He still does. He is still full of surprises – for individuals, for families, for churches, and even for nations.

John Piper writes, *"There is a pride in the predictions of human beings based on human calculations of human knowledge about human factors. There is a pride in such predictions that God does not like – even when made by Christians! It is a practical atheism. It does not allow for the Living Lord of the universe who turns things around – out of the blue!"* It's true today, and it was true in the first century. Imagine what it must have been like for the believers in the first century. Jesus was gone. The religious leaders were still in charge. They were condoning – and initiating – persecution of the church. The Romans were still in control of the country. Everyone was against these followers of Jesus! They were battling the belief that it is what it is.

Peter was in the town of Lydda – about twenty miles northwest of Jerusalem. He was there to visit the church in the town. It had either been started by residents of the town who had been in Jerusalem at Pentecost nine years earlier, or by believers who scattered from Jerusalem after the stoning of Stephen five years earlier. Peter had come to town to encourage them in their faith. He met a man by the name of Aeneas who had been paralyzed for eight years. Aeneas had heard of the healing miracles of Jesus when He was travelling the Judean hillside. But Aeneas hadn't needed healing when Jesus was in the hillside. Today was a different matter, but Jesus was no longer there. So, "it was what it was". Imagine the hopelessness of this one who had been bedridden for eight years! Then – out of the blue – Peter came passing by and said, *"Aeneas, Jesus Christ heals you! Get up, and roll up your sleeping mat!"* Instantly, Aeneas was healed! Imagine the joy. Imagine his euphoria! The whole town saw him walking around, but i would venture that was after he jumped up and down in the air! Jesus may have been out of sight, but He sure wasn't gone. It no longer "was what it was". Jesus had healed Aeneas – for the glory of the Father, and for the spread of the gospel. We read, *"the whole population turned to the Lord."* Not only was one life transformed, but an entire town! And the word spread from there… another ten miles toward the coast to the city of Joppa.

Tabitha was already a believer. She apparently had an active ministry to the widows of Joppa as a couturier. She had become ill and died. She was already being prepared for burial when the believers sent two men to fetch Peter. The entire region knew about how Jesus had raised Lazarus from the dead. Now they had heard how He had healed Aeneas through Peter, and they immediately believed that Jesus could still raise the dead. They believed that "it was NOT what it was" – because of Jesus. And God's plan was for Tabitha to "get up!" God responded to the faith of the believers and the obedience of Peter in a way that aligned with His perfect plan.

This is the only instance recorded in Scripture where Jesus worked through Peter to raise someone from the dead. Jesus hadn't called Peter to an itinerant ministry of raising the dead to life; He had called him to make disciples. In this instance, God chose for this one to be raised from the dead. His plan will not always look the same. His plan will not always be to bring about physical healing – but it will always be about bringing glory to the Father. If the healing doesn't occur on this side of eternity, it will always occur on the other side. Don't forget that Jesus sees with an eternal perspective and He works all things *"together for the good of those who love God and are called according to His purpose for them"* (Romans 8:28), and always for His glory. Trust Him to do the same thing in your circumstance and in your life.

Jesus is as much alive today as He was in the first century. He is able to do a lot more today than we are often willing to see or receive. He has surprises in store for us of which we have never dreamed. There were two characteristics that were evidenced in that early church that we have seemingly lost today. If we would see Jesus work in the same power He demonstrated that day in Lydda and in Joppa, perhaps He is waiting for us to turn to Him in the same way. Luke wrote, "*So the church throughout all Judea and Galilee and Samaria had peace and was being built up. And walking in the fear of the Lord and in the comfort of the Holy Spirit, it multiplied* (Acts 9:31 ESV). First, they walked in a holy fear of the Lord. They believed in a Lord God who is infinitely holy and infinitely powerful. They knew that He was not to be trifled with. They had seen the storms stilled. They had seen Ananias and Sapphira fall dead. You do not make light of this God. He is the "I AM that I AM", and He is greater than whatever is.

Second, they walked in the comfort of the Holy Spirit. That comfort is much like being in the eye of a hurricane. In the eye you are experiencing a calmness and a peace in the midst of mighty power. We walk in the center of a fearsome power, but as we do, we can have the calm and confidence that we are in His presence. When we walk in that place, there is no circumstance or situation that can withstand His power. "It is what it is" can't stand up to "I AM that I AM". He alone is an immutable force... and so He will be... until He returns!

* * *

29

HE GOES BEFORE US

In Caesarea there lived a Roman army officer named Cornelius, who was a captain of the Italian Regiment. He was a devout, God-fearing man, as was everyone in his household. He gave generously to the poor and prayed regularly to God. One afternoon about three o'clock, he had a vision in which he saw an angel of God coming toward him. "Cornelius!" the angel said. Cornelius stared at him in terror. "What is it, sir?" he asked the angel.
And the angel replied, "Your prayers and gifts to the poor have been received by God as an offering! Now send some men to Joppa, and summon a man named Simon Peter. He is staying with Simon, a tanner who lives near the seashore." As soon as the angel was gone, Cornelius called two of his household servants and a devout soldier, one of his personal attendants. He told them what had happened and sent them off to Joppa.
Acts 10:1-8

* * *

Approximately nine years have passed since the Day of Pentecost. Saul has just recently departed for Tarsus. God has just raised Tabitha from the dead through the ministry of Peter, and he is still about thirty miles away in Joppa. The door of faith has been opened for the Jews in Jerusalem and Judea, as well as the Samaritans, and the Father has empowered Peter to use the "keys of the Kingdom" to unleash His Spirit to dwell among those peoples (as we saw in chapter 21 of this book). God is now preparing to open the remaining door to the Gentiles, first here in Caesarea through Peter, then soon to be followed in Syria and Cilicia through Saul.

. . .

God's ways are most definitely not our ways (Isaiah 55:8). He will accomplish His purpose in His way (Isaiah 46:9-11). He has the capacity to be at work in all places at all times. He is not confined by space or time (Psalm 139:7-12). He is always at work preparing us for what He is preparing for us. And this day in Joppa and Caesarea was no exception. We'll look in our next chapter at how God was preparing Peter at Simon the tanner's house in Joppa (Acts 9:43). While at the same time, He was preparing for the work in Caesarea.

Most of the Roman soldiers in the Iudaean province were locally recruited. They tended to be more like mercenaries than professional soldiers. But the Centurion – Cornelius – led a contingent of one hundred professional soldiers that had been recruited and trained in Rome. This was an elite fighting force that was stationed in Caesarea because that is where Pilate and those who ruled the land lived. Remember that Romans, for the most part, were polytheistic pagans – worshipping many gods. Luke tells us that Cornelius was "God-fearing". He was not a Jewish proselyte, but he apparently prayed to Jehovah God and worshiped Him, albeit perhaps not exclusively. Interestingly, he was probably never taught by a rabbi as to "how" to pray to God. He prayed as best as he knew how – with a sincere heart. Also, he, uncharacteristically as an officer of the oppressing military force, gave gifts of charity to the oppressed poor. And as Luke points out, he did so generously.

In many respects, Cornelius was a model of religious respectability. On the outside he looked like many today, and on the inside he also looked like many – he did not yet have a true relationship with God. But unlike many today, he knew that his religious devotion was not sufficient to save him. Many today are satisfied that their character and good works will earn them a place in heaven, because they have no concept of their own sin or of God's grace. Cornelius, on the other hand did, and he was asking God to show him the way of salvation. God, by His grace, chose to hear the prayer of Cornelius. He will always respond to the prayer from the heart that is sincerely seeking Him.

Warren Wiersbe tells the story of John Wesley, who in many ways resembled Cornelius. "*Wesley was a religious man, a church member, a minister and the son of a minister. He belonged to a religious club at Oxford, the purpose of which was the perfecting of the Christian life. He served as a missionary, but even as he preached to others, he had no assurance of his own salvation. On May 24, 1738, he reluctantly attended a small meeting in London where someone was reading aloud from Martin Luther's writings on the Book of Romans. 'About a quarter before nine,' Wesley wrote in his personal journal, 'while he was describing the change which God works in the heart through faith in Christ, I felt my heart strangely warmed.'"* At that moment, Wesley surrendered his life to Christ, trusting Him alone for salvation. He stepped from religious beliefs into a relationship with Christ. The result was a revival that swept many into the Kingdom of God!

God sent one of His heavenly "soldiers" – an angel, and Cornelius immediately snapped to attention. The angel instructed Cornelius to send for Peter. Being the good military man that he was, Cornelius immediately obeyed.

Peter was God's man for this assignment. Very possibly, there were others who were closer to Caesarea than Peter. Philip may have already made his way back up the Mediterranean coast from Gaza. Saul had just sailed out of Caesarea not that long ago, and God could have orchestrated a visit while Saul was still in the city. And yet, God's plan involved Peter. Remember, Peter "held" the "keys to the Kingdom". The Father had ordained for him to be the one to open the door of faith to the Gentiles. And God was simultaneously at work in Peter's heart to prepare him to do just that. It would take an adjustment in Peter's life. It would require him to step out of his "comfort zone". It wouldn't have been as great of a stretch for Saul, or even Philip. But God's work wasn't about the worker's comfort. That's why God does not, most often, call the equipped, He equips the called (Hebrews 13:21). That's why He empowers us through His Spirit – the same Spirit who goes before us to make a way.

Most of you who are reading this book would be considered Gentiles – just like me. i am certain that as you look back on your life, you can "see" spiritual markers where God was divinely orchestrating events that He would use in your life for you to enter into His salvation – through His saving grace. But it is worthy to point out that this moment in Caesarea – and in Joppa – God was at work preparing the way for the door of faith to be opened to us. The obedience of Cornelius put in motion the means through which the door of faith was opened to you – and to me. Obedience that was as simple as sending two servants and a soldier to bring a message to Peter. In many respects, for a person of Cornelius' rank and position that was a small thing. But the ripple effect touches you and me today.

God is still at work preparing us for what He is preparing for us. No matter how small – or large – it may seem, trust Him and take the step. We have no idea what the ripple effects will be down the way… until He returns.

* * *

30

BEING PREPARED FOR WHAT'S AHEAD

The next day as Cornelius's messengers were nearing the town, Peter went up on the flat roof to pray. It was about noon, and he was hungry. But while a meal was being prepared, he fell into a trance. He saw the sky open, and something like a large sheet was let down by its four corners. In the sheet were all sorts of animals, reptiles, and birds. Then a voice said to him, "Get up, Peter; kill and eat them." "No, Lord," Peter declared. "I have never eaten anything that our Jewish laws have declared impure and unclean." But the voice spoke again: "Do not call something unclean if God has made it clean." The same vision was repeated three times. Then the sheet was suddenly pulled up to heaven. Peter was very perplexed. What could the vision mean? Just then the men sent by Cornelius found Simon's house. Standing outside the gate, they asked if a man named Simon Peter was staying there. Meanwhile, as Peter was puzzling over the vision, the Holy Spirit said to him, "Three men have come looking for you. Get up, go downstairs, and go with them without hesitation. Don't worry, for I have sent them." So Peter went down and said, "I'm the man you are looking for. Why have you come?" They said, "We were sent by Cornelius, a Roman officer. He is a devout and God-fearing man, well respected by all the Jews. A holy angel instructed him to summon you to his house so that he can hear your message." So Peter invited the men to stay for the night. The next day he went with them, accompanied by some of the brothers from Joppa.

Acts 10:9-23

* * *

God's timing is perfect – in His preparation and His invitation. The messengers from Cornelius were already en route and would soon arrive. Peter was on the roof resting before the noon meal. He was hungry. His stomach was probably growling. He began to dream about food. So God spoke to him in a language that would clearly speak to him at that moment. God was preparing Peter to not only receive the messengers, but also, to receive their invitation – which was truly His invitation. And God completed His preparation just as the messengers arrived.

As i write this, i am mindful of a personal experience that occurred just last week. Ten days ago, God began to stir my wife's and my hearts regarding a change in direction that we believed He was wanting to make within our small group. We planned to discuss it with the leaders of our group over our weekly meal that immediately precedes our discussion time. We love the members of our group and our leaders and wanted to make sure that the change truly was being Spirit-led and not "Ken and LaVonne led". Two hours before the starting time of our group, i received a call from our leader. God was stirring his heart that we needed to make a change. He was calling to see what we thought and what that new direction might be. He also was thinking that we needed to make a change that very night. Wasn't that a coincidence? NOT! We all immediately knew that God was speaking to all of our hearts and confirming the change of direction, and had already given us the plan of what that new direction was to be. Only God can orchestrate events with such perfect timing! You, too, have probably experienced similar "coincidences" in your life. The reality is that when we are walking according to the Spirit of God, there are no "coincidences". Our steps are being ordered by a Sovereign God who has a perfect plan, and He is orchestrating events for the accomplishment of that plan. Such was the case that day in Joppa.

As Peter's dream began, he knew right away that the voice that was speaking to him was that of the Lord. It is interesting that his first response was *"No, Lord!"* That answer reminds us of the same Peter who we all know never hesitated to speak up to Jesus. Do you remember the night in the upper room when Jesus was washing His disciples' feet? He came to Peter, and he refused, saying, *"No, Lord, You will never wash my feet"* (John 13:8). Though a lot had occurred in Peter's life since that night in the upper room, his flesh nature still was given to responding in a similar way. That is a reminder to each of us that we also can quickly be influenced by our flesh nature. Our initial response too often is born out of our flesh and not out of our spirit. We, like Peter, need to make sure that our response is Spirit-led. Also, we need to be mindful that when we know that the Lord is leading us to do something, the response can never be "No, Lord". Those two words can't go together in one sentence. Either

Jesus is Lord, and the answer is "yes", or the answer is "no" because He is not our Lord.

God will always reveal His will and purpose to us in a way that will enable us to understand. He is not in His heaven hoping we will figure it out. He will make it abundantly clear in a "language" that we will clearly understand. If we are in any doubt, all we need to do is ask Him to give us eyes and ears to see and hear Him clearly. Too often, the reason we are not clear is because we don't like what He has told us to do – not unlike Peter's first response.

The distinction between foods that were clean and those that were unclean was a major point of contention between Jews and Gentiles – not only in that day, but also for the centuries that had passed before, and those that have passed since. In that light, the Lord was directing Peter in a truth that He had already taught His apostles one day in Galilee while He was with them. He had just rebuked the Pharisees for being more concerned about their food laws and ceremonial cleaning laws than they were about the condition of their hearts and truly honoring God. Then He had turned to the crowd and said, *"All of you listen," He said, "and try to understand. It's not what goes into your body that defiles you; you are defiled by what comes from your heart"* (Mark 7:14-15). Right after that, Jesus led His disciples into a house to get away from the crowd, and *"His disciples asked Him what He meant…. 'Can't you see that the food you put into your body cannot defile you? Food doesn't go into your heart, but only passes through the stomach and then goes into the sewer.' (By saying this, He declared that every kind of food is acceptable in God's eyes.) And then He added, 'It is what comes from inside that defiles you. For from within, out of a person's heart, come evil thoughts, sexual immorality, theft, murder, adultery, greed, wickedness, deceit, lustful desires, envy, slander, pride, and foolishness. All these vile things come from within; they are what defile you.'"* (Mark 7:17-23)

It is interesting to remember that Mark penned his Gospel account from the eyewitness testimony of Peter. The parenthetical note about the acceptability of "every kind of food" is an indication from Peter that he now knew that what Jesus had taught all of His disciples that day in Galilee was the same truth He had taught him through the dream this day in Joppa.

So here are the take-aways for us to carry with us in our journey… until

He returns. First, we will never know the truth of any situation until we have heard from God. That which He calls clean, can never be unclean; and that which He calls unclean, can never be called clean. The world – or the religious leaders – don't set the rules, God does! Second, He will reveal His Truth, His purpose and His plan in a way that is clear, and in a way that is timely. When God has revealed a truth to you, be watchful – He is preparing to lead you into a situation where you will need to apply it! Third, the correct response to God when He directs is, "Yes, Lord!" – and never "no". He is preparing you and guiding you in what's ahead. Follow Him… because the messengers have come for you. They are at the door – and His time is now.

* * *

31

CAN ANYONE OBJECT?

They arrived in Caesarea the following day.... As Peter entered his home, Cornelius fell at his feet and worshiped him. But Peter pulled him up and said, "Stand up! I'm a human being just like you!" So they talked together and went inside, where many others were assembled. Peter told them, "You know it is against our laws for a Jewish man to enter a Gentile home like this or to associate with you. But God has shown me that I should no longer think of anyone as impure or unclean. So I came without objection as soon as I was sent for. Now tell me why you sent for me." Cornelius replied, "Four days ago I was praying in my house.... Suddenly, a man in dazzling clothes was standing in front of me. He told me, 'Cornelius, your prayer has been heard, and your gifts to the poor have been noticed by God! Now send messengers to Joppa, and summon a man named Simon Peter....' So I sent for you at once, and it was good of you to come. Now we are all here, waiting before God to hear the message the Lord has given you." Then Peter replied, "I see very clearly that God shows no favoritism. In every nation He accepts those who fear Him and do what is right. This is the message of Good News for the people of Israel – that there is peace with God through Jesus Christ, who is Lord of all.... He is the one all the prophets testified about, saying that everyone who believes in Him will have their sins forgiven through His name." Even as Peter was saying these things, the Holy Spirit fell upon all who were listening to the message. The Jewish believers who came with Peter were amazed that the gift of the Holy Spirit had been poured out on the Gentiles, too. For they heard them speaking in other tongues and praising God. Then Peter asked, "Can anyone object to their being baptized, now that they have received the Holy Spirit just as we did?" So he gave orders for them to be baptized in the name of Jesus Christ....

Acts 10:24-48

* * *

At the beginning of all of this, Cornelius did not have a saving relationship with God. He knew within his heart that there was one true God. He knew that the one true God was not any one of the countless gods that were recognized by his people, the Romans. The gospel had not yet come to the Romans. They were, what we would call today, an "unreached people group" – without knowledge of the gospel, or access to the gospel from within their own people. There was a growing desire within Cornelius' heart to know this one true God, and he began to search. He knew that he must search outside of his Roman people group.

Cornelius was like every one of us. His Creator created him with the innate need for relationship with Him. Cornelius was a successful officer within the greatest army that existed in the world at the time. The Romans dominated the known world. Cornelius had great reason to be content with what he had achieved in life. And yet, he knew that there must be more. God not only created him with the need; He also gave him a desire to seek that "something more". As Cornelius responded to that desire and began to diligently seek the one true God, He directed his steps – because God "*rewards those who sincerely seek Him*" (Hebrews 11:6). God directed him to seek the "Jehovah God" of the Jews. Cornelius began to pray to Him – not yet truly knowing Him. God answered his prayer and led him, in an extraordinary way, to the truth whereby he could enter into a personal saving relationship with the one true God. Then through this one, and the family and friends gathered with him, God opened the door of the gospel to the entire unreached people group (the Romans) and all of the unreached people groups that were or forever would be (the ends of the earth). As i've said before, God wasn't just hoping he would figure it out! He, who created him with the need to know God, gave him the desire to seek Him, and directed his path to find Him through His messenger, having also directed the steps of His messenger to seek him. Peter said, "*I see very clearly that God shows no favoritism. In every nation He accepts those who fear Him*" (verse 34-35). God was prepared to work wonders to bring Cornelius to the gospel – and the gospel to Cornelius.

Luke writes in verse 31 that Cornelius told Peter that the angel said to him, "*Cornelius, your prayer has been heard, and your gifts to the poor have been noticed by God! Now send messengers to Joppa, and summon a man named Simon Peter....*" This implies that the prayers were for God to send him what he needed in order to be saved. God accepted his prayer and his "groping for truth" in his life, and worked wonders to bring the saving message of the gospel to him. Paul describes this "groping for truth" when he says, "{God} *made from one man every nation of mankind to live on all the face of the earth, having determined their appointed times and the boundaries of their habitation, that they would seek God, if perhaps they might grope for Him and find Him, though He is not far from each one of us*" (Acts 17:26-27 NASB).

Through his journey to seek God, Cornelius shed any objection that he had toward God. He had shed the objections of false religion, self-sufficiency, selfish ambition, and pride. Through Peter's journey to follow His Lord, he had shed his objections of religious pride, ethnic bigotry and personal prejudice, such that he came to Cornelius *"without objection"*. Most importantly, God Himself had no objection! The Father sent the Son to redeem a lost world to Himself – peoples of every tribe, language and nation. There was, however, one objection – and that objection existed within, of all places, the body of believers – the church! Those who were the recipients of God's grace had somehow come to believe that they were uniquely qualified to receive God's grace, while others (the Gentiles) were not. Their objection was a direct contradiction to the idea of grace. Grace is unmerited favor extended to all. No one can have a corner on grace, or it ceases to be grace.

Our objections can be expressed passively or aggressively, or both. They can be voiced wantonly and selfishly through our self-serving remarks and actions – even within the church – that disparage being obedient to our Lord's commission for fear that it will take away from our own needs or wants being met. Or, even more often, they can be expressed passively, through our failure to be obedient to what God has called us to do. The first century church needed to shed its objections – and the same is true for us today.

First, no human being is excluded from the saving grace of the gospel. No one is less deserving than another. We are ALL undeserving! No one is to be spurned, shunned, rejected, or despised because of his/her ethnic origin or race or culture or physical traits. Followers of Jesus should have no part in the kind of renewed racism that is cropping up around our nation today. Second, within every ethnic people group around the world, there are people being prepared by God to seek Him as they call out through prayer to a God who they do not yet know. Therefore, we are to go! We cannot stay where we are. For some of us, it will be to the other side of the world; for others of us, it will be to the other side of the street.

Cornelius would not have been saved if no one had taken the gospel to him. And no one will be saved today without the gospel. Also, we must be full of hope and expectancy that God is still at work making connections between the "groping" of unreached peoples and those willing to take the gospel to them.

The Jewish believers who came with Peter stood in amazement as the gift of the Holy Spirit was poured out on the Gentiles. Peter asked them, *"Can anyone object to their being baptized?"*

We, too, can no longer object. God is still working wonders to bring the unreached to the gospel – and the gospel to the unreached. So, let us wash our minds and our mouths of all racial slurs and ethnic put-downs, and be done with all alienating behaviors. Let's be the Peter for some waiting Cornelius. Let's be the good Samaritan for some ethnic outcast. And, let's be the hands of Christ for some untouchable leper… until He returns.

* * *

32

THE LITTLE CHURCH THAT COULD

Meanwhile, the believers who had been scattered during the persecution after Stephen's death traveled as far as Phoenicia, Cyprus, and Antioch of Syria. They preached the word of God, but only to Jews. However, some of the believers who went to Antioch from Cyprus and Cyrene began preaching to the Gentiles about the Lord Jesus. The power of the Lord was with them, and a large number of these Gentiles believed and turned to the Lord. When the church at Jerusalem heard what had happened, they sent Barnabas to Antioch. When he arrived and saw this evidence of God's blessing, he was filled with joy, and he encouraged the believers to stay true to the Lord. Barnabas was a good man, full of the Holy Spirit and strong in faith. And many people were brought to the Lord. Then Barnabas went on to Tarsus to look for Saul. When he found him, he brought him back to Antioch. Both of them stayed there with the church for a full year, teaching large crowds of people. (It was at Antioch that the believers were first called Christians.) During this time some prophets traveled from Jerusalem to Antioch. One of them named Agabus stood up in one of the meetings and predicted by the Spirit that a great famine was coming upon the entire Roman world. (This was fulfilled during the reign of Claudius.) So the believers in Antioch decided to send relief to the brothers and sisters in Judea, everyone giving as much as they could. This they did, entrusting their gifts to Barnabas and Saul to take to the elders of the church in Jerusalem.

Acts 11:19-30

* * *

Saul had a hand in planting the church in Antioch – albeit unintentional. His persecution of the church in Jerusalem, and the stoning of Stephen, as he held the cloaks of the persecutors, led to the scattering, that led to the planting of this new church. It is a reminder that what the enemy intends for evil, God can use for good (Genesis 50:20). God was planting Antioch to be a strategic center that He would use for the advancement of the gospel throughout Asia.

The capital of Syria, three hundred miles north of Jerusalem, Antioch boasted a population of half a million people which made it the third largest city in the Roman Empire, surpassed only by Rome and Alexandria. A busy port and a center for luxury and culture, Antioch attracted all kinds of people, including wealthy retired Roman officials who spent their days chatting in the baths or gambling at the chariot races. With its large cosmopolitan population and its great commercial and political power, the general populace wanted for very little, including a Jewish Messiah. Antioch was also a very wicked city, perhaps eclipsed only by Corinth. Though all of the Syrian, Greek and Roman deities were honored in the city, the principal shrine was dedicated to Daphne, whose worship included immoral rituals. It was a city filled with every epicurean delight of the day.

Antioch presented to those scattered believers a very different field for evangelism, but they were armed with the Word of God on their lips and the Spirit of God in their hearts. As a result, *"a large number of these Gentiles believed and turned to the Lord."* The response was so significant that the elders of the church in Jerusalem commissioned Barnabas to go to Antioch to find out what was happening among the Gentiles. Gratefully the elders sent an encourager, one who was filled with faith and the Holy Spirit, so he did not go to control a mission, but to encourage a Spirit-filled movement. Through his encouragement, the church continued to grow and multiply, and there was now need for another shepherd to nurture and disciple this growing flock.

Barnabas could have easily sent word back to the elders in Jerusalem with a request for them to send someone to assist him. But Barnabas knew that God had commissioned Saul to minister to the Gentiles, so he didn't take the easy route of sending a messenger to Jerusalem, he took the "road" of greater effort and traveled personally to Tarsus. Remember, Barnabas had not seen Saul for seven years, and they had only actually been together for a few weeks in Jerusalem. Yet, he knew by faith that Saul was God's person for the job. God had used Barnabas to encourage and pour into

Saul's life in Jerusalem, and now the Lord was giving him more opportunity to do the same, as together they now co-labored in Antioch for a year.

Remember that Jesus had instructed Saul for three years in the wilderness of Arabia. He had equipped him as His apostle to make disciples of the Gentiles and to teach them to obey everything He commanded. For the past seven years, the Lord had continued that work of molding and shaping Saul as He prepared him now for this work in Antioch. Luke tells us that it was in Antioch *"that the believers were first called Christians."* In that day, it distinguished the believers as followers of Jesus. They became known as a people that sought after, followed and radiated Jesus. Unfortunately, due to our own actions, and those of many generations before us, the term "Christian" has lost a great deal of significance over the years, and now simply describes a culture, a tradition, a parentage or a religion, instead of a relationship with the One whose name we bear.

One of the first ways that the believers began to demonstrate their faith in Christ was through the giving of their financial resources to assist their persecuted brothers and sisters in Judea through an impending famine. They knew that to whom much has been given, much is required. They knew that the gospel had been given to them at a cost of great price – the shed blood of Jesus – and the message had been brought to them also at a cost of great price – the blood of the martyrs. They knew that whatever they gave paled in comparison to the price the Judean believers had given for them – so everyone gave as much as they could. And it is interesting to note one of the great ironies – that when they sent their gifts to Jerusalem, they did so through Barnabas and Saul (the one who was now bringing relief back to the very church that he had persecuted).

Most of us are by-products of that little church that could. Perhaps not of the financial relief that they sent to Judea, but definitely of the Good News that they sent throughout Asia and Europe. God used a handful of seeds that were sent out from a persecuted church that were, in turn, multiplied by a little church that could. God used them to touch a world for time and eternity. And He intends to do the same through us, if we too will be the little church that can… until He returns.

* * *

33

LORD, WHAT ABOUT HIM?

About that time King Herod Agrippa began to persecute some believers in the church. He had the apostle James (John's brother) killed with a sword. When Herod saw how much this pleased the Jewish people, he also arrested Peter. (This took place during the Passover celebration.) Then he imprisoned him, placing him under the guard of four squads of four soldiers each. Herod intended to bring Peter out for public trial after the Passover. But while Peter was in prison, the church prayed very earnestly for him. The night before Peter was to be placed on trial, he was asleep, fastened with two chains between two soldiers. Others stood guard at the prison gate. Suddenly, there was a bright light in the cell, and an angel of the Lord stood before Peter. The angel struck him on the side to awaken him and said, "Quick! Get up!" And the chains fell off his wrists. Then the angel told him, "Get dressed and put on your sandals." And he did. "Now put on your coat and follow me," the angel ordered. So Peter left the cell, following the angel. But all the time he thought it was a vision. He didn't realize it was actually happening. They passed the first and second guard posts and came to the iron gate leading to the city, and this opened for them all by itself. So they passed through and started walking down the street, and then the angel suddenly left him…. At dawn there was a great commotion among the soldiers about what had happened to Peter. Herod Agrippa ordered a thorough search for him. When he couldn't be found, Herod interrogated the guards and sentenced them to death….
Acts 12:1-19

* * *

Several years ago, i participated in a wilderness safety, survival and security training in the mountains of Idaho with about thirty other people. Though i didn't know most of the folks going into the training, a shared experience like that creates a bond that sticks with you for the rest of your lives. Two of those folks – a husband and wife – and i were teamed together for several of the exercises. They – like the rest – will forever hold a special place in my heart. Over the years since then, i have seen God use this couple – Steve and Laura – in phenomenal ways in the advancement of the message of the Good News across the globe. He has ordered their steps and worked through them to have eternal impact for the Kingdom. In the midst of that activity, Steve was diagnosed with liver cancer. In recent months, he was in and out of the hospital – until one day the Lord delivered him from his frail body and took him home to heaven. The physical battle was intense – and while we prayed for healing, we also prayed for grace and strength, and restorative rest in the midst of the battle. One of their prayer requests was that God would grant Steve the time on this side of glory to finish a specific project that He had placed before him to do. By His grace, God granted Steve with that time, and he and his son were able to complete the project before God took him home.

In times like those, we tend to want to ask God, why them? Why are they having to walk through this difficult journey? And, if we were to be totally honest – and if we are walking through a difficult journey ourselves – we may sometimes want to ask God, why are we walking through this, while others are not seemingly needing to carry such a heavy burden? If you ask the latter question, you are in good company. You're asking the same question Peter asked Jesus.

You will recall that toward the end of the last chapter of John's Gospel, Jesus told Peter the manner in which he would die. It would be a painful and brutal death. Peter's immediate response was to direct the Lord's attention to John and ask, *"Lord, what about him?"* (John 21:21 CEV). This wasn't the first time, or the last, that followers of Jesus endeavored to compare themselves to other believers to determine whether they or the other person got the better deal. Peter wanted to know if his death was going to be in a manner that was more or less brutal than John's. Prior to this, the disciples often speculated as to which one of them would have the greatest position in the Kingdom. As the new church emerged, the widows were squabbling over who was receiving more attention or care from the apostles.

This idea of comparing ourselves to others didn't start with them. It started with Cain comparing the way God accepted Abel's offering to the way He refused to accept his. It continued with the competition that developed between Rachel and Leah for greater favor from God. And it didn't stop with them. How often do we compare ourselves to other followers of Jesus and ask:

- Why did Jesus heal him/her and not me?
- Why am i needing to walk through this betrayal and loneliness and others are not?
- Why am i walking through such great financial difficulty when others seem to be so much more successful?
- And so on.

Or allow me to frame the question in a slightly different way. But before i do, allow me to take a quick side road in Roman history. Tiberius was the Roman Emperor when Jesus was crucified. Upon his death in 37 A.D., Caligula became Emperor. His reign, however, was short-lived and he was assassinated in 41 A.D. There was a political struggle in Rome and Herod Agrippa backed the right man. Thus, when Claudius became the new Roman Emperor, he withdrew the current prefect (of which Pontius Pilate had been the fifth in a long line) from the rule of the Iudaean province, and replaced him with his ally Herod Agrippa. Soon after becoming the puppet King, Herod Agrippa arrested the apostles James and Peter in order to gain favor with the Jewish religious leaders.

Now, back to the question. James and Peter weren't doing anything illegal. As a matter of fact, they were doing exactly what Jesus had told them to do. They were both making disciples. The church in Jerusalem prayed for the release and safety of both men with equal fervency. But James was killed, while Peter was miraculously delivered from prison by an angel. Now where is the fairness or the equity in that? Does it mean that God loved Peter more than He loved James?

And what about us? One is miraculously healed of a terminal illness, and yet another suffers and dies? One seems to prosper in all that he/she does, and yet another who is working equally as hard can't seem to get ahead? Or why is one couple able to have children and another can't? The list of comparisons can be unending. And as we make those comparisons, it can often appear that God is very unfair.

. . .

In the case of Peter, John and James, the Father ordained for them to walk in very different paths. But you and i – and every follower since them – have been enriched by all three of their lives, their ministries and their testimonies. God was at work – and continues to be – through each one of their lives and through their very different paths.

It is imperative that we remember how Jesus responded to Peter, when he asked his question. Jesus replied, *"If I want him to remain alive until I return, what is that to you? As for you, follow Me"* (John 21:22 NLT). Jesus was acknowledging that all of our paths will be different. Even John's path would not be easy. But regardless of our path, we are to follow Him. And if we follow Him, we will end up right where He wants us to be. Paul encouraged the believers in Corinth when he wrote, *"…our Lord Jesus Christ … will sustain you to the end…"* (1 Corinthians 1:7-8 ESV). Take heart and strength in that promise! Our Lord Jesus Christ will sustain us. He will comfort us. He will enable us. He will encourage us. He will strengthen us. He will carry us. He will hearten us. To the end! And it will end. And it will end in His glory! His plan and purpose will be fulfilled. Trust His word. Trust His promise. Trust Him!

No matter what you are walking through today – good times or hardship – remember Jesus' words – *"As for you, follow Me!"* And remain faithful to do so… until He returns.

* * *

34

GOD DOESN'T SHARE HIS GLORY

Now Herod was very angry with the people of Tyre and Sidon. So they sent a delegation to make peace with him because their cities were dependent upon Herod's country for food. The delegates won the support of Blastus, Herod's personal assistant, and an appointment with Herod was granted. When the day arrived, Herod put on his royal robes, sat on his throne, and made a speech to them. The people gave him a great ovation, shouting, "It's the voice of a god, not of a man!" Instantly, an angel of the Lord struck Herod with a sickness, because he accepted the people's worship instead of giving the glory to God. So he was consumed with worms and died.

Acts 12:20-23

* * *

Just a few reminders – some of which are from our last chapter. Herod Agrippa was the grandson of Herod the Great. In 41 A.D., the new Roman Emperor Claudius rewarded Herod for his loyalty by placing him as puppet King over the Iudaean province, which included Judea, Samaria and Idumea (encompassing the lower two-thirds of what is the modern day nation of Israel). His grandfather had governed this region as a client kingdom under the authority of the Roman Emperor, as had Herod Archelaus, his uncle. Between Archelaus and Agrippa, a succession of seven Roman prefects had governed the region. Agrippa's rule only lasted for four years, but he was a cunning and ambitious ruler. He parlayed his favor with Caesar Claudius (and Caesar Caligula before him) to bring about the banishment of his uncle, Herod Antipas, and the merging of the provinces he had ruled (Galilee and Perea) into Iudaea. He was the last Herodian to govern the region. Upon his death, the entire region returned to direct Roman rule.

The cities of Tyre and Sidon were not under the rule of Herod Agrippa. They were a part of the Phoenician province under the direct control of Rome. The Phoenician and Iudaean provinces enjoyed strong commercial relations with one another. Tyre and Sidon relied heavily on the corn, oil and wine that they imported from Iudaea. Apparently, Agrippa had become angry with the people of the two cities due to some perceived affront. Since both regions were under Roman rule, Agrippa was prohibited from seeking a military solution – but, he was free to pursue an economic one. He was threatening to withhold the vital food exports that the two cities needed. The two cities quickly resolved to seek peace with Agrippa over their affront by employing the tactic of flattery. The representatives knew that their plan would have better success if they sought out an ally within Agrippa's court. Apparently, they found one in Blastus, Herod's chamberlain and personal assistant – more than likely, by bribing him.

Josephus records that on the day of their appointment, Agrippa wore *"a garment made wholly of silver, of a truly wonderful texture…."* On the morning that he entered the theater where their audience was to take place, the risen sun reflected brilliantly off of the garment. *"There the silver of his garment, being illuminated by the fresh reflection of the sun's rays, shone out in a wonderful manner, and was so resplendent as to spread awe over those that looked intently upon him."* Apparently, the motivation of their mission, combined with the spectacle that he made through the garment that he wore, caused *"his flatterers* to cry *out, one from one place, and another from another, that he was a god."*

The men of Tyre and Sidon worshiped pagan gods. Though their statements and accolades were an abomination, they had no understanding of how they were profaning a Holy God. But Agrippa knew. He had been schooled in the Law given through Moses. He knew that only One was due worship, honor and reverence. He knew that to receive such flattery was sinful and blasphemous. Yet, he neither rebuked them nor rejected their impetuous and irreverent flattery. Instead, he received it unto himself and took pleasure in it. He arrogantly accepted worship that is only due to the Almighty God and, in so doing, attempted to keep it for himself. Instead of giving glory to God, he retained the glory for himself. But God will not be mocked. He will not share His glory with anyone else! (Isaiah 48:11). Instantly, an angel of the Lord struck Herod, and five days later he died. It's interesting to note that God did not strike him dead because he was responsible for having the apostle James killed. Herod will be accountable for that act on the Day of Judgement, but he wasn't immediately put to death for that reason. He was struck dead because he attempted to rob God of His glory.

God is jealous for His glory! When we are jealous for our glory, it is the sin of our selfish pride. But it is not sinful for God to be jealous for His glory, because He alone is worthy of glory and all glory is due Him. We see God's zeal for His glory evidenced throughout all of Scripture:

- **God chose His people for His glory (Ephesians 1:4-6).**
- **God created us for His glory (Isaiah 43:6-7).**
- **God called Israel for His glory (Isaiah 49:3; Jeremiah 13:11).**
- **God rescued Israel from Egypt for His glory (Psalm106:7-8).**
- **God raised up Pharaoh to show His power and glorify His name (Romans 9:17).**
- **God defeated Pharaoh at the Red Sea to show His glory (Exodus 14:4).**
- **God spared Israel in the wilderness for the glory of His name (Ezekiel 20:14).**
- **God gave Israel victory in Canaan for the glory of His name (2 Samuel 7:23).**
- **God did not cast away His people for the glory of His name (1 Samuel 12:20,22).**
- **God saved Jerusalem from attack for the glory of His name (2 Kings 19:34).**
- **God restored Israel from exile for the glory of His name (Ezekiel 36:22-23).**
- **Jesus sought the glory of His Father in all He did (John 7:18).**
- **Jesus told us to do good works so that God gets glory (Matthew 5:16).**
- **Jesus said that He answers prayer that God would be glorified (John 14:13).**
- **Jesus endured His final hours of suffering for God's glory (John 12:27-28).**
- **God gave His Son to vindicate the glory of His righteousness in forgiving us (Romans 3:25-26).**
- **God forgives our sins for the glory of His Name (Isaiah 43:25, Psalm 25:11).**

- **Jesus receives us into His fellowship for the glory of God (Romans 15:7).**
- **The ministry of the Holy Spirit is to glorify the Son of God (John 16:14).**
- **God instructs us to do everything for His glory (1 Corinthians 10:31).**
- **God tells us to serve in a way that will glorify Him (1 Peter 4:11).**
- **Jesus will fill us with fruits of righteousness for God's glory (Philippians 1:9, 11).**
- **All are under judgment for dishonoring God's glory (Romans 1:22-23; Romans 3:23).**
- **Jesus is coming again for the glory of God (2 Thessalonians 1:9-10).**
- **Jesus' ultimate aim for us is that we see and experience His glory (John 17:24).**
- **Even in wrath God's aim is to make known the wealth of His glory (Romans 9:22-23).**
- **God's plan is to fill the earth with the knowledge of His glory (Habakkuk 2:14).**

Allow this to serve as a reminder for each one of us today. First, let us be mindful that all glory is due to God alone. The next time someone attempts to give the glory to you, pass it on to the One to whom it is due. It can be tempting to hold onto it and allow our egos to be stroked. But don't make the same mistake Agrippa made. We are but servants of the Most High God – all honor and praise is due to Him – and Him alone!

Second, remember that God created us for His glory. He redeemed us for His glory. He orders our steps for His glory. He has placed our feet on the path we are currently walking on for His glory. Even the wilderness that we may currently be walking in is ultimately for His glory. So, hold onto this truth, no matter where you are, or what is happening… until He returns:

For everything comes from Him and exists by His power and is intended for His glory. All glory to Him forever! Amen.
(Romans 11:36)

* * *

35

A SENDING CHURCH

Among the prophets and teachers of the church at Antioch of Syria were Barnabas, Simeon (called "the black man"), Lucius (from Cyrene), Manaen (the childhood companion of King Herod Antipas), and Saul. One day as these men were worshiping the Lord and fasting, the Holy Spirit said, "Appoint Barnabas and Saul for the special work to which I have called them." So after more fasting and prayer, the men laid their hands on them and sent them on their way.
Acts 13:1-3

* * *

The leaders of the church at Antioch gathered to fast, pray and worship – seeking clear guidance from the Lord. The church was at a point in their history when they needed a word from God about their next crucial step. i doubt that they realized what the Holy Spirit would say, and how monumental that step would be – God was about to use them to change the world forever.

And what a diverse group it was! Barnabas (the "son of encouragement") was a Levite from the island of Cyprus. Simeon was a dark-skinned Gentile believer from Africa. Lucius was probably a Cyrenian Jew who was one *"of the believers who went to Antioch from Cyprus and Cyrene"* {to begin} *"preaching to the Gentiles about the Lord Jesus"* (Acts 11:20-21). Manaen, who we will probe a little further in a moment, was raised in the luxury of the court of Herod the Great. Saul, a Jewish scholar from Tarsus in Cilicia, was a former persecutor of the church. None of them were originally from Antioch. All of them came from very different backgrounds. They were different ethnicities and races. They spoke different languages. They had very different "religious" backgrounds. They truly only had one thing in common – and that was that they were all followers of Jesus – who were prepared to go wherever He led. He had led them all to Antioch for this season and for His divine purpose. He had brought them together with a heart to follow Jesus and a heart to lead this newly-formed church in how to send out witnesses to places as diverse as the ones from which they had come. At least three of them would go out from this place – Barnabas and Saul, who we see being sent out in this passage – and Lucius, who we later read was with Paul in Corinth (Romans 16:21). We don't know what subsequently happened with Simeon and Manaen, though we know they had a heart to go because God had sent them to Antioch. God may have kept them there to shepherd this church that He was raising up to be a sending church – sending forth witnesses of His gospel to the ends of the earth.

We have already begun to probe the lives of Saul and Barnabas and seen how God had uniquely ordered their steps in preparation for what He was going to do through them in the years ahead. God had also been uniquely preparing the other three, through the twists and turns of their life journeys – twists and turns that no one could have ever imagined would lead to this place at this moment.

Let's look specifically at the life of Manaen. Historians of the early church tell us that when Herod the Great attained the summit of his power, he sought the counsel of an Essene by the name of Manaen, whom he had known as a boy. It is believed that through their friendship, Herod offered to be the patron of his son (or grandson), who also was named Manaen. It would have been a significant adjustment for Manaen to leave the stern purity of the life of the Essenes to now enter into the pomp and luxury of the court of Herod, and to be raised as the foster brother of Herod's sons – Antipas and Archelaus. This was followed by an even greater change when all three boys were sent to receive their educations in Rome. After receiving his education, Manaen continued to be attached to the royal household, having adopted the life and principles of those with whom he lived. The bond between Manaen and Antipas was apparently strong, so that when Herod the Great died, Manaen moved with Antipas as he became the client king over Galilee and Perea. Manaen appears to have turned a blind eye to Antipas' incestuous marriage to Herodias, but the teachings of John the Baptist apparently still had some effect on him. As time went on, several in the court of Antipas became disciples of John, and, soon after, others became disciples of Jesus. It would appear that the witness of these disciples had an ever-increasing influence on Manaen, as it did on others in the household. The imprisonment of John brought him into closer contact with those in the household of Antipas, who himself "heard John gladly." The turning point in Manaen's life may possibly have been the beheading of John. It is not known how much longer he remained in court after that event. Antipas was banished and exiled to Spain soon after Agrippa became King. But it is likely that Manaen left sometime before that – probably when he became a follower of Jesus. It could have been through the influence of Chuza, the manager of the Kings' household, and his wife, Joanna, prior to Jesus' crucifixion, or it may have occurred sometime soon after.

It is here in this passage in Acts that we have the first actual mention of Manaen. Though most of us would struggle to remember his name, we are recipients of his influence. He was one of the leaders of the church that God used to send out Barnabas and Saul with the witness of the gospel that was subsequently spread around the world – and at some point arrived to each one of us. He was a great encourager and supporter of Saul in that endeavor. There is a strong probability that Manaen's influential relationships with the Herodians and Romans proved to be beneficial in assisting Saul in his ministry and travels throughout the years. Luke's life as a follower of Jesus also appears to have begun at Antioch. (There are some who would go further and contend that Lucius and Dr. Luke are the same person.) Regardless, Manaen was more than likely Luke's source for many of the facts about the history of John the Baptist, and the details of multiple generations of Herodian rule, which he incorporated into his Gospel account.

We never know how God will use the experiences and relationships in our lives to further His purpose and plan through our lives. We must think of ourselves as an arrow being sent by the bow in the hands of the Master Archer. His aim is true. He always hits His target. He has shaped each of us uniquely as arrows, fittingly suited for the path and the target. We may have been designed for different purposes with different backgrounds, different ethnicities, different languages, and different races. But we have all been crafted as an "arrow" for His purpose. We have all been sent! None of us have been crafted to remain in the quiver. None of our churches have been planted to be permanent waiting rooms. These men led their church to lay their hands on Barnabas and Saul and "let them loose" (send them on their way). May that be true of each of our churches… and each of our lives… until He returns!

* * *

36

GREATER IS HE THAT IS IN US

Afterward they traveled from town to town across the entire island until finally they reached Paphos, where they met a Jewish sorcerer, a false prophet named Bar-Jesus. He had attached himself to the governor, Sergius Paulus, who was an intelligent man. The governor invited Barnabas and Saul to visit him, for he wanted to hear the word of God. But Elymas, the sorcerer (as his name means in Greek), interfered and urged the governor to pay no attention to what Barnabas and Saul said. He was trying to keep the governor from believing. Saul, also known as Paul, was filled with the Holy Spirit, and he looked the sorcerer in the eye. Then he said, "You son of the devil, full of every sort of deceit and fraud, and enemy of all that is good! Will you never stop perverting the true ways of the Lord? Watch now, for the Lord has laid his hand of punishment upon you, and you will be struck blind. You will not see the sunlight for some time." Instantly mist and darkness came over the man's eyes, and he began groping around begging for someone to take his hand and lead him. When the governor saw what had happened, he became a believer, for he was astonished at the teaching about the Lord.

Acts 13:6-12

* * *

When the Word of God is proclaimed, you can be assured that the enemy will send his representatives to try to oppose and pervert the truth, and try to discourage the proclaimer. That is a good reminder why God hasn't called us to be "Lone Ranger" followers. He has placed us within a body of believers and most often sends us out in teams of two or more, just as He did His disciples in Luke 10, so that we can encourage, exhort and uphold one another. But even more importantly, Jesus did not send us out alone. He gave us His Holy Spirit to dwell within us so that by Him we are empowered to be His witnesses (Acts 1:8). And John wrote to remind us: *"He who is in you is greater than he who is in the world"* (1 John 4:4 ESV). Jesus knows who and what we will encounter. He has known it since before the beginning of time and He has given us all that we need to overcome it.

Such was the case that day in Paphos. God in His sovereignty orchestrated that four men would encounter one another in the governor's court in this Roman capital of Cyprus. The first was a man named Joseph, who had become Barnabas. God had gifted him to be an encourager and an exhorter. Barnabas had the ability to enable those around him who were down to be lifted up. However, he wasn't "Pollyannaish", dispensing a hollow hope built on a substanceless foundation. He was an ambassador of the hope, assurance and encouragement that is built on the substantial Truth of God. It was that Truth that had given him the confidence to bring Saul before the apostles in Jerusalem when they feared him. It was that Truth that had enabled him to know that he was to bring Saul to Antioch to disciple those new believers. It was that Truth that now gave him the courage and the boldness to stand before a demon-filled sorcerer.

The second was a man named Saul, who in Paphos became known as Paul. The name "Paul" means "small or little". Some contend that he took that name as an act of humility, but all would agree he changed his name as a clear reminder to all that he was no longer Saul, the persecutor of the church, he was now Paul, servant of Christ. Paul was a student and a bold proclaimer of Truth. He had studied the Scripture at the feet of some of the best Jewish Scholars. He had travelled throughout the wilderness of Arabia being schooled by none other than Jesus Himself. And He had the Spirit of Christ dwelling within him. He could proclaim the Truth with confidence because he knew the One from whom it had come. He could proclaim the Truth boldly because he knew the One who had called him to carry it forth.

The giftedness of these two men complimented one another. The encouraging nature of Barnabas opened doors through which Paul was able to speak apostolic words of Truth. The prophetic nature of Paul provoked Barnabas to even greater understanding of the Truths of God which enabled him to be an even greater exhorter and encourager. God knew exactly what each of these two men needed and sovereignly brought them together for His purpose.

The third was a man named Bar-Jesus, who became known as Elymas. This instrument of deceit and fraud was a Jewish sorcerer. Talk about an oxymoron! The Jews were chosen and set apart by God to be His people, but this sorcerer – this dispenser of black magic – had chosen to be a servant of Satan. Apparently his assignment from the evil one was to keep the governor from ever accepting the Truth by blinding him and frustrating the attempts of Barnabas and Paul to proclaim the Truth to him. That continues to be Satan's strategy today.

The fourth was a man named Sergius Paulus, the governor of Cyprus. Sergius Paulus was a seeker of Truth. He had invited Barnabas and Paul to visit him because he wanted to hear and know the Truth. The enemy did not want that to happen. He never does! Elymas distracted the governor with his magic, his lies and his interruptions. But Satan knew that he was a defeated foe – and he remains a defeated foe. As the liar that he is, he had never told Elymas that his efforts would ultimately fail. Thus, his instrument, Elymas, was on the losing side of the battle. He may have appeared to be victorious for the moment, but his victory was short-lived. It always is! Satan will never prevail – no matter how dark things may look at the moment. Our Almighty God is the Sovereign Victor!

God, through His Spirit, enabled Paul to boldly confront the lies with Truth. As a result, the eyes of Sergius Paulus were opened, and the eyes of Elymas were blinded. God in His sovereignty even used the defeat of the deception of Elymas to bring Himself glory. What Satan had intended for evil, God used for His glory (Romans 8:28; Genesis 50:20). God still does – and He always will.

Are you being confronted by an "Elymas" who is spreading lies and attempting to defeat you today? Remember, *"He who is in you is greater…."* Has God brought a "Sergius Paulus" across your path who needs to hear God's Truth today? Be the "Barnabas" or the "Paul" that he/she needs to hear from, and remember, *"He who is in you is greater…."* And He will always be… until He returns.

* * *

37

THEY JUDGED THEMSELVES TO BE UNWORTHY

Paul and his companions then left Paphos by ship for Pamphylia, landing at the port town of Perga.... But Paul and Barnabas traveled inland to Antioch of Pisidia. On the Sabbath they went to the synagogue for the services. After the usual readings from the books of Moses and the prophets, those in charge of the service sent them this message: "Brothers, if you have any word of encouragement for the people, come and give it." So Paul stood, lifted his hand to quiet them, and started speaking. "Men of Israel," he said, "and you God-fearing Gentiles, listen to me. The God of this nation of Israel chose our ancestors and made them multiply and grow.... Then the people begged for a king, and God gave them... David.... And it is one of King David's descendants, Jesus, who is God's promised Savior of Israel! ....The people in Jerusalem and their leaders did not recognize Jesus as the one the prophets had spoken about. Instead, they condemned Him, ...but God raised Him from the dead! ...The promise was made to our ancestors, and God has now fulfilled it for us, their descendants, by raising Jesus.... We are here to proclaim that through this Man Jesus there is forgiveness for your sins. Everyone who believes in Him is made right in God's sight – something the law of Moses could never do." ...The following week almost the entire city turned out to hear them preach the word of the Lord. But when some of the Jews saw the crowds, they were jealous; so they slandered Paul and argued against whatever he said. Then Paul and Barnabas spoke out boldly and declared, "It was necessary that we first preach the word of God to you Jews. But since you have rejected it and judged yourselves unworthy of eternal life, we will offer it to the Gentiles...." When the Gentiles heard this, they were very glad and thanked the Lord for His message; and all who were chosen for eternal life became believers. So the Lord's message spread throughout that region.

Acts 13:13-49

* * *

In their day, it was the custom within the synagogues for Jews who were visiting from distant cities to bring a word of greeting and encouragement. Thus, those who were gathered that Sabbath day in the synagogue in Antioch of Pisidia were extending that customary courtesy to Paul and Barnabas. Paul began his message to those gathered in the synagogue in the same way that Stephen had (Acts 7), by recounting their history. He began with the ancestors – Abraham, Isaac and Jacob – and unfolded the history of the Chosen People of God. There were two primary truths in his message. The first truth was that everything in the history of Israel and the prophecies pointed to, and was leading up to, the coming of Jesus and the redemptive work that would be accomplished through His death and resurrection. The second truth in his message was that the underlying story throughout it all is God's story. Sixteen times in his message, Paul emphasized the truth that God is the central Actor in history. He was telling them that there is a great and glorious God. Know Him. Reckon with Him. Think about Him. He was saying that God is the main Worker in history. He is the explanation for, and the meaning of, everything!

We live in an age where most people do not believe that to be true. We have become a superficial and naive age. It is superficial and naive to discuss events and never acknowledge their most important connection – namely, their connection with God and His purposes. Let's look at it. Almost all news reports are superficial. Almost all history books are superficial. Almost all public education in America is superficial. Almost all editorial and news commentary is superficial. Why? Because of the complete disregard for God – who is the main Reality in the universe, the explanation behind everything, and without which all understandings are superficial. When we disregard the "Main Thing", we have made whatever it is superficial.

Someone may say, "Oh, that's just religion. You can't expect all news, or history, or education to be about religion." It's not religion. It's reality. If you want to be a Christian, it means believing that God is the main Actor in world events – that He is the most important Factor in all matters. Paul was talking to unbelievers here. He was evangelizing. And part of what he was trying to do was show them a way of looking at the world that sets the stage for the gospel – namely, that it is God's world. He made it. He owns it and everyone in it. He works in it. He is guiding it to His appointed purpose. Everything, without exception, has to do with God, and gets its main meaning and purpose from God.

One of the most amazing confirmations of the truth of the gospel is the way Jesus fulfilled so many prophecies made hundreds of years before His coming. In fact, to understand who Jesus Christ really is, we need to remember that He is not like a rabbit pulled out of a hat with no warning. He didn't just pop up in history with no meaning. Instead He is like a treasure chest of gold at the end of a centuries-long treasure hunt with lots of "clues" and markers pointing to Him along the way.

Let's look at a few of those "clues". In Genesis, God said to Abraham, "*All the families of the earth will be blessed through you*" (Genesis 12:3). So the earliest hope and expectation was that through the people of Israel some amazing blessing would come to the entire world. Three generations later, a promise was made to one of Abraham's great grandsons, Judah. "*The scepter will not depart from Judah, nor the ruler's staff from his descendants, until the coming of the One to whom it belongs; the One whom all nations will obey*" (Genesis 49:10). So the promise became more specific: the blessing will come to the world ("all the families") through a Ruler, and that Ruler will be of the house of Judah, one of Abraham's great grandsons.

Then several hundred years later. God gave a king to Israel, by the name of David, from the house of Judah. Before David died, God spoke to him through the prophet Nathan saying, "*When you die and are buried with your ancestors, I will raise up one of your descendants, your own offspring, and I will make His kingdom strong. He is the One who will build a house – a temple – for My name. And I will secure His royal throne forever*" (2 Samuel 7:12-13). God was not speaking of a temple built with hands, He was speaking of a temple – and a Kingdom – that would last forever. And the ruler to come, who would bring blessing to the nations, would be a Son of David and sit on the throne of David. Then came the prophet Isaiah who made the prediction even more specific: "*For a Child is born to us, a Son is given to us. The government will rest on His shoulders. And He will be called: Wonderful Counselor, Mighty God, Everlasting Father, Prince of Peace. His government and its peace will never end. He will rule with fairness and justice from the throne of His ancestor David for all eternity. The passionate commitment of the Lord of Heaven's Armies will make this happen!*" (Isaiah 9:6-7). Then the prophet Micah added that this Child, born of the house of David, would be born in Bethlehem and would have His origin from ancient days (Micah 5:2).

. . .

How was this Ruler going to bring blessing to the entire world like God had said to Abraham? God revealed that answer through the prophet Isaiah seven hundred years before Jesus was born: *"He was pierced for our rebellion, crushed for our sins. He was beaten so we could be whole. He was whipped so we could be healed. All of us, like sheep, have strayed away. We have left God's paths to follow our own. Yet the Lord laid on Him the sins of us all"* (Isaiah 53:5-6). But that sounds like it's the end of Him – dying as a Sacrificial Lamb in the place of sinners so they could go free. How does He rule forever on the throne of David if He is dead? Isaiah goes on to make clear that He does not stay dead. God says, *"I will give Him the honors of a Victorious Soldier, because He exposed Himself to death. He was counted among the rebels. He bore the sins of many and interceded for rebels"* (Isaiah 53:12).

So hundreds of years before Jesus was born, we are told by God in the Scriptures that Jesus would be of the house of Judah. He would live a life of righteousness, but He would be accused with the transgressors. He would be put to death for the sins of many. He would rise from the dead and sit down on the throne of His father David at God's right hand. And He would rule there, spreading blessing to all the families of the earth until He is acknowledged as the Lord of all the nations. So when Jesus came onto the scene two thousand years ago, He was not like a rabbit out of the hat – a total surprise with no preparation, and nothing in history to give Him meaning. Instead He was like a treasure chest of gold at the end of a long treasure hunt with dozens of clues along the way of what He would be like and what He would mean.

And He really is the Treasure. To know Him and be known and loved by Him is worth more than all this world has to offer. And that's the way Paul spoke to his listeners. He used the Old Testament history and prophecy to show that the Messiah was to rise from the dead and reign as the Son of David and never die again. Then Paul proclaimed, *"through this Man Jesus there is forgiveness for your sins. Everyone who believes in Him is made right in God's sight."* He said you have been "made right" – acquitted, cleared, pardoned. Your condemnation has been lifted. You can become a clean slate. That's what Jesus means: He means freedom!

Those in the synagogue that day never expected that they would receive that message when they invited Paul to speak. It was as if their blinders had been removed. They had now heard the story behind the story. They had heard the substance and the connection. They were no longer left to view things superficially and naively. They had now heard the whole truth. Thus, there was only one thing left to do – accept it. The people begged them to return the following week. There must have been much discussion throughout the week, because almost the entire city turned out to hear them the following week.

But seeing the size of the crowd, the religious leaders became jealous. Crowds had never turned out like that to hear them teach! So they slandered Paul, disputed the truth and swayed the Jews to reject the truth. In their rejection, they judged themselves to be unworthy of the precious gift of eternal life. Eternal life was never a gift they could earn or merit. It is not a gift that any one of us will ever be worthy to receive. It is a gift given by God's grace. But by rejecting the truth – and by rejecting the gift – they adjudicated themselves to an eternity separated from God. They committed the one sin that can never be forgiven – they rejected Jesus. If we reject Jesus there is no eternal life with God. God's grace can overcome every sin except rejection of His grace. If we walk away from His grace and reject His Son, we have judged ourselves to be unworthy. And that is what many of the Jews did that day. But Luke tells us that many Gentiles believed that day, and the gospel spread throughout the region.

God has created all things for His redemptive purpose. He is at work in and through all things to draw His creation back to Himself. He is the reason and His purpose is behind all things – even those things that the enemy has intended for evil. None of us are worthy of His redemption. But by His grace, every event and circumstance has ultimately been permitted to point us to His redemptive purpose. At the end of the day, the only thing that will judge anyone as unworthy is rejection of Him and His truth. We have been called – like Paul and Barnabas – to point others to His truth. May He find us faithful to do so… until He returns.

* * *

38

FROM LAUDING TO LOATHING

When the crowd saw what Paul had done, they shouted in their local dialect, "These men are gods in human form!" They decided that Barnabas was the Greek god Zeus and that Paul was Hermes, since he was the chief speaker. Now the temple of Zeus was located just outside the town. So the priest of the temple and the crowd brought bulls and wreaths of flowers to the town gates, and they prepared to offer sacrifices to the apostles. But when the apostles Barnabas and Paul heard what was happening, they tore their clothing in dismay and ran out among the people, shouting, "Friends, why are you doing this? We are merely human beings – just like you! We have come to bring you the Good News that you should turn from these worthless things and turn to the living God, who made heaven and earth, the sea, and everything in them. In the past He permitted all the nations to go their own ways, but He never left them without evidence of Himself and His goodness. For instance, He sends you rain and good crops and gives you food and joyful hearts." But even with these words, Paul and Barnabas could scarcely restrain the people from sacrificing to them. Then some Jews arrived from Antioch and Iconium and won the crowds to their side. They stoned Paul and dragged him out of town, thinking he was dead. But as the believers gathered around him, he got up and went back into the town. The next day he left with Barnabas for Derbe.

Acts 14:11-20

* * *

The journey from lauding to loathing can be particularly painful. At one moment, everyone loves you (or so it would appear), and in the next, everyone seemingly despises you. Just ask Jesus. On Sunday, the crowd was cheering, *"Hosanna"*; then on Friday, they were shouting, *"Crucify Him!"* Or ask Paul. On one day, the crowd laid wreaths at his feet, then only a few days later, they left him for dead after stoning him. In neither instance had Jesus nor Paul done anything to warrant such a dramatic and violent change of opinion. Jesus deserved to be worshiped, but never deserved to be crucified. Paul didn't deserve to be worshiped (and he corrected the people for doing so), but he did not "deserve" to be stoned. It is amazing to see how quickly – and how easily – the crowd could be moved from emotive praise to relentless persecution and utter abandonment.

But then again, it isn't amazing. Jesus was never surprised. John writes this about Jesus, as He began His itinerant ministry: *"Now when He was in Jerusalem at the Passover Feast, many believed in His name when they saw the signs that He was doing. But Jesus on His part did not entrust Himself to them, because He knew all people"* (John 2:23-24 ESV). Jesus "knew all people": He knows what is in our hearts. He never sought the approval of men; He sought only the approval of the Father. Paul later wrote about himself: *"Obviously, I'm not trying to win the approval of people, but of God. If pleasing people were my goal, I would not be Christ's servant"* (Galatians 1:10). i have never experienced physical persecution, but i have experienced emotional abandonment. i have experienced the emotional withdrawal that felt like loathing, where previously there had been support, encouragement – and even praise. To that degree, i can relate to Paul's experience – and perhaps you can as well.

In the verses immediately preceding this passage, we are introduced to a man there in Lystra who had been crippled from birth. Paul saw the man and *"realized he had the faith to be healed"* (Acts 14:9). So Paul told him to stand up and walk. The crowd had just witnessed that miracle as we begin this passage in verse 11. The crowd went wild with excitement. They knew this man. He had been crippled all of his life. Miraculously, he was now able to walk. The crowd then made the mistake of attributing this man's healing to Paul and Barnabas. Upon seeing and hearing the crowd's reaction, Paul and Barnabas swiftly redirected the crowd's praise to the One who truly had healed the crippled man and was worthy of their praise and worship. They were careful to not make the mistake that too often we can make – and that is to allow some of that praise to fall on us. Paul and Barnabas knew that they were servants and instruments of the Most High God; they knew that anything praiseworthy was His work and not theirs.

. . .

Let's take an important sideroad: In the midst of his statement to the crowd, Paul says, *"In the past He permitted all the nations to go their own ways, but He never left them without evidence of Himself and His goodness."* How many of us have wondered about the salvation of those who do not have access to the gospel? What will happen to the people who have never heard the Name of Jesus? First, that question must compel us to go – just like Paul and Barnabas were doing – to tell the people who have not yet heard the Good News of the gospel. It has been my experience that those who accuse God of being heartless in condemning to death those who are dead in their sin and have not heard about Jesus are the very same people who are making the least effort to make Him known. Second, Paul is giving us insight into the work that God has already begun to draw them to Himself. This is not intended to keep us from going – rather, to encourage us to expedite our obedience. Well, if the people don't have the spoken word or the written Word, what do they have? God gave them a witness. What was it? I love this: "*... He sends… the rain and good crops and gives… food and joyful hearts.*" Do you know what that's known as? His providence. They're not excusable. You say, "But they don't have any written Word." That's all right. They have the word written in their hearts, and the visible creation and the providence of God. Every man in this world is responsible for the knowledge of God, for God has written it in his conscience. God has revealed it in the creation, and He continues to reveal it in His providence.

Back to the passage – soon after, some of the religious leaders who had stirred up the crowd in Antioch of Pisidia and Iconium did the same thing here in Lystra. They sowed seeds of discord through false accusations. Remember, those who were sowing the discord were truly seeking to maintain the status quo of their positional power. The gospel was a threat to their status quo. And regrettably the people were easily deceived. They stoned the one that only a few days earlier they had worshiped as if he was a god, dragged what they thought was his lifeless body out of town, and left him for dead. *"But as the believers gathered around him, he got up and went back into the town."*

That prompts two further sideroads: first, did Paul die or did the people only think he was dead? i believe he died. You should know that there are those who would disagree with me in that regard. But, in his second letter to the church in Corinth, Paul wrote, *"I was caught up to the third heaven fourteen years ago. Whether I was in my body or out of my body, I don't know – only God knows…. But I do know that I was caught up to paradise and heard things so astounding that they cannot be expressed in words, things no human is allowed to tell"* (2 Corinthians 12:2-4). i don't believe the crowd left him half-dead. i believe that he was dead, and as the believers gathered around him, God raised him from the dead! Why? Because he had not yet completed the assignment that God had for him on this earth. Which immediately prompts the second question – why, then, did God allow him to be stoned to the point of death? Paul answered that question in his letter to the Galatians: *"Don't be misled – you cannot mock the justice of God. You will always harvest what you plant"* (Galatians 6:7). Paul was permitted to harvest that which he had planted. He had ordered the stoning of Stephen and watched on as the evil deed was transacted. God permitted him to go through the same experience – but then brought him back to life and allowed him to live to tell about it. Why did he have to go through that pain even now after he had become a follower of Jesus and an apostle? Salvation guarantees that we will not suffer the eternal consequences of our sin, but it does not guarantee that we won't suffer the penalty for our actions on this side of eternity. As Paul wrote – what we sow, we reap. This was the temporal consequence for sin that he could not escape. And there was a continuing reminder of that sin through the lasting "thorn in the flesh" (2 Corinthians 12:7) from which Paul suffered for his remaining days. His "vision of paradise" and his "thorn in the flesh" were both born out of the stoning and the death that resulted. But God used even those things, in addition to raising him from the dead, to bring glory to His Name.

But as we close, let's come back to the lessons for us – because hopefully, you've never been a part of stoning anyone, and prayerfully you will never be stoned. You may however have the crowd turn against you – simply because you are being obedient to what the Father has directed you to do. The Son experienced death on the cross, and Paul experienced stoning. The Father gave them both the grace to endure for the sake of His mission. He never abandoned them. And even though both of them experienced a loathing to the point of death, He raised them both from the dead for His purpose. The bottom line for us is we need to trust Him. He will not forsake us. He will give us the grace and strength to walk through the pain. For most of us, it will have absolutely nothing to do with death – but it could include friends who walk away from us and relationships that are severed. We will feel betrayed and abandoned – and hurt. But if we know we have been faithful to do what God has told us to do – and have not sinned against "our neighbor" in any way – then we must trust God even in the outcome – even when it hurts. Our God who was able to raise Jesus and Paul from the dead is able to heal the pain of our hurt.

. . .

A mentor once told me, "Be sure to pass along all the praise to God when it comes, as well as all of the pain and criticism when it follows." When you are following Jesus, lauding can quickly become loathing. Pass them both on to Jesus and keep following Him… until He returns.

* * *

39

BE SURE TO REPORT THE PRAISES

Finally, they returned by ship to Antioch of Syria, where their journey had begun. The believers there had entrusted them to the grace of God to do the work they had now completed. Upon arriving in Antioch, they called the church together and reported everything God had done through them and how He had opened the door of faith to the Gentiles, too. And they stayed there with the believers for a long time.

Acts 14:26-28

* * *

The church at Antioch in Syria was Paul and Barnabas' sending church (chapter 35). Almost two years had passed since the church had commissioned them to go and sent them out. The church had provided the financial resources needed in order for them to go. They prayed for them throughout their journey – praying for divine opportunities for the spread of the gospel, for anointing in their preaching, for the nurture of new believers, for the new churches being planted, for safety and health in their travels, and so on. The church undergirded the work in every way. The church made it possible for them to go. The church was as much a part of the mission journey as if they had actually traveled with Paul and Barnabas. God's calling on Paul and Barnabas to go was also a calling on the church to send them and "go" with them. And now they had returned. They were two of the most beloved people in the life of the Antioch church. They looked a little worse for wear. Now the way they returned to the church and the way the church received them would be just as important – if not more – than the way they had been sent out.

. . .

Paul and Barnabas would have been the first to tell you that they could not have gone without the prayers and support of the Antioch church. The church had entrusted them to the grace of God. By His grace, God had called them to the journey. By His grace, He had gone before them to prepare hearts to receive the seeds of the gospel. By His grace, He had provided them with "people of peace" at each of the synagogues along the way who invited them to speak and thereby opened the door for them to be able to preach the Good News. By His grace, He gave them peace to continue when their traveling companion, John Mark, unexpectedly bailed out on them in Perga (Acts 13:13). By His grace, He gave them power to defeat Elymas, the sorcerer – the instrument of Satan. By His grace, He granted them favor with Governor Sergius Paulus, as they witnessed his personal salvation and thereafter experienced his favor as they continued to travel throughout the island. By His grace, He opened a wider door for the spreading of the Gospel among the Gentiles in Antioch of Pisidia and beyond. By His grace, He brought glory to His Name through the healing of the crippled man in Lystra. By His grace, He raised Paul from the dead after the stoning. By His grace, God raised up elders in every church that was planted. And by His grace, He permitted them to safely return to Antioch. In these ways, and in many others, the Spirit of God had gone before them in their travels and led them through each and every twist and turn.

The sending church needed to hear this report. They needed to know how their prayers had been answered. They needed to know how God had worked through them for the furtherance of His mission. They needed to have the opportunity to praise God and glorify Him through their worship and thanksgiving over the great things He had done. The sending church needed to love on Paul and Barnabas. They had "come home" weary from their travel. They had returned somewhat beaten and bruised. They had arrived back home with "empty tanks" having constantly been pouring into others. The church needed to be used by the Lord to fill them back up, to encourage them, to minister to their woundedness and their weariness. The church needed to be an oasis at the end of a long and vigorous journey.

Paul and Barnabas not only needed to share God's answers to prayer and to be ministered to themselves. They needed to pour from themselves into the church. They needed to use the experiences they had to better equip the church to reach the nations right there in Antioch. They needed to better equip the church in how to support and undergird those who would be sent out from her midst in the days to come. They needed to help the church better prepare the others that God was calling for them to send from within the body. They needed to help the church see her ever growing role in carrying out Christ's Great Commission to the nations.

"And they stayed there with the believers for..." over a year to do just that. They stayed and picked up their work of pastoring and discipling the people. It was during that time that Paul wrote his letter to the Galatians. And in that letter, he gives all the glory to God for what they had seen Him do.

As we close, let's look at a statement in the first part of the passage. They had been *"entrusted... to the grace of God to do the work they had now completed."* Note the last word – "completed". You know what that means? It means they did it. God said, "Go do it" and they did it. They completed it. All too often when God says, "Go do it", we don't do it. Or, if we start, we don't finish it. But there are some in the history of the church that God told to do it, and they did. Paul and Barnabas were two of them, They came back to report that the work – that specific portion for which they had been sent out – was completed!

When i come to the end of my life or the day that Christ returns – whichever comes first – and He says to me, "Ken, did you finish the course? Did you fight the good fight? Did you keep the faith? Did you complete the work that I called you to do? i pray that i will be able to say, "Yes, Lord, i completed the work that You gave me." And i pray that you will be able to say the same – for the honor and glory of God.

In the meantime – until He returns – let's be faithful to give Him praise as we bear witness and report on the great work He has done!

* * *

40

IT SEEMED GOOD TO THE SPIRIT

While Paul and Barnabas were at Antioch of Syria, some men from Judea arrived and began to teach the believers: "Unless you are circumcised as required by the law of Moses, you cannot be saved." Paul and Barnabas disagreed with them, arguing vehemently. Finally, the church decided to send Paul and Barnabas to Jerusalem, accompanied by some local believers, to talk to the apostles and elders about this question.... When they arrived in Jerusalem, Barnabas and Paul were welcomed by the... apostles and elders. They reported everything God had done through them. But then some of the believers who belonged to the sect of the Pharisees stood up and insisted, "The Gentile converts must be circumcised and required to follow the law of Moses." So the apostles and elders met together to resolve this issue.... Everyone listened quietly as Barnabas and Paul told about the miraculous signs and wonders God had done through them among the Gentiles. When they had finished, James stood and said, "Brothers, listen to me. Peter has told you about the time God first visited the Gentiles to take from them a people for himself.... And so my judgment is that we should not make it difficult for the Gentiles who are turning to God...." Then the apostles and elders together with the whole church in Jerusalem chose delegates, and they sent them to Antioch of Syria with Paul and Barnabas to report on this decision. The men chosen were two of the church leaders – Judas (also called Barsabbas) and Silas. This is the letter they took with them:

"This letter... is written to the Gentile believers in Antioch, Syria, and Cilicia. Greetings! We understand that some men from here have troubled you and upset you with their teaching, but we did not send them! So we decided, having come to complete agreement, to send you official representatives... to confirm what we have decided concerning your question. For it seemed good to the Holy Spirit and

to us to lay no greater burden on you than these few requirements: You must abstain from eating food offered to idols, from consuming blood or the meat of strangled animals, and from sexual immorality. If you do this, you will do well…."
Acts 15:1-29

* * *

Whenever God is at work, there will always be people who attempt to put their mark on the work. They will endeavor to either add to, or take away from, the gospel. Often times, it is not an intentional attempt to distort the gospel; rather, it is borne out of our personal, cultural or traditional influences. In the case of the men from Judea, they believed that one could not be saved apart from the requirements of the law of Moses. Though they themselves had received salvation by believing in Jesus, they also believed that the laws they had followed since birth were a part of their salvation. They were mixing their personal religious experiences with salvation through Christ, and teaching a distorted gospel. You might say they were practicing syncretism by adding the gospel to their existing beliefs, instead of the gospel replacing their existing beliefs. In essence they were saying that a Gentile had to first become a Jew in order to become a Christian. Simply trusting in Jesus Christ wasn't sufficient; they also had to obey Moses.

Peter himself had learned that salvation is not determined by whether or not one eats meat, or whether one eats pork or doesn't eat pork. Salvation is not dependent upon whether we gather to worship on Sunday, or the Sabbath, or another day. It is not the result of keeping the Law, going through a ritual, or joining a church. We are all sinners before God, for whom Christ died on the cross. He was buried and rose again. He paid the price and extends His salvation to us by His grace which we receive through faith. There is one need, and there is but one gospel – with nothing to be added to or subtracted from it.

The church can still be guilty of trying to add to it today, particularly when we begin to elevate our traditions (whether old or new) to having equal importance to the gospel – i.e. what we wear when we gather to worship, our style of musical worship, the liturgical order of our worship gathering, and so forth. Allow me to use a missional example. For decades, the modern missionary movement from the western church exported a gospel heavily influenced by our western culture. We taught new believers that worship involved meeting in rectangular church buildings, sitting on uncomfortable benches, listening to a preacher that was flanked by notice boards that showed the hymns to be sung on one side, and last week's offering and attendance on the other side. And we built that rectangular building in the midst of villages surrounded by round mud huts, singing songs that were as foreign to the heart cries of the culture as our English language was. But we were convinced that all of that was a part of being a Christian church. We were teaching people from other cultures how to become a westerner in order to be a Christian. Gratefully, the Spirit of God awakened the realization that we must strip away our culture and traditions from the preaching and practice of the gospel as we are making disciples. Just as we have been freed from the Law of Moses, we are freed of the customs and traditions.

But also, whenever God is at work, there will be those who attempt to turn our focus away from the gospel and toward a myriad of other issues. Some will be as trivial as the color of the carpet in the church, the type of coffee we serve, or the Bible translation we use. Others will seek to turn our attention from the gospel to lesser doctrinal issues, such as the ongoing Calvinist-Arminian debate, or political issues – either inside or outside of the church – which cause us to shout at one another across the aisle either literally or figuratively.

The council in Jerusalem was seeking to resolve both an essential doctrinal issue, as well as a fellowship issue. At the conclusion of their deliberation, James stood up and summarized the council's understanding of what they believed God would have the church do. Just as a quick reminder: James was the half-brother of Jesus. He had not come to believe in Jesus until after He rose from the dead. James had grown up with Jesus. He had lived with Him as his brother for twenty-something years, and yet, he had rejected Him as Savior until the final days before Jesus ascended into heaven. In the eighteen years that had passed since His ascension, James had become a leader in the Church in Jerusalem. At the timeframe of this passage, he had already written the Epistle of James to the Jewish believers throughout the Roman provinces, exhorting them to endure in their faith. Now, on behalf of the council, he was speaking to the Gentile and Jewish believers, exhorting them to live out their lives in a way that signified their belief in Christ.

Gentile culture was characterized by idolatry and immorality – not unlike our world today. The early church leaders were admonishing the Gentile believers to walk in a manner worthy of the gospel, just as Paul himself did: *"Live as citizens of heaven, conducting yourselves in a manner worthy of the Good News about Christ"* (Philippians 1:27). That meant that they had to walk in the righteousness of Christ and abstain from any practice of idolatry or immorality -- or even the appearance of it. Thus, they should not even eat any food that had been presented to idols.

To the Jewish believers the council was saying: "God has not placed the burden of the Law upon the Gentiles – and you, as Jews, have no need to do so either." Jesus' blood had been shed for Jew and Gentile alike. One did not need to become like the other to partake in the grace of God. Rather, each needed to receive the gift of God by faith.

Further, just as the Jewish and Gentile believers were to walk in a manner worthy of the gospel, they were to walk in a manner that promoted unity within the body. The new church was a mixture of Jewish-background believers and Gentile-background believers. That church did a great deal of eating together and practicing hospitality. The idea that wherever two or more believers are gathered there is food, is not a new idea! The church leaders were calling upon the Gentile believers to make dietary concessions – to abstain from eating blood, as well as meat from animals that died by strangulation. Those concessions were for the purpose of promoting unity within the body, and presenting a united witness to a lost world.

Yes, we must continue to seek the Spirit and the Scriptures to make sure that we are not adding anything to, or taking anything away, from the gospel. We must come to the same place as those elders and apostles that *"it seem{s} good to the Holy Spirit and to us to lay no greater burden on you than"* this. At the same time, we would do well to learn that problems and differences of opinion will still arise within the church. Those differences can either be a point of dissension and division or an opportunity for growth in a healthy way. How many hurtful fights and church splits could be avoided if we took time to listen to the Spirit to hear "what seems good and right to the Holy Spirit"?

Jesus told us that the world would know that we are His disciples by the love we have for one another (John 13:35). God has opened a wide and effective door of ministry (1 Corinthians 16:9) for us to take the gospel of His grace to a condemned world. But there are forces at work in the church even today that want to close that door. They emphasize those things that would divide us and divert us. Let us learn from the early church in Jerusalem to listen only to God's Word and His Spirit that we might together continue to walk through that wide and effective door… until He returns.

* * *

41

WHO WAS RIGHT?

After some time Paul said to Barnabas, "Let's go back and visit each city where we previously preached the word of the Lord, to see how the new believers are doing." Barnabas agreed and wanted to take along John Mark. But Paul disagreed strongly, since John Mark had deserted them in Pamphylia and had not continued with them in their work. Their disagreement was so sharp that they separated. Barnabas took John Mark with him and sailed for Cyprus. Paul chose Silas, and as he left, the believers entrusted him to the Lord's gracious care. Then he traveled throughout Syria and Cilicia, strengthening the churches there.
Acts 15:36-41

* * *

John Mark was the son of a woman named Mary. It was their family's home in Jerusalem to which the apostle Peter went when the angel led him out of prison (Acts 12:12). Apparently theirs was an affluent family that employed servants – at least one (Acts 12:13). Peter appears to have had a close association with the family. The servant girl recognized his voice, and there was a group of believers gathered in the home at that very moment, praying for Peter's deliverance from prison. Peter subsequently refers to Mark as "my son" (1 Peter 5:13), indicating that he may have been the one who first led Mark to Christ. Peter was, without question, Mark's primary source for his Gospel account.

But, regrettably, to this point, as we move chronologically through Scripture, every time we have seen Mark, he is running away and abandoning those he is following. The first time was when he abandoned Jesus. Mark confesses his abandonment in his Gospel account. He writes, *"One young man following behind was clothed only in a long linen shirt. When the mob tried to grab him, he slipped out of his shirt and ran away naked"* (Mark 14:51-52). The unnamed young man is Mark himself. But in all fairness to him, all of Jesus' disciples abandoned Him in the garden and ran away. However, Mark is the only one that we are told *"ran away naked"*!

The next time we see him, he is accompanying Barnabas and Saul from Jerusalem to Antioch (Acts 12:25), and then as they are sent out by the church in Antioch on their first missionary journey. Mark was Barnabas' cousin (Colossians 4:10), and he journeyed with them as their assistant (Acts 13:5). When Saul (now Paul) and those traveling with him arrived in Pamphylia, we are told that Mark left them and returned to his home in Jerusalem (Acts 13:13).

Luke does not tell us why Mark abandoned them, but his departure came right after what appears to have been a fruitless time in Cyprus (Acts 13:4-12). To that point, they had seen a limited response to the gospel, and they had experienced strong demonic opposition through Elymas, the sorcerer. It is very possible that Mark was discouraged at the difficulty of the journey and decided to return to the comforts of his home. By the way, it is also very possible that God prompted him to return to Jerusalem to protect him from the persecution in Lystra that Paul and Barnabas would suffer. Perhaps God was protecting him for another day. Remember, we will seldom know all that God, in His sovereignty, has protected us from.

All of that brings us to where we are in this passage. Paul and Barnabas have agreed that they need to return to the cities in which churches were planted during their first missionary journey, in order to encourage the new believers. Barnabas wanted to forgive Mark's earlier failure and again bring him with them. His motivation was not only their family relationship, but more importantly, Barnabas, as we know, was an encourager. He was a nurturer. This "son of encouragement" (Acts 4:36) wanted to give Mark another opportunity to prove himself and serve the Lord. i, for one, am grateful for the "Barnabases" in my life who have not given up on me, but have been willing to go the second and third mile – and beyond – with me when i failed. Just as Barnabas had been willing to stand with Paul when it was unpopular to do so (Acts 9:27), he was insisting that they to do the same for Mark.

. . .

Paul, on the other hand, was just as adamant that they not take Mark. Pioneering missionary work requires dedication, resolve, and endurance. Paul saw John Mark as a risk to their mission. After all, he had deserted them on their prior journey and shown weakness. Paul believed their mission was too important, and the work too demanding, to bring someone along who had proven to be unreliable.

As the discussion continued, the two men "disagreed strongly", and neither one was willing to compromise. Here were two dedicated men who were both being used by God in great ways. As we saw in the last chapter, they had just helped bring about unity between the Jewish and Gentile believers; and yet, they could not settle their own disagreement. Their solution was for them to divide the territory and separate. Barnabas would take John Mark with him to Cyprus, and Paul would take Silas with him through Syria and Cilicia to encourage the believers in those churches.

So, who was right? That's probably the wrong question! It really doesn't make much difference. Perhaps both of them were right in some ways, and both of them were wrong in other ways. We know that John Mark ultimately did succeed in the ministry, and that Paul came to love and appreciate him. Paul later calls him a "fellow worker" (Philemon 1:24), and near the end of his life sends a request to Timothy from a Roman prison: "*Bring Mark with you when you come, for he will be helpful to me in my ministry*" (2 Timothy 4:11).

Where there had once existed one missionary team, there were now two! If God had to depend upon perfect people to accomplish His work, He would never get anything done. By His grace, He uses our limitations and imperfections for His good purpose – even our disagreements! Good and godly people in the church will disagree. Paul looked at Mark through the lens: "What can he do for God's work?" Barnabas, on the other hand, asked: "What can God's work do for him?" Both questions are right and important as we follow Jesus. But sometimes it is difficult to walk in that balance.

The key is that in our disagreement that we do not become disagreeable. There is no indication that either of these men – Paul or Barnabas – ever succumbed to "name-calling", or "talking trash" about the other. They did not separate to pout, or go their own way. They honored God even in their separation and, through it, the work was multiplied.

Regrettably, over the years, there have probably been more churches started as the result of church splits than there have been through intentional church planting – at least in the U.S. In too many instances, the splits have resulted in churches that were borne out of animosity, instead of a love for the gospel. When Paul and Barnabas went their separate ways, they did not do so with hearts filled with bitterness and hostility. Their passion for God and His work was never extinguished. They both earnestly sought to follow God with their whole hearts. And as they did, He led them to go their separate ways in a way that multiplied the work, rather than hurt the work.

Even in disagreement, they honored God. They were mature enough in their walk with God to know that the issue was not – "who was right?" – the issue was – "will you follow Me wherever I lead?" We would do well to learn that lesson and follow their lead. Disagreements will arise. Let's be faithful to seek the truth of God's Word in all things, to treat one another with love and respect, and to follow Jesus wherever He leads – even if our paths look different. If we do, we will be able to look back, as Paul later did, to see how God has worked it all for our good and His glory! And He has promised that He always will… until He returns.

* * *

42

WHO IS YOUR TIMOTHY?

Paul went first to Derbe and then to Lystra, where there was a young disciple named Timothy. His mother was a Jewish believer, but his father was a Greek. Timothy was well thought of by the believers in Lystra and Iconium, so Paul wanted him to join them on their journey. In deference to the Jews of the area, he arranged for Timothy to be circumcised before they left, for everyone knew that his father was a Greek. Then they went from town to town, instructing the believers to follow the decisions made by the apostles and elders in Jerusalem. So the churches were strengthened in their faith and grew larger every day.

Acts 16:1-5

* * *

It had been slightly more than two years since Paul and Barnabas had been in Lystra. It was there that Paul had been stoned and left for dead. They had returned to Lystra a few months later on their way back to Antioch, in order to encourage and strengthen the new believers. On one of those initial visits, Paul had met a young man by the name of Timothy, who had then come to faith in Christ. Timothy was the product of a mixed marriage – which was very common in that region. His mother Eunice was a Jew and his father was a Greek Gentile. Eunice and his grandmother Lois had also come to faith through the witness of Paul. In the ensuing two years, all three members of the family had grown in their walk as followers of Jesus and were esteemed by the other believers and well known for their faith. There is, however, no record that Timothy's father came to faith in Christ.

. . .

Seeing Timothy's spiritual growth and maturity, and hearing the good report from the churches, Paul invited him, now in his late teens or early twenties, to join Silas and him on this missionary journey. He would serve as their assistant, in a similar capacity to that which John Mark had served Paul and Barnabas. Perhaps this was another reason that God had led Paul and Barnabas to go their separate ways – so that Paul could disciple Timothy along the journey.

When Timothy decided to go with Paul and Silas, he was immediately confronted with a crisis of belief. That will often be true for us when we take a step of faith that God has placed before us. We will encounter something or be forced to make a decision that will reveal whether we truly believe what God has said. Timothy's crisis of belief stemmed from the fact that in order to join Paul on the trip, Timothy would need to be circumcised. Having been raised by a Greek father, he had not been circumcised as a boy.

An important question for us is – why did he need to be circumcised? Paul had only recently aided the elders and apostles at the Church in Jerusalem in coming to the decision that Gentile believers did not need to be circumcised in order to be saved. So, it was not an issue of salvation. But Paul's ministry was to both Jews and Gentiles – and he was shepherding the new believers to walk in unity with one another. He was nurturing Timothy to also serve in a shepherding role. If Timothy was to serve in that role, he would be working with both Jews and Gentiles in the churches. If Timothy was not circumcised, it would create contention among the Jewish believers. And obviously, contention would disrupt the unity of the body.

Paul described the principle behind this well in his first letter to the believers in Corinth:

"Even though I am a free man with no master, I have become a slave to all people to bring many to Christ. When I was with the Jews, I lived like a Jew to bring the Jews to Christ. When I was with those who follow the Jewish law, I too lived under that law. Even though I am not subject to the law, I did this so I could bring to Christ those who are under the law. When I am with the Gentiles who do not follow the Jewish law, I too live apart from that law so I can bring them to Christ. But I do not ignore the law of God; I obey the law of Christ. When I am

with those who are weak, I share their weakness, for I want to bring the weak to Christ. Yes, I try to find common ground with everyone, doing everything I can to save some. I do everything to spread the Good News and share in its blessings."
(1 Corinthians 9:19-23)

Timothy and Paul could have debated the issue with the Jewish believers that Timothy was not under the law of Moses. But those energies would have been expended to the detriment of the proclamation of the gospel and the nurturing of the church. In order to be a servant of Christ to all the believers, Timothy – under Paul's leadership – knew that it wasn't the law of Moses that he was under, but rather, the law of Christ. Timothy knew that he couldn't follow Christ – by following Paul – if he was not circumcised. He could not become a stumbling block and faithfully serve his Lord (Romans 14:13-15). As Warren Wiersbe writes, *"It is a wise spiritual leader who knows how and why to apply the principles of the Word of God – when to stand firm and when to yield."*

In later years Paul told Timothy, "*Work hard so you can present yourself to God and receive his approval. Be a good worker, one who does not need to be ashamed and who correctly explains the word of truth*" (2 Timothy 2:15). He counseled Timothy, his "*dear son*" (2 Timothy 1:2), from a heart of love, wanting Timothy to stand firm in his own faith and to lead others well.

In the years that followed, Timothy played an important role in the spread of the gospel, and the expansion and strengthening of the churches. He traveled with Paul and often served as his special ambassador to "trouble spots" in the work, such as Corinth. He became the shepherd of the Church in Ephesus, and joined Paul in Rome shortly before the apostle was martyred.

Paul invested his life into Timothy. He heeded his own counsel: *"What you have heard from me in the presence of many witnesses entrust to faithful men, who will be able to teach others also"* (2 Timothy 2:2). He entrusted truth to men like Timothy who in turn taught others. Men, all of us need to be investing our lives into "Timothys". Ladies, you need to be investing your lives into "Loises". Just as we have received from others, we are to give.

• • •

So who is your Timothy? Or, who is your Lois? Who are the ones that God has placed in your path to encourage, to mentor and disciple in the truth of God and the work of the ministry? You are never too young, and you are never too old. Continue to be faithful to do so… until He returns.

* * *

43

A MACEDONIAN CALL

Next Paul and Silas traveled through the area of Phrygia and Galatia, because the Holy Spirit had prevented them from preaching the word in the province of Asia at that time. Then coming to the borders of Mysia, they headed north for the province of Bithynia, but again the Spirit of Jesus did not allow them to go there. So instead, they went on through Mysia to the seaport of Troas. That night Paul had a vision: A man from Macedonia in northern Greece was standing there, pleading with him, "Come over to Macedonia and help us!" So we decided to leave for Macedonia at once, having concluded that God was calling us to preach the Good News there.

Acts 16:6-10

* * *

God orders our steps and our stops. Just ask Paul. Time and again Paul was either in the midst of a journey, or preparing to make one, when God stopped him in his tracks and redirected him. It started on the road to Damascus. He was headed there for one purpose, and God gave him a totally different mission. And that redirection changed the trajectory of his life from that point forward. Through those twists and turns this unlikely candidate became the apostle to the Gentiles. Now, the Holy Spirit was preventing him from going where he planned to go and redirecting him to the unplanned and the unforeseen. Paul was sovereignly prevented from entering into the provinces of Asia and Bithynia, and now found himself in the seaport town of Troas on the shore of the Aegean Sea. Paul had never planned to go to Troas – at least on that journey.

. . .

But then again, just ask Silas. He was a leader in the Church in Jerusalem. The elders of the church selected him and Judas Barsabbas to return with Paul and Barnabas to the Church in Antioch in Syria – to help bring the report from the Jerusalem Council (Acts 15:22). Little did he know that Barnabas and Paul would end up having a disagreement that would lead him to accompany Paul on this missionary journey. A brief trip that he thought would last for just a few weeks to a place just three hundred miles away would become a three-plus-year journey into Europe that would cover thousands of miles and result in the planting of churches in Philippi, Berea and Corinth. i sure hope he packed enough socks and underwear!

And we can also ask Timothy. Paul invited this "late-teen, early-twenty-something" to assist him and Silas in the work they would be doing in the churches in Galatia, Phrygia, Pamphylia and Asia. All of this was within a one hundred mile radius of his home. i'm fairly certain he had given some specific parameters for the trip to Timothy's mother Eunice. And those parameters wouldn't have included the Greek and Macedonian provinces of Europe. But then God redirected their steps, and we now have the letters written to encourage the churches that were planted as a result in Philippi, Thessalonica and Corinth – letters that the Spirit of God uses to encourage and teach us even to this day.

We can even ask Dr. Luke. The three men encountered Luke in Troas. They hadn't even planned to go to Troas. We don't know if Luke was already a follower of Christ, or if the physician became a follower as a result of the witness of Paul. But regardless, he became a "fellow laborer" (Philemon 1:24) and boarded the boat with them that took them to Neapolis (Acts 16:10). The Gospel of Luke and the Book of Acts represent twenty-five percent of the New Testament. Would we even have them, if Luke hadn't gotten on the boat? Before you quickly remind me that those Books were a part of God's plan – so, of course, we would have them – i merely want to point out that they were a product of Luke walking in "the steps and stops" that God set before him.

Their journeys had all looked different – and yet, God had ordered their steps for this moment to receive His call to Macedonia. And that day, after having closed so many other doors, God used a vision to redirect them to *"come over to Macedonia and help us!"*

. . .

None of it was "per chance". It was all the result of the activity of a sovereign God who had chosen them and called them – and set their feet in motion – long before they ever realized He had.

As i look back over my own life, i am reminded of significant redirections that i have seen God bring about in my personal journey, some of which pre-date my salvation. There are many, but i will name three specifically. The first is when he redirected me to attend a different university three weeks before classes were to begin. For months i had been enrolled to attend the University of Florida in Gainesville (Go Gators!). But at the last minute, He prompted me to enroll at Florida Atlantic University in Boca Raton (home to the Burrowing Owls!). Go figure! But unbeknownst to me, it was a redirect that would ultimately lead me to marry the help-mate that He had created specifically for me. Then twelve years later, God used my wife as a part of His work to bring me to faith in Him. Soon thereafter, God gave us a clarion call to serve Him in vocational ministry. i can tell you that was nowhere on my career plan! Then twelve years after that, He gave us our own Macedonian call to step out from where we were and join Him on a "Genesis 12 journey" that subsequently has led to the writing of this series of books. What would have happened if i had gone to Gainesville? i have no idea! But i know that this is the path God had for me.

You, too, can look back and see how God has ordered your steps and redirected your path. You can look back and see the twists and turns in the pathway. None of us can see the ones that are still up ahead. But we can be confident in the One who directed Paul, Silas, Timothy and Luke that day in Troas. He has a Kingdom purpose in mind. It is a journey that He will use to fulfill His purpose for our lives – and through our lives. Those men could no more imagine what God had in store for them, than we can today.

You may be at a place very similar to the one these men were just a few days prior to their arrival in Troas. Every door along your path seems to be closing. Every way you have turned has led you to a "dead end". You may be on the edge of discouragement. You may be saying, "God, I saw this going differently!" And you may be wondering if you can keep going on. Stay the course – Troas is just up ahead. And God has a Macedonia to which He is leading you. Keep your eyes on Him and the path He has set before you. Watch for His activity and His vision. He will make it clear. And He will be faithful to lead you all of the way… until He returns.

* * *

44

A MERCHANT BELIEVES

We boarded a boat at Troas and sailed straight across to the island of Samothrace, and the next day we landed at Neapolis. From there we reached Philippi, a major city of that district of Macedonia and a Roman colony. And we stayed there several days. On the Sabbath we went a little way outside the city to a riverbank, where we thought people would be meeting for prayer, and we sat down to speak with some women who had gathered there. One of them was Lydia from Thyatira, a merchant of expensive purple cloth, who worshiped God. As she listened to us, the Lord opened her heart, and she accepted what Paul was saying. She and her household were baptized, and she asked us to be her guests. "If you agree that I am a true believer in the Lord," she said, "come and stay at my home." And she urged us until we agreed.

Acts 16:11-15

* * *

This moment marks the beginning of a new epoch in the history of the gospel. Up to this point, the gospel had not gone further west than Asia Minor. In fact, on this journey, as we've already seen, Paul's original intention had been to stay in Asia, but God had changed his plans. As a result, Paul was able to witness the salvation of the first person in Europe. All of those who would subsequently come to faith over the centuries in Europe would in fact come after her. And as we'll see in a moment, her influence would not stop there.

Philippi was a Roman colony in Macedonia situated ten miles inland from the port of Neapolis. It had become the home to the Roman governor of the province, and was situated at the eastern end of the Via Egnatia. The highway was one of Rome's massive accomplishments, built on the backs of slave labor. It stretched 490 miles from the Adriatic Sea to the Aegean Sea – which created efficient access for the Roman military force and made it the major trade route over land from Italy to Asia. Thus, Philippi had become a strategic center – politically, commercially, militarily, and culturally.

Paul's first stop in any town or village was always the synagogue, but there does not appear to have been a synagogue in Philippi. Jewish custom required that there be at least ten men for the founding of a synagogue, so apparently there were not ten Jewish men that lived there. However, there was a group of Jewish women, or more than likely, Greek Gentile proselytes, that gathered for prayer along the riverbank. It would appear that Paul's call to Macedonia through the vision of a man, actually was God's response to the prayers of a gathering of women!

One of those women – Lydia – was a successful merchant from Thyatira. She was a seller of purple cloth. There is no mention of Lydia having a husband, so we can presume that she was either a widow, or a freeborn single woman. She had apparently moved to Philippi in order to ply her trade. Thyatira was the trade center for indigo dyes, situated in Asia Minor. It was one of the cities that the Holy Spirit had prevented Paul and Silas from visiting. Later in Scripture, we discover that a church was planted in Thyatira (Revelation 2:18). Though Paul was never able to visit the city in any of his missionary journeys, God apparently had a different plan to establish His church there. And that plan may possibly have included Lydia to be the one to bring the gospel back to her hometown.

God was already at work through His Holy Spirit drawing these women to Himself. Lydia had apparently already turned from the paganism of the world in which she lived, and was seeking to know and worship the one true God, even though she had not yet heard the gospel. This is another reminder like the Ethiopian eunuch (Chapter 22) and Cornelius (Chapter 30). If there is a pagan who in his/her heart honestly seeks to know God, He will reveal Himself in the fullness of the gospel to that individual. God knows exactly what He is doing, and He knows exactly where the seeking hearts are. He will never shut Himself off from a willing seeking heart. He will move heaven and earth to get to that seeking heart. As God told Israel through Moses: "*If from there you seek the*

Lord your God, you will find Him if you seek Him with all your heart and with all your soul" (Deuteronomy 4:29 NIV). God will always meet a seeking heart.

Lydia's salvation story is another great example of God's providence and His care for believers. God rerouted Paul and his traveling companions, while at the same time He also ensured that Lydia would be in the right place at the right time to encounter Paul and hear the Good News of Jesus. But Lydia not only sought the Lord, she listened.

Some people have ears but they don't hear. An example is the situation on the road to Damascus – Saul heard the voice of Jesus and fell down, whereas his traveling companions perceived a voice but did not hear. That's too often the case. People hear without listening. While Jesus was on earth He encountered the Pharisees often. They too heard, but they refused to listen. They were like people who choose to attend a concert or a great musical extravaganza wearing blinders and earplugs. They had no idea what was going on. They didn't see the truth when He stood in their presence and when He spoke they never listened to Him. But that's not the case with Lydia.

As Paul was speaking, Lydia heard the gospel of Jesus Christ, and *the Lord opened her heart*. As soon as she believed, Lydia was baptized, along with the rest of her household. She was obviously a woman of great influence – not only on others within her community, but upon her entire household as well. Whether "her household" refers only to her family, or if it included her servants, is unclear from the biblical account.

Seven years after this time in Philippi, Paul wrote a letter to the Church in Rome. He admonished the believers as to their behavior and told them not to be slothful in business, but rather to be fervent in spirit, and to serve the Lord (Romans 12:11). One can't help but wonder if he was thinking of Lydia when he wrote those words.

After Lydia's conversion and baptism, she insisted that Paul and his friends come stay at her home, if they judged her to be "*a true believer in the Lord*" (verse 15). Luke says that "*she urged us until we agreed,*" which indicates the fervency of her request. The missionaries did indeed judge Lydia to be a true believer, and her home became their place of lodging while they remained in Philippi. But her home became more than that – it also became the meeting place for that starting church. As we'll see in Chapter 46, Luke remained in Philippi to help nurture those that God was adding to this brand new church.

So, let's relook at the guiding hand and empowering work of the Spirit of God through all of this. God closed door after door to lead Paul and his traveling companions to this place – at just the right time. God worked in Lydia's life to bring her to Philippi, and began to work in her heart that she might seek Him. Out of that small prayer gathering, a church was formed in Lydia's home that became the launching pad for the gospel throughout Europe and beyond. Eleven years later, Paul would write this church, while he was imprisoned in Rome, with this admonition: "*I am certain that God, who began the good work within you, will continue His work until it is finally finished on the day when Christ Jesus returns*" (Philippians 1:6).

God began a good work in the life of a merchant who believed – and the ripple effects continue… until He returns.

* * *

45

A JAILER IS SET FREE

A mob quickly formed against Paul and Silas, and the city officials ordered them stripped and beaten with wooden rods. They were severely beaten, and then they were thrown into prison. The jailer was ordered to make sure they didn't escape. So the jailer put them into the inner dungeon and clamped their feet in the stocks. Around midnight Paul and Silas were praying and singing hymns to God, and the other prisoners were listening. Suddenly, there was a massive earthquake, and the prison was shaken to its foundations. All the doors immediately flew open, and the chains of every prisoner fell off! The jailer woke up to see the prison doors wide open. He assumed the prisoners had escaped, so he drew his sword to kill himself. But Paul shouted to him, "Stop! Don't kill yourself! We are all here!" The jailer called for lights and ran to the dungeon and fell down trembling before Paul and Silas. Then he brought them out and asked, "Sirs, what must I do to be saved?" They replied, "Believe in the Lord Jesus and you will be saved, along with everyone in your household." And they shared the word of the Lord with him and with all who lived in his household. Even at that hour of the night, the jailer cared for them and washed their wounds. Then he and everyone in his household were immediately baptized. He brought them into his house and set a meal before them, and he and his entire household rejoiced because they all believed in God.

Acts 16:22-34

* * *

The movement of the Holy Spirit at the riverbank was quickly followed by an attack of the evil one. He did not like "his territory" being invaded by the Spirit of God. In the verses immediately preceding this passage, we read that Paul and Silas repeatedly encountered a slave girl who was possessed by a demon (Acts 16:16-21). She earned a lot of money for her masters by telling fortunes. One day, Paul commanded the demon – in the name of Jesus Christ – to come out of the woman. Instantly it left her – and with it, so did her ability to tell fortunes – as did her ability to make money for her masters. The masters dragged Paul and Silas before the authorities to be punished. And as we read here, a mob quickly formed to do them bodily harm. In light of their own religious and racial prejudices the Roman officials acted rashly without investigating the matter fully. Remember – Paul and Silas were both citizens of Rome which meant that they could not be beaten or harmed until the matter had been properly adjudicated. But the officials failed to do so, and instead, ordered the jailer to severely beat them and throw them into prison.

Here is an important lesson for us. Paul and Silas were wrongfully accused, wrongfully judged and wrongfully punished. But instead of complaining or calling upon God to right these wrongs and judge their enemies, these men prayed and praised God – at the top of their lungs. They weren't shouting their complaints; they were declaring their praise. God responded by shaking the foundations of the prison, opening the doors and loosening their chains – not only those of Paul and Silas, but of every prisoner in the place. They could have all fled to freedom, but instead they all remained right where they were. An awe of God came over all of the prisoners and it overshadowed any fear that they had of their Roman captors. i can't help but wonder how many of the other prisoners came to faith in Christ that night.

But Paul's attention was fixed on the jailer – the one for whom Christ had placed them in the jail. Roman law stated that if a guard lost a prisoner, he would receive the same punishment the prisoner would have received. Potentially there could have been some pretty severe punishments awaiting that host of prisoners. So the jailer was prepared to take his own life instead of facing the shame and penalty of their escape. A hard-hearted vindictive person could have easily justified taking vengeance on his persecutor by allowing the jailer to take his own life. But Paul rightly realized that the jailer was really the prisoner – imprisoned by his own sin. Paul was already the freed man – set free from the bondage of sin. Paul knew that he was no more worthy of the grace extended to him through the compassion of Christ on the Damascus road than this cruel jailer. So Paul shouted out, *"Don't kill yourself!"*

. . .

The power of God seized the jailer's attention, but it was the grace and compassion of God as expressed through His servants that brought the jailer to the recognition of his need for a Savior. It wasn't the supernatural power of the earthquake that God used to draw him to Himself; it was the spirit of humility, grace and kindness that drew him to the gospel. We would do well to remember that! Yes, God sometimes works in might and in power, but most often, He works through the fruit of His Spirit – love, joy, peace, patience, kindness, goodness, faithfulness, gentleness and self-control (Galatians 5:22-23) – that cannot be otherwise explained apart from Him.

Having witnessed the unexplainable, he asked, *"What must I do to be saved?"* Paul declared the simple truth of the gospel, and he believed. Then the members of his household heard and believed. And then all of them were baptized. An evening that had begun with the jailer subjecting Paul and Silas to severe beatings ended with him washing their wounds and caring for them.

How many of us would have anticipated that ending to this story? How many of us would have been that forgiving and compassionate toward the jailer? It's easy, as we read this, to get focused on the way God shook the jail and miss the gracious way that two men, under the control of the Holy Spirit, who were wrongfully beaten, graciously responded to those who had beaten them.

So here is what the jailer learned that day – and here is what Paul and Silas "preached" that day – not only through their words, but also through their actions:

- Being a Christian means recognizing that there is a great God who created all things and all persons for His glory – to display the greatness and beauty and power of who He is.
- Being a Christian means recognizing that every person exists to bring glory to God. This is our reason for being. This is the meaning of human life – to reflect back to God and to reflect to each other the glory of our Maker and all His attributes, by loving Him, trusting Him, thanking Him, and obeying Him.
- Being a Christian means recognizing that we have all failed to do this. We have all fallen short of living for His glory. We have exchanged it for other values we preferred, and so we have scorned His glory. The Bible calls it sin. And we are all guilty.

- Being a Christian means recognizing that we are all therefore condemned justly by God to eternal punishment for the infinite guilt of dishonoring an infinitely glorious God.
- Being a Christian means recognizing that the love of God moved Him to send His Son, Jesus Christ, into the world to provide eternal life for helpless sinners. When Jesus died for sinners, He became our ransom, our substitute, and the vindication of God's glory on our behalf.
- Being a Christian means we have gone beyond recognizing those truths, we have repented of our sin and turned to Jesus by faith, believing that all that He is, is all that we need.

Through the power of the gospel, the jailer was set free. But there are many who are still imprisoned in their sin, waiting to hear this powerful truth through our words – and through our actions… until He returns.

* * *

46

ARE WE TURNING THE WORLD UPSIDE DOWN?

Now when they had passed through Amphipolis and Apollonia, they came to Thessalonica, where there was a synagogue of the Jews. And Paul went in, as was his custom, and on three Sabbath days he reasoned with them from the Scriptures, explaining and proving that it was necessary for the Christ to suffer and to rise from the dead, and saying, "This Jesus, whom I proclaim to you, is the Christ." And some of them were persuaded and joined Paul and Silas, as did a great many of the devout Greeks and not a few of the leading women. But the Jews were jealous, and taking some wicked men of the rabble, they formed a mob, set the city in an uproar, and attacked the house of Jason, seeking to bring them out to the crowd. And when they could not find them, they dragged Jason and some of the brothers before the city authorities, shouting, "These men who have turned the world upside down have come here also, and Jason has received them, and they are all acting against the decrees of Caesar, saying that there is another king, Jesus." And the people and the city authorities were disturbed when they heard these things. And when they had taken money as security from Jason and the rest, they let them go.

Acts 17:1-9 (ESV)

* * *

The church in Philippi was continuing to grow. The household of Lydia, combined with the household of the jailer, had now formed the nucleus of a budding church. It was time for Paul, Silas and Timothy to continue on their journey to spread the gospel to other cities in Macedonia. It appears that Luke did not go with them, but remained in

Philippi for a short period to shepherd those that God was raising up to be the leaders of the church.

Paul and company traveled to Thessalonica. The city was so named after the step-sister of Alexander the Great, and was another prominent city of its day. Three rivers flowed from the city into the Aegean which made it another major seaport for trade and transportation. It was a "free city" which meant that it had an elected citizens assembly and it had no Roman garrison stationed within its walls.

There were obviously more than ten Jewish men in Thessalonica because there was a synagogue in the city. Paul labored at his tentmaking trade through the week, but on the Sabbath, as was his practice, he went to the synagogue seeking out devout Jews and Gentiles, "God-seekers" and proselytes. He returned for two more Sabbaths, each time using the Scriptures to share the gospel message of Christ's death, burial and resurrection.

After three weeks of ministry, Paul saw a large number of people believe, especially Greek proselytes and women of influence. Among the men were Aristarchus and Secundus, who would later travel with Paul, as well as Jason, who welcomed Paul and company to lodge in his home. But seeing the spread of the gospel, the unbelieving Jews became envious, formed a mob and began to incite a riot against this infant church. They declared, *"These men who have turned the world upside down have come here also."*

The reputation of Paul and Silas – and more importantly the reputation of the gospel – preceded them. The only part of that statement that they got wrong was that truly the gospel was turning the world "right side up". A world that had become disoriented and blinded by sin had now been transformed by the Light of the world and was being turned to face heavenward and bring worship, honor and glory to God. And that work which had already begun in other cities in Europe and Asia was now taking place right here in Thessalonica!

The Jews sought to bring Paul and Silas before the city council under false accusations that were very similar to those used against Jesus. He had truly been the One to turn the world "right side up" that day when He rose from the grave. Now these two men who He was using to continue His work were also being falsely accused of disturbing the peace and promoting treason against Caesar.

Unable to find Paul and Silas, the Jews turned to Jason and some of the other new local believers and brought them before the council declaring them to be guilty of treason by virtue of their newly professed belief in Jesus. These believers were now in turn being accused of "turning the world upside down". Jason was forced to post a bond and guarantee that Paul and Silas would leave the city and not return. This was Satan's attempt through the unbelieving Jews to hinder the work that the Spirit of God had begun. But though Paul and Silas would be forced to leave, they all were soon to discover that what God begins, He continues and brings to completion (Philippians 1:6).

Paul himself wrote regarding these believers and their boldness despite the persecution:

So you received the message with joy from the Holy Spirit in spite of the severe suffering it brought you. In this way, you imitated both us and the Lord. As a result, you have become an example to all the believers in Greece – throughout both Macedonia and Achaia. And now the word of the Lord is ringing out from you to people everywhere, even beyond Macedonia and Achaia, for wherever we go we find people telling us about your faith in God. We don't need to tell them about it, for they keep talking about the wonderful welcome you gave us and how you turned away from idols to serve the living and true God. And they speak of how you are looking forward to the coming of God's Son from heaven – Jesus, whom God raised from the dead.
(1 Thessalonians 1:6-10)

So what about us – is anyone accusing us of turning the world upside down? Are the truth we are declaring and the actions we are demonstrating enough of an indictment of our belief in Christ to make the unbelieving world take notice and be in an uproar? Is that true in our own lives personally, like it was in Paul and Silas? Is that true in the witness of our church, like it was in the church of Thessalonica? Is that true in our witness as the larger body of Christ? It was true in the first century because the believers reflected the One who they followed. Does the world around us see Him in our lives? Or have we become content to blend in? Have we become more fearful of the world in which we live instead of the One true God who is worthy of our reverent fear and awe? Have we become content in maintaining the status quo? Or are we truly committed to following the One who turned the world "upside down"?

The believers in the Church in Thessalonica are a part of that great crowd of witnesses that surrounds us (Hebrews 12:1). Will we become that same *"example to all believers"* that they were? Will *"the word of the Lord ring out from us to people everywhere"* as it did from them? Will others find that wherever they go, that *"people tell them about our faith in God, and how we serve the living and true God"*? Will the world *"speak of how we are looking forward to the coming of God's Son"*? Will the world even notice if we have been here? i pray that we will be found faithful in following the example of the church of Thessalonica as we follow Jesus in *"turning the world upside down"* – or rather, "right side up" – until He returns.

* * *

47

AN UNKNOWN GOD

While Paul was waiting for them in Athens, he was deeply troubled by all the idols he saw everywhere in the city. He went to the synagogue to reason with the Jews and the God-fearing Gentiles, and he spoke daily in the public square to all who happened to be there.... Then they took him to the high council of the city. "Come and tell us about this new teaching," they said.... So Paul, standing before the council, addressed them as follows: "Men of Athens, I notice that you are very religious in every way, for as I was walking along I saw your many shrines. And one of your altars had this inscription on it: 'To an Unknown God.' This God, whom you worship without knowing, is the one I'm telling you about. He is the God who made the world and everything in it....From one man He created all the nations throughout the whole earth.... His purpose was for the nations to seek after God and perhaps feel their way toward Him and find Him.... For in Him we live and move and exist.... And since this is true, we shouldn't think of God as an idol designed by craftsmen from gold or silver or stone. ... Now He commands everyone everywhere to repent of their sins and turn to Him. For He has set a day for judging the world with justice by the man He has appointed, and He proved to everyone who this is by raising Him from the dead." When they heard Paul speak about the resurrection of the dead, some laughed in contempt, but others said, "We want to hear more about this later." That ended Paul's discussion with them, but some joined him and became believers. Among them were Dionysius, a member of the council, a woman named Damaris, and others with them.

Acts 17:16-34

* * *

After leaving Thessalonica, Paul preached the gospel in the city of Berea. News that the gospel had spread to Berea reached the Jews in Thessalonica and they traveled there to disrupt the work. Despite their disruption, there were many who believed in Jesus. But the new believers sensing the danger that Paul was in, encouraged him to leave the city. Some of the believers traveled with him as he departed from Berea and journeyed to Athens, while Silas and Timothy remained in Berea to disciple the new believers.

Paul was waiting for Silas and Timothy to arrive in Athens. While waiting, he went to the synagogue on the Sabbath and spent the remaining days in the market of the public square, probably selling tents, all the while sharing the Good News of Jesus. As he walked throughout the city, Paul witnessed their many objects of worship. He saw their altars, their idols and their temples. As a matter of fact, they even had an altar to the "Unknown God". The Athenians didn't want to leave anyone out. Everything and anything had become the object of their worship – except the One true God.

Paul saw the many objects of their worship because he was looking for them. A few years ago, a group of us gathered in New York City to discuss how believers in the U.S. can more effectively share the gospel with the growing number of people groups that God is leading to live in this country – people from most every language, tribe and nation. We were being challenged that Christ's Great Commission includes not only going to the ends of the earth, it also includes reaching out to those who are our immediate neighbors.

In the course of our gathering, we were challenged that we need to open our eyes, our ears and all of our senses as we walk through our cities and neighborhoods, and discover all of the many people – and different people groups – that God is placing within our regular traffic pattern. We were challenged that typically we walk through life with our heads down and our blinders on – we look but we don't see, and we hear but we don't listen. If we would truly be witnesses, we must first be open to witness all that is going on around us – and *who* is around us. When we remove the blinders, we begin to see and learn more about the people who are around us. We also begin to see the objects of worship of those around us – just like Paul did.

• • •

We need to be "seeing" literally. Just as Paul did. We need to open our eyes to see the literal altars, idols and temples that are around us, and gain insight into the beliefs of our neighbors, asking God to enable those insights to be a bridge to share the Good News. God enabled Paul to see the altar to the "Unknown God" in order that he might better understand the spiritual hunger of the Athenians and use the altar as a bridge to introduce them to the One true God.

But also, we need to be attuned to see figuratively. First, we are to watch for the altars. Altars are not the object of worship; they are a means of worship. We often think of an altar as a structure upon which an offering or sacrifice is made. Most Christian churches have a place or a structure that is referred to as the altar – and so do the Buddhists, the Hindus, the Jews and the Paganists – to name just a few. In Christian churches, it is often the place (most often at the front of the church) to which people are invited to come to pray or make a public commitment to Christ. But altars are not only physical structures or places, they can also be metaphorical. Altars can be those commitments in our lives that we are unwilling to give up regardless of the pain and destruction they may cause to others. For example, over the years i have encountered men and women engaged in ministry who became so wrapped up in the ministry that the activity of ministry became an altar on which their family and family relationships were sacrificed and destroyed. Causes of any kind, no matter how worthy, can become an altar, when we allow the pursuit of the cause to control us. Addictions can be altars. Far too many lives have been sacrificed and destroyed on the altar of addiction.

Second, we are to watch for the idols. They are the object of worship. Sometimes altars can become idols as well. In our walk with Christ, our service to Him can be an altar on which we express worship to Him. But we must guard making our service the object of our worship. That danger comes into play when we become focused on what we are doing, rather than the One who is the reason for what we are doing.

But there are many other idols we can worship. Money is "at" or "near" the top of the list for many. That is why Jesus spoke so often about money. Money is one of those things of which we can never have enough. When my wife and i were first married and starting out, we would frequently look at each other and say, "All we need is $10,000." Interestingly enough, once we had the $10,000, then all we needed was another $10,000, and so on!

. . .

Another common idol – which often goes hand-in-hand with money – is success. It can be success in anything – a career, a hobby, a pass-time (such as sports), a relationship, a possession, a goal, and so on. We have elevated anything to an idol when the pursuit of "it" has become all-consuming. There is only one object worthy of our worship and all-consuming pursuit – and that is the Almighty God. Anything that we have placed before Him has become an idol.

Third, we are to watch for the temples. They, too, can become the object of our worship. We can become so preoccupied with the temple that we lose sight of why it exists to begin with. We know that Paul wrote, "*Don't you realize that your body is the temple of the Holy Spirit, who lives in you and was given to you by God?*" (1 Corinthians 6:19) But we can lose sight of the continuation of that verse: "*...You do not belong to yourself,*" and become so focused on maintaining our bodies that we begin to worship them! Or – and i have seen this too many times – we elevate the place that we worship to the degree that it is all about the beautiful building, or the beautiful fixtures, or the wonderful programs – and totally miss the true object of our worship. Another example is creation itself. We see the beauty of God's creation and begin to worship it. That was a common practice among the Athenians, and it is still all too common today.

Most of those who heard Paul as he addressed the council did not believe. But Luke writes, "*some joined him and became believers. Among them were Dionysius, a member of the council, a woman named Damaris....*" The Holy Spirit used the "bridge" of the altar to the "Unknown God" to draw some of those who heard to faith in Jesus. The fact that Dionysius and Damaris are mentioned by name indicates that they were prominent in Athens and/or were somehow known to Luke's original readers in the early church. Some commentators assert that Damaris was the wife of Dionysius, but that is pure speculation.

As we close this chapter, let us be mindful to be watchful for the objects of worship of those who are all around us. And be watchful – and responsive – to the way the Holy Spirit would lead us to walk across the bridges that He has provided to share the Good News. Just as it was in Athens, there will be some who are just across the bridge waiting to hear... until He returns.

48

THE CORINTHIAN CHURCH

Then Paul left Athens and went to Corinth. There he became acquainted with a Jew named Aquila, born in Pontus, who had recently arrived from Italy with his wife, Priscilla. They had left Italy when Claudius Caesar deported all Jews from Rome. Paul lived and worked with them, for they were tentmakers just as he was. Each Sabbath found Paul at the synagogue, trying to convince the Jews and Greeks alike. And after Silas and Timothy came down from Macedonia, Paul spent all his time preaching the word. He testified to the Jews that Jesus was the Messiah. But when they opposed and insulted him, Paul shook the dust from his clothes and said, "Your blood is upon your own heads – I am innocent. From now on I will go preach to the Gentiles." Then he left and went to the home of Titius Justus, a Gentile who worshiped God and lived next door to the synagogue. Crispus, the leader of the synagogue, and everyone in his household believed in the Lord. Many others in Corinth also heard Paul, became believers, and were baptized. One night the Lord spoke to Paul in a vision and told him, "Don't be afraid! Speak out! Don't be silent! For I am with you, and no one will attack and harm you, for many people in this city belong to Me." So Paul stayed there for the next year and a half, teaching the word of God. But when Gallio became governor of Achaia, some Jews rose up together against Paul and brought him before the governor for judgment. They accused Paul of "persuading people to worship God in ways that are contrary to our law." But just as Paul started to make his defense, Gallio turned to Paul's accusers and said, "Listen, you Jews, if this were a case involving some wrongdoing or a serious crime, I would have a reason to accept your case. But since it is merely a question of words and names and your Jewish law, take care of it yourselves. I refuse to judge such matters." And he threw them out of the courtroom. The crowd then grabbed Sosthenes, the leader of the synagogue, and beat him right there in the courtroom. But Gallio

paid no attention. Paul stayed in Corinth for some time after that, then said goodbye to the brothers and sisters and went to nearby Cenchrea.
Acts 18:1-18

* * *

After Paul completed the work that the Holy Spirit had for him in Athens, he went to Corinth. Bear in mind that there would always be more work to be done in Athens. But God gave those assignments to others – like Dionysius and Damaris. Paul's part was completed. God orders our steps according to His purpose for His season. Those "seasons" have different durations. His work will continue until He returns – but our role in the work is to do what He has put before us to do for the season that He has placed us there to do so. When that season comes to an end, He will show us. As He does, we are to follow Him. That is exactly what Paul was doing.

Corinth's reputation for wickedness was known throughout the Roman Empire. With a population of 200,000 people, the city was the capital of the province of Achaia, and a center for trade – of all types – and travel. Money, vice, and philosophies of all varieties found a home in Corinth. There were many philosophers and teachers of false religions in Corinth preying on an easily swayed and superstitious population. When you live in a city built on the fulfillment of feelings and desires instead of truth, you'll fall for anything because you stand for nothing.

One way that Paul distinguished himself from the plethora of religious hucksters in the city was by supporting himself as a tentmaker. Soon after he arrived in the city, he met Aquila and Priscilla, who were also tentmakers. We don't know if they were already followers of Jesus when Paul met them, or if they surrendered their lives soon after. But they quickly became co-laborers with Paul – not only in tentmaking, but also in the spreading of the gospel in the city. With their hands, hearts and home, they dedicated themselves to the work of the Lord. When Silas and Timothy arrived from Macedonia, they brought with them financial aid from the church in Philippi (2 Corinthians 11:9), which enabled Paul to spend more of his time preaching the gospel.

As was Paul's practice, he had begun his teaching in Corinth in the synagogue. But many of the Jews opposed and insulted him. One notable exception was Crispus, the leader of the synagogue, who, together with everyone in his household, came to believe in Christ, and became a part of the new church of Corinth. Paul viewed the rejection by the Jews as a release from God to preach the gospel among the Gentiles.

God led Paul to a Gentile proselyte by the name Titius Justus who soon believed in Jesus and opened his home for the new believers to gather for the worship of God and the teaching of the gospel. Titius Justus lived right next door to the synagogue, so the Jews had a "ringside seat" to witness the many who were coming to faith and being baptized. Though Jewish opposition grew, God did not lead Paul to leave Corinth as He had in Thessalonica and Berea. God encouraged Paul and affirmed His direction for him to stand firm and remain faithful in that which He had placed before him: *"For I am with you, and no one will attack and harm you, for many people in this city belong to Me."*

So Paul stood firm for the next eighteen months – not only confident in the promise of God, but also in the presence of His Spirit. You and i would do well to heed that lesson. There will be times in our journey when circumstances will be pressing in on us. We may be tempted to throw in the towel and move on. But be mindful, we're not done until God says we're done. We must stand firm and rely on the promise and presence of God. Throughout my time in ministry, God has taken me to a word of admonition He directed me through when He first called me into vocational ministry. The word comes from the epistle that Paul wrote to the Colossians. As he closes the letter, he writes a "by-the-way-type" word of admonition to a man by the name of Archippus. He says, *"Take heed to the ministry which you have received in the Lord, that you may fulfill it"* (Colossians 4:17 NASB). My paraphrase is: "Stick with it until I tell you otherwise, that you may complete what I have called you to do."

Luke records one example of God's protection over Paul there in Corinth. Apparently, the arrival of a new governor from Rome, by the name of Gallio, gave the unbelieving Jews hope that Rome might declare this new "Christian sect" illegal. So they illegally assembled a mob and forcefully brought Paul before their new governor, making false accusations about him. But even before Paul was able to make any defense, Gallio turned to Paul's accusers and *"threw them out of the courtroom"*. Paul didn't need to raise a defense – his Defender raised up one to come to his defense! The crowd then turned on the new leader of the synagogue who had brought the charges – Sosthenes – and *"beat him right there in the courtroom."*

. . .

Before you grieve for Sosthenes – take heart. Sosthenes became a follower of Christ sometime soon after that beating. Sosthenes wrote the first letter to the new church in Corinth on Paul's behalf (1 Corinthians 1:1). So, he not only became a follower, but also a co-laborer. God truly does work in mysterious ways – and in ways we would never anticipate – or even ask or think (Ephesians 3:20).

Be mindful of these truths as you continue in your journey. The same God who protected Paul, who defended him, who encouraged him, and who directed him – goes before you – and He will be faithful to do so… until He returns.

* * *

49

WHAT DOES YOUR BAPTISM MEAN?

Now a Jew named Apollos, a native of Alexandria, came to Ephesus. He was an eloquent man, competent in the Scriptures. He had been instructed in the way of the Lord. And being fervent in spirit, he spoke and taught accurately the things concerning Jesus, though he knew only the baptism of John. He began to speak boldly in the synagogue, but when Priscilla and Aquila heard him, they took him aside and explained to him the way of God more accurately. And when he wished to cross to Achaia, the brothers encouraged him and wrote to the disciples to welcome him. When he arrived, he greatly helped those who through grace had believed, for he powerfully refuted the Jews in public, showing by the Scriptures that the Christ was Jesus. And it happened that while Apollos was at Corinth, Paul passed through the inland country and came to Ephesus. There he found some disciples. And he said to them, "Did you receive the Holy Spirit when you believed?" And they said, "No, we have not even heard that there is a Holy Spirit." And he said, "Into what then were you baptized?" They said, "Into John's baptism." And Paul said, "John baptized with the baptism of repentance, telling the people to believe in the one who was to come after him, that is, Jesus." On hearing this, they were baptized in the name of the Lord Jesus. And when Paul had laid his hands on them, the Holy Spirit came on them, and they began speaking in tongues and prophesying. There were about twelve men in all.

Acts 18:24 – 19:7

* * *

After his exoneration by Governor Gallio, Paul remained in Corinth for a short while before he departed, taking Timothy, Aquila and

Priscilla with him. Silas appears to have remained in Corinth for a short while after Paul's departure. (We then lose track of Silas for about ten years until he joins Peter in Rome.) Paul and his companions traveled across the Aegean Sea, departing from the port of Cenchrea and arriving in Ephesus. Paul remained there only a short while and then sailed to Caesarea Maritima, probably still accompanied by Timothy. Aquila and Priscilla, however, remained in Ephesus to disciple the new believers and assist the newly forming church (Acts 18:18-23).

About one year after Paul had departed from Ephesus, Apollos arrived. Ephesus, with its 300,000 inhabitants, was the capital city of the Roman province of Asia and an important commercial center. Thanks to its thriving harbor, the city grew wealthy on trade. Thanks to the temple of Diana, considered to have been one of the seven wonders of the world, the city attracted hosts of visitors. Cultic prostitution was an important part of temple worship, and hundreds of "priestesses" were available in the temple.

Apollos arrived in Ephesus from Alexandria, a center of education and philosophy with a large Jewish community. He had been well-schooled in the Scriptures (the Old Testament). He obviously had a boldness, a confidence and an eloquence in speech. He was well equipped to share the truths that he had learned. The only problem was that he did not yet know the whole gospel.

While Apollos was receiving his education in Alexandria, he had learned the truths that John the Baptist had proclaimed. John had preached about the coming salvation through the Messiah. He had even preached about a future baptism of the Holy Spirit (Matthew 3:11). But remember, none of those two prophecies had yet been fulfilled when John was beheaded. He believed by faith, but never witnessed it by sight – and at the time, neither had his disciples. So that was the message that Apollos had heard in Alexandria – and up until now, he had not yet personally heard the rest of the Good News himself. He had not yet believed in Jesus – because he had not yet heard about Jesus' redemptive work!

But God had arranged for him to encounter Priscilla and Aquilla in Ephesus, that he might hear *"the way of God"* – *"more accurately"* and more completely. As a result, Apollos came to faith and truly believed. He was then baptized himself. Luke tells us that it then seemed good to the believers in Ephesus – and to the Holy Spirit – to send him to Corinth. Two of those believers who would have encouraged him to go to Corinth were Aquila and Priscilla. The new church in Corinth was close to their heart. They knew that Silas was no longer there. They probably believed that Apollos' understanding of the Scriptures would be of great help in the spiritual nurturing of that "very young" church. So off Apollos went.

Soon after Apollos left for Corinth, Paul returned to Ephesus – now on his "third missionary journey" through Asia and Europe. He encountered twelve men who had been discipled by Apollos before he himself had trusted in Jesus. When the men told Paul that they had not yet heard of the Holy Spirit, he knew that they had not yet truly been born again. They had been baptized and were seeking to be religious, but they had not yet heard the complete gospel of the saving work of Jesus. Therefore, they had not yet had an opportunity to fully receive the free gift of salvation.

In the first century, a person's baptismal experience was a clear indication of his or her spiritual condition. You had the baptism of John, which was a baptism of repentance under the Old Covenant, looking forward to the arrival of the coming Messiah. It had been important before the arrival of Jesus because it acknowledged the need for a Savior and the promise of His soon arrival.

Once Jesus began His earthly ministry, you then had the baptism being performed by His disciples, confirming Christ's arrival, but still looking ahead to the death, burial and resurrection of Christ, to be followed by the arrival of the Holy Spirit. Finally, you had the baptism that occurred on and following the Day of Pentecost, acknowledging the completed work of salvation through Christ and the indwelling presence of His Holy Spirit. The pattern was clearly established once the gospel made its way to the Gentiles, as recorded in Acts 10:43-48:

- sinners hear the Word of God,
- they repent of their sin and believe in Jesus Christ,
- they immediately receive the Holy Spirit, and
- they are baptized as a testimony of their salvation.

A person's baptismal experience today is also a clear indication of his or her spiritual condition. Baptism is not a part of salvation; it follows our salvation. There can be no salvation apart from the saving work of Jesus through His death, burial and resurrection (1 Corinthians 15:3-4). Then once we repent and believe by faith in Jesus, He seals our salvation by indwelling us with His Spirit (Ephesians 1:13-14). We then follow Christ in water baptism as an act of obedience – He told us to be baptized; and as an act of witness – bearing public testimony of the salvation we have already received by grace.

This account is an important reminder for us – not only for ourselves – but for those that God will lead us to disciple in the days ahead. It isn't sufficient for us to be passionate and bold in declaring only a portion of the gospel as Apollos was initially doing. In his enthusiasm, he led these twelve men to only have partial understanding – a partial understanding that still left them without a saving relationship with Jesus. Left in that condition, those men would have probably passed that *fatal* flaw – that incomplete truth – on to others. But God in His sovereignty brought Paul into their lives, so that they could hear the entire gospel.

We must be faithful to communicate the full story of salvation. Jesus told us, *"Go and make disciples of all the nations, baptizing them in the name of the Father and the Son and the Holy Spirit. Teach these new disciples to obey all the commands I have given you"* (Matthew 28:19-20a). Once they have become disciples, we must baptize them and teach them to obey ALL that He commanded. So that they in turn can do the same. And as we do, He told us we can be certain of this: *"I am with you always, even to the end of the age"* (Matthew 28:20b). Yes, He will be with us and empower us to bear witness to the full story of His salvation … until He returns.

* * *

50

THE EPHESIAN CHURCH

A solemn fear descended on the city, and the name of the Lord Jesus was greatly honored.... So the message about the Lord spread widely and had a powerful effect.... About that time, serious trouble developed in Ephesus concerning the Way. It began with Demetrius, a silversmith who had a large business manufacturing silver shrines of the Greek goddess Artemis. He kept many craftsmen busy. He called them together... and addressed them as follows: "Gentlemen, you know that our wealth comes from this business. But as you have seen and heard, this man Paul has persuaded many people that handmade gods aren't really gods at all.... I'm not just talking about the loss of public respect for our business. I'm also concerned that the temple of the great goddess Artemis will lose its influence and that Artemis... will be robbed of her great prestige!" ... Soon the whole city was filled with confusion. Everyone rushed to the amphitheater, dragging along Gaius and Aristarchus, who were Paul's traveling companions from Macedonia. Paul wanted to go in, too, but the believers wouldn't let him. ... Inside, the people were all shouting, some one thing and some another. Everything was in confusion. In fact, most of them didn't even know why they were there. The Jews in the crowd pushed Alexander forward and told him to explain the situation. He motioned for silence and tried to speak. But when the crowd realized he was a Jew, they started shouting again and kept it up for about two hours.... At last the mayor was able to quiet them down enough to speak. "Citizens of Ephesus," he said. "...You have brought these men here, but they have stolen nothing from the temple and have not spoken against our goddess. If Demetrius and the craftsmen have a case against them, ...they can be settled in a legal assembly. I am afraid we are in danger of being charged with rioting by the Roman government, since there is no cause for all this commotion." ...Then he dismissed them, and they dispersed.

Acts 19:17-41

* * *

Paul remained in Ephesus for three years. Throughout that time, he and the Ephesian church remained focused on the main thing – preaching the gospel and making disciples – through their words and their actions. The Lord Jesus was honored, the gospel spread widely and more were added to the Kingdom.

Paul did not arouse the opposition of the silversmiths by picketing the temple of Diana or staging anti-idolatry demonstrations. All he did was teach the truth daily and send out those who were coming to faith in Christ to do likewise to the lost in the city. Paul and the followers of "The Way" were declaring the true God, and pointing people to cleansing and purity through the free grace of God. And the Holy Spirit was drawing more people to faith each day.

Demetrius, the other craftsmen and sellers, as well as all of the leaders and purveyors of false religion, were promoting idolatry and immorality – motivated by greed and selfish ambition. As more and more people began to follow Christ, those who made a living from the worship of Diana began to see a decline in their income. The silversmiths were much more motivated by their concern for their jobs and declining incomes than they were about Diana and the temple. But they were cunning enough to not make that known; instead, they chose to use the art of manipulation. Demetrius made use of the two things the Ephesians loved the most – the honor of their city and the greatness of their goddess and her temple.

Demetrius was able to use those two passions to stir many in the city into an uproar – an uproar that became a riot. A crowd of about 25,000 shouting people began to make their way to the amphitheater. Along the way, they intended to seize Paul, but, being unable to find him, they seized two of his traveling companions – Gaius and Aristarchus, believers from Macedonia. When Paul learned what had taken place, he wanted to enter the amphitheater, but the believers, as well as some of the city leaders, wisely counseled him to stay away.

Most of the people in the amphitheater had no idea what was taking place or why they were there. They had been caught up in the emotion of the moment – and there is nothing more dangerous than an emotionally-charged, disoriented crowd.

Prior to this riot, the Jewish leaders had become envious of the popularity of Paul and The Way. They were losing adherents at a troubling rate which was, in turn, diminishing their bases of power and income. These leaders apparently saw this crowd as an opportunity for them to gain an upper hand over The Way. So they pushed one of their leaders – Alexander – forward to speak to the crowd. No doubt he wanted to tell the crowd that the Jews did not endorse Paul and The Way. They, too, wanted to see them stopped from making any further inroads into the city.

But Alexander's appearance only aroused the crowd even more, causing the deafening shouts to continue for two more hours. The crowd knew that the Jews also did not approve of the idols and did not honor Diana. The Ephesians saw the Jews as interlopers into their way of life, as much as, or maybe even more than, the followers of The Way. The only thing protecting the Jews was the Roman law that gave them freedom of religion.

Finally, it was the mayor of the city that was able to quiet down the crowd – and the mayor's interruption was motivated politically for his own self-preservation. Ephesus had been designated as a "free city" by Rome with its own elected citizens assembly. Rome extended that privilege merely as a concession, and would have welcomed any excuse to revoke that privilege. If Rome chose to do so, the mayor would be out of a job. So, he chose to use the same tactics to calm the crowd that Demetrius had employed to arouse them. He, too, reminded them of the greatness of their city and of their goddess.

The mayor declared that Paul and The Way were innocent of any crime. Rather, he accused Demetrius and the craftsmen of acting in an unlawful manner and admonished them to seek lawful remedy if there truly were any valid complaints.

The crowd was dismissed, and no doubt returned to their homes congratulating themselves for their success in defending their great city and their famous goddess. Regrettably, it is doubtful that the event caused many –

or any – to question the truthfulness of their own beliefs, or the truths being preached by Paul. Jesus once said, *"You can enter God's Kingdom only through the narrow gate. The highway to hell is broad, and its gate is wide for the many who choose that way. But the gateway to life is very narrow and the road is difficult, and only a few ever find it"* (Matthew 7:13-14). All too often, it is much easier to believe a lie and follow the crowd, than to take a stand for the truth.

Today Ephesus is gone, and so is the world-wide worship of Diana. The city and the temple are gone, as is the silversmiths' guild. But the Good News of Christ lives on. And we are recipients of the truth that arose out of that Church in Ephesus. We have the Epistle to the Ephesians, as well as First and Second Timothy. Ten years after Paul left the city, the apostle John came to pastor the church. But the church subsequently drifted from its first love – Jesus (Revelation 2:1-7).

There are important lessons for us to glean from this church and this experience. The church thrived as they remained faithfully focused on their Lord and His gospel purpose. They didn't spend their time demonstrating against the immorality of the day; they spent their time sharing the gospel. They didn't spend their time debating the false religions of the day; they spent their time sharing the gospel. They didn't spend their time fighting off false attacks; they entrusted those to God and kept sharing the gospel.

In a day that we as the church have become better known for what we are against than what we are for, we too would be wise to heed the warning to return to our first love – Jesus. And share His gospel – in word and deed – until He returns.

* * *

51

EACH ONE RAN THEIR RACE – PART 1

When the uproar was over, Paul sent for the believers and encouraged them. Then he said good-bye and left for Macedonia. While there, he encouraged the believers in all the towns he passed through. Then he traveled down to Greece, where he stayed for three months. He was preparing to sail back to Syria when he discovered a plot by some Jews against his life, so he decided to return through Macedonia. Several men were traveling with him. They were Sopater son of Pyrrhus from Berea; Aristarchus and Secundus from Thessalonica; Gaius from Derbe; Timothy; and Tychicus and Trophimus from the province of Asia. They went on ahead and waited for us at Troas. After the Passover ended, we boarded a ship at Philippi in Macedonia and five days later joined them in Troas, where we stayed a week.

Acts 20:1-6

* * *

This passage is one of those sections of the Bible that would be easy for us to avoid, or even skip over – just another list of names and places, most of which are hard to pronounce. Yet, if we believe that every line of God's Word is not only inspired by Him, but is also a gift from Him, then there is treasure that He would have us glean from this travelogue. Let's take a few minutes to look at the eleven companions of Paul that are mentioned here.

Timothy and Erastus

While in Ephesus, Paul had received distressing news regarding the church in Corinth. It prompted him to dispatch Timothy – with his pastoral heart -- to deliver a letter of correction (now known as 1 Corinthians). Timothy subsequently returned to Ephesus with continuing concerns about the Corinthian church, which included a significant personal offense against Paul and a challenge to his authority by one unnamed individual. When Timothy returned to Ephesus, he brought with him a man by the name of Erastus.

Erastus was the city treasurer in Corinth (Romans 16:23), and a new believer in Jesus Christ. Erastus was an influential man in the city. His duties likely included the upkeep of civic buildings, city streets, and city services, as well as the collection of public revenue. In that role, he also would have been called upon to settle public disputes. Erastus came to faith through Paul's second missionary journey (Chapter 48) and had become a leader within the Corinthian church. He apparently joined Timothy to bring further first hand witness to Paul of the continuing turmoil in Corinth.

In spite of his prominent rank, Erastus appears to have regarded ministry as his top priority. He left his work in Corinth to ask Paul to help bring healing to the division within the church, and then subsequently was used to spread the gospel into other lands. He did not, however, neglect his public duties, but rather, was a servant of the people, such as Paul describes in Romans 13:3-4.

While Paul was in Ephesus – before the riot – he felt compelled by the Holy Spirit that he must go to Jerusalem (Acts 19:21). In many respects, his face was set like flint toward Jerusalem, in much the same way that Jesus had set His face toward that city (Isaiah 50:7; Luke 9:51). The Father clearly had His purpose in mind. And though Paul, unlike Jesus, did not know all of what the Father's plan included in Jerusalem, he knew that he must be about the journey. He also knew, however, that he must first spend some time – a final time – with the churches that had been planted in Macedonia, Greece and Asia before going to Jerusalem. He sent Timothy and Erastus on ahead to Macedonia, while he concluded his time in Ephesus (Acts 19:22).

Titus and Trophimus

After the riot, Paul bid the Ephesian believers farewell and departed for Macedonia. He travelled through Troas, with the hope that he would see Titus there. Titus, you will recall, was a Greek from Antioch. He was led to the Lord by Paul, whereupon he served as Paul's secretary and interpreter. Titus accompanied Paul to the council held in Jerusalem, regarding the implications of the Mosaic laws upon Gentile believers (Chapter 40). Although Paul had encouraged the circumcision of Timothy, in order to render his ministry acceptable among the Jews (Chapter 42), he did not encourage Titus to do the same, so as not to seem in agreement with those who would require it of Gentile believers.

In light of the concerns that Timothy and Erastus reported about the church in Corinth, Paul decided to send them another letter – referred to as his "severe letter" (2 Corinthians 7:8-9) – the contents of which we do not know. Paul decided to send this letter through a different courier this time. It would require someone with a different gifting than Timothy. God led Paul to send Titus to Corinth as the courier of the "severe letter" with the commission to strongly admonish the Corinthian saints.

Paul was hoping to meet Titus in Troas and get a full report of what had taken place in Corinth. But when Paul arrived in Troas, Titus was not there (2 Corinthians 2:12-13). So he decided to continue his travels on into Macedonia to catch up with Timothy and Erastus. Paul and Titus finally caught up with one another somewhere in Macedonia. Paul was overjoyed by Titus' report. The Corinthian church had responded with repentance, prompting Paul to write another letter to them (that we now know as 2 Corinthians). Titus couriered that letter to Corinth accompanied by a larger entourage. Paul would later join Titus in Corinth for three months. From Corinth, Paul then sent Titus to organize the collections of alms for the Christians at Jerusalem. Titus was a troubleshooter, a peacemaker, an administrator, and a missionary.

Trophimus was a Gentile believer from Ephesus. He, too, had come to faith through Paul's ministry, and had witnessed the activity of God throughout Paul's three years in that city. It is believed that he was one of the members of the entourage that accompanied Titus to Corinth, as together they delivered the letter of 2 Corinthians to the church. This would indicate Paul's high level of trust in Trophimus. He then traveled with Paul from Corinth through Macedonia, into Asia, and onward by sea to Jerusalem.

Paul apparently wanted the church leaders in Jerusalem to hear

Trophimus' testimony about the work in Ephesus. As a result, the Jewish leaders in Jerusalem saw Paul and Trophimus in each other's company in the city, from which they fabricated the accusation that Paul had "*brought Greeks also into the Temple, and....defiled this holy place*" (Acts 21:28). That accusation is what led to Paul to be assaulted in the courts of the Temple by the Jewish mob, followed by his arrest and imprisonment by the Romans. Trophimus would rejoin Paul in his later journeys, after Paul was liberated from his first imprisonment in Rome.

Aristarchus

Aristarchus came to faith in Christ during Paul's trip to Thessalonica (Acts 17), and accompanied him on his third missionary journey. He was one of the two men seized by the crowd in Ephesus during the riot and placed before the mob in the amphitheater. Despite what had happened in Ephesus, Aristarchus continued with Paul through Macedonia and Achaia, and was there at Troas when the disciples came together, despite the attempts made by the Jews to stop the mission (Acts 20:3). Aristarchus remained close to Paul even after this, joining Paul in his voyage as a prisoner to Rome, after being locked up in Caesarea for two years (Acts 24:27). Aristarchus is mentioned as a "fellow prisoner" by Paul (Colossians 4:10; Philemon 24), showing his resolve to remain faithful no matter what trials came his way. He wasn't necessarily a great speaker, leader, or teacher. There's not even one recorded word from his mouth in Scripture. Yet, through these brief glimpses, we see a faithful follower of Christ, whose conduct can be an inspiration for the majority of us today. Let us not forget that a faithful Christian is not necessarily one who is remembered or recognized by the most men for their conduct and good works, but by God. While being a "Paul" is a great thing, let us be content with being an "Aristarchus", a Christian who didn't let trials and tribulations discourage him, but faithfully pressed toward the goal.

We'll pick up with the stories of the rest of these men in the next chapter. But in the meantime, we would do well to follow the lead of those that we have already seen and faithfully press toward that same goal – the upward calling of our Lord Jesus Christ… until He returns.

* * *

52

EACH ONE RAN THEIR RACE – PART 2

When the uproar was over, Paul sent for the believers and encouraged them. Then he said good-bye and left for Macedonia. While there, he encouraged the believers in all the towns he passed through. Then he traveled down to Greece, where he stayed for three months. He was preparing to sail back to Syria when he discovered a plot by some Jews against his life, so he decided to return through Macedonia. Several men were traveling with him. They were Sopater son of Pyrrhus from Berea; Aristarchus and Secundus from Thessalonica; Gaius from Derbe; Timothy; and Tychicus and Trophimus from the province of Asia. They went on ahead and waited for us at Troas. After the Passover ended, we boarded a ship at Philippi in Macedonia and five days later joined them in Troas, where we stayed a week.

Acts 20:1-6

* * *

Let's pick up from where we left off in the last chapter.

Secundus

Next on the list is Aristarchus' fellow countryman Secundus. Both men came from Thessalonica, but they were probably two very different men. Aristarchus' name was connected with aristocracy, the ruling class. It's likely that he came from a wealthy and powerful family. His is just the kind of name that would be given to a nobleman. We can suppose that he was a man of higher station. Secundus, on the other hand, was a common name for a slave. It meant "Second." Slaves were often not called by their true names. The first-ranking slave in a household would have been called Primus; the second-ranking slave was often called Secundus. So, there they were - Aristarchus and Secundus, one probably a nobleman and the other probably a slave. Yet, side by side they served the Lord and the apostle Paul. This true fellowship between noblemen and slaves was a scandal to many in the Roman world; they found it hard to believe that they sat together and served together in church. Yet they did, because they both believed that who they were in Jesus Christ was more important than who they were thought to be in this world.

It has rightly been said that the ground is level at the foot of the cross. There is no one from such a high station of life that they don't need Jesus. There is no one from such a low station of life that Jesus can't lift them up. Everyone – both high and low – must humble themselves and come through the same gate of faith to Jesus. It doesn't matter if you are an Aristarchus or a Secundus – Jesus is your only way, and same way for all.

Sopater and Gaius

We know the least about Sopater. He was a Gentile background believer from Berea who traveled with this group back into Asia.

Another one of Paul's traveling companions was Gaius of Derbe. Derbe was a city in Galatia in Asia Minor. It is very probable that Gaius came to faith in Christ through Paul's first missionary journey. It seems that Gaius joined this traveling band while they were in Greece and assisted Paul throughout this journey through Asia.

Tychicus

Another one of Paul's companions on the way from Corinth to Jerusalem is Tychicus. He was a native of Asia Minor. Paul calls him a *"much loved brother"* and a *"faithful servant"* of the Lord (Ephesians 6:21). He is characterized as being an encourager (Ephesians 6:22), which is evidenced by the fact that he was with Paul during his first and second Roman imprisonments. He also was trustworthy; Paul entrusted him to deliver his epistles to the Ephesians and Colossians and to bring news of the apostle to those congregations (Colossians 4:7-8).

In traveling to Colossae, Tychicus accompanied Onesimus, the former slave who was returning to Philemon. No doubt, Tychicus, as a trusted companion to Paul, was able to emphasize the need for grace in receiving Onesimus back home (Philemon 17).

Tychicus also served as "interim pastor" in both Crete and Ephesus, so that Titus and Timothy, respectively, could visit Paul while he was in prison. It is believed that Paul was describing Tychicus when he wrote, *"a brother who has often proved to us in many ways that he is zealous, and now even more so because of his great confidence in you"* (2 Corinthians 8:22).

Silas and Luke

Lastly we see that Silas and Luke have reunited with the group. Silas rejoined Paul in Corinth, and they all reunited with Luke in Philippi. Then while the others all went ahead to Troas, Silas and Luke remained with Paul in Philippi for five more days until the Passover had concluded.

Like i said at the outset of the last chapter, it would be easy to skip over this list of names and places. But we need to see this unique group of men that God brought together for His purpose. They were men from Judea, Syria, Cilicia, Asia, Macedonia and Achaia. They were Gentiles and Jews. They were public officials, commoners, aristocrats and slaves. They represented a diversity of backgrounds, languages and cultures. But they all had three things in common.

First, they were all fully-devoted followers of Jesus. They were all sinners whose lives had been transformed by the saving grace of Christ – and they were completely sold out to Him.

Second, with the exception of Silas, they all appear to have come to faith through the ministry of Paul. And all of them – even now as co-laborers – have been discipled by Paul. Paul didn't forget about these men once they came to faith, he continued to pour his life into them. Each one of them were now being used by God to disciple others and extend His Kingdom throughout Europe and Asia. They were making disciples who were making disciples... who were making disciples.

Third, each one, in obedience to God's direction in their lives followed Him without regard for personal safety, comfort or wealth. They were threatened by the Jews. They would soon be persecuted by the Romans. They dealt with disagreement and division within the church. And yet, they ran their race in such a way to obtain the prize (1 Corinthians 9:24).

We would do well to remember that God has also brought us together for His purpose. We come from different countries, cultures and languages – just like this group of eleven. Let's be faithful to follow their lead and run the race in such a way to obtain the prize… until He returns.

* * *

53

PERSUADED TO GO

The next stop after leaving Tyre was Ptolemais, where we greeted the brothers and sisters and stayed for one day. The next day we went on to Caesarea and stayed at the home of Philip the Evangelist, one of the seven men who had been chosen to distribute food. He had four unmarried daughters who had the gift of prophecy. Several days later a man named Agabus, who also had the gift of prophecy, arrived from Judea. He came over, took Paul's belt, and bound his own feet and hands with it. Then he said, "The Holy Spirit declares, 'So shall the owner of this belt be bound by the Jewish leaders in Jerusalem and turned over to the Gentiles.'" When we heard this, we and the local believers all begged Paul not to go on to Jerusalem. But he said, "Why all this weeping? You are breaking my heart! I am ready not only to be jailed at Jerusalem but even to die for the sake of the Lord Jesus." When it was clear that we couldn't persuade him, we gave up and said, "The Lord's will be done." After this we packed our things and left for Jerusalem. Some believers from Caesarea accompanied us, and they took us to the home of Mnason, a man originally from Cyprus and one of the early believers. When we arrived, the brothers and sisters in Jerusalem welcomed us warmly.
Acts 21:7-17

* * *

As we have already seen in Chapter 51, while Paul was in Ephesus the Holy Spirit compelled him to go to Jerusalem (Acts 19:21). It would be Paul's last journey to Jerusalem. And not unlike Jesus' last journey to Jerusalem, Paul stopped at multiple points along the way. He used the journey to encourage many of the churches that God had allowed him to be a part of planting. This journey had been about "watering" – and in some instances "pruning" – the churches that had already begun, more than it had been about "sowing" new seeds.

Along the way, he stopped in Miletus and invited the elders from Ephesus to come meet with him. When they arrived he declared, *"I am bound by the Spirit to go to Jerusalem. I don't know what awaits me, except that the Holy Spirit tells me in city after city that jail and suffering lie ahead…. And now I know that none of you to whom I have preached the Kingdom will ever see me again"* (Acts 20:22-23,25). He then encouraged them to shepherd the flock over which the Holy Spirit had appointed them as leaders. Having done so, they prayed together… and cried together – knowing they would not see one another again. Then they escorted him on his way (Acts 20:36-38).

Upon arriving in Tyre in Syria, he met with the local believers and stayed with them for a week. The believers there "kept on saying to him" that he should not set foot in Jerusalem (Acts 21:4). In Caesarea, a man named Agabus, who had the gift of prophecy, after having bound himself with Paul's belt, said to Paul, *"The Holy Spirit declares, 'So shall the owner of this belt be bound by the Jewish leaders in Jerusalem and turned over to the Gentiles'"* (Acts 21:11). Luke records that all of Paul's traveling companions – including Luke – as well as the local believers *"all begged Paul not to go to Jerusalem"* (Acts 21:12).

To which Paul responded: *"Why all this weeping? You are breaking my heart! I am ready not only to be jailed at Jerusalem but even to die for the sake of the Lord Jesus"* (Acts 21:13).

With few exceptions, most everyone was trying to persuade Paul to NOT go to Jerusalem. Most everyone included his closest companions like Luke and Silas. It included the elders of the churches. It included the evangelist Philip (Acts 21:8). It included Agabus the prophet. Most everyone was telling him not to go… EXCEPT the Holy Spirit. The Holy Spirit had clearly told Paul to go to Jerusalem.

So, what do you do when you know God has told you to do one thing and most everyone else – including those who are the closest to you – is telling you to do the exact opposite?

• • •

A number of years ago i read the book *"The Dream Giver"* by Bruce Wilkinson. It was a very timely read because, at the time, God was directing us to step out by faith on a journey into the unknown. It was unknown for us, but God clearly knew where the journey would lead.

Bruce Wilkinson writes in his book that when God leads you to leave your "Land of Familiar" – that place where you currently are, that place that is comfortable – and go to a new land – a "Land of Promise", you will pass through a Wilderness. That Land of Promise can be a gloriously inviting place – or it can be a difficult place. The key is that it is the place that you know God has told you to go – and to do anything less would be disobedience to God. That is exactly what Paul was doing – he was going to a place – physically and figuratively – that he knew God had told him to go.

As you take that journey and step into the Wilderness, Bruce writes that you will encounter three types of people along the way. You will encounter the "Bullies" who try to drive you back to Familiar, the "Buddies" who love you but are less than enthusiastic because they can't understand what you are doing, and the "Busters" who will encourage you each and every step along the way. Bullies and Buddies will always try to persuade you that there is another way – a better way. And they'll either try to bully you into submission, or sweet talk you into submission.

The Bullies are most often driven by a fear of what your journey of faith will do to them. They are concerned about the repercussions they will experience as a result of your decision. Or, they are driven out of grief. They are grieving a personal loss resulting from your journey. The Buddies are trying to save you heartache or difficulty. They have designated themselves to be your "holy spirit" because they believe they have your best interest in mind. They don't want you to go through the pain, and as your friend, they don't want to go through it either. An important distinction is that Bullies and Buddies do NOT have a word from God. They are leaning on their own understanding (Proverbs 3:5).

Busters, on the other hand, have sought the Lord with you. They may not like what they hear, but they know that they – like you – need to trust the One from whom they have heard it. They too have come to that place that to do anything different would be disobedience to God. Busters will do whatever they can to help you and encourage you along the way. Busters will also be your best prayer intercessors.

. . .

Over the years, we've encountered all three. Regrettably, the Busters stand in the minority – but what they lack in numbers they make up for in resolve. And i am grateful to God for each and every one that He has brought across our path! My prayer continues to be that i will be the Buster that God would have me be to others as they walk their personal faith journey. This series of books has in fact been written for that purpose.

Paul was not persuaded to depart from the path that God had set before him, because he had already been "persuaded" by God to walk that path. God had given him a clear word with a clear confirmation by His Spirit. i have intentionally used the word "persuaded" instead of the word "compelled". i have done so because i want it to be clear that Paul had a choice. He could have chosen to be disobedient to God and go his own way. The Bullies and Buddies would have supported that decision.

But Paul chose to walk by faith according to God's Word empowered by His Spirit. Paul himself later writes, *"For this reason I also suffer these things; nevertheless I am not ashamed, for I know whom I have believed and am persuaded that He is able to keep what I have committed to Him until that Day"* (2 Timothy 1:12 NKJ). Paul was "persuaded" to go because he knew that God was trustworthy and able to keep that which Paul had committed to Him – his own life – until the day of Christ's return. And He still is... and always will be... until He returns!

* * *

54

THE RIGHT CITIZENSHIP

The commander brought Paul inside and ordered him lashed with whips to make him confess his crime. He wanted to find out why the crowd had become so furious. When they tied Paul down to lash him, Paul said to the officer standing there, "Is it legal for you to whip a Roman citizen who hasn't even been tried?" When the officer heard this, he went to the commander and asked, "What are you doing? This man is a Roman citizen!" So the commander went over and asked Paul, "Tell me, are you a Roman citizen?" "Yes, I certainly am," Paul replied. "I am, too," the commander muttered, "and it cost me plenty!" Paul answered, "But I am a citizen by birth!" The soldiers who were about to interrogate Paul quickly withdrew when they heard he was a Roman citizen, and the commander was frightened because he had ordered him bound and whipped.
Acts 22:24-29

* * *

Paul's arrest had been precipitated by false accusations and misunderstandings. The *"whole city"* had been rocked by the accusations (Acts 21:30). A riotous crowd was trying to kill Paul when the Roman regiment arrived to bring order. The Jews had falsely accused Paul of bringing the Gentile Trophimus (Chapter 51) into the Temple, which he had not. The commander (Claudius) mistakenly thought Paul was an Egyptian rebel leader, which, of course, he was not. So Claudius ordered that Paul be bound in chains and taken to the fortress. Just before he was taken inside, Paul was granted permission to speak to the crowd. He spoke to them in Hebrew, so Claudius was unable to understand any of what Paul was saying.

. . .

The riotous crowd that was gathered in the courtyard of the fortress quieted down to listen as Paul told them the story of his conversion. They continued to listen while he told them that Jesus was the Messiah. But when he told the crowd that the Lord had told him to tell the Good News to the Gentiles, the crowd erupted. No devout Jew would have anything to do with the Gentiles! Had Paul not uttered that one word, he might have been released. Paul knew that, but he had to be faithful in his witness, no matter the cost. He knew that it was better for him to be a faithful prisoner than it would be for him to be a freed man who had failed to speak truth.

Claudius had no idea why the crowd was again rioting, but he ordered that Paul be taken inside and whipped, so that he might confess his crimes. That brings us to this particular passage in Acts. Claudius was about to have his soldiers commit a crime. A crime for which Claudius would have, at the very least, been discharged from his position. The soldiers would have themselves been beaten, if not also discharged from service. It was no small act to violate the rights of a Roman citizen.

Claudius, acknowledging his error, arranged to have Paul brought before his accusers – the Jewish high council. Claudius would ensure that this time there would be no riotous crowd. He wanted to know exactly what the trouble was all about so that he could officially charge Paul under his rights as a Roman citizen. Secondly, Claudius needed to have official charges so that he could support the action he had already taken against Paul. (He needed to cover his back against any possible repercussions!)

As Paul stood before the high council, the members quickly divided – Pharisees versus Sadducees – over whether Paul stood accused of anything. Quickly Claudius realized that no one was expressing any crime for which Paul should be charged. But as the debate became more animated, Claudius was afraid they would tear Paul apart. *"So he ordered his soldiers to go and rescue him by force and take him back to the fortress"* (Acts 23:10).

Later that night the Lord appeared to Paul in his jail cell and said, *"Be encouraged, Paul. Just as you have been a witness to me here in Jerusalem, you must preach the Good News in Rome as well"* (Acts 23:11). God had just given

Paul an irrefutable word. He was going to Rome! He would preach the Good News in Rome! He may have currently been sitting in a jail cell in Jerusalem, but the Lord God was going to move heaven and earth to accomplish His purpose through Paul. From that moment until he "preached in Rome", Paul became invincible. There wasn't a power on earth – or outside of this earth – that could keep him from accomplishing God's purpose. God did not give Paul a *conditional* word; He gave him an *absolute* word.

There would be numerous times between that moment in the jail cell and the moment that he would first preach in Rome that Paul would have good reason to question whether that, in fact, was going to take place! But on each of those occasions all Paul would need to do was remember the word God had given him. That is as true for us as it was for Paul. When God gives you a promise, hold onto it! Write it down! God is not a man that He should lie (Numbers 23:19). Nothing and no one can keep God from fulfilling His promise!

God's promise was to be tested in Paul's life as soon as the next morning. A group of more than forty men made an oath before the leading priests and elders that they would not eat or drink until they had killed Paul. They sought the assistance of the priests by requesting that a message be sent to Claudius to bring Paul back before the council. They planned to kill Paul along the way. But Paul's nephew learned of the plot and informed Claudius. Claudius wisely directed two of his officers to take Paul that very evening, under an armed guard of almost five hundred soldiers, to Caesarea. (Acts 23:12-24). Think about it – when God makes a promise He backs it up with all the resources that are needed to bring it about. He arranged for Claudius to provide five hundred soldiers to protect Paul! And He also provided a horse so he wouldn't have to walk! (Acts 23:24).

Claudius sent Paul together with a letter to the Governor of the Iudaean province – Marcus Antonius Felix. (By the way, Felix was the seventh governor over Iudaea after Pilate, and the fourth after Agrippa (Chapter 33). No one seemed to be able to hold that job for very long.) The letter said, "*This man was seized by some Jews, and they were about to kill him when I arrived with the troops. When I learned that he was a Roman citizen, I removed him to safety. Then I took him to their high council to try to learn the basis of the accusations against him. I soon discovered the charge was something regarding their religious law – certainly nothing worthy of imprisonment or death. But when I was informed of a plot to kill him, I immediately sent him on to you. I have told his accusers to bring their charges before you"* (Acts 23:27-30).

We'll pick up with the story in the next chapter. But here's what we need to see thus far. Throughout his ministry – and even now as he began this leg of his journey that would subsequently lead to Rome – God demonstrated that He had uniquely equipped Paul to be the missionary to the Roman Empire. Even Claudius came to realize that Paul was a remarkable man. He was a learned man who spoke Greek. He was not the common crook or rebel leader that Claudius first thought. His Greek training had given him a global worldview. His Hebrew training in the Mosaic Law and prophecies had prepared him to interpret the law in the light of Christ and His redemptive death and resurrection. His Roman citizenship opened doors throughout the empire and ultimately these doors to Rome.

God has uniquely prepared and equipped each and every one of us for the mission He has set before us. You may not speak Greek, Hebrew, Aramaic or Latin – but you speak the language that you will need to accomplish God's purpose. You may not have formal training in the Scriptures, but you have the knowledge that you will need to communicate the gospel and fulfill the mission God has for you. You may not have Roman citizenship, but you have just the citizenship that you will need – you're a citizen of the Kingdom! As a result, the same Holy Spirit who dwelt within Paul dwells within you. Yes, you have all of the ability that you need to accomplish God's purpose through the indwelling presence of His Holy Spirit (Acts 1:8). And you have the same mandate that Paul had – to go and make disciples.

Nothing can prevent us from accomplishing that purpose – except ourselves. We're citizens of the Kingdom. So let's take a pointer from Paul and trust our God to lead us, protect us, empower us and direct us – each and every step of the way… until He returns.

* * *

55

THE CASE FOR THE PROSECUTION

"I will hear your case myself when your accusers arrive," the governor told him. Then the governor ordered him kept in the prison at Herod's headquarters. Five days later Ananias, the high priest, arrived with some of the Jewish elders and the lawyer Tertullus, to present their case against Paul to the governor. When Paul was called in, Tertullus presented the charges against Paul in the following address to the governor: "You have provided a long period of peace for us Jews and with foresight have enacted reforms for us. For all of this, Your Excellency, we are very grateful to you. But I don't want to bore you, so please give me your attention for only a moment. We have found this man to be a troublemaker who is constantly stirring up riots among the Jews all over the world. He is a ringleader of the cult known as the Nazarenes. Furthermore, he was trying to desecrate the Temple when we arrested him. We would have judged him by our law, but Lysias, the commander of the garrison, came and violently took him away from us, commanding his accusers to come before you. You can find out the truth of our accusations by examining him yourself." Then the other Jews chimed in, declaring that everything Tertullus said was true.

Acts 23:35 – 24:9

* * *

Marcus Antonius Felix had been the Roman governor of Iudaea for approximately six years. He was said to have the disposition of a slave and the power of a tyrant. Emperor Claudius had appointed Felix governor in about 52 AD. He governed Iudaea until about 60 AD when he was recalled to Rome to answer for disturbances in the province and irregularities in his rule. Felix's home base was Caesarea Maritima, just like the kings, prefects and procurators of that province before him.

Affairs between the Jewish people and their Roman rulers deteriorated under Felix's governorship. He was well known for his cruelty and licentious behavior. His predisposition to receiving bribes further led to a great increase in corruption and crime throughout the province. The years of his rule were marked by internal feuds and disturbances, which he was known to put down with brutal severity.

In general, the Iudaean populace mistrusted him. There had been a Sadducee by the name of Jonathan, who had been instrumental in helping Felix secure his appointment as governor. Initially Jonathan was a counselor and confidant to Felix, helping him navigate relations with the Jews. When the High Priest Ananias was sent to Rome in 52 AD, Felix named Jonathan to replace him. In his role as High Priest, Jonathan continued to counsel Felix to change his ways if he wanted peaceful relations with the people and favor from Rome. Jonathan truly wanted Felix to succeed and feared that the governor's actions would cause the Jewish leaders to complain to Caesar. But Felix tired of Jonathan's criticism. As a result, he persuaded one of Jonathan's most faithful friends to kill him. Soon thereafter, Ananias returned to the role of High Priest.

In fairness, Felix had little experience ruling when he was originally given the position. He was born a slave, became a freedman, then was quickly elevated to a high government official. Felix's brother Pallas was one of Emperor Claudius' most trusted ministers and probably obtained the governorship for Felix. While governor, Felix fell in love with Drusilla, the beautiful daughter of King Agrippa. At the time of their meeting, she was the wife of Azizus, king of Emesa. She and Felix conspired together for her to divorce Azizus so that the two of them could marry.

Ananias was the High Priest in Jerusalem from 47-52 and 53-59 AD. In 52 AD he was sent to Rome by Quadratus, legate of Syria, to answer a charge of oppression brought by the Samaritans, but Emperor Claudius acquitted him. On his return to Jerusalem, he resumed the office of high priest which had just been vacated by Jonathan's untimely demise. He was a typical Sadducee – wealthy, haughty, unscrupulous, fulfilling his sacred office for purely selfish and political ends, anti-nationalist in his relation to the Jews, and friendly to the Romans. He would later die an ignominious death, being assassinated by the popular zealots at the beginning of the last Jewish war.

Tertullus was a well-known "prosecuting attorney" in the province. He had certainly argued in Roman court many times before. The Jews had employed him to state their case before Felix. More than likely, he was a Hellenistic Jew. The high council had not needed a lawyer to try Paul in their own court, but after Claudius had secretly moved Paul to Caesarea, they had no choice. They required an expert in Roman law to present their case accordingly. With only a matter of days to prepare, Tertullus was their choice.

After dispensing with the customary – and completely baseless – flattery, the lawyer set forth his unjust charges. First, he charged that Paul was creating disturbances among Romans throughout the empire to stir up sedition – an offense against the Roman government. Second, he charged that Paul was the ringleader of a rebellious sect known as the Nazarenes. It is interesting to note that the lawyer did not refer to the "sect" as Christians. That term was already being used in many parts of the province, but for Tertullus to do so would imply that the Jews' were acknowledging Jesus as the Christ (the Messiah). Third, he charged that Paul had attempted to profane the Temple (by bringing a Gentile into it), a crime that the Jews themselves were permitted to punish.

Additionally, Tertullus included subtle insinuations against Claudius Lysias, intended to imply that the Romans had unnecessarily escalated the matter. He was intimating that if Claudius had handled the situation properly Felix would never have had to be called upon to adjudicate this disturbance. But now that it had been escalated, he clearly indicated that the charges against Paul had implications for the entire empire. When he was done, *"the other Jews chimed in, declaring that everything Tertullus said was true."* He lied… and they swore to it!

It was a formidable attack against Paul. On one side stood an unscrupulous religious leader represented by a crafty attorney, presenting their case before a crooked judge who was ultimately looking for a bribe. On the other side was a near-blind missionary who had been falsely accused. The cards were stacked in favor of the prosecution – or so they thought. Because no one in the room, except Paul, had the spiritual eyes to see that God was on his side!

. . .

Paul was His ambassador on His mission, journeying according to His plan. The outcome of this trial had been settled long ago. God had already declared His verdict. "My servant Paul is going to Rome to preach My gospel" (Acts 23:11). No "trumped up" charges were going to change that. No eloquence on the part of the attorney was going to make any difference. And Ananias and Felix were impotent to do anything about it.

You may be in a place right now that feels like that "court room" did for Paul. You may feel like the cards are stacked against you. Follow Paul's lead. God is right there with you. Hold onto the promise He has given you and trust Him to lead you through all of the details. He's the Judge… and the Jury. This is all going to end according to His verdict and His plan. Watch Him work… and trust that He will… until He returns.

* * *

56

A DIVINE DELAY

...Paul said, "I know, sir, that you have been a judge of Jewish affairs for many years, so I gladly present my defense before you. You can quickly discover that I arrived in Jerusalem no more than twelve days ago to worship at the Temple. My accusers never found me arguing with anyone in the Temple, nor stirring up a riot in any synagogue or on the streets of the city. These men cannot prove the things they accuse me of doing. But I admit that I follow the Way, which they call a cult. I worship the God of our ancestors, and I firmly believe the Jewish law and everything written in the prophets.... Ask these men here what crime the Jewish high council found me guilty of...." At that point Felix, who was quite familiar with the Way, adjourned the hearing and said, "Wait until Lysias, the garrison commander, arrives. Then I will decide the case." He ordered an officer to keep Paul in custody but to give him some freedom and allow his friends to visit him and take care of his needs. A few days later Felix came back with his wife, Drusilla, who was Jewish. Sending for Paul, they listened as he told them about faith in Christ Jesus. As he reasoned with them about righteousness and self-control and the coming day of judgment, Felix became frightened. "Go away for now," he replied. "When it is more convenient, I'll call for you again." He also hoped that Paul would bribe him, so he sent for him quite often and talked with him. After two years went by in this way, Felix was succeeded by Porcius Festus. And because Felix wanted to gain favor with the Jewish people, he left Paul in prison.

Acts 24:10-27

* * *

Tertullus had accused Paul of treason – but there were no witnesses and there was no evidence to support such a charge. If Paul was guilty of treason, he should be put to death. But once Felix had heard the charges against Paul as presented by Tertullus (Acts 24:2-9), he clearly saw that there was no basis for those charges. Legally Felix should have let Paul go free right there and then. He didn't even need to hear Paul's defense. The prosecution had failed to make its case!

But Felix, above all else, had learned how to be a politician. He did not want to needlessly antagonize the religious leaders. In order to retain his position as governor of the province, he needed to keep peace with the Jews. And in order to keep peace with the Jews, he needed the religious leaders to see him as an ally – at least in this matter – and not as an adversary. He was more concerned about doing what was politically expedient than he was about doing what was right. He was quite content to keep Paul unjustly imprisoned because it fulfilled his end purpose. Though he said that he wanted to hear from Claudius Lysias before he made any decision about Paul, there is no indication that Claudius was ever asked to give such a report at any time over the two years that followed.

Over the course of the next two years, Paul repeatedly had opportunity to preach the Good News to Felix and Drusilla. But on each occasion Felix would put off making any decision until "the next time". As Luke writes, particularly as time went on, part of the reason for Felix continuing to keep Paul imprisoned was his hope that Paul would give him a bribe. He even made it easy for Paul to arrange a bribe by allowing his friends *"to visit him and take care of his needs."* But no bribe every materialized, so Paul remained a prisoner.

It would have been customary for Felix to release Paul from prison when he was turning over rule of the province to Porcius Festus. But even on that occasion, Felix was more concerned about the political capital he was earning by keeping Paul imprisoned than he was with doing the right thing.

But if we read all of this at face value and attribute Paul's extended imprisonment to the decisions of Felix, we will have missed the whole point. This was God's plan, not Felix's. This delay was a part of the plan that the Holy Spirit confirmed when He told Paul that he would *"preach the Good News in Rome*" (Acts 23:11). Paul would not only preach to Romans in Rome; he would preach to Romans along the way.

In Chapter 22, we looked at divine appointments, but here we witness a divine delay. Divine delays are not necessarily momentary – though they can be. The divine delays that i'm talking about are those seasons that appear to go on for what feels like an eternity. Often, there is no apparent reason for what is causing the delay.

Scripture is full of people who were delayed by God. Abraham and Sarah waited twenty-five years for the son God promised to give them. Jacob worked for Laban for fourteen years in order to receive the hand of Rachel in marriage. Joseph waited thirteen years to rise from the pit of his imprisonment to the throne room of Pharaoh. The Israelites wandered in the wilderness for forty years before they entered the Promised Land. Fifteen years passed between the time that David was anointed king and the time he actually ascended to the throne. The one hundred twenty disciples waited eight days in the upper room for the Holy Spirit to be poured out upon them. And Paul remained imprisoned for two years by Felix.

What are we to do while we wait in that waiting room of delay? i know the simple answer is "trust God". But what more has God shown us through the life of Paul and others in Scripture.

First, embrace the promise God has given you. And if you don't have a promise, ask Him for one! God is at work through every detail of our lives to bring glory to His Name. We have the tendency to live with the myopic view that everything is about us. It isn't! God created the heavens and the earth and all of us who dwell within it for His purpose – not ours. Everything we have is from Him. Our very lives belong to Him. Every person that i mentioned from Scripture received a promise from God – Abraham and Sarah were told they would have a son, Jacob was promised that his descendants would be as numerous as the dust of the earth, Joseph was promised that his family would bow before him, the Israelites were promised a land in which they would worship God, David was promised the throne, the disciples were promised the Helper, and Paul was told he would preach in Rome. Keep God's promise before you and don't let go of it.

. . .

Second, remember that a delay is not inactivity. We must walk in obedience, doing all that God has placed before us to do, while we are awaiting the fulfillment of His promise. For Abraham, it included rescuing his nephew. For Joseph, it included being a faithful steward in prison. For David, it included slaying the giant Goliath. For the disciples, it included worshiping in the Temple under the watchful eyes of the very leaders who had arranged to have Jesus crucified. For Paul, it involved preaching to Felix and Drusilla. Delays are rarely times to just sit back; more often they are a time to press forward in what we know God has called us to do. There is always a temptation to step out on our own to try and find a shortcut around the delay. Abraham and Sarah attempted to do that. Their efforts resulted in the birth of Ishmael, when God's promise was Isaac. Don't sit idly by. Take the path God puts before you. But make sure it is His path.

Third, acknowledge that His timing is perfect. God is at work in ways we will never know to accomplish His purpose in His perfect timing. We all know that the Holy Spirit came upon the disciples in that upper room on the Day of Pentecost – but, as we already saw in chapter 6, let's remember why it was significant that the Holy Spirit came on that day. Pentecost is a Greek name. The Jews called it the "Festival of the Harvest". The festival celebrated the first fruits of the harvest season. With the arrival of His Holy Spirit on the "Festival of the Harvest", God was signifying that the harvest of the first fruits of salvation had now begun. Three thousand were baptized that day. The church was birthed. His harvest had begun – on the "Festival of the Harvest". A word that the Lord gave me years ago is *"I am the LORD; in its time I will hasten it"* (Isaiah 60:22 ESV). His timing is perfect. He will delay until then, and He will hasten it on the day.

There is an end to the delay. It ends with His promise being fulfilled and Him being glorified. No matter how much time it takes, no matter how long you have been delayed in the waiting room, remember He will complete what He has begun! Hold onto that promise… until He returns.

* * *

57

AN APPEAL TO CAESAR

Three days after Festus arrived in Caesarea to take over his new responsibilities, he left for Jerusalem, where the leading priests and other Jewish leaders met with him and made their accusations against Paul. They asked Festus as a favor to transfer Paul to Jerusalem (planning to ambush and kill him on the way). But Festus replied that Paul was at Caesarea and he himself would be returning there soon. So he said, "Those of you in authority can return with me. If Paul has done anything wrong, you can make your accusations." About eight or ten days later Festus returned to Caesarea, and on the following day he took his seat in court and ordered that Paul be brought in. When Paul arrived, the Jewish leaders from Jerusalem gathered around and made many serious accusations they couldn't prove. Paul denied the charges. "I am not guilty of any crime against the Jewish laws or the Temple or the Roman government," he said. Then Festus, wanting to please the Jews, asked him, "Are you willing to go to Jerusalem and stand trial before me there?" But Paul replied, "No! This is the official Roman court, so I ought to be tried right here. You know very well I am not guilty of harming the Jews. If I have done something worthy of death, I don't refuse to die. But if I am innocent, no one has a right to turn me over to these men to kill me. I appeal to Caesar!" Festus conferred with his advisers and then replied, "Very well! You have appealed to Caesar, and to Caesar you will go!"

Acts 25:1-12

* * *

It had been two years, but the Jewish leaders still wanted to kill Paul. He may have been out of sight, but he hadn't been forgotten. It appears that at their first meeting with the new governor, Porcius Festus, the Jewish leaders told him their accusations against Paul.

It is noteworthy to see how the priests and elders interacted with their new governor. First, they asked him to transfer Paul to Jerusalem. They were hopeful that as a new governor, Festus would acquiesce to their request as a sign of good faith for future relations, and they would be able to successfully execute their original plan to kill Paul. Second, after the first attempt failed, they followed Festus back to Caesarea requesting that he immediately convene a trial. But no mention is made of a lawyer accompanying them. Apparently they felt that Tertullus' representation before Felix had proven to be inadequate and ineffective, so they were confident that they could do no worse representing themselves before their new governor.

Very quickly, as the religious leaders made their accusations against Paul, it became obvious to Festus, just as it had been to Felix, that Paul wasn't guilty of any crime under Roman law. So here he was – just like Pontius Pilate and Felix before him. Festus' assignment from Rome was to maintain peaceful control over this occupied nation. He was directed by his superiors in Rome to not do anything that could disrupt the peace or make the Roman occupation more tenuous. Before him stood the religious leaders of the occupied people pressuring him to find a man guilty of baseless charges. If he found in favor of Paul, he would alienate the Jews and potentially disrupt the peace of what was already a tenuous occupation. If he found Paul to be guilty, he would be sentencing a man to death that he knew wasn't guilty of any crime. At that moment, he blamed Felix for having left him with that "no-win" dilemma.

Since no Roman law was broken, Festus' resolution was that Paul should be returned to Jerusalem to be tried in the Temple court. Though that remedy would not provide the religious leaders with the legal means to execute Paul, it would enable them to arrange to have him killed while he was being transported back to Jerusalem. So Festus' solution was more than acceptable to the Jews.

But Paul's response to Festus' resolution totally caught the new governor off guard. He appealed to Caesar! As we saw in Chapter 54, Roman citizenship came with various perks. One of those perks was that citizens had the right to appeal a decision to a higher authority. And the decisions of governors, such as Festus, could be appealed to Caesar himself. Decisions appealed to local authorities could often take as long as one to two years due to administrative backlogs. As you can imagine, the Emperor's backlog was even greater.

Once a citizen had requested an appeal to a higher authority, the process could not be negated by a lower authority. So, for example, once Paul appealed to Caesar, Festus was powerless to do anything further. He could no longer require that Paul be taken to Jerusalem. He was powerless to do anything regarding Paul, other than keep him under guard awaiting transport to Rome.

In many respects, Paul's appeal to Caesar provided Festus with the best solution to his "no-win" dilemma. He was now powerless to make any decision regarding Paul – therefore he no longer was compelled to do anything to this innocent man for fear of how the Jews would respond. And the Jews could no longer hold him responsible, because he was powerless to make a decision!

But it's important for us to remember that this wasn't Festus' plan. It wasn't even Paul's plan. This was God's plan. Long before there was a Caesar, and long before there was a Paul, God had orchestrated that Paul would have the ability to appeal unto Caesar. He had put all the mechanisms in place for Paul to be able to make that appeal. And it wasn't simply for the protection of Paul; it was for the furtherance of God's plan – that Paul preach the Good News in Rome!

God has promised that He will make a way where there seems to be no way. The prophet Isaiah wrote:

I am the Lord, who opened a way through the waters,
making a dry path through the sea…
I will make a pathway through the wilderness.
I will create rivers in the dry wasteland.
(Isaiah 43:16,19)

He will do whatever it takes to accomplish His purpose in and through our lives. He'll make a dry path across a Red Sea, or He'll use an unsuspecting Caesar and a process of appeal.

If you find yourself in one of those situations where you're not sure how or where to turn, allow God to lead you in the path that He has set before you – your equivalent of an appeal to Caesar… or a dry pathway through a sea… or a river in a dry wasteland. He's already prepared it. And He will continue to do so… until He returns.

* * *

58

I AM ALMOST PERSUADED

A few days later King Agrippa arrived with his sister, Bernice, to pay their respects to Festus. During their stay of several days, Festus discussed Paul's case with the king. "There is a prisoner here," he told him, "whose case was left for me by Felix.... I was at a loss to know how to investigate these things, so I asked him whether he would be willing to stand trial on these charges in Jerusalem. But Paul appealed to have his case decided by the emperor. So I ordered that he be held in custody until I could arrange to send him to Caesar." "I'd like to hear the man myself," Agrippa said. And Festus replied, "You will – tomorrow!" So the next day Agrippa and Bernice arrived at the auditorium with great pomp, accompanied by military officers and prominent men of the city. Festus ordered that Paul be brought in. Then Festus said, "King Agrippa and all who are here, this is the man whose death is demanded by all the Jews, both here and in Jerusalem. But in my opinion he has done nothing deserving death. However, since he appealed his case to the emperor, I have decided to send him to Rome. But what shall I write the emperor? For there is no clear charge against him. So I have brought him before all of you, and especially you, King Agrippa, so that after we examine him, I might have something to write. For it makes no sense to send a prisoner to the emperor without specifying the charges against him!" Then Agrippa said to Paul, "You may speak in your defense." So Paul, gesturing with his hand, started his defense.... Agrippa interrupted him. "Do you think you can persuade me to become a Christian so quickly?" Paul replied, "Whether quickly or not, I pray to God that both you and everyone here in this audience might become the same as I am, except for these chains." Then the king, the governor, Bernice, and all the others stood and left. As they went out, they talked it over and agreed, "This man hasn't done anything to deserve death or imprisonment."

And Agrippa said to Festus, "He could have been set free if he hadn't appealed to Caesar."
Acts 25:13 – 26:32

* * *

King Agrippa II was the great grandson of King Herod the Great. His father, King Agrippa I had ruled the Iudaean province from 41 to 44 AD. So Agrippa II had been a teenage boy in this palace in Caesarea when his father ruled. Agrippa II was now the client ruler over several cities in Galilee, Perea and four smaller territories, while Festus, as governor, was the ruler over the Iudaean province. Though the two men had different titles, they held equal rank in the hierarchy of Roman rule.

This was a cordial visit by Agrippa II to welcome the new governor of Iudaea. His sister (and incestuous lover), Bernice, accompanied him on the visit. It was a very timely visit in light of Paul's imprisonment. Coming from Rome, Festus was not knowledgeable about the religious beliefs of the Jews. His predecessor Felix had the advantage that his wife, Drusilla, was a Jew and therefore was able to counsel him as to Jewish beliefs. By the way, she was the sister of Agrippa II and Bernice. They were the fourth generation of their family to live in this region – and all of the generations were well-versed in Judaism though their practice of those beliefs varied. They used that understanding to curry favor with the people, while more often choosing to personally embrace Greco-Roman culture and religion. Festus knew that Agrippa and Bernice would be able to provide him with an insight into Jewish beliefs that he lacked.

Festus was struggling with what explanation he should give to Caesar for sending Paul to him. He truly wanted to understand why the Jews were trying to kill Paul. But he also knew that he would look foolish before the Emperor if he was unable to provide official charges for a trial in Rome. Thus, he seized the opportunity to ask Agrippa for his advice.

Festus arranged to have Paul present his case in the amphitheater. In honor of Agrippa and Bernice, it was arranged with great pomp, including military officers and prominent men from the city. The amphitheater was filled with people – more for Agrippa's sake than Paul's – but still, it provided a great audience to hear Paul's message.

. . .

Paul acknowledged Agrippa's understanding of these matters by saying, *"I know that you are an expert on all Jewish customs and controversies"* (Acts 26:3). He then proceeded to explain that he had been a Pharisee and a persecutor of those who followed the Way until he encountered Jesus on the Damascus road. Paul told Agrippa what Jesus had said to him: *"For I have appeared to you to appoint you as My servant and witness. Tell people that you have seen Me, and tell them what I will show you in the future. And I will rescue you from both your own people and the Gentiles. Yes, I am sending you to the Gentiles to open their eyes, so they may turn from darkness to light and from the power of Satan to God"* (Acts 26:16-18). Then Paul said, *"And so, King Agrippa, I obeyed that vision from heaven.... I teach nothing except what the prophets and Moses said would happen – that the Messiah would suffer and be the first to rise from the dead, and in this way announce God's light to Jews and Gentiles alike"* (Acts 26:19, 22-23).

At that point, Festus interrupted Paul because it all sounded like craziness to him. *"But Paul replied, 'I am not insane, Most Excellent Festus. What I am saying is the sober truth. And King Agrippa knows about these things. I speak boldly, for I am sure these events are all familiar to him, for they were not done in a corner! King Agrippa, do you believe the prophets? I know you do!'"* (Acts 26:25-27) Agrippa interrupted him, saying, *"You almost persuade me to become a Christian"* (Acts 26:28 NKJ). Paul then replied, *"Whether quickly or not, I pray to God that both you and everyone here in this audience might become the same as I am, except for these chains."*

Agrippa, Bernice, Festus and all the others then stood and walked out saying, *"This man hasn't done anything to deserve death or imprisonment. He could have been set free if he hadn't appealed to Caesar."*

Sadly, they had heard, but they had not listened. Paul was more than likely the only "free" man in the amphitheater that day. He had turned to Jesus on that Damascus road and received forgiveness for his sins. He had been redeemed from sin and death. His was not the plight to be pitied. But Agrippa, Bernice, Festus and, more than likely, all of the others were walking out of that place still under the bondage of their sin.

Agrippa had "almost" been persuaded. But "almost" is what had prevented him from being set free. Paul wasn't the prisoner; the rest of them were. Prayerfully we will one day learn that some of those assembled that day did surrender their lives to Christ, but there is no indication that any of them did so – on that day, or any day thereafter. But here's the thing, Paul wasn't responsible for how anyone responded. His responsibility rested with being obedient to the "heavenly vision" – to proclaim the Good News.

That day wasn't about Paul being set free; it was about the others being given the opportunity to be set free spiritually. God had promised that Paul would preach the Good News in Rome, and the journey had begun with the opportunity to preach it to an amphitheater full of Romans in Caesarea. As we continue in our journey, it would be good for us to be mindful – and obedient – to proclaim the Good News so that the captives we encounter are set free. Let's be found faithful to that heavenly vision… until He returns.

* * *

59

EVEN THOUGH THE SHIP MAY GO DOWN

When the time came, we set sail for Italy.... Aristarchus, a Macedonian from Thessalonica, was also with us.... The next day when we docked at Sidon, Julius was very kind to Paul and let him go ashore to visit with friends so they could provide for his needs. Putting out to sea from there, we encountered strong headwinds that made it difficult to keep the ship on course, so we sailed north ... landing at Myra, in the province of Lycia. There the commanding officer found an Egyptian ship from Alexandria that was bound for Italy, and he put us on board. ... We struggled along the coast with great difficulty and finally arrived at Fair Havens, near the town of Lasea. ...The weather was becoming dangerous for sea travel because it was so late in the fall, and Paul spoke to the ship's officers about it. "Men," he said, "I believe there is trouble ahead if we go on – shipwreck, loss of cargo, and danger to our lives as well." But the officer in charge of the prisoners listened more to the ship's captain and the owner than to Paul. ...The terrible storm raged for many days, blotting out the sun and the stars, until at last, all hope was gone. ...Finally, Paul called the crew together and said, "Men, you should have listened to me in the first place and not left Crete. You would have avoided all this damage and loss. But take courage! None of you will lose your lives, even though the ship will go down. For last night an angel of the God to whom I belong and whom I serve stood beside me, and He said, 'Don't be afraid, Paul, for you will surely stand trial before Caesar! What's more, God in His goodness has granted safety to everyone sailing with you.' So take courage! For I believe God. It will be just as He said. But we will be shipwrecked on an island." ...So everyone escaped safely to shore.

Acts 27:1-44

* * *

Paul wasn't the only prisoner being transported to Rome in the charge of a Roman centurion named Julius. But it would be safe to assume that he was the only prisoner who was a Roman citizen. The others were more than likely prisoners who were being sent to Rome to become gladiators. Rome's lust for blood was insatiable. Romans found armed combat to the death to be very entertaining, so the need for new gladiators was endless. They were brought to Rome from the far corners of their empire. They were men without hope headed to their deaths in the Colosseum at the hands of other gladiators or in the jaws of wild beasts. This was a group that needed to hear about the grace of God – and before the journey was done, they would witness it first-hand.

Paul was also accompanied by two companions – Dr. Luke and Aristarchus from Thessalonica (Chapter 51). Both of these men would have also been Roman citizens – which afforded them the right to be able to travel with Paul on this journey. As citizens, however, their passage would not have been paid for by Rome; the three of them (including Paul) would have needed to pay their own way. Given Paul's unique circumstance, the centurion granted him the freedom to go ashore in Sidon to visit friends and obtain the needed financial provisions – not only for the voyage, but also for expenses he would incur when he subsequently arrived in Rome. Whether Julius' kindness was motivated by compassion or the financial gain that would result from Paul's visit ashore is not clear.

After sailing to Myra, Julius arranged passage for all of them on an Egyptian vessel bound for Rome. Delays in the journey pushed them into late fall, well past the ideal season for sailing to Rome. It was Paul that expressed safety concerns to the ship's officers, recommending that they find a safe harbor to weather the winter. But the ship's owner and captain, motivated by personal avarice, assured Julius that the journey could be made. Given the option of listening to experienced sailors or a Jewish tentmaker, Julius opted for the former.

Ultimately the ship was battered by gale-force winds that raged for days *"blotting out the sun and the stars, until at last, all hope was gone."* Even the experienced seamen had now lost hope. It was then that Paul gathered all the men on the ship – seamen, prisoners, soldiers and companions – telling them to take courage. God had again reminded Paul that he would *"surely stand trial before Caesar"* and *"God in His goodness"* had promised the *"safety to everyone sailing with"* Paul. Everyone who stayed on the ship would be saved. The One who can still the waves and the storm had assured them that they would not perish.

This moment reminds me of the night when Jesus and the disciples were crossing the Sea of Galilee and a storm arose.[1] The disciples had learned that night, as must we, that storms are a part of the journey. If God is sovereign over all things – which He is – then the storms of our life, at the very least, have been permitted by Him, and in some instances have been orchestrated by Him. All for the purpose that He desires to accomplish in and through our lives for His glory.

There is an important difference between that night for the disciples on the Sea of Galilee and this journey for Paul and his companions on the Mediterranean Sea that gives us added insight. God had given those now journeying on the Mediterranean Sea an opportunity to escape the storm. Paul had warned the ship's captain and owner not to sail on – but they had made the decision to go ahead despite the warning. On the Sea of Galilee, the disciples didn't have any choice. On the Mediterranean Sea, Paul and the prisoners didn't have a choice, but the others did – and they had chosen poorly. Jesus stilled the storm on the Galilean Sea. This group had to weather the storm on the Mediterranean Sea. Their actions had caused them to endure the storm – even the "innocent ones" like Paul.

But still God extended His grace to everyone – all two hundred seventy-six on board – even those who had chosen poorly. They experienced two weeks of a violent storm, as well as damage to the ship and cargo, that all could have been avoided. But no one perished – they all made it safely to shore.

So it is worthwhile to repeat these truths that we must always remember when we find ourselves in the midst of a storm.

1. **Hold onto the promise that God gave you before you encountered the storm (or while you were in the midst of the storm)**. God had promised Paul the safety of everyone who remained on the ship. We must hold on to the promise He gave us before the storm, in the midst of the storm, and after the storm has passed. He is trustworthy! What He says will be accomplished!

. . .

You may be going through a storm right now. It may be health-related… or financial… or you may find that you are unemployed. Whatever the storm is, hold on to His promise. It may not be a storm of your making – it may in fact be a storm that has arisen because of your obedience to God. Hold to His promise. If He has not given you a specific promise about this particular storm – whatever it is – Jesus has promised you that He will never fail you or abandon you! (Hebrews 13:5)

If you find that you are in a storm because of your disobedience, repent and turn to Him. Trust Him to lead you out of the storm to safe shores – though perhaps somewhat bruised

2. **Take comfort in His presence in the midst of the storm**. Now granted, we can only take strength from that fact if we are truly walking in His presence, and we haven't headed off doing our own thing. In those times, it's difficult to take comfort in His presence – because we have probably walked away from Him. But the good news is, if we repent of our disobedience and seek His forgiveness, we have then entered back into His presence. And we not only have the assurance of His promise, we have the assurance of His presence.

3. **Your Master is more powerful than your storm**. There is not anything outside of His view. There is not anything taking place in our lives that is beyond His *capacity* to know what needs to be done to make it right. AND, there is nothing beyond His *capability* to make it right. Every storm we will ever encounter will ultimately experience defeat at the hands of God.

4. **Your Master will use your storm to bring Himself glory**. More than likely, He will not still your storm in the way you expected – or perhaps in the way you would have preferred. But one fact stands above all the rest – He will still the storm and bring you to safety in the way that brings Him the greatest glory! And we may not understand what that is on this side of heaven. But hold to His promise that He *"causes everything to work together for the good of those who love God and are called according to His purpose for them"* (Romans 8:28).

Even though the ship may go down, trust the faithfulness of God. Encountering His faithfulness will often involve storms! Why? Because in the storms we come to realize our total dependence upon Him. And at the end of the day, that's a good place to be – totally dependent upon Him – even if the ship goes down.

---

1. Walking With The Master, Ch. 29, Mark 4:35-41

60

EVEN THE SNAKE WAS POWERLESS

Once we were safe on shore, we learned that we were on the island of Malta. The people of the island were very kind to us. It was cold and rainy, so they built a fire on the shore to welcome us. As Paul gathered an armful of sticks and was laying them on the fire, a poisonous snake, driven out by the heat, bit him on the hand. The people of the island saw it hanging from his hand and said to each other, "A murderer, no doubt! Though he escaped the sea, justice will not permit him to live." But Paul shook off the snake into the fire and was unharmed. The people waited for him to swell up or suddenly drop dead. But when they had waited a long time and saw that he wasn't harmed, they changed their minds and decided he was a god. Near the shore where we landed was an estate belonging to Publius, the chief official of the island. He welcomed us and treated us kindly for three days. As it happened, Publius's father was ill with fever and dysentery. Paul went in and prayed for him, and laying his hands on him, he healed him. Then all the other sick people on the island came and were healed. As a result we were showered with honors, and when the time came to sail, people supplied us with everything we would need for the trip. It was three months after the shipwreck that we set sail on another ship that had wintered at the island – an Alexandrian ship with the twin gods as its figurehead.

Acts 28:1-11

* * *

Two hundred seventy-six people arrived safely on shore that day in the midst of a torrential rain, clinging onto planks or debris from the broken up ship. Remember that many were prisoners being sent to Rome for punishment. Yet the people of the island greeted them all with open arms of kindness and compassion.

It was early to mid-November. It was biting cold and those that had washed up on the shore were soaked. The first order of business was to build a fire for warmth. Many hands made light work as everyone – those who had been shipwrecked, together with those who lived on the island – searched for and gathered dry wood for the fire. As Paul added his armful of sticks to the pile, a poisonous snake crawled out of the fire, biting him and affixing itself to his hand. The residents, believing Paul to be a criminal, concluded that justice was seeking its revenge. *"A murderer, no doubt!"*

They expected Paul to fall dead as a victim of his "crimes". These pagan people, uninitiated in the gospel, uninformed about Christianity in any sense, and having no idea of the revelation of God, had a sense of right and wrong. They had a sense of justice and a sense that sin gets punished. They were thinking, "Aha, if he dies, look, he must be a murderer." In other words, there is a right and a wrong, and when you are wrong there are consequences.

They had a sense of morality. They had an understanding of sin – and the penalty for sin. Where did that come from? Paul would later write to the believers in Rome, *"God shows His anger from heaven against all sinful, wicked people who suppress the truth by their wickedness. They know the truth about God because He has made it obvious to them"* (Romans 1:18-19). Their sense of morality and sin was God-given.

God has also planted a sense of goodness and kindness in a man's heart (such as what the Maltese expressed to those who washed ashore), as well as a sense of morality. The residents on Malta had an understanding of goodness and evil even though they did not yet know God. It began for them, just as it did for everyone, when Eve and Adam took a bite of the fruit in the garden and received the knowledge of good and evil. That's why God would hold the Maltese people – and all people – responsible for their activities and their actions. *All have sinned – and all have fallen short of the glory of God* (Romans 3:23). And the people knew clearly that *the wages of sin is death* (Romans 6:23). They already knew that! They didn't need to be told that! But now they were about to hear and experience the Good News – that *the gift of God is eternal life through Christ Jesus* (Romans

6:23). This shipwreck was all a part of God's plan and grace to bring the message of the gospel to that island.

The people watched, as Paul shook off the snake. They fully expected his hand to swell up and for him to fall over dead at any moment. Usually such a snake bite would create a panic and the person who had been bitten would be running around and flailing in horror. But Paul was calm – and as they watched, they saw that he was unharmed. The only death to occur was that of the snake being burned up in the fire. Seeing that Paul was unharmed by the snake bite, the residents decided that he was no ordinary man. They were wrong when they thought him to be a god, but they were right that he was no ordinary man – he was a redeemed man.

Here was the picture for them – and for us. Paul was a criminal – he was a sinner – just like each and every one of us. And the guaranteed outcome of sin is death. BUT, God in His grace made a way for us to be redeemed through the shed blood of His Son. If we have received His gift of grace by believing in His Son by faith, our sins have been forgiven and the consequence of death has been defeated. Sin no longer has power over us. Regrettably, we still have a capacity to sin, but God has assured us that *if we confess our sins to Him, He is faithful and just to forgive us of our sins and cleanse us from all unrighteousness* (1 John 1:9).

The picture of the snake – a reminder of that serpent in the Garden of Eden -- being shaken off and burned in the fire is a reminder that Satan is a defeated foe. And one day he will be burned up in the fire. We do not live in fear of him or in panic over his power over us. He is powerless over us – not because of anything we can do – but because we have been redeemed by the blood of the Lamb, and we are indwelt by His Holy Spirit.

Over the next three months, the residents of the island – as well as the survivors of the shipwreck – all had more opportunity to hear and witness the power of the gospel as Paul, Luke and Aristarchus preached and lived it out. But nothing was more powerful in communicating that truth than that first day when they witnessed that the snake was powerless.

. . .

The same is true for us. A watching world will be most attuned to listen to the gospel when they see for themselves that sin and Satan are powerless over us. Live out the gospel through your action – and then add words… until He returns.

* * *

61

PROCLAIM THE GOOD NEWS BOLDLY

The brothers and sisters in Rome had heard we were coming, and they came to meet us at the Forum on the Appian Way. Others joined us at The Three Taverns. When Paul saw them, he was encouraged and thanked God. When we arrived in Rome, Paul was permitted to have his own private lodging, though he was guarded by a soldier. Three days after Paul's arrival, he called together the local Jewish leaders. He said to them, "Brothers, I was arrested in Jerusalem and handed over to the Roman government, even though I had done nothing against our people or the customs of our ancestors. The Romans tried me and wanted to release me, because they found no cause for the death sentence. But when the Jewish leaders protested the decision, I felt it necessary to appeal to Caesar, even though I had no desire to press charges against my own people. I asked you to come here today so we could get acquainted and so I could explain to you that I am bound with this chain because I believe that the hope of Israel – the Messiah – has already come." They replied, "We have had no letters from Judea or reports against you from anyone who has come here. But we want to hear what you believe, for the only thing we know about this movement is that it is denounced everywhere." So a time was set, and on that day a large number of people came to Paul's lodging. He explained and testified about the Kingdom of God and tried to persuade them about Jesus from the Scriptures. Using the law of Moses and the books of the prophets, he spoke to them from morning until evening. Some were persuaded by the things he said, but others did not believe. And after they had argued back and forth among themselves, they left with this final word from Paul: "... I want you to know that this salvation from God has also been offered to the Gentiles, and they will accept it." For the next two years, Paul lived in Rome at his own expense. He welcomed all who visited him, boldly proclaiming the

Kingdom of God and teaching about the Lord Jesus Christ. And no one tried to stop him.
Acts 28:15-31

* * *

The day arrived when their ship docked in Italy at the port of Puteoli, one hundred twenty-five miles southeast of Rome. After remaining in the port town for a week and regaining their "land legs", Julius and his soldiers led Paul and the rest of the company by foot to Rome along the Appian Way. About forty-three miles outside of Rome, they encountered a group of believers looking for Paul. Apparently word had already reached the believers in Rome that Paul was coming. After traveling another ten miles they encountered a second group. The journey from Jerusalem to Rome had taken slightly less than three years, including Paul's two-year imprisonment in Caesarea. After all of the difficulties he had experienced along the way, seeing these believers as he approached Rome was a great encouragement to Paul.

One does have to wonder about the centurion Julius, as well as the rest of the soldiers. They had been traveling with Paul, Luke and Aristarchus – in very close quarters and through very difficult circumstances – for more than six months. But through it all, Paul and his companions had remained confident in God's promise and steadfast in His mission. The soldiers had heard the gospel preached a countless number of times – and they had seen it lived out minute-by-minute for many months. They had witnessed God's healing power at work through Paul, and God's miraculous protection when the snake bit him. Scripture does not tell us whether Julius, any of the other soldiers, or any of the other prisoners came to faith during their time together. But one thing we know for certain is that if they did not come to faith, it was not for lack of witness or opportunity.

After arriving in Rome, Paul stayed in his own private lodging for two years. God graciously provided the resources for him to be able to do so. Throughout the time, he preached the Good News – first to the Jews and then to the Gentiles. He received anyone who wanted to discuss the things of the Kingdom of God. Throughout the time, he was chained to a guard who was relieved every six hours. The guards had no choice but to listen to Paul as he preached, taught, and prayed. It would be no surprise to one day learn that some of them entered into the Kingdom as a result (Philippians 1:13-14).

. . .

Throughout his time in Rome, Paul was surrounded by men that he continued to pour his life into – Timothy, John Mark, Luke, Aristarchus, Epaphras, Justus and Demas. And he discipled the churches from a distance as he wrote his letters to the Philippians, Ephesians and Colossians, as well as his letter to Philemon.

Luke's account concludes before Paul's case was heard by Caesar. Apparently he was released and was able to resume his ministry travels – back to Greece, Macedonia, Asia and Crete, as well as into Spain (Romans 15:24). Wherever he went, he was faithful to preach the Good News to all. Five years after his release from Rome, he was again arrested – this time in Troas – and transported back to Rome. Scripture is silent as to the specific details surrounding this arrest.

But we do know that this time he did not live in his own lodging; he was chained in a prison and treated like a criminal (2 Timothy 1:16; 2:9). This time he was not surrounded by believers (2 Timothy 4:9-16); they appear to have abandoned him, except for Luke. And this time, his imprisonment didn't end in his being released; it ended in death. Because he was a Roman citizen, Paul was not crucified on a cross, but he was beheaded by orders of Emperor Nero.

The Holy Spirit did not inspire Luke to write the Book of Acts that we might simply know the early history of the church. He gave us this Book to encourage the church, in every age, to be faithful to the Lord to carry the gospel to the ends of the earth.

Jesus commissioned us to go boldly and proclaim the Good News throughout Jerusalem, Judea, Samaria and the ends of the earth. The early church took that mandate seriously and went – with all boldness – to wherever the Holy Spirit led them. Which brings us, most importantly, back to the promise that Jesus made, just before He ascended to sit at the right hand of the Father. It is the promise that James, Stephen, Peter, Paul and so many others carried with them until their last breath –

"Be sure of this: I am with you always, even to the end of the age."
(Matthew 28:20)

Wherever you are in your journey, hold onto that promise. Whatever circumstance, whatever trial or whatever battle you are walking through, walk according to that promise. Whether you are surrounded by others who are encouraging you, or you have been abandoned and are walking alone, do not let go of that promise. Stay the course. Finish the race. Fulfill the ministry He has given you… until He returns!

* * *

BEFORE YOU GO...

PLEASE HELP ME BY LEAVING A REVIEW!

i would be very grateful if you would leave a review of this book. Your feedback will be helpful to me in my future writing endeavors and will also assist others as they consider picking up a copy of the book.

To leave a review, go to:
amazon.com/dp/1734193085

Thanks for your help!

* * *

COMING SEPTEMBER 18, 2020

Little Did We Know

… Eyewitnesses to the Advent

A collection of **twenty-five short stories for the Advent season** from some familiar and some not-so-familiar people. Experience anew the truth of the glorious arrival of the Baby in the manger through the lens of these **fictional first-person accounts** of the prophecies and events heralding the birth of Jesus. Some of the characters may be fictional, but **the truth they tell is very real!**

* * *

Not Too Little To Know

… Children who witnessed the Advent

Experience the Advent through the eyes of ten children who witnessed the glorious arrival of the Promised One. Join Isaac, Salome, Sarah, Yanzu and others in their journeys as they share their own fictional eyewitness accounts of the prophecies and events surrounding the birth of Jesus. **Some of the characters may be fictional, but the truth they tell is very real!**

This illustrated chapter book has been written for ages 8 and up. It is a companion to ***Little Did We Know***, a collection of short stories written for teens and adults. Though both books stand alone, their stories intertwine into a delightful Advent journey for the entire family.

COMING FEBRUARY 19, 2021

The One Who Stood Before Us

… Eyewitnesses to the Resurrection

A collection of **forty short stories** for the **Easter** season from some familiar and some not-so-familiar people. Walk with those who walked with Jesus — some as **followers**, some as **friends** and some as **foes**. Join them on the three year journey that led to the cross … but didn't stop there. **Experience the miracles they witnessed, the truth they learned, and the One they came to know**. Some of the

characters in these fictional first-person accounts may be unreal, but **the truth they all tell is very real!**

AND

Through the Eyes of a Prisoner

A novel
about the mission of God

COMING FALL 2021

* * *

For more information, go to
wildernesslessons.com or kenwinter.org

ALSO BY KENNETH A. WINTER

Though the Eyes of a Shepherd

A Novel — **Shimon was a shepherd boy when he first saw the newborn King in a Bethlehem stable.** Join him in his journey as he re-encounters the Lamb of God at the Jordan, and follows the Miracle Worker through the wilderness, the Messiah to the cross, and the Risen Savior from the upper room. Though Shimon is a fictional character, we'll see the pages of the Gospels unfold through his eyes, and **experience a story of redemption – the redemption of a shepherd – and the redemption of each one who chooses to follow the Good Shepherd.**

Though the Eyes of a Spy

A Novel — **Caleb was one of God's chosen people** – a people to whom He had given a promise. Caleb never forgot that promise — as a slave in Egypt, a spy in the Promised Land, a wanderer in the wilderness, or a conqueror in the hill country. We'll see the promise of Jehovah God unfold through his eyes, and **experience a story of God's faithfulness – to a spy who trusted Him – and to each one of us who will do the same.**

* * *

Other Books in the Lessons Learned In The Wilderness series

*Each of the six books in the series contains 61 chapters, which means that the entire series is comprised of 366 chapters — **one chapter for each day of the year.** The chapters have been formatted in a way that you can read one chapter each day or read each book straight through. Whichever way you choose, allow the Master to use the series to encourage and challenge you in the journey that He has designed uniquely for you so that His purpose is fulfilled, and His glory is made known.*

The Journey Begins (Book #1)

God's plan for our lives is not static; He is continuously calling us to draw closer, to climb higher and to move further. In that process, He is moving us out of our comfort zone to His land of promise for our lives. That process includes time in the wilderness. Many times it is easier to see the truth that God is teaching us through the lives of others than it is through our own lives.

"***The Journey Begins***" is the first book in the "***Lessons Learned In The Wilderness***" series. It chronicles those stories, those examples and those truths as revealed through the lives and experiences of the Israelites, as recorded in the Book of Exodus in sixty-one bite-sized chapters.

As you read one chapter per day for sixty-one days, we will look at the circumstances, the surroundings and the people in such a way that highlights the similarities to our lives, as we then apply those same truths to our own life journey as the Lord God Jehovah leads us through our own wilderness journey.

The Wandering Years (Book #2)

Why did a journey that God ordained to take slightly longer than one year, end up taking forty years? Why, instead of enjoying the fruits of the

land of milk and honey, did the Israelites end up wandering in the desert wilderness for forty years? Why did one generation follow God out of Egypt only to die there, leaving the next generation to follow Him into the Promised Land?

In the journeys through the wildernesses of my life, i can look back and see where God has turned me back from that land of promise to wander a while longer in the wilderness. God has given us the wilderness to prepare us for His land of promise, but if when we reach the border we are not ready, He will turn us back to wander.

If God is allowing you to continue to wander in the wilderness, it is because He has more to teach you about Himself – His Person, His purpose and His power. "**The Wandering Years**" chronicles through sixty-one "bite-sized" chapters those lessons He would teach us through the Israelites' time in the wilderness as recorded in the books of Numbers and Deuteronomy.

The book has been formatted for one chapter to be read each day for sixty-one days. Explore this second book in the "**Lessons Learned In The Wilderness"** series and allow God to use it to apply those same lessons to your daily journey with Him.

Possessing the Promise (Book #3)

The day had finally arrived for the Israelites to possess the land that God had promised. But just like He had taught them lessons throughout their journey in the wilderness, He had more to teach them, as they possessed the promise.

And so it is for us. Possessing the promise doesn't mean the faith adventure has come to a conclusion; rather, in many ways, it has only just begun. Possessing the promise will involve in some respects an even greater dependence upon God and the promise He has given you.

"**Possessing the Promise**" chronicles the stories, experiences and lessons we see recorded in the books of Joshua and Judges in sixty-one "bite-sized" chapters. The book has been formatted for one chapter to be read each day for sixty-one days.

Explore this third book in the "**Lessons Learned In The Wilderness**" series and allow God to use it to teach you how to possess the promise as He leads you in the journey with Him each day.

Lessons Learned In The Wilderness Series: Books 1-3

THE LESSONS LEARNED IN THE WILDERNESS COLLECTION - VOLUME 1

The first three books in the ***Lessons Learned In The Wilderness*** series are also available in a three-book collection as an **e-book** boxset or as a **soft-cover print** volume. We will walk with the Israelites as God enabled them to overcome the challenges of their exodus from Egypt, their wanderings in the wilderness, and finally, the giants they faced in possessing the Promised Land. Throughout each step from Exodus through Judges, we will seek to learn the lessons God would teach us through their journey.

The collection includes:

The Journey Begins
The Wandering Years
Possessing The Promise

* * *

For more information about these books, including how you can purchase them, go to
wildernesslessons.com or kenwinter.org

ABOUT THE AUTHOR

Ken Winter is a follower of Jesus, an extremely blessed husband, and a proud father and grandfather – all by the grace of God. His journey with Jesus has led to him to serve over the past three decades on the pastoral staffs of two local churches — one in West Palm Beach, Florida and the other in Richmond, Virginia, as well as in the role of vice president of mobilization with the International Mission Board of the Southern Baptist Convention.

Each step of Ken's journey with Jesus has been a part of a continuing Genesis 12 journey. God has always been faithful to reveal the next step when Ken and his family have stepped out by faith on the path He has set before them. Today that journey continues as Ken labors as a bond-servant of the Lord Jesus Christ in the proclamation of the gospel through his writing to the end that every person may be presented complete in Christ.

To read Ken's weekly blog posts go to kenwinter.blog.

* * *

And we proclaim Him, admonishing every man and teaching every man with all wisdom, that we may present every man complete in Christ. And for this purpose also I labor, striving according to His power, which mightily works within me.
(Colossians 1:28-29 NASB)

PLEASE JOIN MY READERS' GROUP

Please join my Readers' Group in order to receive updates and information about future releases, etc.

Also, i will send you a free copy of ***The Journey Begins*** e-book — the first book in the ***Lessons Learned In The Wilderness*** series. It is yours to keep or share with a friend or family member that you think might benefit from it.

It's completely free to sign up. i value your privacy and will not spam you. Also, you can unsubscribe at any time.

Go to kenwinter.org to subscribe.

* * *

Made in the USA
Columbia, SC
05 January 2021

30255391R00417